Breathing Life
into Family Ancestors

about the Ritchhart, Dean, Bush,

O'Malley, Schmidt, McConnell

and other associated Families

by

Delbert A. Ritchhart

AuthorHouse™
1663 Liberty Drive
Bloomington, IN 47403
www.authorhouse.com
Phone: 1-800-839-8640

First published by AuthorHouse   08/25/2011

ISBN: 978-1-4634-4350-4 (sc)
ISBN: 978-1-4634-4351-1 (ebk)

Library of Congress Control Number: 2011913264

Printed in the United States of America

DEDICATION

This book is dedicated to my children, grandchildren, great grandchildren and future descendants. My hope and inspiration in writing this book has been that they will some day appreciate my efforts, find enjoyment in following through with the research and, ultimately break through some of those remaining "brick walls" that still confront and confound me.

Table of Contents

Prologue

This is a book that represents a summary of family history that I have collected over the past ten years of part time genealogical research. It is a book that I hope will be of interest to my children, grandchildren and future generations. Most of my children and grandchildren don't presently have much interest in genealogy, but I am convinced that as they grow older they will have a greater appreciation for family history and what I have compiled in this book. To be very honest, I didn't develop any interest in family history until I was almost sixty years old.

I owe that to a fortunate coincidence. Around 1995 I received a letter in the mail that was promoting a book about the Ritchhart family history. In summary it was a solicitation for $50 for a book that the author was selling entitled *Richhart Ritchhart Ritschard—A Swiss-German Family From 1500 Until 1993*. My first thought was that this was a come-on deal like some I had seen previously that just contained general information about the Ritchhart name, where the name originated, a Coat of Arms photo, short bios of some Ritchharts that had achieved some degree of recognition; but nothing specific about family lines. The letter did mention a Library of Congress Catalog Card Number, so I got on the internet, entered the number on the home web page for the Library of Congress and, sure enough, the book did exist and seemed to be legitimate. Therefore, I decided it was worth a chance and ordered a copy.

When I received the book in the mail and skimmed over it, I was absolutely thrilled. It not only had detailed information about the Ritchhart family dating back to the 1500s, it had my father's name and that of each of his ancestral line dating back for fifteen generations. I didn't know it then; but I was hooked for life on genealogy!

Shortly after that I purchased the software application Family Tree Maker and started entering information about my family. Being so fortunate as to have most of the work already done on the Ritchhart surname, I was able to branch out and work on both of my mother's parent's and my dad's mother's ancestors. I also filled in a lot about my direct line that was not included in the book.

I was so excited about the book that I bought copies for each of our three daughters and for my brother. I also told several cousins about the book. In the process of ordering the books and getting started with my genealogy, I talked on a couple occasions on the phone with Bettye Richhart, author of the book. My contact with Bettye continued over the next few years and when Joanne and I left the Washington D.C. area following my retirement from Lockheed Martin, we stopped in the Ft. Worth area and spent the evening with Bettye and Jim Richhart. I marveled that she had two file cabinets full of research data. I now have one file cabinet and am well on my way to two! I have made references in this book to living people; but have only written more detailed accounts of ancestors or family members who are deceased. Thus, the reason I have written a section about my sister; but not my brother.

I must acknowledge the patience and understanding of my wife, Joanne, with the thousands of hours that I have spent doing genealogy over the last ten plus years. She was also very understanding during our trip across country from Virginia to California when I retired. Not only did we stop to visit Bettye and Jim; but we stopped in Chillicothe, Ohio; Noblesville, Indiana and Carthage, Missouri where we visited the local cemeteries looking for headstones of my ancestors and met with Ritchhart distant relatives. Interestingly, in Chillicothe we met one of the three Ritchhart brothers who were still actively farming land that had been in the family name for over 100 years. More amazing was the fact they were all nearly 80 years old! I am thinking that if I don't dedicate a little more time to finishing this book, I will be 80 years old and it still won't be done!

I hope that future generations enjoy the fruits of my labor.

Conditions in Europe Stimulating Emigration

Within our immediate families both the Schmidt and Ritchhart ancestors were of German heritage. Frederic Schmidt lived in the region of Württemberg and came to America in 1848. Christian Ritschhard was Swiss German and came to America from the Hilterfingen/Oberhofen area in 1750. Peter O'Malley lived in Mayo County, Ireland and also came to this country around 1850. Such a trip in those times was long, treacherous, expensive and was filled with many unknowns. Why would anyone attempt such a journey? We don't know for sure; but by examining the conditions in their native lands and America at the time, we can perhaps gain some insight into what might have motivated them.

SWITZERLAND IN THE 1750s

Because a number of Swiss had been leaving their homeland for other countries, particularly America; the government became very concerned about losing valuable income from taxes. Decrees had been issued as early as 1720 making it very difficult to sell land and leave the area without permission. An "emigration tax" was levied so as to provide compensatory income to the local Cantons (states). There is some evidence that Christian and his family "stole away in the night" to avoid paying the tax and trying to obtain permission to leave—probably because they doubted they could obtain such authorization.

During Bettye Richhart's visit to Switzerland in 1985, residents in Oberhofen told her that in the mid 1700s, about the time Christian and his family left Switzerland, the economic situation was very depressed. The vineyards, that had long supported the families in the village, had become diseased and it was almost impossible to economically survive in the area. The vineyards had been the main source of income for the residents for hundreds of years. We visited the area in 2003 and noted the fact that there was very little level land on the northern shore of Lake Thun where Oberhofen and Hilterfingen are located. Other than grapes, there wouldn't be many other agricultural crops that could be grown in that area and in those days most people lived off the land. Even in 2003 when we visited, many vineyards still existed in the area.

If the economic situation wasn't itself a strong enough motivation to leave the area, that was also a time when Switzerland was making a great effort to rid itself of the troublesome group called "Anabaptists." Among their beliefs were complete separation of state and church, voluntary church membership, and of great importance to the state, their refusal to bear arms. These Anabaptists were the victims of systematic persecution, especially in the cantons of Bern (which included Oberhofen & Hilterfingen) and Zürich." Many of these Anabaptists, also later known as Mennonites, emigrated to America from Germany, Switzerland and Holland seeking freedom to pursue their religious beliefs.

GERMANY

Like Switzerland in the 1750s, Germany in the 1850s was suffering from an economic crisis which was fueled by an agrarian crisis. "During the years 1846–1849 several economic crises overlapped an agrarian crisis of the years 1846–47. The harvests of 1845 and 1846 were very poor. In addition a potato blight raged. As a result of grain and potato scarcity the cost of basic commodities dramatically increased, especially in the spring of 1847." (*Economic Crisis in Germany*, Rudiger Hachtmann, translated by James Chastain). This resulted in high unemployment, especially among tradesmen. Frederic Schmidt was a butcher, and with scarce crops to feed livestock, it is likely that the need for butchers was markedly reduced. Severe depression, unemployment and failure of the liberal revolutionary movement in 1848 sent about 4 million Germans to the United States between the 1840 and 1880s.

The coincidences of these major crises, combined with other political factors, resulted in the 1848 Revolution in Germany. Following on the heels of similar events in France, the people in the loosely formed alliance of German states began demanding additional freedoms. There was also a great wave of political asylum seekers who left Germany in 1848 after the failed Revolution. It was January of 1848 when Frederic traveled from the Württemberg area to the French port city of Le Havre and boarded the Probus bound for New York City in America.

Terrain near Oberhofen along North Shore of Lake Thun

IRELAND

Much has been written about the various potato famines that plagued Ireland, one of the worst being in the period 1845–1850. I read parts of *The Great Hunger; Ireland 1845–1849* by Cecil Woodham-Smith and was stricken by the sheer hopelessness the Irish people faced. The British government expected the large landowners and overseers to each care for their own renters; however, the problem was so great and so widespread that some type of higher level government assistance was required. When it didn't happen, people starved to death because there simply wasn't any food or any work to earn money to buy food. What little reserves most families had was quickly eaten up when the new crops failed because of the blight.

Land in County Mayo was typically very rocky so they made fences alongside the fields that they cleared.

A Typical County Mayo Farm with Rock Fences

The book finally got so depressing I stopped reading. I don't think any of us can imagine how something like that could happen—but it did!

Since Peter and Julia O'Malley's first child was born in Pennsylvania in 1854, I assume they were married in 1852–53 and probably arrived in this country only a few years earlier. That would have meant they married at around 18 years of age and arrived in America at the tail end of the potato famine.

Since I have not been able to trace them back to a specific village or parish in Mayo County or to identify their parents; there are several possibilities regarding Peter and Julia's emigration. One or both of them could have lost their parents, as around one million people died during the famine. It is possible that their parents came with them; but I haven't uncovered any evidence of that in any of the documents I have researched. While it is still a possibility, I think it is unlikely.

I think that they probably went to the Scranton, Pennsylvania area because other family or friends had already settled there and written back to them in Mayo county. Early in my research I thought they might have come to America as indentured servants, but I later learned that practice essentially ended around 1820. I know from census data that Peter lived and worked as a farmer in the Salem, Wayne County, Pennsylvania area just outside Scranton for about ten years before moving to Scranton, where he worked in the mines. The fact Peter and his family appeared in both the 1860 and 1870 census as a family unit with their own residence tends to further support the theory that they were not indentured.

In some cases the Overseers of some Irish tenants would pay tenants' fare to America just to rid themselves of the burden of trying to support some of the people who were their responsibility. The move of the family from Pennsylvania to Mason County, Illinois in 1880 could have been for a couple reasons. First, the railroads were pushing across the county following the completion of the transcontinental railroad in 1869 and we know from the 1880 census that Peter worked for the railroad in Mason County, Illinois. Secondly, there was good farmland in Illinois and people were migrating westward following the development of roads and railroads. It is also likely that a friend or even relative might have written them about Mason County.

COME TO THE PROMISED LAND

Troubling conditions in Switzerland in the 1750s and Germany and Ireland in the 1850s might have been enough to drive Christian, Frederic, and Peter and their families to emigrate, however, why would they have chosen America as their destination? Throughout most of the 18th century emigration was officially a crime, but at the beginning of the 1700s there was a scheme encouraged by the Council of Bern to petition the British to allow the establishment of a Swiss settlement in Pennsylvania or Virginia. By doing this, the Swiss were hoping to get rid of the paupers and members of the Baptist, Anabaptist and Mennonite dissident religious groups. Although this plan failed initially; it was basically what did happen a few years later.

Because the Anabaptists had arrived in America as early as the 1680s, they were sending word back to their homeland about the great opportunities this new land offered. Many of the Mennonites traveled to America via Germany and the Netherlands; and some even ventured as far as Russia before eventually making their way to America. They, of course, made friends along the way and encouraged them to follow when they arrived in the new country. Many from Ireland had also emigrated earlier to America and were, likewise, sending word home about the great opportunities America provided.

Thus, it was both the "pull" coming from the glowing reports from America; and the "push" of economic hard times, famine, rebellions and various forms of persecution that caused most emigrants to move to the new promised land.

I did find that there were other Ritschards in the Reading, Pennsylvania area where Christian and his family first settled upon arriving in America. Thus, it is entirely possible that Christian and Magdalena were drawn to that area by reports from relatives who had arrived there earlier.

Likewise, there were other O'Malley, Maloy and Malia families (as noted in other portions of the book, I believe Peter and Julia's surname was spelled various ways before finally becoming "O'Malley" in the late 1800s) in the general Scranton, Pennsylvania area in the 1750s when Peter and Julia arrived there from County Mayo. There were also a large number of Irish families in that area who might have sent word back to others in their homeland about the opportunities in and around Scranton.

In the case of Frederic Schmidt, who landed in New York City and stayed there for a few years before moving on to Indianapolis, the choice of New York was probably a decision of convenience. During the mid-1800s, New York was the major port for European immigrants where there were large communities of almost every immigrant nationality: Italian, German, Irish, English and others. Thus, an immigrant could find a degree of comfort in knowing there would be a community with whom they could assimilate, who spoke the same language, and had the same traditions. The fact that Frederic and Maria moved on to Indianapolis after only three years in New York City seems to provide further evidence that New York City was only a destination of convenience. I am assuming that once they heard from other Germans about the job opportunities and large German community in Indianapolis, which included German churches, newspapers, and social clubs, they left New York.

The Ritschharts, Ritschards of Switzerland

Prior to Christian Ritschhart and his family emigrating from Switzerland in 1750, his family had lived in the Hilterfingen-Oberhofen area for at least 200 years. This lineage is traced in Bettye Richhart's book *Richhart Ritchhart Ritschard—A Swiss-German Family From 1500 Until 1993*. Bettye did the work on the family history covering the period following their arrival here in America. However, she hired a Swiss genealogist to search Swiss records and trace Christian's ancestors back to the 1500s. Apparently Swiss records are quite good; but being written in German makes research difficult for one who doesn't know the language.

When Joanne and I were planning our trip to Switzerland in 2003, I asked Bettye for the names of any contacts she might still have in Oberhofen or Hilterfingen. She gave me the name of Alfred Ritschard as being someone she had visited with during her trips there and who seemed knowledgeable about his family's history. I wrote Alfred a letter asking to set up an appointment with him during our visit. I received a reply several weeks later from Beatrice Frey, who explained that her Grandfather had passed away. Since her Grandmother did not speak English, she passed the letter on to Beatrice, whom she knew did understand English. Apparently Beatrice had refined her English by the fact she worked as a research assistant at the University in Bern, where many of her fellow workers spoke English. She was willing to meet with us and show us around the area. Another plus that facilitated communication was the fact Beatrice had internet at home. Thus, we arranged for her to meet us in Oberhofen in October 2003.

Beatrice & Del on Oberhofen Pier

As we pulled into the dock opposite the Oberhofen Castle on Lake Thun there on the dock was the bright smiling face of Beatrice.

Since we were within only a few yards of the Oberhofen Castle, we proceeded over there and looked around the exterior of the Castle, but did not take the internal castle tour. The castle dates back to 1130 when it was known as The Monastery of Interlaken and over the years it had been a major source of employment for many Ritschards. At least three generations of Ritschards served as castle bailiff in the late 16th century, early 17th century time frame.

The castle gradually fell into disrepair until 1926 when it was purchased by an American lawyer, William Measey of Philadelphia. It remained under his care until 1940 when the castle administration was transferred to the canton of Bern. Since 1952 it has been under the control of the Bernese Historical Museum.

Hilterfingen Church

We had asked Beatrice to pick out a place for lunch, so we took a short five minute drive over to a lovely restaurant on the lake. Our major visit planned for the afternoon was to the Hilterfingen Church and there directly above us, as we sat on the restaurant patio, was the church! Beatrice couldn't have picked a better location for lunch. Here we were sitting at the water's edge on a beautiful day with a sailing regatta underway on the lake and a perfect view of the Church we were going to visit following lunch. To top it off, the food was delicious.

Having some time to talk to Beatrice, we learned she was a single mom and that she worked in Bern as a research assistant in the University of Bern. I would guess that she was in her mid to

Beatrice at her Grandfather Alfred Ritschard's grave

late 30s. Her mother was babysitting so she could only stay with us until 2 p.m. when her mom had to leave. After lunch, we didn't even have to move our car. We walked across the street and up a stairway to the church grounds.

Beatrice took us first to the church cemetery, which was on the far side of the church. The grounds were beautifully decorated with both live and cut flowers. I don't think I have ever seen a more colorfully decorated cemetery. Beatrice pointed out the grave and headstone of her Grandfather, Alfred, whom I originally wrote regarding our visit.

In looking around at several headstones it was apparent that most of the people in the cemetery had died within the past 100 years. Considering that the church was built in the mid-1700s, that seemed strange. However, we learned that due to the sparse amount of usable land in Switzerland, cemeteries are basically turned under about ev-

Del points out the Ritschhart Family Crest

ery 100 years so the land can be reused. After spending a short time in the graveyard, we moved to the inside of the church—a move I was anxiously awaiting as I wanted to see the large wooden plaque that I had read about in Bettye Richhart's book. In 1731 thirty-two of the church families donated this huge plaque, depicting Moses and the Ten Commandments, to the church. Each of the thirty-two families' names, their position within the church and coat of arms were inscribed around the sides of the plaque—eight of those families being Ritschharts. Ironically, Beatrice didn't know the plaque existed. We had read that church attendance among the Swiss is very low and Beatrice's comments reinforced that fact.

The plaque was huge, probably six or seven feet in height and about five feet wide. It must have weighed several hundred pounds. After we had studied the plaque and the church's

interior for sufficient time, we departed and bid Beatrice farewell, so that she could get back and relieve her mother by 2 p.m.. Since it was a beautiful day and the boat didn't leave to go back to Interlocken until around 3:30 p.m., we wandered through the villages back to the Castle and took the full tour. Not only was the Castle interior and its furnishings impressive; but the surrounding gardens were beautiful.

When it came time to depart and catch the boat, I felt that the stay had been entirely too short. I would have liked to have met more of the Ritschards, looked at church records, and spent more time wandering the streets and through the castle. Perhaps there will be a second chance some day.

As we cast off and headed back toward

Six Ritschhart Family Crests line the left edge of the plaque

Oberhofen Castle Gardens

The Beautifully Restored Sitting Room

Oberhofen Castle

The Ritschhart Crest—one of eight on the
mural in Hilterfingen Church

Interlocken I looked forward to the next day's venture. When Christian and Magdalena decided to marry they chose to cross this same lake and venture about two miles inland to the Church at Almsoldingen. It was a beautiful 10th-century church situated in a quaint rural setting. It was reported to be one of the most beautiful structures in the Lake Thun area when it was built. I would be taking the train around Lake Thun the next day to visit that same church.

The next day I boarded the train for about a forty minute ride into Thun. There I boarded a bus for Almsoldingen. Since there is both an Almsoldingen and Allmendengen in the same general area, which I only learned when trying to catch the correct bus, it was a little confusing. I have to once more give the Swiss credit for their efficiency. As I got off the train to catch the bus; there was a bus station, train station and Lake Thun boat terminal all within about a quarter mile radius. I managed to get onto the correct bus and after nervously watching each stop for about 20 minutes we got to Almsoldingen. As I got off the bus and gazed up the road, I was relieved to see a large church that looked like the picture I had seen in Bettye Richhart's book. As I got closer to the church, I realized that in order to get a better angle for a photo I needed to go down one of the lanes leading to a small farm house. As I got into position to take the above photo I could hear the tinkling of bells around the necks of the cows and the goats in the field. The thought crossed my mind that this setting wasn't radically different from that in 1733, when Christian and Magdalena were here to get married! Yes, there was an occasional car that came by on the winding road leading to the church and there were light poles that wouldn't have existed then; but the quaint, serene, rural setting still existed.

The Church at Almsoldingen

Church Interior and Choir Loft

When I entered the church, it was very stark; but there was a certain majesty about the high ceilings, interior rock walls and the large tapestry draped on a side wall. There were now chairs in place of benches or simple pews that probably once existed; but once again, not much was different from what I imagine it had been like almost 270 years earlier! I had hoped to run into a caretaker or clergyman to ask them to relate some of the history of the church; but despite wandering all through the church and around the grounds and adjacent cemetery, I never saw anyone. However, I could appreciate why someone would travel two miles across the lake and two miles inland to be married in this beautiful setting and church.

After staying about an hour, I reversed my route and made my way back to the station, had some lunch and caught the train home. I enjoyed having the opportunity to, in a sense, travel back in time and enjoy a setting very much the same that my 5th great-grandfather and grandmother had experienced.

Proving Our Swiss Heritage

When Joanne and I traveled to Switzerland in 2003 we had a marvelous time and I was totally consumed with visiting the castle where Ritschharts/Ritschards had been the bailiffs for three generations, meeting Beatrice whom I believed to be a distant relative, and seeing the huge plaque in Hilterfingen Church with the Family Crests of eight Ritschhart families who had contributed to donating the plaque. While I had made arrangements for Beatrice to meet us and show us around, I hadn't pushed hard enough to meet with other family members in the area. I had suggested this to Beatrice and hoped she would take the lead; but I should have allowed another day for our visit and scheduled visits with other Ritschards.

Another aspect of our Swiss visit that I overlooked didn't occur to me until we had been home around 6 years. As I learned more about DNA and its use in identifying family relationships, it dawned upon me that I might be able to use it to prove a family relationship with Beatrice and the Ritschards still in Hilterfingen and Oberhofen, from whence Christian Ritschard and his wife, Magdalena, and their children emigrated in 1750.

I was by no means an expert in DNA; but had learned enough to know that I was going to have to find a male Ritschard who would agree to provide a DNA sample. The Y chromosome is passed totally within the males—from father to son to grandson, etc. Because the surname never changes (or rarely changes) it is easier to trace the lineage. On the other hand, the X chromosome is passed from mother to son and daughter; but is only passed on by the daughter. This is much more difficult to trace over several generations because the women marry and their names change. So, I decided if we were going to prove anything, I needed to see if Beatrice could locate a male relative with the Ritschard surname, who would agree to take the test.

Since there was a fee of over $100 for processing the DNA, I decided that if I offered to pay for the test, I would increase the chance of getting a volunteer to come forward. Beatrice was a Ritschard through her mother's side of the family, so it would have to be one of her mother's brothers, her maternal grandfather, one of his brothers or a male offspring on any of those.

I sent an e-mail to Beatrice explaining all of this and asked if she could find me a volunteer. Within a couple weeks I received a positive reply from her that she had a cousin Ulrich Ritschard, the son of her mother's brother. Practically the same day I put the test kit in the mail to Ulrich. There are several different levels of DNA tests: 12-marker, 25-marker, 37- and 67-marker were the most common. As the number of markers tested increases, the more refined the testing. Thus, the 67 marker test provides a higher degree of assured relationship than a 12-marker test. However, because Ritschard/Ritchhart is a fairly uncommon surname the higher marker tests aren't quite so important to prove relationships. If the surname were Jones, Johnson or Smith; one would definitely want to use the 67-marker test. I also did it for economics, as the 25- and 37-marker tests were in the $200 range. Ironically, as I write this a year later, they no longer give the 12- or 25-marker tests because the 37-marker is now $109.

I eagerly awaited the news from Ulrich that he had performed the cheek swab and returned the samples to the testing lab in the enclosed pre-addressed envelope. About three weeks after mailing him the packet I received an e-mail that the package had been returned to the testing lab. Now I had to patiently wait for about a month for the lab processing and to get the results. Since I had paid for the test, Family Tree DNA would provide the results to both Ulrich and me. In about three weeks I received initial results via e-mail. The certificate and official results arrived in the mail about a week later. At first I was disappointed in the results, as it revealed only an 11 out of 12 marker match. I was expecting a perfect 12 for 12 match of markers. The results arrived in May 2009 and the Southern California Genealogy Society Annual Jamboree was in mid-June in Burbank. I had planned to attend and knew that Family Tree DNA was usually one of the vendors in attendance in the Exhibit Hall. Additionally, their president, Bennett Greenspan, normally gave two or three presentations during the two and a half day conference.

During one of the breaks I was fortunately enough to corner Bennett at his display booth. I explained my concern and he immediately went into his database on his laptop computer and looked at the specifics of my test and Ulrich's test. He explained that because the one marker that was different in our tests in more inclined to mutate over time and because we were both from such a very rare haplogroup—I could be assured we were related!

An interesting sidelight to the story relates to the fact that I later learned that Ulrich was a senior executive with United Bank of Switzerland (UBS) responsible for their operations in the Middle East. Thus, while it was the proper tactic for me to offer to pay for the DNA test; he could well have afforded to pay for the test!

Ulrich Ritschard

Ironically, later that year in November, Ulrich and a friend stopped in San Diego and had lunch with us. They had been on a cruise through the Panama Canal and the tour ended here. They were driving up to Las Vegas for a few days before flying back to Switzerland.

I used the term haplogroup, which requires some explaining if you are not DNA savvy. Without getting too technical (even if I could) a haplogroup can be thought of as major branches on the family tree of Homo sapiens. These branches characterize the early migrations of population groups. Therefore, haplogroups are usually associated with a geographic region. Haplogroup G, to which both Ulrich and I belong, is the most rare of all haplogroups; thus the fact we both come from a very rare haplogroup and that the one marker that differs in our two dna tests is prone to mutate—led the President of Family Tree DNA to state that "you two are definitely related." I asked him if it would help to do a 37-marker test on Ulrich (my earlier test was a 37-marker test) and he said, "No, the 11 out of 12 marker match is sufficient proof of your relationship."

Interestingly, the oldest skeletons confirmed by ancient DNA testing as carrying haplogroup G date only from the 7th century and were found in present-day Bavaria, Germany.

As time goes on, hopefully Ulrich and I will learn of more and more Ritchharts or Ritschards whose DNA matches ours.

The Ritchhart Family

Christian and his family settled in Reading, Burks County, Pennsylvania in 1750. As discussed earlier, this was probably because friends and/or relatives had come there earlier and sent encouraging word back about the area. Also William Penn had been spreading the word throughout England and other parts of Europe encouraging people to emigrate to America and settle in Pennsylvania. They remained in that area until around 1768 or 1770 when they set upon a migration that they and their descendants would continue for another 170 years. This migration followed the routes of transportation that had been developed or were developing in conjunction with the westward move of the population.

They first moved to the Shenandoah Valley, likely following river routes. They settled there near Harrisonburg, in what is now Rockingham County, and remained until around 1797. We must remember these were turbulent times with the Revolutionary War spanning the period of 1776 to 1779. Thus, they were living in Virginia throughout the formulative years of America!

Again following the waterways, they moved on to Ohio and settled on the Scioto River at the mouth of Deer Creek. *The History of Ross and Highland Counties Ohio* indicates their move was by flat boat, down the Ohio River to where Portsmouth now stands, then heading up the Scioto to the mouth of Deer Creek. Apparently they arrived there on October 10, 1797.

The Ritchharts established some very permanent roots in Ohio. In fact, part of the land that was originally purchased in 1797 is still in the hands of Ritchharts at this time (2010). Additionally, there are numerous Ritchharts currently living in and around Chillicothe, Ross County, Ohio. When Joanne and I came through there in 1999, we stopped and visited the current farm that is a part of the land originally purchased in 1797, and visited with several Ritchharts.

Downtown Chillicothe

Around 1829, Polly Ritchhart moved to Hamilton County, Indiana following the death of her husband, John. Among the children accompanying her was Andrew. It is likely that this

Original Ritchhart Farm House

move of little under 200 miles was made by waterway or by wagon. The family remained in Noblesville, Indiana until around 1880 when Andrew's oldest son Wesley moved to Jasper County, Missouri. Again, we are not certain how the move was made; but it was probably by wagon. The transcontinental railroad had been completed but didn't go through the Jasper

Wesley and Mary Ritchhart

County, Missouri area. It was here in Carthage, Missouri that my father was born to Wesley and Mary's son, Alonzo, and his wife, Grace. We also stopped and visited Ritchharts in Carthage, Missouri where a fairly large contingent of Ritchharts still reside. Alonzo and Grace had moved to Colorado in 1901 by train; but they moved back to Carthage around late 1908–early 1909. My dad was born in 1910. They then moved back to La Junta, Colorado near where I was later born in 1937.

To complete the Ritchhart's migration all the way to the west coast, Alonzo's brothers Orville and Sanford moved to California around 1915. Thus, it took about 165 years from the time Christian Ritschard settled in Pennsylvania, until Orville and Sanford Ritchhart settled in California. Following are the approximate durations in the various states as the generations moved westward Pennsylvania—20 years, Virginia—27 years, Ohio—32 years, Indiana—51 years, Missouri—21 years. Thus, the average time between moves was about 27 years or slightly more than one generation.

Orville Ritchhart

It appears that the Ritchharts were predominantly farmers until my father's era. Although they were raised on a homestead, neither my father nor any of his brothers became farmers nor did the two sisters marry farmers. None of the Ritchhart cousins whom I know of were farmers. However, back in Chillicothe, Ohio where we visited Ritchharts, many of them are still farming. Others we met were in the sheriff's department and teachers.

The Ritchhart families, not unlike most of their peer families, were large. Starting with my grandfather, Alonzo, and going back four more generations; they averaged about 8 children per family. Because the farmers always wanted to have lots of boys to help on the farm, the Ritchharts were quite fortunate. Over those five generations two thirds (26) of the children were boys. My family was also two boys and a girl; but it ended there. My siblings and I have five girls and two boys and my three girls have six girls and two boys. Perhaps the good lord knew that we weren't farmers anymore so boys weren't as necessary! Needless to say, I am quite happy with the way it all turned out.

The last five generations of Ritchharts starting with my grandfather were very hearty, with an average lifespan of 74 years. Quite remarkable for those days. In fact, Alonzo, his father and grandfather had an average lifespan of 83 years—truly amazing considering their lives spanned the period 1818 to 1959. In 1900 life expectancy was 30 years, in 1985 it was 62 years and even today is just 83.

ALONZO RITCHHART—MY PATERNAL GRANDFATHER

Clifford Ritchhart's family history listed his father's name as Alonzo Francis vice Frank. Interestingly, Alonzo and Grace had a child who died in infancy whose name was listed on his headstone as Frances (actual name Adell Frances). Some sources, including Alonzo's obituary, listed his birthdate as November 5, 1867, but his father's Civil War pension and a journal kept by Michael Wagner (his grandfather on his mother's side) show it as Nov 3.

Alonzo Ritchhart

Alonzo moved to Colorado with the Bush family. Shortly after that they were married in La Junta. They moved back to Carthage in late 1908–early 1909, when Clifford was about five. Paul was born in May 1908 in La Junta, thus the reason I say it must have been late 1908. They only stayed about two years and then moved back to La Junta. This was probably in 1911, as my dad was born in Carthage in Nov 1910, and I imagine they would have waited a few months before traveling across country with a new baby.

After moving back to La Junta they homesteaded southeast of La Junta. After homesteading about three years, they sold the property and moved back into town. It is interesting, however, that the land patent in Bent County was dated 1919. I am speculating they didn't actually file for the patent until they were getting ready to sell the property. They lived there until Grandma died. Grandpa then went to California to live with his daughter Lillian, in Modesto, until he passed away. However, he come back once to visit because I recall going to a football game with my dad and he when my brother Dean was playing for Las Animas and I was in college. That would probably have been in the fall of 1955.

I recall my grandfather at the age of about 78 (when I was about 8) as being a very stern old German. He would laugh occasionally, but I don't think he was particularly tolerant of young kids in his older age. He was hard of hearing and would sit next to the radio to listen to the news with his ear up very close to the speaker and his hand behind his ear acting like a reflector. A young boy we played with when we visited lived directly across the street and was always scared to death of our grandpa. He never wanted to play in our yard, thus, we always played at his house; which was great because he had lots of toys—a big treat for us.

To supplement his income Grandpa had a single coin operated gas pump on the back portion of the property for several years. There was a bell to ring if a customer needed help. My brother and I could never resist ringing the bell which annoyed my grandpa because he would come out, expecting to see a customer. We knew we shouldn't ring the bell; but it was always too big a temptation for 5 and 8 year olds!

We liked going to visit because the La Junta Creamery, where they made and sold ice cream, was next door. We would always pester mom and dad until they gave us five cents to get an ice cream cone. That didn't usually come until we had gotten the "We're not made of money and it doesn't grow on trees" lecture. Then came the big decision as to which flavor. I recall lemon and banana as being my favorites.

Grandpa would usually walk down to the park in the middle of town every morning to sit on the bench and chat with his "old cronies," who also congregated there each day. It was only about a two block walk. As I recall, he would be there an hour or two and then come on back home for lunch. He had a cane, which had white and black on it to signify a blind person or person with poor sight. Grandpa always used a straight edge razor to shave and would hone it with a leather strap. He also had a harmonica, which my brother and I always liked to play with. I assumed grandpa played it, but don't remember ever hearing him play.

I don't think my grandparents ever had a car. They had horse and buggys when they first moved to La Junta and while on the homestead, but I don't think they ever had a car when they moved into town.

We didn't spend a lot of time with Grandma and Grandpa Ritchhart because we didn't live in La Junta. We lived in California and Oklahoma during my 1st and 2nd grade years, my folks divorced near the end of my 3rd grade year, and grandma died when I was 15. We lived in La Junta part of my 4th and 5th grade years after my folks separated and Dean and I did see them some when my dad would pick us up and take us to their home.

DELBERT BUSH RITCHHART—MY FATHER

To the best of my knowledge my father was the first Ritchhart in his line of the family to attend college. He and his brother Paul "Dutch" were outstanding football players in high school. Dutch was two years ahead of my dad in school; but he never went on to college. I am not sure why he didn't; but I learned from my cousin Paul Allen, Dutch's son, that his dad always had a bit of resentment about his younger brother getting to go to college while he didn't. I am almost certain that the decision wasn't made by Grandma and Grandpa Ritchhart, because they didn't have the money to send them to school. My dad went on a football and baseball scholarship and worked his way through. In fact he worked for two years after graduation from high school before going to college. He might have been given a little money by grandma and grandpa; but I doubt that it was much. I think it was a combination of my dad getting a scholarship and

Delbert Bush Ritchhart

working for two years to save money that got him into college I don't have a lot to base this on; but I think my dad was probably also a better student — which could also have been a factor in getting a scholarship. Very recently (2010), I ran across a very surprising bit of information about my father. I didn't have a copy of his birth certificate, so I sent to the state of Missouri to get a copy. A few weeks later I received this letter in the mail, opened it and didn't recognize the information and set it aside; thinking possibly it was junk mail or sent in error. Later I read through it again more carefully and realized it was my dad's birth certificate that I had ordered. His name is listed as Delmar Bush Ritchhart. I have never in my life heard the name Delmar associated with my dad, or anyone else in the family. I speculate that one of two things happened. Either he was given the name Delmar and the family and relatives later decided they didn't like it and Delbert was better, or it was a mistake. The Doctor heard Delmar and that is what he wrote on the certificate. In either case, they probably wouldn't have bothered to get the certificate changed.

My dad was the fourth of five children and I am sure he benefited from that. Clifford was the oldest and it fell upon him to be the "man of the family" when Grandpa wasn't there — which was frequently. Clifford, who was seven years older than my dad, wrote an account of his life growing up and it related his having had a rough life as a young man. He could only attend school if he wasn't needed to work on the farm, thus, his education was very much neglected. However, by the time my dad was in school, his parents had left the farm and moved into town. Therefore, his education progressed normally. That might have been why he was a better student, as I am sure that Paul's education was also impacted by having to work on the farm. I recall my dad telling me about working in a restaurant in Boulder throughout his college days. The owner was a supporter of Colorado University athletics and allowed my dad to work his schedule around classes and his football and baseball practices and games. When I was going to school in Boulder my dad took me to the restaurant and it was still owned by the same family. Ironically they moved the restaurant up "on the hill" next to the campus while I was in school. I have racked my brain but can't remember the name of the restaurant. The restaurant name was the family's last name.

My dad majored in education, studying to be a coach. He was selected to the All-Conference football team his junior and senior years — playing guard one year and end the other. He was drafted by the Detroit Lions and played for them in 1936 and 1937 as a center on offense and linebacker on defense. One of his major accomplishments his rookie year was intercepting a pass against the New York Giants and running it back 92 yards for a touchdown. When he left school in 1936 he was still a few credits short of getting his degree. He came back the following summer and completed his course work for his degree.

His pay with Detroit was $100 per game, which was good money in those days; but nothing comparatively to the types of salaries NFL players get today.

I am not sure whether he left the Lions because they didn't ask him back or he could make better money teaching; but he went into teaching and coaching in 1938. His first job was in Fruita, Colorado near Grand Junction. The following year he moved to another coaching job in Lamar, Colorado just a few miles from the nearby towns where he and my mother grew up.

The war then interrupted and he went into the Navy under the Navy V-5 program. He was a graduate of the program that produced what was commonly referred to as "90-day wonders." That was because they were commissioned as an officer after only 90 days of training! He was assigned to St. Mary's Pre-flight Training School as an instructor. The Navy placed heavy emphasis on physical fitness training for their aviators and my dad's background made him a perfect fit as an instructor. After little over a year there he was reassigned to Cordell, Oklahoma where the Navy had another base. That tour was cut short when WW II ended and he was released from the Navy.

I believe it was while he was in the Navy that my father began drinking heavily, a problem that would plague him the remainder of his life.

My dad always made sure that my brother, Dean, and I had athletic gear—whether it was footballs and basketballs or baseball gloves and balls. The neighborhood kids always wanted us to come out and play because we had all the sports equipment.

Shortly after leaving the Navy my dad got a job as an athletic director for the Veterans Hospital at Ft. Lyon, Colorado—just outside my mom's home town. Not long after that he and my mother separated—my dad's drinking being the problem. He moved into a boarding house, continued working at Ft. Lyon and we would still see him on a regular basis. At one time my mother and father got back together; but it only lasted a few weeks. His drinking continued to get worse and he lost a couple jobs until he finally hit bottom my junior year in High school.

I was playing baseball in Garden City, Kansas—having been recruited, along with about four other players from outside the Kansas area. I hadn't seen my dad for about a year and had no idea where he was. One Sunday I received a call at the boarding house where I was staying and it was from him. He asked me to come down and see him at a hotel in Garden City where he was staying.

I went down to see him and it was one of the saddest and most shocking times of my life. He looked like a bum. He was working on the railroad as a laborer repairing tracks. They were working in the vicinity and somehow he found out where I was, He had lost a finger in an accident on the railroad—probably because he was drunk. A couple of the players I roomed with had driven me to the hotel and I was totally embarrassed to admit this was my father.

I had a chance to talk privately with him and can't remember exactly what I said; but I am sure he knew I was very disappointed in him and the depths to which he had sunk. I think it must have had a big impact on him because within a year he had sobered up and gotten a job back in Colorado He attended most of my football, basketball and baseball games my Senior Year and seemed on the road to recovery. Throughout my college years he lived in Denver, where he had gotten a job as the Youth Activities Director at Lowry Air Force Base. He came to see me almost every weekend and regularly provided me with some funds to help out with my school expenses.

He prided himself upon regularly attending AA meetings and having been sober for a couple years. He remained sober for over 15 years. Unfortunately, however, he resumed drinking and this led to his taking his own life at the age of 71.

A few years earlier he had been drinking and came home one night only to fall asleep in his car. It was a very cold winter night. Both feet got frostbite and he had to have part of one foot amputated and the other leg had to be amputated at the knee. Although he had a prosthesis for the amputated leg and could walk, the wounds on the other foot wouldn't heal and he was in constant pain. This let to further drinking and eventually to his taking his own life one night alone in his room.

I think he always meant well and he tried hard to overcome his alcoholism; but in the end it ended his life early.

I always had a hard time dealing with his alcoholism because I couldn't understand why an educated person would knowingly do that to himself. It wasn't until years later when I came to realize that it is a disease and not, as I thought, a character weakness.

My dad wasn't a demonstrative person; but I know that he loved me and was proud of my accomplishments. Despite his alcoholism and the financial and emotional problems his divorce from my mother caused our family—he tried to be a good father and I loved him for that.

Preface

The following article "Beginnings" was written by my Uncle Clifford. It relates some information regarding what he was told about the family history; but, most importantly, it chronicles his life growing up in Colorado. He was the oldest of six children, one of whom died as an infant. When his parents (my grandparents) homesteaded South of La Junta, he had to assume a lot of responsibility at a very early age. During the winter months he was the "man of the house" as his dad usually stayed in town working other jobs to support the family, as not much farming could be done in the winter.

Some of Clifford's facts about the family's early history do not agree with the later research that I have conducted. However, all genealogists learn that, while passed down family history can be extremely helpful, it sometimes has errors. Considering the extensive research resources we now have at our disposal, as opposed to his times, the information is surprisingly good and very helpful.

I am deeply indebted to my two cousins, Ken and Eugene Ritchhart, for giving me permission to publish their dad's writings. Ken gave me a copy of "Beginnings" several years ago during a visit to their home in Indianapolis. It provides a fascinating insight into what life was like in the early 1900s, especially as a homesteader.

Beginnings

by Samuel Clifford Ritchhart

As far back as we can trace the Ritchhart name we find an ancestor named Christian Ritchhart. He came to this country by way of Switzerland from Germany. His family settled in Pennsylvania. He was quite wealthy and went back several times and brought other immigrants to this country. Finally he was arrested, imprisoned, and his wealth confiscated.

My grandfather was Wesley Ritchhart, son of Andy and Mary Booth Ritchhart. He married Mary S. Wagner, whose parents were Michael Wagner and Harriet Goldman Wagner. Wesley Ritchhart enlisted in the Civil War at the age of 19 in Noblesville, Indiana. He was in the Calvary where he was trained to be a veterinarian. He served in four major battles including Sherman's famous march to the sea. Veterinary work became his life's profession although he met with much opposition from men who were trained in veterinary schools.

Samuel Clifford Ritchhart
(Photo courtesy of Kenneth Ritchhart)

After being discharged from the service he returned to Noblesville and was married to Mary S. Wagner December 20, 1866. They lived for a time in Noblesville where their nine sons were born, two of them dying in infancy.

Those who survived were: Alonzo Francis (my father), Alvin, Frank, Kurt, Orville, Sanford, and Harry. When my father was a young man, in the early 1880s, the family moved to Carthage, Missouri. Here he met my mother, Grace Bush.

Mother graduated from high school in Carthage. Some of her friends were the Hooker girls who were cousins of the Minklers. She often attended the Church of God with the Hooker girls, although her family were Methodists.

Grandpa Bush was in poor health with an asthmatic condition and the climate in Missouri made this condition worse. The family of children were nearly grown and they decided to move to Colorado where many people went for this health problem as well as tuberculosis. There were many tuberculosis sanatoriums in Colorado at this time, and people came from all over the country because the Colorado climate was good for these ailments. The children in the Bush family were: Adel, who married Holmes Simonton, Grace, my mother, Bert and Leslie. Holmes Simonton was much older than Adel and he operated a store and was in charge of the Post Office in La Junta where the Bush family settled.

The Bush family rented railroad cars to move their household goods, animals, and machinery. Railroads were the primary mode of travel in those days. There was no other way unless you went over land in a covered wagon. After arriving in La Junta the family bought a house near town, on Harriet Ave. Bert and Les did team work, dray work and general hauling to support the family. The move did not prove successful as far as grandpa was concerned. Before he died he gave me his billfold with twelve dollars in it.

Alonzo Ritchhart moved along with the Bush family to help them and also because he was interested in Grace. After keeping company for some time they were married January 1, 1902 and began living on what was known as the Greenlee ranch where I was born May 31, 1903.

This ranch was northwest of La Junta. Dad worked as a cattle feeder. Later Mother and Dad bought a home in the east part of town and moved there. It was while living here that Dad was employed driving a beer wagon with two big black horses. This was long before the days of Prohibition. It was while living here that my sister Lillian, two and one-half years younger than I, was born. When she was old enough she and I began attending the Methodist Sunday School. One Sunday morning we got lost and couldn't find the church. I saw a man and asked him the way to the church. I introduced myself: "I am Clifford Ritchhart and this is my little sister Lillian." A few days later Dad was in the bank and a man asked him if he had two children and related the story.

When I was about five, my parents decided to move back to Carthage. Dad sold our home to Mr. Klein who had a grocery store across the street from where we lived. Many years later Mr. Klein's son Henry became mayor of La Junta.

Dad became employed on Colonel Phelps' ranch north of Carthage. We lived for a short time in a small portion of the large ranch house. Here I started to school in a one room white school house. All eight grades were taught here. Later we moved into a smaller house because the work in the large house was too much for mother; also, Paul Wesley (Dutch) was born about this time. Mother also developed some heart trouble. There were several employee houses on this ranch. One of them was empty and wheat was stored in it. Lillian and I had lots of fun one day moving the wheat all over the house. Needless to say we got into trouble for our efforts. It wasn't nearly as much fun putting it all back.

After living in Missouri for about a year Mother and we children made a trip back to La Junta to visit Mother's family. Uncle Bert said Uncle Les had a contract to supply sand and gravel for a large irrigation project southeast of La Junta. They had several men working for them with their teams and wagons since it was too big of a job for the two of them. Of course I would go with them. One morning Uncle Les had to see the dentist. He told me to take his team and go along with the rest of the men and he would catch up with us along the way. We were getting the gravel from the river bed. I drove the team and wagon into the gravel pit just as big as anyone else. Then I grabbed a shovel and started trying to shovel sand in the wagon box. I don't remember just how much sand I managed to get into the wagon. I'm sure it wasn't much. When the men had their wagons loaded they all came over and finished loading my wagon. We had pulled out of the river bottom and were well on our way when Uncle Les caught up with us. The weather was quite cold and we were all walking along side our wagons. My team was crowding the wagon ahead and the wagon tongue bumped the dump boards and caused sand to sift out of the wagon. I jumped up on the brake beam of the wagon to get the lines in order to hold my team back. My foot slipped off the brake beam. I grabbed the side of the wagon bed but couldn't hold on and fell with my feet and body under the wagon. The wheel, which was about three and one-half inches wide, ran over me between my hip bones and my ribs. This put me out of circulation for quite a while. Uncle Les took his sheep-skin coat and wrapped me in it and laid me on the load of sand until we could get to our destination. The men let him unload first, then he took out across country for grandma's house where mother was. I was in bed a few days and had no permanent damage. This was my first close brush with death. Soon after this we returned to Carthage.

It wasn't long until Dad became disenchanted with his work on the Colonel Phelps ranch and he rented the Berry place. The owner was a relative of R.L.Berry, a pioneer Church of God minister. This was a nice place—only about a half mile from the river where I liked to fish. I wasn't supposed to go down to the river alone but one day I did. It was a happy and proud time for me—I caught a catfish that was at least eighteen inches long. I draped it over my shoulder and took it home. We all enjoyed a good mess of fish.

I had a mile and a half to walk to school, however, this was a larger school but still only one room with all eight grades. Sometimes the older boys gave the teacher a bad time. She always seemed to be able to keep things under control. One day a young man got the whipping of his life—the teacher would not stand for his foolishness. When the weather was snowy and bad Dad would hitch up the old bay mare (our buggy horse) to a sleigh and take me to school. A real treat this was. It was something special and lots of fun.

During the summer I would plow, driving three horses to a riding plow which Dad had hitched up, or plow corn with one horse hitched to a double shovel. This I disliked as the corn was too tall to plow with a cultivator. It was hot, dusty and dirty.

While we were living on the Berry farm I had another close encounter with death. Dad was short of horses that were necessary to get the work done. His brother, Uncle Alvin, had more horses than he needed so he offered to let Dad use a mule he wasn't using and said Dad could keep him as long as he needed him. He was a mean critter. He and Dad had a few encounters, but Dad always came out the victor.

I went with Dad when he went to get the mule. Uncle Alvin did not use him because he was so mean. They kept him tied in the barn and carried water to him instead of letting him out to water. We had taken a wagon with two horses. Dad unhitched one of the horses and put the mule in her place. Dad wouldn't let me get back in the wagon until he saw how the mule was going to behave. He had run off with one of my cousins and wrecked things. I walked and led the other horse until Dad was sure everything was alright.

Dad had used the mule several times. One day he went into the stall to harness the mule and he tried to put Dad out of the stall. Dad had put the harness over his back when he started kicking. Dad had to get out of the stall. He reached up on the wall and took down the pole strap. A pole strap is a long heavy broad strap which hangs from the horse collar and goes between the horses two front legs under the belly band. It has a large ring which the britchen strap snaps into and the other end has a loop which goes over the end of the neck yoke. This is used so the horses can hold back the wagon. During plowing it is not used. Dad used this to whip the mule and Dad gave him the whipping of his life. In the fracas the harness fell off the mule and under his feet. Dad whipped him until he could go into the stall and pick up the harness, straighten it out and put it back on the mule.

Dad was pretty well caught up and it was thrashing time. He was helping a neighbor. He had told me to put the horses in the barn at noon and feed them, tie the horses, but not to bother about the mule. I wasn't very familiar with him although I had worked him on the riding plow. I put the grain in the grain boxes, led the horses into the barn and tied them. Then I decided I should tie the mule rather than leave him loose. He was in a single stall. I went to put the halter on him and turned to go out when he turned and struck me in the mouth with his left foot. I fell cross way in the stall, between his front and rear feet. Of course this knocked me out. The mule continued stomping and kicking. The other children heard the commotion and saw my plight and called mother. She was able to reach under the partition and pull me out from under the mule from the other stall which was empty. She carried me to the house and called the country doctor. He stitched up my chin, but I had lost my three front teeth. I was without them until I was about fourteen. These were very unhappy years for me. All through school the kids thought it was funny and called me "snaggle tooth." My worst time was after we moved back to Colorado and Dad was farming north-east of La Junta near Bent's old fort. I don't know what Uncle Alvin did with the mule after we sold out and left.

When we lived on the Berry place I always went to Sunday School in the schoolhouse where I went to school. One Sunday morning as I was going out the gate to go to Sunday school, my cousin Lester came riding in on his burro to spend the day with me. They lived around five or six miles south of us. I asked Lester to go to Sunday School with me but he refused. I told him that I would see him when I got back. When I returned I was in a hurry and as I came through the yard gate I snagged one of my pant legs. Boys at that time did not wear long pants—they wore knickers. Well, as might be expected I was in trouble. First for not staying home and spending the day with Lester, whom I liked very much and we were about the same age, second because I tore my trousers. We did spend a very pleasant afternoon and in the evening he got on his burro and went home.

My parents were Methodists. Dad used to sing in the choir. He had a beautiful tenor voice. The story is told of a little boy who was asked what his dad did. He answered, "Well, he's a Christian but he doesn't work at it very much." Dad seldom went to church and objected to my going into the ministry. I really feel that it was for this purpose that I was born. I always had a lot of respect for the church and attended when I could. I do not remember whether this happened before I went to the ranch or not, but one Sunday just before Easter I went forward and joined the Methodist church. I don't know just what I expected but I had some standards I felt a Christian should live by. I soon became disenchanted with the way the kids in my Sunday School class lived. They didn't meet my expectations so I quit. Some time later Dr. Bulgin, a nationally known evangelist, was holding a tabernacle meeting in La Junta. I went forward again but again didn't receive much help. This turned me pretty much against the church until later.

I was about seven years old when my parents decided to sell out and move back to La Junta. There Dad and Uncle Les farmed together southwest of La Junta and north of old Fort Bent. Here we had quite a long distance to walk to school. It was Dutch's first year of school. Again it was a white frame school with all eight grades. It seemed that none of us kids liked the teacher and we sought ways to get rid of her, but none of them seemed to work. In fact, some of them backfired and we nearly got in trouble.

The farming was all done with horse power, however; someone had a big tractor that Dad and Uncle Les hired to plow their sugar beet ground. This tractor was very crude compared to those used now. They planted about two hundred acres of beets and two hundred acres of hay. Four hundred acres was a lot of ground to farm with horses. Dad had to buy horses, cows, and farm equipment and this required quite an outlay of money. They were doing quite well: the beet and hay crops were good. It was while here that they decided to go south and look for homestead land. This was probably a big mistake for all involved in this project, for no one of them stayed any longer than it took to get a deed to the land.

On this farm we lived in a large square two story house which was a good half mile off the highway which at that time was the most traveled road from La Junta to Las Animas and on east. There was also a large two story square house on the highway. Both houses were just alike and had been built by the same person. There was a boy living in the house on the highway about my age. We spent quite a bit of time together. We would get water from the irrigation ditch and ditch it into a prairie dog town and drown out the prairie dogs. They were everywhere and were a nuisance. The folks would not let me keep any of these pests around so my friend would take them home with him. Their yard became a regular prairie dog town. They became quite domesticated and made pretty good watch dogs. When any one would come on the place they would sit beside their hole on their hind legs and bark like you would never believe.

Farming at that time required quite a few horses and also some hired help. Dad had one hired man and Uncle Les had one. These were on a regular basis. During beet hauling more help was required.

Dad's man was a Bohemian. I don't remember his name now but Dad called him the Bohunk. He was rather tall and slender and a pretty nice sort of a guy. We had a little grey mare we called Doll. She was a pretty nice horse but not too hefty for heavy work. She was a nice saddle horse, at least most of the time. One day the Bohunk saddled her up for some reason. He was a pretty good rider but this time Doll wasn't in the mood to be ridden—she threw him in a pile. As he left the saddle the front of his britches caught on the saddle horn (pants did not have zippers then but buttons), and ripped one leg of his pants from the top to the bottom. It was funny but not to him. Boy was he mad and embarrassed. His face was red as a red beet and his eyes big and flashing with rage. He would have killed the horse if he thought he dared. He got up and got back on her and rode her. Dad took her with us when we moved to the homestead.

I mentioned earlier about living on a farm near old Fort Bent. In the early days this was a trading post when Indians were still around. The fort was owned and operated by the Bents. They had three forts out west. There was another one west of Lamar, Colorado on the bank of the Arkansas River which was at one time the boundary between Mexico and the United States. Mexico owned the land south of the river. This fort would care for a wagon train and a little farther west was Fort Lyons. A cavalry unit was stationed there. Colonel Chivington was in charge of this unit, he signed the peace treaty with the Indians at Fort Bent and later Chivington Colorado was named for him. The third fort of the Bents was near the foothills of the mountains, which also was a trading post.

While we were living at Lamar I got acquainted with Colorado Senator Hamm from Las Animas. We had several visits about "the good old days" in the Arkansas Valley. He was acquainted with the two brothers, Englishmen, who owned the J.J. Ranch where I had worked as a young man. Their name was Jones and Jones. They later sold the ranch to Tate and Hardy. Hardy later sold his part to Tom Tate who owned the ranch when I was working there. The two Jones boys were instrumental in getting the Bent County courthouse in Las Animas. Dad's homestead was mostly in Bent County, however, 80 acres were in Las Animas county and Trinidad is the county seat.

The Old Bent's Fort near where Dad farmed—about seven miles east of La Junta—has in recent years been completely rebuilt and is now a very nice historical place to visit. We came by there just before the official opening and went through it. They have many interesting things to see.

There are several old English Land Grants in the abstract office in Lamar and I had the privilege of seeing them when we pastored the church in Lamar. I also saw the remains of the old Bent's Fort near there. The outline of the entire fort is still there. I have often wondered why this fort was not restored instead of the one near La Junta. It is of more historical interest than the other one and ought to be restored.

HOMESTEADING

It was while we were living north and east of La Junta, near Bent's Fort, that the folks got the idea of homesteading on some government land that was available for that purpose. I do not know whose idea it was nor just all the people included, but they all got together and decided they would meet at Las Animas on a certain day. Those in the group that I know were: Mother and Dad, Uncle Les and his family (I mentioned earlier that Uncle Les and Dad were farming together), Uncle Bert and his family, the Prunty family who were related to Uncle Les's wife. Oscar Olson from La Junta homesteaded about the same time and I am not sure whether he was in this group or not and there could have been others. Oscar Olson was an old bachelor. After they met in Las Animas they all went south together in a small wagon train over the helium flats. This was a cattle trail from Texas to Dodge City, the rail head, where they shipped their cattle to Kansas City.

The first stop was somewhere in this area, however, the men did not find enough suitable land so they moved on. This part of the country was pretty well infested with wild animals such as wolves and coyotes. Men had been attacked by them, and this had a bearing on their moving on. As they traveled south they also moved west into Muddy Valley. The next stop where they looked for land was on a homesteader's place. His name was Bud Gant and he had a rather large pond where he permitted us to camp. Bud went with the men to look for land. There were several other homesteaders in this area whose names I do not recall. Most of the men found land joining each other. Oscar Olson joined Dad on the west, Uncle Bert joined Dad and Oscar on the north, Uncle Les joined Dad on the east and ran south of Dad's place. Prunty's land was east of Uncle Les. All the land was pretty close to Muddy Creek, which ran

Ritchhart Homestead 2010

through Les's and Dad's place and on south west through the corner of Uncle Bert's place. However, Dad and Uncle Bert were the only ones who had running water. This proved to be trouble. When it was fenced the range cattle would strip the fence to get to the water.

After staking their land they had to return to the county seat and file on the parcels of land. Each person was allowed 320 acres. Then they were given a certain amount of time (a year I think) to build a house, fence a certain amount of land and have 40 acres under cultivation and live on it for so many months out of each year for four years. These requirements must be met at certain intervals of time before you could prove upon the claim, which means, get a clear title to the land.

Dad bought a 16x16 foot frame building, took it down in sections, and hauled it to the claim on a hay wagon and reassembled it. This was our home. Dad later built a kitchen on the west. All of them built frame houses except Uncle Les. He built a stone house. He was our closest neighbor.

When we moved to the homestead mother was unable to go with us but came about a month later. My little sister Frances had been born with a poor heart and had to be close to a doctor. It was a happy day for me when mother could finally come out. Dad had taken the other small children with him when he went to get mother. I had to stay and look after the stock. It took three days to go to town, get what was needed and get back.

After we moved out there we had corrals to build to hold the livestock. We also had to build a barn. I hauled load after load of rock for the barn. In one sense of the word we had a better barn than a house. The stone was laid up with mud for mortar then to keep the rain from washing the mud from around the rocks they would point it up with mortar made from gypsum stone which was pounded into a powder, then put into a large vat and burned. It would boil like water. We would dig a trench, place the vat over the trench, then build a fire in the trench and cook the powder. It was then mixed with sand to make the mortar. This also made a good plaster inside of the home. One homesteader who moved in after we did, northeast of Dad's place, built a sod house. This makes a rather warm house.

After we got our fencing done it was time to start the spring farming. Dad had a sod plow. A sod plow had a rather flat blade and rods in place of a mole board. Dad would plow three rounds then we would drop the seed by hand real close to the land side. Then, when you would plow the next furrow the grain was primarily in a crack and with the grass upside down, it held the moisture and we had a bumper crop. Because of the sod the farmers were unable to cultivate the crop but they could harrow it until it began to get some growth. After the first year it was different. The sod was soft and mellow and could be cultivated.

The second spring on the homestead we were plowing and getting ready for planting. We were short on horse power, so we would plow then hitch the horses to the harrow and harrow the ground so it would not dry out, thus preserving the moisture. One day two burros showed up at our place. We inquired around to find out who they belonged to but no one seemed to know anything about them. Of course I tried them out for riding and they rode ok except when you would slide back on their hips and put your heels in their flanks—then could they buck. If they could throw you they would, or they would run under the fence and you were off. The fences had only two wires. One day Oscar Olson was at our place and I was telling him about the burros and he tried his skill at riding one. He was considered a pretty good rider, but he had about as much success as I did, which was not too bad but neither was it the best. Dad had two sets of single buggy harness so I proceeded to fit these harness to the burros. I found they would work so I continued to work them by hitching them to the harrow and as Dad plowed I harrowed. The burros continued to stay around and I continued to work them. We had our spring plowing and harrowing about done and ready for planting. Then one morning we went out and the burros were gone. We never saw them again and no one seemed to have seen them. Where they came from or where they went remains a mystery.

We had to haul our drinking water and what we used for the house. The stock could drink from the creek. We later dug a well and lined it with rock but the water was not good for household use. A neighbor, two miles south, had a drilled well and many of the settlers hauled water from his place for domestic use.

Dad dug a cellar beside the house for storage of good and vegetables. We always had a large garden and plenty of vegetables. We had lots of chickens, several brood sows, and usually a couple hundred little pigs to sell at weaning time for which we got about $2.00 apiece. We also had several milk cows. After Dad got things going it became necessary for him to go to La Junta and get work. He would work for the Santa Fe Railroad.

One day Dad told me to saddle old Doll and go over to one of the neighbors a few miles east and see if he would take mother and the baby Frances to town for the baby was sick. He had the only automobile in the whole country. On my way home Doll got the foolish idea that she wanted to get rid of her rider. I don't know what happened to her any more than the Bohunk did, but she took off bucking and jumping here and there. The tree cactus was everywhere. I rode for dear life. I did not want to find myself in one of these cactus bushes. She finally gave up and I rode her back to the road, got off and walked and led her for a ways. I hurt so bad I couldn't ride any more, nor could I hardly walk. She had hurt me more than any bucking horse I ever rode. That was the last time she ever bucked with me. She was the same horse I was riding later when I was lost in a snowstorm and almost froze to death.

The homesteader took Mother and Frances to La Junta. This was the last time I saw my baby sister alive. Her death hit me very hard for this was my first encounter with death. Grandpa Bush had died but I was so small that it did not affect me. Then too, Grandma Ritchhart died in Missouri but we were in Colorado so this did not affect me either. I got to know Grandma and Grandpa Ritchhart while we were in Missouri and of course when we went to town we went to their house. One thing I didn't like was their water. They had a chain pump on the porch over a cistern. The water came from the house roof and was rain and snow water filtered through a charcoal filter. To me it tasted terrible. On the farm we had good well water. In town they did not have city water as we do today.

It was on the homestead that I learned to ride and rope and handle cattle. My father and Uncle Les had quite a few cattle and when Dad or Uncle Les was gone it was my responsibility to look after them. Most of the land was open range and cattle could roam far. One afternoon

Uncle Les and his family were in town and Dad was working in town so mother told me that I had better go after the cattle. It had started to snow and we needed to get the cattle home before it stormed. We had not moved to town for the winter as we sometimes did. I saddled my horse and rode off south. I enquired about the cattle at a homestead shack I came to but the man had not seen them and advised me to forget the cattle and return home as it was getting dark and snowing harder. I had ridden this land so many times and I was sure I knew every foot of it. I turned northeast for a short distance. Suddenly I realized that nothing looked familiar. I was lost! I turned around on my horse and was going to try to follow his tracks back but the wind and heavy snow had erased them. I was well aware that others had been lost and frozen to death on these prairies. Realizing my lost condition, I dismounted, knelt in the snow and prayed, as far as I know, my first prayer, asking God to guide me home and I promised the Lord to serve him the best that I knew how. Quite some time later, with a weary horse, I reigned up at home where mother helped unsaddle my tired, weary horse and turned her loose. I was riding on Doll, the horse that had given me such a bad time earlier. Mother helped me to the house and carried in snow and rubbed it on my half frozen body. I spend about a week in bed recovering. The cattle also found their way home and to shelter. I did not forget the promise I had made to God. I have spent a lifetime trying to fulfill that promise.

The last year before the homestead was proved up I was the only one who was there much of the time. Mother and the other children had gone to town so they might go to school. Mother had had to have surgery and the expense of Frances' death made more bills than a homesteader could stand and Dad had to go to town for work. From then on Dad did not spend too much time on the homestead. At times mother was with us kids, and at other times it was just me.

In fencing the required amount of land it required that we spend considerable amounts of time in the hills cutting cedar posts. The government required the posts be a certain distance apart and not less than two strands of barbed wire. We also managed to keep a generous supply of cedar wood on hand to load up and haul to town when we would have to make a trip. We sold the posts at the coal yard. This gave the folks a little extra cash.

During the summer we had plenty of vegetables. We always had a large garden and mother canned all she could. However there were times she was in town and when winter came we were often short of food and money was scarce. Many times mother would make what she called "thickened soup." She would put a pan of milk on the stove to heat. Then take flour and make a thickening, much as you would do for gravy, only it was not nearly as thick. She would then add some butter. Then a paste like substance of flour, milk and seasoning and spoon it out in small balls in the hot milk and cook until it was done. This would be our supper. Many times this was my evening meal when I was alone. They would also buy canned salmon by the case since it was the most inexpensive food available—perhaps about 10 cents per can or less by the case.

As I said before it took three days to make a round trip to La Junta and back: one day to go, and a day to shop and let the horses rest and one day to return. If we brought back a load of freight for the store, it would take until dark, then deliver the freight the next day. I do not recall what the folks would get for bringing back a load of freight. During melon season we would take a load of melons. They would sell for about 10 cents apiece. Size didn't matter.

I had been on the homestead alone most of one summer looking after things and doing the farming. If I had not, Dad could not have proved up or gotten a title to the homestead. Dad had traded a horse, Old Fly, for a wagon load of corn to feed the hogs. So if I went any place I had to ride one of the horses I had been working. Uncle Les was quite a horse trader. He had traded for a saddle horse. One day he asked me if I would like to have this horse. He was a pretty nice horse. I told him that I had no money. He said we could work that out, and that I could have the horse for around $20.00 and that I could work it out at my convenience. There were times when I was up early, had my chores done and headed for the hills for a load of wood as Uncle Les was going to the barn to milk. I would get home before dark with my wood. You see we would never let our wood supply get low. I arrived home in time to do my chores, eat supper, then if it wasn't too late I would spend the evening with Uncle Les and Aunt Jennie. Well, I had dealt for the horse, took him home, and then Dad unexpectedly came out from town to see how things were going and if I was keeping up the work. Dad saw the strange horse in the pasture and immediately wanted to know where that horse came from. I said that it was my horse. He wanted to know where I got him. I explained the deal. He informed me in no uncertain words that I couldn't keep the horse and had to return him immediately. Then he gave Uncle Les a going over for selling me the horse and said we had too many animals to feed as it was.

One Sunday morning when we were all at the homestead the folks were going to Sunday School and church which was being held in the school house. I did not want to go with them. For some reason I wanted a horse so I could go horseback. I do not recall the reason. However Dad refused me the horse and I refused to go with them. Dad whipped me unmercifully, in fact he whipped me twice. We both refused to give in. I went to the barn and hid in the hay in the manger. As far as I can remember the folks finally went on without me.

Now, I don't want to do Dad an injustice. He is no longer here to defend himself. I have tried, with God's help, to be a better Dad to my children. I know that I have failed miserably on many points. I do love my children very much. I have not spent as much time with you as I should have. I was not able to help you as much in your education as I would have liked, but I tried to see that you had a better education than I did and each day I pray God's blessing upon each of you.

Harvesting our crop was quite crude. For the row crop Dad built what was called a sled and it was pulled by one horse. It was narrow enough to go between the rows of grain and about six feet long with a cutter blade and an arm made from a 2x4 cut down to a much smaller size on the end of the sled and this arm straddled the row of grain. As one stepped off the other stepped on and was on his way, and so it went. When this was finished and as we needed the fodder for feed we shucked the corn or topped the maize. The grain was stored and fodder was fed to the cattle.

We would also take a team and a long chain and pull out the tree cactus, haul them in and burn the stickers off and feed them to the cattle. The cattle would really go for them. We would also stack Russian thistles when they were green and tender, scattering salt in the stack as we went and the cattle ate them well. I didn't like to stack them for they were hard to handle and hard to tromp down as you stacked them. We usually had about 50 acres of Sudan grass for feed which I would cut with a scythe and rake with a hay fork. There were no thrashing machines anywhere in the country so the grain had to be thrashed by hand. We used what was called a flail. This was made from a straight pole about five feet long with a short heavier piece of wood about 18 inches. This short piece was fastened to the longer piece with a small piece of rope or a thong so as you held the long pole in your hand and as you would swing it with your arms this short piece would hit the ground and beat out the grain. When we wanted to thrash some grain we spread it out on a large tarp or piece of canvas, put the heads of grain on the canvas, take the flail and start swinging it so the short piece of wood would hit the grain and eventually you had it all beat out. Then to separate the grain from the chaff we would do this on a windy day. We would take a grain shovel or a bucket and pitch the grain into the air and the wind would carry the chaff away and the grain fell back on the canvas. Of course the corn was shelled by hand. This process was only done to get the seed to plant.

While living on the homestead I was intrigued by the round up wagons and riders from the JJ Ranch. They always made camp just east from our place. Here they had plenty of water for their horses and could replenish their water supply for the mess wagon and for drinking. This was the last water available until reached what was known as the Alkalis. This was a water hole with a lot of alkali in it and not good for animals or human consumption.

The range cattle were a menace to the homesteader, especially if the water was on the homestead land, which it often was. Especially during dry weather, many times they would break through the fence to get water and when we would chase them out they would sometimes strip a fourth of a mile of fence, which had to be repaired. The cattle were spooky to people and especially to our dog old Towser. He was a very good watch dog both for cattle and coyotes. Both were in abundance. Antelope were also in abundance for a while north and east of our place. We never killed any but they were soon killed off by homesteaders or crowded out.

Our post office was the Moffatt Post Office, some distance north of our place. We would get mail once or twice a week. The post master was also a homesteader. He had several boys and a pack of hound dogs. Their big sport was hunting and chasing coyotes, killing them, and selling the hides.

Our only grocery store was west of us. This was opened after Dad homesteaded. When it was necessary to go to La Junta we would always bring back a load of freight for the store. Where the store was known as Harbordale.

The homesteader had very little social life as we today know it. During the summer when one of the settlers went to town they would bring back a 300 pound block of ice. Neighbors from far and near would all gather for a get together and make ice cream. Everyone had all the ice cream and cake they could eat. Some would bring milk, others cake, and every one had an enjoyable time. Some would sit around and visit, others got out in Skipyard and played party games such as Scip to Ma Lou and Miller Boy. Everyone went home having had an enjoyable evening. O yes, you wonder how they got home from town with the ice? Getting ice was the last thing they bought before starting on that lone journey home. The ice was wrapped in paper, then a tarp wrapped around it, then well covered with bed blankets. You would be surprised just how little melted on that long trip home. When the weather began to get too chilly for outdoor games a family about two or three miles east of us had a piano and a couple young people. We would dress in our Sunday best, mount our horses, and ride over to our next door neighbors. It didn't matter whether you could sing or not, we all gathered around the piano to sing. They only had one song book and that was a hymnal of some kind. Therefore, the evening was spent mostly in singing hymns. Often some refreshments were served, such as a piece of cake and a glass of milk before we all returned home. This was mostly just young people. This was where I wore my first pair of long pants except for overalls.

As I said before, I was intrigued by the round up wagons that stopped close to our place. I well remember watching them at round up time come by our place and camp just east of our homestead for the night. The crew included a cook, who also drove the wagon, and eight or ten riders with twice as many horses for each rider had two horses and he changed horses at noon. Also one man who was the horse wrangler. He was responsible for looking after the horses. The horses not being ridden were turned out to graze. This was the only food they had to go on. I thought this was the life and I looked forward to the day I could be one of those riders. However, by the time I went to work for the ranch this type of rounding up cattle was virtually over. We never were away from the ranch over night.

My education while on the homestead was quite erratic. I spent very little time in school. The school house was much like the schools I had attended: a one room accommodating the children who were able to attend. Most young children were able to go. It was also the only place of worship in the country. An old homesteader whose name I do not recall did the preaching. Usually the attendance was small.

The folks had moved to town for the winter. In the fall at deer hunting time Dad wanted to go deer hunting. Dad knew I had a heavy rifle 44 caliber, so he brought a box of shells for it. I don't know just who all went but there was Uncle Bert and his son Heber who was a little younger than I, and Uncle Les, Dad and I. Dad took my gun so I was left without one. I guess it didn't make much difference, we did not get a deer. Some other hunters who were camped near our camp did. They shared a mess of meat with us. After season I went to town.

When the folks moved to town in the fall so Dad could work for the winter sometimes he would work for the railroad and sometimes at the sugar factory at Swink. In Swink we lived in a tent south of the sugar factory. Here I attended school until time to move back to the homestead in the spring and get ready for spring planting, so I started school late—after the crops were in—and left early so we could get ready to plant again. When we moved to La Junta Dad either had a place rented and had a job at the railroad or rented a house and got a job. Early in the spring it was back to the homestead. Sometimes Dad moved back with us and sometimes he didn't. Usually he didn't.

One spring we were moving back and Dad stayed in town. Uncle Bert was moving us, and Uncle Les had come to town with his hay wagon to take home a load of bailed wheat straw. Uncle Bert had our furniture and belongings in his beet wagon with a cow tied behind the wagon and a calf in uncle Les's wagon. Also, Mother and all four of us kids. We had not traveled far when it began to rain. The road got muddy and slick. We had reached what was called the divide and Uncle Les was forced to unload most of his load of straw. It began to snow. We were finally able to make it to a place called Mackmain. This was a camping place and a rather large cap rock to the north. Here we prepared to camp. Mother and the other children caught a ride back to town with the mail hack. We rustled wood, took care of the livestock the best we could and bunked in for the night. There was somewhat of a natural fire place in the cap rock. We had good shelter and dry wood. The next morning the snow was quite deep. We started out but progress was slow. Someone had to go ahead of the wagons to keep them out of the ditch. By noon we had traveled about eight miles. We stopped at a Mexican goat ranch and they let us prepare some hot food. Here we left the furniture, put four horses on a virtually empty wagon and by late that night we had made it to uncle Bert's place. Here we unloaded all we could as Uncle Les still had about two or more miles to travel before he reached home. The next day was a reasonably nice day. The sun came out but it was cold. Uncle Bert and I left to go back and get the wagon and the furniture. We each rode one of the horses. We made it back by night. I do not recall how long it was before mother and the other kids, Lillian, Dutch, and Del, were able to get home to the old cold shack.

On the south side of the farmland on the homestead was a large well or shaft and water was within about 10 feet from the top, or in other words it had about thirty feet of water in it. No one knew who put it there. This water was full of alkali, however, Dad had the big idea of some day putting in a pump and using it for irrigation. This was right beside the road and high enough that water would run in all directions on the farm land. One day one of Uncle Les's calves disappeared and he was sure that it had gotten through the fence and fell in this well. Dad and Uncle Les took 2 or 3 hay hooks and made a grab hook and began fishing around in the well. They didn't find the calf but they did find the well pretty well filled with cow hides. Cattle rustlers would find a nice looking young beef, kill and dress it out, and roll up the hide, tie it with wire and throw it in the well. Then they could take the meat to town and sell it. They could not sell the hides because they had brands of the owners. We had seen wagons stop in that area as they passed by but thought nothing of it. This well was some distance from the house, then too, there were times when no one was home, especially when we had moved to town for the winter. Uncle Les went in and filled this well with dirt and boy, was Dad ever mad, and he and Uncle Les really had it out. However, Dad finally got over it. He and Uncle Les never did get along any too well except when they were farming together after we came back to Colorado from Missouri.

It seemed that Dad and I began to grow farther and farther apart. At one time I planned to run away but changed my mind. I later left and went to work at the Fred Harvey House's dairy. The Harvey House was a large restaurant with sleeping rooms on the second floor along beside the railroad tracks in La Junta. At that time La Junta was a bustling railroad town and many passengers as well as employees of the railroad ate and slept there. After working at the dairy for a while I was offered a job as busboy in the dining room at the Harvey House. This required that I be dressed up, carry out the dirty dishes, etc. then one evening I was told that we would be waxing the dining room floor after it closed. This took all night. It had to be done by hand as there was no such thing as power tools for this purpose. I decided I didn't want any more of this so I quit. It was near the Fourth of July so I bought some fire works for the kids at home and caught a ride home. I was glad to be back home, but soon became restless. I went back to La Junta and get a job working for Art Holbrook, east of La Junta plowing beets, and working a beet puller.

When I left the homestead Dad came out from town and sold off most of his livestock. He had two young horses, halfgraythers, one was black and gray, the other a dapple grey. I bought dapple grey. I had broken the black horse to ride before I left. When I got a job on the ranch I bought the black horse, Bob, from Dad. He was one of the best grayhorses anywhere around. I later bought the grey. He had been turned loose on the range for quite some time and had become undomesticated. When the folks finally left the homestead Dad turned the gates open and let the livestock that was left run loose. They rented a house in La Junta, a two story brick house on Raton just east of the city park. They lived here for quite some time and it was here that Betty Jane was born. I was in wheat harvest in Kansas. When I returned home I found an addition to the family, a little baby sister. Dad finally bought a house on the corner of Cimarron and second street where they made their home until mother passed on.

IN BETWEEN TIMES

My grandmother Bush had remarried to a Mr. Turner and they were living in the basement apartment of the North La Junta School and doing the janitorial work for the school. It was while I was working for Art Holbrook that Grandpa Turner died. After this I stayed with Grandma Turner for a while and went to school. I was in the fifth grade and had been for several years. Because I was never able to stay in school a full year, not because of my grades, they would not pass me on to the next grade as they do now. I also worked on Saturday at a grocery store and delivered groceries with one horse and wagon, and after school during the week I worked for a man who ran a dairy a couple blocks west of the school house. I also took some of the money I earned working for Art Holbrook and had teeth put in where the mule had knocked them out. My life was pretty well mixed up at this time.

When I came back in town after leaving the homestead for good, I was passing a grocery store in La Junta and saw a sign in the window "Boy Wanted." This grocery store also had a bakery and I was hired to help there. This is where I first started to learn the bakery trade. It was fall and I worked there till harvest time in Kansas. A man came to La Junta to find help in his harvest field. I was making $6 a week and he offered me $6 a day to go with him to Kansas to work in the harvest. I talked to my boss and he told me to go so I went to Lewis, Kansas and worked for two different farmers before I came back. I had pulled some muscles in my shoulders and needed to first let them heal. About this time a carnival came to town and of course I went to the carnival. The man who was running the Ferris Wheel had just lost his helper and asked me to help him. So I put the people in and let them out of the seats. He then wanted me to go along with them. I did go to Lamar and Dodge City but when they left Dodge I left the carnival and got a job north of Dodge City on a farm helping with the thrashing. From there I went home and got a job as a carpenter's apprentice at the railroad where we built and repaired box cars. Here we were to work with an experienced journeyman but my boss put two apprentices together to work and he nearly lost his job and we did lose ours.

From here I went to work for the J J Ranch. Life on the ranch was what I had often dreamed of, however, it was not an easy life. It was much like life on the Homestead but still different by many ways. I was used to doing many things we had to do. We were expected to be able to do most anything from riding, wrangling cattle, to farming. Riding the range one had to be prepared for most anything including bad weather.

On one occasion I was caught in a severe rain storm. The darkness became intense I could not see. My horse stopped and refused to move, even when I spurred him. I got off only to find we had come upon an anchor wire for a corner post. I led him around the wire, mounted him and proceeded on my way. I soon came to a homesteader's shack with an old shed in the back. I rapped on the door and asked if I could spend the night in the shed. I had disturbed their sleep and of course they wanted to know who I was and what I wanted. I told them who I was, a rider from the JJ ranch, and then asked if I might take shelter in their shed. They told me that the shed was not fit to sleep in and for me to turn my horse loose and then I could sleep on the floor. I unsaddled my horse, put my saddle rope around his neck so I could catch him the next morning, threw my saddle on the floor for a pillow, and after they gave me some bedding I was ready to sleep for the rest of the night. In the morning they gave me breakfast of biscuits, bacon, eggs, and coffee. My horse was grazing not too far away in a draw south of the house. With the rope on him he was easy to catch. I led him back to the house, saddled him and was soon on my way.

Remnants of JJ Ranch

The owner of the ranch was Tom Tate. Most of the help were Mexicans. The only other Americans on the ranch was Tom Tate's brother's son and Everett Phoebus the ranch foreman. His wife was also Spanish. Tom Tate was a bachelor. Tom also owned a store in Higbee, which was a very small town with only a store, an implement store, dance hall, and a hotel. His brother ran the store. The hotel also was owned by Tom but Bill Lander ran it. Old Bill Eddy was the cook for the mess house and a handyman. He had a boy called Little Bill who was in every one's hair. He was a real nuisance. We always kept a horse in the corral called the rustling horse. Young Bill would take him out and when we needed him he was gone.

This cattle ranch not only did farming but they also had some sheep. They did not graze or herd the sheep but they were bought and fattened and shipped to market. This is the way hay and grain not needed for the cattle and horses was disposed of and provided a good income for the ranch.

I helped trail the last sizeable herd from the ranch to the stock yards for shipping. The stock yards at that time were south west of La Junta on the Santa Fe rail siding toward Trinidad. After arriving at the stock yards the cattle had to be brand inspected before they could be shipped. This ran into considerable amount of work. The cattle were all placed in one large pen and as the inspector checked the brand on each cow it was cut out from the rest of the cattle and let out of the pen to be placed into a separate pen. This required several pens. It also required a man on each gate so when the inspector called out a certain brand those working the gates would know which gate to open. All cattle with the brand J J were placed in one pen, these were to be shipped. Cattle with other brands were turned over to the owners, or turned back on the range. Then there were some with long hair and the brand was not clearly visible. They had to be run through the chute, the hair clipped, then the brand was visible.

We were nearly through and two of us were on the main gate when the inspector cut out a longhorn steer. We opened the gate. Then the inspector called out not to let him out. He was crowding the open gate pretty fast. When we swiftly closed the gate we caught his head and long horns in the gate, breaking his horns in the middle of his head. He backed out, but was he ready for a fight! He ran every one out of the pen. He eventually quieted down but he created a lot of excitement for a while, and was finally run through the chute. So much for that.

Tom Tate also owned a horse ranch up the Purgatory river west from the JJ ranch. This was called the I L horse ranch. This required a horse round up in which I did not participate. This required much more skill than working cattle. The horses were brought to the J J ranch to be branded, castrated, etc. Kit Carson's brother always did the castrating. He lived south of Smith Canyon. Tom sold a herd of horses and had to deliver them to the stock yards southwest of La Junta. After delivering the horses we rode into town. There had been a lot of rain for several days and the Arkansas river was flooding out of its banks. This turned out to be what is known as the Pueblo or the '21 flood. Much of Pueblo was under water, all of north La Junta was under water and much damage was done. Aunt Del, mother's sister, lived close to the river in north La Junta and their house had a lot of water in it and the furniture was ruined. I also went to see the folks. We stayed in town until quite late before starting back to the ranch which meant we had to ride after dark.

There were three of us and instead of following the main traveled road we went south on what was known as the Belue Road. This road led to the cattle ranch's southwest corner. We then swung our horses south east across the prairie to pick up the JJ road. We knew there was a barbed wire fence somewhere in this area, belonging to a homesteader. Our intention was to stay far enough north so as to avoid this fence. The night was pitch dark. I was riding a black horse, and on the right of the other two riders. We were riding in a slow lope when my horse ran into the fence on an angle. He jumped to the left and into the other rider. I felt the wire on my right chaps. My horse was cut pretty bad. I was not hurt but my chaps protected my leg and they were pretty badly torn. My pants were also some protection for me. We rode slow until we reached Higbee where we got Bert Tate (Tom's brother) out of bed to get us some Iodine from the store. When we reached the ranch we washed the blood off (it was frothing pretty bad) and applied the iodine. The next morning I caught the horse and applied creosote. He healed up real good, however the hair all came off because of the creosote. I then kept it greased good with bacon grease which I got from the boss's wife Edna. This kept the scab soft and he healed without leaving a scar.

There was lots of work to be done besides riding. They had lots of alfalfa, corn, wheat and cane to be irrigated and cared for. I helped cut and stack the hay, both alfalfa and prairie hay, also cut and stack some cane. This is another story.

We had the cane cut and raked and one day Everett (the boss) told me to take some of the Mexicans and stack the cane. We had to be through by Saturday noon as the boys wanted to go into town and get ready for the dance Saturday night at Higbee. Things were going pretty well. I had climbed on the stack to help so we could finish by noon and get the equipment to the house, when Tony drove up in the hay wagon and told Talono to take the push rake and go over to the hay field and bunch up hay for him to haul to the feed yards for the sheep. I asked him who had told him to have Talono to take out from his work. Tony said I did. I told Tolono he couldn't go as we had to finish this job. Tony began to curse me and call me all kinds of names (Whan, who had been on the stack with me, had gotten off the stack to clean up around the stack) I slid down the side of the stack and when I touched ground Whan hit me in the jaw which sent me to the ground. When I came back to my feet I had a slivered piece of 2x4 in my hand. Whan then ran and jumped in the wagon with his nephew Tony and left us to finish up and he helped Tony with his load of hay. It was needless to say I was pretty mad. We managed to get all the equipment to the house or where they were supposed to be. I put the horses in the corral and headed for the bunk house when I met Everett. He wanted to know what was wrong. I told him that I had just quit and wanted my time. He still insisted on knowing what was wrong. I then asked him who ran this outfit, him or those Mexicans. He informed me that he did and again asked what wrong. I told him. He fired them all except Talono who had stayed to help finish up and get the equipment to the house. Everett told me to go to the corrals and water the sheep I think. We had about 500 head. While I was watering the sheep Talono came to me and told me that I had better lay low for the Mexicans, who had been fired were out to get me. I passed this information on to Everett. He said not to worry, he thought we could take care of them if it came to a show down, which it never did.

Another thing that had to be done by the ranch hands was to ride what we called the bog. This meant to ride the river bank. This river was a very treacherous river because of the quicksand. Cattle would go to the river for water and often get bogged down in the quicksand and were unable to get out without help. Whoever rode the river and found a cow critter unable to get out would take his saddle rope, throw it over the head and around her neck, fasten the rope to the saddle horn and pull her out. Sometimes after we removed the rope she would refuse to get up. Usually she had worn herself out trying to get out of the sand by herself. We would take her by the tail and help her up. If we didn't help her up she would lay there and die. And if we did help her up she would very often try to turn around and fight us and fall down again, so when we tailed her up she would run, jump on our horse and drive away as she tried to chase us. This was also true of the cows that had been brought in during round up that were thin and would bear a calf in the spring. We always had to check these cows and many times we would find a cow that had delivered a calf and was too weak to get back on her feet.

We would tail her up on her feet and she would try to fight us and fall down. We would carry the calf over by our horse, lay it down, go back and tail her to her feet, and run pick up the calf and get on our horse and ride toward the corral. The cow would follow. They were placed in a pen with shelter and plenty of feed.

I was paid $30.00 per month and the pasture of my horse. For this $30.00 we had to furnish our own gear, that is saddle, rope, snaps, spurs, etc. If we broke a rope we had to replace it. I don't remember what a rope cost, not too much, but a good pair of boots cost about a month's wages. Also you furnished your own slicker (rain Coat) if you wanted one, I did not have one.

There were other things that had to be done on the ranch, and we had to be pretty good riders. When we saddled up each morning we usually had a pretty good bucking contest or rodeo. Most of the horses had to go through this process, then they were good for the rest of the day. If we were riding a horse pretty hard then we changed horses at noon. One morning I saddled my horse in a hurry as I would be gone all day. Everett told me to run the horses out of the alfalfa field into the pasture before I left. I led my horse to the gate, opened it, and mounted my horse. Before I could get set in my saddle he came apart and threw me quite hard, then ran to the corral. I caught him again, mounted him, and drove the horses into the pasture, all the while trying to gain control of his head and he trying to throw me. As long as you hold their head up they can't buck.

I had heard a lot about this horse and that no one could ride him. Everett had assigned him to me, which was a put up deal. However this was the first time he had bucked with me and the boys had been disappointed up till now. The boys got quite a kick out of this. He hadn't been ridden for quite some time. I left the ranch headed south, and I rode him hard all day, arriving back at the ranch about 9 p.m. He was still determined to be the victor. He had not forgotten that he had thrown me that morning. However, he never gave me any more trouble. We each had our own mounts. No one else was allowed to ride another man's horse. However, one of the Mexicans caught him when no one was around and tried to ride him. I caught him at it and we had it out.

The rule of the ranch was for one to be a good rider he had to rope, snub, and saddle a wild horse, get on and ride him without any help.

One Sunday morning I saddled my own horse Bob, rode south to the old homestead in search of the dapple grey horse I had bought from Dad and he was running loose. My mission was to find this horse, take him back to the ranch and break him to ride. I found him with a bunch of horses and ran him into the corral on uncle Bert's old place which had been abandoned for a long time. I guess this was one of the most foolish things I ever did. I roped this horse, snubbed him to a post, removed my saddle from old Bob and saddled this grey horse, got on him, cut him loose and rode him there in the corral with no one around for help. If I had gotten into trouble, or gotten hurt no one would have known where I was. However, things went pretty well. I rode him without any trouble. I took him back to the ranch and broke him to ride. When we got back to the ranch and as soon as we arrived Everett wanted me to go up to the north pasture and bring in the milk cows. So I saddled the grey horse, mounted him again and boy did he ever give me the ride of my life. He bucked everything out of my pants pockets. He turned out to be a good horse with lots of endurance, but he never got over bucking when you first mounted him but after he had his buck out he was good for all day. Before I left the ranch I sold him and the fellow who bought him broke him to work. He turned out to be just as good in the harness as he was under the saddle.

Tom Tate owned the old Greenlee Ranch southwest of La Junta where dad was cattle feeder when I was born. Tom had some Mexicans farming it. One morning in the fall Everett told me that I was to take the tractor and ensilage cutter and go to this ranch and help fill the silos. There were two large ones and this would take two to three weeks. I wasn't too thrilled about this. I didn't care too much for these people. They had been at the ranch some time earlier and had gone to the hills for a couple loads of cedar wood. When they left my spurs disappeared. I had always left them with my saddle gear. I was positive one of these Mexicans got away with them. They were a beautiful pair of spurs: lady leg shank, silver and bronze with a star rowel. However, it became my job to live with these people for at least two weeks. They were nice people. They had nice horses and harness and were very neat. The women were nice housekeepers and cooks. I never ate so much chili before in my life. They nearly set me on fire. Their fried chicken was cooked after being rolled in chili. This turned out ok but I never found my spurs. I was glad to get back to the old ranch on the Purgatory River.

There was also the other side of the coin. Many evenings when the work was done we would saddle our horses and ride up Smith Canyon, to a swimming hole and go swimming. This was a nice place with an outcropping of rock on one side about 8 or 10 feet high which sufficed as a diving place. This hole was large and deep with a good sand bottom and shore. The river was no good for the water was seldom very clear and it contained lots of quicksand. It was said that at one time in the early days a cavalry unit was crossing the river and bogged down and all were lost. This is how it became known as the Purgatory River, meaning the river of lost souls.

When we were on the homestead we had to ford the river as there was no bridge at Higbee at that time. In crossing the river Dad nearly lost one of his horses. The water was higher than usual. The horse went down. Her head went under the water. Dad jumped off the wagon, grabbed her head and held it up. The other horse had good footing and pulled the wagon and by Dad helping they managed to make it across. When there was more wagons than one trying to cross-the river they crossed one wagon at a time. The quick sand shifts by crossing one wagon. The others could swing usually a little upstream and cross ok. They later built quite a long bridge across this river. When we boys at the ranch crossed this wooden bridge we raced our horses across and about every one for quite a distance knew that the boys at the ranch were on the move.

We were not supposed to work Sundays, however sometimes this became a necessity, but on Sundays we usually had something planned. This did not include the Mexicans but was usually boys who lived around this part of the country. Sometimes it was just going and spending the day with one of them or we would have a bull riding spree. We had a black bull and I had tried to ride him a couple times. Notice I said "tried." He was a bad one. He threw me into a barbed wire fence, tore my clothes and skinned and cut me up pretty bad. They took him to the Rocky Ford fair and he came back unridden. We decided we would try to ride him, one would try each Sunday. If he couldn't ride him he was turned loose until the next Sunday. After they had all had their turn and no one had succeeded they told me it was my turn. I told them I had tried before and didn't care to try again. They said, "We didn't get to see you, therefore; you have to take your turn just as the rest of us." So they roped him, put the surcingle on him (a surcingle is a broad leather strap with a hand hold, buckling over the bull's back and under his belly). I got all set and they let him go. I wasn't sure I was going to make the ride but I did, which was a victory for me. This was the last time anyone at the ranch tried to ride him as far as I know. I never did any contesting at the rodeo but we all did a lot of it just for the fun of it.

The ranch had a rodeo grounds south of the river. It was not the kind you see on TV. They had corrals for the animals that were to be ridden but no chutes There was a track with no fence around it. When a rodeo was planned it was advertised by word of mouth. People came from far and near, for barbecuing before the rodeo. The ranch would kill a fat steer or two for barbequing. To do this they had a large pit, not too wide but rather deep and long where would put logs and let them burn for about two days or until they had a heavy bed of coals that were red hot. The beef was cut into rather small chunks, placed in a large metal vat, along with a good supply of onions, and covered with a heavy lid. This was placed in the pit and well covered with dirt for about two days. This way the meat retained all its flavor. A chuck wagon was pulled alongside the pit from which the meat was served. Of course there was always plenty of beans, coffee and bread. There was always a big crowd with wagons, hacks, and some who came horseback. Usually there were quite a few Mexicans. This they called Guyo Day or Rustler day. The Mexicans had a great time. They would bury a rooster in the middle of the track with its head and feet above the ground. They would line up on their horses about a quarter of the track away. When the shot was fired, or the signal given, they raced their horses and as they passed the rooster they would swing down and try to get the chicken. Then the other riders would try to take it from the rider who had it. Sometimes it would take a couple laps around the track as they did not always get the chicken the first lap. The one coming in with the largest piece of the chicken was the winner, and they were usually a bloody mess. This has been outlawed now on the grounds of cruelty to dumb animals. The Rocky Ford fair rodeo was just over and some of their riders came to the ranch for this occasion.

One I remember well was a man by the name of Curly Lewis. He was from Dead Man's Canyon which was way south and some east from Dad's homestead. He usually took top honors in bronc riding. He asked me to go with him on a trip to Madison Square Garden. He wanted to take a bunch of bucking horses and he would put on a horse bucking show along the way. He would ride any horse they brought to him or his own. All I would have to do was to help take care of the horses, help him saddle up and he would do the riding. I would get no salary, only my expenses. I turned him down. Another bronc rider was Cuddle Ridner. He came to the rodeo in a bright red shirt. He was thrown from his horse and landed in a mud puddle and boy was he embarrassed. They also had some bucking horses from the Rocky Ford fair.

Jim Brezlin was a good friend of mine, also of Granddad Glatz, however I did not know the Glatz family until quite some time later. Jim was an old bachelor who had a small place up the river south. He ran a few cattle. Jim had lived with the Indians in his early life and he could do most anything the Indians could. He could spin his own wool into thread and weave rugs as well as saddle blankets. He would braid horse hair into beautiful bridles and reins, saddle quirts and cinches. He always rode with one and said his horse never had a cinch sore. He could chip arrows, and braid saddle quirts. He gave me a beautiful handmade shot loaded quirt. I did not know where it disappeared to. One day it just turned up missing. Jim used to come and stay at the ranch for a while during the winter months and hunt coyotes. He would usually be around when we were working cattle at the corral and pick up the hair we had cut from the brush end of the cow's tail. This is the way we could tell which cows had been worked and which had not. When I went to Kansas city to go to Bible Training school in 1924 I shipped out with some cattle from the ranch on a stock train. Jim Brezlin shipped some cattle also so we went together. This was good for me for I could never have found my way around by myself.

The corrals were made from cedar posts placed close together making a solid post fence or stockade. They were originally tied at the top with rawhide and when it dried it drew the posts tight and made the fence very solid. The corrals were getting to where they needed repairs. One day we were dehorning cattle. We had let a cow critter out of the chute and she ran blindly into the fence, not through it, but she did quite a bit of damage. Tom had taken it upon himself to do the repair job. Well, he was all bent over working away, the seat of his pants as tight as a drum when we released an old cow from the chute. We had just removed her horns. She made a run for Tom. We were all scared but there was nothing we could do for it all happened so fast. We were all sure she was going to hit him right in the seat and drive him right into those posts, however, she stopped just short of him, blew snot all over his back end and started twisting her head trying to gore him; but her horns were gone. She did him no damage but she gave us all quite a scare, but after it was over it became very funny. Tom always had a pipe in his mouth, but hardly ever smoked it. Sometimes it was upside down. He always bit the stem tight in his teeth. This made him talk somewhat through his nose. His nephew called him snorts. Tom was a rather old man, but he had started out at the age of about 15 wrangling horses, rounding up wild or range horses, trailing them into Kansas and on east, selling them to farmers.

We usually did not ride without a side arm. I had a white handle, small caliber six gun. No one had a 45. They may have had a 38 or 45 frame on a 32 on a 38 frame. These were more accurate and they did not bounce so bad when fired. I did not have a saddle rifle. They were lighter and shorter than an ordinary rifle, a 30-30 was very handy for coyotes or wolves and both were bad on the cattle. A gun was not used like you see in the wild west movies. However they can get one into trouble if you aren't careful. They were carried for protection from animals.

Sometimes I didn't carry mine and didn't have it when I needed it one day. I was moving a herd of cattle alone. Among them was a bull that had given me trouble, in fact, he was a troublesome animal. I was moving them along a fence line and had about 20 feet of my saddle rope dragging to use as a prod. The end of it had a knot, then some fringe. I could use it pretty well to sting a cow. This bull had threatened me several times but had never made his threat good. He turned sideways, head toward the fence, shook his head and bellowed and pawed the dirt with his front feet. I threw my rope under handed and caught him on the nose. He made a run at my horse, hit him in the breast, picked his front up and he came down with his front feet on the other side of the fence. He then hit him in the side as I stepped off on the other side. He then hit my horse in the right hip with his horns. I managed to break off a fence post to do battle but as I came around the back of my horse and he saw me he ran off into the herd. I stepped on the fence, reared my horse with the reins, and be came down clear of the fence.

By this time some of the cattle had began to turn back. I stepped back on my horse and rode out to head them back. As I swung my horse to the right and myself into the saddle I saw blood running down his right rear leg. I dismounted and found the right hip split wide open. If I would have had my gun there would probably have been a dead bull. He was mean to other animals. Several horses had been gored but no one knew before now what was happening to these horses, however none had been so badly hurt. I took my horse in, put some healing powder on him and turned him loose.

Sometimes in moving cattle and they wouldn't move but just bunch up, especially if you were trying to get them to cross the river, if someone pulls his side arm and fires a shot into the air, they will get moving. Old Bill Eddy carried his gun more than any one. He drank quite a bit. I have found him lying on the ground or in a ditch so drunk he couldn't sit in the saddle. I would get him on his horse, take him to the bunk house, unsaddle his horse, and let him sleep it off. Bill has threatened to shoot me on several occasions. This was during the days of prohibition, but there was always plenty of bootleg to be had. I never drank. I didn't like the stuff. I and another fellow bought a bottle together one time. I guess he drank it, I don't know, but that was the only time.

Once in a while there would be a church service somewhere and I would usually try to attend. A gun can get one into trouble very easy. One day there were three men, none from the ranch, and they got into some kind of trouble and had a shoot out, all three men were killed, also one or two of their horses. They were found later but no one seemed to know anything about their trouble.

A fellow by the name of Wesley Evers West lived on a parcel of land belonging to the ranch. He had both pasture land and farm land rented. We at the ranch had to cross some of this land on occasion. One day he met me at the gate near the main irrigation ditch which belonged to the ranch and ordered me off the place. He also told me that he didn't want any one from the ranch crossing his place. When I got back to the ranch I told Everett what had happened, then asked him what had gone wrong. Everett said that he didn't know but that he was going to find out, and we were to cross or pass through his place any time we needed to. A short time later the revenue officer arrested him for having a still. Several barrels of mash, and bootleg gin. He went to prison and I do not know what happened to his family.

One of my early ambitions was to bulldog a steer from the running board of a car. This was never attempted. One day I was trying to ride a young white faced bull. When I hit the ground I lit flat on my back and his front feet straddled my chest, his hoofs scraping the hide on both sides of me. The old saying is: "God watches over babies and fools. I can truly say the Lord surely did His share of watching over me, I also liked to trick ride and bulldog steers. Both required a good horse.

One day in the spring, about March I think, the weather was quite bad and I had been out in it most of the day I had brought in a cow and her calf. I tied my horse at the gate and had gone to the bunk house for something. When I came back my horse was gone. I made several inquiries and no one knew anything about him, nor had they seen him. Everett told me not to worry that he had probably gone to pasture. I did worry. He was still saddled and bridled and I didn't want him out in the storm with them on. About 3 a.m. in the morning Everett called me and said to get dressed, the ranch house was on fire. This was a large U-shaped house with a bell tower and a bell. The tower had burned off and let the bell fall to the cement floor which woke up one of the men sleeping in the north wing. The house burned to the ground. We managed to save the office furniture in the office. Tom Tate was not on the ranch. He was in town. The fire had to have been set. About 10 a.m. that morning Wes Evers, who had been living on some ranch property came riding in on my horse. It was thought by many that he had set the fire. No one had ever seen him on the ranch. He was deeply in debt to Tom. We searched through the ruins when Tom got home looking for his ledger with all his records but not a trace of the ledger could be found. We were not able to get a satisfactory answer as to why he had taken my horse. No one had even seen him on the ranch. It was thought by Everett that he had slipped away unseen, then if anything went wrong setting the fire my horse would be found and suspicion placed on me. This was foolish for I slept in the house where the boss lived. I also ate my meals with him and his family. He had three children, two boys and one girl. When Everett left the ranch they moved to La Junta and he worked at the Safeway store. They lived just a couple doors south from us when Kenny was small and Edna used to keep him at times for mother.

We didn't usually have to work on Sunday. One night it was so hot that I rolled up my bed mattress and carried it outside, rolled it out on the ground and went to sleep. The sun woke me up. I rolled up my mattress and carried it back into my room which I shared with Edna's father. I threw the mattress back on the bed and crawled in. Pretty shortly Edna's dad jumped up and yelled: A Rattler! A rattle snake crawled out of my bed and disappeared through a hole in the adobe wall.

After the fall roundup the cattle for shipping were put in what we called the school section until time for shipping. This was what we might call a holding pen for the cattle, it was easy then to get them together when it was time to market them. This was a section of land north of the ranch. It was a little hard to get to from the south but it was pretty flat, and wasn't too high, only rough and rugged with narrow rocky trails leading to the top. This required good sure footed horses. The ranch had many good and fast horses, but this required that they be sure footed also, for one miss-step could be disastrous. There were times when I wasn't sure my horse would make it, especially when a rock would give way around my horse's feet. It required a horse whose rear feet tracked with the front feet. This means that when the horse found a good solid footing for the front feet the rear feet must be placed on the same spot. The Psalmist tells us:"He maketh my feet like hinds feet and setteth me upon my high places." The hind or deer is one of the most sure footed of animals. and this was what was required of our horses.

After leaving the ranch I went to town with the folks. They lived on south Raton in a two story brick house. I went to work for Uncle Les and Uncle Bert. They did a lot of team work. One day I left my gun laying on the dresser. Mother picked it up and it went off and shot a hole in the wall. Dad raised a fuss so I had to get rid of the gun. Another time after I had secured a job in the bakery I came home one evening to find that a neighbor boy had been shot with my gun. Dutch and some of his friends were going rabbit hunting and Dutch was going to use my 22 which was in the coat closet, but instead of getting the 22 he brought out this big rifle which was lever action. They found the safety and released it. One of the boys leveled it, pointing it out the back door and pulled the trigger just as Scott Gale, our neighbor, stepped across in front of the door and he was hit, not striking the bone or he would have lost his leg. He later became a doctor. I got rid of all my guns except a 22 which was still there when mother died and we were going through the things at home.

La Junta (circa 1940)
(Note the Train Depot and rail yards in the upper portion of the photo)

Some time after leaving the homestead Dad sold the house. Later he sold the land to George Stout, a cattle man that also bought the homestead where we got our drinking water. Mr. Stout came out there after we left and bought up a lot of land for grazing cattle. He wanted Dad's land because of the water on it. I did not know when Dad sold the land. It was many years later that mother told me that Dad had reserved the mineral rights. After Dad passed away we were able to lease the mineral rights to the Standard Oil of California for $1.00 per acre, which was divided among the children.

POSTSCRIPT

Uncle Clifford went on in life to become a Minister of the Church of God. He and his wife, Marianna Glatz, had three boys and a girl who, unfortunately died at the age of seven. All of the boys developed into outstanding individuals. Ken was a highly respected architect in Indianapolis and has become a very close friend over the past several years. I really never knew him as a child, as our paths only crossed on one or two brief occasions. Arthur was a student at the University of Colorado the same time as I was and he and his wife, Jerri, were nice enough to treat me to a home-cooked meal a couple times while we were students. Our paths also crossed occasionally on campus. I didn't meet Gene until 1999 when we stopped in Indianapolis to visit with Ken and his second wife Jeannette. Ken and Jeannette were both widowed and met while both were hospice caregivers for their respective spouses. I had the good fortune to meet all of the kids and grandkids of the three families at the family reunion they held outside Colorado Springs in 2009.

When my father passed away in 1982, Uncle Clifford and Marianne were retired, living in Canyon City, Colorado. I asked him to perform the graveside service for his brother. My brother and I picked him up in Pueblo on our drive down from Denver for the service in La Junta. That gave us a few hours to chat on the way to and from the service. Unfortunately, that was the last time I saw him, as he passed away a few years later. I am sure that he was an outstanding minister, as he could certainly emphathize with the trials and tribulations that others encountered in life.

(Front) Marianne, Clifford, Arthur; (Back) Patricia, Ken

Four generations of "1st Born" Ritchharts
Alonzo, Ken, Clifford and Linda

The Bush Family

Although I haven't done nearly the amount of research about the Bush side of the family as the Ritchharts, from the information I have dating back three generations, they were also farmers. I believe the family heritage was German; but have not been able to trace the Bush line all the way back to Germany. As far as I could trace them back was to Virginia, then they moved to Kentucky, to Missouri and on to Colorado; where my grandfather and grandmother (Grace Bush) were married.

Grace's father, Samuel, was told by doctors to move to Colorado for health reasons. But he died just six years later at the relatively young age of 51. I cannot find any evidence of his burial in the La Junta area; however, his wife is buried there. She remarried and is listed as Lillian Turner. I do recall visiting "Aunt Dell" in North La Junta. She was Grandma Ritchhart's sister.

Also, when we had my father's funeral in La Junta in 1981, I recall a couple ladies that came up to me and said they were part of the Bush family. I think they were children of Aunt Dell's.

I have a theory about my father's given name. Since his mother had a sister Adell, who went by the name Dell; and a brother, Elbert, who went by the name Bert—she combined the names for Delbert! I have no proof whatsoever about this; but it sounds logical and makes a good story!

Samuel & Lillian Bush

GRACE BUSH RITCHHART—MY PATERNAL GRANDMOTHER

The wedding announcement in the Carthage newspaper stated that Grace moved with her parents from Carthage, Missouri to La Junta, Colorado in the fall of 1901. According to the written accounts of Clifford Ritchhart, Alonzo accompanied the Bushes to Colorado to help them move because of his attraction to Grace. I would also assume they must have had some wedding plans since they were married within about 4–5 months of moving to Colorado.

Dean and I always liked our Grandma Ritchhart. She was always very good to us and a very kind person. She worked part time at the swimming pool, which was about a half mile walk from their home. We always liked to go with her to work because we got to swim free. This was in a time when there were no private swimming

Grace Bush Ritchhart

pools and only a few of the larger towns had a pool. We never got a pool in Las Animas until I was in high school. We would go with her when she opened the pool, spend all day swimming and then go home with her. I recall when I first learned to swim I could only swim underwater. The shallow area of the pool was separated from the deep area by metal bars with a separation between them. Being very small, I could swim between the bars from one area into the other. In hindsight that was a very dangerous design because, potentially, people could get stuck between the bars and drown.

As long as I can remember, Grandma cooked on a coal burning stove. She was a very good cook; but food was always very basic; mostly meat, potatoes and vegetables, with some chicken now and then. Whenever she made potatoes, mashed or boiled, they were always mixed with turnips. I think this came from their German heritage. They had a built-in booth in the kitchen where we ate if there was only three or four of us. Otherwise, we sat around the dining room table. The house only had five rooms. Two bedrooms, a living room (which when their kids lived at home had been used as a bedroom), dining room and kitchen. They had an outhouse for several years; but later got indoor plumbing and a bathroom.

As I related earlier, Grandma and Grandpa never owned a car. They lived within about two blocks of downtown where they could walk to get groceries and do other shopping. I think Grandma even walked to the Methodist church, where she was very active. I imagine friends would drive them if the weather was bad. When they lived on the homestead, a horse, or horse and buggy was their transportation. They never had much money and their only child to go to college was my dad, who got a football scholarship. I recall that both Grandma and Grandpa had false teeth, which was very common for people in those days.

Grace Ritchhart died at the relatively young age of 66 from arteriosclerosis. (hardening of the arteries).

Four Generations of Women (circa 1924)
Lillian Logsdon Bush, Grace Bush Ritchhart, Lillian Ritchhart
Rumsby and (baby) Margaret Rumsby

The O'Malley Family

It was 1850 in Mayo County, Ireland. The potato famine had been ravaging the country for almost five years. There was little or no food to eat for most families and no jobs to be had. Over 1 million people had died of disease or starvation. The western counties of Ireland, including Mayo, had been particularly hard hit. It was in this setting that fifteen year old Peter Malia was faced with the decision of continuing to try and survive in his homeland or to take a risk on going to America. Others from his area, and possibly some relatives, had already settled in this land of promise and sent back letters encouraging others to join them. We don't know if his parents had survived the famine or wanted to emigrate to America. I did find some fairly good evidence that he may have traveled with friends on the *Young Queen* from Galway—arriving April 24, 1847 in New York. I matched the names of three of the people on that boat with census records in Wayne County, Pennsylvania. Could be a coincidence; but I don't think so. During those times, it was not unusual to find a widowed mother or father living with one of their children. In looking at all the Pennsylvania and Illinois census data for Peter and Julia this was not the case.

Julia McNally, about the same age as Peter, also likely faced the same challenges. Did she and Peter travel together, did they meet on the ship, or did they meet after arriving in America? Once again we are not sure; but I surmise that it was probably the latter. It would have been unusual for two 15 year olds to marry at that age, so I am guessing they met a few years after arriving in America and married in 1852 or 1853 when they were 17 or 18. Their first child, John, was born in 1854. In those times when birth control didn't exist, Catholic or not, most first children were born within the first year of marriage. In 1860 they are listed as Peter and Julia Maloy with children John, Mary and Hannah in the Salem, Pennsylvania census. Salem was a small community just a few miles west of Scranton. Peter's occupation is listed as "farmer." It is interesting that almost all of their neighbors listed on the census page where they are listed have about the same value for real estate and personal property.

It is significant that Peter and Julia went to a very small farming community outside Scranton. That strongly suggests that they already knew someone there—probably from their townland or village in Ireland from whence they came. Most immigrants who didn't already know someone in America went to larger, more well known cities where there were known settlements of people from their homeland. In checking the census listings for Salem Township, there were a large number of people from Ireland.

Peter and Julia are listed with the surname of Malia in the 1870 census, along with children John, Joanna (often interchangeable with Hannah), Sarah, Walter and Ellen. Peter was listed as a miner and the value of his real estate had increased from $200 to $900. Peter also shows up in the Scranton City Directory in 1867–68.

Interestingly, Scranton was incorporated as a city in 1866. The Scranton area had extensive mining and the Scranton Brothers had developed the process of making steel rails for the railroads and their plant was in Scranton. Peter and Julia were probably drawn to Scranton by the prospect of higher wages working in the mines.

In the 1880 Census, taken in June, Peter and Julia O'Maly and children, Walter, Ella and Michael are in Sherman Township, Mason County, Illinois and his occupation is laborer on the railroad. Since many people in Scranton worked for the railroad, it appears that Peter left the mines to work for the railroad which would have enabled him to get reduced fares to move his family to Illinois. This is borne out by the fact the Scranton City Directory for 1879–80 listed Peter's occupation as brakeman on the railroad. It is interesting to note that the 1880 Census in Mason County had John and Sarah O'Malley in the same household with Thomas Hyland and his wife Mary, John and Sarah's sister. Thomas and Mary have a daughter Isabella, who is five months old. It is likely, therefore, that Thomas and Mary were married in 1879. It is possible they had moved to Mason County, Illinois ahead of Mary's parents and the other children.

Peter and Julia lived in Mason County the remainder of their years. Of interest, the 1880 Census had the spelling of Peter's surname as O'Mally. Thus, the name progressed from Maloy in 1860, to Malia in 1870, to O'Mally in 1880 and eventually O'Malley. At first I thought these variations were just errors by the enumerators or due to the fact neither Peter nor Julia could read or write English. However I later learned that several sources within Ireland indicate that Malia is a variant of O'Malley often used—and there were many other variants as well.

This was also true of many other Irish names. One source indicated that around 1880 the British government decided to standardize the spelling of all variants of surnames and decreed that O'Malley was to be the standardized spelling used by all of the clan. I am guessing that the word of that decree spread to America and that many Irish residents of America decided to also comply with the standardization. This seems to coincide roughly with the change in spelling that we have observed.

In *County Mayo, Ireland Achill Parish, Some Baptismal Transcriptions with Index* by William G. Masterson he stated the following: "I have attempted to constitute families from the records by standardizing the father's surname to fit the majority of the baptismal records. As an example: the surname O'Malley, Maley, Malley and Malia may be found under the predominant surname for the family… It appears that Malley was used for several years at the beginning of the records and then it became Maley for a few years and then reverts to Malley."

Another source, *The Surnames of Ireland* by Edward MacLysaght, states, "…O'Malley is one of the few O names from which the prefex was seldom dropped. In Mayo, however, it was called Melia." Thus, we have two different sources citing various spellings of O'Malley in County Mayo.

Peter died in 1893 and Julie in 1906 and the spelling of the surname on the headstone was O'Malley for both of them. They are buried in St. Fredericks Cemetery in Manito, Mason County, Illinois. I have tried to locate death certificates or any other records for Julia and Peter in Mason County; but thus far have been unsuccessful. I also tried to get any church records. Initially, the diocese in Peoria, Illinois had no archivist and, therefore, could not search their records. However, they later acquired an archivist; but their best efforts did not reveal any records for Peter or Julia.

Peter and Julia O'Malley's Headstone

WALTER WILLIAM O'MALLEY

Walter was born to Peter and Julia in Scranton, Pennsylvania on July 17, 1867. Thus, he was around 13 years old when they moved to Mason County, Illinois. It was here that he met Mary Elizabeth Earhart, who was about two years younger than he. We don't know for sure their exact wedding date; but it was probably late 1885 or early 1886, for their first child, Mary Loretta, was born in November of 1886. Walter would have been 18 or 19 and Mary Elizabeth 16 or 17. Their second child, Walter Lee, was born in January of 1889. We don't know what Walter's occupation was; but it is likely that he worked on a farm or as a laborer. Unfortunately, three years after giving birth to Walter Lee, Mary Elizabeth died. We aren't certain when; but Walter abandoned the children, moved to St. Joseph, Missouri and they became wards of the County and were raised by Walter's sister, Sarah, and her husband Thomas McCabe. It is possible that Walter tried to care for the children for a year or so; but a Petition was filed by D.C. White for guardianship of the children ages 8 and 6 on 28 December 1894 because their father was not caring for their needs and had moved out of the county. That same date a petition was also filed by D.C. White and Thomas McCabe for Mary Elizabeth's estate of about $500. The 1900 Federal Census showed Walter and Mary living with Sara and Thomas McCabe, their five children, and their grandmother Julia O'Malley.

I find it very surprising and unusual that both set of grandparents to Mary and Walter Lee were living in Mason County at the time the children were legally made wards of the County. They might have shared in helping Sara and Thomas raise the children; but no mention is made of either set of grandparents in the legal petitions, nor did they appear to make any effort to obtain guardianship of the children.

Stories passed down from Walter Lee to his children and grandchildren aren't very positive of the treatment Mary and Walter received from the McCabes, Thomas in particular. Apparently Thomas wasn't very supportive of educating the children. He viewed a woman's role in life as bearing children, caring for them and taking care of the home; not totally atypical for those times. Walter Lee was only allowed to attend school if there was no work to do on the farm. Thus, his education was hit and miss.

Walter William apparently moved to St. Joseph, Missouri and in 1900 married Bessie Morey and had a second family of five children. He was listed as a laborer-packer in the 1900 census and in 1910 as a bartender. While I was doing some research regarding Thomas and Mary Hyland about a year ago I stumbled upon a very interesting fact. As I was observing the 1920 Census page containing the data on Thomas and Mary, I happened to scan down the page to see if any of their neighbors might be relatives. Listed two door away was Walter, Bessie and four children. As I further examined the data it revealed that Thomas was a watchman with the railroad and Walter was a laborer with the railroad. I surmise that Prohibition in 1918 ended

Walter William O'Malley

his bartending and Walter's brother in law, Thomas, wrote that he could arrange a job for him with the railroad in Denver. That must not have worked out very well, in many ways, because in the 1930 census Bessie and the children were back in St. Joseph. She was listed as "Married" but Walter was not listed. I thought perhaps he was still working in Denver so I did a search for him in the 1930 census records. The results were some of the most startling since I started doing research over ten years ago—he was a prisoner in Leavenworth Federal Penitentiary! You have to commit a federal crime to be assigned to a Federal Prison. It turns out that he and his family probably returned to St. Joseph from Denver around 1925. Having been a bartender previously, he must have decided to pursue a similar line of work; however, it was during prohibition time and peddling booze was a violation of the Prohibition Act which had been passed in 1918. Thus, he was convicted by the Federal Court of the Western District of Missouri and began spending his one year and one day sentence on September 16, 1929. With time off for good behavior, he was released on July 6, 1930. He had good company as Al Capone, Machine Gun Kelly and the Bird man of Alcatraz were there at the same time. The facilities must have been very new as the prison wasn't totally completed until 1930.

We can all expect to find some "black sheep" in our family histories; but this discovery was a little more than I expected. If there was a positive side to the story, it was the fact that I obtained around 35 pages of Walter's files from the Federal Bureau of Prisons, including the above photo.

MARY LORETTA O'MALLEY

Mary O'Malley Dean

Shortly after Mary turned 18 (1904–05), we believe she left Mason County and the McCabes and went to Denver and attended stenography school. While I have known for many years that Mary went to Denver when she left Mason County, I was never sure why she chose Denver. It turns out that her Aunt Mary O'Malley, who married Thomas Hyland, had moved to Denver from Mason County. Thus, it is likely that Mary heard good things about Denver through the family network and decided to go there. The 1910 Census listed her living just a few blocks west of the Capitol and her occupation was "stenographer."

Interestingly, her father and mother's birth places are listed as New York and Pennsylvania;

which are the birth places of Thomas and Sarah McCabe. Pennsylvania and Illinois are the birth places of her real mother and father, Walter and Mary Elizabeth.

In 1909 a young man from a small farming and ranching community in southeastern Colorado came to Denver to work in the state brands office as a clerk, recording and investigating cattle brands. Probably within a few months of moving to Denver he met Mary O'Malley. Since he worked at the capitol and she lived within a few blocks of the capitol; it is likely they met at some event near the State Capitol. In 1911 they were married and shortly thereafter moved back to Las Animas, where Arthur had grown up.

Mary and Arthur spent the remainder of their lives in Las Animas, Colorado. Interestingly, Mary and Arthur had four children and they were all born in St. Frances Hospital in Denver, Colorado. Once again, it seemed very unusual for a woman in a small southeastern Colorado town to travel almost 200 miles to have her babies born. It seems even more unusual when we all know that predicting when children will be born is a very inexact science, which was even more true in the early 1900s. It seems likely that Mary could only have done this because she had an aunt in Denver, with whom she could stay until labor started and she had to go to the hospital. Of course Arthur couldn't accompany her, as he had to stay and tend to the farm work or later to his job. I have several letters that were exchanged between Mary and Arthur during her trips to Denver. Most people today would wonder why they didn't just call each other on the phone. In those days not everyone had phones and if you did, long distance phone calls were relatively expensive and many people only called long distance during emergencies or at special occasions like Christmas.

In addition to raising their own four children, Mary and Arthur raised her brother's boy, Lee. Lee's mother died shortly after he was born. Despite the fact Mary and Arthur already had three children, they took Lee in and raised him until he was about twelve years old. I find it very interesting that Mary and her brother were raised by an Aunt and then Mary raised her brother's child.

In a recent conversation with my brother, Dean, he related a story grandma had told him about knowing Molly Brown of "Unsinkable Molly Brown" fame. I didn't take the story too seriously until a few weeks later while going through some of my files doing some genealogy research. I was reading through an old newspaper clipping about the death of one of grandma's cousins, Elizabeth Moll. The closing line of the obituary stated that, "She was the niece of J.J. Brown, wealthy mining man, whose widow died last October." Since Dean's comments were fresh in my mind, I decided to "Google" J.J. Brown to see if he could have any connection to Molly Brown. Yes, he had been her husband and she had lived in the Leadville and Denver areas of Colorado. My research revealed that Molly died in October of 1932 and Elizabeth died in May of 1933; thus, the statement in the obit that J.J.'s "widow died last October" was totally compatible with all the facts. It is very believable, therefore, that grandma knew the "Unsinkable Molly Brown" because she was the aunt of her cousin, Elizabeth.

Grandma Dean was probably the most influential person in my life. That influence took several forms. She was always there for you whenever you had a problem or you just wanted to talk. She had that quality of putting you at ease and never overreacting to anything. Thinking back,

I think she learned that from her own experiences.

She always loved it when we had rain and thunder. She would sit on the front porch and just rock in her chair and watch the sky light up. As with most children, I didn't like the thunder because it sounded rather menacing, especially combined with the flashes of lightning. She taught me to enjoy nature in action and that it was nothing to fear. In fact, as time went on, I too looked forward to those times, especially sharing them with her.

If we needed money as kids, we could usually get a dime or a quarter from Grandma; but we always had to earn it. She always had chores to be done, whether it was to rake up the leaves in the yard or carry out the trash or go to the store to pick up something for her. She was a devout Catholic and in later years when she couldn't make it to mass because of illness, she would always give me something to put in the collection and a dime for me to get an ice cream. Now that I think back on it, I believe it was also a subtle bribe to encourage me to go to church.

When my brother was in high school many of his friends were Methodists and they had a very active youth program, which was somewhat lacking at the St. Mary's Catholic Church. I believe the youth program helped entice my brother into attending the Methodist church. I was sure that Grandma would get very upset with this; but in her infinite wisdom, she didn't. She could understand his reasoning and realized this would probably be a passing infatuation that would change with time. Sure enough, after a year or so, he was back to attending church at St. Mary's.

In my sophomore year we moved in with Grandma and Grandpa. My mother claimed it was so we could take care of them; but I think it was more of the opposite—so they could take care of us. Financially, I don't think we were making it, as it seemed we moved whenever the rent came due. That might be a bit of an exaggeration; but not much. My mom did help out and do most of the cooking , washing, and cleaning; but without their support I am not sure what we would have done. In today's world, we could easily have become homeless. Then when my mother had a mental breakdown my Junior year, we were totally dependent on my grandparents. They sent Mary Jane, who was around six, to live with my Aunt Frances and her husband, Paul, in Pittsburgh, Pennsylvania. Despite not being in very good health, my grandmother was always a rock solid support; as was grandpa.

Being a grandparent myself now, I have a much greater appreciation for the sacrifices they made on the behalf of my mother, brother , sister and me. Not only was it a financial burden; but they totally gave up their privacy. We were six people in a three bedroom, 1400 square foot house with one bathroom!

Once both Dean and I left for college, my grandparents rented out that house and moved into a small apartment. I think they did that for financial reasons, as once my grandmother passed away, my mother and grandpa moved back into the house where they remained until my grandfather's death.

WALTER LEE O'MALLEY

According to Walter Lee's granddaughters Betsy Smith and Marilee Kapsa, Walter ran away when he was 15 and went to St. Joseph, Missouri where he was taken in by a Catholic Boy's home run by the Christian Brothers. This was about the same time that his sister, Mary, left and

Walter Lee O'Malley

went to Denver. Once Mary had saved up enough money in Denver, she is reported to have sent Walter Lee the money to join her in Denver. Extensive searches of the federal census for both 1900 and 1910 failed to locate Walter Lee. He does show up in the 1920 census in Salt Lake City. We also know that he was married to Elizabeth Kyle in Denver in 1914.

Uncle Lee, as we always called him, was about three years younger than his sister, Mary. He would usually come to Las Animas about every year to visit. Now that I know more about their lives as children, I think that drew them closer than most siblings, because of the difficult times they shared in their childhood. We all liked Uncle Lee.

He was very friendly and personable and always took time to talk with the children He was always nicely dressed in a suit and we thought perhaps he was one of those "rich uncles." After the early 1950s, I don't recall him coming to visit again. He may have; but perhaps I just don't recall.

After Uncle Lee and Elizabeth Kyle married in Denver on November 28, 1914 they moved to Las Animas where Marion was born. Around 1920 they moved to Salt Lake, where Lee was born, and he remained there until around 1937, when he moved to Twin Falls, Idaho. I believe he worked in sales for farm implements most of his life. Then he moved to Peoria, Illinois where he worked for Caterpillar during the early war years. He moved back to Salt Lake around 1940.

Uncle Lee died in May of 1961 in Phoenix, Arizona, two months after his sister, Mary, passed away. I seem to recall that he was in poor health the last few years in Phoenix; because he didn't attend his sister, Mary's, funeral or come to visit when she was very ill.

Despite the fact his wife died when he was still a young man of 32, he never remarried. When his wife died, shortly after giving birth to their third child Lee, he asked his sister Mary to raise Lee and he put his two daughters, Marion and Elizabeth, into a boarding school in Salt Lake City. After Lee got to be about 12 years old, he moved back home with his dad and sisters. In later life Lee admitted that it was a tough transition for him and, in some ways, he resented being taken away from his life with Mary, Arthur and their children. He always referred to Mary as "Mama" because she was the only mother he ever knew. I am not sure why; but ,while living with the Deans, Lee was called "Jim." My mother and grandparents always talked abut Jim O'Malley—not Lee O'Malley.

LEE O'MALLEY—HIS SISTERS AND NIECES

I recall meeting Lee a couple times when he came back to visit Grandma and Grandpa Dean. I think one time was shortly after WW II ended. He was in the Army and met his future wife, Heather, while in Australia during the war. Then as an adult I met Lee a couple more times; once when he lived in Brea in the Los Angeles area and then when he and Heather lived on Orcas Island off of Seattle.

Lee O'Malley

Lee was very handsome and had a wonderful speaking voice. He wanted to be an actor and had a few bit parts in movies in Hollywood, but gave that up and worked in the Aerospace Industry. He did remain active in local drama groups throughout most of his life. I always enjoyed Lee very much. Heather and Lee had two children, Leigh and Marion Elizabeth, who went by "Ebey." I only met them the one time we went to Brea. My mother grew very fond of Ebey while she was attending school in Colorado. My brother, Dean, who lived in the Seattle area the same time Jim and Heather were on Orcas Island, got to know Jim and all of his family very well. In fact , Jim lived with Dean and Evelyn for a couple weeks one time when Heather went back to Australia to visit her family.

My mother always spoke fondly of Lee's sisters, Marion and Elizabeth, and kept in touch with them; but I only had the chance to meet Marion, and at that time she was suffering from Alzheimer's. I have, however, gotten to meet with three of Marion's daughters: Marilea, Melanie and Betsy. I met Marilea and Melanie once each; but I have met with Betsy twice and correspond with her regularly about family history matters. They are all very personable and outgoing and we had a fun time exchanging stories about the O'Malley family the one time we were able to all get together.

I have recently talked and corresponded by e-mail with Lee and Heather's son, Leigh. In the hopes of being able to trace Peter O'Malley back to Ireland, I thought I might find a connection through the use of DNA. However, as explained earlier, I needed to identify an O'Malley male who was a descendant of Peter O'Malley. Leigh met all the criteria and was nice enough to agree to provide a DNA sample. Thus far, however, there has not been a match that provides us any insight as to Peter's parents or which village in County Mayo he came from. However, with the rapid growth in popularity of DNA's use in genealogy, I am are still hopeful.

THE MOZINGO FAMILY LINE—A SLAVE CONNECTION?

In May of 2010 I happened to be reading a genealogy blog which included a reference to an article by a Los Angeles Times reporter entitled "In Search of the Meaning of Mozingo." Recognizing the name Mozingo as being one of my ancestors, I read the blog and then pulled up the article in the LA Times. The essence of the article was that the reporter, Joe Mozingo, had traced his family history and had traveled back to several states including Virginia, Kentucky, North Carolina and Indiana to interview relatives, do other research and write a three-part series in the newspaper about his experiences.

Joe's research led him to the conclusion that:

> "Every Mozingo in America probably descended from Edward Mozingo, a 'Negro man' who lived in the Tidewater region of Virginia in 1644. I could trace myself only as far back as Spencer (Mozingo), who first showed up as a white adult in a 1782 census in the Piedmont (region of Virginia)."

Further research by Joe revealed that a person referred to as "Mozingo" in the diary of a cousin of James Madison had been sold on March 23, 1790 for 60 francs. While his first name, Spencer, was not used in connection with this specific entry; previous and later diary entries strongly suggest that it was Spencer who was sold.

This finding definitely sparked my interest to determine if I could find any connection between Spencer and my Mozingo ancestors. I quickly sent an e-mail to Joe and asked him about a reference he had made in his article about an online Mozingo family database. He promptly responded and told me the database was maintained by Samie Melton of Dallas and could be found at www.angelfire.com. I went to the web site and, in a very short time, determined that my great-great-grandmother, Mary Elizabeth Mozingo, was Spencer Mozingo's great-great-granddaughter. Mary's daughter Mary Elizabeth Earhart was the first wife of Walter William

O'Malley, my great-grandfather who spent time in Leavenworth Prison for bootlegging. Thus, Spencer was my 5th great-grandfather. For someone who always was told he was English, Irish and German this was quite a revelation! Interestingly, a few months later I viewed a taped interview with one of the most respected professional genealogists in the United States and she claimed that a very significant percentage of Americans are descendants of slaves and don't know it either because there aren't any records revealing the relationship or, if there are records, they don't want to admit it. She went on to explain that this "descendency from slaves" exists because owners and slaves, to put it politely, frequently "intermixed" socially.

Interestingly enough, a few months after learning about the family's "Mozingo Connection," I was contacted by a lady from Illinois, whose grandfather had been given some books by a neighbor. Two documents had only recently been found by her father in an atlas which was one of the books. One of the documents was an adoption certificate, showing that Mary Elizabeth Earhart, my great-grandmother, was adopted by Frank and Mary Earhart. Thus, the Mozingo heritage was never passed down to her descendents. In a way I was disappointed, as it sort of ruined a good story!

Mary Mozingo Earhart's Headstone
(Headstone in Pleasant Hill Cemetery, Forest City, Illinois of Mary Elizabeth Mozingo Earhart Gilmore, whose gggrandfather was the black slave Spencer Mozingo.)

My Visit to Mason County, Illinois

In April of 2009 the San Diego Genealogical Society was making a week-long trip to the Allen County Public Library in Ft. Wayne, Indiana to do genealogical research. Second to the Mormon Family History Library in Salt Lake City, the Allen County Public Library has the largest collection of family history research material in the United States. I also had a strong desire to go to the Mason County area to do more research on my ancestors on the O'Malley side of the family who had lived there in the mid-to-late-1800s. Since I had some expiring frequent flyer miles I decided to combine both trips. In fact, there was a third leg to the trip, to research Joanne's ancestors who lived in Indianapolis.

Entering Mason County

I flew into Chicago, as it was only about a three-hour drive from there to Mason County and when I completed my research in Ft. Wayne, it would only be a couple hours back to Chicago. After arriving in Peoria, near Mason County, around midnight, I got an early start the following morning and headed first for Manito, which is in the Northeastern part of the County. I was fortunate in that it looked like the day was going to be perfect—not a cloud in the sky and mild temperatures.

I knew that my gggrandparents, Peter and Julia O'Malley, and their daughter were buried in Manito. Having researched addresses ahead of time and bringing my portable GPS unit with me, helped considerably in finding locations with little wasted time. I drove to St. Frederick's Cemetery's back entrance and parked. I walked inside the fence and immediately spotted the headstone of Peter and Julia. Directly adjacent was a headstone for their daughter Sarah, her husband Tom McCabe and their son Walter. Tom and Sarah raised my grandmother and her brother when their mother died very young and their father essentially abandoned them. After taking some photos, I looked around at surrounding graves to see if I recognized any other names. Not recognizing any, I proceeded to go to the front entrance to take more photos.

St. Frederick's Cemetery

Knowing that I had a 10 a.m. appointment at the Havana Library, I then drove on to Forest City, which was in the direction of Havana. I knew there were more ancestors who had lived there and were buried in the Pleasant Hill Cemetery. I arrived in Forest City and spotted the Post Office. I thought I knew where the cemetery was; but since it was about three miles from

Pleasant Hill Cemetery

town in a rural area, I wanted to make sure of the directions. When I inquired in the post office, the only customer there said his parents were buried in the same cemetery and he confirmed that the road I thought would lead me there was, in fact, correct. I found several headstones of interest; but the most significant was of Frank and Mary Elizabeth Mozingo Earhart, my gggrandfather and gggrandmother. They were my maternal grandmother Mary O'Malley Dean's grandparents. The cemetery was on a hill (obviously Pleasant Hill) overlooking miles and miles of farmland in every direction.

As I looked around at the surrounding land, I had this strong feeling that the land that my grandmother and her brother inherited from Mary Elizabeth and Frank had to be nearby; but not having been to the records office yet, I wasn't sure exactly where it lie.

I was now about 9:15 p.m. and I was about 20 minutes from Peoria, so I finished taking photos of headstones and departed.

As I entered Havana, which was the county seat for Mason County, it was very much as I expected—a few blocks of downtown commercial area, a courthouse with memorials to local war veterans surrounded by a tree-lined residential area; which, in turn, was surrounded on all sides by farm land. It was typical of most mid-Western farm towns.

Downtown Havana

As I visit various locations where my ancestors lived, I always take a few moments to reflect and try to visualize what it was like when they lived in the area. I try to visualize what it looked like in their time—what has changed and what remains the same. In Havana, the courthouse was relatively new and there had been upgrades to the commercial part of town; but many of the homes and downtown buildings probably hadn't changed much. A considerable effort had obviously been made to maintain the cobbled downtown streets just as they had been 100 plus years ago. Some of the farmhouses I saw outside of town also probably dated back at least 100 years.

The library was just a block from downtown and typical of most small town libraries. It was built in 1896. Peter wouldn't have seen it as he died in 1893; but Julia would have been able to enjoy it for about ten years. Unfortunately, the local genealogist whom I expected to meet at 10 a.m. didn't show up until just before noon; but the librarian was very helpful and I busied myself researching the old newspapers and other documents looking for obituaries or any other data. Unfortunately, I didn't find much of interest; but I at least satisfied myself that I had done the best I could to see if any obituaries existed for Peter or Julia. When my contact showed up later, she was very helpful in directing me to the courthouse in search of land records. She also

Havana Library

gave me some leads regarding other small newspapers in outlying Mason County communities that were potential sources of the obituaries I was seeking.

I couldn't help but notice during the couple hours I spent in the library that it was certainly well-used and a center of activity, especially by children. The librarian knew all the kids by name, and asked about how their mothers and fathers were doing. The same was true of the little cafe across the street where I went for lunch. The waitress knew every-

one in the cafe and in most cases didn't ever have to ask what they wanted to order because many of them obviously came in frequently and ordered the same thing. It reminded me of the small farm community where I grew up.

The day had already been successful with my visits to the two cemeteries; but it was made even more so when I visited the county records office. The lady was extremely helpful and within about ten minutes I had located the transaction records for the land that my grandmother and

her brother inherited. The land was originally owned by Frank Earhart, whose headstone I photographed at Pleasant Hill Cemetery outside Forest City. When he died it passed to his wife, Mary Elizabeth. She later remarried John Gilmore and then when she passed away in 1933, it was left to my grandmother, Mary Dean, and her brother, Lee O'Malley. They kept it until 1946 and then sold it. Knowing the tract number for the land, I then obtained directions to the land from the very helpful clerk.

Family Farmland

Much as I suspected when I was standing at Pleasant Hill Cemetery, I was only a half-mile from the farm site. Just one-half mile past the cemetery, on the same road, was the land. Since it was only about 20 minutes from Havana, I backtracked toward Forest City and drove to see the land. There were no structures on the land; but as you will note in the photograph, there were structures on the adjoining property.

McCabe Home in Forest City

Since I was back in the vicinity of Forest City, there were a couple of locations that I had not visited earlier in the morning due to time constraints. One was the home where Tom and Sarah McCabe had lived. During the years that they raised my grandmother and her brother they lived on a farm. However, they later moved into town and Tom took a job with the lumber yard. Once again my GPS took me right to the home. Interestingly, when I got to the home I noticed a St. Patrick's Catholic church just about a block down the street. Knowing from church and burial records that the McCabes were Catholic, I checked out the Church to see if it had been existence when they lived there. Sure enough, the church signage indicated that it had been established in 1865. It was obvious, however, that the church structure was fairly new—probably having either torn down and rebuilt or expanded and renovated the original church.

Having had a very successful day in Mason County I headed for Springfield, Illinois, about a two hour drive away.

St. Patrick's Catholic Church

The Dean Side of the Family

My mother's maiden name was Dean, thus the connection to the Dean side of the family. I had always been told that the Deans (also spelled Deane) originally came from England. Turns out that it was a family story that proved to be true.

The name "Dean" appears to be English in origin, having traced the family back to John Dean, who was born and lived in England. John and Elizabeth Dean had a son, Richard, who was born in England in 1698. We are not certain of the year; but Richard emigrated to America and settled in Henrico County, Virginia near Richmond. Since his son Edward was born in 1718 in Henrico, it is likely that Richard came around 1715 when he would have been about 17 years old. Both Richard and his wife Sarah died in Henrico County—he in 1748 and she in 1751. Their son Edward moved to Halifax County where he met and married Rebecca Abney about 1738.

Edward died in 1761 and it is likely that Rebecca died shortly thereafter, because court records show that in October 1763 they did "bind out" as orphans four of their sons, Charles, Joshue, Edward and William. Essentially they were being indentured as apprentices to people who would care for them and teach them a trade. Their oldest son, John, was about 18 years old at the time and he married Keziah Smith in 1761, the same year his father died. John appeared to have a lot of problems handling his debts as court records reveal several claims against him by other individuals in Halifax County, including one by his mother and another by his brother-in-law Ironically, despite his debt problems, he was appointed Sexton of the Antrim Parish at a salary of 400 pounds in 1769. The last record of John in Fairfax County was a sale of land in 1772.

It is likely that John and Keziah moved to North Carolina around 1772 following the sale of their land. Records show that John died in 1775 in Surry County, North Carolina. Surry County is about 200 miles southwest of Richmond—near Winston-Salem, just across the border between Virginia and North Carolina. John and Keziah had six children: John, Winnie, Thomas, Job John, Keziah and Amasa. Some family trees show up to eight, but it appears that there was some duplication of names. I believe Winnie must have died relatively young, as she was not listed in her mother's will in 1787.

Following the death of Keziah in 1787, it appears that most of the children departed North Carolina within the next few years. John and Amos both died in Wayne County, West Virginia. which is about 150 miles NNW of Surry County. Since John was the oldest and Amasa the youngest, it is likely that John took care of Amasa, who was only 13 when their mother died.

Thomas, Job John and Keziah all moved to Kentucky and all died there. Interestingly, Lawrence County Kentucky is only about 50 miles from Wayne County, West Virginia where John and Amasa lived. Washington County is another 200 miles due west. As with most of the immigrant migration patterns, the moves seemed to be almost every generation. They were relatively short moves and generally westward. Then 45 years later, Edward Maxwell Dean moved to Texas. My great grandfather, Thomas Franklin, and his brother, James Bingham, then moved to Colorado in 1879, three years after Colorado gained "statehood," to help their uncles, John,

Peyton and Stephen Jones on the JJ Ranch. At that time the JJ Ranch was one of the largest cattle ranches in the United States. In January of 1882 the Jones Brothers sold the ranch to the Prairie Cattle Company for $625,000. The sale included 300 horses, 55,000 head of cattle and use of the water holes that the Jones brothers had bought or homesteaded. The Prairie Cattle Company was owned by a group of investors in Edinburgh, Scotland and was organized under law of Great Britian.

James C. Jones, owner of the JJ Ranch

If you are familiar with either the book or TV Series *Centennial*, you will recognize a lot of similarity about the drive of the cattle to Colorado by the Jones brothers, the involvement of English and Scots in early Colorado and several other aspects of the story. In fact, James Michener, the author of *Centennial*, was married to a woman from Las Animas, Colorado and came to Las Animas on occasion while writing the book *Centennial*. While there he interviewed people, including Marshal Dean, the son of James Bingham Dean, about the JJ Ranch and development of the cattle industry in Colorado. Knowing this, and the role my ancestors played in the settling of Colorado, I watched the *Centennial* series of tapes again several months ago from a much more personal perspective. In part, I viewed the portion about the development of the cattle industry as a story of my ancestors.

James Bingham's father was Spear Catlett Dean, my great-great grandfather. Spear was married to Sarah Marshall (Jones) Dean. Sarah's brothers were the Jones brothers, who drove the cattle from Texas and built up the JJ Ranch. According to stories passed down within the family, Sarah was the great-aunt of General George Catlett Marshall of WW II fame. He later became Secretary of State and developed the Marshall Plan, which was crucial to the recovery of Europe following WW II. However, I have done some preliminary checking through census records and haven't yet been able to identify the connection between Sarah and General Marshall.

When Thomas and James Bingham got to the JJ Ranch they envisioned a great life of being "cowboys." Unfortunately, as family lore goes, they were put to work doing mundane things like digging ditches and mending fences. Later they were promoted to breaking horses and working the cattle

Sarah Marshall Jones Dean

on the JJ Ranch. After the cattle and ranch were sold in 1882 to the Prairie Cattle Company, Thomas and J.B. tried to "prove up" on land in Smith Canyon. However, they could not

get title to the land and were considered "squatters." Supposedly, the Prairie Cattle Company had some enforcers to discourage "squatters," so they moved to Las Animas. It was about this time that Thomas met Ida Britton, whom he married in 1885.

Ida had come to the Las Animas area in 1881 from Missouri with her parents, Thomas and Effie. This was verified in an article in the *Bent County Democrat* dated April 23, 1937. She was one of the founding members of The Half Century Club (also called the Pioneer Club) and the paper had interviewed them as to when they came to Colorado. The members had all lived in Colorado for 50 years or more. Supposedly she came here in a covered wagon. I don't have a direct source for that—only word of mouth from my mother. When they first arrived, they lived at Prowers

Thomas Franklin Dean

Station, near Ft. Lyon, where her father, Thomas Britton, worked for the Santa Fe Railway Company and at one time was in charge of a hundred men doing construction work. After two years they moved to Las Animas where he engaged with Carter and Lambert in supplying meat to Ft. Lyon. He held various public offices in Las Animas including deputy sheriff, town marshal, police magistrate and was still in public service when he died in 1928.

Thomas Dugan Britton

IDA BRITTON DEAN

I was fortunate to have known my "Grandma Jane." She still lived in the house on Locust and when I was about 11 or 12 years old, I would go over weekly and pump her drinking water from the well. She didn't like drinking the faucet water because she said it didn't taste as good. I have a 38 caliber Smith and Wesson pistol that belonged to her. The patent date on it is 1889, but I am not sure when it was made.

She was not a very big woman, probably about 5'4". She was always very pleasant and would always spend some time sitting and talking with me whenever I went to pump water for her.

In 1952 at the Old Settlers contest in La Junta she was recognized as the registered attendee having the 18th longest longevity of being a resident of Colorado.

Thomas and Ida tried farming for a while and were granted a land patent in 1901 for land just south of the present cemetery. It is likely that he "homesteaded" the land for a few years before filing for the land patent. The farming must not have been very successful or he decided that

Ida Britton as a Young Lady (circa 1882)

wasn't his calling, as he had a butcher shop for a short time. There is also some evidence that the land flooded frequently, being adjacent to the Purgatory River. Then in the fall of 1899 he became one of Bent County's first Sheriffs. He was elected Sheriff again in 1901 and was in office when he passed away of appendicitis in 1905 at the young age of 44.

In my files I have a series of letters between Frank, while he was Sheriff, and people in Sundance, Wyoming (northeast corner, near North Dakota border). His brother Jessie worked on a ranch outside of Sundance and, apparently after getting his seasonal pay, went to town, got drunk, got in a fight and eventually it evolved into a gun fight and he was killed. Frank corresponded with the Sundance Sheriff, Jessie's employer, and a couple other observers to get the details of how Jessie was killed. They brought Jessie's body back to Las Animas and buried him in the Cemetery in the Dean section. The letters are an interesting read and suggest that he was shot in the back by a card player who he had gambled with.

Ida Dean (circa 1945)

ARTHUR DEAN—MY MATERNAL GRANDFATHER

Thomas and Ida's first child, Arthur, was born in 1886. Arthur, my grandfather, was a man of many talents. He wasn't a big man in stature, probably standing about 5′9″ and weighing about 160 pounds; but he eventually became a big man in southern Colorado. He attended the Las Animas school system and was a good student. He then attended Clark Business School in Pueblo, Colorado for a couple of years before going to work for the local bank as a bookkeeper. While in Business School his father died from appendicitis. Around 1909 Arthur moved to Denver, where he worked for the branch of the Secretary of State's office that provided oversight for all the registered brands in Colorado. It was there that he met the very attractive Irish lass by the name of Mary O'Malley. They were married in July of 1911 in Denver and shortly thereafter moved back to Las Animas. I believe he worked for the bank again for a short time and then began farming and ranching. He continued doing than until 1926 when he became under sheriff to Dan Gates. Many will remember Dan's son, Curtis, who for a time sang with the Sons of the Pioneers and later had the memorable role as "Festis" on the TV Series *Gunsmoke*. One day while serving as under sheriff, he and Dan received a call from the police in the neighboring town of Lamar to be on the alert for a man who had stolen a car, then filled it with gas and left without paying. He and a passenger were headed their way on Highway 50. They set up a roadblock in town, but the suspects ran it and headed south out of town. The driver made the mistake of turning into a dead end. Grandpa and Dan came in behind them, got out of their car and tried to stop the young man. However, he decided to run through them. They drew their guns and fired as he raced past them. He was hit and killed.

The victim's parents pressed charges of murder. Dan and Arthur were tried; but in a very short trial the judge dismissed the case. Needless to say, the incident made big headlines in the quiet little town of Las Animas. I recall my grandpa also telling me about another time when they chased some robbery suspect out of town and ended up, with guns drawn, tracking him down on foot. Shots were exchanged and while Dan kept the suspect occupied, grandpa circled around behind (just like in the Western movies) and got the draw on the suspect, who was captured without injury to anyone.

Arthur Dean

It was about midway during his term as under sheriff that Art became heavily involved in the effort to get a dam built on the Arkansas River east of Las Animas. This was needed to provide badly needed flood control and a reliable source of irrigation for farming in southeastern Colorado. He soon became the point man on the effort to get the dam built, an objective many thought was hopeless.

Le Roy Boyd, a writer for the local newspaper described very well the challenge, and Art's role, in his column. Following one of the dam project meetings, *"I told Art that the federal government would never build Caddoa dam, and when Art looked at me in a queer sort of manner I began to support my arguments with what I considered some pretty good facts. Art Dean, though, wouldn't take 'no' when it came to Caddoa dam. He just simply wouldn't be licked and I remember when everybody around here thought there was no use to press the matter further, Art only grinned and kept on working... We raised some money in town here once to help pay expenses for those trips (to Washington D.C. to lobby for the dam). but while Art never said anything about it, I wouldn't be surprised if he dug down into his own pocket for funds to pay some of his expenses. And there was one thing about Art on those trips which no doubt helped him to get official consideration. He didn't bluff or bluster. He was once a cowboy out here on the range, and when he went to Washington he didn't put on striped pants and a frock coat or a white tie and tails. He remained a cowboy in Washington, just as he had been out here in Colorado, and I'm sure the high and mighty brass in Washington were impressed by his direct approach and honesty of purpose... Art isn't a fellow to push himself forward or to tell the world what he has done and that might happen again on April 1. I hope not, for if any person has been responsible for getting Caddoa dam it has been Art. In recognition of that fact, Mac of the* Leader *once suggested in his column that the project be called 'Caddoa Dean Dam,' but it was officially given the name of John Martin dam after the congressman who was in office at the time it was started. But here's another idea. According to the plans that have been announced for April 1, a plaque is to be placed at the dam bearing the names of about 30 "men of vision" who worked to get the project. With all due respect to everybody who worked for the dam, I'm wondering how it would be to have just one name on that plaque. And let it be ART DEAN."*

In a letter from Ed Dean, the son of grandpa Dean's cousin Marshall Dean, were the following comments about grandpa (Art Dean): "Arthur never forgot a name, everyone in Southeastern Colorado knew him and he became well acquainted with President Roosevelt, who once said on seeing the back of his head, 'Stand up Art Dean, I'd know you anywhere.' As I understand it, Roosevelt was visiting Colorado by train, probably campaigning, and en route back to Washington D.C. The train picked up some of the local politicians in La Junta and they rode with him down to the vicinity of where the John Martin Dam was to be built. Included in the group was Art Dean. Roosevelt came into the car to speak with these local politicians and saw the back of Art's head (or perhaps his hat) and made his comment. Local stories also claim that Art Dean and President Roosevelt were visiting and someone announced a Cabinet meeting and Roosevelt said, 'Tell them to go to hell, Art and I are visiting.' I would like to think that was true; but believe that has to be taken with a grain of salt, as it seems like too much of an exaggeration for a small town cowboy lobbyist to command that amount of Roosevelt's attention."

Arthur S. Dean—Bent County Treasurer 1932–1938
(The desk in the photo was still in the Court House when I toured it in 2010)

Art continued as Under Sheriff until 1932, when he ran for and was elected County Treasurer. He served in that office until 1938, when he was defeated despite the key role he was playing in working to get Caddoa Dam approved. It isn't entirely clear what he did in the interim between then and 1944, when he was appointed Postmaster. I think he returned to ranching during that time.

The election of 1944 brought Roosevelt his fourth term of office. Because of his health it is doubtful that he would have run, except the U.S. was now at war on two major fronts. Art Dean was a staunch Democrat, but it wasn't a change of administrations that led to his appointment as Postmaster, Roosevelt having already been in office for twelve years. However, it probably didn't hurt that Arthur had gotten to know both Roosevelt and senior Democratic leaders in Colorado through his leadership role in lobbying for the new dam. It is interesting to note, however, that Colorado was one of only eight states that voted for Dewey, the Republican candidate.

Art continued as the Las Animas Postmaster until 1952 when Eisenhower and the Republicans came into office. It was in late 1952 that his mother, Ida, passed away. She was 83 years old. I remember being part of a conversation between Grandpa and Grandma Dean after the new Postmaster had been appointed. He had offered Grandpa some sort of mundane job down in the basement of the Post Office or he could deliver mail on one of the rural routes. Grandpa surmised that the new postmaster assumed that he would turn down both options. However, he chose to deliver the mail on the rural route. Although he was 66 years old by then, he needed something to do and this was a perfect job. It only took a few hours a day and left him time to get out to the farm and "help out."

Because he put a lot of miles on the car delivering mail, Grandpa normally got a new car every couple years. Well, it wasn't just the miles that necessitated a new car, it was how he drove it and used it. I recall Grandma getting particularly upset one year just a few months after he had gotten a new car. He had the farm which his sons J.B. and Tom worked. However, he spent most of his spare time out there "helping" them out. He was out in the field with the new car and a cow had delivered a new calf. He needed to get the calf back to the corral near the barn, so he wrapped it in a blanket and laid it on the seat of the car! Needless to say, the blanket didn't prevent the seats from getting badly soiled. Despite having the car cleaned at the dealership, I recall there being a very noticeable permanent stain on the seat. Grandma made him get seat covers!

Additionally, he wasn't the best driver in the world; mostly because he was more interested in looking at the fields to see how the crops were progressing or just taking in the sights. Two of my friends, Max and Ray Wheeler, who lived on a farm that was on his mail route, had a couple humorous happenings that they related to me about Grandpa. He was always pulling up too close on the driver's side to the mail boxes, such that the bottom of the metal box would scrape the front left fender. Thus, he would have these long scratches extending from the headlight all the way to the rear view mirror (another reason his cars didn't last long). Apparently, he got so close one time to the Wheeler's mailbox that he knocked it over. After that he would just stop, get out of the car, open the mailbox laying on the ground and put the mail in. Apparently, he did that for several months before they fixed it and replaced the broken post. They also told of meeting him a few times on the road as they were heading the opposite direction on the road to their house. They said Grandpa would always wave at them and put his head out the window to say "howdy" or some other greeting. Meanwhile the car would veer off the road onto the side of the borough ditch and as they watched in their rear view mirror he would recover and bring the car back up on the road. They were sure that on one of their encounters they would have to tow him out of the ditch; but he always managed to recover in time to get back on the road.

I think he continued with the mail route until around 1955 or 56. It was also about that time, or shortly thereafter, that he sold the farm. Fortunate for him, and grandma, he had a long time friend, Dick Klett, who was about his age and still owned a farm. Dick would come by almost every day and pick up Grandpa in his pickup truck and they would go out to Dick's farm, which was run by his son, and "help out." Young Dick said he had to assign a spare hired man just to go around and fix what Grandpa and Dick had broken, which included towing them out of ditches when they got stuck or repair fences they had broken. He said it was well worth it, however, as that was their life and neither were the type to sit around home.

I came back to Las Animas in November of 1969 from San Jose, where I was assigned with the Navy, for a short visit, and as I pulled up in the front noticed an emergency vehicle. When I got inside they were attending to grandpa, who had become dizzy and taken a fall in the bathroom. They took him to the hospital, he developed pneumonia and died a few days later at the age of 83.

Ed Dean also commented that Art Dean was known as the best storyteller in Southeastern Colorado. I can back that up. I just wish that I had tape recorded some of the stories or taken notes about some of the tales he used to tell. I recall him talking of cattle drives from "Twin Peaks" near Walsenburg where there was a railroad cattle loading lot to south of Las Animas. That was in the days of an "open range" where there were no fences.

Grandpa took me golfing on a few occasions to the golf course in La Junta. The group would consist of Wilson R. Brown (who owned the bank), Shorty Clark (real estate), Grandpa and I. None of them could hit the ball much over 150–180 yards; but it was always down the middle. Meanwhile, I could hit it a ton; but never had any idea where it would go—usually **not straight**. Needless to say we spent a lot of time looking for my ball. He used to very quietly say "Del, you don't have to swing so hard." But, of course, I never listened! That is probably why I only got invited a couple times!

I think the most excited I ever saw him was following the time we played in Grand Junction for the state American Legion Baseball Championship. I pitched a shutout and Larry Turner hit a two-run home run over the fence (most fields we played on didn't have a fence!). Grandpa was so excited after the game he could hardly stand it. He had played baseball as a youth and still had his glove and cleats hanging in the basement. One of my regrets is that I didn't save them. The glove wasn't much bigger than a work glove with a single strap between the thumb and index finger--a real classic.

He had a varied background including working in the Secretary of State's office in charge of brands, was a butcher, was the County Treasurer, was Under Sheriff of Bent County, was the Postmaster, was very active in the Bent Prowers Cattlemens Association, and was a mailman doing rural deliveries; but throughout it all he was a "cowboy" rancher and farmer.

Not until I was an adult did I realize the sacrifices Grandma and Grandpa Dean made for my mom, Dean, Mary Jane and myself. Because of my parents' divorce and my mother's alcoholism, they took us in and we lived with them throughout my high school years, and my mother continued living with them until both of them had passed away. Thus, there were six of us in a three bedroom, one bathroom house of about 1500 sq. ft Now that I am a grandfather, I realize that was not only an additional expense; but a total loss of any privacy.

Grandpa was also always very good about letting me borrow the car once I got a license and started dating. Because we only had the one car, on nights I borrowed it, that meant they were without one. He also let me drive it back to Chicago at Christmas of 1958, when I drove back to see Joanne and meet her parents. I think he also had a pickup truck for the farm by then, so they weren't totally without transportation.

Grandpa and Grandma were both very well respected in the community. He was always very active in politics and was a staunch Democrat. He actually ran for state assembly when he was in his 80s. I think he knew he wouldn't win; but wanted to bring attention to some issues that he believed in. He was the treasurer of the local Irrigation Water control board for many years.

Grandpa liked to hunt and fish and I remember that Grandma had an agreement with him. If he killed it, he cleaned it and she would cook it. But it was clear that she didn't do any cleaning of fish or game! He also liked to play poker and had his periodic night out at the local Elks lodge. When he would get home from the game, having also had a shot or two of bourbon (or maybe three!), Grandma would always chide him that she got half his winnings. They would then go through a regular ritual of him claiming he lost and she owed him money, and she sticking to her guns that he owed her half the winnings. I think most times she won out because he was know as a cagey poker player.

He had a great mind for numbers and was always quizzing Dean and I about numbers related to acres in a section and other figures pertaining to land measurements.

He wasn't much for talking on a telephone. In those days long distance calls were a luxury and something we didn't do very often because of the cost. This might have part of his reason for short phone conversations. On those occasions when Grandma might call one of their children or vice versa, Grandma would give him the phone to say , "Hi." That is about all he would say. As I recall his typical response was "Hi, how are you all doing? ("Fine") Well that's good, we're doing fine--here let me give you back to Grandma." I doubt that he was ever on the phone more than about 15 seconds!

Grandma was the Catholic in the family; but in her later years, due to poor health, didn't go to church often. When she did go regularly, Grandpa only went twice a year. He would go on Easter and Christmas eve. Mass was always at midnight on Christmas eve and we kids loved it because we got to stay up. However, Grandpa would go to bed, get up around 11 p.m. and get dressed, go to church with us and then come home and go back to bed.

He would occasionally offer advice and I recall coming home to visit once when I was in the Navy and was undecided about making the Navy a career. He urged me to stay in the Navy because he thought it would be a better life due to the uncertainties of the economy and the job market at that time. It turned out to be good advice.

Grandpa always wore a Stetson cowboy hat when he got dressed up or a straw hat for work. However, unlike most of today's "cowboy wannabes," he always removed his hat when indoors or in the presence of ladies. Nothing irks me more than to see men in restaurants or other public places with their hats on! I also don't think I ever saw him in anything but cowboy boots. He had everyday boots and dress boots. I guess he did have golf shoes for golf—but that was one of the few times he didn't have his boots on.

Grandpa also liked cigars and chewing tobacco. In his later years he had to have a cancerous growth on his lower lip cut out. I am sure it was caused by the cigars and chewing tobacco. Grandpa also liked to have his bourbon; but I don't think I ever saw him drink it other than straight—either from a shot glass or from the bottle. He had a very wry sense of humor and the first time Joanne came to visit us in Las Animas before we were married, mother asked Grandpa to offer Joanne and I a drink. He went into his room, got the bourbon bottle, came back to the living room and handed the bottle to Joanne with a straight face. My mother almost hit him! He knew better; but was testing Joanne a little and also showing his humorous side.

HELEN JANE DEAN RITCHHART—MY MOTHER

Helen Jane Dean

My mother was a very good athlete in high school, playing basketball, tennis and softball. In fact she was recruited by Bonnie's Beauty School to play basketball for them in the Denver Womens' League. I would characterize the team as semi-professional as they didn't pay the players, but they did provide them incentives to play for the team. My mother earned a certificate as a beautician while playing for the team, and I assume she didn't have to pay for the training she received and might have also received something like room and board. Her sister, Frances, and Swede Thaxton, a High School All-American, were on the team and were also from Las Animas, my mother's home town. Their high school team was the best in the state. She and her sister Frances were the tennis doubles champion of their league in high school and one or the other of them (I am not sure which) was the singles champion. I don't have any clippings about her softball exploits, but I know that she and her best friend coached our summer softball team when I was about 11–12 years old and she could field and throw the softball better than most of the boys on the team.

My earliest memories of my mom were when we lived in a farm house outside Walnut Creek, California. My dad was in the Navy, stationed at the St. Mary's Preflight Training School nearby. She had a victory garden and we grew lots of our own vegetables. I remember her getting me off to school in the mornings and taking Dean and me to church on Sundays. I made my First Communion while we lived there.

Once WW II was over, my dad was released from the Navy and we returned to Colorado. Not too long after that I recall many arguments between my mother and father; his drinking being the prime cause of the conflict. They separated when I was in the 4th grade. My mother, although having been certified as a beautician, never pursued that type work; but she did get a job working for a ladies dress shop. Between whatever she received from my dad and her job we still didn't have much income. We rented a three room apartment and I remember often having nothing but potato soup for dinner. I even recall a few times when we had bread and milk.

We were only in Las Animas a few months until we moved to La Junta, 18 miles away, to live with my aunt Frances and her husband, Paul. They operated an upscale (for La Junta) restaurant. I don't think they were very successful financially, because I recall being told frequently to answer the door and tell the man that my aunt and uncle weren't home. I soon learned these were people trying to collect money that was owed them for restaurant supplies, rent, etc.

My sister, Mary Jane, was born in February 1948. At the age of 11, it didn't occur to me to count how many months since my folks had separated. Even today, I am not sure how long it was; but my dad later claimed that he wasn't Mary Jane's father. I never discussed it with my mother.

We moved back to Las Animas very soon after Mary Jane was born, probably because six of us were too many for the small house Paul and Frances had and they probably wanted a little more privacy. Obviously, my mom didn't have time to work, so we were totally dependent on what child support my father paid. As I recall that was just over $100 a month.

We continued to get by over the next five years or so. Then when I was a sophomore we moved in with my grandmother and grandfather. I am not certain why, but I think it got to the point that we couldn't get by financially any more and it did allow my mom to help look after grandma and grandpa.

My mom was not a very good cook, but she was never forced to be as we always had only the most basic of food. She was, however, very good at baking. When I was playing sports in high school, she always made sure I had a good meal before a game. That was one of the few times I might get a good piece of meat.

I can remember times that I grumbled a little about having to wear patched clothes to school. Her answer: "You might have to wear patched clothes, but they are always clean." She always strived to do the best with what she had. Unfortunately, when I was a Junior in high school (1954), my mother had a mental breakdown and my grandparents had her committed to the state mental hospital in Pueblo. Like my father, she too had developed a drinking problem and I think that contributed to her mental situation. To lighten the burden, my grandparents had Mary Jane go live with my Aunt Frances and Uncle Paul in Pittsburgh. They had long ago given up on the restaurant and had moved back to Paul's home town, Pittsburgh, where he worked for the railroad.

Fortunately, the treatment that my mother received worked very well and she was back home after about three or four months. I have requested the records from the hospital so that I can be more exact as to the diagnosis, type treatment, and length of stay.

Once mother returned home, Mary Jane also came home from Pittsburgh. My mother did very well for several years after her treatment. She remained in Las Animas after Dean and I graduated and went off to college, taking care of Grandpa. Grandma had died in 1961. She lived with Grandpa and took care of him until he passed away in 1969. By this time Mary Jane had also graduated, married and moved up to the Boulder area.

I don't have all my dates correct; there was a short period of time that mother came out to El Cajon, California and stayed with her Aunt Blanche, grandpa Dean's sister. Then she stayed with Emma and Herb Billings in the Pueblo area. She eventually settled in the Longmont area first in a house that she rented in the western part of town, and then in a small apartment about three blocks from town.

Helen Jane Ritchhart

Since she had no job, retirement or income, she lived off of social security and welfare. She did manage to come out to visit Joanne and me in 1962 while we were living in San Diego, and in 1988 she went out to Seattle to visit Dean and Evelyn and Jackii. I flew up and spent a few days with them as well. We also brought her out to California for Cheryl's Wedding in 1984 and again in 1993 for Debi's.

I have my mother to thank for making my genealogy research much easier than for most people. That is because she saved everything! In her final few years almost every time I would visit her in Colorado she would give me a box or two of papers and photos to take. Most of them I didn't even open, I just stored them in the garage. I only took the boxes to appease her and make her happy! Eventually I accumulated several boxes of this "stuff," as did my brother. However, it wasn't until my mother passed away in 1995 and I developed an interest in genealogy that I started going through those boxes to see what I could throw away. Much to my delight there were large numbers of old family photographs, letters, newspaper articles and other memorabilia. Obviously, this information heightened my interest in family history and has been a rich source of information about my grandmother and grandfather and their families.

Unfortunately, similar to my father, my mother also had a relapse from staying sober. In my phone conversations I began noticing signs of this. When I visited I noticed bottles of wine. She wouldn't admit that she was drinking again; but the signs were very obvious. She had moved from Longmont to Loveland and was living there in a three room, second floor apartment. I worried about the walk up the stairs, as there was no elevator; but she seemed to like the location. Finally a combination of her failing health and continued drinking led to moving her into an assisted living facility. I was able to find her a very nice place where she could still have some of her own furniture and it provided meals and on call assistance, if needed.

However, within just a few weeks of her moving in, I got a call that she had been admitted to the hospital. We were living in El Cajon, California at the time, so I flew back to Denver. I found out from the doctor that she wasn't serious and he would be releasing her the next day. I went over to the assisted living facility to pick up some things and when I inquired at the front desk the manager came out and told me that mother couldn't come back to the facility. There was a limitation as to how often a resident could ring the bell and ask for assistance or service and she was far exceeding their limits. The manager claimed she needed a facility that provided full time care—which this place did not.

Well, I don't think I have ever experienced such stress in my life. She was going to be released from the hospital that day; but didn't have anywhere to go! Additionally, I was working and couldn't just take off a week to spend researching and getting her relocated. I went back to the hospital and the doctor agreed to keep her an extra day, thus, I had one day to find her a place. Fortunately, the hospital connected me with a with a county agency that dealt with welfare and seniors. They gave me a list of recommended facilities in the Loveland area. I looked at several that day and found a couple that I thought were very nice. I remember being surprised and impressed with how many facilities for seniors were in this relatively small town.

The good Lord must have been looking out for me that day as the facility I thought was the best had an immediate opening. I was really fortunate as it was not unusual to be on a waiting list for weeks or months for a room in this care facility. Additionally, since the county was going to be paying for her care, they even approved her move to the facility in one day—almost unheard of in most government organizations! Having wrapped this up by around 4 p.m., I then contacted Linda, who lived close by in Fort Collins, and she agreed to bring their van and meet me to move mother's furniture and belongings between the two facilities. I think we finished up around 9 p.m. that night. Needless to say, I slept well that night! I don't recall the exact date; but I think all this took place around February or March of 1995.

In August 1995, we had a big party at Linda's for mother's 80th birthday. All of our kids and their families attended. We hired a limo to pick up mother at the care facility and drive her to Linda's where we had a tent set up and several people there besides just family. Cheryl's girls were in the 7 to 10 age group and they rode with grandma to the house and I am not sure who enjoyed it more—mother or the girls.

Our timing was good, because two months later mother either collapsed or fell in the bathroom of her room at the facility and died from hitting her head.

My mother didn't have what most would judge a very happy life. She endured a lot of hardship, suffered through bouts with alcoholism and never had much materially. However, she never complained and always tried to do the best with what she had. She got a great deal of satisfaction out of the accomplishments of Dean, Mary Jane and myself. Losing Mary Jane was a big blow to her, but that was somewhat offset by finding Jackii. Even though Mother's death cut that relationship short—it meant a lot to her.

Mother was a survivor and her approach to life was truly typified by her statement to Dean and me; "I may have to send you off to school with clothes that are patched; but they will always be clean!"

MARY JANE RITCHHART—MY SISTER

Mary Jane Ritchhart

Since there was 11 years difference in our ages, I don't think I ever got to know my sister as well as I should have. We also had quite a bit of turmoil within the family during Mary Jane's earlier years. She was born in La Junta months after my mother and father separated, thus, she never had a father figure in the house until we moved in with our grandparents when she was about three years old. Then when my mother was put into the Pueblo Mental Hospital, Mary Jane, who was then about six years old, went to Pittsburgh and lived with my Aunt and Uncle, Frances and Paul Gallagher.

Although I never remember her mentioning it, I am sure it must have bothered her that our dad never paid much attention to her. Even though he and our mother were divorced, he still lived in the local area and came by often to pick up Dean and me and spend time with us. He did move to the Denver area around 1955 when I was in college in Boulder. The reason he felt no connection to Mary Jane is because he said he was not her natural father. When I was in college he shared this with me.

Not so Dean and I would think any less of our mother, but because he didn't want to look like such an uncaring person in the eyes of his two sons. Based on my perceptions and intuition, I believe he was correct. I never had the chance to share that with Mary Jane. I always planned to tell her after our mother died, but never had that chance as Mary Jane preceded her in death.

Further reducing the time I had to spend with Mary Jane was the fact that I worked in Gunnison and Poncha Springs following high school graduation and then was away to college the next four years and spent one of those summers in Denver. Mary Jane was a good student, doing exceptionally well in Distributive Education. Her Junior year she won the state competition based on skill at interviewing for a job. She won a trip to the National Competition in Chicago. In her junior high and early high school years she was very enamored with baton twirling with the marching band. She began dating Eldon Johnson, four years her senior, around her Junior year or late as a Sophomore. My mother didn't like Eldon and made life very difficult for the two of them. My mother could be very stubborn at times and this was one of them. In my opinion she didn't think Eldon "came from a good enough family." They weren't from one of the long established families of Las Animas, whom my mother and Grandparents would have known for many years. I think she was also concerned about Eldon being four years older than Mary Jane.

Mary Jane became pregnant the summer of her Junior year in school and my mother had her sent away to a Nun's convent in Canyon City, where the baby was born. The baby was then put up for adoption through Catholic social services. Mary Jane and Eldon didn't have much say as mother was adamant that the baby be given up for adoption. Under the circumstances, I believe it was the best decision for all. Neither Eldon's nor our family had the money to afford to support Eldon and Mary Jane. Mary Jane was only 17 and Eldon was about 21. I don't recall exactly, but I think Eldon had enlisted in the Army and was stationed in the Colorado Springs area. My grandmother and grandfather had enough burden just supporting my mother, brother, and Mary Jane, let along bringing a baby into the picture.

Mary Jane and Eldon did marry after Mary Jane graduated from high school and had spent a year or so in college at Ft. Collins. My mother eventually seemed to accept Eldon. However, their marriage only lasted about four years. I think Mary Jane, not having had much money or nice possessions during her younger years, liked the "good life" and probably tended to push Eldon beyond their means. Following the Army, Eldon, who was a very good student, went to college and became a professor. I think he was completing either a masters or Ph.D. at the University of Colorado while he and Mary Jane were married. He was also doing some teaching.

Mary Jane married John Hayes in 1976 and they lived in the Boulder area. John was an Air Traffic Controller who worked in the Denver Center control station. They seemed to have a very happy life. Mary Jane worked for a farm implement store outside the Longmont area while she and Eldon were married and for a short time after marrying John. She then worked for a travel agency in the Boulder area most of her life with John. Unfortunately she was stricken with lymphoma and died in 1979.

This was a big blow to mother, who really enjoyed having Mary Jane close to where she lived in Longmont. Not too long after Mary Jane died, mother began an effort to locate her granddaughter, the baby that she had Mary Jane give up for adoption. She was very persistent and eventually was able to identify Jacqueline Fitzpatrick as the child. Jackii had been adopted by a couple who lived not far from Canyon City. Mother met both Jackii and Jackii's parents and this was a very positive and happy event for her. Jackii maintained contact with mother over the years and was exceptionally nice to her. She was very proud of Jackii and I know it made her very happy to be able to have located her and to enjoy a positive relationship with her.

Jackii and her husband, Steve moved to the Seattle area in the early 1990s. Eldon Johnson had remarried and was teaching at a college in the area. Additionally, Dean and Evelyn lived there. They established contact with Jackii and I met her during a visit to the area around 1988 when mother was there visiting with Dean and Evelyn. I was very positively impressed with Jackii. She was a tall attractive young lady who seemed very self assured and well adjusted. She was getting a degree in Accounting and became an accountant. She and Steve moved away from the area later and moved to Mount Pleasant, South Carolina. They live there currently (2010) and have two children, Zack and Zoe.

Wirszyla Family—Jackii, Zack, Steve, Zoe

The Schmidt Family

When I initially started researching my wife's family, I knew she claimed that Schmidt was a German name and that her Grandfather's name was Oscar, but didn't have any other data about where her family came from in Europe or when they came to America. Few would argue with the supposition that Schmidt is a Germanic name so I readily accepted that assumption.

In checking census data I was able to work back from Oscar and learn that he was born in Indianapolis and that his parent's names were Frederic and Maria. Census data also revealed that Frederic and Maria's first born, Frederick, was born in New York around 1850. Since Frederic and Maria would have been about 28 and 20 years of age, respectively, I assumed they probably came to this county somewhere between 1845 and 1849. Other census data also revealed that Frederic was from the region of Württemberg and Maria from Bavaria or Prussia. Since their second child, Matilda, was born in Indianapolis around 1852, I assumed that they left New York for Indianapolis around 1851.

Frederick was a very popular name in the Schmidt family. Not only did Frederic and Maria have a son Frederick; but Joanne's father's name was Frederick as was her brother's. In trying to track the original Frederic back to Württemberg, I learned the name Frederic(k) Schmidt in Germany is like John Smith in the United States—it is a very common name, which really complicates research! Although Joanne's father and brother spelled their given name with a "k," from my research I am very confident that her great-grandfather spelled it only with a "c"—Frederic.

Oscar & Joanne Schmidt

Knowing that Frederic and Maria had lived in New York City in 1850, I attempted to find them in the 1850 New York Census or City Directory. My initial efforts were unsuccessful. Finally, following a German Research Association meeting in San Diego in January 2006, one of discussion leaders agreed to help me search. She suspected that the spelling in the census records might be different and asked if I had explored that possibility. I had tried a couple variants like Schmit and Schmitt with no success. After confirming she couldn't find a Frederic Schmidt that matched my information, she suggested we search in New York City for Frederic S with a wild card for the end of the surname (this enables the search engine to look for any name starting in S). We searched and came up with a surprisingly small number of candidates. Much to my surprise and relief, one of the names, Frederick Smith, had a wife Eliza (her given name was Maria Elizabeth) and son Frederick, whose ages and birth places matched that of the people I was researching. Thus, it is likely the enumerator heard "Smith" rather than "Schmidt"—understandable considering that Maria or Frederic's response to the enumerator was probably spoken in a heavy German accent. Lending further credence to our discovery was the fact Frederic's occupation, "butcher," matched that from Indianapolis census and city directory records.

Over the next several years I attempted to identify Frederic in immigration or ship passenger lists. I found many Frederic(k) Schmidts; but none that I could definitely correlate to Joanne's great-grandfather. In early 2010 I happened to be reading an article which mentioned Castle Garden. I had heard of Castle Garden and knew it was used for processing immigrants into New York City prior to the opening of Ellis Island. However, I didn't recall ever searching the Castle Garden database for Frederic. My first efforts provided several Frederic(k) Schmidts; but none that I could confirm with any degree of assurance. I then noticed a feature that allowed you to click on the individual's name and obtain amplifying information in addition to name, arrival date and age. Searching the arrival time frame of 1840–1850, I identified 14 Frederic(k) Schmidts. Starting at the top I began amplifying each of them sequentially. Finally, as I got to the 13th name, I noted evidence that my search might have ended! It listed him as a butcher, age 22, from Württemberg, who departed from Havre, France. The ship arrived on January 18, 1848; which would make his birthdate around 1826. Other records indicated he was born in 1822 or 1823; but it is possible the difference was because of language problems or an attempt for some reason to appear younger.

I was really pleased to make this discovery, thinking this could lead me to learning the name of the city or village in Württemberg he came from and, eventually, the names of his mother and father! These expectations came to a sudden end, however, when I explored the Havre (Le Havre), France emigration records and discovered they only cover the period 1780 to 1840. I now knew how and when he traveled from Europe to America; but nothing that would enable me to pin down exactly where in the Württemberg region he had lived.

Between census records, Indianapolis City Directories and other vital records I learned quite a bit about Frederic, Maria and their family. Oscar's death certificate listed his mother's maiden name as Holliday. However, I talked with the German expert at the Family History Library in Salt Lake City and he said Holliday was not a German name. I have confirmed that by researching listings of German surnames and looking for other Hollidays born in Germany in census records. I have checked other logical sources for Maria's maiden name; but couldn't find any other than the one source—Oscar's death certificate. I am very skeptical about Holliday being her true maiden name; but don't have anything better to go with.

The 1900 Census indicated that 13 children were born to Maria; but only 9 were still living. Cemetery records at Crown Hill Cemetery in Indianapolis included Clarence and Elizabeth in the family plot. I haven't been able to account for the other two children who died young.

Various records list Maria's place of birth as Bavaria and Prussia—somewhat of a conflict since the areas normally associated with Prussia were Poland and the Northeastern fringes of modern day German, while Bavaria is Southeast.

The 1872, 1873 and 1874 City Directories list "Mrs. E. Schmidt" as a midwife. However, the 1887–1890 directories list her as a "physician." In those days the requirements for being designated as a physician were very lenient; thus, I feel certain she was still serving as a midwife, but the title physician sounded more professional and was often used to identify midwives. In any case, she must have been fairly successful, as Frederic died at the very early age of 50 and she seemed to have had no problems in raising the remaining children at home. Her obituary also stated that she was "one of the most prominent German charity organization workers in the city…," which implies that she was probably doing well financially.

The 1900 Federal Census and her obituary both indicate that she immigrated into this county in 1847. Combined with the fact we know Frederick arrived in 1848, that lends credence to my assumption that they met and married in New York rather than having married prior to coming to America. I checked immigration records, including Castle Garden, and couldn't find any record of a Maria or Elizabeth Holliday of German nationality arriving in 1847 (or any other likely arrival year).

Frederic and Maria's son, William H. Schmidt, was the Treasurer of Marion County and apparently also a druggist. He was also listed in the book *The Germans of Indianapolis: 1840–1918* by George Theodore Probst as a member of the Maennerchor Society (translates as Men's Choir). This was a group that promoted music from their homeland that later evolved into a social club and advocates for classical music. Also listed were F. H. and Edward Schmidt, who might have been William's brothers. Maria's obituary stated that her son William was in a sanatorium at the time of her death. He died a year later. Since tuberculosis patients were frequently placed in sanatoriums in those days, that might have been the cause of his illness and death. Interestingly, however, is the fact Maria's cause of death was listed as tuberculosis; but she apparently died at home.

Other sons of Frederic and Maria worked for travel agencies, were druggists, and Joanne's grandfather, Oscar, became a very successful insurance broker in the Chicago area and Joanne's father, also Frederick, was a lawyer in Chicago.

I would like to have been able to track Frederic and/or Maria back to their home town or village and to identify their parents; but, thus far, have been unable to make that connection.

Frederick Henry Schmidt

FREDERICK HENRY SCHMIDT

Joanne's father attended Dartmouth, where he played basketball and obtained a law degree. Following graduation he returned to the Chicago area and practiced corporate law there for the remainder of his career. Within two years of returning to Chicago, Fred met and married Frances McConnell. They had three children, Joanne, Betty Jean and Fred.

Fred was a very outgoing personable man. He was a big man, standing about 6′ 1″ and weighing in excess of 250 pounds. I think his weight contributed to the health problems that he suffered. At a relatively early age he suffered a heart attack and then when he was about 66 years old (July 1974) he suffered a stroke that left him partially paralyzed. This, combined with having diabetes, resulted in his having a leg amputated.

Shortly after Fred's stroke the family talked him and Frances into moving to the San Jose area. Besides us, Betty Jean also lived there and we felt they should be closer so that we could help out. They bought a nice condo unit in a golf course community on the southeastern outskirts of San Jose. Unfortunately the strain of taking care of Fred, who was almost totally confined to bed, was too much for Frances and she died in her sleep in January 1978, less than three years after coming to California.

Fred obviously couldn't live on his own, so the condo was sold and he moved in with his son, Fred, and his family in the San Diego area. That didn't work out well and one day he just disappeared. Finally, the family had to hire a detective to find him. He was living in his old Men's Club in Chicago that he had belonged to when he was practicing law. He had been charging his expenses. After paying his expenses, we brought him back to an assisted living facility in the San Jose area near where Betty Jean was living. He remained there until he passed away in 1982.

JOANNE SCHMIDT RITCHHART

Joanne attended New Trier High School in Willmette, Illinois where she was a very accomplished member of their synchronized swim team and was Vice President of their Senior Class. After graduating, she attended the University of Colorado. We met Joanne's Freshman year. My roommate was in a class with Joanne and when I asked him to get a date for a friend of mine coming to visit for the weekend, he picked Joanne. I had another date; but we took a liking to one another and began dating shortly thereafter We continued dating and became engaged just prior to the Christmas holidays her sophomore year. Joanne didn't enjoy school very much, so at the end of the semester (January 1958) she left CU and entered United Air Lines Flight Attendant Training. Upon graduation she was domiciled in Chicago; but managed to get assigned to flights to Denver very frequently on weekends throughout my Junior and Senior years.

She attended so many of my baseball games in Boulder that my baseball coach was convinced she still lived in Boulder. Following my graduation from CU and completing Navy Officer Candidate School in November 1959, we were married in Evanston, Illinois.

Joanne Frances Schmidt

We had three girls, Cheryl, Debi and Linda. Joanne was an exceptional military wife, providing a solid foundation for the family that required my frequently being gone on six-month deployments, as well as other short-term assignments away from home. Joanne started working when we were stationed in Taipei, Taiwan in 1965. She had an excellent job supervising all flight attendants for China Airlines. This involved screening, hiring, training and supervising all flight attendants. Since the airlines flew to Seoul, Korea; Manila, Philippines; Tokyo, Japan; Bangkok, Thailand; Singapore and Hong Kong; she made frequent trips to those cities to observe the attendants and check on support services at those various air terminals. She had an interesting experience when she returned from one of those flights. When she went through immigration in Taipei they noted that her visa had expired. They required her to leave the country on the next flight, which was to Hong Kong. She had to remain there for a couple days until we could get her visa renewed.

She had many other jobs throughout our time in the Navy; but frequently had to start over in a new location when we were transferred.

Finally, after we retired and moved to the San Diego area, she went into real estate and was able to successfully stay with that career for about 14 years. After returning to the San Diego area in 1999 following my retiring from Lockheed Martin in Bethesda, Maryland, she became interested in "stamping." "Stamping" is actually a craft which involves making greeting cards using a wide variety of techniques. Joanne became a very accomplished "stamper" and frequently taught classes at the stamping supplies store where she worked part-time. She often gives a packet of her cards to friends as gifts, but the recipients rarely send the cards to anyone else. They keep them and display them because they claim the cards are too beautiful to give away. It looks very likely that this craft will be perpetuated within the family, as she has sparked the interest of one daughter and at least two granddaughters in this hobby.

Throughout some very trying years involving frequent moves and my absences on military and business assignments, Joanne has been a loving wife, a wonderful mother and grandmother and the real foundation of our family.

ELIZABETH JEAN SCHMIDT

Betty Jean was born on 29 August 1940 in Evanston, Illinois. During the time that I knew her she went by the names of Betty Jean and later, Betty. I first met Betty in a rather unusual manner. Early in my Sophomore year at CU my roommate asked me to go out with a blind date as a favor to a girl he met in one of his classes. Her sister was visiting her and was a Senior in high school. I agreed, went on the date, the girl went back to her home and that was the end of the

Betty Schmidt Wolf

story—I thought. Several months later I met Joanne when she was on a blind date with a friend of mine who was in Boulder for the week end. My same roommate that had lined me up with the blind date with Betty Jean invited Joanne as the blind date for my friend.

A couple months after I began dating Joanne she asked me about the blind date that I gone out on earlier in the year. I couldn't imagine how she knew about the blind date. She then told me that my blind date was her sister! Somehow she made the connection; but I didn't.

Betty went to the University of Michigan and studied physical therapy; but left school after her Junior year. She married Fred Wolf, whom she had dated in High school, in 1961. Fred and Betty had two boys, Fred and Jeffrey.

Unfortunately, the marriage did not go well and Betty divorced Fred in 1969. Shortly after the divorce Betty decided she wanted to move to Germany. This caused some problems with custody of the boys. Initially, both Jeff and Fred went with Betty to Germany; but shortly afterward, Fred went back with his father. Betty pursued further education as a physical therapist, gained accreditation and then was employed in that field. Betty enjoyed Munich and put Jeff into German schools. They both became very fluent in the German language.

Betty developed some medical problems that had to do with blood clots in her legs around 1974. Joanne and Betty talked and decided it was best for Jeff to come back and live with us in Cupertino, California where I was assigned to Naval Air Station Moffett Field. Jeff was about 8 at the time and it was quite an adjustment, not only to moving back to the United States; but living with three girls. They shared one bathroom and I remember some conflicts over who tied up the bathroom the most!

Betty finally returned to the San Jose area early in 1975, somewhat in an effort to get better medical care. She overcame her medical problems and decided to stay in the San Jose area. Her German Physical Therapist certification was not recognized in California so Joanne and I convinced her to get into real estate. She obtained her license and became a very good real estate agent—continuing in that field until her bout with cancer forced her to stop.

Betty met Armin Kampman a few years after settling in Cupertino and they married in April 1979. Armin claimed to be a successful businessman, but soon after they were married I think Betty learned that was far from the truth. In fact, we loaned him money that was later paid back with some of his paintings at about the time Betty was divorcing him. I can't recall exactly how long the marriage lasted; but I think it was less than two years.

Finally, her luck with men changed when she met Al Estabrook. In my eyes Al was a very unlikely match with Betty. Al was a retired butcher, with no education beyond high school. He was a "good old boy" type person. He was low key and very easy going. In the end I think that turned out to be the secret to their happiness together. Betty had a very strong personality and could be dominant at times. Al just played along and whatever Betty wanted was fine with him.

I first met Al when I was on a business trip to the San Jose area around 1998. He seemed like a nice enough guy; but didn't seem like someone who matched up well with Betty. However, as I stated at Al's memorial service, "Al grows on you." The more I saw of Al, the better I liked him.

Al owned a very nice large home in the hills on the eastern side of San Jose. Eventually, he sold the house and moved in with Betty in a condo in the Saratoga area. Somewhere around 2002 we talked Al and Betty into moving to San Diego where they bought a nice home about one mile from us in the Rancho Bernardo area.

We teased Betty that she was trying to kill off Al with all her sporting and athletic endeavors. She and Al hiked Mount Kilimanjaro, went on 50-mile bike outings and several other vigorous outdoor activities. Joanne claimed that Betty was the family's "Auntie Mame" because she was always doing something venturesome. In addition to these aforementioned adventures, she once sailed as the only woman on the crew in the "TransPac" sailboat race from the West Coast to Hawaii and participated in a 100-mile bike race in the Lake Tahoe area. She was also recognized on the cover of a sailboat racing magazine for her accomplishments as a female sailor.

Betty had made a very good transition into the local real estate market and she and Al were very happy in their new home. Unfortunately, she was diagnosed with ovarian cancer late in 2004. She put up a strong battle; but finally succumbed to the cancer in March 2006.

Al had been fighting cancer even before Betty was diagnosed. He seemed to be in remission, but it came back shortly after Betty's death and he died in February 2007.

The McConnell Family

Joanne's mother was a McConnell; in fact she was the youngest of eight children born to Russell McConnell and Mary Myrtle Dye. Russell was a lawyer and was probably a staunch advocate of the Libertarian Party. He lobbied most of his life against income tax and was very much against government controls. Apparently, he was born and given the name Norman Russell; but later changed it to Russell Norman. Family legend has it that the McConnell name is Scotch Irish; but I have not been able to trace their ancestry back to Europe.

Russell McConnell

I must thank Valerie Wolf for much of the information I have about the McConnell family. Valerie's husband, Jeff Wolf, is the grandson of Frances McConnell and Fred Schmidt. Russell's mother's (Margaret Stitt) side of the family traces back to Ireland on both her paternal and maternal sides of the family. James Stitt was born in Antrim, Ireland in 1750 and Cromwell McVitty, Margaret Stitt's maternal great-grandfather, was born in Dublin, Ireland in 1729. However, another great-grandfather on her mother's side was born in Germany.

Russell was born in Henry County, Illinois, which is about 100 miles southwest of Chicago. He, or he and his family, moved to McPherson, Kansas when he was about 18 years old. He must have entered the University of Michigan a couple years later, as he graduated from law school in 1894, when he would have been about 26 years old. About two years later he married Mary Myrtle Dye in Oklahoma City. All eight of their children were born while they lived in Oklahoma City, where he practiced law. He and Mary must have moved to the Chicago area in the 1915–20 time frame. The 1930 census listed his occupation as Commercial Lawyer.

Joanne remembers she, her sister and her mom taking the train from Chicago to Las Angeles to visit Russell, Mary and her Aunt Edith around 1950. Thus, the McConnells probably moved to California from Illinois in the late 1940s. Mary passed away in 1960 and Russell in 1965. It didn't occur to me until I was writing this chapter that Joanne and I lived in San Diego from 1962–64 and no mention was ever made of her grandfather living in Los Angeles. We knew her Aunt Carol lived in Laguna Beach and visited her in 1960 and again in 1962, but not her grandfather. Joanne said that her mom never talked much about her parents.

FRANCES LOIS MCCONNELL

I first met Joanne's mother and father in December of 1957. We had just become engaged; I had only met them one other time when they came out to Colorado to bring Joanne to school her Sophomore year. I think they wanted to get to know me better so I was invited out between Christmas and New Year's. My two roommates, Roger Kinney and Lloyd (Porky) Manown, drove out with me. They stayed at the Phi Gam house at Northwestern University, just a short distance away, and I stayed with the Schmidts. I think Joanne's mother and father were concerned that we would get married and expect them to support us at school. I also know they weren't real happy with their daughter choosing this small-town boy from a divorced family, with no money, and on top of that being a Catholic. Looking back on it as a parent, I don't really blame them. I think I reassured them I had no intention of getting married until after graduation.

Frances McConnell Schmidt

Despite their reservations about me, they were very hospitable and I had a very nice time throughout my stay with them. I also got to meet others of the family, including Joanne's brother and sister; Joanne's dad's sister, Min; and Frances's brother, Vincent.

Frances was a very attractive lady. In fact, when Fred sufferred a heart attack at a relatively young age, she enrolled in the John Robert Powers modeling program so as to have a backup career if Fred had another attack and died.

She enjoyed entertaining and was very good at it, something that she passed on very well to her daughters. She came to Hawaii in September of 1960 just prior to Cheryl's birth. In fact, Joanne had a check-up with the doctor and then we were going to pick up her mom. The doctor examined her and told us to go immediately to the hospital. I then picked up her mom at the airport and when we arrived home and called about Joanne, Cheryl had been born. We had a drink to celebrate and headed to the hospital.

CAROL MCCONNELL LISCOM

Other than Joanne's mother, the McConnell branch that I got to know best was Joanne's Aunt Carol and her daughters, Joanne and Joyce. As I mentioned, Carol lived in Laguna Beach just a couple blocks from the beach. My second assignment in the Navy was to Air Intelligence School in Alamada, California. From there we were assigned to Hawaii, but before we left I

Joanne Liscom Pawlo

had to attend a short two- or three-day school in San Diego. Joanne was pregnant with Cheryl and stayed with Carol while I attended school. I then drove back up to Laguna Beach and we stayed a couple more days before returning to Alamada and then on to Hawaii. Carol's husband had passed away in 1957. They had a daughter, Joanne, who was just a year older than my wife, Joanne. She was engaged to Bob Pawlo and the two of them got married a couple months after our visit.

Carol was a devout Christian Science church member and I recall Joanne having to sneak into the bedroom or bathroom to take the medications that her doctors were prescribing during her pregnancy.

In 1968 we were based at nas Moffett Field in the San Jose area. By this time Joanne and Bob had moved to the Marin County area just north of San Francisco where he was a dentist. We went up a couple times to visit them as their children were about the same ages as ours. On one occasion Joanne was having a severe dental problem while I was on deployment. She talked with Bob and he had her and the girls come up on the weekend and he took care of her dental work.

McConnell Family Reunion in Los Angeles (circa 1953)
(Back row: Joyce & Don Davies, Rusty & Inez McConnell, Mary & Russell McConnell, Edith McConnell, Family Friend, Katie Crowder—Edith's daughter, Art McConnell
Front Row: Carol McConnell Liscom, Amelia Liscom, Joanne McConnell, Joyce's baby Dru, Bill Liscom, Betty Ann Crabtree—Edith's daughter)

Later, around 1983, when we were living in McLean, Virginia, Bob and his son, Ron, came and stayed with us for a few days. Ron was interested in the Naval Academy and I had arranged a visit and tour of the campus in Annapolis. Ron must have liked what he saw, as he was accepted and graduated from the Naval Academy. He wanted to be an aviator, but following graduation there were no flight training openings. They sent him to San Diego on a temporary assignment until they could get him into flight school. By that time we had retired from the Navy and were living in San Diego. Most of the summer that he was in San Diego he spent the weekends at our house. We had a nice pool to lounge around, it beat bachelor officer quarters on the base, and he had someone to pal around with, as he had become friends with our daughter, Debi.

We have met all of the Pawlo children; but got to know Ron and his sister, Mindy, the best. We still keep up with Joanne and Bob and see them occassionally.

I got to know Joanne's Pawlo's sister, Joyce, only through phone conversations. In researching the McConnell family she shared my interest in family history and provided me quite a bit of information. In turn, I sent her everything that I had and had obtained from Valerie Wolf. She and her husband, Don Davies, lived on the East Coast in Marblehead, Massachusetts. The times we talked on the phone she always seemed very energetic and very appreciative of the work I was doing on the McConnell family history. Unfortunately, as I was writing this chapter, I received an e-mail from Don notifying us that Joyce passed away the previous week.

I met Vincent McConnell, Joanne's uncle, a couple times at Joanne's parents'. I believe he also attended our wedding. I didn't get to know him well, but remember that he was very friendly and seemed to be a very nice person.

Musings

In this chapter of the book I have compiled some of my thoughts about various aspects of my life that I thought future generations (and perhaps the present) might find interesting. They not only reflect some of my personal experiences and feelings; but are representative of the time period in which they occurred.

Del Ritchhart—The Author (2008)

Where I Lived

Following is a synopsis of my military assignments and the locations and/or residences where I lived. Needless to say I have moved around a lot. I would guess that I have moved over 50 times in my life—around thirty of those having been by Joanne and I during our married life.

Shorter moves within a city are not reflected below. For instance I lived in seven different houses within Las Animas from the time I was 10, following the divorce of my parents, until I was 15 when we moved in with my grandparents. I think we frequently moved when the rent came due!

Joanne and I always like to say "Even though we moved a lot, it never got easier—but we did get better at it!" We moved once from Cupertino, California to Monterey, California two days before Christmas and had a tree up and decorated and the house in pretty good order by Christmas Eve. We moved to San Diego in 1984 and by July 1999 had moved five times, which included living in three different homes in San Diego, one in Westlake Village, California and one in Vienna, Virginia.

I served in the U.S. Navy from 1959 to 1984.
Attended Officer Candidate School in Newport, RI July 1959–Nov 1959

Following is a list of major assignments:

Air Ground Officers School, Jacksonville, FL	Nov 1959–Feb 1960
Air Intel Trng Ctr, Alameda, CA	Mar 1960–May 1960
VP-28 Barbers Point, Hawaii	May 1960–Oct 1962
VP-31 Air Intelligence Officer & NFO Instructor, San Diego, CA	Oct 1962–Aug 1964
Defense Intelligence School, Anacostia, Washington D.C.	Sep 1964–May 1965
Taiwan Defense Command, Taipei, Taiwan	Jul 1965–Jun 1967
FASO/VP-31 Student, NAS North Island, Coronado, CA	July 1967–Dec 1967
VP-9, NAS Moffett Field, Sunnyvale, CA	Jan 1968–Jul 1969
Naval Postgraduate School, Monterey, CA	Oct 1969–Dec 1970
FAW-8, NAS Moffett Field	Jan 1971–Aug 1971
Tactical Training, Team/FAW-10, NAS Moffett Field	Aug 1971–Jun 1973
Naval War College, Newport, RI	Jul 1973–Jul 1974
COMPATWINGSPAC, NAS Moffett Field	Aug 1974–Sep 1975
VP-31 Student, NAS Moffett Field	Oct 1975–Feb 1976
XO/CO VP-9, NAS Moffett Field	Mar 1976–Mar 1978
CINCPATFLT (Air Ops), Makalapa, Hawaii	Mar 1978–Jun 1981
Office of Legislative Affairs, Washington D.C.	Jul 1981–Jan 1984

Following retirement from the U.S. Navy in January 1984 I entered the civilian world as follows:

Booz Allen & Hamilton, San Diego, CA	Jan 1984–May 1988
DAR Associates (Consulting)	Jun 1988–Sep 1989
Lockheed Corporation, San Diego, CA	Oct 1989–March 1993

Lockheed Corporation, Calabasas, CA   April 1993–March 1994
Lockheed Martin Corporation, Bethesda, MD   March 1994–July 1999

RESIDENCES. Following is a list of early years residences/schools:

May '37–July 1937	Las Animas, CO
July '37–Dec 1937	Detroit, MI (Father playing pro football for Lions)
Dec '37–Aug 1938	Las Animas, CO
Aug '38–July 1939	Fruita, CO (father coach at High School)
July '39–July 1942	Lamar, CO (father coach at High School)
July '42–Sep 1942	Chapel Hill, NC (father attended V5 Program Officer Training)
Sep '42–Jun 1944	Concord, CA (father stationed at St. Marys Preflight Trng w/Navy)
Aug '44–May 1945	Cordell, OK (father still in Navy)
Sep '45–Jan 1946	La Junta, CO (Lincoln Grade School)
Jan '46–May 1947	Las Animas, CO (Fry Grade School, Dad at Ft. Lyon)
May '47–June 1948	La Junta, CO (Park Grade School)
June '48–May 1950	Las Animas, CO, Columbian School (grade school and Jr. High)
Sep '50–May 1955	Las Animas (Bent County High School)
Sep '55–May 1959	Boulder, CO (Univ of Colorado)
May '59–July 1959	Denver, CO (lived with father and worked at brick yard)
July '59–Nov 1959	Newport, RI, (Officer Candidate School)
Nov '59–Jan 1960	1900 Lakeshore Blvd., Jacksonville, FL (AGO School)
Feb '60–May 1960	748 Lincoln Ave, Alameda, CA (Air Intelligence Training Center)
May '60–Aug 1960	91-431 Ft. Weaver Road, Ewa Beach, HI (VP–28)
Aug '60–May 1961	5852-A Fulmar, Ewa, HI (VP–28)
May '61–Oct 1961	BOQ MCAF Iwakuni, Japan (VP-28 deployment)
Oct '61–Oct 1962	5781-A Erne, Ewa, HI (VP-28)
Oct '62–Aug 1963	705 3 Rd St., Apt D, Imperial Beach, CA (VP-31)
Aug '63–Aug 1964	1427 Signal, Imperial Beach, CA (VP-31)
Aug '64–June 1965	6504 Berkshire Dr., Alexandria, VA (Defense Intelligence School)
July '65–July 1967	161-6 Lanyali, Tien Mou, Taipei (U.S. Taiwan Defense Command)
Sep '67–Nov 1967	520 D St., Coronado, CA (Navy School—Survival and FASO)
Nov '67–Dec 1969	3298 Woody Lane, Milpitas, CA (VP-31 and VP-9)
Dec '69–Dec 1970	3200 White Circle, Marina, CA (PG School—MS Management)
Dec '70–May 1972	924 Providence Ct., Cupertino, CA (FAW-8/10)
May '72–July 1973	Cupertino, CA (FAW-10/TTT)
Sep '73–June 1974	55 Boulevard Terrace, Middletown, RI (Naval War College)
Aug '74–July 1978	10383 Noel, Cupertino, CA (CPWP/VP-9)

July '78–Nov 1980	98-1285 Kaonohi, Aiea, HI (CINCPATFLT)
Nov '80–Jun 1981	57 Halawa Dr., Honolulu, HI (CINCPATFLT)
Aug '81–Oct 1983	7722 Lewinsville Rd., McLean, VA (Navy Legislative Affairs)
Oct '83–Nov 1983	6171 Leesburg Pike, Falls Church, VA
Nov '83–Jan 1984	6948 Camino Amero, San Diego, CA
Jan '84–Nov 1985	2027 Hidden Crest Dr., El Cajon, CA (Booz•Allen)
Nov '85–Sep 1992	1238 Hidden Mtn. Dr., El Cajon (Booz•Allen)
Sep '92–Jun 1993	17544 Plaza Otonal, San Diego (Lockheed)
Jun '93–Mar 1994	Westlake Village, CA (Lockheed)
Mar '94–April 1999	2748 Pembsly Dr., Vienna, VA (Lockheed Martin)
July 1999	3017 Hightower Place #107, Vienna, VA
July '99–Present	17544 Plaza Otonal, San Diego (Retired)

My Teenage Years

Originally, this article was written in response to questions submitted to me by my granddaughter, Jamie, for a college class she was taking.

SCHOOL EXPERIENCES

I attended high school at Bent County High School in Las Animas, Colorado; a town of about three thousand people and only one stop light. We had a class of about 70 when we graduated. I always enjoyed school throughout the years from grade school through college and graduate studies, probably because I was fortunate enough to be a good student. Our school had a basic curriculum that included algebra, English, chemistry, physics, history, civics, physical education, language (Spanish or Latin), and social studies. Because we were such a small school, if you wanted advanced mathematics like trigonometry or calculus, you took it by extension class from one of the universities. You were assigned a class period to do the work and one of the math teachers was assigned to be your counselor, but essentially you self-taught yourself. I took both trig and calculus that way. If you were taking "engineering college preparatory" type classes there was a loophole that you didn't have to take Spanish or Latin. I used that loophole, but to this day regret that I didn't take Spanish. We usually always had an hour for "study hall" each day. I made good use of that to get most of my homework done. This was especially important as I played football, basketball and baseball, so was spending two to three hours a day after school at practice throughout the whole school year. There were some nights each week when I also had to spend some time at home completing homework, but I never found it to be a burden.

MY FAMILY LIFE

My mother and father both grew up in small towns that were 18 miles apart. Their parents were basically farmers or ranchers and neither would be considered wealthy. In fact my father's family would probably have been considered poor. They never owned an automobile in their life and my father was the first in his family to ever get a college degree. My mother's father and mother were highly respected in the community and would be considered middle-class. Although my father's family was German, they were 3rd generation and I don't remember any specific cultural practices or traditions that they followed. If there were any cultural influences during my teen years it was to work hard and be a good citizen.

My parents divorced when I was about ten years old and that had a strong influence on my life. Divorce was not very common in those days and it was a bit of a stigma to come from a divorced family. It was always something I was embarrassed about. It was also a tremendous financial burden. My mother worked for a couple years following the divorce, as I believe she only got about $150 a month in alimony/child support. My constant hope and prayer was that my parents would somehow get back together. They did remarry when I was 14 years old; but it only lasted a few months. Finally, when I was a freshman at Bent County High School, my mother, brother, sister and I moved in with my mother's parents in a three-bedroom, one bathroom house. That provided some stability to our lives, as we had been renting and moving from house to house in Las Animas, seemingly moving every time the rent came due.

624 Locust, Las Animas, Colorado

At one time we had lived in five separate houses/apartments in four years. Teenagers were expected to obey and respect their parents and to live by the rules. Rarely were we out later than 10 p.m. at night and during the weekdays it was closer to 9 p.m.. There were no drugs in those days. If there was any vice it was smoking. Since most of the people I hung out with were athletes, none of us smoked. Meals were always eaten together as a family at breakfast and in the evening.

JOBS AS A TEEN

Most of the kids I knew had jobs in the summer and some throughout the year. Because of necessity, I started working younger than most. I had a morning paper route, which I did on my bicycle, starting at the age of 12.

I had just started the 7th grade and that year was probably my poorest year in school for grades throughout my career, because I didn't have time to do homework. I can remember on many occasions giving my mother my monthly paper route earnings of about $14 because it was needed for food. I never resented or thought much about having to work, it was just what needed to be done.

Throughout my high school years I always had a job—most of the time I had two or three jobs. One summer I worked at the Safeway during the day and had two night jobs cleaning the local Utilities Company office and cleaning a doctor's office. Over the years I also worked in a gas station and had some farm labor jobs.

During the school year I usually worked 8 hours on Saturdays at the gas station or Safeway and about 10 hours a week in the evenings. During the summers I usually worked 40 to 50 hours a week.

The summer between my Junior and Senior year in high school I was recruited by the Garden City, Kansas semi-pro baseball team to work and pitch for their team. My day job was running a jackhammer at a construction site. I have discussed the details about this job in another chapter.

The four years I was in college, I always had a job, both during the school year and in the summer months. The lesson I learned from all the various jobs I had was—"I don't want to do this the rest of my life. I am going to get a college degree and learn to use my head rather than my brawn!" When I retired at age 62, it occurred to me that I had held some type of job for 50 continuous years.

CLOTHING STYLES OR FADS

I won't say that clothing styles had no influence where I lived; but it certainly didn't have much influence. What I wore was driven more by affordability than style. Most guys wore jeans, and there were NO designer jeans. These were basic Levis that you bought at Penny's or Sears. I can remember complaining about having to wear jeans which had been patched with the "iron-on" patches where they had been torn playing baseball or falling on my bike. My mother's reply was that we might have to wear patches; but our clothes were always clean and that was the important thing. I had one sport coat that had been given to me, and one white shirt. I am sure that other kids in school, especially the girls from families with better incomes, were more style-conscious. Rarely did I see a girl in slacks or jeans—they wore dresses. If there was an overriding style it was to be neat, clean and conform.

I do recall at one time when I was about 12 that it was "the thing" to roll up your jeans to form about a four inch cuff and to roll up your t-shirt sleeves. In the summers at that time most boys just wore plain white t-shirts.

Interestingly, to this day I rarely wear jeans and my daughters will often ask me why I don't wear them. I think it is because that is the ONLY thing I wore throughout my whole youth.

I did, however, become aware of style when I went away to college. In particular I recall that the really hip guys had this particular style light jacket that was tan with a distinct high collar. However, it was about $35 and that was not in my budget. Finally, in my junior year I was able to splurge and buy one of those and I figured I had really arrived!

I also learned what Bermuda shorts were in college and bought a pair. That summer in Las Animas I actually believe I was the first person to EVER wear Bermudas in that town. I got a lot of funny looks from people! If you know much about a farming community and farm work; bermudas aren't very practical!

I have often been amazed how someone today in the stylish jeans with the "tattered" look with holes in the legs would have been viewed in my day. The statement one would have been making in those days is, "This is all I can afford—I can't even afford to patch the holes!" There would not have been a teen alive in that day who would want to admit to his or her peers that they couldn't afford something better. However, because most of this generation is so much more affluent; they don't run the risk of people viewing them as not being able to afford something better. Therefore, they are viewed as making a fashion statement by wearing tattered and torn garments rather than being viewed as someone who is too poor to afford something better.

FRIENDS

My friends were mostly guys that I played sports with in school. To this day I still correspond with and see four of them on a fairly regular basis. Our free time hangouts were the City Pharmacy and Rexall drug store soda fountains. It was sort of a "Happy Days" (the tv show with Fonzie and his friends) atmosphere. In the evenings on the weekends three, four or five of us would all pitch in a quarter or fifty cents apiece for gas and ride around the main part of town (all of about 4 square blocks). Some nights we would load up the back seat with water balloons and throw them at other cars that were also "cruising" around. This eventually would lead to water balloon fights among three or four cars. When it would get too carried away, the sheriff would tell us to quit. It always worked because he knew all our parents and would threaten to tell them. None of us wanted that to happen. Dating was also a very important part of our high school years, especially as we got to be juniors and seniors. You weren't really a part of the "in" crowd unless you were going "steady." You knew a girl was going steady because the boy gave her his class ring. She would then wrap tape around the bottom of it and put it on a chain around her neck. The tape was to keep the chain and the ring from rubbing thin where they interfaced. You also knew everyone that was going steady through the "grapevine" (gossip). It was always hot news whenever a couple started going steady or broke up from going steady. I can remember three or four fights at school between friends of mine, and it was always over a girl. If a couple were going steady, the guys didn't take kindly to any of the other guys hitting on their girl. I did go steady throughout my senior year (but never got in any fights). However, she went to college about 70 miles from where I went to college and the relationship died away my freshman year in college. She is now married to one of my best friends from high school.

PROBLEMS OR DISAPPOINTMENTS

I always loved school, had lots of friends, was an honor roll student, editor of the High School Annual, a class officer, quarterback of the football team, an All-state basketball player, went steady with one of the most popular girls in school, etc.

However, my biggest problems as a teenager were internal family problems. As I mentioned, my parents were divorced and both became alcoholics. It wasn't quite as troubling to me about my father, because we didn't live with him. However, my junior year in high school my mother got so bad she had to be committed to a mental institution in a town 90 miles away. Fortunately, my grandparents were there to care for us and to be a steadying influence on our lives. In fact, I have often thought back at how fortunate I was to grow up in a small town near my grandparents. Had we lived in a large city with no family support structure, I am convinced we would have ended up homeless. Only as I have become an adult have I realized how much my grandparents sacrificed by taking us in and housing us for over eight of their prime years. What few problems I might have encountered with my social life as a teen were totally overshadowed by the internal family problems. In many ways school was a pleasant diversion from the situation at home.

The Role of Sports in My Life

From the earliest that I can remember I have always been interested in sports. I can recall going to the gym with my dad when I was about four or five years old and he was coaching at Lamar High School. I remember being excited about playing with all the different types of balls—basketballs, footballs, softballs and volleyballs. We always had sports equipment available because my dad was a good athlete, having played both baseball and football at the University of Colorado and then professional football for the Detroit Lions. He then coached for a couple years before going into the Navy where he was also involved in athletics. He was an instructor in physical conditioning for aviators during their pre-flight training phase. When he was stationed in Cordell, Oklahoma during my second grade year we lived across the street from the grade school which had an outdoor basketball court. My brother and I were always very popular because we had a basketball. The bigger kids tolerated us and would let us play because we provided the ball.

My first real organized sports were basketball, football and softball when I was in the fifth grade at Lincoln Grade School in La Junta, Colorado. We played against the other grade school in town in all three sports. Amazingly, I still know a couple of the kids I played on the same teams with even though the next year I moved eighteen miles away to Las Animas. I then competed against them, as they were our chief rival in high school sports. I still have a couple newspaper articles about our grade school games. I was a pitcher in softball, a forward in basketball and quarterback in football—the same positions I played in high school.

SOFTBALL/BASEBALL

Throughout my grade school and junior high years almost all of my free time involved sports in some way. In the summers I started playing organized softball when I was about ten or eleven. I was always one of the best hitters, fielders and pitchers in town, albeit a small town. The league games were usually played in the evenings and were a major source of entertainment for the townspeople. The Midget League included boys 12 and under. The Juniors went from 13 to 18 and then there was an adult league. Both the Midget and Junior leagues were organized according to churches. We had teams from the Methodist, Presbyterian, Baptist, Catholic, Anglo-Catholic and Christian churches. We had a relatively large Mexican/Hispanic population; thus the Catholics had two teams—Mexican Catholics and Anglo-Catholics. That wouldn't be tolerated in today's society, but in those days it was accepted as quite normal. The best teams were those that had the best pitcher. I played for the Anglo-Catholics, where Joe Brooks and I shared pitching and catching duties.

The Christians were our top rivals, as Glen Richeson was a very fast pitcher. I didn't throw as hard as Glen, but I had better control and usually didn't walk as many batters. That combined with the fact we had more good hitters than the Christians, meant that we usually won the league each summer; but it was always close.

At the end of the season there was usually a regional tournament where the top two or three teams in each of the towns in Southeastern Colorado played to see who got to send a team to the state tournament. When I was twelve, Lamar beat us; but they asked Joe Brooks and I to join their team to go to the state championship in Colorado Springs. Joe played catcher and I was in the outfield. However, in the semi-final game Lamar's best pitcher wasn't doing so well so they brought me in to pitch. I pitched very well and we won. That meant that we got to play in the championship game. I was selected to pitch that game and I remember feeling ill before the game. My mother humored me a little; but insisted I would be all right when the game started, because she knew it was just nerves. Sure enough I was fine, pitched the whole game and we won the State Championship.

Lamar decided to try and go to the National Tournament; but it had already been completed. The National Champs were Okmulgee, Oklahoma. Lamar challenged them to play a game for the national title; but they declined to play us. I don't disagree with them as they had already won the national title—why risk losing it if they didn't have to! A couple weeks after the tournament, Lamar held a luncheon awards ceremony to present trophies to all of us who were on the team. My Grandpa Dean drove me to Lamar and I remember being quite excited to get the trophy. It stands about seven inches high and is probably one of the smallest of the many I won throughout my years of sports competition—but I still have it and it is probably the one of which I am most proud.

During my high school years I moved up to the Junior League and continued to play in the league every summer. Frequently, I and a couple of the better Junior league players were asked to play for the adult teams when they didn't have enough players. However, baseball started coming into my life when I was around 14 or so. Las Animas formed an American Legion team, which played other American Legion teams within the Southeastern Colorado area. I remember being one of the youngest (and smallest) players my first year and I usually played second base or outfield. As I got a little older I started pitching. Then my sophomore year in high school several of us convinced the school to form a baseball team. There was a lot of resistance from the track coach, because a few of his best track men were baseball players. A deal was finally worked out that we could have a team, but only if the track men who played baseball spent the first hour of practice on track and then moved over to the baseball field. We did very well and our Senior year actually won the league but lost in the State playoffs. I played both shortstop and pitched.

I think the most memorable baseball game I ever played was the summer of my Sophomore year in high school. We won the American Legion league and qualified to go to Grand Junction to play for the State Championship in our division. Grand Junction was known as a baseball hotbed and had a wonderful baseball park and team. We were all in awe of this field that looked like a real major league park with grass and outfield fences. The ballparks we played in were all dirt and had no outfield fences. There were no odds makers for that level game, but I would guess that Grand Junction had to be 5 to 1 favorites to beat us. It was to be a two-day, best two out of three game event. I was scheduled to pitch the first game against their best pitcher, Lloyd "Porky" Manown. We went about four innings scoreless and in the top of the fifth Larry Turner, our best hitter, hit a homer over the right center field fence to put us ahead 2–0. I ended up pitching a shutout and we won the game. My mother, brother and grandfather had driven over for the game. I will never forget how excited and proud my grandfather was following the game. He was not one to show a lot of emotion, but it was the most excited I ever saw him in my whole life and that made me feel good. Unfortunately, we weren't very deep in pitching and Grand Junction had another good pitcher. The next day we were scheduled for two 7-inning games. Grand Junction won the first game about 4–1 behind the pitching of John Douglas and they then pitched him in the second game. They won again and, thus, were the State Champions. Ironically, my winning that first game came to the attention of the baseball coach at the University of Colorado, which led to him later offering me a baseball scholarship.

Interestingly, I was on the freshman baseball team at the University of Colorado with both John Douglas and Porky Manown. John Douglas didn't make the varsity the following year, and Porky always claimed that John's arm was injured by pitching those two games in a row against us and he was never the same quality of a pitcher after that.

The summer following my Junior year in high school, Larry Turner and I were recruited by the Junior Chamber of Commerce of Garden City, Kansas to play baseball for their city's Ban Johnson League team. Ban Johnson was the first president of the American League and was instrumental in starting the Ban Johnson league in the 1930s in Kansas for young aspiring baseball players. When I played, it seems that the age limit was 25; but it is now 22. We played teams from throughout western and central Kansas. Most of the players played for college teams in the area during the school year, although that was not a requirement. Still being in high school, Larry and I were among the younger players in the league. The Jaycees provided us with a job and arranged a boarding house where we could live. The employers who provided the jobs understood that we would need some time off for practices and games. Larry and I lived in a very nice boarding house with three other players who had been recruited—two from Denver and one from Oklahoma. Most of the remainder of the players on the team were from Garden City and lived at home.

Unfortunately, I was assigned the most difficult job of all the out-of-town players. I worked for a construction company that was expanding the local telephone office and I had to run a jackhammer all day tearing up a concrete pad in the area to be expanded. Even for a 17-year-old, it was such physically demanding work that I found it difficult to be fresh and strong in the evenings when I was expected to pitch for the team. The other guys were painting the interior of a local school—a much less physically demanding job! After about a month to six weeks, I left and returned to home in Las Animas because they either wouldn't or couldn't find me another more suitable job.

However, the best thing that came out of that experience was meeting Roger Kinney. Roger had been recruited out of Denver and was an infielder. He and I became friends and, upon realizing that we both planned to attend the University of Colorado, agree to be roommates at CU. We roomed together our Freshman and Junior years at school and developed a close friendship that still exists today—almost 55 years later.

Throughout my college years, I played baseball in the summer for the Lamar Town Team. Lamar was a town about 35 miles east of Las Animas near the Kansas-Colorado border. They were part or a league of about 6 or 8 teams in southeast Colorado—southwest Kansas area. We

Del Ritchhart—University of Colorado 1958

played most of our games at night, thus it involved lots of driving and being able to get off work early for the travel. Fortunately, there were a couple other guys in Las Animas who also played for Lamar and we could share the driving. My employers were also very understanding and good about my leaving work early on game days. One of the benefits we received for playing for Lamar was from one of their supporters who owned a gas station. Each time we had a game, we could stop at his station and fill up with gas for free.

The quality of ball wasn't particularly good, but it kept us in shape in the summer for college ball. However, there was a pitcher whom I pitched against twice in that league by the name of Ron Herbal who later made it to the big leagues and played for the San Francisco Giants. His record was 12–9 with the Giants in 1965. Unfortunately the quality of the coaching wasn't very good either and probably reduced my effectiveness as a pitcher in college. I believe it was the summer between my sophomore and junior years in college that I was pitching for Lamar in the small west central Kansas town of Leoti. They had a big left-handed American Indian who was a very good pitcher. He and I locked up in a pitchers duel which went 12 or 13 innings and we both pitched the complete game. That following year at CU I had a lot of arm problems and I really think it was the result of having thrown that long game. A manager with any reasonable baseball knowledge on either team would have limited someone of that age to no more than nine innings. No one thought about "pitch count" in those days. I am sure each of us probably threw at least 150 pitches in that game. Few pitchers today ever go beyond 100 pitches! I should also have known better; but at that age you are indestructible and can do anything. If I have any regrets about my baseball years it is that I should have taken better care of my arm and not thrown that 13-inning game and that I didn't start playing baseball sooner. I started playing organized softball at around 9 or 10 years of age; but didn't begin playing baseball until I was around 14, and that was only a couple times a week. We played softball of some sort almost every day! Consequently, I was a very, very good hitter in softball; but not nearly as good a hitter in baseball. In college, I was a good enough hitter my senior year to play first base whenever I didn't pitch, but I still wasn't a very good baseball hitter compared to my softball skills.

I played three years of varsity baseball at the CU and was the number two starting pitcher. My sophomore year I had about a 5–1 record; but the last two years probably had a record of around 6–10. I didn't have an overpowering fast ball, but got by mostly on good control and changing up my speeds.

My baseball coach at CU was Frank "Chief" Prentup. The name Chief came from the fact he was of Native American descent. Chief and my dad had been stationed together when they were in the Navy and I am sure that helped in my relationship with Chief. He was very demanding, but taught us more than just how to play baseball. He did his best to teach us how to be good productive citizens—something more coaches should do today. He had a very positive and lasting impact on my life.

BASKETBALL

I played my first organized basketball in the fifth grade for Lincoln Grade School in La Junta, Colorado and I continued playing it through my freshman year in college and into my early years in the Navy. I recall playing on the "lightweight team" (under 100 lbs) at Columbian Junior High in Las Animas. We played against other "lightweight teams" from surrounding towns. In high school I didn't develop as quickly as a some of my other classmates, thus, I didn't make the varsity until my Junior year. My Senior year we won our league and got to play in the State Tournament in Denver. We won our first two games to get into the championship game. Unfortunately for me, near the end of the second game I tore all the lateral ligaments in my left ankle and had to undergo surgery the morning of the championship game. I had played very well in those games, scoring 14 points in each game. Fortunately, the guys who filled in for me played well and Las Animas won the State Championship against Fort Morgan. Even though I missed that last game, I was named, along with two of my teammates, to the All-State Team.

My freshman year at CU I went out, along with about 120 other players, for Freshman Basketball. We had about 6 or 7 players who had been given scholarships, but they were going to carry about 15 players on the team. I can recall the anxiety of going over to the gym in the evening about every two days to see if my name was still on the list, as each day they whittled down the number. I made the final cut and, due to injuries, transfers, or quitting, by the end of the bas-

Del Ritchhart—1955

ketball season we only had about 12 players left. I wasn't invited to be on the varsity the next year, quite simply because I wasn't good enough. I later continued playing basketball through my early years in the Navy and became a much better player, ending up being the number-two scorer in the military league in Taiwan when I was about 28 years old. My regret in basketball is that I didn't have the arm and leg strength to be a good shooter until I matured and gained some weight. In high school and college I was 6′1½″ and about 140 to 160 lbs. Later at around 175–180 lbs, I had the arm and leg strength to become a much better shooter.

FOOTBALL

We played one football game against the other grade school in La Junta when I was in the fifth grade and I still have the newspaper clipping about the game. I ran for one touchdown and Larry Barksdale ran for the other and we won the game. Since we didn't have pads, I think it must have been touch football rules. I can't imagine them letting us play tackle without pads, although we did that as kids all the time.

We had a team in Junior High; but I don't think I was on the first team. I was about 5′6″ and weighed around 98 pounds at that time. We practiced on a hard dirt field, as the only grass field in town was the high school football field. We thought it was great to go to the high school to scrimmage the freshman team because it didn't hurt so much when you fell on grass rather than hard dirt! Once again, I was later in developing size and strength in high school and didn't make the varsity until my Junior year. I played mostly halfback on defense, but about the second game of our Junior year was put into the starting quarterback position because the regular quarterback, Joe Brooks, threw the passes so hard that the receivers had trouble holding on to them. Also, Joe was a very good runner and could serve the team better as a running back. We had a very good record our Senior year and beat out biggest rivals, La Junta, twice. Unfortunately, we couldn't beat Lamar and finished second to them in the league.

Del—Quarterback & Defensive Halfback

When I was at CU the Athletics Business Manager was a man by the name of K.O. Lam. He had been an outstanding running back at CU and played on the same team as my dad. He had also been stationed with my dad in the Navy.

K.O. approached me three or four times when I was at CU and tried to get me to try out for football, as I had pretty good speed and, of course, he knew my dad had been a very good player. It was never much of a temptation for me, however, as I probably only weighed around 150 pounds as a Sophomore and Junior and I watched enough of the football practices to know there was a lot of hard hitting going on out there! I stuck to my baseball.

I think I learned a lot from all my years of competing in sports. You learn a lot about yourself, your ability to handle pressure, to work hard and to be disciplined. You learn that you don't always win and how to handle defeat. Good athletes hate to loose, but still know how to demonstrate good sportsmanship after losing. My mother frequently commented that she had been around lots of good athletes in her life and she "never saw one that liked to lose!"

As a sports fan I still enjoy watching baseball and football. I enjoy watching the finals of the college basketball season tournaments, but am not a big fan of professional basketball. I know a lot of people think baseball is too slow a game, but if you understand all the tactical thinking and fine points of the game it can be a great spectator sport.

"First" Experiences

Understandably, I think most of the young people today take a lot of what they have for granted. This short chapter is a recollection of some of the "firsts" in my life. Perhaps a reminder to later readers that times have certainly changed!

Airplane ride—My first airplane ride was when I was 22 years old. I had joined the Navy toward the end of my senior year in college and was scheduled to report in Newport, Rhode Island about a month after graduation. Since I had a car and Joanne and I were to be married in Chicago shortly after graduation from Officer Candidate School in November, I drove the car from Colorado to Chicago in July and left it with Joanne. I then flew from Chicago to Newport. I really don't remember much about the flight and don't think I had much anxiety.

TV Viewing—The first television I ever saw was around 1951 when I was 14 years old. Because it was so new and relatively expensive, many people in my hometown of Las Animas, Colorado would stand outside the local hardware store that sold TVs and watch through the window in the evening. In the early years there wasn't much programming during the day. The reception we did get came through a series of relay towers from Denver which was almost 200 miles away. Today's viewers would declare it totally unacceptable because it was so "snowy," but we were totally amazed at this modern marvel. We didn't actually own a set in our home until a couple years later.

English Muffin—I had my first English Muffin when I was 20 years old. Joanne and I had gotten engaged just before Christmas of my Junior year in college. Having not yet met her parents, I drove back to Chicago during Christmas break with two of my roommates to meet the Schmidt family. I was very impressed that they served this extravagant "special toast," which I was sure only very rich people could afford. I had never seen an English Muffin before and don't think I ever had one again until after we were married.

Pizza—Las Animas, where I grew up, never had a pizza restaurant; so the first time I had pizza was when I went away to college in Boulder in 1955. It was reserved for Sunday evenings, when we would splurge and go out to one of the few local restaurants that served pizza. In fact when I took Cheryl, Debi and Linda back to a high school reunion in Las Animas around the year 2000, Cheryl decided to call and order pizza when we arrived at the motel, only to find out there still were no pizza restaurants in Las Animas!

Shaving—I didn't start shaving until I was a Freshman in college, and I probably didn't really need to start then. However, since most all my peers had started in high school, I was too embarrassed to wait any longer. As a younger child I had watched my Grandpa Ritchhart shave with a straight edge razor. I later tried that; but quickly gave up after cutting myself a couple times. To this day I don't know how men used those straight edge razors!

Personal Radio—We had a radio in the house; but the first radio that I owned as my own was given to me as a high school graduation present by my then girlfriend, Betty Jean Holt. It was a combination portable and plug in which served me well throughout my college years.

Personal Camera—My Aunt Frances owned a camera, but I don't remember our family having one throughout my junior high and high school years. Thus, the only photos that I have of myself during those years were the annual school photos. The first camera I owned was given to me by Joanne for my college graduation. It was an Argus C-3.

Car—I always wanted a car in high school, but we couldn't afford it, so I borrowed my grandfather's car for dates. I once was tempted to buy a car that was for sale for $300 at the local used car dealer, but my mom convinced me otherwise. I recall her words that the "$300 was the cheap part." Then came all the expenses for insurance, gas and repairs. I am glad I took the advice. I did finally buy a car my Junior year in college with some help from my father. It was a Chevrolet 4-door, probably about a 1948 model. I almost made it through my senior year when it threw a rod. Just before I graduated, my dad traded in his 1955 Chevy Impala for a new car with the understanding the dealer didn't have to put any money into it and would sell it to me at a good price. Joanne and I had that car until about 1962.

Car Accident—My first accidents didn't involve another car and I really think should be blamed more on my uncles, Paul and J.B., than me. I was about 11 and Uncle Paul though I should learn to drive. It was a Buick, around a 1932 model with a floor shift. I did all right driving the three or four blocks from the house to the restaurant they owned. As I approached the restaurant, I was planning on parking parallel to the curb in front of the restaurant since there were no other cars there. However, at the last minute he said "Turn into the parking lot and park there." Well, I made the turn but didn't slow down and hit a tree straight on about the time he reached over and hit the brake. Fortunately cars had bumpers in those days and all it did was bend the bumper a little and scare me to death. He did make me drive back home, but I never drove again for several years.

Alcoholic Drink—I think the first time I had a drink, I was in college and was home for the summer. In those days you could drink 3.2 beer if you were 18. There were a couple hangouts in the adjacent town of La Junta and some of us went there one night. I think I had one beer and thought that was a big deal. I still recall that the brand was "Walters." It was a local beer made in Pueblo, Colorado.

Girlfriend—The first girl I remember being infatuated with was when I was in the fifth grade in La Junta. Her name was Lois Fullerton. I recall giving her a bag of those little valentine mints and a card on Valentines Day. Of course, I got teased by all the guys for having a "girl friend." I think the first girl that I ever dated more than once was a girl that lived about two blocks from our house. Her name was Carole Greene. I was 16 and had just gotten my driver's license. I can't remember why I stopped dating her, but I think it was because her family moved away from Las Animas a few months after we started dating.

Kiss—The first girl I ever kissed was a girl by the name of Janice Netherton. I think I was 15 years old and was a freshman. There were three couples of us just cruising around town and we were in the back seat with another couple who were "making out." So, the stage was well set for me to get my first kiss. I remember the relief of getting past my shyness and fear of rejection more than I remember anything about the kiss.

Job—My first job, other than doing chores or yard work for my grandmother, was a paper route. I started delivering the Rocky Mountain News in Las Animas when I was about 12 years old. There were three routes and the other two kids (brothers) lived across the street from me. I would get up around 6 a.m. and ride my bike about three blocks to pick up the papers that had been dropped on the street corner on the highway by the Greyhound bus driver. They were in two large bundles that just fit in each of the canvas bags that were wrapped around the handle bars. I then peddled back to the house across the street, took them inside and the three of us would fold them into a small square so they could be thrown like a Frisbee onto the porches. If the weather was bad we had to put them into plastic bags—which was a real pain. I had the least desirable route because the oldest of the two brothers was the boss and he and his brother got the main part of town. I got the area "across the tracks" where most of the roads weren't paved. It was where the population was mostly Hispanics. In the rainy season or the winter it was particularly bad because the mud would coat the tires to the point they wouldn't turn because it would jam under the fenders of the bike. There were times I would have to carry the bike and papers through certain areas. I think I only had to deliver about 40–50 papers, but I had to hustle to get them delivered, get home and pick up my books and some breakfast and ride my bike about six blocks to school. There were a few times I was tardy because of the paper route. Once or twice, my mother borrowed my grandparents' car and drove me because of snowstorms. The worst part about being a paper boy was collecting. We had to go door-to-door once a month and collect the $1.50 or so for the month's subscription. There were often times people were at home, but wouldn't answer the door because they didn't want to pay you or didn't have the money. It would usually take almost a week of going after school to the homes to eventually collect from everyone. I think we got something like fifteen cents a month for each customer. Thus, I made about $7.50 for probably about 50 hours of work (which included the time to collect the money). I had never thought of it until this moment that I am now writing this, but I was making about fifteen cents an hour. Of course, three years later I was only making $.35 an hour working at Safeway, which was about average for those days.

Shortly after starting to deliver papers, I got a job setting pins at the bowling alley. I worked at nights when they had league bowling. Each team had five players and a match consisted of three lines (a line being 10 frames). We got five cents a man for each line. Thus, in an evening we made $.75. If some of them bowled an extra line of "potts" for money, we would earn about $1 in the evening. They started about 7 p.m. and ended about 8:30 p.m..

I had these two jobs most of my two years in junior high. It probably wasn't a coincidence that my grades were the worst I ever had those two years. The only time I had for school work was immediately after school when I wasn't practicing basketball, football or collecting for the paper route.

Big Failure—I think the first thing I can ever remember failing at was in college. I was a pretty good high school student, especially in math. My mother always said she wanted me to be an engineer so when I went off to college and had to declare a major, it was engineering. Well, I was also playing freshman basketball and baseball and working about three hours a day at the bakery in the cafeteria, while carrying 17 semester hours in six courses. My job was cleaning the bakery in the evening after they shut down. Have you ever tried to sweep flour? If not, take my word, it is very difficult and time consuming. After my first semester I think my GPA was around 1.4 or something near that. I studied hard when I had time; but the classes didn't come easy and would have been a challenge to me even if I wasn't working or playing sports. Fortunately, the coach realized that the job was taking more time than he had anticipated, so they switched me out of that job. Thank heaven! Just prior to the end of the semester I realized that this wasn't working and I couldn't afford to flunk out of school. I didn't really have anyone around to advise me so I sought out help at the counseling center. They gave me some tests to determine my interests and finally, in desperation, I took the easy road and went into preparing to teach and be a coach. My GPA the next semester, again taking 17 hours of classes, jumped to 3.0 and I felt greatly relieved. I do recall Frank Prentup, my baseball coach, trying to get me to go into business school. This was my sophomore year and he sensed that, while engineering might have been too tough for me, I was still a good enough student to make it in the business school. I think my final overall college GPA was around 3.4 on a 4.0 scale.

College Life

As long as I can remember I always assumed I was going to college. My mother always wanted me to be an engineer—either because she thought it was a very respected profession or because they made good money. It was likely a little of each. I think it was also because I was always good at math. I started getting serious about college in my Junior year of high school. We took the SATs and began applying for scholarships. I was approached by some of the local men of the community, one whom had attended West Point, as to whether I would be interested in West Point if they could get me an appointment. I said, yes, without a second thought because it was a free education and I had no idea how I was going to pay for college. I was also encouraged by my grandfather.

Midway through my Senior year I received notification that I was the 1st alternate nominee of Congressman Chenowith, our congressional representative. I was directed to go to Fitzsimmons Army Hospital in Denver (200 miles away) and take the academic, physical and physical fitness aptitude tests. I did very well on them, particularly the physical fitness, but had a glitch with the physical. When I was being examined at Fitzsimmons I had volunteered that as a 12-year-old I had Osgood-Schlatter Disease. This is a calcification and associated tenderness on the knee just below the kneecap. It was caused by being hit there by a baseball, but can occur in children ages 10–15 just through repeated physical activity. I was treated, which just consisted of putting the leg in a full cast for six weeks. The inactivity allowed the calcification and tenderness to go away. The notice from the Army indicated that I was entitled to a reexamination, but when I received the notice I had just sustained torn lateral ligaments in my ankle during the State High School Basketball Tournament (which our team went on to win). The ankle had been operated on and was in a cast. I figured when I went to get the knee reexamined they would ask about the ankle and that would disqualify me. My mother had been recently put into a mental hospital, so there were lots of distractions for my grandpa and grandma, thus I never responded to the reexamination offer. Talking in later years with military doctors, they assured me I would have been accepted, as neither injury was considered disqualifying. However, I have no regrets. I enjoyed my Navy career very much.

My senior year I applied to two or three colleges in Colorado—the University of Colorado being my first choice since both my father and uncle had gone there and played sports. I was awarded a Tuition and Fee Academic Scholarship to CU and received a letter from the baseball coach offering to get me a job that would pay room and board. CU baseball didn't have much money, so that was about the best they could do. It turned out that both the baseball coach and the athletic business manager had known my dad. He had played football at CU with the business manager and was in the Navy during WW II with both of them. I think they both knew my dad had become an alcoholic and was not doing well and knew I could use any help they could provide. I think my Uncle J.B., who was in Denver at the time, still had a few contacts at CU and did some lobbying for me. Anyhow, I worked that coming summer for a contractor tearing up the old narrow gauge railroad lines that ran from Alamosa, Colorado over the continental divide to Poncha Springs, and managed to save about $500. When I left for CU I had the Academic Scholarship, a promise of a job and $500 and knew that I couldn't expect any monetary support from home.

My mother didn't have enough to live on and my grandmother and grandfather had enough to just support themselves, my mother, brother and sister. As a good friend of mine drove up to the house to pick me up and head for Boulder my Freshman year, I vividly recall my mother saying that if things didn't work out in Boulder, I could always come back home and go to the junior college in the adjacent town. While that potential outcome was more likely than I ever realized, it never entered my mind that I would do that. I was going to graduate from the University of Colorado one way or the other! I really think that all the successes I had enjoyed in high school, both academically and athletically, provided me an inner confidence so that getting through college both financially and academically was just another challenge to be conquered.

When Leo Hayward and I headed for Boulder, everything both of us needed for the school year fit in his car easily. I had a few clothes, a portable radio and a baseball glove. Leo, being a Junior had a few more belongings, but not many. I laugh today when kids arrive at the school with a truck full of clothes, sound systems, televisions, refrigerators, computers, etc. I arrived and moved into Hallett Hall, where my counselor was the Freshman Basketball Assistant Coach. Leo said the next day we had to go to the adjacent girls dorm and hang around outside until we saw some good looking girls who needed help carrying suitcases and moving into their room. I recall meeting a tall attractive blond from Texas and a short dark-haired Jewish girl from New York. Coming from Las Animas, I don't believe I had ever met anyone who was a Jew as we didn't have any Jewish people in Las Animas. Later that year I went to a dance at the student union and that Jewish girl (whose name I can't remember) taught me to jitterbug—something I had never done in my life. Over the years, I have really enjoyed dancing and wish I had the opportunity to thank her for getting me off on the right foot (get the pun). Ironically, the blond girl, Nancy Johnson, and I crossed paths frequently at CU over the ensuing years. I never dated her but she was very nice and I had a couple classes with her. I still recall she was from Midland, Texas.

The job I was given to earn my room and board was cleaning up the bakery in the Student Union in the evening after they closed. The biggest challenge and main part of the job was to sweep the floors which were covered with flour. If you have ever tried sweeping flour you know it is extremely fine and isn't easy to sweep. I think I was expected to do the job in about two hours, but it frequently took much longer than that. I was enrolled in Engineering with a full load of about 16 hours. Additionally, basketball tryouts started very soon after school started.

College was a very enjoyable time for me, with the exception of my troubles with academics my first semester. In my final year, I had a scholarship which paid tuition and fees, worked in the dorm for room and board, my books were paid by the athletic department and I worked at the gym and made around $150 per month and I was dating a wonderful girl who later became my wife. I had never had it so good!

Interesting Experiences in the Navy

SIGNING UP

As graduation neared during my senior year at the University of Colorado it became obvious to me that I needed to make a decision regarding the military. If I did nothing I would probably receive my draft notice in the mail sometime very near my graduation date. However, serving a stint, albeit only two years, as an Army enlisted man didn't appeal to me much. Since my father had been an officer in the Navy during WW II, that had a natural appeal to me. Coincidentally (or perhaps not) the Navy had a recruiting table set up outside the student union for about a week in April or early May and I talked with them. I expressed strong interest and was told to report to a Federal Building in Denver for a physical and to actually sign on the dotted line.

During the interview process in Denver they asked me which branch of the Navy I was interested in. Not knowing one branch from another, they explained a couple options, one of which was to be an Air Intelligence Officer. When I asked what type work an AI did, it was explained that he was the guy you see in the war movies who stands up in front of the pilots getting ready to go on a mission and briefs them about their targets, enemy defenses and other details. That sounded good to me so I put that down as my first choice!

VP28 P-2V5 Neptune

After attending Officer Candidate School for about four months in Newport, Rhode Island, I was commissioned as an Ensign and assigned to an aviation indoctrination school in Jacksonville, Florida. Joanne and I were married in Chicago on the Saturday after I graduated from OCS and we had to be in Jacksonville by midnight on Sunday so I could start school on Monday morning. Not much time for a honeymoon!

The school lasted from the end of November through early February, just long enough to learn that all of Florida isn't as warm as we thought. Jacksonville can get pretty chilly during the winter months—even for newlyweds! We were then off to Alameda, California for another school to learn how to be an Air Intelligence Officer. We arrived there in mid-February, but since the school didn't start until the first part of March they sent about five of us out on the Aircraft Carrier *Bon Homme Richard* to observe flight operations for a week. I learned that I made a good choice when I decided not to become a sea-going line officer as I fought sea sickness most of the time.

By the middle of April we had completed the school and were assigned to a P-2V Neptune squadron at NAS Barber's Point in Hawaii. Some of my classmates and their wives were sent to Hawaii aboard the cruise ship Luraline. We weren't quite so fortunate and were assigned to *USNS* (U.S. Navy Ship) *Horace Mann*. It was all right; but not exactly a luxury liner! Once again I proved not to be much of a sailor and spent a lot of time munching crackers and trying unsuccessfully not to get seasick. Joanne, on the other hand, was about five months pregnant and didn't have a single problem with the voyage.

OPERATION DOMINIC—NUCLEAR TESTING

I had many interesting experiences that first two and a half years in the Navy, but probably the most memorable involved participating in the 1962 Nuclear Tests conducted by Navy Task Group, Joint Task Force Eight. Our squadron operated out of Johnson Island and Christmas Island during about a two-month period when both air-dropped and missile-fired nuclear weapons were detonated for testing purposes. Our mission was to patrol the waters near where the weapons were to be detonated to ensure there weren't any ships in the area that might be harmed by the detonations or radiation. I was airborne in a P-2V during at least two of the tests and was on the ground for another 4 or 5 of them.

When I was on the ground at Christmas Island the weapons were dropped from an Air Force B-52 and detonated above the ocean about 30 miles from the island. Everyone on the ground had to muster and be accounted for prior to each drop. We were given dark goggles to protect our eyes from the brightness of the flash and we were told to face away from the blast so as not to risk eye injury. The island was ringed with powerful speakers which broadcast the countdown from 25 seconds to 0 prior to the actual detonation. It was a great lesson in physics as we experienced the bright flash, the wind from the overpressure and the heat on the backs of our necks from the huge amount of power generated. Lastly we would hear the loud boom! Then the most amazing experience was to turn around after about 30 seconds and observe the awesome sight of the mushroom cloud. Although it somewhat resembled a large cumulus cloud, it was much different because of the powerful churning that you could observe as ice crystals formed on the outer edges and the white cloud swirled inwardly as if driven by a huge blender. We were all required to wear little dosimeters about ½ inch think and the diameter of a silver dollar around our necks throughout our total involvement in the tests. They absorbed any radiation and provided a cumulative reading of the amount of radiation, if any, that you had experienced during the testing. Each person who participated in the tests had a special entry made in their medical records to ensure that their medical history would be closely monitored throughout their career. They told us that there was a certain amount of radiation that could safely be tolerated; but I have often wondered why we always had to muster in open areas of the island before the detonations rather than being inside where there would be some shielding? I never had any health problems later that could be traced to the testing; but there were some Air Force pilots who had to fly near the mushroom clouds to collect air samples who did. The high altitude detonations carried by the missiles from Johnson Island created so much light that people in Australia were able to observe a bright glow in the sky that, because of refraction, radiated across the upper atmosphere. The missile detonations above Johnson Island were also seen by people in Hawaii as it would turn night into day for a few seconds and it was preceded by an eerie red glow. Joanne and other wives gathered on the beach to observe this phenomenon on the nights when it was announced that the detonations would take place.

Because of my job as an Air Intelligence Officer, I was one of the few people allowed to remain on Johnson Island when two of the tests were conducted. A missile with a nuclear warhead was fired from a launch pad at the end of the island. It proceeded many miles into the sky above the island and then detonated. I was on board the specially configured radar tracking ship anchored at the pier which monitored and controlled the testing. After the detonation we were allowed to go on deck to observe the churning cloud and watch what looked like daylight slowly return to night. A second test that I observed had to be aborted because the missile started to veer off course. In that case the missile tracking ship sent a signal which blew up the missile and warhead; but there was no nuclear explosion.

When we were airborne for the test, we had to be sure that the aircraft was on a heading directly away from the blast at the time of detonation. This was to ensure that our eyes would be protected from looking directly at the blinding flash of light, even though we still had to wear dark goggles. It also ensured that the aircraft would present a small "tail-on" profile to the overpressure from the blast. Obviously, we carefully synchronized our watches to make sure we knew when the blast would take place.

I have often been sad that I don't have photographs of this experience; but we were forbidden from even having a camera in our possession. I do still have a copy of the Honolulu newspaper with huge front-page headlines and a photo of the eerie glow that lit up the sky from one of the Johnson Island missile tests. I am probably one of a select few people alive today who observed these tests and as time goes on there will be even fewer of us.

NAVY LEGISLATIVE AFFAIRS

Everyone who is fortunate enough to have command of a ship or squadron normally cites that as the most memorable and rewarding tour of their career. I enjoyed my tour as Commanding Officer of VP-9 and have a lot of fond memories of the people I worked with and accomplishments of the squadron, but I don't think it was the most interesting tour I had. That would have been my last tour in the Navy when I was Head of the Legislative Liaison Department and Deputy Director of Navy Legislative Affairs. I held each position for about a year. This tour exposed me to how the Washington D.C. Navy leadership really functions as apposed to theoretically how they function.

The Chief of Legislative Affairs (CLA) and the Chief of Information & Public Affairs (CHIN-

FO) both work directly for the Chief of Naval Operations (CNO) and the Secretary of the Navy (SECNAV). These two people are at the top level of leadership of the Military and Civilian branches of the Navy and they don't always agree on which policies the Navy should adopt.

Every morning my boss and three or four other Admirals would meet with the CNO, inform him what the major issues were within their domain of responsibility, provide recommendations and receive guidance. About three days a week CLA and CHINFO plus four or five top civilian Navy leaders would meet with SECNAV for the same purpose. Interestingly, however, the guidance they received on some occasions might be somewhat at odds with the guidance from CNO. This could create a bit of a quandary for CLA and CHINFO and required them to be very skilled "tight rope walkers" and politically astute. My boss, while I was the Deputy, was trying to decide whether to become a Lutheran priest when he left the military, so took 7 to 10 days of vacation on two separate occasions to attend Lutheran retreats. This required that I attend the meetings with CNO and SECNAV in his stead. Fortunately, I was never put in the position of receiving contradictory guidance, although I was once called in with 6 to 8 other top Navy officers and told to prepare a recommendation of which programs to cut if we were directed by Congress to make a huge cut in the budget. I don't remember the exact amount, but it was on the order of half a billion dollars. Fortunately, I didn't have to identify the specific programs, only comment on the political impact from the congressmen whose districts and states would be impacted most by the cuts. Fortunately, the cut never came about.

SENATOR WARREN RUDMAN

By virtue of our positions in Legislative Affairs we were frequently required to escort individual Senators, Congressmen or delegations of several members and/or staff on investigative trips. I was fortunate early in my OLA tour in 1983 to be asked to take Senator Warren Rudman, a Republican from New Hampshire who was a key member of the Senate Appropriations Committee, on a trip to Italy, Turkey and Greece. The purpose was to observe a joint United States, Italian, Turkish amphibious landing off the coast of Turkey.

We flew commercial to Naples, Italy where we were met by Admiral Bill Crowe, who was Commander Allied Forces Southern Europe and later ended up being Chairman of the Joint Chiefs of Staff (JCS). From there we and several U.S. and Italian Generals and Admirals flew by U.S. Military aircraft to Turkey. We were placed in cars of a motorcade to take us about 5 miles from the airport to our hotel in town. Our car was about a 1965 Chevrolet and the other cars in the motorcade were of similar vintage. When we arrived at our hotel we couldn't take the elevator to our floor as the power was out in that sector of town due to planned conservation measures. It was soon dark and I was forced to "feel" my way around to try and take a shower and get dressed for a dinner being hosted by the Turkish Military. I then made my way to Senator Rudman's room just a couple doors down from mine. When I knocked he replied "come on in." He was still sitting in the chair and not yet dressed for the dinner. I had to chuckle when he said, "I'm not moving until the lights come on. I'm not going to break my neck stumbling around in the dark!" Fortunately, the lights came on shortly and we arrived at the event in a timely manner.

Following the amphibious landing the next day, a Navy helicopter flew the Senator and me out to the Aircraft Carrier *USS J. F. Kennedy*. A few days earlier Kennedy Air Wing pilots had shot down two MIGs from the Libyan Air Force who had made aggressive moves in the vicinity of the carrier. We were fortunate to be briefed on the shoot-down by the Commanding Officer of the squadron who shot down the aircraft. He was also one of the pilots credited with a MIG kill. After having dinner with Rear Admiral Jim Service, the Task Force Commander, we toured the ship and were up past midnight on the bridge watching a night underway replenishment from a supply ship.

The next morning we were flown by helo into Athens, Greece. This was our one day of relaxation on the trip and the Naval Attaché had lined up an embassy driver and car and hired a local tour guide to show us around Athens. I don't believe anyone could have possibly seen more of Athens in the time that we had. As I recall we started about 9:30 a.m. and didn't finish until around 10 p.m.. We flew out commercial the next day back to Washington D.C. I will comment that we flew First Class on the commercial flights because congressional rules allow congressmen to fly First Class on international flights. That certainly made the trip much more pleasant.

I was fortunate to take Senator Rudman on another trip of about a week to Hawaii, Japan, the Philippines and Okinawa. The most memorable event of that trip was when we flew from Okinawa to Manila. Two days earlier former Philippine President Akino was assassinated as he got off the airplane in Manila returning from a period in exile. My office called me in Okinawa and told me we weren't to do anything in regard to our scheduled trip the next day to Manila until guidance was received from the State Department. Later that evening we were told that the Senator should proceed with the trip as scheduled. We had very tight security the two days we were in Manila. In fact there were security guards at the front door of the very prestigious Manila Hotel where we stayed and on the floor where were housed. We made a call on the U.S. Ambassador and were briefed on the security situation in Manila and the Philippines before proceeding with the other scheduled stops on our visit.

Senator Rudman was a wonderful person and Joanne and I were fortunate to get to know him fairly well, including having him to our home in McLean, Virginia for dinner on one occasion. When we departed on our first trip he told me that he would carry his own luggage—that wasn't my responsibility. My duties were to schedule the trip and all associated visits, to provide transportation and try and keep him on schedule. Prior to a trip I would go to his office a couple times to get his input, review the schedule and then get his final approval. He was very personable and very considerate of others. I recall having dinner with Rear Admiral Gerald MacKay and his wife, Linda, while we were in Japan. The Senator was a smoker and Linda would have physical reactions to smoke and it adversely affected her lungs. Senator Rudman was very careful to go out to the large porch at the MacKay's quarters whenever he desired to smoke. As a matter of routine, prior to lighting up he would normally ask people with him if they objected to his smoking.

When I retired from the Navy, Senator Rudman send me a U.S. flag that had been flown over the Capitol and a framed photograph of Jefferson Memorial with the cherry blossoms in bloom. He was a very good amateur photographer and his photograph proudly hung in our home for years.

When I was back in the Washington D.C. area with Lockheed Martin Corporation years later, I met and had lunch with Senator Rudman. He had retired from the Senate and was working for a law firm in Washington D.C. I also was invited to his book signing when *Combat: Twelve Years in the U.S. Senate* was released. He gave me a copy endorsed

"To Del, With good wishes and great memories!"

Warren B. Rudman.

I took several other members of congress and their staff members on trips during my two-year tour in Legislative Affairs, but I hold dear the opportunities I had to interface with Senator Warren Rudman.

BOB HOPE'S 80TH BIRTHDAY

I had only been assigned to Navy Legislative Affairs a few months when we received an invitation in the mail that was like none we had ever received before or would ever receive. It was in honor of Bob Hope's 80th birthday. Joanne and I were two of 24 guests invited by VADM and Mrs. Ed Waller, Superintendent of the Naval Academy, to join in honoring Bob Hope and celebrate his birthday. VADM Waller had been my boss during an early assignment in Patrol Aviation and was directly responsible for my being assigned to Navy Legislative Affairs. Both of our previous assignments had been in Hawaii where he was Commander of 3rd Fleet and I was on the Commander in Chief, Pacific Fleet Staff. We had become friends socially in Hawaii and I believe that was why we were invited.

As most people are aware, Bob Hope dedicated most of his Christmas holidays to go overseas and perform for deployed military troops. Thus, he was highly respected by everyone in the military. I believe he was coming to the Naval Academy to either be honored during the graduation ceremonies or to be the graduation speaker—I can't remember for sure which. Since this coincided with his 80th birthday the Wallers decided to have a special dinner party for him.

The evening started with cocktails aboard the Superintendent's Yacht *Astral* sailing on the Severn River adjacent to the Academy. However, the Hopes did not join us for cocktails. Toward the end of the cruise a very amusing incident occurred. A large yacht was returning from sea, going the opposite direction as our boat, and it was occupied by a number of younger people who had obviously been partying. As they came abeam of us, two or three of the gals on the boat removed their bikini tops and shouted to ensure they got the attention of all of the guests on our boat! I am certain VADM and Mrs. Waller were very embarrassed by this, but most everyone just took it in stride as a prank. We then returned to the dock at the Academy and were bused back to Buchanan House, the Superintendent's quarters where we had the opportunity to be introduced to Bob and Dolores Hope and then have dinner.

Guests included: Supreme Court Justice Sandra Day O'Connor, who was also the former Governor of Maryland; The Secretary of Defense, Cap Weinberger; Maryland Governor Harry Hughes; Maryland Congresswoman Marjorie Holt; Secretary of the Navy, John Lehman; Admiral James Holloway, former Chief of Naval Operations; Bruce Laingen, Ambassador and 14-month hostage during the Iranian Hostage Crisis of 1978–81; Admiral Bobby Inman, former Deputy Director of the CIA; two other civilians whose positions I don't know; Captain Bud

Edney who was Commandant of Midshipmen at the Academy; and Joanne and I. We were obviously "out of our league" and I am sure many of the people who read the guest list wondered who we were and why we were invited. It was a very enjoyable evening and certainly a memorable event in our lives.

Jobs I Have Held

In other chapters of the book I have mentioned several of the jobs I have had, but thought it might be interesting to talk about them in a chronological order and as a singular topic.

My first job was my paper route in Las Animas when I was in the 7th grade. I delivered the *Rocky Mountain News* daily in the morning. One of my best friends, Clark Billings, who was a couple years older than me, managed delivery for Las Animas and was in need of someone to cover the third route in town. We had three delivery boys, Clark, his brother Jim and me. I didn't realize it when I took the job; but there was a real drawback to my route—it was the only one that included areas that didn't have paved streets. Thus, when it rained or snowed, I had to peddle my bike through the mud which would stick to the tires and soon build up so thick that it would impact with the fenders and block the wheels from turning. Sometimes I could clear it with a stick, but often times I just had to pick up the bike and carry it until I could get to a paved area.

As I recall, I would get up around 6 a.m. and get dressed and peddle about two blocks to where the Greyhound Bus dropped off the papers. There were usually two large bundles. I would put one on each side of the canvas bags that wrapped around the handlebars and hung on either side of the front wheel. On Sundays, when the paper was extra large; it usually took two trips to get them to Clark and Jim's house, where we folded them. Fortunately, that was directly across the street from where we lived. We would normally get them folded into the bags on the bike to commence our route around 6:45 a.m.. The route took about 45 minutes to an hour, so we would be back home to get ready for school around 7:15 a.m.. I think I earned around $12 to $15 a month and, in addition to delivering the papers, we collected monthly from the customers.

About that same time I learned from a couple friends about setting pins at the bowling alley. The town had a men's bowling league which competed about four nights a week. They used four of the five lanes in the bowling alley. A match was three games and there were five men on a team. Each bowler paid 25 cents a line to bowl and the pen setters got 5 cents of that. Two teams would compete and they would use two lanes. Usually we had one pin setter per lane, thus he would make 25 cents per game or 75 cents for the night. A game would take about 30 minutes. Following the match, some of the bowlers would stay for "pots" which was for money. We would usually make another 25 to 50 cents for that which would usually wrap up around 9:30 p.m.. So, for 2½ to 3 hours of work we would make $1 to $1.25.

Since I got up at 6 a.m. and didn't get to bed until around 10 p.m., there wasn't much time for homework and my grades showed it.

While I was in High school I had several jobs. For a couple years the jobs included working at Safeway. Our store was in the middle of the main block in town. We didn't have a separate parking lot, so people parked on the street as close to the store as they could get. We had two check-out stands and during busy times always had a "bagger" at the stand bagging the groceries. In almost every case we would also carry them out to the customer's car—even if it was a block away. In fact, our manager insisted that we carry the groceries home for two or three ladies that lived within a couple blocks of the store. I know it is incredible; but no one ever thought about putting the bags in a cart and pushing it to the car. Carts weren't allowed outside the store.

Rather than wait for people to show you their car, we just asked which direction on the street and their license number. Rarely did a customer not know their license number, either because they thought it was important or to be sure the groceries got in the correct car!

When the checkstands weren't real busy, we would stock shelves. Once or twice a week, the Safeway supply truck would come and we had to unload our resupply order into the storage area in the back. This was quite a process. We had large, heavy conveyor track which we would connect together so that the truck driver could place the cases of supplies on it in the truck and the case would roll by gravity down into the storage area. Fortunately, there was a system to how the trucks were loaded. Canned vegetables in an area, canned fruit, canned juices, etc. We used the same system for stacking the cases of cans, boxes, and bottles in the back storage area. Thus, we would add extensions or orient the conveyors to deliver each category of supplies to the isle leading to the area where it was to be stacked.

The trucks normally arrived at our store around 6:30 a.m. before the store opened. I would like to think it was because I was a good worker, but I almost always was selected to work when trucks had to be unloaded. This was not the #1 choice job of any of the guys who worked at the store! I say guys, because I don't remember any women working at Safeway the couple years I worked for them. We had about four men who worked full time and then five or six boys who were part-time doing stocking and carry-out like I did.

Saturday was always our busiest day of the week. Many of the farmers lived several miles from town and only came to town on Saturday to shop. We normally closed around 5, but on Saturday night stayed open until 8 p.m.. We would be very busy until around 7:30 p.m. and then a couple of us would start getting the "closing" tasks done so we could get out of the store and head for the dance or to pick up our date. These tasks including sweeping the floor and then oiling them. The floor was made with a soft wood that would absorb the oil. We had large wide broom-like devices that were made of a cloth substance like a mop. They were used for applying the oil to the floor.

Since the store was closed on Sundays and the fresh vegetable bins weren't refrigerated, we had to store all the vegetables in the large walk-in cooler in the back storage area. Additionally, the bins had to be scrubbed with soap and water. We had to be careful not to be too aggressive with our "closing" tasks because John Wilburn, the store manager, rightfully insisted that the customers should have full, unimpeded access to all items until the store was closed. If a customer walked through the door at 1 minute before closing, we were not allowed to remove any items from the bins or shelves until that person finished their shopping. However, that didn't keep us from throwing some real glares at people who walked in the door just before closing! We learned, however, how to get quite a bit done in that last 30 minutes before closing, yet ensure the customers (and John) were kept happy.

Then once that last customer was out the door the work really got done! It was undoubtedly the most productive 30 to 45 minutes of the entire week. John and the other full time men must have chuckled to themselves watching the young part-time guys flying around getting all those "closing" tasks completed so they could hit the road for some Saturday night fun. We tried to be done by 8:30 p.m., but it was sometimes 8:45 p.m. before we finished.

During the summer I sometimes had baseball games in the evening which required me to leave early. Often times we had to drive two or three hours for the game and had to be there around 5:30 p.m. to warm up. John was always very understanding and would work around my schedule.

In high school I also worked for the Las Animas Gas Company doing janitor work in the evenings after they closed. This consisted mostly of sweeping the floors, emptying the wastebaskets and doing a little dusting. I could do it in around 45 minutes. Each Saturday I would go down and wash the windows. Since that was also one of my tasks at Safeway, I was a very good window washer.

For a few months I also cleaned a doctor's office each evening. That was a larger area than the gas company and took a little longer. They also had venetian blinds on all the windows and they were very hard to clean. I don't remember if I quit that job or got fired; but it was probably by mutual agreement. I don't think my cleaning was up to their standards.

I can also remember that there were a few times I forgot to clean the gas company's and/or the doctor's office. Wes Pyle, who managed the gas company was unbelievably understanding. When I think back I can't understand how I could "forget" to do a job that was 5 days a week! I can only write it off to being a teenager who also had sports, school, other jobs and a girlfriend that all took time.

When I was only around 14, I worked for Cliffs Grocery Market. I am not sure how I got the job, but I do remember one of the first tasks I learned to do was to "candle" eggs. Because most of the eggs were purchased directly from local farmers, the eggs had not been through any screening process. To "candle" the egg it is placed in a transparent holder with a bright light behind it. The light penetrates the egg shell such that you can see if there is any solid object in the egg. In particular, it is to ensure that the egg hasn't been fertilized and a small chick is growing inside. You can imagine how unappetizing it would be to crack open an egg and find the embryo of a chick inside!

Had we been able to do a dozen eggs at a time, it would have been an easy job. Unfortunately, the design of the "candle" wasn't that sophisticated—we did one at a time. I am guessing that the term "candling" came from the fact that prior to electricity, candles were used for examining the eggs.

I had a couple "one-time" jobs on farms in the area. One was a couple days driving a tractor with a harrow on the back. I had never done it before, but it didn't take a lot of skill, so with 10 minutes of instruction I was off and running. It was pretty boring because tractors in those days weren't enclosed with stereo systems and air conditioning.

Another job that was a day or two was picking up baled hay and putting it on the back of a flatbed truck. We had a pair on J-shaped metal tongs with wooden handles—one in each hand. We would spike them into either end of the bale and throw it up on the truck where another worker would stack them. The bales weighed in the vicinity of 50 pounds. At the end of the day you slept real well! If it has rained and the bales were wet—you could add another 10 pounds to their weight because the hay really absorbs water. It is jobs like this that convince you to go to college and get an education so you don't have to do that the rest of your life.

Today, of course, they have mechanized the process and there is a piece of machinery with a sloping powered escalator-like device just a little wider than a bale that pulls the bales up the sled onto the flatbed for stacking.

I worked my sophomore year for my uncle, J.B., on the farm. I believe my grandfather owned the farm; but J.B. and his family lived there and worked the farm. My Uncle Tom was also involved; but I am not sure what working relationship they had regarding finances. Their main enterprise was to raise chickens, process them, package them and sell them to grocers for re-sale. However, they also raised turkeys on an open range area a few miles south of the farm. I don't remember that we processed the turkeys in our processing plant—just the chickens. They also had a few head of cattle, some hogs and a couple milking cows.

J.B. would pick me up around 6:30 a.m. in the morning and take me back to the farm, which was directly southwest from the Las Animas football field—just across the railroad tracks. He and I would then load the pickup truck with sacks of grain so I could go feed the turkeys. I was only about 15, but we could get a learner's permit and drive in the rural areas. I would drive to the turkey field and fill the feeders with grain and tow the water trailer to the pump and wait while it filled. I am not sure how big the container was; but it would take on the order of an hour to fill it. I would then tow it back and reconnect it with the water troughs. You had to be very careful when driving through the turkeys because they wouldn't move naturally like most animals when they saw a vehicle approaching. If you honked the horn they would just put their heads up and give you a good "gobble-gobble" and not move an inch. It was unavoidable that we would occasionally run over one because they either weren't smart enough to move or had no fear of vehicles. I think the derogatory term "turkey" was based on observing their behavior.

When they were small we would move them out to the range area in portable sheds. We would jack up the shed and slide a low flatbed with two wheels underneath. While we were towing them someone had to stay inside the shed to keep them from piling up in a corner and suffo-cating some of them. They would "spook" very easily and their natural reaction was to bunch together. They would also do this on the range if a hawk flew over them. If this happened and they were near a fence they would all pack into the fence and if there was a corner that is where they would head. If there wasn't someone to wade in and disperse them, some would get trampled and die. Like I mentioned earlier, the expression "He or she is a real turkey" didn't come about for no good reason!

One day when Tom and I were jacking up a shed getting it ready to move, I was pumping the jack. We put a long metal bar into a receptacle in the jack and used the bar for leverage to pump up the jack. As I was in the process of pushing down on the bar my hands slipped off the bar before the teeth of the jack had engaged to hold the jack at the next height. The weight of the shed immediately forced the bar back up very rapidly. The bar hit me on the jaw and sent me reeling back. I immediately checked for broken teeth and expected my jaw to be broken and about the same time Tom rushed over. Fortunately for me the bar struck me close to its highest possible position as the shed settled to its previous height. Had the bar hit me when it still had several inches further to reach its top position and with the weight of the shed driving it, I am certain it would have broken my jaw and knocked out or broken several teeth!

When I finished feeding and watering the turkeys I would then head back to the farm and do a few chores like cleaning the chicken hutches. This was not a fun job. The chickens were raised in wire pens that had multiple layers and were about six feet high. In that six feet might be three or four layers of chickens. Each layer was about 6 or 8 square feet. Below each layer was a flat pan with an edge about ¾″ high. We would line the pan with newspaper and all the droppings from the chickens went through the wire floor onto the paper. These had to be cleaned every day. I don't remember the exact numbers; but I am guessing there were around 30 or 40 cages with a pan in each to be emptied and clean papers inserted.

We would also inspect the chickens to see if any had developed sores. This was not uncommon because of the heat and close conditions. We had medicine to treat sores and you can imagine in those close confines if an infection developed, it would spread like wildfire if not caught and treated right away. Despite our best efforts there would be a few chickens a week that would die or so sick they had to be removed and killed or put into an isolation pen.

If it was a processing day, which was three or four days a week, I would then go into the small plant and prepare to run the chicken "plucker." The processing was mostly a family operation. My uncle did the killing and soaking of the chickens, I ran the plucker to remove the feathers and my mother would cut them open, clean them and package them. We might have had another person to help with packaging now and then; but the three of us did most of the work.

We had a stainless steel device for killing the chickens and draining the blood. In the top of the device were three or four large funnels about the size of a chicken. The chicken was put in upside down and his head pulled through the narrow end of the funnel at the bottom. Below the funnels was a long trough that was sloped toward one end. Below the low end of the trough was a 50 gallon barrel. With a sharp knife we would then cut off the head of the chicken and leave it hang there in the funnel long enough so that as much blood as possible was removed from the chicken. Obviously, the blood would run down the trough and into the barrel.

The head and legs and innards of the chicken, when it was cleaned by my mother, would also be thrown into the barrel. That combination would then be fed to the hogs. Thus, a very efficient operation with very little waste. Needless to say, this job wasn't for someone with a squeamish stomach!

Once the chicken was killed and the blood sufficiently drained, it would be held by its feet and dipped into hot water whose temperature was constantly monitored and maintained at a specific temperature. If the temperature was too high or the chicken was held in the water too long the skin would get too soft and would tear in the plucking process. I would then take the chicken and do the plucking. The machine was a large round drum about two feet wide and about 18″ in diameter. It had rubber fingers about 4″ in length protruding out of the side of the drum. There was a hood over the top of the drum and extending down the back. This directed the flow of feathers into a catcher on the floor beneath the plucker. The drum was driven by a motor so that it rotated at a moderate speed. I would then hold the chicken against the fingers in such a manner as to remove the feathers; but not with too much pressure so as to protect the skin from tearing. There was a sequence of moves that I made to ensure each portion of the chicken's feathers were removed. The last move was to remove the pin feathers on the tail of the chicken. I believe I could step up to a "plucker" today and still repeat the sequence of moves that I did about a hundred times a day. I am certain they have a much easier and more sophisticated way to process chickens today. Surely, the "plucker," as I knew it, doesn't exist today.

I think the "normal" quitting hour was around 5 p.m.. However, it seems to me we normally didn't quit at the "normal" time! I vividly remember one of those times. I was a member of the High School Band and we had several practices within a couple weeks time for a special marching band competition being held in Pueblo or Colorado Springs. We had to attend a minimum number of practices or we couldn't go on the trip. I had already missed one practice earlier and mentioned to J.B. that I needed to get off at 4:45 p.m. so I could get across the street to the football field for the practice. As that time approached we were working on some task in the lot just beside the processing plant. I could see the band assembling across the tracks on the football field and reminded him a couple times about the practice. He kept putting me off with something like "just a few more minutes." To the best of my recollection it was around 5:30 p.m. when we finished and I was too embarrassed to show up that late. I didn't get to go on the trip with the band because of missing that practice.

Another experience I recall was a day of cutting alfalfa. I think the field was near where we had the turkeys. He took me out, showed me how to run the cutter and told me he would be back later when he figured I would have the cutting complete. Everything went fine for a few hours, but I hit a very rough area and suddenly I noticed that the cutting arm had fallen back to about a 140 degree angle from the tractor instead of the normal 90 degree angle. I immediately stopped the tractor and got off. I looked it over and came to the conclusion I had broken it and was going to be in big trouble. Fortunately, J.B. showed up within about an hour. I told him what happened and was surprised when he didn't get upset. Instead he had me help him pull the arm back into the 90 degree position and reinsert the frame back into the "breakaway" coupler. It was designed to do just what it did when the cutting arm hit something unusually solid. Needless to say, I was very relieved.

I recall another event that happened within a week or so of my starting to work on the farm for J.B. We had the pickup truck parked directly in front of the processing plant because I think they had just unloaded some supplies and put them in the shed. He told me to get in the truck and move it up so we could get better access to the front door of the plant. I had only learned to drive a few days earlier—that's my excuse and I am sticking with it! I got into the truck and immediately turned the key to start the truck. That might have been alright if the last person in the truck had left it in neutral gear. Unfortunately, the gear had been left in reverse so that when I turned the key the truck jumped back and impacted the frame of the door—knocking it out of place. I should have first either put the gearshift in neutral or held my foot on the clutch. Since most of you reading this don't know what a clutch is—I will explain it. With manual transmissions the driver had to press in the clutch (located to the left of the brake) with his left foot before shifting gears. This essentially put the transmission into neutral while you shifted to the next gear. Well, J.B. lost his temper, sent me inside to clean the chicken pens and told me he was going to take the cost of the repairs out of my wages. Tom calmed him down and tried to console me a little and assure me it wasn't going to take much to repair the door. I am not sure if it was later that day or the next day, J.B. recanted about docking my pay.

My pay for 5 or 6 days a week of around 10 hours a day was $10 per week! The going wage at that time was around 35 cents an hour and I was getting about 20 cents an hour. However, to J.B.'s credit that was better than nothing and my mother and I needed anything we could make at that time. I also think that he wasn't making much off the farm and the chicken processing and had to cut his costs as close as possible. There is however, an old adage that says "Never work for relatives." In hindsight that is probably pretty good advice.

Another job that I had the summer of my senior year was working at the Standard Gas Station. I believe Leo Hayward, who was two years older than me but was a good friend, got me the job. Leo had worked there for several years and was well-respected by the owner.

I didn't know much about cars, but with a little training learned how to change oil and lubricate a car, fix flat tires by patching the tube, pump gas and to do simple maintenance like replace radiator belts. Nowadays all car tires are tubeless; but in my time all tires had an inner tube. The tube held the air that kept the tire inflated. If a nail or something penetrated the tire and tube, the tube had to be taken out and patched. I was paid 50 cents an hour—a step up from the 35 cents I had been getting at Safeway.

In those days it was unheard of for anyone to fill their own gas tank. We were trained to almost run out when a car pulled so that when the driver rolled down the window we were immediately there to inquire how much gas he wanted and if there was any other service he needed. We always told them to release the hood (in older cars we could release it from outside) so we could check to see if he needed oil and to make sure his radiator belt didn't have any cracks or signs of wear. There were no credit cards then, but many of the people were regular customers and had an account which they paid monthly.

Probably the most difficult job we had was to repair tractor tires. Most people don't realize that tractor tires are filled with a liquid so as to provide extra weight and traction to the tractor. If the tire needed repair it would usually be removed from the tractor by the farmer and brought into our station. It wasn't an easy chore just moving the tires around, as they weighed several hundred pounds. To repair the tire the fluid mixture in the tire had to be pumped out into 50-gallon barrels where it was stored until the tire was patched and ready for the fluid to be reinserted. These tires also had metal rims that were about 2 to 3″ wide that clamped in place around the outside edge of the wheel, between the wheel and the tire. The rims were under a lot of tension and if not carefully handled could spring off the wheel and severely injure or even kill a person. In fact, while I was working at the station a man in an adjacent town was killed by a rim while he was repairing a tire. Needless to say, we used extra caution when working with rims.

Our owner was very good at his trade and insisted that the service we provided was always of high quality. I still remember what I learned from him about washing cars. He would always roll down each window a couple times and wipe off the window and top edge. When you wash a car the water gets into the window linings around the edge of the window and dampens those linings that hold the window snug within the window frame. If those linings aren't dried then each time the window is rolled up and down residual moisture goes onto the window. We were taught to dry off those linings inside the window frame and to roll each window up and down a couple times to ensure all the moisture was removed. Since then I always check the windows when I get the car washed and have never experienced anyone who dried off those window linings like we did in 1955!

About midway through the summer following my Senior year, I was recruited to play in a softball tournament in Longmont, Colorado along with several guys I knew from my home town. Most of them were already in college. I think it was a weekend tournament, so I got time off from the station and got a ride up to Longmont with some friends. While there a couple of the guys I knew from Las Animas told me about the great job they had working on a railroad near Gunnison, Colorado. They were making $1.25 an hour plus double that for overtime. Since I was desperately trying to save as much as I could for college, this seemed like a great opportunity to me. I called my mom, asked her to please let my boss know that I was leaving for this opportunity and to please box up some clothes and mail them to me in Gunnison. I have felt guilt ever since about abruptly leaving that job, but the opportunity was just too good to pass up. I rode back to Gunnison with Glen Richeson and Max Wheeler, who were both working for the company that had the contract to remove the narrow gauge tracks and ties. My first day on the job was the following day. We met and were driven out to the worksite. The job of removing the rails, plates and spikes was accomplished by using an engine with three cars. Each car had a metal "A-frame" which supported a cable used to pull the rails up onto the cars. The first car behind the engine had a powered winch attached to the cable. As the rails behind the train were pulled up onto the cars the train moved ahead a short distance and repeated the process of pulling up the rails behind it. Once the three cars were filled, the train and crew would proceed to a siding ahead where the cars were unloaded.

The great motivator for the crew was that we got paid for 8 hours work whenever the three cars were filled. Most days that only took about 5 to 6 hours. Then the two or three volunteers who agreed to help unload got paid overtime for the hour or so it took to offload the rails.

It was standard practice for the a new hire to work his first day or two with the boss. This was essentially an evaluation to see if you were a good worker and could handle the type of hard work. We worked on the tracks ahead of the train pulling up spikes. Our tool for doing that was a 35-pound crowbar device with a claw on the end that fit around the spikes like a claw hammer does with the head of a nail. There was a small four-wheel car that also worked ahead of the train pulling most of the spikes that attached the rail, and the supporting plates beneath the rail to the ties. The machine couldn't pull all of the spikes because the engine and three cars still had to pass over that portion of the tracks. Also, there were some spikes that might be slightly bent or too embedded into the tie for the mechanical "puller" to engage. Those were left for the boss and me (or other recruits) to dig out with our 5-foot claw bar. The few spikes that were purposely left attached so the train could pass safely were then pulled by another worker working behind the train, so that the rails could be detached and pulled up on to the cars.

That first day or two were the most physically demanding days I ever worked in my life! Nearing the end of the day that 35-pound bar felt like it weighed 75 pounds and, even though I was young and very active athletically, every muscle in my body ached.

I was really relieved when I had "passed" the evaluation and got to work behind the train with the majority of the crew. However, that didn't mean that the job was now a "piece of cake." Underneath the rail on each tie was a 12-pound plate through which the spikes were driven to attach the rail to the tie. These plates were carried by us and thrown into the last car 6 or 8 at a time. I realize you can multiply; but that was 75 to almost 100 pounds each trip! I used to know exactly how many plates a day each person carried, but I know it was between 1.5 and 2 tons of plates a day.

At the time I started to work we had a crew of around 6 or 8, not counting those who were on the engine and cars. They were mostly college football players who were attending Western State University in Gunnison, Colorado. Three of them I knew from my home town. We were all hard workers and that was the reason the job was usually completed in well less than 8 hours.

The portion of the narrow gauge that we were removing ran from Gunnison up over the Continental Divide down into Poncha Springs and then on to Canon City. Obviously, as we progressed removing the track, the start point each day changed. The first week or so I bunked in with Glen and a couple of his roommates, as Glen was going to be a Freshman at Gunnison and had already gotten a room. However, it became necessary to move closer to the job site. The company put us up in a motel at the western base of Poncha Pass. The only drawback is that the motel didn't have running water. Each night when we got home—after working as hard as we did in hot weather—we really needed a bath! Being improvising young men, we noted that there was a stream about 50 yards behind the motel, so we put on our bathing suits, grabbed some soap and a towel and took our bath in the stream. One had to really be dirty and dedicated to cleanliness to get in that very cold water each night! It might have been 80 degrees outside, but this was water coming out of the mountains from melting snow. I think there were some nights that we would all have rather skipped the encounter with that ice water, except we had to live in close quarters with one another.

We were always amazed by the extremes to which tourists, railroad buffs and other people would go in order to take photos of us tearing up this railroad. We would be high up in the mountains in very remote areas and as we progressed around a bend there would be someone with a camera taking photos of us, and the wild life that was abundant. Sightings of elk, deer, and coyotes were almost a regular occurrence.

As we neared the summit of the pass, it became necessary again to move into a location ahead of the train. The company put us up in a small hotel in Poncha Springs on the eastern side of the mountain leading to Poncha Pass. At the top of the pass was a fairly significant railroad facility which included a large turntable where the engine could be placed on it and turned 180 degrees so as to face the other direction.

Now that we were staying at a location well ahead of our work site, each day after completing work we had a small four-wheel powered flat car that we would ride down the hill to Poncha Springs. One of the first days we did that I did something very stupid that could have ended me up in the hospital. As we were descending the track we came to a switchback area. I could see that the track made a big loop and came back directly below our position, so I jumped off, as we weren't going very fast, and told them I would run down the hill and meet them below after they made the big loop down and back. I started running down the hill, not realizing how steep it was. Somehow I managed to stay on my feet until about halfway down, when gravity and speed overcame my ability to stay upright. I tumbled head over heels for about 30 feet. Fortunately, it was not a rocky area and there weren't any trees. I was a little skinned up, but made it to the bottom in time to jump back on the car as it passed. I took a little ribbing for my clumsy exhibition.

About the time we shifted over to Poncha Springs, it was August and time for football practice to start at Western State. That meant that we lost the bulk of our workers. The boss went to the employment office and hired some replacements. The first day they were on the job the three or four of us who remained from the original crew realized it was going to be a long day. Instead of finishing the job in 5.5 or 6 hours, it took the full 8 hours. These guys weren't going to work any harder than they had to! Also, they didn't want to work overtime to unload the cars at the end of the day. This was the only good news, because all of we "regulars" enjoyed that opportunity to get paid double-time.

After we had been working just a few days out of Poncha Springs, I returned from work one day and had terrible stomach pains. I found a doctor's office and he gave me something to take. As I recall, I stayed in the hotel the next day, but wasn't getting any better. The next day I informed the crew chief that I was quitting and going home. I think the combination of not feeling good, getting closer to school starting in September and the fun having gone out of the job now that the core of our work team had started football practice, led me to that decision. I had also talked with my mom on the phone and, being a concerned mother, she wanted me to come home. I boarded a bus that day and returned home.

I had saved $500, which is what I had in the bank when I started school at the University of Colorado in September.

When I went to college, I had a Tuition and Fees Scholarship based on my high school grades. The baseball coach said he would get me a job that would pay for my room and board. The $800 I had saved that summer was to cover the remainder of my expenses. I arrived a couple days before school started and was assigned to Hallett Hall. Within a couple days I learned that I had been assigned to work cleaning the bakery in the student union in evenings as my room-and-board job. As I related earlier when discussing my college years, this turned out to be a much more time-consuming job than my coach anticipated. Flour would be all over the floor of the bakery and one of the tasks including sweeping and mopping the floor. Sweeping flour isn't very easy. It is so fine that it is very difficult to get it all with a broom. It should probably be vacuumed, but I wasn't given a vacuum as one of my tools—just brooms. I don't remember exactly how long I kept the job, but I reluctantly finally went to the coach to tell him that it was taking much longer than I had been told would be necessary to work each day. In addition, I was a freshman in engineering and playing both basketball and baseball. I was finally relieved of that job and was given jobs to do within the athletic department.

The jobs at the athletic department continued throughout my four years of college and consisted of a variety of different tasks. The most challenging was to clean up the gymnastics room each morning before classes started. I would get up around 6 or 6:30 a.m. and walk the 2 or 3 blocks to the gym. Mats would be all over the floor of the room as would the chalk that gymnasts put on their hands for a good grip on the rings and bars. That chalk was about as difficult to sweep as flour. I would sweep off each mat individually and stack them in a corner of the gym. Once I had that completed, I would then wipe down all the equipment and then sweep the floor. The toughest challenge of the job was the morning alarm clock. They didn't have snooze alarms in those days and, unfortunately, there were several mornings I would hit the alarm button, roll over for "just a minute more of sleep" and wake up an hour later. Thus, some mornings the job wasn't as thorough as it should have been and a couple times it didn't get done at all. Winters were particularly tough when snow was on the ground and it was cold and dreary.

I also had the task of filling the soap dispensers in the locker rooms. They used liquid soap which worked on a gravity basis. There were containers located high on the walls of the showers that were about a gallon in size and could be filled from the top. Through connecting pipes they fed down and along the wall where the men could dispense the soap by pushing a button. This job was actually assigned to a couple of the basketball players who were on scholarship, but they didn't have to actually do the work. Essentially it was their job on paper, but someone else like me would do the work for them.

On Sunday mornings following home football games a large group of us would gather in the stadium and sweep all of the rows and aisles. Each of us was normally assigned a few sections to sweep. We could work longer if we wanted, but, as a minimum, had to complete our assigned sections.

On Saturdays during football season, a select number of baseball players had the privilege of selling programs. This was a highly desirable job, as we made pretty good money in a relatively short time. Programs were a quarter, of which we kept a nickel. Thus, for every 100 programs sold we made $5. On really good days, like Oklahoma games, we would make as much as $50 in 3 or 4 hours of work. That was great money in those days! On the average, however, we probably made about $30 a game. My sales pitch was "Programs, programs! You can't tell the players from the goal posts without a program!" Not too original, but lots of people got a kick out of it and bought a program from me.

One Saturday, another player and I decided to be real enterprising and go down into Boulder and sell programs early, well before game time. The games usually started at 1 p.m. and we would start selling around 10:30 a.m. or so. This day we got our programs around 9 a.m. and walked the five or six blocks to the downtown area and went from store to store and along the sidewalk. I think we might have sold about 75 each and decided we wouldn't do that again. The small return wasn't worth the effort.

By the time I got to be a Junior and Senior, the equipment manager, Lee Akins, had taken a liking to me and I worked a lot for Lee. Before football and basketball practice the players would drop by the equipment room and be issued shirts, jocks, socks and trunks, or pants. These were all items that were washed each day and had to be issued on a daily basis. Before games the equipment included the game uniforms. When I wasn't occupied with my own practices, I would help Lee issue equipment, which was actually an easy job, but a job you had to earn and work your way into. Lee also had a bit of a drinking problem and sometimes didn't show up on time. Those were times I covered for him and bailed him out. I think this is also part of the reason he took a liking to me! I am almost certain that his bosses knew about his problems, but he was such an institution within the athletic department and such a nice person that they overlooked it.

After living in the dorms my Freshman year with Roger Kinney and Merle Weitz, the three of us found an apartment across the street from the northwest corner of the campus and recruited a fourth roommate, Porky Manown. We lived there for two years, with Jim Suplizio replacing Merle the second year when Merle graduated. My senior year I became a counselor in Baker Dorm. I was assigned a wing on the three-story dorm that was mostly occupied by "jocks." Being one of them I think they thought I would be a good choice. In return for being a dorm counselor I received room and board. This meant that all the money I earned working for the Athletic Department was spending money. The athletic department also bought my books the last two years, so I had room and board, tuition and fees, books and about $100 a month. I had never had it so good!

Around the middle of my Freshman year, I noticed that I appeared to be getting overpaid. At the end of each week we would fill out a time card with the number of hours worked each day. I don't remember exactly what we made, but I think it was around $1.50 per hour. I would log 20 hours and get a check for $40 or log 15 hours and get a check for $30. Finally, I went in to the Athletic Business Manager's office, where we turned in the cards and told the secretary, Miss Ecke, about the problem. She thanked me and sent me on my way. However, this continued to happen so I went in again and showed her my last paycheck and that the hours were more than I had put on my time card. This time she took me into the office of Kayo Lam, the Athletic Business Manager. I knew Kayo, because my dad and he had played football together at CU and were stationed together when they were in the Navy during WW II. He had introduced himself to me one of the first days after I arrived at CU my first year. Being careful not to admit he was doing anything wrong, he explained to me that he noticed how exact I was in reporting my time—always down to the quarter hour, whereas most of the other players always rounded up to the next hour. He also noted that I was working more hours than many of the others, but always recording fewer hours than they were. He was merely "adjusting" my hours so that I was being fairly compensated in relationship to the others. Basically, I was a bit naive and very honest in reporting my hours. The others had learned the "system" early and knew that it was almost expected they would "fudge" a bit on their hours. I think Kayo soon realized that I hadn't caught on to the system, so he was helping me out. I know that he also knew I really needed the money.

After graduation, I had some time to kill until heading across country to Newport, Rhode Island to start Officer Candidate School in August. I went down to the employment office in Denver and was immediately given a lead with a brick company in Denver. They needed a laborer to help plant bushes on a large hill on a side of their property. It was a sloping hill that was about 40 yards by 40 yards. My partner was a school teacher who took this on as a summer job. I think when the brick company realized I was a college graduate, they decided to expand my job a little. Thus, some days I would be assigned to make deliveries of brick to worksites. So, I might spend half a day planting and half a day delivering.

One day I had a pickup truck and it was filled to the top edge of the truck bed with bricks. I am sure the weight exceeded the limits of what the truck was designed to carry. As I was proceeding along the road to the delivery location, I had a flat tire and pulled over to the side. As I recall, I either had a small jack that couldn't handle the weight of the bricks or no jack at all. While I was standing there surveying the situation a truck with a couple Hispanics (they were called Mexicans in those days) pulled up behind me and asked if they could help. They quickly pulled out a big jack and had the tire changed within a few minutes. Needless to say, I was relieved and very grateful.

The school teacher and I finished planting the hill about the time I needed to leave and start driving across county to leave my car with Joanne in Chicago, before flying on to Newport. A couple years later I was in Denver and happened to drive by that hill where we had planted the bushes. They were all dead. We had told them they were going to need a sprinkler system to keep the plants alive. Obviously, they never got around to putting one in. All that work for nothing.

Following Officer Candidate School and being commissioned an Ensign in the U.S. Navy, I spent 24 years in the Navy. Throughout that time we had assignments in Jacksonville, Florida; Alameda, California; Honolulu, Hawaii; San Diego, California; Alexandria, Virginia; Taipei, Taiwan; Coronado, California; San Jose, California; Monterey, California; back to San Jose, California; Newport, Rhode Island; back again to San Jose, California; again to Honolulu, Hawaii; and, finally, Washington, D.C.

We then moved to San Diego where I took a job with the Consulting firm of Booz-Allen & Hamilton in 1984. I worked there until mid-1987 when I got a consulting job with General Dynamics Laser Laboratory. The lab's primary project was to design a blue-green laser to be mounted on an aircraft for communicating with submarines operating hundreds of feet beneath the surface of the water. They needed the defense department to fund an additional $25 million for the program or the lab was going to be out of business. I spent about a year taking laser PhDs through the halls of the Pentagon and Congress to get the money funded.

It was a rewarding job in that the two PhDs that I worked with were brilliant scientists, but knew nothing about Congress, the Pentagon or how to get the money authorized and appropriated. We did get the money funded and they were all very appreciative. On more than one occasion they would say to me as we were going down a hall in the Pentagon or in a House of Representatives Office Building, "Don't ever go off and leave us in here. We wouldn't know how to find our way out or how to find the office for the next meeting!"

About the time we got the program funded, I was approached by John Manuel of Lockheed Corporation about a job running a new Field Marketing Office in San Diego. He had been given my name by retired Vice Admiral Ed Waller, who worked for Lockheed Aeronautics. I had worked for Vice Admiral Waller during my Navy career and he knew I was in San Diego.

That turned out to be a very fortunate big break for me. I opened the new office in 1989 with the objective of developing more business for Lockheed at the local Navy Laboratory, Naval Ocean Systems Command (NOSC). After about a year's effort, we were making some progress, but not much. Other than myself and a small Lockheed Company that maintained the Navy's Deep Submergence Rescue Vehicles, Lockheed didn't have any other presence in San Diego. NOSC people liked to be able to pick up the phone, call their contractors, and have the contractor in their office in an hour to talk about an issue or whatever might be on their mind. We couldn't do that with our primary NOSC support companies being in Austin, Texas; Sunnyvale, California; and Nashua, New Hampshire. I suggested buying a local company who had a good rapport and existing contracts with NOSC, but it didn't happen.

My boss, John Manuel, finally decided we needed to close the office as we weren't generating enough business in San Diego to justify the cost of the office. However, a couple of the Lockheed Companies doing business at NOSC—primarily Sanders in Nashua—wanted to keep my services. It was decided that I would continue as a consultant and Lockheed would provide me an office and computer in the building used by the Deep Submergence Rescue Vehicle Company.

I continued in a consultant basis for about a year until, one day, I received a call from John Manuel. About a year before closing the office, John had asked me to come to Corporate Headquarters to fill an opening he had there. Since, we seemed to be doing all right in San Diego and Joanne had a great job in real estate, I asked John if I could just stay in San Diego. He was very graceful and agreed. He was now calling to offer me the same job. The man he hired a year earlier wasn't working out and he needed to replace him. I jumped at the chance. It looked like a very good opportunity and was a much more stable job than consulting.

Before I was formally offered the job it was required that I interview with the Chief Operating Officer of Lockheed, Vance Coffman. Vance and the CEO, Dan Tellup, were required to brief the Lockheed Board of Directors monthly. One of the tasks of my new job was to support this briefing by overseeing the preparation of the briefing slides and back-up data for both Vance and Dan. I had a very good meeting and lunch with Vance and was informed the following day that the job was mine.

I think this is a good time to point out a very valuable lesson that I had learned long ago and that I think was key to being offered the new job with Lockheed. That is, "Never burn your bridges behind you." When John closed my office in San Diego and let me go, albeit to a consultant status, I could have been very upset and reacted negatively. I could have questioned why he hadn't insisted I take the job he had offered me earlier in Calabasas—since he might have know at that time the office might have to be closed. Instead, I made lemonade out of lemons and gracefully accepted the change to a consultant status.

I reported to Calabasas, California, home of the Corporate Headquarters, in March 1993 as Director Programs. I had previously been a Manager, so Director was a promotion. Since we had to buy a house in the new area and rent our Rancho Bernardo home, Joanne stayed in San Diego for about a month and I commuted on the weekends. We settled into our new location and really enjoyed living in Westlake Village where we had a nice condo right on the lake. We had purchased a new electric-powered "cocktail" boat and really enjoyed it.

We had only been there about four months when it was announced that Lockheed and Martin Marietta Corporations would be merging and moving their corporate headquarters to Bethesda, Maryland. About half of the Lockheed corporate employees would be laid off with severance pay and half would move to the new headquarters. This was a bit of a bombshell.

We were part of the group selected to become a part of the new Lockheed Martin and moved in March 1994 to Fairfax, Virginia. This move was about number 30 for Joanne and me since we married in 1959! Throughout all the moves, she was a true trooper. We tried to make each of our new locations a "home" and face each new assignment with a positive attitude. Not many wives could have handled all the moves, separations and burdens as gracefully and successfully as she did.

We purchased a new townhouse near the Vienna metro stop and, once again, settled in to a new location. I was initially assigned to work out of Lockheed Martin's Crystal City offices. Being such a large defense contractor we had to have almost a daily presence within the Pentagon and on Capitol Hill. Crystal City provided good access to both, whereas, operating from Bethesda would have been very cumbersome and inefficient. I was to provide liaison for Business Development issues between the Corporation's legislative and program development people in Crystal City and my boss for Business Development in Bethesda.

Within about six months it became apparent to me that John was being overwhelmed by his new responsibilities as VP Business Development for this enlarged $20-billion-a-year corporation. His span of responsibilities was just too large. We had around 20 marketing field offices spread throughout the country, and many were accustomed to almost daily interface with John—usually on the telephone. More and more they were calling me and asking me to get a message to John or get an answer to a problem from John. About that time it also was becoming obvious that my presence was needed more at Bethesda than at Crystal City, so John had me move there. Shortly after that, John turned over responsibility to me for the 22 Field Marketing Offices and got a promotion to Vice President Domestic Business Development approved for me. In essence, he formalized what I was already doing by assigning me the Field Offices. I still had oversight responsibility for the monthly Board of Directors briefings, but had a man working for me who did most of the detailed work for me on that. I also took over responsibility for Corporate Trade Show Management and had two people directly working that area for me.

John Manual and 10 other corporate Vice Presidents retired three years after we moved to Bethesda. The merger package incentivized the new corporate VPs to stay with the new organization a minimum of 3 years, in exchange for a $1 million guarantee. This was to provide stability for the newly merged corporation. However, the clause also stated they couldn't receive the bonus if they stayed longer than 3 years. Tax laws wouldn't allow them to write off the bonuses as a part of the merger expenses if it were more than 3 years after the merger. For one or two of the younger VPs, they could more than make up that $1 million in the years they had left with the corporation. However, if the VPs were anywhere near retirement age it made economic sense to take the money and run.

This turned out to be unfortunate for me, as I never could develop the sense of rapport and trust with John's replacement that I had with him. I retired in the middle of 1999 at the age of 62. Had the situation been different, I would like to have worked another 2 or 3 years. It was still a great opportunity and very rewarding financially.

After retiring to San Diego, I consulted periodically with Northrop Grumman Corporation for a couple years. Shortly after I retired, it occurred to me that I started working as a paper boy in 1949 and had held some type of job almost continuously for 50 years.

How I Got Involved in Genealogy

I am sure most people sort of evolve into genealogy and an interest in family history. However, I know exactly when and why I became interested. Joanne and I were living in Vienna, Virginia and I was working for Lockheed Martin Corporation, having been transferred there in March 1994. I was 57 years old and hadn't the slightest interest in family history and couldn't even spell genealogy correctly (geneology).

I knew Grandpa and Grandma Ritchhart were of German ancestry, but assumed it was their generation or one generation back when they came to this country. I knew Grandma Dean was Irish and her maiden name was O'Malley, but knew nothing about her parents—not even their names. I knew my great-grandmother Dean, grandpa Dean's mother. I think I had heard that her maiden name was Britton. My mother always said we were English, Irish and German, so I assumed through the process of elimination that the Dean side of the family was English. I knew that my Grandma Dean had a brother, Uncle Lee, whom I had met a couple times. I also knew that my Grandpa Dean had a sister, Blanche, whom I had also met. I didn't know anything about Grandpa Ritchhart's side of the family, but had met Aunt Dell, Grandma Ritchhart's sister. I can't remember any of my grandparents ever telling me much about their parents or siblings.

This all changed one day about a year after moving to the Vienna area. I came home from work that day and had received a letter in the mail which opened with the salutation "Dear Cousin." It then went on for a page telling me all about the book that had been written about the Ritchhart family and that for $45 plus $5 shipping it could be mine. Well, I had received other offers similar in the mail. One that I had ordered, which was only around $15, had some generic information about the Ritchhart name, some history of Germany, why Germans emigrated to America and listed, by state, the addresses and phone numbers of several Ritchharts—a list that had been obtained from phone directories. My first reaction was to toss the letter in the waste basket. However, in reading it over again the author provided her name, address, phone number and e-mail address. Additionally, and this turned out to be the key factor, was a Library of Congress Card Catalog Number.

I had gotten a computer several months earlier and was familiar enough with the web to be able to find the web site for the Library of Congress and to note that there was a box for entering Catalog numbers. Upon entering the number 93-85863 I was able to view a description of the book that was very similar to the information contained in the letter. Now my interest was piqued. Joanne was very skeptical, but the Library of Congress Catalog number helped quell some of her (and my) concerns about this being a "rip off." After sleeping on it a day or two, we decided to order the book. It was still a bit of a leap of faith, but we ordered the book anyhow. The book arrived in a timely manner about two weeks later. I immediately went to the index and found my father's and grandfather's names. Upon going to the pages listed for them, I was reassured to find a list of my dad's brothers and sisters, my aunts and uncles. This gave me some feeling of relief than the $50 might not have been a total waste. I then started to trace back and when I realized there were 14 generations of my line of Ritchharts, going back to 1503 in Switzerland, I was elated. I didn't realize it at the time, but I was now entering the first phase of a genealogist's maturation. That is when one develops an interest in family history. It then evolves into a hobby, which then becomes a passion and then very quickly become an obsession and for many an addiction. I have no scientific proof of this evolution, but the spouses, children and friends of genealogists have all witnessed this progression and will confirm my characterization of the process.

After skimming through the book over the first week or so, I decided that I needed to record this information and add to it the additional details that I knew that weren't in the book. I had read or seen something about computer application programs that one could purchase for this purpose. I did a little more research and decided to purchase *Family Tree Maker*. Now I was on my way to this becoming a hobby—I was quickly entering the next phase of becoming a genealogist.

It is now fifteen years later. I have over 3000 entries in my *Family Tree Maker* program, a two-drawer file cabinet full of folders filled with census sheets, land records, marriage records, photographs, newspaper clippings and various other records. I am president of one genealogy society, a member of two others, have spent a week within the past year at both the Salt Lake City Family History Library and the Allen County Public Library doing genealogical research. I have made two other shorter trips to the Family History Library and spend some time almost every day on something that is genealogy-related. I have been through cemeteries in Virginia, Ohio, Indiana, Missouri and Colorado looking for headstones, recording information and taking photos. Much to the dismay of my wife, other family members, and friends, I will talk about family history whenever given half a chance and can glaze over the eyes of even the most ardent relatives. Even distant family members are not safe, as most family gatherings will include a discussion or presentation by me about family history.

I realize that none of the family share my intense interest in family history, but I keep at it because I know that someday—perhaps after I am long gone—they too will age and develop an appreciation for family history. This belief, right or wrong, keeps me plugging away and, yes, I have completed my maturation as a genealogist—it is truly an obsession! However, I have no regrets of having mailed off that $50 fifteen years ago. Best $50 investment I ever made!

A Timeline Comparison

I find it very interesting to compare major events in our family's history with what was happening here in the United States and in the world at the same time. I think it helps put these events into perspective. It may be that there is no correlation between family history events and the history of our country, but in many cases there is a connection which makes it easier to understand why our ancestors made some of the decisions in their lives that they did.

In looking at the Ritchhart, Dean, O'Malley, Schmidt and McConnell ancestry lines, the Deans arrived in this country the earliest. The came here from England around 1715, give or take a few years. Richard Dean was born in England in 1698 and his eldest son, Edward was born in Virginia in 1718. Thus, I conclude that Richard came to this country a couple years before Edward was born. Interestingly William Penn died in 1718 leaving his sons to be the proprietors of Pennsylvania. William had done a lot to entice Europeans to emigrate to America—Pennsylvania in particular. In 1713 the first America-built schooner was launched in Massachusetts, providing a line of faster ships to bring immigrants to America from Europe. At that time America was still a British Colony, so Richard was merely moving from England to another colony.

About thirty-five years later, in 1750, Christian Ritschard arrived in Pennsylvania from Switzerland. George Washington was a seventeen-year-old county surveyor in Culpeper, Virginia; Mason and Dixon were appointed to survey the Pennsylvania and Maryland boundary; the first coal mine was started in Virginia; and Benjamin Franklin was conducting his experiments with electricity. However, America was still twenty-six years away from declaring its independence from Great Britian. Slaves were coming into America at the rate of about 10,000 per year. In 1755 the first scheduled passenger ship service commenced between America and Britian.

It is only about thirty years later, around 1780, that Thomas McConnell arrived in this county from Scotland or Ireland. In the year 1780 slavery was banned in Pennsylvania, the first state to do so. The American Revolution started in 1776 and in 1883 the British finally recognized America's independence. A village near San Gabriel was named Los Angeles in 1781. Christian Ritschard's son Christian, born in 1739, served in the Dunmore County, Virginia Militia under Captain Jacob Holeman's command. It wasn't until about fifteen or sixteen years after the Revolutionary War ended that Christian and his family went by boat from Virginia and settled in Ross County, Ohio. That was around 1797—six years before Ohio became a state. Christian would have been about 58 years of age then. There is a headstone mounted in Springbank Cemetery for Christian, indicating that he served in the Revolutionary War.

I was told by Wayne Ritchhart during my visit to Chillicothe in 1999, that a man, claiming to be a relative from Utah, paid to have the headstone made and mounted in Springbank. However, there is no solid evidence that Christian was actually buried in that cemetery. My guess is that he was buried somewhere on his farm.

Shortly after Christian and his family settled in Ross County Lewis and Clark set out on their journey to explore the upper reaches of the Missouri and out into the Pacific Northwest and the

Columbia River. President Jefferson was an advocate of westward expansion and the government was also interested in better defining the true extent of the Louisiana Purchase.

The "latecomers" to this country were Peter and Julia O'Malley and Frederic and Maria Schmidt. Peter probably arrived in the late 1840s–early 1850s, settling outside Scranton, Pennsylvania in the little village of Salem in Wayne County. Frederick Schmidt probably also arrived in the late 1840s, settling in New York City. As noted previously these were troublesome times in their respective homelands of Ireland and Germany. The mid-40s saw the Irish potato famine at its worst and in 1848 the failed revolution in Germany prompted large scale emigration to the United States.

It is almost certain that Peter O'Malley, and possibly Julia, had friends from County Mayo living in the Salem, Pennsylvania area. Being such a small and remote location, it is highly unlikely that they just happened to choose that area at random. Interestingly, within a few years they moved into the more populous nearby town of Scranton, probably because work was more plentiful there—both in the mines and the burgeoning steel and railroad industries.

Similarly, Frederick and Maria Schmidt didn't remain for long in New York City. Their first son William was born there in 1850, but around 1851 they moved to Indianapolis. There was a strong and growing German culture in Indianapolis that probably influenced their decision to move. This included German churches, newspapers and social organizations.

Slavery was becoming an issue within the relatively young country and finally erupted into the Civil War in April 1861. This found the Ritchharts in Noblesville, Indiana, and Wesley, along with a couple brothers, enlisted. He was assigned to the cavalry, where he learned the veterinary trade. This served him well later when he returned to civilian life in Indiana and later in Missouri.

My third great-grandfather Edward Maxwell Dean and his family moved to Texas in 1833—twelve years before Texas became a state. Thus, the Deans were in Texas when the war broke out. In 1861 Spear was around 33 years of age and he and his wife, Sara, had six children. The youngest, my great-grandfather Thomas Franklin, was only a year old.

Peter O'Malley was at the prime age of 30, he and Julia had three children and he was still farming in the Salem, Wayne County, Pennsylvania area. However, despite his prime age, there is no record of his involvement in the war.

Frederic and Maria were living in Indianapolis, where he was a butcher and she was a midwife. Frederic, at 40 years of age, was a bit past his prime and they had six children so, as best I can determine, he did not serve in the military during the war.

Colorado became a state in 1876, 100 years after America declared its independence, thus the name "The Centennial State." In 1879, only three years later, my great-grandfather Thomas Franklin went from Texas to Colorado to help his uncles, James, Peyton and Mac Jones, on the JJ Ranch. A couple years later, in 1881, Ida Jane Britton would move to the same area of Colorado with her parents from Missouri. In 1885 Frank and Ida would marry.

I was fortunate to have known "Grandma Jane." Her husband, Frank, died relatively young, so I never had the opportunity to know him. Grandma Jane claimed that she and her parents came to Colorado from Missouri by covered wagon. Train service had begun in the area, but for many it was luxury they couldn't afford.

We only lived about a block from Grandma Jane and one of my chores was to go about once a week to her home and pump her a bucket of water from the well in the back yard. She had running water in the house, but didn't like the taste of "city water." I must admit that cool well water did taste much better than water out of the pipes.

The Spanish-American War only lasted about four months in the latter part of 1898. I believe there were a couple ancestors that participated in this war, but I am still trying to identify them.

WW I didn't seem to have much impact on any of our family lines. My dad was only four when the war broke out and his father, Alonzo, was in his late 40s. My grandfather, Arthur Dean, was at a prime age (28), but wasn't drafted. His sister, Blanche, however served in the U.S. Navy as a Nurse. Joanne's father, similar to my dad, was only six and his father, Oscar, was forty-four with three children. Joanne's grandfather McConnell was forty-six and had eight children.

The great depression hit in 1929 and all the nation's banks were closed by President Roosevelt in 1933. My dad and Joanne's dad were in college in 1933 and as we emerged from the great depression into WW II they were both at a prime age to be drafted. My dad

Blanche Dean

joined the Navy through the V5 program which permitted college graduates to go through an abbreviated "officer training" that led to commissioning as an Ensign. They were frequently referred to as "90-day wonders," because their training was about three months long. Joanne's dad was deferred because of eyesight problems. Grandpa Dean was too old to be drafted but both of his sons, J.B. and Tom, served during WW II.

J.B. was an officer in the Marines and Tom was with the Seabees building the ALCAN (Alaska/Canada) Highway. Lee O'Malley, who was raised by Grandma and Grandpa Dean, was in the Army and was seriously wounded during the war.

I am not sure about the McConnells, but Joanne's mother had about three or four brothers who would have been in the prime age group for the draft and I am sure

J.B. Dean

several probably served. Most families were impacted in one way or another by WW II. They either had fathers, brothers or sons (and in some cases daughters) in the military and/or were impacted by the rationing. Many items including auto tires, sugar, meat, butter, and other foods were rationed. Families were issued a book of stamps each month and purchases of rationed items could only be made if you had a stamp. When you ran out of stamps, you tried to borrow from friends or family or you did without.

The Korean War spanned the period 1950 to 1953, a time when I was in high school. However, when I graduated from college in 1959, the draft was in full force and the Vietnam War was in its early stages. Rather than be drafted and be an enlisted "ground pounder," I decided to enlist in the Navy and was accepted into Officer Training in Newport, RI, commencing in August 1959, three months after graduating. I completed Officer Candidate School and was com-

P-3s on the Flight Line in Cam Ranh Bay, South Vietnam

missioned an Ensign on November 21, 1959. A week later Joanne and I were married and the following day we left Chicago for my first assignment in Jacksonville, Florida. I would later serve in Patrol Squadron NINE in 1969 flying support missions out of Cam Ranh Bay in South Vietnam. Typically, we would take off out of Cam Ranh Bay and fly directly up into the Gulf of Tonkin and provide a couple hours of support to our aircraft carriers. We would patrol the areas out to a couple hundred miles around them, providing them intelligence about any ships in that area. We would then proceed south along the coast of Vietnam looking for suspected North Korean infiltration boats that might be smuggling guns, supplies and soldiers into South Vietnam. We would continue around the southern tip of South Vietnam and then land at Utapao, Thailand. The U.S. had a huge airfield there that supported B-52s that flew bombing missions over North Vietnam. The Navy also had a small portion of the base which support our P-3 Orion operations in support of "Market Time"—that was the name given to our air and surface patrols to stop North Vietnamese infiltration into the south.

I am in the foreground right with other members of my crew enjoying the beach during time off in Cam Ranh Bay, South Vietnam—what a way to fight a war!

A Day off At Cam Ranh Bay

One of my most surreal experiences was attending the outdoor movies in Cam Ranh Bay. We would be sitting in the bleachers with our popcorn and soda watching the movie, while in the distant background we could see the flashes of artillery and gunfire as the war continued. How often in your life would you be watching an outdoor movie with a real war going on as a distant backdrop?

The Vietnam War finally ceased in 1973, ending over 14 years of conflict. It was a very unpopular war with many of the U.S. populace, who saw no real reason for the U.S. involvement and loss of tens of thousands of lives. The U.S. military was frustrated because they had to fight with one hand tied behind their backs as the "rules of engagement," dictated by their civilian bosses, wouldn't let them attack sites in North Vietnam where much of the war supplies were being manufactured, stored and shipped to the south. In the beginning years of the war President Eisenhower and other government leaders justified the war based on the "Domino Theory." This theorized that if we let North Vietnam take over South Vietnam, they, with backing from Communist China, would continue taking over all of Southeast Asia—one country at a time.

Hopefully, this chapter helps bring into perspective some of the world events that surrounded the lives of our ancestors during their move to America and for some years after.

Charts, Trees and Reports

This chapter contains Pedigree Charts and Register Reports for each of the branches of the Ritchhart and Schmidt families that are discussed earlier in the book. They contain the myriad facts that I have accumulated in researching these individuals. The Pedigree Charts depict the relationships between the various individuals.

The Register Reports also contain notes that I made for many of the individuals. Some of the notes are to explain the rationale for conclusions or decisions I made about an ambiguity in the individual's life. Other notes are anecdotal in nature—perhaps relating an event in their life.

It is my hope that future generations will find these notes helpful in continuing the research and filling in the many holes that still exist in detailing the ancestry of these families. I am certain that all of the assumptions I have made are not correct and that future research will expose these flaws and correct them.

I have attempted to provide source documentation for all of my facts, thus assisting one in trying to resolve conflicting information. When I first started researching I was too anxious to just record all the information I could find and didn't spend as much effort on also providing the source data. However, I soon learned the necessity of sourcing the facts and, thereafter, was much more dedicated to providing sources for all the data I entered.

Facts, the source of which are either World Family Trees or *Public Member Trees*, should be viewed with some skepticism. Other people have entered the data on Ancestry's *Public Member Trees* or public trees of other genealogical websites and in most cases haven't provided any source documentation. In some cases the information may be accurate. I have usually included World Family Tree or Public Member Tree information if I don't have anything with a better source.

EXPLANATION OF REGISTER REPORT SUPERSCRIPTED FOOTNOTES

The superscript numbers following names of individuals at the start of paragraphs and subparagraphs denote the generation of the individual (i.e., the first individual listed in each Register Report is 1, the next 2, etc.). However, superscripted footnotes in other parts of the Register reports refer to the source for that associated information. A chronological listing of sources, with a description of the source, follows each respective Register Report.

Pedigree Chart for
Delbert Bush RITCHHART

Delbert Bush RITCHHART
b: 02 Nov 1910
m: 01 Aug 1936 in Las Animas, Bent, Colorado, USA
d: 18 Feb 1981 in Denver, Colorado, USA

Alonzo Francis RITCHHART
b: 03 Nov 1867 in Indiana, USA
m: 01 Jan 1902 in La Junta, Otero, Colorado, USA
d: 27 May 1959 in Stanislaus, California, USA

Wesley RITCHHART
b: 30 Jun 1842 in Noblesville, Hamilton, Indiana, USA
m: 20 Dec 1866 in Noblesville, Hamilton, Indiana, USA
d: 23 Mar 1921

Andrew RITCHHART
b: 11 Jun 1818 in Ross, Ohio, USA
m: 16 Jun 1841 in Hamilton, Indiana, USA
d: 24 Dec 1897 in Hamilton, Indiana, USA

John RITCHHART
b: 31 Mar 1780 in...
m:
➡ **165**

Mary (Polly) HEINRICH
b: 06 May 1782
d: 1837 in Hamilton,...

Mary BOOTH
b: 17 Nov 1817 in Stokes, North Carolina, USA
d: 28 Sep 1873 in Fall Creek, Hamilton, Indiana, USA

George BOOTH
b: 1774 in Virginia, USA
m:

Mary MCANALLY
b: 1785 in North Carolina,...
d: 04 Feb 1861 in...
➡ **165**

Maria Sibilla WAGNER
b: 11 May 1840 in Brownsville, Union, Indiana, USA
d: 20 Jan 1916

Michael WAGNER
b: 13 Jul 1808 in Lancaster, Pennsylvania
m: 07 Dec 1839 in Union, Indiana, USA
d: 17 Apr 1893

George Michael WAGNER
b: 15 Jul 1771 in Upper...
m:
➡ **166**

Magdalena MOYER
b: 1777
d: 1844

Harreata Aena GOLDMAN
b: 10 May 1818 in Gettysburg (Berks County), Pennsylvania
d:

Johanns GOLMANN
b:
m:

Anna Marie ELLNABERGER
b:

Grace Azetta BUSH
b: 17 Nov 1879 in Carthage, Jasper, Missouri, USA
d: 28 Jan 1952 in La Junta, Otero, Colorado, USA

Samuel Shelton BUSH
b: 27 Jan 1852 in Hart, Kentucky, USA
m: 19 Apr 1876 in Jasper, Missouri, USA
d: 08 Jun 1907 in La Junta, Otero, Colorado, USA

John Harding BUSH Jr.
b: Abt. 1807 in Hart, Kentucky, USA
m: 1839
d: 19 Jul 1894 in Jasper, Missouri, USA

John Hardin BUSH
b: Abt. 1776 in Virginia,...
m: 1803 in Kentucky, USA
➡ **166**

Ann BASS
b: 1775 in Virginia, USA
d: 25 Oct 1853 in Hart,...
➡ **167**

Abergale Abigal WARDRIP
b: 25 Jan 1812 in Kentucky, USA
d: 10 Feb 1883 in Jasper, Missouri, USA

Reese WARDROPE
b: 1793 in North Carolina,...
m: Bef. 1812 in Kentucky,...
➡ **167**

Catherine WADDLE
b: 1787 in Cincinnati,...
d: 19 Dec 1854 in Hart,...
➡ **168**

Lillian Perdida LOGSDON
b: 01 Mar 1860 in Iowa, USA
d: 01 Jan 1929 in La Junta, Otero, Colorado, USA

George W. LOGSDON
b: Abt. 1822 in Kentucky, USA
m:
d: 15 Feb 1883

Susan LINDER
b: Abt. 1826 in Kentucky, USA
d: 23 Dec 1899

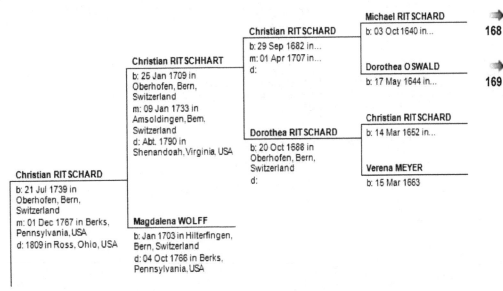

Michael RITSCHARD
b: 03 Oct 1640 in...

→ **168**

Christian RITSCHARD
b: 29 Sep 1682 in...
m: 01 Apr 1707 in...
d:

Dorothea OSWALD
b: 17 May 1644 in...

→ **169**

Christian RITSCHHART
b: 25 Jan 1709 in
Oberhofen, Bern,
Switzerland
m: 09 Jan 1733 in
Amsoldingen, Bern,
Switzerland
d: Abt. 1790 in
Shenandoah, Virginia, USA

Christian RITSCHARD
b: 14 Mar 1652 in...

Dorothea RITSCHARD
b: 20 Oct 1688 in
Oberhofen, Bern,
Switzerland
d:

Verena MEYER
b: 15 Mar 1663

Christian RITSCHARD
b: 21 Jul 1739 in
Oberhofen, Bern,
Switzerland
m: 01 Dec 1767 in Berks,
Pennsylvania, USA
d: 1809 in Ross, Ohio, USA

Magdalena WOLFF
b: Jan 1703 in Hilterfingen,
Bern, Switzerland
d: 04 Oct 1766 in Berks,
Pennsylvania, USA

John RITCHHART
b: 31 Mar 1780 in
Shenandoah, Virginia, USA
m:
d: Mar 1829 in Ross, Ohio,
USA

164

Maria Elizabeth PENTZ
b: Dec 1747 in Berks,
Pennsylvania, USA
d: 1803 in Ross, Ohio, USA

Jesse Mc ANALLY
b: North Carolina, USA
m:
d:

Mary MCANALLY
b: 1785 in North Carolina,
USA
m:
d: 04 Feb 1861 in Wayne,
Hamilton, Indiana, USA

169

Mary WRIGHT
b:
d:

John Jacob WAGNER

b: 1700 in Rauschenberg,
Hesse Nassau, Prussia,
Germany
m: 1721 in Pennsylvania,
USA
d: 11 Aug 1761 in Upper
Bern, Berks, Pennsylvania,
USA

Anna Sophia ENGLE

b: 1702 in Germany
d: Pennsylvania, USA

John Jacob WAGNER

b: 04 Oct 1729 in Upper
Bern, Berks, Pennsylvania,
USA
m:
d: 13 May 1800 in Upper
Bern, Berks, Pennsylvania,
USA

George Michael WAGNER

b: 15 Jul 1771 in Upper
Bern, Berks, Pennsylvania,
USA
m:
d: 29 May 1829

164

**Catharine Magdalena
SCHOCK**

b: 11 Jan 1738 in Berks,
Pennsylvania, USA
d: 20 Aug 1820 in Upper
Bern, Berks, Pennsylvania,
USA

Unk BUSH

b: Abt. 1752
m:
d:

John Hardin BUSH

b: Abt. 1776 in Virginia,
USA
m: 1803 in Kentucky, USA
d: 1850

164

Daniel Marsh NOE

b: 29 May 1787 in Caldwell,
Essex, New Jersey, USA
m:
d: 11 Jul 1869 in New
Albany, Franklin, Ohio,
USA

Daniel Marsh NOE

b: 1815 in New Jersey,
USA
m:
d: 23 May 1892 in Putnam,
Ohio, USA

Mary (Polly) WILLIAMS

b: 28 Jul 1793 in New
Jersey, USA
d: 02 Jan 1879 in New
Albany, Franklin, Ohio,
USA

Ann BASS

b: 1775 in Virginia, USA
m: 1803 in Kentucky, USA
d: 25 Oct 1853 in Hart,
Kentucky, United States

Jane SMITH

b: 02 Aug 1815 in New
Jersey, USA
d: 19 Jan 1888 in Putnam,
Ohio, USA

← **164**

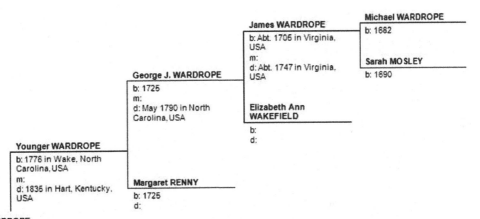

Michael WARDROPE

b: 1682

169 →

James WARDROPE

b: Abt. 1705 in Virginia,
USA
m:
d: Abt. 1747 in Virginia,
USA

Sarah MOSLEY

b: 1690

George J. WARDROPE

b: 1725
m:
d: May 1790 in North
Carolina, USA

**Elizabeth Ann
WAKEFIELD**

b:
d:

Younger WARDROPE

b: 1776 in Wake, North
Carolina, USA
m:
d: 1835 in Hart, Kentucky,
USA

Margaret RENNY

b: 1725
d:

Reese WARDROPE

b: 1793 in North Carolina,
USA
m: Bef. 1812 in Kentucky,
USA
d: 10 Aug 1854 in Hart,
Kentucky, USA

Ann R REECE

b: 1765 in North Carolina,
USA
d: 1855

← **164**

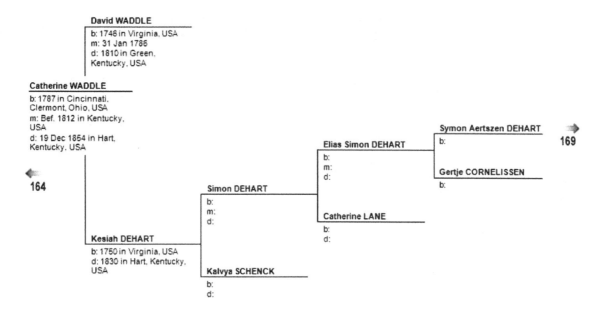

David WADDLE

b: 1746 in Virginia, USA
m: 31 Jan 1786
d: 1810 in Green,
Kentucky, USA

Catherine WADDLE

b: 1787 in Cincinnati,
Clermont, Ohio, USA
m: Bef. 1812 in Kentucky,
USA
d: 19 Dec 1854 in Hart,
Kentucky, USA

164

Kesiah DEHART

b: 1750 in Virginia, USA
d: 1830 in Hart, Kentucky,
USA

Simon DEHART

b:
m:
d:

Kalvya SCHENCK

b:
d:

Elias Simon DEHART

b:
m:
d:

Catherine LANE

b:
d:

Symon Aertszen DEHART ➡

b:

169

Gertje CORNELISSEN

b:

Michael RITSCHARD

b: 19 Sep 1605 in Oberhofen, Bern,
Switzerland
m: 16 Nov 1629 in Hilterfingen,
Bern, Switzerland
d:

Michael RITSCHARD

b: 03 Oct 1640 in Hilterfingen, Bern,
Switzerland
m: 06 Mar 1668 in Oberhofen, Bern,
Switzerland
d:

⬅
165

Katrina BAUMGARTNER

b: Abt. 1608 in Hilterfingen, Bern,
Switzerland
d: Mar 1648 in Hilterfingen, Bern,
Switzerland

Hans OSWALD

b: 04 Oct 1613 in Hilterfingen, Bern, Switzerland
m: 1642 in Oberhofen, Am Thunersee, Bern, Switzerland
d:

Dorothea OSWALD

b: 17 May 1644 in Oberhofen, Bern, Switzerland
m: 06 Mar 1668 in Oberhofen, Bern, Switzerland
d:

165

Madlena SPRING

b: 09 Jan 1625 in Hilterfingen, Bern, Switzerland
d:

Michael WARDROPE

b: 1640
m:
d:

Michael WARDROPE

b: 1682
m:
d: 1775

167

Aart Symonsz DEHART

b:
m:
d:

Symon Aertszen DEHART

b:
m:
d:

168

Gerritjen STOFFELS

b:
d:

Pedigree Chart for
Helen Jane DEAN

Helen Jane DEAN

b: 06 Aug 1915 in
Denver, Adams,
Colorado, USA
m: 01 Aug 1936 in Las
Animas, Bent,
Colorado, USA
d: 28 Oct 1995 in
Loveland, Larimer,
Colorado, USA

Arthur Spear DEAN

b: 22 Oct 1886 in Las
Animas, Bent,
Colorado, USA
m: 25 Jul 1911 in
Denver, Adams,
Colorado, USA
d: 01 Dec 1969 in Las
Animas, Bent,
Colorado, USA

Mary Loretta O'MALLEY

b: 14 Nov 1886 in
Forest City, Mason,
Illinois, USA
d: 14 Mar 1961 in Las
Animas, Bent,
Colorado, USA

Thomas Franklin DEAN

b: 15 Nov 1860 in
Weatherford, Parker,
Texas, USA
m: 23 Dec 1885 in Las
Animas, Bent,
Colorado, USA
d: 29 Jun 1905 in Las
Animas, Bent,
Colorado, USA

Ida Jane BRITTON

b: 13 Nov 1868 in
Bernard, Nodaway,
Missouri, USA
d: 18 Oct 1952 in Las
Animas, Bent,
Colorado, USA

Walter William O'MALLEY

b: 17 Jul 1867 in
Scranton, Lackawanna,
Pennsylvania, USA
m: Abt. 1885
d: 05 Feb 1937 in St
Joseph, Andrew,
Missouri, USA

Mary Elizabeth EARHART

b: 26 Apr 1869 in est
Mason Co., Illinois
d: 06 Mar 1892 in
Forest City, Mason,
Illinois, USA

Spear Christopher DEAN

b: 18 Jun 1829 in...
m: 12 Jul 1853 in Red...
d: 11 May 1908 in...

Sarah Marshall JONES

b: 15 Oct 1835 in...
d: 28 Jul 1935 in...

Thomas Dugan BRITTON

b: 25 Jun 1846 in...
m: 30 Jul 1866 in...
d: 26 Nov 1928 in Las...

Effie Melissa MOLER

b: 22 Mar 1848 in
Wabash, Indiana, USA
d: 17 Jan 1929 in Las
Animas, Bent,
Colorado, USA

Peter O'MALLEY

b: Abt. 1835 in Mayo....
m: Bet. 1852–1853 in...
d: 1893 in Manito,...

Julia MCNALLY

b: Jan 1835 in Mayo,
Ireland
d: Apr 1906 in Manito,
Mason, Illinois, USA

Franklin EARHART

b: 1825 in Ohio, USA
m: 09 Nov 1865 in
Mason, Illinois, USA
d: 1879 in Forest City,
Mason, Illinois, USA

Mary Elizabeth MOZINGO

b: 15 Apr 1844 in Green
Castle, Indiana
d: 11 Jul 1933 in Forest
City, Mason, Illinois,
USA

Edward Maxwell DEAN → **171**

b: 21 Apr 1799 in...

Sarah Jane DEAN

b: 1805 in Kentucky,...

Erasmus JONES II → **172**

b: 19 Dec 1799 in...

Christianna BOND → **173**

b: 1802 in Gates,...

Isaac Newton BRITTON → **173**

b: 03 Mar 1806 in...

Vanda Ellen FOUTS → **174**

b: 01 Feb 1811 in...

William Mannass MOLER → **175**

b: 02 Nov 1807 in...

Clory Ann STINGLEY → **176**

b: 28 Jun 1811 in...

Name:
b:
m:

Name:
b:
d:

Name:
b:
m:

Name:
b:
d:

* EARHART
b:
m:

Name:
b:
d:

John MOZINGO → **177**

b: 1810 in Kentucky,...

Sarah MARTIN

b: 1815 in...

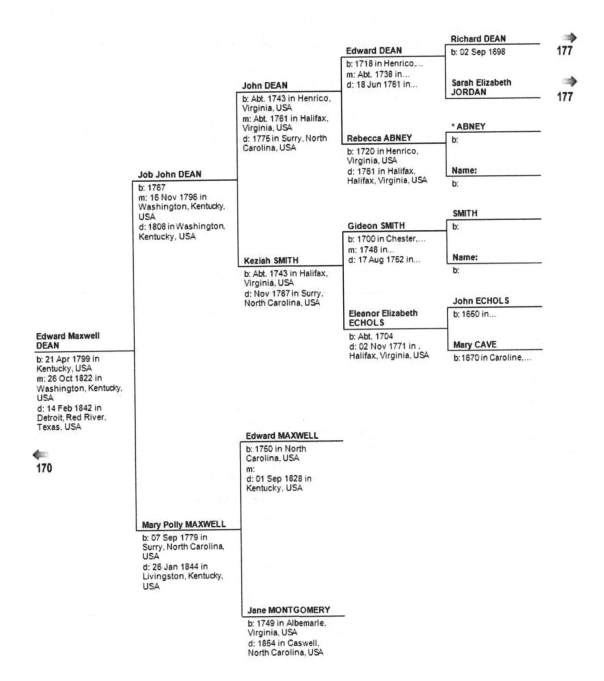

Edward Maxwell DEAN

b: 21 Apr 1799 in Kentucky, USA
m: 26 Oct 1822 in Washington, Kentucky, USA
d: 14 Feb 1842 in Detroit, Red River, Texas, USA

← 170

Job John DEAN

b: 1767
m: 16 Nov 1796 in Washington, Kentucky, USA
d: 1808 in Washington, Kentucky, USA

Mary Polly MAXWELL

b: 07 Sep 1779 in Surry, North Carolina, USA
d: 26 Jan 1844 in Livingston, Kentucky, USA

John DEAN

b: Abt. 1743 in Henrico, Virginia, USA
m: Abt. 1761 in Halifax, Virginia, USA
d: 1775 in Surry, North Carolina, USA

Keziah SMITH

b: Abt. 1743 in Halifax, Virginia, USA
d: Nov 1787 in Surry, North Carolina, USA

Edward MAXWELL

b: 1750 in North Carolina, USA
m:
d: 01 Sep 1828 in Kentucky, USA

Jane MONTGOMERY

b: 1749 in Albemarle, Virginia, USA
d: 1854 in Caswell, North Carolina, USA

Edward DEAN

b: 1718 in Henrico,...
m: Abt. 1738 in...
d: 18 Jun 1761 in...

Rebecca ABNEY

b: 1720 in Henrico, Virginia, USA
d: 1761 in Halifax, Halifax, Virginia, USA

Gideon SMITH

b: 1700 in Chester,...
m: 1748 in...
d: 17 Aug 1752 in...

Eleanor Elizabeth ECHOLS

b: Abt. 1704
d: 02 Nov 1771 in, Halifax, Virginia, USA

Richard DEAN

b: 02 Sep 1698

→ 177

Sarah Elizabeth JORDAN

→ 177

* ABNEY

b:

Name:

b:

SMITH

b:

Name:

b:

John ECHOLS

b: 1650 in...

Mary CAVE

b: 1670 in Caroline,...

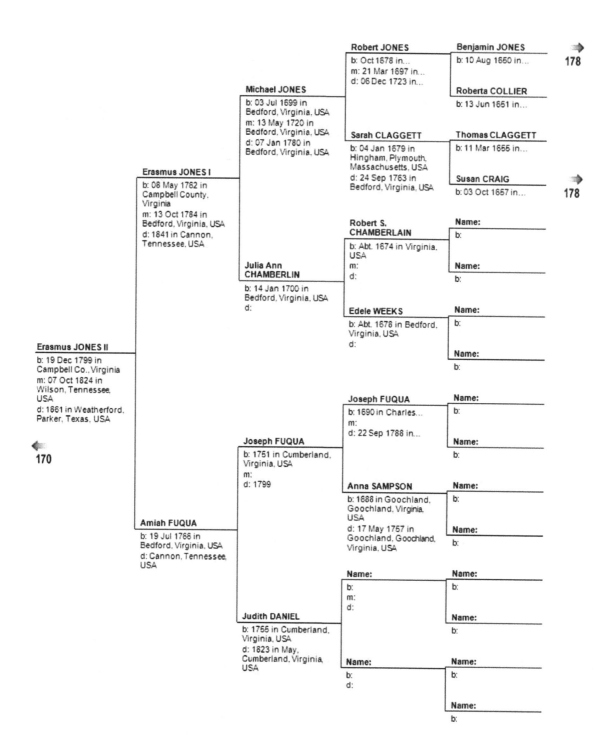

Erasmus JONES II
b: 19 Dec 1799 in Campbell Co., Virginia
m: 07 Oct 1824 in Wilson, Tennessee, USA
d: 1861 in Weatherford, Parker, Texas, USA

◀
170

Erasmus JONES I
b: 08 May 1762 in Campbell County, Virginia
m: 13 Oct 1784 in Bedford, Virginia, USA
d: 1841 in Cannon, Tennessee, USA

Amiah FUQUA
b: 19 Jul 1766 in Bedford, Virginia, USA
d: Cannon, Tennessee, USA

Michael JONES
b: 03 Jul 1699 in Bedford, Virginia, USA
m: 13 May 1720 in Bedford, Virginia, USA
d: 07 Jan 1780 in Bedford, Virginia, USA

Julia Ann CHAMBERLIN
b: 14 Jan 1700 in Bedford, Virginia, USA
d:

Joseph FUQUA
b: 1751 in Cumberland, Virginia, USA
m:
d: 1799

Judith DANIEL
b: 1755 in Cumberland, Virginia, USA
d: 1823 in May, Cumberland, Virginia, USA

Robert JONES
b: Oct 1678 in...
m: 21 Mar 1697 in...
d: 06 Dec 1723 in...

Sarah CLAGGETT
b: 04 Jan 1679 in Hingham, Plymouth, Massachusetts, USA
d: 24 Sep 1763 in Bedford, Virginia, USA

Robert S. CHAMBERLAIN
b: Abt. 1674 in Virginia, USA
m:
d:

Edele WEEKS
b: Abt. 1678 in Bedford, Virginia, USA
d:

Joseph FUQUA
b: 1690 in Charles...
m:
d: 22 Sep 1788 in...

Anna SAMPSON
b: 1688 in Goochland, Goochland, Virginia, USA
d: 17 May 1757 in Goochland, Goochland, Virginia, USA

Name:
b:
m:
d:

Name:
b:
d:

Benjamin JONES
b: 10 Aug 1650 in...

Roberta COLLIER
b: 13 Jun 1651 in...

Thomas CLAGGETT
b: 11 Mar 1655 in...

Susan CRAIG
b: 03 Oct 1657 in...

Name:
b:

Name:
b:

Name:
b:

Name:
b:

Name:
b:

Name:
b:

Name:
b:

Name:
b:

Name:
b:

Name:
b:

➡
178

➡
178

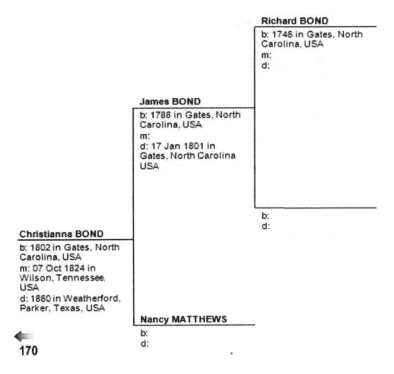

Richard BOND

b: 1746 in Gates, North
Carolina, USA
m:
d:

James BOND

b: 1788 in Gates, North
Carolina, USA
m:
d: 17 Jan 1801 in
Gates, North Carolina
USA

b:
d:

Christianna BOND

b: 1802 in Gates, North
Carolina, USA
m: 07 Oct 1824 in
Wilson, Tennessee,
USA
d: 1860 in Weatherford,
Parker, Texas, USA

Nancy MATTHEWS

b:
d:

170

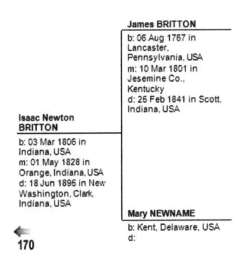

James BRITTON

b: 06 Aug 1767 in
Lancaster,
Pennsylvania, USA
m: 10 Mar 1801 in
Jesemine Co.,
Kentucky
d: 25 Feb 1841 in Scott,
Indiana, USA

**Isaac Newton
BRITTON**

b: 03 Mar 1806 in
Indiana, USA
m: 01 May 1828 in
Orange, Indiana, USA
d: 18 Jun 1895 in New
Washington, Clark,
Indiana, USA

Mary NEWNAME

b: Kent, Delaware, USA
d:

170

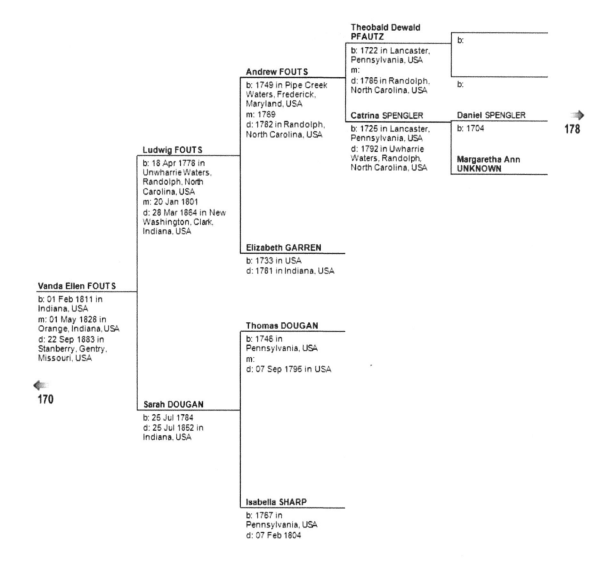

Theobald Dewald PFAUTZ
b: 1722 in Lancaster, Pennsylvania, USA
m:
d: 1785 in Randolph, North Carolina, USA

b:

b:

Andrew FOUTS
b: 1749 in Pipe Creek Waters, Frederick, Maryland, USA
m: 1769
d: 1782 in Randolph, North Carolina, USA

Catrina SPENGLER
b: 1725 in Lancaster, Pennsylvania, USA
d: 1792 in Uwharrie Waters, Randolph, North Carolina, USA

Daniel SPENGLER
b: 1704

Margaretha Ann UNKNOWN

178

Ludwig FOUTS
b: 18 Apr 1776 in Unwharrie Waters, Randolph, North Carolina, USA
m: 20 Jan 1801
d: 28 Mar 1864 in New Washington, Clark, Indiana, USA

Elizabeth GARREN
b: 1733 in USA
d: 1781 in Indiana, USA

Vanda Ellen FOUTS
b: 01 Feb 1811 in Indiana, USA
m: 01 May 1828 in Orange, Indiana, USA
d: 22 Sep 1883 in Stanberry, Gentry, Missouri, USA

170

Thomas DOUGAN
b: 1746 in Pennsylvania, USA
m:
d: 07 Sep 1795 in USA

Sarah DOUGAN
b: 25 Jul 1784
d: 25 Jul 1852 in Indiana, USA

Isabella SHARP
b: 1767 in Pennsylvania, USA
d: 07 Feb 1804

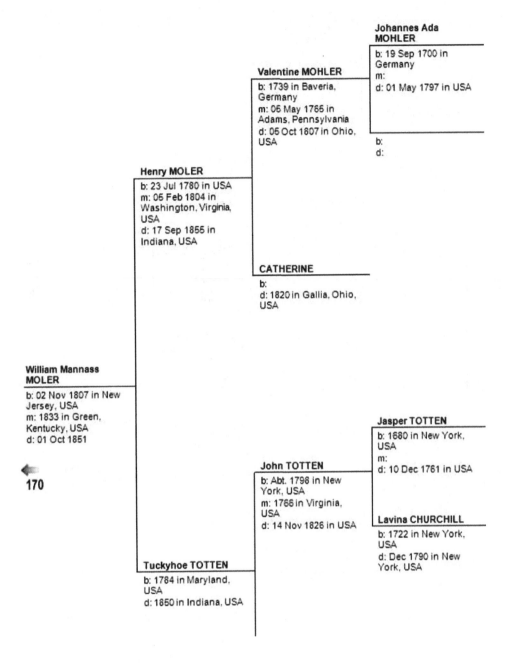

Johannes Ada MOHLER

b: 19 Sep 1700 in Germany
m:
d: 01 May 1797 in USA

b:
d:

Valentine MOHLER

b: 1739 in Baveria, Germany
m: 05 May 1765 in Adams, Pennsylvania
d: 05 Oct 1807 in Ohio, USA

Henry MOLER

b: 23 Jul 1780 in USA
m: 05 Feb 1804 in Washington, Virginia, USA
d: 17 Sep 1855 in Indiana, USA

CATHERINE

b:
d: 1820 in Gallia, Ohio, USA

William Mannass MOLER

b: 02 Nov 1807 in New Jersey, USA
m: 1833 in Green, Kentucky, USA
d: 01 Oct 1851

170

Jasper TOTTEN

b: 1680 in New York, USA
m:
d: 10 Dec 1761 in USA

John TOTTEN

b: Abt. 1798 in New York, USA
m: 1766 in Virginia, USA
d: 14 Nov 1826 in USA

Lavina CHURCHILL

b: 1722 in New York, USA
d: Dec 1790 in New York, USA

Tuckyhoe TOTTEN

b: 1784 in Maryland, USA
d: 1850 in Indiana, USA

George STINGLEY

b: 12 Sep 1763 in USA
m: 1783 in Virginia,
USA
d: 28 Mar 1838 in USA

Leonard STINGLEY

b: 07 May 1785 in
Virginia, USA
m: 09 Sep 1810 in
Virginia, USA
d: 05 Sep 1863 in
Missouri, USA

Sebastian HAGLER

b: 1735 in Switzerland
m: 1757 in Hardy,
Grant, Virginia
d: 15 Dec 1802 in USA

Chlorie HAGLER

b: 14 Jul 1757 in USA
d: 1830 in Green,
Adams, Ohio, USA

Eve HIRE

b: 29 Sep 1742 in
Tulpehocken, Berks,
Pennsylvania, USA
d: 02 Nov 1833 in
Green, Adams, Ohio,
USA

Leonard HYER

b: 15 Jun 1695 in St....

➡ **178**

Clara Grace LUTZLER

b: 1705 in Basel, ...

➡ **179**

Clory Ann STINGLEY

b: 28 Jun 1811 in
Green, Adams, Ohio,
USA
m: 1833 in Green,
Kentucky, USA
d: 04 Apr 1895 in
Jewell, Kansas, USA

⬅ **170**

Sebastian HAGLER

b: 1735 in Switzerland
m: 1757 in Hardy,
Grant, Virginia
d: 15 Dec 1802 in USA

Leonard HAGLER

b: 1765 in West
Virginia, USA
m: 1796 in Virginia,
USA
d: 18 Jan 1831 in Ohio,
USA

Eve HIRE

b: 29 Sep 1742 in
Tulpehocken, Berks,
Pennsylvania, USA
d: 02 Nov 1833 in
Green, Adams, Ohio,
USA

Leonard HYER

b: 15 Jun 1695 in St....

➡ **178**

Clara Grace LUTZLER

b: 1705 in Basel, ...

➡ **179**

Mary HAGLER

b: 1790 in Hardy,
Bedford, Virginia, USA
d: 1850 in Winterset,
Madison, Iowa, USA

**Mary Susannah
PETERSON**

b: 06 Jan 1767
d: 03 Apr 1861 in Ohio,
USA

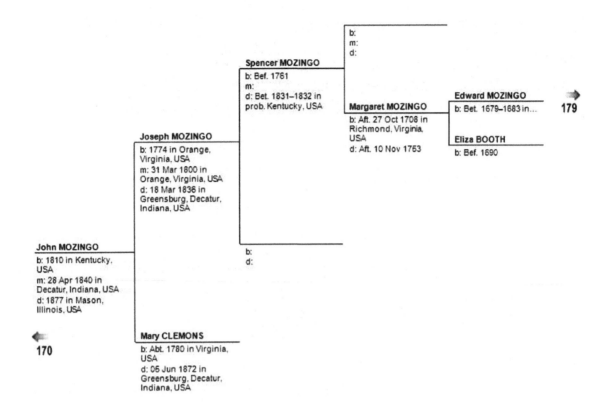

Spencer MOZINGO
b: Bef. 1761
m:
d: Bet. 1831–1832 in
prob. Kentucky, USA

b:
m:
d:

Margaret MOZINGO
b: Aft. 27 Oct 1708 in
Richmond, Virginia,
USA
d: Aft. 10 Nov 1753

Edward MOZINGO
b: Bet. 1679–1683 in...

179

Eliza BOOTH
b: Bef. 1690

Joseph MOZINGO
b: 1774 in Orange,
Virginia, USA
m: 31 Mar 1800 in
Orange, Virginia, USA
d: 18 Mar 1836 in
Greensburg, Decatur,
Indiana, USA

John MOZINGO
b: 1810 in Kentucky,
USA
m: 28 Apr 1840 in
Decatur, Indiana, USA
d: 1877 in Mason,
Illinois, USA

b:
d:

170

Mary CLEMONS
b: Abt. 1780 in Virginia,
USA
d: 06 Jun 1872 in
Greensburg, Decatur,
Indiana, USA

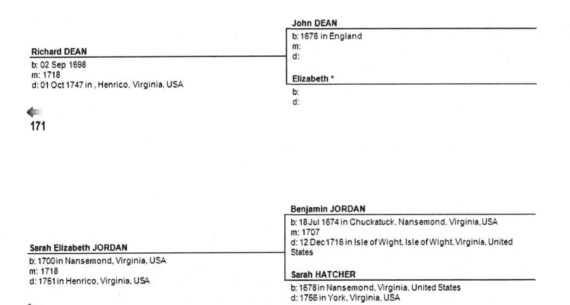

John DEAN
b: 1678 in England
m:
d:

Richard DEAN
b: 02 Sep 1698
m: 1718
d: 01 Oct 1747 in , Henrico, Virginia, USA

Elizabeth *
b:
d:

171

Benjamin JORDAN
b: 18 Jul 1674 in Chuckatuck, Nansemond, Virginia, USA
m: 1707
d: 12 Dec 1716 in Isle of Wight, Isle of Wight, Virginia, United
States

Sarah Elizabeth JORDAN
b: 1700 in Nansemond, Virginia, USA
m: 1718
d: 1751 in Henrico, Virginia, USA

Sarah HATCHER
b: 1678 in Nansemond, Virginia, United States
d: 1756 in York, Virginia, USA

171

Benjamin JONES

b: 10 Aug 1650 in Hingham, Plymouth, Massachusetts, USA
m: 02 Nov 1676 in Hingham, Plymouth, Massachusetts, USA
d: 1729 in Hingham, Plymouth, Massachusetts, USA

Robert JONES

b: Abt. 1608 in Reading, Berkshire, England
m: 15 Jan 1649 in Hingham, Plymouth, Massachusetts, USA
d: 17 Nov 1691 in Hingham, Plymouth, Massachusetts, USA

Elizabeth ALEXANDER

b: 1628 in Reading, Berkshire, England
d: 25 Sep 1712 in Hingham, Plymouth, Massachusetts, USA

172

Susan CRAIG

b: 03 Oct 1657 in Hingham, Plymouth, Massachusetts, USA
m: 05 Oct 1676 in Hingham, Plymouth, Massachusetts, USA
d: 17 Apr 1751 in Hingham, Plymouth, Massachusetts, USA

Harvey CRAIG

b: 02 Jun 1633 in Hingham, Plymouth, Massachusetts, USA
m: 01 Nov 1655 in Hingham, Plymouth, Massachusetts, USA
d: 03 Apr 1710 in Hingham, Plymouth, Massachusetts, USA

Margaret HOLMES

b: 10 Aug 1634 in Hingham, Plymouth, Massachusetts, USA
d: 27 Oct 1705 in Hingham, Plymouth, Massachusetts, USA

172

Daniel SPENGLER

b: 1704
m:
d: 1728 in Estonia

Hans Casper SPENGLER

b: 20 Jan 1684 in Weiler, Ahrweiler, Rhineland-Palatinate, Germany
m:
d: 28 Apr 1760 in Paradise, York, Pennsylvania, USA

Judith ZEIGLER

b: 1684 in Weiler, Alb-Donau-Kreis, Baden-Württemberg, Germany
d: 1730 in Paradise, York, Pennsylvania, USA

174

Leonard HYER

b: 15 Jun 1695 in St. Gallen, Switzerland
m: 19 Apr 1793 in Germany
d: 12 May 1722 in West Virginia, USA

Anton HEYER

b: 16 Feb 1662 in Switzerland
m: 15 Dec 1690 in Switzerland
d: 1754 in Switzerland

Anna Elizabeth RUFLIN

b: 1669 in Switzerland
d: 1754 in Switzerland

176

Clara Grace LUTZLER

b: 1705 in Basel, Basel-town, Switzerland
m: 19 Apr 1793 in Germany
d: 1722 in Hampshire, Virginia

Rudolph LUTZLER

b: Abt. 1677 in Switzerland
m:
d: 1758 in Virginia, USA

Barbara HEIER

b: 1679 in Switzerland
d: 1737 in Switzerland

176

Edward MOZINGO

b: Bet. 1679–1683 in Old Rappahannock, VA
m: Bef. 27 Oct 1706 in Richmond or Westmoreland, Virginia, USA
d:

Edward MOZINGO

b: Bef. 1644
m: Bef. 04 Sep 1685 in Old Rappahannock, VA
d:

Margaret /PIERCE BAILEY

b: Bef. 1669
d: Aft. 30 Jul 1711 in North Farnham Parish, Richmond, Virginia, USA

177

Pedigree Chart for
Frederick Henry SCHMIDT

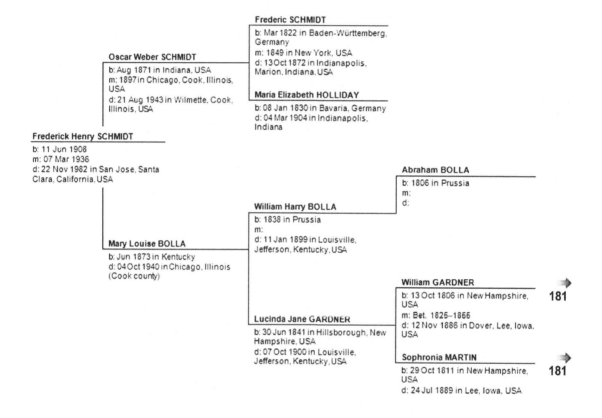

Frederic SCHMIDT
b: Mar 1822 in Baden-Württemberg, Germany
m: 1849 in New York, USA
d: 13 Oct 1872 in Indianapolis, Marion, Indiana, USA

Oscar Weber SCHMIDT
b: Aug 1871 in Indiana, USA
m: 1897 in Chicago, Cook, Illinois, USA
d: 21 Aug 1943 in Wilmette, Cook, Illinois, USA

Maria Elizabeth HOLLIDAY
b: 08 Jan 1830 in Bavaria, Germany
d: 04 Mar 1904 in Indianapolis, Indiana

Frederick Henry SCHMIDT
b: 11 Jun 1908
m: 07 Mar 1936
d: 22 Nov 1982 in San Jose, Santa Clara, California, USA

Abraham BOLLA
b: 1806 in Prussia
m:
d:

William Harry BOLLA
b: 1838 in Prussia
m:
d: 11 Jan 1899 in Louisville, Jefferson, Kentucky, USA

Mary Louise BOLLA
b: Jun 1873 in Kentucky
d: 04 Oct 1940 in Chicago, Illinois (Cook county)

William GARDNER
b: 13 Oct 1806 in New Hampshire, USA
m: Bet. 1825–1866
d: 12 Nov 1886 in Dover, Lee, Iowa, USA

181

Lucinda Jane GARDNER
b: 30 Jun 1841 in Hillsborough, New Hampshire, USA
d: 07 Oct 1900 in Louisville, Jefferson, Kentucky, USA

Sophronia MARTIN
b: 29 Oct 1811 in New Hampshire, USA
d: 24 Jul 1889 in Lee, Iowa, USA

181

Benjamin Jacob GARDNER

b: 21 May 1726 in Hingham,...
m: 24 Nov 1748 in Hingham,...
d: 20 Jul 1786 in Hingham,...

→ **182**

Esekiel GARDNER

b: 15 Dec 1751 in South Liberty,
Plymouth, Massachusetts, USA
m:
d: 18 Apr 1828 in Bedford,
Hillsborough, New Hampshire, USA

Rachel SMITH

b: 02 Jan 1731 in Hingham,
Plymouth, Massachusetts, USA
d: 01 Jul 1802 in Abington,
Plymouth, Massachusetts, USA

Ezekial GARDNER

b: Abt. 1780 in Bedford,
Hillsborough, New Hampshire, USA
m:
d:

Betsy CHUBBUCK

b: 15 May 1759 in Abington,
Plymouth, Massachusetts, USA
d: 1838

William GARDNER

b: 13 Oct 1806 in New Hampshire,
USA
m: Bet. 1825–1855
d: 12 Nov 1886 in Dover, Lee, Iowa,
USA

← **180**

Mary NESMITH

b:
d: Bet. 1840–1850

Amos MARTIN

b: Abt. 1761
m:
d: 09 Dec 1840 in New Hampshire,
USA

Sophronia MARTIN

b: 29 Oct 1811 in New Hampshire,
USA
m: Bet. 1825–1855
d: 24 Jul 1889 in Lee, Iowa, USA

← **180**

Samuel SMITH

b:
m:
d:

Samuel SMITH

b:
m:
d:

PRISCILLA

b:
d:

Nancy SMITH

b: 08 Jan 1772 in Topsfield,
Washington, Maine, USA
d: 20 Jan 1828 in New Hampshire,
USA

Rebekah TOWNE

b:
d:

Benjamin GARDNER

b: 07 Apr 1666 in
Hingham,Plymouth,Massachusetts,
USA
m:
d: 30 Jun 1736 in Hingham,
Plymouth, Massachusetts, USA

Benjamin GARDNER

b: 15 May 1700 in Hingham,
Plymouth, Massachusetts, USA
m: 24 Jun 1725 in
Hingham,Plymouth,Massachusetts,
USA
d: 1760 in Plymouth, Plymouth,
Massachusetts, United States

Sarah DUNBAR

b: 1674 in
Hingham,Plymouth,Massachusetts,
USA
d: 12 Feb 1761 in
Hingham,Plymouth,Massachusetts,
USA

Benjamin Jacob GARDNER

b: 21 May 1726 in Hingham,
Plymouth, Massachusetts, United
States
m: 24 Nov 1748 in Hingham,
Plymouth, Massachusetts, United
States
d: 20 Jul 1786 in Hingham,
Plymouth, Massachusetts, United
States

181

Joanna JONES

b: 29 Mar 1705 in
Hingham,Plymouth,Massachusetts,
USA
d: 06 Oct 1793 in Hingham,
Plymouth, Massachusetts, United
States

Pedigree Chart for
Frances Lois MCCONNELL

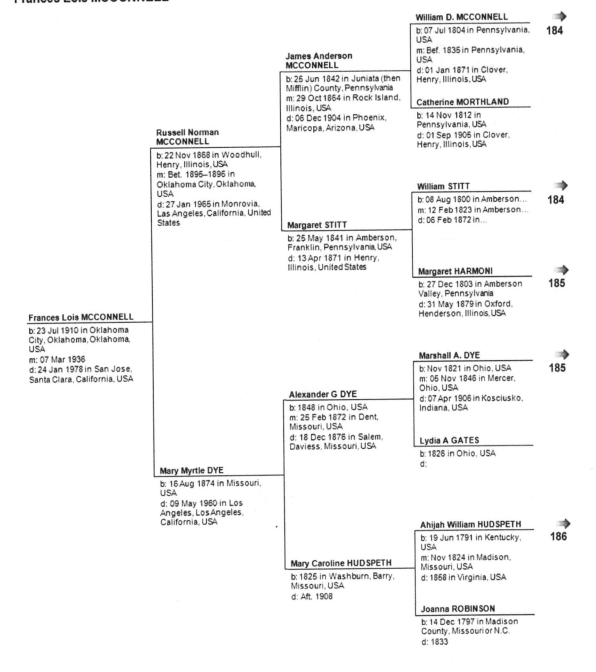

Frances Lois MCCONNELL
b: 23 Jul 1910 in Oklahoma
City, Oklahoma, Oklahoma,
USA
m: 07 Mar 1936
d: 24 Jan 1978 in San Jose,
Santa Clara, California, USA

Russell Norman MCCONNELL
b: 22 Nov 1868 in Woodhull,
Henry, Illinois, USA
m: Bet. 1895–1896 in
Oklahoma City, Oklahoma,
USA
d: 27 Jan 1965 in Monrovia,
Las Angeles, California, United
States

James Anderson MCCONNELL
b: 25 Jun 1842 in Juniata (then
Mifflin) County, Pennsylvania
m: 29 Oct 1864 in Rock Island,
Illinois, USA
d: 06 Dec 1904 in Phoenix,
Maricopa, Arizona, USA

William D. MCCONNELL
b: 07 Jul 1804 in Pennsylvania,
USA
m: Bef. 1835 in Pennsylvania,
USA
d: 01 Jan 1871 in Clover,
Henry, Illinois, USA
184

Catherine MORTHLAND
b: 14 Nov 1812 in
Pennsylvania, USA
d: 01 Sep 1905 in Clover,
Henry, Illinois, USA

Margaret STITT
b: 25 May 1841 in Amberson,
Franklin, Pennsylvania, USA
d: 13 Apr 1871 in Henry,
Illinois, United States

William STITT
b: 08 Aug 1800 in Amberson...
m: 12 Feb 1823 in Amberson...
d: 06 Feb 1872 in...
184

Margaret HARMONI
b: 27 Dec 1803 in Amberson
Valley, Pennsylvania
d: 31 May 1879 in Oxford,
Henderson, Illinois, USA
185

Mary Myrtle DYE
b: 16 Aug 1874 in Missouri,
USA
d: 09 May 1960 in Los
Angeles, Los Angeles,
California, USA

Alexander G DYE
b: 1848 in Ohio, USA
m: 25 Feb 1872 in Dent,
Missouri, USA
d: 18 Dec 1876 in Salem,
Daviess, Missouri, USA

Marshall A. DYE
b: Nov 1821 in Ohio, USA
m: 05 Nov 1846 in Mercer,
Ohio, USA
d: 07 Apr 1906 in Kosciusko,
Indiana, USA
185

Lydia A GATES
b: 1826 in Ohio, USA
d:

Mary Caroline HUDSPETH
b: 1825 in Washburn, Barry,
Missouri, USA
d: Aft. 1908

Ahijah William HUDSPETH
b: 19 Jun 1791 in Kentucky,
USA
m: Nov 1824 in Madison,
Missouri, USA
d: 1858 in Virginia, USA
186

Joanna ROBINSON
b: 14 Dec 1797 in Madison
County, Missouri or N.C.
d: 1833

Thomas MCCONNELL

b: Abt. 1776
m:
d: 03 Oct 1843

William D. MCCONNELL

b: 07 Jul 1804 in Pennsylvania,
USA
m: Bef. 1835 in Pennsylvania,
USA
d: 01 Jan 1871 in Clover,
Henry, Illinois, USA

◀
183

Eleanor UNKNOWN

b: Abt. 1764
d: 04 Jan 1840

William STITT

b: 1735 in Antrim, Northern
Ireland
m:
d: 1791 in Franklin,
Pennsylvania, USA

James STITT

b: 1750 in Antrim, Ireland
m: Ireland
d: 1844

Elizabeth MORRISON

b: 1735 in Pennsylvania, USA
d: 1755

William STITT

b: 08 Aug 1800 in Amberson
Valley, Franklin, Pennsylvania,
United States
m: 12 Feb 1823 in Amberson
Valley, Franklin, Pennsylvania,
USA
d: 06 Feb 1872 in Henderson,
Illinois, USA

◀
183

Sarah A. DAVISON

b: 1758 in Down, Northern
Ireland
d: 1853 in Amberson, Franklin,
Pennsylvania, USA

John Ludwig HARMONI

b: 17 Mar 1734 in Hebron,
Nassaudillenberg, Germany
m: 1772 in Fannett, Franklin,
Pennsylvania, USA
d: 23 Nov 1831 in Amberson,
Franklin, Pennsylvania, USA

Henry HARMONI

b: 05 Oct 1776 in Amberson
Valley, Franklin, Pennsylvania,
USA
m: 04 May 1801 in
Chambersburg, Franklin,
Pennsylvania, USA
d: 30 Jan 1856 in
Chambersburg, Franklin,
Pennsylvania, USA

Elizabeth Ludley LOWE

b: 14 Oct 1752 in Talbot,
Maryland, USA
d: 17 Aug 1831 in Amberson
Valley, Franklin, Pennsylvania,
USA

Margaret HARMONI

b: 27 Dec 1803 in Amberson
Valley, Pennsylvania
m: 12 Feb 1823 in Amberson
Valley, Franklin, Pennsylvania,
USA
d: 31 May 1879 in Oxford,
Henderson, Illinois, USA

Cromwell MCVITTY

b: 1729 in Dublin, Ireland
m: 1770
d: 03 Sep 1813 in Caernarvon,
Lancaster, Pennsylvania, USA

183

Nora Anna MCVITTY

b: 26 Feb 1775 in Amberson,
Franklin, Pennsylvania, USA
d: 07 Jan 1843

Margaret MCCURDY

b: 1746 in Franklin,
Pennsylvania, USA
d: 07 Mar 1833

Andrew S DYE

b: 13 Jun 1744 in Cranbury,
Middlesex, New Jersey, USA
m:
d: 05 Jul 1835 in Newton,
Miami, Ohio, United States

Andrew A DYE

b: 25 Dec 1774 in Miami, Ohio,
USA
m: 1795
d: 03 Apr 1838 in Concord,
Miami, Ohio, USA

Sarah MINOR

b: 1747 in Winchester,
Frederick, Virginia, USA
d: 1810 in Jollytown,
Washington, Pennsylvania
United States

Stephen W DYE

b: 1798 in Miami, Ohio, USA
m: 06 Jan 1821 in Miami, Ohio,
USA
d: 1832

Jane GUTHRIE

b: 1778 in Greene,
Pennsylvania, USA
d:

Marshall A. DYE

b: Nov 1821 in Ohio, USA
m: 05 Nov 1846 in Mercer,
Ohio, USA
d: 07 Apr 1906 in Kosciusko,
Indiana, USA

183

Elizabeth MCCOLLOUGH

b:
d: 1828

George Washington HUDSPETH

b: Abt. 1766 in Granville, North
Carolina, USA
m:
d: 06 Aug 1827 in Washington,
Missouri, USA

Ahijah William HUDSPETH

b: 19 Jun 1791 in Kentucky,
USA
m: Nov 1824 in Madison,
Missouri, USA
d: 1858 in Virginia, USA

183

Sarah WOODS

b: Bet. 1770–1780 in North
Carolina, USA
d: Aft. 1830

Generation 1

1. **CHRISTIAN***[1]* **RITSCHHART**[1,2] was born on 25 Jan 1709 in Oberhofen, Bern, Switzerland[1,3]. He died about 1790 in Shenandoah, Virginia, USA[1,3]. He married **MAGDALENA WOLFF** on 09 Jan 1733 in Amsoldingen, Bern, Switzerland[2,3]. She was born in Jan 1703 in Hilterfingen, Bern, Switzerland[2,3]. She died on 04 Oct 1766 in Berks, Pennsylvania, USA[3].

Notes for Christian RITSCHHART:
According to notes from Clifford Ritchhart, Christian (he spelled it Christjohn) was a wealthy man but ran into some problems and had his wealth confiscated. However, I haven't found any information that would confirm that.

The following was taken from FTM CD 267 *German and Swiss Settlers in America, 1700–1800s*: "According to a report from the Landvogt of Oberhofen, Christen Ritschard, of Oberhofen, in spite of all warnings and in spite of his vows, has emigrated to America (Pennsylvania). His family consisted of his wife, 5 children, and his 80-year-old mother-in-law. Joseph Gyger of Hilterfingen, Ritschard's brother-in-law, with his wife and one child, left the country with him. They left secretly, by night, and went to Basel, in order to take ship there. They were pursued by the Landvogt as runaways, and orders were given that they should be transported back. Ritschard had secretly sold his small property. The present owner is to pay over the emigration tax for this Ritschard, according to the valuation of the property." This piece was dated April 1750.

There is a possibility that Christian and his family were Anabaptists (later known as Mennonites). Interestingly many Germans from the Palatinate and Holland were also Anabaptists. We do know from researching the tax lists for Berks County in 1767 and *Berks County Marriages 1730–1800* that there were other Ritscharts in the county. Ulrich Ritschard was listed having 100 acres, 2 horses and 2 cattle in 1767. Several were listed in the marriage records, both male and female, with a wide range of spellings including Ritschert, Ritshart, and Ritshert.

The *Annals of Southwest Virginia 1769–1800* indicate that Christian Richards owned 138 acres on Terry's Creek. This was dated 3 December 1783. That is located about 25 miles southwest of Roanoke. According to Ethel Beieler Gould who authored *Genealogy of the family of Jacob Blessing I of Pennsylvania and Virginia*, Christian started writing the Haus Book in 1750 which was continued by his son Christian Ritschard III. The book is deposited at the Pennsylvania State Library, call # GEN RI5. It is also on film #468306, item 3 at Salt Lake City Genealogical Library (translated into English by George Seiffort).

Christian RITSCHHART and Magdalena WOLFF had the following children:

      i. MAGDALENA[2] RITSCHARD was born on 22 Oct 1733.

      ii. CHRISTAIN ANNA RITSCHARD was born on 03 Sep 1735.

  2 iii. ELIZABETH RITSCHARD[2,4] was born on 24 Aug 1738 in Oberhofen, Bern, Switzerland[2,4]. She died in 1800 in Washington, Virginia, USA[4]. She married JACOB

BLESSING in 1750 in Pennsylvania, USA[4], son of John BLESSING and Barbara. He was born about 1728 in Baden-Württemberg, Germany[2,4]. He died on 30 Apr 1790 in Virginia, USA.

3   iv. CHRISTIAN RITSCHARD[3] was born on 21 Jul 1739 in Oberhofen, Bern, Switzerland[4]. He died in 1809 in Ross, Ohio, USA[5,6]. He married (1) MARIA ELIZABETH PENTZ on 01 Dec 1767 in Berks, Pennsylvania, USA[4]. She was born in Dec 1747 in Berks, Pennsylvania, USA[4]. She died in 1803 in Ross, Ohio, USA[6]. He married (2) SOPHIA TIMMONS in 1804 in Ross, Ohio, USA. She was born on 07 Jul 1780 in Oberhofen, Bern, Switzerland[4]. She died on 18 Nov 1855 in Ross, Ohio, USA.

     v. DOROTHEA RITSCHARD was born on 08 Jan 1741. She married RITH.

Generation 2

2.   **ELIZABETH[2] RITSCHARD** (Christian[1] RITSCHHART)[2,4] was born on 24 Aug 1738 in Oberhoffen, Bern, Switzerland[2,4]. She died in 1800 in Washington, Virginia, USA[4]. She married **JACOB BLESSING** in 1750 in Pennsylvania, USA[4], son of John BLESSING and Barbara. He was born about 1728 in Baden-Württemberg, Germany[2,4]. He died on 30 Apr 1790 in Virginia, USA.

Notes for Jacob BLESSING:

Supposedly arrived in this country about 1754. He migrated to Berks Co, PA then to Virginia and then to Missouri as per Ethel Gould's book *Genealogy of the Family of Jacob Blessing 1—of Pennsylvania and Virginia.* Jacob and his family lived along Holman's Creek in Dunmore County (became Shenandoah County in 1778), Virginia as early as 1780. Jacob was in the militia of Dunmore County during the Revolutionary War. His unit was called out to repel the British invasion during the Revolutionary War of the Virginia colony in 1780–1781. His unit was under the Command of Capt. Jacob Holman. The list of Militia is printed in *Revolutionary War Records, Vol. 1, Virginia*, page 607 by Gaius Marcus Brumbaugh. (Of interest, Christian Ritschard was also in this same militia unit.) His head-stone in Springbank Cemetery in Ross County, Ohio indicates he was a Revolutionary War Veteran.

Jacob BLESSING and Elizabeth RITSCHARD had the following children:

4   i. JACOB[3] BLESSING[2,4,7] was born in 1756 in Berks, Pennsylvania, USA[2,4,7]. He died in 1830 in Washington, Virginia, USA[4,7]. He married in 1783 in Virginia, USA[4]. He married in Shenandoah, Virginia, USA[4]. He married (4) ELIZABETH MESSERSMITH in 1783 in Wythe, Virginia, USA[4,7], daughter of John Nicholas MESSERSCHMIDT and Maria Dorothea REITZELIN. She was born in 1765 in Botetourt, Virginia, USA[4,7]. She died in 1834 in Smyth, Virginia, USA[4,7]. He married (5) Nancy. She was born in 1750[4].

     ii. ELIZABETH BLESSING[2,4] was born in 1759 in Berks, Pennsylvania, USA[2,4]. She married GEORGE WEAVER on 20 Dec 1782 in Shenandoah, Virginia, USA[4].

     iii. BARBARA BLESSING[2,4] was born in 1761 in Berks, Pennsylvania, USA[2,4].

iv. MARY MAGDALENA BLESSING[2,4] was born on 10 May 1763 in Berks, Pennsylvania, USA[2,4]. She died in Greene, Ohio, USA[4].

v. LEWIS BLESSING[2,4] was born in 1765 in Berks, Pennsylvania, USA[2,4]. He died on 24 Aug 1825 in Woodland, Greene, Ohio, USA[4].

vi. CHRISTIAN BLESSING[2,4] was born in 1767 in Berks, Pennsylvania, USA[4].

vii. JOHN BLESSING[2,4] was born in 1770 in Shenandoah, Virginia, USA[2,4]. He died on 30 Jul 1828 in Greene, Ohio, USA[4].

viii. HENRY BLESSING[2,4] was born in 1772 in Shenandoah, Virginia, USA[4].

ix. ABRAHAM BLESSING[2,4] was born on 03 Jul 1778 in Shenandoah, Virginia, USA[2,4]. He died on 31 May 1858 in Greene, Gallia, Ohio, USA[4].

x. CATHERINE BLESSING[2,4] was born in 1787 in Shenandoah, Virginia, USA[4]. She died in 1860 in Washington, Virginia, USA[4].

xi. CHRISTINA BLESSING[2,4] was born in 1789 in Shenandoah, Virginia, USA[4].

Notes for Christina BLESSING:

Mother would have been over 50 when she was born. Somewhat questionable.

3. **CHRISTIAN**[2] **RITSCHARD** (Christian[1] RITSCHHART)[3] was born on 21 Jul 1739 in Oberhofen, Bern, Switzerland[4]. He died in 1809 in Ross, Ohio, USA[5,6]. He married (1) **MARIA ELIZABETH PENTZ** on 01 Dec 1767 in Berks, Pennsylvania, USA[4]. She was born in Dec 1747 in Berks, Pennsylvania, USA[4]. She died in 1803 in Ross, Ohio, USA[6]. He married (2) **SOPHIA TIMMONS** in 1804 in Ross, Ohio, USA. She was born on 07 Jul 1780 in Oberhoffen, Bern, Switzerland[4]. She died on 18 Nov 1855 in Ross, Ohio, USA.

Notes for Christian RITSCHARD:

Christian and his family moved in 1796–97 and settled at the mouth of Deer Creek. Ohio was not yet a state so it was still the Northwest Territories. However, the county of Hamilton had been formed in 1792 and encompassed the area. In 1796 Adams County was formed followed in 1799 by Ross County. In 1803 Ohio became a state. Thus, records could be found in any of at least three counties: Hamilton, Adams or Ross.

I have a photo which I took of his headstone in Stoneybank Cemetery in July 1999. The headstone says he was born in 1744 and died in 1807. I believe the headstone is incorrect. When we visited Chillicothe and talked with Fred Ritchhart, he indicated that a relative from Utah had come there and had the headstone provided by the Government because Christian was in the Revolutionary War with the Virginia Militia. I later confirmed in *Revolutionary War Patriots of Ross Co., Ohio* by the Sons of the American Revolution, Arthur St. Clair Chapter, Chillicothe, Ohio, that he was in Captain Jacob Holeman's Company of the Dunmore County (now Shenandoah) Virginia Militia. This qualifies us for membership in the SAR and DAR (depending on gender). However, if I had paid attention to the headstone and photos I took of it when we visited Ross County in 1999, I would have known this earlier. On the headstone it says :"Dunmore CO VA Militia Rev War;" thus, proving we sometimes miss the obvious.

The book *History of Ross and Highland Counties, Ohio* published in 1880 contained the following: "Christian Ritchhart and family, consisting of wife, and his daughters Mary and Elizabeth, emigrated from Rockingham County, Virginia in 1797. They journeyed down the Ohio River on a flat-boat until arriving where Portsmouth now stands; thence pushed up the Scioto on a keel-boat to the mouth of Deer creek, where they arrived on the tenth day of October 1797. Here he settled and resided for two years, when, on account of sickness, which then prevailed to so great an extent on the bottoms, he settled on Spring bank, where he lived the remainder of his life. About ten years after his settlement his wife died, and he afterwards married the widow Timmons, by whom he had two children, Frederick and Anna. He purchased a tract of land of between twelve and thirteen hundred acres, on Deer creek, and his sons also settled on this tract, except Abraham, who died in Noble County, Indiana. His daughters, Mary and Elizabeth became the wives respectively of John Moyers and Philip Minear, who was one of the earliest settlers of Union."

I viewed *Revolutionary War Records* by Gaius Marcus Brumbaugh and viewed a listing of the men in the Denmore County Militia under the command of Capt. Jacob Holman. Both Jacob Blessing and Christian Richards were listed. While I am happy that the Ross County Sons of the American Revolution have published a book confirming Christian as a Revolutionary War Veteran, if this is the evidence, it may be a little questionable.

Christian RITSCHARD and Maria Elizabeth PENTZ had the following children:

5   i. MARIA ELIZABETH[3] RITSCHARD[8] was born on 03 Oct 1768 in Virginia, Rockingham Co.[8]. She died on 27 Feb 1835 in Ross, Ohio, USA (buried Springbank Cemetery)[8,9]. She married PHILLIP MINEAR on 24 Mar 1803 in Ross, Ohio, USA[4], son of John MINEAR and Marie URSALA. He was born on 31 Mar 1761 in Bucks, Pennsylvania, USA[4]. He died on 17 Oct 1846 in Ross, Ohio, USA[4,8,9].

6   ii. CHRISTIAN RITSCHARD was born on 12 Jul 1770. He died in 1824 in Ross, Ohio, USA. He married Mary Magdalena * on 17 Oct 1797 in Shenandoah County, VA. She was born about 1773[8]. She died in 1831 in Ross, Ohio, USA (buried in Springbank Cemetery)[8].

    iii. BARBARA RITSCHARD[10] was born on 08 Jan 1773[11]. She died on 06 Sep 1831 in Ross, Ohio, USA[11]. She married CHRISTIAN MOYER JR. on 12 May 1798 in Shenandoah, Virginia, USA[11].
    Notes for Barbara RITSCHARD:
    Some lists of the family, especially on World Family Tree do not include Barbara. She was on the DAR Ross County Chapter records.

    iv. MARY MAGDALENA RITSCHARD[8] was born on 10 Feb 1776[12]. She died on 06 Sep 1831 in Ross, Ohio, USA[12]. She married ABRAHAM JOHN MOYERS on 14 Feb 1797 in Shenandoah, Virginia, USA.

7   v. JACOB RICHHART[4,10] was born on 19 Feb 1778 in Shenandoah, Virginia, USA[4,10]. He died on 23 Dec 1836 in Ross, Ohio, USA[4]. He married (1) ELIZABETH GRIFFITH on 01 Jul 1819 in Ross, Ohio, USA[4]. She was born on 06 Jun 1796 in Sissex Co., DE. She died on 22 Sep 1839 in Ross, Ohio, USA. He married (2) ROSANA NOLAND on

28 Apr 1800 in Ross, Ohio, USA[4]. She was born in 1800[8].

8   vi. JOHN RITCHHART[4,8,13,14,15] was born on 31 Mar 1780 in Shenandoah, Virginia, USA[14,15,16]. He died in Mar 1829 in Ross, Ohio, USA[4,14,15]. He married MARY (POLLY) HEINRICH[8]. She was born on 06 May 1782[13]. She died in 1837 in Hamilton, Indiana, USA[8,15,17].

9   vii. HEINRICH (HENRY) RITSCHARD was born on 06 May 1782. He died on 17 Jan 1837 in Ross, Ohio, USA. He married SUSANNAH LAWYER. She was born on 05 Sep 1793. She died on 16 Oct 1829 in Ross, Ohio, USA[8].

    viii. CATHARINA RITSCHARD[18] was born on 18 Feb 1785[1]. She died on 22 Mar 1785.

10 ix. ABRAHAM RITSCHARD was born on 16 Feb 1786 in Shenendoah, Virginia, USA[6,19]. He died in 1876 in Noble, Indiana, USA (Probably Noblesville, IN)[6]. He married (1) BETSY FARROW on 25 Sep 1810 in Ross, Ohio, USA[6,19]. She died in 1818 in Ross, Ohio, USA[6,19]. He married (2) NANCY CASKEY on 07 May 1818 in Ross, Ohio, USA[19].

Notes for Sophia TIMMONS: Bettye's book quotes an author who thought Sophia's maiden name could have been Mitz. The Family Tree from Kathleen Bridges lists her name as "Sophia Mitz Timmons."

Christian RITSCHARD and Sophia TIMMONS had the following children:

11. x. FREDERICK FERDINAND RITSCHARD[8] was born on 18 Mar 1805 in Ross, Ohio, USA[4]. He died in 1869 in Ross, Ohio, USA[4]. He married (1) ELIZABETH GULLICK on 26 Apr 1827 in Ross, Ohio, USA[4], daughter of Ferdinand GULICK and Hannah Bell LEIGH. She was born on 22 Jan 1808 in Ross, Ohio, USA[4]. She died on 15 Jun 1840 in Ross, Ohio, USA[4]. He married (2) TEMPERANCE WOLF on 26 Apr 1827 in Ross, Ohio, USA[4]. She was born in 1805 in Ross, Ohio, USA[4]. He married (3) LEAH BARNHART on 13 Mar 1851 in Ross, Ohio, USA[4], daughter of William Henry BARNHART and Mary Polly MAY. She was born in 1830 in Ohio, USA[4].

    xi. ANNA RITCHHART[8] was born on 21 Feb 1807. She died on 05 Jun 1883 in Polk, Iowa, USA. She married JAMES ALEXANDER WOODS on 13 Sep 1827 in Ross, Ohio, USA[4]. He was born in 1807 in Ohio, USA[20].

Notes for Anna RITCHHART: The book *History of Ross and Highland Counties, Ohio* lists the two children of Christian and "the Widow Timmons" as Frederick and Anna (vice Aumain). I did find a number of references in "One World Tree" to Aumain. It is likely that Anna was a nickname that she used.

Generation 3

4. **JACOB**[3] **BLESSING** (Elizabeth[2] RITSCHARD, Christian[1] RITSCHHART)[2,4,7] was born in 1756 in Berks, Pennsylvania, USA[2,4,7]. He died in 1830 in Washington, Virginia, USA[4,7]. He married in 1783 in Virginia, USA[4]. He married in Shenandoah, Virginia, USA[4]. He married (4) **ELIZABETH MESSERSMITH** in 1783 in Wythe, Virginia, USA[4,7], daughter of John Nicholas MESSERSCHMIDT and Maria Dorothea REITZELIN. She was born in 1765 in Botetourt, Virginia, USA[4,7]. She died in 1834 in Smyth, Virginia, USA[4,7]. He married (5)

Nancy. She was born in 1750[4].

Jacob BLESSING and Elizabeth MESSERSMITH had the following children:

    i. ABRAHAM[4] BLESSING[4] was born on 25 Jun 1785 in Shenandoah, Virginia, USA[4]. He died in 1833 in Smyth, Virginia, USA[4].

    ii. MARY BLESSING[4] was born on 22 Jun 1786 in Shenandoah, Virginia, USA[4]. She died on 12 Feb 1866 in Cass, Missouri, USA[4].

    iii. CATHERINE BLESSING[2,4] was born in 1787 in Shenandoah, Virginia, USA[4]. She died in 1860 in Washington, Virginia, USA[4].

    iv. ISAAC BLESSING[4] was born in 1790 in Shenandoah, Virginia, USA[4].

    v. REBECCA BLESSING[4] was born in 1794 in Washington, Virginia, USA[4]. She died in 1853 in Fulton, Arkansas, USA[4].

    vi. JACOB BLESSING[4] was born in 1798 in Shenandoah, Virginia, USA[4].

    vii. DAVID BLESSING was born in 1802 in Washington, Virginia, USA.

    viii. SUSANNAH BLESSING[4] was born on 12 Jul 1804 in Washington, Virginia, USA[4]. She died in 1875[4].

    ix. SOLOMON BLESSING[4,7] was born in 1805 in Washington, Virginia, USA[4,7].

    x. ELIZABETH BLESSING[4] was born in 1807 in Washington, Virginia, USA[4].

    xi. ANN BLESSING[4] was born in 1810 in Washington, Virginia, USA[4].

    xii. JOHN BLESSING[4] was born in 1811 in Washington, Virginia, USA[4].

5. **MARIA ELIZABETH**[3] **RITSCHARD** (Christian[2], Christian[1] RITSCHHART)[8] was born on 03 Oct 1768 in Virginia, Rockingham Co.[8]. She died on 27 Feb 1835 in Ross, Ohio, USA (buried Springbank Cemetery)[8,9]. She married **PHILLIP MINEAR** on 24 Mar 1803 in Ross, Ohio, USA[4], son of John MINEAR and Marie URSALA. He was born on 31 Mar 1761 in Bucks, Pennsylvania, USA[4]. He died on 17 Oct 1846 in Ross, Ohio, USA[4,8,9].

Phillip MINEAR and Maria Elizabeth RITSCHARD had the following child:

    i. RACHEL[4] MINEAR[4] was born on 21 Feb 1802[4].

6. **CHRISTIAN**[3] **RITSCHARD** (Christian[2], Christian[1] RITSCHHART) was born on 12 Jul 1770. He died in 1824 in Ross, Ohio, USA. He married **MARY MAGDALENA*** on 17 Oct 1797 in Shenandoah County, VA. She was born about 1773[8]. She died in 1831 in Ross, Ohio, USA (buried in Springbank Cemetery)[8].

Notes for Mary Magdalena *:
Name spelled Maddilina in *Revolutionary War Patriots*.

Christian RITSCHARD and Mary Magdalena * had the following child:

12.   i. PHILLIP[4] RITCHHART was born in Dec 1804.

7. **JACOB**[3] **RICHHART** (Christian[2] RITSCHARD, Christian[1] RITSCHHART)[4,10] was born on 19 Feb 1778 in Shenandoah, Virginia, USA[4,10]. He died on 23 Dec 1836 in Ross, Ohio, USA[4]. He married (1) **ELIZABETH GRIFFITH** on 01 Jul 1819 in Ross, Ohio, USA[4]. She was born on 06 Jun 1796 in Sissex Co., DE. She died on 22 Sep 1839 in Ross, Ohio, USA. He married (2) **ROSANA NOLAND** on 28 Apr 1800 in Ross, Ohio, USA[4]. She was born in 1800[8].

Notes for Jacob RICHHART:

Was a Captain in the War of 1812. Genealogy.com record of *Rosters of Ohio Soldiers War of 1812* lists him as serving from 7/28/1813 to 8/18/1813. He headed a Ross County Company. Henry Ritchhart was listed as a Private in his company. That was probably Jacob's brother who was two years younger. The *History of Springbank and Yellowbud Community* states that, "Jacob was a captain in War of 1812, his brothers all members of his company." Henry (Heinrich) was born on 3/31/1780 and would have been 33.

Was probably the Ritchhart who changed his name from Ritschard to Ritchhart because all his children's names are spelled Ritchhart and that is the way he was listed in the military records for the War of 1812.

The land purchases were in Piqua County, which is well north of Ross Co., but he apparently lived, died and was buried in Ross Co. Perhaps he purchased the land for his children or that land office controlled the land in Ross Co.—I am not sure which. According to the *History of Ross and Highland Counties* he, his father and grandfather came in 1796 to Ross Co.

Jacob RICHHART and Elizabeth GRIFFITH had the following children:

13.   i.   JACOB[4] RITCHHART[21] was born on 16 Jun 1822 in Ross, Ohio, USA. He died on 24 Nov 1882 in Athens, Ross Co., Ohio. He married (1) EMMALIZA DUNNING on 15 Feb 1849 in Ross, Ohio, USA[22]. She was born in 1833[8]. She died on 10 Oct 1858 in Yellowbud, Ohio[8]. He married (2) ANN DUDLEY ROWLAND on 24 Nov 1859 in Ross, Ohio, USA[21], daughter of William Dudley ROWLAND and Bethenia LYONS. She was born on 28 Apr 1839 in Terre Haute, Vigo, Indiana, USA. She died on 30 Oct 1926 in Chillicothe, Ross, Ohio, USA.

      ii.   HIRAM RITCHHART[8] was born on 14 Aug 1825 in Union, Ohio, USA. He died on 26 Sep 1890 in Ross, Ohio, USA. He married REBECCA A. MACE on 22 Feb 1853 in Ross, Ohio, USA[5,21]. She was born in Aug 1833. She died in Mar 1901 in Ross, Ohio, USA.

            Notes for Hiram RITCHHART: I took a photo of the headstone in Springbank Cemetery for Hiram and his wife Rebekah. It was a very large and probably expensive headstone that was well weathered. *The History of Ross and Highland Counties Ohio*, pg. 268, states that Hiram was born in Union, inherited 105 acres from his father. He farmed south of the old place near Andersonville, seven miles north of Chillicothe. He was city treasurer of Union for some fifteen years and a member of Patrons of Husbandry. He was considered one of the substantial farmers of the area, a leading and useful citizen of the town of Union. He was of German stock. Hiram and Rebecca had a childless marriage. He left the land to his nephew namesake, Hiram Ritchhart. The book *History of Ross and Highland Counties* adds that, although childless, they raised one of his brother Jacob's children and one of his wife's cousins, Jessie Mace.

14   iii.   PENELOPE RITCHHART[8] was born on 28 Dec 1827[9,23]. She died on 29 Dec 1892 in Ross, Ohio, USA[9]. She married (1) JACOB S. MORRISON in Ross, Ohio, USA[8]. He was born on 23 May 1821. He died on 22 Jul 1891 in Ross, Ohio, USA[23]. She mar-

ried (2) ANTHONY SIMMS DAVENPORT on 13 Jan 1848 in Ross, Ohio, USA[22], son of Bazzle DAVENPORT and Sarah EVANS.

15   iv.   ELIZABETH RITCHHART[8] was born on 04 Jan 1832. She married SAMUEL PINTO. He was born in 1828[5]. He died in 1891 in Ross, Ohio, USA[5].

Jacob RICHHART and Rosana NOLAND had the following child:

16.   v.   ABRAHAM RITCHHART was born in 1804 in Ross, Ohio, USA. He died on 20 Jan 1853 in Ross, Ohio, USA. He married (1) CYRENE WROUGHTON on 11 Sep 1842 in Ross, Ohio, USA. She was born in 1820. She died on 18 Aug 1844 in Ross, Ohio, USA. He married (2) LETHA BROWNING on 23 Mar 1848 in Ross, Ohio, USA[8,22]. She was born on 04 Apr 1819. She died on 09 Mar 1892 in Ross, Ohio, USA.

8.   **JOHN[3] RITCHHART** (Christian[2] RITSCHARD, Christian[1] RITSCHHART)[4,8,13,14,15] was born on 31 Mar 1780 in Shenandoah, Virginia, USA[14,15,16]. He died in Mar 1829 in Ross, Ohio, USA[4,14,15]. He married **MARY (POLLY)HEINRICH**[8]. She was born on 06 May 1782[13]. She died in 1837 in Hamilton, Indiana, USA[8,15,17].

Notes for Mary (Polly) HEINRICH: The family trees I got from Kathleen Bridges gave Polly's birthdate as 1784, and Bettye Richhart's book indicated "Polly died in Hamilton Co. IN in 1837 at the age of 53." (which would also indicate she was born in 1784).

Polly moved to Hamilton County after John died. She probably did this because John's brother Samuel had moved to Hamilton County earlier; thus, she had family there to provide support. In the *Family Maps of Hamilton County* 977.256 E7b; Polly is listed as owning almost two full sections of land outside Noblesville. In fact she owned the land on both sides of the road surrounding Lowry Cemetery. Samuel and Abraham Ritchhart also owned large tracts in the same area near the intersection of E136th St. and 110th St. The patent date on the Patent Map is listed as 1837. However, that is the year she died. I speculate she owned the land earlier; but the patent didn't get approved until later. Abraham and Samuel's patent dates were also 1837.

John RITCHHART and Mary (Polly) HEINRICH had the following children:

17.   i.   SAMUEL B.[4] RITCHHART[13,24] was born in 1806 in Ohio, USA[15,25,26]. He died on 17 Apr 1858 in Hamilton, Indiana, USA[15,25,26]. He married SALLY COVERDALE on 21 Oct 1828 in Ross, Ohio, USA[22], daughter of Purnell COVERDALE and Charlotte. She died on 03 Nov 1848 in Hamilton, Indiana, USA[25].

     ii.   JOHN RITCHHART[13,17] was born in 1810 in Ross, Ohio, USA[27]. He married (1) NANCY GULICK on 06 Feb 1828 in Ross, Ohio, USA[28]. He married (2) MARY NICHOLS on 21 Jan 1831 in Ross, Ohio, USA[28].

          Notes for John RITCHHART:
          The Land patent that I have listed in the Media section of John's father, John, probably belongs to this John. The date of the Land Patent is 1835 and John (Sr.) died in 1829. Also the land was not listed in the probate of his will.

     iii.   POLLY (MARY) RITCHHART[13] was born about 1810. She married REUBEN COVERDELL on 23 Aug 1841 in Hamilton, Indiana, USA.

18. iv. ANDREW RITCHHART[4,13,14] was born on 11 Jun 1818 in Ross, Ohio, USA[4]. He died on 24 Dec 1897 in Hamilton, Indiana, USA[14]. He married MARY BOOTH on 16 Jun 1841 in Hamilton, Indiana, USA[29], daughter of George BOOTH and Mary MCANALLY. She was born on 17 Nov 1817 in Stokes, North Carolina, USA[4,30]. She died on 28 Sep 1873 in Fall Creek, Hamilton, Indiana, USA[4,30].

v. CORNELIUS RITCHHART[13,31] was born about 1822. He died in 1845 in Hamilton, Indiana, USA.

Notes for Cornelius RITCHHART: Bettye Richhart's book lists the fifth child as Collins, but notes that the headstone at the cemetery only had a "Collins." Since no other records were found for Cornelius or Collins, they could be one and the same—perhaps Collins being a nickname for Cornelius?

9. **HEINRICH (HENRY)**[3] **RITSCHARD** (Christian[2], Christian[1] RITSCHHART) was born on 06 May 1782. He died on 17 Jan 1837 in Ross, Ohio, USA. He married **SUSANNAH LAWYER**. She was born on 05 Sep 1793. She died on 16 Oct 1829 in Ross, Ohio, USA[8].

Notes for Heinrich (Henry) RITSCHARD:
Heinrich must have later changed the spelling of his name to Richhart, which is how his children's names are spelled. I took a photo of his headstone when I visited Chillicothe in July 1999. Other facts say he died in 1836, but his headstone says 1837. It was a very new headstone. He served in the War of 1812 with his brother Jacob, who was a Captain. Henry was a Private in the 2nd Regiment, Ohio Militia.

Heinrich (Henry) RITSCHARD and Susannah LAWYER had the following children:

i. BARBARA[4] RITCHHART was born on 23 Jan 1809 in Ross, Ohio, USA.

ii. KATHERINE RITCHHART was born on 26 Jan 1811 in Ross, Ohio, USA.

19. iii. WILLIAM RITCHHART was born on 13 Dec 1816 in Ross, Ohio, USA. He died on 18 Mar 1857 in Morgan, Illinois, USA. He married ELEANOR NICHOLS on 07 Aug 1842 in Pickaway, Ohio, USA. She was born on 22 Apr 1826. She died on 13 Jan 1910 in Jennings, Jefferson Davis, Louisiana, USA.

iv. HENRY RITCHHART was born on 27 Sep 1829 in Ross, Ohio, USA.

v. SUSANNA RITCHHART.

10. **ABRAHAM**[3] **RITSCHARD** (Christian[2], Christian[1] RITSCHHART) was born on 16 Feb 1786 in Shenandoah, Virginia, USA[6,19]. He died in 1876 in Noble, Indiana, USA (Probably Noblesville, IN)[6]. He married (1) **BETSY FARROW** on 25 Sep 1810 in Ross, Ohio, USA[6,19]. She died in 1818 in Ross, Ohio, USA[6,19]. He married (2) **NANCY CASKEY** on 07 May 1818 in Ross, Ohio, USA[19].

Abraham RITSCHARD and Betsy FARROW had the following children:

i. ALLEN[4] RITCHHART[6,19] was born on 09 Dec 1812 in Ross, Ohio, USA[6,19]. He died on 25 Nov 1888 in Kosciusko, Indiana, USA[6,19].

ii. JOHN RITCHHART[19] was born in 1818 in Ross, Ohio, USA[32]. He married (1)Sally Ann. She was born about 1835 in Ross, Ohio, USA. She died about May 1850 in Hamilton, Indiana, USA[33]. He married (2)HESTER ANN PALMER in 1850. She was born in 1828 in

Delaware, USA[34].

Abraham RITSCHARD and Nancy CASKEY had the following children:

    iii. ABRAM RITSCHARD was born in 1819.

    iv. SAMUEL RITSCHARD was born in 1828.

    v. ADAM RITSCHARD was born in 1829.

11. **FREDERICK FERDINAND**[3] **RITSCHARD** (Christian[2], Christian[1] RITSCHHART)[8] was born on 18 Mar 1805 in Ross, Ohio, USA[4]. He died in 1869 in Ross, Ohio, USA[4]. He married (1) **ELIZABETH GULLICK** on 26 Apr 1827 in Ross, Ohio, USA[4], daughter of Ferdinand GULICK and Hannah Bell LEIGH. She was born on 22 Jan 1808 in Ross, Ohio, USA[4]. She died on 15 Jun 1840 in Ross, Ohio, USA[4]. He married (2) **TEMPERANCE WOLF** on 26 Apr 1827 in Ross, Ohio, USA[4]. She was born in 1805 in Ross, Ohio, USA[4]. He married (3) **LEAH BARNHART** on 13 Mar 1851 in Ross, Ohio, USA[4], daughter of William Henry BARNHART and Mary Polly MAY. She was born in 1830 in Ohio, USA[4].

Frederick Ferdinand RITSCHARD and Elizabeth GULLICK had the following children:

20.   i. JOHN M.[4] RICHHART[4] was born on 27 Oct 1829 in Ross, Ohio, USA[4]. He died on 21 Aug 1891[4]. He married MARY ELLEN VIRGINIA DE CAMP on 10 Oct 1861 in Middleton, Logan Co., Illinois[35], daughter of Parter DE CAMP and Kaziah HAINES. She was born on 29 May 1843 in Illinois, USA. She died on 10 May 1917 in Raymond, Pacific, Washington, USA.

    ii. WILLIAM RICHHART[4] was born about 1830.

Generation 4

12. **PHILLIP**[4] **RITCHHART** (Christian[3] RITSCHARD, Christian[2] RITSCHARD, Christian[1] RITSCIIIIART) was born in Dec 1804.

Phillip RITCHHART had the following child:

21.   i. BENJAMIN ALLEN[5] RITCHHART.

13. **JACOB**[4] **RITCHHART** (Jacob[3] RICHHART, Christian[2] RITSCHARD, Christian[1] RITSCHHART)[21] was born on 16 Jun 1822 in Ross, Ohio, USA. He died on 24 Nov 1882 in Athens, Ross Co., Ohio. He married (1) **EMMALIZA DUNNING** on 15 Feb 1849 in Ross, Ohio, USA[22]. She was born in 1833[8]. She died on 10 Oct 1858 in Yellowbud, Ohio[8]. He married (2) **ANN DUDLEY ROWLAND** on 24 Nov 1859 in Ross, Ohio, USA[21], daughter of William Dudley ROWLAND and Bethenia LYONS. She was born on 28 Apr 1839 in Terre Haute, Vigo, Indiana, USA. She died on 30 Oct 1926 in Chillicothe, Ross, Ohio, USA.

Notes for Jacob RITCHHART: According to Bettye Richhart's book, Probate Case #6938 in Ross Co. records that on Oct 3, 1882, Jacob, age 60, was brought into court by his brother, Hiram, and two doctors. Jacob was declared legally insane and hospitalized at the Athens Lunatic Asylum. One month and 21 days later, Jacob died. It appears from court records that Jacob suffered from depression rather than insanity. The report states that he displayed a weakness from unwillingness to take sufficient food; he expressed a desire to die. He had experienced a business loss with his farm. It was reported in the family health history that he did not have epilepsy, though his half-sister had it.

Jacob RITCHHART and Emmaliza DUNNING had the following children:

    i. JOSEPHINE[5] RITCHHART was born in Sep 1850.

    ii. INEZ RITCHHART was born in 1852[21]. She married SPENCER WILLIS on 16 Oct 1873 in Ross, Ohio, USA[21].

    iii. EMMA RITCHHART was born in 1854. She married R. G. MCCOY on 21 Sep 1876 in Ross, Ohio, USA[36].

22   iv. JACOB RITCHHART[37] was born in Oct 1858 in Ohio, United States[37]. He died in 1940 in Ross, Ohio, USA. He married EDNA JANE NEAL on 03 Jan 1889 in Ross, Ohio, USA[21,36], daughter of James Monroe NEAL and Anna Mariah CAMPBELL. She was born in Feb 1866 in Lawrence, Lawrence, Ohio, USA[37]. She died on 05 Oct 1944 in Ross Co., OH[38].

    v. HIRAM RITCHHART was born in Jun 1858. He died on 16 Oct 1858.

    Notes for Ann Dudley ROWLAND: Both the 1870 and 1880 census list her as Anna; but they also listed the kids names with nicknames. Thus, her name could have been Ann, but she preferred Anna.

Jacob RITCHHART and Ann Dudley ROWLAND had the following children:

    vi. MINNA RITCHHART was born in Dec 1860 in Ohio, USA. She died on 25 Feb 1861.

23   vii. IDA PENELOPE RITCHHART[4,39,40] was born on 08 Feb 1862 in Andersonville, Ross, Ohio, USA[4]. She died on 15 Feb 1942 in Circleville, Pickaway, Ohio, USA[4]. She married WILLIAM ELBRIDGE NORRIS on 02 Sep 1880[4,36], son of John G. NORRIS and Elizabeth BUXTON. He was born on 27 Mar 1860 (Monroe T, Perry Co., OH). He died on 08 Jan 1945 in Walnut, Pickaway, Ohio, USA.

    viii. LILLY RITCHHART was born about Jan 1864 in Ohio, USA. She died on 03 Feb 1866.

    ix. JOHN P. RITCHHART[41] was born about Dec 1864 in Ohio, USA.

    x. ELIZABETH RITCHHART[41] was born in 1867 in Ohio, USA.

    Notes for Elizabeth RITCHHART: Listed in 1880 census as Lizzie, which I assume was her nickname for Elizabeth.

    xi. ALICE REBECCA RITCHHART[41] was born in 1869 in Ohio, USA.

    Notes for Alice Rebecca RITCHHART: Name could be Rebecca Alice. 1870 census listed as "Alice" and the 1880 census listed her as Rebecca (Richhart).

    xii. OTTA RITCHHART was born in 1874 in Ohio, USA.

14. **PENELOPE[4] RITCHHART** (Jacob[3] RICHHART, Christian[2] RITSCHARD, Christian[1] RITSCHHART)[8] was born on 28 Dec 1827[9,23]. She died on 29 Dec 1892 in Ross, Ohio, USA[9]. She married (1) **JACOB S. MORRISON** in Ross, Ohio, USA[8]. He was born on 23 May 1821. He died on 22 Jul 1891 in Ross, Ohio, USA[23]. She married (2) **ANTHONY SIMMS DAVENPORT** on 13 Jan 1848 in Ross, Ohio, USA[22], son of Bazzle DAVENPORT and Sarah EVANS.

Notes for Jacob S. MORRISON: His surname might be Morison according to *History of Ross and Highland Counties*.

Jacob S. MORRISON and Penelope RITCHHART had the following children:

     i. ELIZABETH[5] MORRISON[8] was born about 1860 in Ross, Ohio, USA[8].

     ii. EMMA MORRISON[8] was born about 1865 in Ross, Ohio, USA[8].

Anthony Simms DAVENPORT and Penelope RITCHHART had the following children:

     i. EDWARD[5] DAVENPORT[8] was born about 1848 in Ross, Ohio, USA[8].

24   ii. FLORA ALICE DAVENPORT[42] was born in 1850 in Ohio, USA[42]. She married JOHN TOLMAN MACK. He was born in 1847 in New York, USA[42].

     iii. MARY DAVENPORT was born about 1850 in Ross, Ohio, USA.

15. **ELIZABETH[4] RITCHHART** (Jacob[3] RICHHART, Christian[2] RITSCHARD, Christian[1] RITSCHHART)[8] was born on 04 Jan 1832. She married SAMUEL PINTO. He was born in 1828[5]. He died in 1891 in Ross, Ohio, USA[5].

Notes for Elizabeth RITCHHART: According to *History of Springbank and Yellowbud Community*, Elizabeth's older four siblings (one by her father's first wife) deeded 103 acres to her in 1850. That would have been in the year following the death of her mother, Elizabeth.

Samuel PINTO and Elizabeth RITCHHART had the following children:

25   i. IDA[5] PINTO was born about 1852 in Ross, Ohio, USA[5]. She married JOHN FENTON.

26   ii. SAMUEL PINTO was born about 1853 in Ross, Ohio, USA[8]. He married SARAH O.

     iii. CHARLES H. PINTO[5] was born about 1858 in Ross, Ohio, USA[5].

     iv. MARY M. PINTO was born about 1861[5]. She married CHARLES H. WISEMAN.

     v. JACOB A. PINTO was born about 1865 in Ross, Ohio, USA[5]. He married NELLIE.

     vi. WILLIAM R. PINTO[8] was born about 1867 in Ross, Ohio, USA[5,8]. He married MARY.

16. **ABRAHAM[4] RITCHHART** (Jacob[3] RICHHART, Christian[2] RITSCHARD, Christian[1] RITSCHHART) was born in 1804 in Ross, Ohio, USA. He died on 20 Jan 1853 in Ross, Ohio, USA. He married (1) **CYRENE WROUGHTON** on 11 Sep 1842 in Ross, Ohio, USA. She was born in 1820. She died on 18 Aug 1844 in Ross, Ohio, USA. He married (2) **LETHA BROWNING** on 23 Mar 1848 in Ross, Ohio, USA[8,22]. She was born on 04 Apr 1819. She died on 09 Mar 1892 in Ross, Ohio, USA.

Abraham RITCHHART and Letha BROWNING had the following children:

     i. JOSEPH[5] RITCHHART was born in 1849 in Ross, Ohio, USA. He died on 27 Feb 1860 in Ross, Ohio, USA.

     ii. CYRENA RITCHHART was born in 1851 in Ross, Ohio, USA.

17. **SAMUEL B.[4] RITCHHART** (John[3], Christian[2] RITSCHARD, Christian[1] RITSCHHART)[13,24] was born in 1806 in Ohio, USA[15,25,26]. He died on 17 Apr 1858 in Hamilton, Indiana, USA[15,25,26]. He married **SALLY COVERDALE** on 21 Oct 1828 in Ross, Ohio, USA[22], daughter of Purnell COVERDALE and Charlotte. She died on 03 Nov 1848 in Hamilton, Indiana, USA[25].

Notes for Samuel B. RITCHHART: While still in Ohio, Samuel was listed as one of three recipients of the deed for the first recorded land for a school in the Springbank/Yellowbud community. The land was recorded on February 15, 1839 and was on the public highway from Chillicothe to Franklintown. His relative Steven Minear was also listed. They were both School Directors.

Enlisted on August 19, 1862 for the Union Army, Indiana Militia as a private.

Either Samuel or his son, William, were the first to change the spelling of the name from Ritchhart to Richhart. Samuel was probably the first Ritchhart to move to Hamilton County. Polly, wife of Samuel's brother John, moved to Hamilton County after John died. They were living in Ross County, Ohio at the time.

Samuel owned land near Noblesville and adjacent to land owned by Polly and Abraham Ritchhart. All of their land has the same date (1837) listed as the patent date. The land surrounds the current location of Lowry Cemetery.

It appears that one of Samuel's skills was as an Appraiser. I found a couple entries in the *Hamilton County, IN Complete Probate Records 1829–1855* where he was listed as the appraiser of an estate.

Samuel B. RITCHHART and Sally COVERDALE had the following children:

     i. PRUSCILLA[5] RICHHART[25] was born in 1830 in Ohio, USA[25].

     ii. MARY M. RICHHART[25] was born in 1831 in Ohio, USA[25].

27   iii. WILLIAM RICHHART[24]. He died in 1869 in Hamilton, Indiana, USA[24]. He married (1) MARGARET LAYTON. He married (2) Mrs. COLBURN.

     iv. BOZE RICHHART.

     v. NANCY RICHHART.

18. **ANDREW[4] RITCHHART** (John[3], Christian[2] RITSCHARD, Christian[1] RITSCHHART)[4,13,14] was born on 11 Jun 1818 in Ross, Ohio, USA[4]. He died on 24 Dec 1897 in Hamilton, Indiana, USA[14]. He married **MARY BOOTH** on 16 Jun 1841 in Hamilton, Indiana, USA[29], daughter of George BOOTH and Mary MCANALLY. She was born on 17 Nov 1817 in Stokes, North Carolina, USA[4,30]. She died on 28 Sep 1873 in Fall Creek, Hamilton, Indiana, USA[4,30].

Notes for Andrew RITCHHART: Wesley Ritchhart showed on his 1920 Census data that his father was born in Indiana. My guess is that he was incorrect and the other data showing he was born in Ohio is correct. However, Wesley's Death Certificate also indicated his father, Andrew, was born in Indiana. It also indicated his mother was Mary Sterns vice Mary Booth. The 1880 Census had Wesley's last name as Richart vice Ritchhart. His next door neighbor was his brother Charles, whose last name was also spelled Richart. At least the enumerator was consistent.

Andrew purchased 160 acres of land on March 15, 1837 in Hamilton County.

The *Hamilton Co Marriage Records 1837–45* in the Allen Co. Library had the date June 16, 1841; but I am guessing that is the date the marriage was recorded and not the actual marriage date. The minister was Craig Moses. Also, Joseph Boothe attested for the marriage on May 24, which would have been three days prior to the marriage.

Andrew's will was proved on 29 Dec 1897. Legatees: children Wesley, Charles, Julia Roudybush, Eliza Dailey/Daley/Daily; children of deceased daughter Mary Stern; Children of deceased son Jesse. Also mentioned Dr. Loftin; Loftin & Evans. Executors: Charles Ritchhart and William Booth. Witness Thomas E. Kane & William H. Boswell.

Notes for Mary BOOTH: The 1920 census for Orville G. Ritchhart shows his mother's birthplace as Pennsylvania.

Notes from Clifford Ritchhart listed his GG Grandmother Booth (Schooler) Ritchhart. The 1920 U.S. Census for Wesley shows his father's and mother's places of birth as being Indiana. The 1860 Census only lists 6 children, with Julia being the youngest at nine months of age. Missing were William, John, Nancy Jane and Andrew. It is possible they died young.

Andrew RITCHHART and Mary BOOTH had the following children:

28.   i. WESLEY[5] RITCHHART[43,44,45,46,47,48,49,50] was born on 30 Jun 1842 in Noblesville, Hamilton, Indiana, USA[51]. He died on 23 Mar 1921 (S Maple Carthage, Missouri)[4,52]. He married (1) MARIA SIBILLA WAGNER on 20 Dec 1866 in Noblesville, Hamilton, Indiana, USA[53], daughter of Michael WAGNER and Harreata Aena GOLDMAN. She was born on 11 May 1840 in Brownsville, Union, Indiana, USA[54]. She died on 20 Jan 1916 (Carthage, Jasper, Missouri, USA)[51]. He married (2) MARY FRYE on 06 Nov 1917 (Carthage, MO after death of first wife), daughter of unknown parents. She was born in 1851 in Illinois, USA[55].

    ii. ELIZA ANN RITCHHART[4,14] was born on 20 Apr 1844[4,14]. She married (1) FRANCIS DAILEY on 11 Sep 1890 in Hamilton, Indiana, USA[18]. She married (2) MICHAEL FERTIG in Jan 1863 in Hamilton, Indiana, USA[18].

    iii. WILLIAM RITCHHART[4,14] was born on 30 Jun 1846[4,14]. He died on 30 Jul 1846[18].

    iv. JOHN FLETCHER RITCHHART[4,14] was born on 12 Jun 1847[4,14,18]. He died on 07 Nov 1847[18].

    v. JESSE RITCHHART[4,14] was born on 09 Sep 1848[4,14,18]. He died before Mar 1894 in Hamilton, Indiana, USA (listed as deceased in father's will dated March 1894)[18,56].

    vi. MARY ELIZABETH RITCHHART[4,14,18] was born on 15 Nov 1850[4,14,18]. She died before Dec 1894 in Hamilton, Indiana, USA (listed as deceased in father's will dated 12 Mar 1894)[18,56]. She married * STERN.

29 vii. CHARLES RITCHHART[14,57,58,59,60,61,62] was born on 16 Apr 1853 in Noblesville, Hamilton, Indiana, USA[14,18,60]. He died on 11 Oct 1931 in Noblesville, Hamilton, Indiana, USA[18]. He married MARIAH GEORGE on 13 Feb 1887 in Noblesville, Hamilton, Indiana, USA[18], daughter of James GEORGE and Maranda SINCLAIR. She was born about 1855 in Indiana, USA[63]. She died on 03 Dec 1940 in Noblesville, Hamilton, Indiana, USA.

viii. MARY (NANCY) JANE RITCHHART[18] was born on 20 Apr 1856[4,14,18]. She died on 04 May 1856[18].

ix. ANDREW RITCHHART[4,14,18] was born on 04 Aug 1857 in Hamilton, Indiana, USA[4,14,18]. He died on 12 Apr 1860[18].

x. JULIA A. RITCHHART[4,18] was born on 07 Sep 1859[4,14,18]. She married JESSE ROUDEBUSH.

19. **WILLIAM**[4] **RITCHHART** (Heinrich (Henry)[3] RITSCHARD, Christian[2] RITSCHARD, Christian[1] RITSCHHART) was born on 13 Dec 1816 in Ross, Ohio, USA. He died on 18 Mar 1857 in Morgan, Illinois, USA. He married **ELEANOR NICHOLS** on 07 Aug 1842 in Pickaway, Ohio, USA. She was born on 22 Apr 1826. She died on 13 Jan 1910 in Jennings, Jefferson Davis, Louisiana, USA.

William RITCHHART and Eleanor NICHOLS had the following children:

i. BALIS ALVA[5] RICHHART was born on 24 Sep 1850 in Morgan, Illinois, USA.

ii. JOHN WALTER RICHHART was born on 16 Jul 1852 in Morgan, Illinois, USA.

30 iii. WILLIAM Z. RICHHART[64] was born on 12 May 1857 in Morgan, Illinois, USA. He married MARY ELIZABETH TOLLY on 19 Nov 1879 in Shelby, Illinois, USA. She was born on 07 May 1860 in Illinois, USA.

20. **JOHN M.**[4] **RICHHART** (Frederick Ferdinand[3] RITSCHARD, Christian[2] RITSCHARD, Christian[1] RITSCHHART)[4] was born on 27 Oct 1829 in Ross, Ohio, USA[4]. He died on 21 Aug 1891[4]. He married **MARY ELLEN VIRGINIA DECAMP** on 10 Oct 1861 in Middleton, Logan Co., Illinois[35], daughter of Parter DE CAMP and Kaziah HAINES. She was born on 29 May 1843 in Illinois, USA. She died on 10 May 1917 in Raymond, Pacific, Washington, USA.

John M. RICHHART and Mary Ellen Virginia DE CAMP had the following children:

i. MALINDA C.[5] RICHHART[35] was born in 1862 in Logan, Illinois, USA. She died in 1888 in Madriver Township, Ohio.

ii. HIRAM RICHHART[35] was born about 1864.

iii. FREDRICK RICHHART[35] was born in 1865 in Yellow Bud, Ross Co., Ohio.

iv. JOHN PHILLIP RICHHART[35] was born on 11 Sep 1867 in Yellow Bud, Ross Co., Ohio.

v. LUCY ELLEN RICHHART[35] was born on 09 Feb 1871 in Yellow Bud, Ross Co., Ohio.

vi. CHARLES LESLIE RICHHART[35] was born on 14 Nov 1874 in Yellow Bud, Ross Co., Ohio. He died in Dec 1941.

vii. MARIAN WALTER RICHHART[35] was born in 1876 in Yellow Bud, Ross Co., Ohio. He died in Mar 1878 in Pickaway, Ohio, USA.

viii. GEORGE WILLIAM RICHHART[35] was born on 17 Mar 1878 in Wayne, Pickaway, Ohio, USA. He died on 09 Oct 1959 in Phoenix, Maricopa, Arizona, USA. He married MABLE BERTHA KERSEY on 17 Aug 1904 in Vancouver, Clark, Washington, USA[35], daughter of Albert Henry KERSEY and Clara Ellen WRIGHT. She was born on 02 Nov 1888 in Camas, Clark, Washington, USA. She died on 28 Aug 1969 in Lowell, Penobscot, Maine, USA.

ix. CORA BEATRICE RICHHART[35] was born on 12 Mar 1881 in Pickaway, Ohio, USA.

Generation 5

21. **BENJAMIN ALLEN[5] RITCHHART** (Phillip[4], Christian[3] RITSCHARD, Christian[2] RITSCHARD, Christian[1] RITSCHHART).

Benjamin Allen RITCHHART had the following child:

    31   i. ALFRED OLIVR[6] RITCHHART.

22. **JACOB[5] RITCHHART** (Jacob[4], Jacob[3] RICHHART, Christian[2] RITSCHARD, Christian[1] RITSCHHART)[37] was born in Oct 1858 in Ohio, United States[37]. He died in 1940 in Ross, Ohio, USA. He married **EDNA JANE NEAL** on 03 Jan 1889 in Ross, Ohio, USA[21,36], daughter of James Monroe NEAL and Anna Mariah CAMPBELL. She was born in Feb 1866 in Lawrence, Lawrence, Ohio, United States[37]. She died on 05 Oct 1944 in Ross Co., OH[38].

Jacob RITCHHART and Edna Jane NEAL had the following children:

      i. EMMA[6] RITCHHART[37,65] was born in Dec 1889 in Ross, Ohio, USA[37]. She died on 15 Nov 1967 in Chillicothe, Ross, Ohio, USA[37].

    32   ii. HIRAM C. RITCHHART[8,37,65,66] was born on 19 Apr 1891 in Ross, Ohio, USA. He died on 15 Jul 1941 in Ross, Ohio, USA. He married EDITH JEANETTE ROLL in 1919 in Greenup, Kentucky, USA. She was born on 23 Aug 1891 in Ross, Ohio, USA. She died on 03 Jun 1977 in Ross, Ohio, USA.

      iii. MAE A. RITCHHART[37,65] was born in Nov 1893 in Ross, Ohio, USA. She died in 1967.

      iv. CLEO M. RITCHHART[37,65] was born on 19 Feb 1895 in Ross, Ohio, USA[37]. She died on 22 Jul 1948 in Ross, Ohio, USA[37]. She married UNK BOYLES.

      v. JACOB NEAL RITCHHART[37,65] was born in Dec 1898 in Ross, Ohio, USA. He died in 1954[37].

      vi. RUTH RITCHHART[37,65] was born in 1903 in Ross, Ohio, USA[37].

      vii. DOROTHY RITCHHART[37,65] was born on 14 Feb 1905 in Ross, Ohio, USA[37]. She died on 07 Sep 1987 in Chillicothe, Ross, Ohio, USA[37].

23. **IDA PENELOPE[5] RITCHHART** (Jacob[4], Jacob[3] RICHHART, Christian[2] RITSCHARD, Christian[1] RITSCHHART)[4,39,40] was born on 08 Feb 1862 in Andersonville, Ross, Ohio, USA[4]. She died on 15 Feb 1942 in Circleville, Pickaway, Ohio, USA[4]. She married **WILLIAM ELBRIDGE NORRIS** on 02 Sep 1880[4,36], son of John G NORRIS and Elizabeth BUXTON. He was born on 27 Mar 1860 (Monroe T, Perry Co., OH). He died on 08 Jan 1945 in Walnut, Pickaway, Ohio, USA.

Notes for Ida Penelope RITCHHART: On a couple census records, she was listed as Lovy, which I assume was a nickname.

William Elbridge NORRIS and Ida Penelope RITCHHART had the following children:

      i. CLARENCE ELBRIDGE[6] NORRIS[4] was born on 06 Aug 1881[4]. He died on 12 Apr 1975[4].

      ii. RAY RITCHART NORRIS[4] was born on 26 Apr 1883 in Ross, Ohio, USA[4]. She died on 18 Apr 1885 in Ross, Ohio, USA[4].

    iii. BERTHA ELIZABETH NORRIS[4] was born on 07 Oct 1884 in Ross, Ohio, USA[4]. She died on 04 Apr 1886 in Ross, Ohio, USA[4].

    iv. HOMER GLADSTONE NORRIS[4] was born on 15 Jan 1887 in Ross, Ohio, USA[4]. He died on 28 Aug 1918 in Ross, Ohio, USA[4].

    v. LEONA ALICE NORRIS[4] was born on 25 Feb 1889 in Ross, Ohio, USA[4]. She died on 21 Mar 1936 in Jackson, Jackson, Michigan, USA[4].

    vi. JESSIE MAY NORRIS[4] was born on 14 Mar 1891 in Ross, Ohio, USA[4]. She died on 08 Nov 1982 in Circleville, Pickaway, Ohio, USA[4].

    vii. FLORENCE ELIZABETH NORRIS[4] was born on 26 Jan 1893 in Ross, Ohio, USA[4]. She died on 19 Apr 1975 in Little Walnut, Pickaway, Ohio, USA[4].

    viii. TERESA SCIOTO NORRIS[4] was born on 10 Feb 1895[4]. She died on 25 Jul 1973 in Cheverly, Prince George's, Maryland, USA[4].

    ix. WILLIAM WALDO NORRIS[4] was born on 20 Jan 1898 in Ross, Ohio, USA[4]. He died on 12 Apr 1976 in Columbus, Franklin, Ohio, USA[4].

    x. ELSIE MARIE NORRIS[4] was born on 28 Sep 1899 in Ross, Ohio, USA[4]. She died on 11 Jun 1923 in Washington, Pickaway, Ohio, USA[4].

    xi. HOWARD BUXTON NORRIS[4] was born on 23 Jan 1902 in Ross, Ohio, USA[4]. He died on 23 May 1995 in Circleville, Pickaway, Ohio, USA[4].

    xii. ROBERT EARL NORRIS[4] was born on 26 Sep 1903 in Ross, Ohio, USA[4]. He died on 10 Aug 1992 in Columbus, Franklin, Ohio, USA[4].

24. **FLORA ALICE[5] DAVENPORT** (Penelope[4] RITCHHART, Jacob[3] RICHHART, Christian[2] RITSCHARD, Christian[1] RITSCHHART)[42] was born in 1850 in Ohio, USA[42]. She married **JOHN TOLMAN MACK**. He was born in 1847 in New York, USA[42].

John Tolman MACK and Flora Alice DAVENPORT had the following children:

    i. JOHN D.[6] MACK[42] was born in 1875 in Ohio, USA[42].

    ii. ALICE R. MACK[42] was born in 1877 in Ohio, USA[42].

    iii. ETHEL B. MACK[42] was born in 1879 in Ohio, USA[42].

25. **IDA[5] PINTO** (Elizabeth[4] RITCHHART, Jacob[3] RICHHART, Christian[2] RITSCHARD, Christian[1] RITSCHHART) was born about 1852 in Ross, Ohio, USA[5]. She married **JOHN FENTON**.

John FENTON and Ida PINTO had the following child:

    i. MARSHALL[6] FENTON[8].

26. **SAMUEL[5] PINTO** (Elizabeth[4] RITCHHART, Jacob[3] RICHHART, Christian[2] RITSCHARD, Christian[1] RITSCHHART) was born about 1853 in Ross, Ohio, USA[8]. He married **SARAH O**.

Samuel PINTO and Sarah O had the following children:

    i. BESSIE[6] PINTO[8].

    ii. WILLIAM PINTO[8].

    iii. SAMUEL PINTO[8].

iv. LETRIN PINTO[8].

27. **WILLIAM**[5] **RICHHART** (Samuel B.[4] RITCHHART, John[3] RITCHHART, Christian[2] RITSCHARD, Christian[1] RITSCHHART)[24]. He died in 1869 in Hamilton, Indiana, USA[24]. He married (1) **MARGARET LAYTON**. He married (2) Mrs. **COLBURN**.

William RICHHART and Margaret LAYTON had the following children:

33   i. ELI A.[6] RICHHART[24] was born on 15 Nov 1859[24]. He married ELLEN LAUDIG in 1880 in Hamilton, Indiana, USA[24], daughter of Jonas LAUDIG and Catherine CAYLOR.

   ii. SAMUEL E. RITCHHART[24].

   iii. MARY RITCHHART[24].

   iv. WILLIAM RITCHHART[24].

   v. NANCY RITCHHART[24].

28. **WESLEY**[5] **RITCHHART** (Andrew[4], John[3], Christian[2] RITSCHARD, Christian[1] RITSCHHART)[43,44,45,46,47,48,49,50] was born on 30 Jun 1842 in Noblesville, Hamilton, Indiana, USA[51]. He died on 23 Mar 1921 (S Maple Carthage, Missouri)[4,52]. He married (1) **MARIA SIBILLA WAGNER** on 20 Dec 1866 in Noblesville, Hamilton, Indiana, USA[53], daughter of Michael WAGNER and Harreata Aena GOLDMAN. She was born on 11 May 1840 in Brownsville, Union, Indiana, USA[54]. She died on 20 Jan 1916 (Carthage, Jasper, Missouri, USA)[51]. He married (2) **MARY FRYE** on 06 Nov 1917 (Carthage, MO after death of first wife), daughter of UNK and UNKNOWN. She was born in 1851 in Illinois, USA[55].

Notes for Wesley RITCHHART: Served in the Indiana Regiment for four years. Spent two years in the infantry and two in the calvary, where he learned to be a veterinarian. According to obituary was with General Sherman on his famous "march to the sea," and was in two Kilpatrick raids—the Rusaw raid and the McCook raid. In Ancestry.com located his civil War Pension Request (image 1542) dated Mar 1, 1880 (served 1861–65). Application no. 347527, Certificate No. 288630. It appears he was in the Indiana 39th Inf, 8th Cavalry. He enlisted on Aug 31, 1861 in Indianapolis. He reenlisted on February 19, 1864. Mustered out July 20, 1865.

Had nine children by Mary Wagner, seven of whom survived him. Had a farm northeast of town, but moved to Carthage in his later years. After Mary Wagner died in Jan 1916, he remarried Mary H. Sanders in Nov 1917.

The obituary commented that he was, "A man of high integrity, loyal to his friends, of sterling worth as a citizen. Wesley Ritchhart was an exemplary citizen. His sons are all men of standing in the communities in which they live, showing the careful home training given by their father."

Photo of tombstone indicates born in 1841; but Bettye Richhart's book indicates born in 1842. His Civil War Pension shows that he turned 70 in 1912, thus his correct birthdate should be 1842. Also his pension application has his DOB as 1842.

1920 Census reflects Wesley at age 77 in Jasper County, Missouri. Roll T625-922, Pg 6B, Ed: 86, Image 908. Source genealogy.com search. It indicated that he rented his home.

Must have moved to Carthage in 1887 according to his wife's obituary data.

Have a copy of the bill for his burial from the Knell Undertaking Co. It totals $253 with the biggest part being $185 for the casket.

Was admitted from Jan 1918 to July 1919 to the U.S. National Home for Disabled Volunteer Soldiers in the Los Angeles area for prostate problems and arteriosclerosis. His wife Mary stayed in San Diego, probably with her son, Orville, who lived there. The home was in Sawtelle, which was between Santa Monica and Culver City. It is no longer listed as a separate city; but was more likely an area. The National Homes for Disabled Volunteer Soldiers was instituted following the Civil War. The purpose of these homes was to provide a place for disabled American soldiers and sailors to live. Admission to a home was voluntary and soldiers could request which home they wanted to live in. Since admission was voluntary, soldiers could also choose when they wanted to leave, both temporarily and permanently. There were twelve of these homes throughout the U.S. There was one in Illinois, which would have been closer, but they probably chose to come to California because their son was nearby in San Diego.

Notes for Maria Sibilla WAGNER: Orville Ritchhart's 1920 Census form indicated his mother was born in Pennsylvania. However, other records indicate she was born in Indiana. The Jan 7/8, 1920 Census for Jasper County, Carthage, MO indicated Mary and her parents were born in Illinois. Her obituary indicated she had lived in Jasper county for 29 years and in Carthage for 15 of those years. Thus, she must have moved there in 1887.

Wesley RITCHHART and Maria Sibilla WAGNER had the following children:

34   i.   ALONZO FRANCIS[6] RITCHHART[4,52,67,68,69,70,71,72,73,74,75,76,77] was born on 03 Nov 1867 in Indiana, USA[67]. He died on 27 May 1959 in Stanislaus, California, USA[52,67]. He married GRACE AZETTA BUSH on 01 Jan 1902 in La Junta, Otero, Colorado, USA (5 p.m. wedding followed by dinner)[78], daughter of Samuel Shelton BUSH and Lillian Perdida LOGSDON. She was born on 17 Nov 1879 in Carthage, Jasper, Missouri, USA[4,69,77,79,80,81,82,83,84]. She died on 28 Jan 1952 in La Junta, Otero, Colorado, USA[4,83,84].

35   ii.   ALVIN E. RITCHHART[85,86,87,88,89] was born on 06 Sep 1870 in Hamilton, Indiana, USA[90]. He died on 05 Sep 1951 (Carthage, Jasper Co., Missouri). He married HATTIE MAY CARR on 09 Mar 1892, daughter of William Winston CARR and Martha Emily ARRINGTON. She was born on 09 May 1873 in Jasper, Missouri, USA[91]. She died on 22 Oct 1948 in Jasper, Missouri, USA[11,88,89,90,92].

36   iii.   CURTIS ANDREW RITCHHART[51,93,94] was born on 05 Sep 1871 in Noblesville, Hamilton, Indiana, USA[54]. He died on 08 Jan 1942 in Madison, Jasper, Missouri, USA (Buried in Oak Hill Cemetery)[54]. He married PEARL BURDETTE PENNY on 19 Dec 1895 (Bride's Parents' home in Carthage, MO (8 P.M.)[11,54,95], daughter of Orsmus Nelson PENNEY and Eliza Althea TAYLOR. She was born on 24 Feb 1875 in Licking, Ohio, USA[54,96]. She died on 01 Dec 1946 (Carthage, Jasper Co., Missouri)[54].

37 iv. FRANKLIN LESTER RITCHHART[97] was born on 19 Mar 1873 in Noblesville, Hamilton, Indiana, USA[97,98,99,100,101,102]. He died on 25 Mar 1955 (Carthage, Jasper Co., Missouri). He married ADA CHARLOTTE CARR on 23 Jan 1898 (Home of bride's parents in Carthage, Missouri), daughter of William Winston CARR and Martha Emily ARRINGTON. She was born on 02 Nov 1880 in Carthage, Jasper, Missouri, USA[100,102,103]. She died on 22 Mar 1951 in Carthage, Jasper, Missouri, USA[92].

v. SANFORD OSCAR RITCHHART[104] was born on 27 Feb 1875 in Noblesville, Hamilton, Indiana, USA[104]. He died on 13 Sep 1959 in Los Angeles, California, USA[105,106]. He married MARY about 1927. She was born about 1877 in California.

Notes for Sanford Oscar RITCHHART: The California Voter Registration Index had Sanford in Coalinga, CA when he was 29 years old. That equates to 1904/05. The 1920 Federal Census had him in Tehachapi, CA (40 mi SE of Bakersfield). It indicated that he rented his home and was single. On his WW I draft registration in September 1918 his occupation was laborer on the Southern Pacific RR. I would assume that he was doing the same when he was in Mojave in 1916; but that the RR work moved westward toward Tehachapi and he moved there to continue working on the RR.

vi. ORVILLE G. RITCHHART[107] was born on 26 Mar 1877 in Noblesville, Hamilton, Indiana, USA. He died on 06 Mar 1932. He married CLARE E. *. She was born in 1877 in Canada.

Notes for Orville G. RITCHHART: 1920 Federal Census showed him in San Diego, CA. It indicated he owned his home at 3984 Illinois St. He was a journeyman plumber.

vii. ARYD RITCHHART[108] was born on 26 Mar 1877. She died on 17 Aug 1877 (believe died at birth as twin of Orville)[108].

Notes for Aryd RITCHHART: A letter from Kathleen Bridges to Dean Ritchhart in 1992 listed notes from the diary of her great grandfather. In those notes Aryd was listed as Aryaette (not sure about spelling—diary hard to read) with a date of 26 March, 1877 and that he was the twin of Orville. However, other sources list Aryd's birthday as Feb 1875 which is Sanford's birthday. It is likely he was a twin of Orville's; but that he died about 6 months after their birth.

viii. FREDDIA W. RITCHHART[109] was born on 24 Sep 1881. He died on 18 May 1884.

Notes for Freddia W. RITCHHART: Previous records listed name as Frd? and as a son. The journal of Michael Wagner listed as Freddia (son).

38 ix. HARRY ELMER RITCHHART[110,111,112] was born on 27 Nov 1884 in Indiana, USA[110]. He died on 12 Apr 1954[108]. He married (1) MARIL BETH HOUSTON on 20 Sep 1904 in Carthage, Jasper, Missouri, USA[113], daughter of * HOUSTON and Sadie *. She was born in 1885 in Ohio, USA[114].

Notes for Mary FRYE: The 1920 census shows that Mary's parents were both born in Illinois.

29. **CHARLES**[5] **RITCHHART** (Andrew[4], John[3], Christian[2] RITSCHARD, Christian[1] RITSCHHART)[14,57,58,59,60,61,62] was born on 16 Apr 1853 in Noblesville, Hamilton, Indiana, USA[14,18,60]. He died on 11 Oct 1931 in Noblesville, Hamilton, Indiana, USA[18]. He married **MARIAH GEORGE** on 13 Feb 1887 in Noblesville, Hamilton, Indiana, USA[18], daughter of James GEORGE and Maranda SINCLAIR. She was born about 1855 in Indiana, USA[63]. She died on 03 Dec 1940 in Noblesville, Hamilton, Indiana, USA.

Notes for Charles RITCHHART:
Charles was living in the adjacent farm to his father, Andrew, in the 1880 Census. Just up the road was living George Wagner, whose wife was married to his brother, Wesley. Charles was named as co-executor of his father's will along with William Booth. Andrew's wife's maiden name was Booth, so William was probably a brother or other close relative. Notes for Mariah GEORGE: The 1880 Federal Census for Noblesville included Mariah's sister in her household. She was May George, age 35, listed as a servant. However, I don't find a May George listed in any other census.

Charles RITCHHART and Mariah GEORGE had the following children:

    i. MARY[6] RITCHHART was born in 1877 in Indiana, USA.

39 ii. EARL RITCHHART[115,116] was born about 1881 in Indiana, USA[115]. He married EMMA P. FISHER on 26 Sep 1906 in Hamilton, Indiana, USA[116]. She was born about 1885 in Indiana, USA[115].

    iii. CECILE RITCHHART. She married JAMES C. ESSINGTON on 31 Aug 1898 in Hamilton, Indiana, USA[59].

30. **WILLIAM Z.**[5] **RICHHART** (William[4] RITCHHART, Heinrich (Henry)[3] RITSCHARD, Christian[2] RITSCHARD, Christian[1] RITSCHHART)[64] was born on 12 May 1857 in Morgan, Illinois, USA. He married **MARY ELIZABETH TOLLY** on 19 Nov 1879 in Shelby, Illinois, USA. She was born on 07 May 1860 in Illinois, USA.

William Z. RICHHART and Mary Elizabeth TOLLY had the following child:

40 i. LEVI WILLIAM[6] RICHHART was born on 20 Oct 1880 in Macon, Illinois, USA. He died on 17 Jul 1937 in Fort Worth, Tarrant, Texas, USA. He married LELA ARMFIELD PLYLER on 20 Feb 1901 in Acadia Co., LA. She was born on 23 Oct 1876 in Statesville, Iredell Co., North Carolina.

Generation 6

31. **ALFRED OLIVR**[6] **RITCHHART** (Benjamin Allen[5], Phillip[4], Christian[3] RITSCHARD, Christian[2] RITSCHARD, Christian[1] RITSCHHART).

Alfred Olivr RITCHHART had the following child:

41 i. WARREN HARRY[7] RITCHHART.

32. **HIRAM C.**[6] **RITCHHART** (Jacob[5], Jacob[4], Jacob[3] RICHHART, Christian[2] RITSCHARD, Christian[1] RITSCHHART)[8,37,65,66] was born on 19 Apr 1891 in Ross, Ohio, USA. He died on 15 Jul 1941 in Ross, Ohio, USA. He married **EDITH JEANETTE ROLL** in 1919 in Greenup,

Kentucky, USA. She was born on 23 Aug 1891 in Ross, Ohio, USA. She died on 03 Jun 1977 in Ross, Ohio, USA.

Notes for Hiram C. RITCHHART: Apparently Hiram inherited the farm on Stone Rd. from his Uncle Hiram, who had no children. This piece of land is part of the original patented land that immigrant Christian bought in 1797. This land is described in the 1900 Census as being in North Union, lying north and east of the Clarksburg Pike. Descendants of Hiram were still farming the land in July 1999 when Joanne and I visited there. The house built by Hiram was occupied by Wayne, Renick, and Floyd. Wayne later died on Sep 17, 2000. He was ill and not at the home when we were there. We visited with Renick and Floyd was delivering hay the day we were there. Despite the fact they were 76 and 72 they were still actively farming. The land had been farmed and owned by Ritchharts for 202 years.

Notes for Edith Jeanette ROLL: I note that Edith is listed with two different middle names. I am guessing they are both correct. I will bet she went by Janet or preferred it. Janet is also shorter for carving on a headstone than Jeanette!

Hiram C. RITCHHART and Edith Jeanette ROLL had the following children:

    i. PEARL[7] RITCHHART[117] was born on 05 Nov 1918 in Chillicothe, Ross, Ohio, USA. She married UNK SHEWALTER.

    Notes for Pearl RITCHHART: Joanne and I met Pearl in July 1999 when we stopped in Chillicothe to visit the Ritchhart farm and meet with Daniel, Renick, Floyd and Fred Ritchhart. I can't remember for sure, but believe it was Nelson Ritchhart and his wife whom we also met. They were living in the Ritchhart farmhouse, whereas Renick and Floyd lived in another farmhouse just up the road.

    ii. WAYNE RITCHHART[117,118,119,120] was born on 27 Jun 1921[120]. He died on 17 Sep 2000 (Chillicothe, Ross, Ohio, USA)[118,120].

    iii. RENICK R. RITCHHART[121] was born on 06 Dec 1923 in Ross, Ohio, USA[121]. He died on 19 Dec 2004 in Piketon, Pike, Ohio, USA[120,121].

    Notes for Renick R. RITCHHART: We met Renick in July 1999 in a meeting arranged by Renick's nephew Daniel. He lived just down the road from the "Ritchhart" farm house that was on the original property. His brothers Floyd and Wayne lived with him in the house. All three were still single and were in their late 70s and still working. Floyd was delivering some grain and we didn't get to meet him. Wayne was ill and in the hospital. Wayne later passed away. Renick's youngest brother, Fred, lived just down the road in a little house directly across the road from a small one room schoolhouse which the Ritchharts had all attended. Fred gave us a tour or the school. About half mile back toward the main road Nelson and his wife lived in the Ritchhart farmhouse just across from the Original farmhouse. I took photos of both. Thus there were three farm houses within about a mile—all on land that the Christian Ritschhard purchased when he moved to Ohio late in the 1700s. The land has since been broken up; but Ritchharts still lived in two of the houses when we were there. Fred lived in a small house (4th) on the same Stone Road.

He was a U.S. Army veteran, serving as a Military Police Officer during WW II. He graduated in 1941 from Union Scioto High School.

    iv. JOHN RITCHHART[117,119] was born on 27 Mar 1925.

    v. FLOYD N. RITCHHART[118] was born on 30 Nov 1927[118]. He died on 25 Nov 2001 (Chillicothe, Ross Co., Ohio)[118].

42 vi. NELSON J. RITCHHART[8,117] was born on 11 Jan 1930. He married BEATRICE IRENE ARLEDGE on 07 Sep 1963, daughter of Harold Woodrow ARLEDGE and Helen *. She was born on 27 May 1943.

43 vii. CHARLES I. RITCHHART[117] was born on 15 Jan 1932 in Ross, Ohio, USA.

    viii. FRED M. RITCHHART[117] was born on 25 May 1935. He married (1) THERESA MARIA WEISENBERGER, daughter of Joseph WIESENBERGER and MARY. She was born on 22 Jul 1947[122]. She died on 21 Apr 2006 in Flagstaff, Coconino, Arizona, USA[122]. He married (2) JOYCE.

Notes for Fred M. RITCHHART: We met and talked at length with Fred in July 1999 when we were in Chillicothe. He had come back a year or so earlier from teaching for years on an Indian reservation in Kayenta, Arizona. He was the youngest of 7 boys and 1 girl. With his return it meant that all 8 of the children were living in Chillicothe, where they were born. Fred had been married twice, Tess and Joyce.

33. **ELI A.[6] RICHHART** (William[5], Samuel B.[4] RITCHHART, John[3] RITCHHART, Christian[2] RITSCHARD, Christian[1] RITSCHHART)[24] was born on 15 Nov 1859[24]. He married **ELLEN LAUDIG** in 1880 in Hamilton, Indiana, USA[24], daughter of Jonas LAUDIG and Catherine CAYLOR.

Notes for Eli A. RICHHART: Eli and Ellen lived for 26 years in Fall Creek Township, Madison County, Indiana. Then moved into a splendid farm house that he built on their 150 acre farm in adjoining Hancock County. They belonged to the United Brethren Church of Mt. Gilead.

Eli A. RICHHART and Ellen LAUDIG had the following children:

    i. WILLIAM S.[7] RICHHART[24]. He married LOLA REDDICK.

    ii. JONAS F. RICHHART[24].

    iii. CLARA M. RICHHART[24].

    iv. RUTH RICHHART[24]. She married LEO NOLAND.

    v. PAUL D. RICHHART[24]. He died before 1917 in Hamilton, Indiana, USA[24].

34. **ALONZO FRANCIS[6] RITCHHART** (Wesley[5], Andrew[4], John[3], Christian[2] RITSCHARD, Christian[1] RITSCHHART)[4,52,67,68,69,70,71,72,73,74,75,76,77] was born on 03 Nov 1867 in Indiana, USA[67]. He died on 27 May 1959 in Stanislaus, California, USA[52,67]. He married **GRACE AZETTA BUSH** on 01 Jan 1902 in La Junta, Otero, Colorado, USA (5 p.m. wedding followed by dinner)[78], daughter of Samuel Shelton BUSH and Lillian Perdida LOGSDON. She was born on 17 Nov 1879 in Carthage, Jasper, Missouri, USA[4,69,77,79,80,81,82,83,84]. She died on 28 Jan 1952 in La Junta, Otero, Colorado, USA[4,83,84].

Notes for Alonzo Francis RITCHHART: Clifford Ritchhart's family history listed his father's name as Alonzo Francis vice Frank. Interestingly, Alonzo and Grace had a child who died in infancy whose name was listed on his headstone as Frances (actual name Adell Frances). Some sources, including his obituary, listed his birthdate as November 5, 1867, but his father's Civil War pension and a journal kept by Michael Wagner (his grandfather on his mother's side) show it as Nov 3.

Clifford Ritchhart claimed that the family moved from Indiana to Missouri in the early 1880's.

Alonzo moved to Colorado with the Bush family. Shortly after that they were married in La Junta. They moved back to Carthage in late 1908–early 1909, when Clifford was about five. Paul was born in May 1908 in La Junta, thus the reason I say it must have been late 1908. They only stayed about two years and then moved back to La Junta. This was probably in 1911, as my dad was born in Carthage in Nov 1910, and I imagine they would have waited a few months before traveling across country with a new baby.

After moving back to La Junta they homesteaded southeast of La Junta. After homesteading about three years, they sold the property and moved back into town. It is interesting, however, that the land patent in Bent County was dated 1919. I am speculating that didn't actually file for the patent until they were getting ready to sell the property. They lived in La Junta until Grandma died. Grandpa then went to California to live with his daughter, Lillian, in Modesto until he passed away. However, he must have come back once to visit because I recall going to a football game with my dad and he when my brother Dean was playing for Las Animas and I was in college. That would have been in 1955 or 1956.

I recall my grandfather at the age of about 78 (when I was about 8) as being a very stern old German. He would laugh occasionally, but don't think he was particularly tolerant of young kids in his older age. He was hard of hearing and would sit next to the radio to listen to the news with his ear up very close to the speaker and his hand behind his ear acting like a reflector. A young boy we played with when we visited lived directly across the street and was always scared to death of our grandpa and never wanted to play in our yard. Thus, we always played at his house which was great because he had lots of toys—a big treat for us.

To supplement his income Grandpa had a single coin-operated gas pump on the back portion of the property for several years. There was a bell to ring if a customer needed help. My brother and I could never resist ringing the bell which annoyed my grandpa because he would come out expecting to see a customer. We knew we shouldn't ring the bell; but it was always too big a temptation for 5 and 8 year olds!

We liked going to visit because the La Junta Creamery was next door where they made and sold ice cream. We would always pester mom and dad until they gave us five cents to get an ice cream cone. That didn't usually come until we had gotten the "We're not made of money and it doesn't grow on trees" lecture. Then came the big decision as to which flavor. I recall lemon and banana as being my favorites.

Grandpa would usually walk down to the park in the middle of town every morning to sit on the bench and chat with his "old cronies," who also congregated there each day. It was only about a two-block walk. As I recall he would be there an hour or two and then come on back home for lunch. He had a cane, which had white and black on it to signify a blind person or person with poor sight. Grandpa always used a straight edge razor to shave and would hone it with a leather strap. He also had a harmonica, which my brother and I always liked to play with. I assumed grandpa played it, but don't ever recall hearing him play.

I don't think my grandparents ever had a car. They had horse and buggies when they first moved to La Junta and while on the homestead, but I don't think they ever had a car when they moved into town.

We didn't spend a lot of time with Grandma and Grandpa Ritchhart because we didn't live in La Lunta, we lived in California and Oklahoma during my 1st and 2nd grade years, my folks divorced near the end of my 3rd grade year, and grandma died when I was 15. We lived in La Junta my 4th and 5th grade years after my folks separated and Dean and I did see them some when my dad would pick us up and take us to their home.

Notes for Grace Azetta BUSH: Grace moved with her parents from Carthage, MO to La Junta, CO in the fall of 1901 according to the wedding announcement in the Carthage newspaper. According to the written accounts of Clifford Ritchhart, Alonzo accompanied the Bushes to Colorado to help them move because of his attraction to Grace. I would also assume they must have had some wedding plans since they were married within about 4–5 months of moving to Colorado.

Dean and I always liked our Grandma Ritchhart. She was always very good to us and a very kind person. She worked part-time at the swimming pool, which was about a half-mile walk from their home. We always liked to go with her to work because we got to swim free. This was in a time when there were no private swimming pools and only a few of the larger towns had a pool. We never got a pool in Las Animas until I was in high school. We would go with her when she opened the pool, spend all day swimming and then go home with her. I recall when I first learned to swim I could only swim underwater. The shallow area of the pool was separated from the deep area by metal bars with a separation between them. Being very small, I could swim between the bars from one area into the other. In hindsight that was a very dangerous design because, potentially, people could get stuck between the bars and drown.

As long as I can remember Grandma cooked on a coal-burning stove with an oven. She was a very good cook; but food was always very basic—mostly meat and potatoes, with some chicken now and then. Whenever she made potatoes, mashed or boiled, they were always mixed with turnips. I think this came from their German heritage. They had a built-in booth in the kitchen where we ate if there was only three or four of us. Otherwise, we sat around the dining room table. The house only had five rooms. Two bedrooms, a living room (which when their kids lived at home was used as a bedroom), dining room and kitchen. They had an outhouse for several years; but later got indoor plumbing and a bathroom.

As far as I know Grandma and Grandpa never owned a car. They lived within about two blocks of downtown where they could walk to get groceries and do other shopping. I think

Grandma even walked to the Methodist church, where she was very active. I imagine friends would drive them if that was required. When they lived on the homestead, a horse, or horse and buggy was their transportation. They never had much money and their only child to go to college was my dad, who got a football scholarship. I recall that both Grandma and Grandpa had false teeth, which was very common for people in those days.

Alonzo Francis RITCHHART and Grace Azetta BUSH had the following children:

44   i. SAMUEL CLIFFORD[7] RITCHHART was born on 31 May 1903 in Rocky Ford, Otero, Colorado, USA[68]. He died on 09 Aug 1989 in Canon City, Fremont, Colorado, USA. He married MARIANNA EVALINA GLATZ on 16 Sep 1926 in La Junta, Otero, Colorado, USA, daughter of Edward William GLATZ and Emma Elizabeth HERWIG. She was born on 02 Jan 1908[120]. She died on 29 Oct 1990 in Murfreesboro, Rutherford, Tennessee, USA[120].

45   ii. MARY LILLIAN RITCHHART[123,124] was born on 16 Jan 1906 in La Junta, Otero, Colorado, USA[124,125]. She died on 28 Jan 1983 in Sacramento, Sacramento, California, USA[126]. She married JAMES RUMSBY about 1923[127], son of James RUMSBY and Louie KIMBALL. He was born on 01 Apr 1902 in Colorado, USA[128,129]. He died on 19 Jan 1983 in Sacramento, California, USA[128,129].

46   iii. PAUL WESLEY RITCHHART[4,69,130,131] was born on 26 May 1908 in La Junta, Otero, Colorado, USA[131,132]. He died in Jun 1964 in Wyoming, USA[133]. He married (1) INEZ JOSEPHINE RITTER about 1930 in Colorado, USA, daughter of Carl Burch RITTER and Dell Reynolds PORTER. She was born on 17 Feb 1908 in Colorado, USA[134]. She died on 06 Dec 1963 in Phoenix, Maricopa, Arizona, USA. He married (2) SUSIE SANTA DELORENZO on 29 Dec 1951[135]. She was born on 02 Sep 1911 in La Junta, Otero, Colorado, USA[4,136]. She died on 03 Feb 1988 in La Junta, Otero, Colorado, USA[137].

47   iv. DELBERT BUSH RITCHHART[69,79,138] was born on 02 Nov 1910 (Carthage, Missouri)[69,70,79,84]. He died on 18 Feb 1981 in Denver, Colorado, USA[84]. He married HELEN JANE DEAN on 01 Aug 1952 in Raton, Colfax, New Mexico, USA (Remarried)[139], daughter of Arthur Spear DEAN and Mary Loretta O'MALLEY. She was born on 06 Aug 1915 in Denver, Adams, Colorado, USA (2:53 p.m., St. Joseph's Hospital)[140,141,142,143]. She died on 28 Oct 1995 in Loveland, Larimer, Colorado, USA[137,142,144].

    v. ADELL FRANCES RITCHHART[4] was born in Apr 1915 in La Junta, Otero, Colorado, USA. She died on 01 Jan 1916 (Died as young child prior to 1st birthday.)[145].

Notes for Adell Frances RITCHHART: Cemetery plot records indicate "Frances Ritchhart died 1/1/1916 and was buried on 11/15/1944." Later analysis indicates that she was buried (probably right after her death) in a lot owned by Lester Bush, Grace's brother, and then moved to its present location in Nov 1944. Grandma Ritchhart's obituary indicated she was preceded in death by "a daughter Adell Frances Ritchhart. Adell died in April of 1915." Since plot records show her death as 1/1/1916 and I know from other sources that she was less than 1 year old, I am speculating that she was born in April 1915 rather than that being her death date. Her head stone also reads "1915–1916" which also indicates she was born in 1915.

vi. BETTY JANE RITCHHART was born on 04 Jul 1919 in La Junta, Otero, Colorado, USA[79,146,147]. She died on 04 May 1993 in Newark, New Castle, Delaware, USA[148]. She married (1) JOHN T. LINEHAN on 04 May 1945[149], son of Joseph Aloysius LINEHAN and Mary Louise HOLMES. He was born in 1920 in Seymour, New Haven, Connecticut, USA. She married (2) BILLY GLENN about 1939.

Notes for Betty Jane RITCHHART: Betty first married Billy Glenn, also from La Junta. During the war he was sent to Panama with the engineers (I speculate it might have been the Sea Bees). According to Margaret Rumsby Barton, Betty had to qualify for a Civil Service job before she could join him in Panama. She later qualified and went to Panama. Margaret said she thought Betty had a miscarriage while in Panama and that contributed to their later divorce. Then in 1945 she married Jack Linehan. Joanne and I once stopped and saw Betty and Jack in Newark, Delaware in 1964, when I was going to Intelligence school at Anacostia in the D.C. area.

I had her birth year listed as 1916 initially, but the *Social Security Death Index* indicated 1919 and the 1930 Census data and her obituary confirm 1919. Betty never had any children from either marriage.

According to her obituary, "Betty J. Linehan, former editor of *Delaware Woman*, the Business & Professional Women of Delaware's magazine, died Tuesday of cancer at home. Mrs. Linehan, 73, of 38 Augusta Drive, Chestnut Hill Estates, and Bailey Island near Brunswick, Maine, was active in the businesswomen's organization for several years and was magazine editor for three years. She operated a Vanda Beauty Counselor cosmetics franchise and recruited, trained and supervised 130 women in Delaware and the vicinity. Mrs. Linehan had worked for U.S. Geological Survey in Newark for several years and was a saleswoman at Strawbridge & Clothier at Christiana Mall for the past year. She and her husband, John T., a bird expert and biologist, led ecology trips for the past 20 years to South and Central America, Africa, Europe and throughout the United States. She was active in Beta Sigma Phi sorority and was its 1969 Girl of the Year. During WW II, she was a civilian supply officer for the Navy in Panama. She spent six months of each of the last 12 years on Bailey Island. She was a member of Holy Family Catholic Church, Newark. She is survived by her husband of 48 years, and a niece... Burial will be in Delaware Veterans Memorial Cemetery, Chesapeake City Road, Summit."

According to a letter from Jack to Ken Ritchhart, Betty lost her speech in 1983 due to throat cancer. They later discovered she also had lung cancer and successfully operated on one lung. However, they later detected it in the other lung, about 9 months before she passed away (on their 48th wedding anniversary).

35. **ALVIN E.**[6] **RITCHHART** (Wesley[5], Andrew[4], John[3], Christian[2] RITSCHARD, Christian[1] RITSCHHART)[85,86,87,88,89] was born on 06 Sep 1870 in Hamilton, Indiana, USA[90]. He died on 05 Sep 1951 (Carthage, Jasper Co., Missouri). He married **HATTIE MAY CARR** on 09 Mar 1892, daughter of William Winston CARR and Martha Emily ARRINGTON. She was born on 09 May 1873 in Jasper, Missouri, USA[91]. She died on 22 Oct 1948 in Jasper, Missouri, USA[11,88,89,90,92].

Notes for Alvin E. RITCHHART: Alvin was Grandpa Ritchhart's brother. I took a photo of his headstone when I visited Carthage, MO in July 1999. We were met at Fasken Cemetery by Ray and Paul Ritchhart. Also there was their Aunt Bernice, who was their dad's sister. Dorothy (Compton) Rees was also there. She was a cousin to Ray and Paul. Dorothy's mother was also a sister of Aunt Bernice and to Ray and Paul's father, Lester. They showed us through the Cemetery and then we took them all to lunch in Carthage. They told us about the Precious Memories Chapel and grounds so we toured there before heading back to Branson.

Alvin E. RITCHHART and Hattie May CARR had the following children:

48　i.　PURL FLOYD[7] RITCHHART[137,150,151,152] was born on 17 Jul 1893 (Carthage, Missouri)[152]. He died in Aug 1975 in Forsyth, Taney, Missouri, USA[137]. He married (1) ELIZABETH *. He married (2) LAURA PERRY on 03 Nov 1929 (Carthage, Jasper, Missouri)[153].

　　ii.　EDITH C. RITCHHART[85,154] was born on 18 Jan 1896 (Carthage, Missouri)[154,155]. She died on 01 Jul 1994 in Garden City, Cherokee, Kansas, USA. She married CLYDE L. WRIGHT on 30 Jun 1925 (Carthage, MO)[156]. He died on 10 Mar 1984 in Garden City, Cherokee, Kansas, USA[156].

　　Notes for Edith C RITCHHART: According to her niece, Kathleen Bridges, Edyth moved to La Junta because of allergies. She lived in a boarding house there and met Clyde, who was with the Santa Fe RR and also living in the boarding house. They later married and lived in the same house on San Juan avenue for 52 years until she moved to Garden City in 1979. In 1992 she was 96 and lived in a retirement home in Garden City, Kansas.

49　iii.　ETHEL GRACE RITCHHART[89,157] was born in Mar 1898 in Missouri, U.S.A[89]. She died in 1960[89,90]. She married BENTON ELVIS CEARNAL on 22 Jun 1924 in Jasper[157]. He was born on 24 Nov 1896[89]. He died in Jan 1972 in Joplin, Jasper, Missouri, USA[89].

　　iv.　CLARENCE HEBER RITCHHART[137] was born in 1900 in Missouri, USA[85,85,154,158]. He died on 27 Feb 1990 in Anderson, McDonald, Missouri, USA[137]. He married EFFIE EULELLIE BASTIN on 27 Jan 1923 in Jasper[159].

　　v.　GLEN W. RITCHHART[85,86] was born in 1913 in Missouri, USA[85,86,87,154].

36. **CURTIS ANDREW**[6] **RITCHHART** (Wesley[5], Andrew[4], John[3], Christian[2] RITSCHARD, Christian[1] RITSCHHART)[51,93,94] was born on 05 Sep 1871 in Noblesville, Hamilton, Indiana, USA[54]. He died on 08 Jan 1942 in Madison, Jasper, Missouri, USA (Buried in Oak Hill Cemetery)[54]. He married **PEARL BURDETTE PENNY** on 19 Dec 1895 (Bride's

Parents' home in Carthage, MO (8 P.M.)[11,54,95], daughter of Orsmus Nelson PENNEY and Eliza Althea TAYLOR. She was born on 24 Feb 1875 in Licking, Ohio, USA[54,96]. She died on 01 Dec 1946 (Carthage, Jasper Co., Missouri)[54].

Curtis Andrew RITCHHART and Pearl Burdette PENNY had the following children:

    i. MAUDE PEARL[7] RITCHHART[54] was born on 08 Nov 1896 in Missouri, USA[54]. She died on 11 Jul 1967 (Carthage, Jasper Co., Missouri)[54]. She married (1) GEORGE W. POLLARD on 08 Nov 1917[54]. He was born on 16 Mar 1880 in Texas, Missouri, USA[160]. He died on 07 Jan 1951 (Carthage, Jasper, Missouri, USA)[54,160].

    ii. TAYLOR ALONZO RITCHHART[54] was born in 1898 in Kansas, USA[54]. He died in 1898[54].

50   iii. CURTIS BURCH RITCHHART[54] was born on 24 Oct 1916 (Carthage, Jasper Co., Missouri)[54]. He died on 21 May 1993 in Joplin, Jasper, Missouri, USA[54]. He married LONA LEA DRESSLAER on 05 Oct 1936 (Jasper County Courthouse/Carthage, Missouri, USA)[54]. She was born on 22 Jun 1914 in Sheldon, Barton County, MO[54]. She died on 14 Mar 2006 in Joplin, Jasper, Missouri, USA.

    iv. LONA LEA RITCHHART.

37. **FRANKLIN LESTER[6] RITCHHART** (Wesley[5], Andrew[4], John[3], Christian[2] RITSCHARD, Christian[1] RITSCHHART)[97] was born on 19 Mar 1873 in Noblesville, Hamilton, Indiana, USA[97,98,99,100,101,102]. He died on 25 Mar 1955 (Carthage, Jasper Co., Missouri). He married **ADA CHARLOTTE CARR** on 23 Jan 1898 (Home of bride's parents in Carthage, Missouri), daughter of William Winston CARR and Martha Emily ARRINGTON. She was born on 02 Nov 1880 in Carthage, Jasper, Missouri, USA[100,102,103]. She died on 22 Mar 1951 in Carthage, Jasper, Missouri, USA[92].

Notes for Franklin Lester RITCHHART: Have a photograph of Frank's headstone in Faskin Cemetery in Carthage, MO (Jasper County). I took it in July of 1999 while traveling across country visiting family burial sites and homesteads. Frank and Alvin married sisters Ada and May Carr.

Moved to Carthage when Frank was 12 years old.

Notes for Ada Charlotte CARR: When she was 4 she moved to the home she later inherited from her parents. When they celebrated their 50th anniversary they had lived in that same home for 44 years.

Franklin Lester RITCHHART and Ada Charlotte CARR had the following children:

51   i. EDNA MAMIE[7] RITCHHART[11] was born on 28 Apr 1900. She died on 18 May 1996 (Carthage, Jasper Co., Missouri)[161]. She married WALTER MARVIN COMPTON on 12 Aug 1921 in Mt. Vernon, Lawrence, MO. He was born on 20 Mar 1900 in Lawrence, Missouri, USA. He died on 01 Jan 1968 (Carthage, MO).

    ii. FERN A. RITCHHART was born in Jul 1903. She died on 26 Mar 1904 (Carthage, Missouri).

     Notes for Fern A. RITCHHART: Notes from a Carthage Newspaper in 1904 announced that nine-month old Fern had died.

52   iii. LESTER CARR RITCHHART[118,162] was born on 21 Jan 1906 in Jasper, Missouri, USA[120,163]. He died on 11 Aug 1995 in Jasper, Jasper, Missouri, USA[118,120]. He married IRENE MAE TILLER on 14 Feb 1925 in Jasper, Missouri, USA. She was born on 08 Aug 1907[11,118]. She died on 24 Jan 1998 in Jasper, Jasper, Missouri, USA[118].

    iv. BERNICE ALBERTA RITCHHART[164] was born on 29 Mar 1910. She married (1) CARL W. CHAPMAN on 08 Sep 1963 (Carthage, Jasper Co., Missouri). He was born on 26 Aug 1908[165]. He died on 23 Dec 1971. She married (2) HARRY DUDLEY KUNAU on 27 Apr 1933 in Carthage, Jasper, Missouri, USA (Carthage, MO, at the Harbour home on Clinton St.)[164,166]. He was born on 15 Sep 1900. He died on 20 Jul 1956.

    Notes for Bernice Alberta RITCHHART: I met Bernice along with her nephews Raymond and Paul Ritchhart and her niece Dorothy Rees in Carthage, MO in July 1999. Her father was Grandpa Alonzo Ritchhart's brother. She is my 1st cousin, once removed. She remembered her Uncle "Lon" (Alonzo).

38. **HARRY ELMER**[6] RITCHHART (Wesley[5], Andrew[4], John[3], Christian[2] RITSCHARD, Christian[1] RITSCHHART)[110,111,112] was born on 27 Nov 1884 in Indiana, USA[110]. He died on 12 Apr 1954[108]. He married (1) **MARIL BETH HOUSTON** on 20 Sep 1904 in Carthage, Jasper, Missouri, USA[113], daughter of * HOUSTON and Sadie *. She was born in 1885 in Ohio, USA[114].

Harry Elmer RITCHHART and Maril Beth HOUSTON had the following children:

    i. ELENOR[7] RITCHHART[111,167,168] was born in 1915 in Missouri, USA[111,167,168]. She married UNK MURREL.

    ii. FERN RITCHHART[114,114] was born in 1908 in Missouri, USA[114,114].

    Notes for Fern RITCHHART: Fern was not with her family in the 1920 census when she would have been about twelve years old, but her sister Elenor was. Perhaps Fern died sometime after the 1910 census.

39. **EARL**[6] RITCHHART (Charles[5], Andrew[4], John[3], Christian[2] RITSCHARD, Christian[1] RITSCHHART)[115,116] was born about 1881 in Indiana, USA[115]. He married **EMMA P. FISHER** on 26 Sep 1906 in Hamilton, Indiana, USA[116]. She was born about 1885 in Indiana, USA[115].

Earl RITCHHART and Emma P. FISHER had the following child:

    i. MARTHA L.[7] RITCHHART[169] was born on 12 May 1912 in Hamilton, Indiana, USA[169].

40. **LEVI WILLIAM**[6] RICHHART (William Z.[5], William[4] RITCHHART, Heinrich (Henry)[3] RITSCHARD, Christian[2] RITSCHARD, Christian[1] RITSCHHART) was born on 20 Oct 1880 in Macon, Illinois, USA. He died on 17 Jul 1937 in Fort Worth, Tarrant, Texas, USA. He married **LELA ARMFIELD PLYLER** on 20 Feb 1901 in Acadia Co., LA. She was born on 23 Oct 1876 in Statesville, Iredell Co., North Carolina.

Levi William RICHHART and Lela Armfield PLYLER had the following children:

53   i. CLARENCE LEON[7] RICHHART was born on 22 Jan 1902 in Moweaqua, Shelby, Illinois, USA. He married MARIE LUCILLE GIRDWOOD on 09 Nov 1924 in Tarrant, Texas, USA.

ii. PAUL KENNETH RICHHART was born on 05 Nov 1910 in Ricardo, De Baca, New Mexico, USA.

Generation 7

41. **WARREN HARRY**[7] **RITCHHART** (Alfred Olivr[6], Benjamin Allen[5], Phillip[4], Christian[3] RITSCHARD, Christian[2] RITSCHARD, Christian[1] RITSCHHART).

Warren Harry RITCHHART had the following child:

   i. JOHN WARREN[8] RITCHHART.

42. **NELSON J.**[7] **RITCHHART** (Hiram C.[6], Jacob[5], Jacob[4], Jacob[3] RICHHART, Christian[2] RITSCHARD, Christian[1] RITSCHHART)[8,117] was born on 11 Jan 1930. He married **BEATRICE IRENE ARLEDGE** on 07 Sep 1963, daughter of Harold Woodrow ARLEDGE and Helen *. She was born on 27 May 1943.

Notes for Nelson J. RITCHHART: Nelson his wife and one daughter lived on Stone Road when the *History of Springbank and Yellowbud Community* was written. I believe we visited them when we were there in 1999.

Nelson J. RITCHHART and Beatrice Irene ARLEDGE had the following children:

54   i. TERESA[8] RITCHHART[8] was born on 09 Nov 1963[170]. She married JOHN ALLEY.

55   ii. MICHELLE RITCHHART[8] was born on 03 Oct 1967[170]. She married TIMOTHY DYKE.

   iii. JEANNETTE RITCHHART[8] was born on 23 Jun 1970.

43. **CHARLES I.**[7] **RITCHHART** (Hiram C.[6], Jacob[5], Jacob[4], Jacob[3] RICHHART, Christian[2] RITSCHARD, Christian[1] RITSCHHART)[117] was born on 15 Jan 1932 in Ross, Ohio, USA.

Charles I. RITCHHART had the following child:

56   i. DANIEL[8] RITCHHART was born in Ross, Ohio, USA. He married PAULA.

44. **SAMUEL CLIFFORD**[7] **RITCHHART** (Alonzo Francis[6], Wesley[5], Andrew[4], John[3], Christian[2] RITSCHARD, Christian[1] RITSCHHART) was born on 31 May 1903 in Rocky Ford, Otero, Colorado, USA[68]. He died on 09 Aug 1989 in Canon City, Fremont, Colorado, USA. He married **MARIANNA EVALINA GLATZ** on 16 Sep 1926 in La Junta, Otero, Colorado, USA, daughter of Edward William GLATZ and Emma Elizabeth HERWIG. She was born on 02 Jan 1908[120]. She died on 29 Oct 1990 in Murfreesboro, Rutherford, Tennessee, USA[120].

Notes for Samuel Clifford RITCHHART: I always knew him as "Uncle Clifford," thus he went by his middle name. He wrote a very informative and interesting paper about his family history which has been invaluable in piecing together the Bush and Ritchhart family history from the time they came to La Junta. I obtained a copy of it from his son, Kenneth.

Uncle Clifford retired in Canyon City, Colorado where he had been a minister (Church of Christ, I believe). When my father passed away I asked Clifford to perform the service. My brother Dean and I drove from Denver to Pueblo, where we met up with him. Then the three of us drove to La Junta for the service.

Notes for Marianna Evalina GLATZ: *Social Security Death Index* lists her DOB as Jan 2,

1908 vice 1907 as other records show.

Samuel Clifford RITCHHART and Marianna Evalina GLATZ had the following children:

57   i.   KENNETH FRANCIS[8] RITCHHART was born on 26 Oct 1927 in Rocky Ford, Otero, Colorado, USA[171]. He married (1) LEONA VIVIAN BARKER on 24 Aug 1947 in Liberal, Seward, Kansas, USA, daughter of John Cleveland BARKER and Ollie Vivian MORRIS. She was born on 30 Jul 1928 in Grey, Beaver Co.,Oklahoma[172,173]. She died on 24 Apr 1994 in Noblesville, Hamilton, Indiana, USA. He married (2) DOROTHY JEANNETTE SHEEK on 09 Aug 1997 in Indianapolis, Indiana, daughter of Ralph Waldo SHEEK and Ruby BILLINGSLY. She was born on 05 Dec 1929 in Indianapolis, Indiana.

     ii. PATRICIA JEAN RITCHHART was born on 05 Dec 1931. She died on 10 Jan 1938 in Satanta, Haskell, Kansas, USA.

58   iii. ARTHUR AUGUST RITCHHART was born on 22 Oct 1934 in La Junta, Otero, Colorado, USA. He died on 21 Mar 1993 in Seattle, King, Washington, USA[137]. He married GERRY LOUISE CONNAWAY on 22 Dec 1955 in Cedar Rapids, Linn, Iowa, USA, daughter of J. Clarance CONNAWAY and Mabel SEALY. She was born on 26 May 1935 in Stratton, Kit Carson, Colorado, USA.

59   iv. CLIFFORD EUGENE RITCHHART was born on 23 Feb 1945 in Liberal, Seward, Kansas, USA[68]. He married WILDENA RUTH COLLINS on 05 Jun 1965 in Lamar, Prowers, Colorado, USA. She was born on 26 Jul 1947 in Garden City, Cherokee, Kansas, USA.

45. **MARY LILLIAN[7] RITCHHART** (Alonzo Francis[6], Wesley[5], Andrew[4], John[3], Christian[2] RITSCHARD, Christian[1] RITSCHHART)[123,124] was born on 16 Jan 1906 in La Junta, Otero, Colorado, USA[124,125]. She died on 28 Jan 1983 in Sacramento, Sacramento, California, USA[126]. She married **JAMES RUMSBY** about 1923[127], son of James RUMSBY and Louie KIMBALL. He was born on 01 Apr 1902 in Colorado, USA[128,129]. He died on 19 Jan 1983 in Sacramento, California, USA[128,129].

Notes for Mary Lillian RITCHHART: Lillian must have left home before she turned 24, as the 1930 census does not show her as a resident with her folks in La Junta. I later learned that she married at age 17.

Lillian had two daughters, Margaret and Betty. Although she died in Sacramento, I initially speculated that she went there for medical care. I thought she would have been buried in Modesto or Bakersfield where she and Jim had lived. Later evidence indicates that she did live in the Sacramento area, Rancho Cordova. In fact, in June 2009 I finally tracked down Margaret and she lived in Rancho Cordova. Her husband, Cliff, who died in 1995, had been in the Air Force and they retired in Sacramento. Margaret confirmed that her parents had moved to the Sacramento area to be near her.

My only recollection of Lillian and her family was when we stopped to visit them in Bakersfield when my dad was assigned to St. Mary's Pre-flight Training School near Walnut Creek, CA about 1943. As I recall, she worked at Penny's. I do remember that she was a very good cook. Even though I was only about 6 at the time, I recall raving for years about the meal we had that evening at their home. In particular, I recall her gravy as being some of the best I ever had. I also saw her again at Grandma and Grandpa Ritchhart's 50th Anniversary celebration when all the family got together in La Junta in January 1952.

Notes for James RUMSBY: According to Margaret Rumsby, her father, Jim, was a machinist apprentice for the Santa Fe RR in La Junta. Around 1925 he, Lillian and their new baby, Margaret, went to California for a vacation and never returned to La Junta. They liked California and the Fresno area so much and jobs were plentiful so they just stayed. Jim's occupation, according to the 1930 census, was a machinist in a lumber mill. Margaret later clarified that was the Sugar Pine Lumber Company. Around 1935 or 36 he got back on with the Santa Fe RR and was transferred to Bakersfield. Later he was hired by the Modesto Empire Traction Company where he eventually retired in the mid-60s.

James RUMSBY and Mary Lillian RITCHHART had the following children:

60   i. MARGARET E.[8] RUMSBY[174] was born in Jul 1924 in Colorado, USA[175]. She married CLIFF BARTON on 04 Apr 1942 in Las Vegas, Clark, Nevada, USA[176], son of Daniel Da Roado BARTON and Winona Rebecca HUNTSMAN. He was born on 21 Apr 1921 in Bigger, Saskatchewan, Canada[176,177]. He died on 25 Sep 1995 in Rancho Cordova, Sacramento, California, USA[176].

61   ii. BETTY LOU RUMSBY[178,179,180,181] was born in Sep 1926 in Fresno, California, USA[182,183]. She married (1) JAMES FRANKLIN KLEINKNIGHT on 12 Aug 1946[184], son of Robert Milo KLEINKNIGHT and Martha Ann MECHAM. He was born on 10 Aug 1925 in Kern, California, USA[185]. He died on 25 Apr 1995 in Fresno, California, USA[184,186]. She married (2) LAURIE D. SWOAP on 22 Apr 1943 in Raton, Colfax, New Mexico, USA. He was born on 07 Jan 1924 (Southern California)[184]. He died on 19 Feb 1944 in Italy (killed in WW II)[184].

46. **PAUL WESLEY[7] RITCHHART** (Alonzo Francis[6], Wesley[5], Andrew[4], John[3], Christian[2] RITSCHARD, Christian[1] RITSCHHART)[4,69,130,131] was born on 26 May 1908 in La Junta, Otero, Colorado, USA[131,132]. He died in Jun 1964 in Wyoming, USA[133]. He married (1) **INEZ JOSEPHINE RITTER** about 1930 in Colorado, USA, daughter of Carl Burch RITTER and Dell Reynolds PORTER. She was born on 17 Feb 1908 in Colorado, USA[134]. She died on 06 Dec 1963 in Phoenix, Maricopa, Arizona, USA. He married (2) **SUSIE SANTA DELORENZO** on 29 Dec 1951[135]. She was born on 02 Sep 1911 in La Junta, Otero, Colorado, USA[4,136]. She died on 03 Feb 1988 in La Junta, Otero, Colorado, USA[137].

Notes for Paul Wesley RITCHHART: Paul was an outstanding football player at La Junta High School. He and his brother, Del, were outstanding backs in the same backfield for one or two years.

Dutch must have moved out on his own prior to turning 22, as the 1930 Census does not show him living with his parents in La Junta.

"Dutch" was incarcerated in the Colorado State Penitentiary from 19 April 1958 to 14 December 1962. I vaguely remember my father telling me it had to do with something fraudulent he did while working as an automobile salesman. His inmate number was 24673, according to "WorldVitalRecords.com."

Found SS Death (SSN 357-05-8358) records for Susie Ritchhart, who lived in La Junta when she passed away on Feb 3, 1988. She was born on Sep 2, 1911, thus she was 76 when she passed away. She was his second wife.

Notes for Inez Josephine RITTER: Interestingly Inez is listed in the 1930 Census as having the last name Ritchhart and living in La Junta, so she and Dutch must have been married prior to 1930. Her age was listed as 22 in April when the census was taken. Dutch (Paul), however, was not listed in that census. Perhaps he was working out of town.

Paul Wesley RITCHHART and Inez Josephine RITTER had the following children:

62   i.   PAUL ALAN[8] RITCHHART[175] was born on 16 Apr 1931[187]. He married BARBARA HALE in 1972 in Denver, Colorado, USA.

63   ii.   MARY ELIZABETH RITCHHART was born on 19 Jun 1933 in La Junta, Otero, Colorado, USA. She married FREDERICK CHARLES BOLSINGER on 18 Jun 1955 in Denver, Colorado, USA, son of Frederick Smith BOLSINGER and UNK. He was born on 30 Jun 1932 in Denver, Colorado, USA.

     Notes for Susie Santa DELORENZO: I was contacted by Cathy, Susan's daughter, as she was doing research on her father, Paul Ritchhart. I shared info with her and put her in touch with her step-brother, Paul Allen. They did later converse on the phone and she met with Paul Allen during a trip to La Junta in 2004.

     Also found her name listed as Santa DeLorenzo on another source. Birth and death dates match with Susan Hyland. It appears that she was born as Santa DeLorenzo; but I am guessing that she went by the nickname Susie. She was married to both Michael Petramala and Paul Ritchhart, so am not sure where the last name Hyland came from.

Paul Wesley RITCHHART and Susie Santa DELORENZO had the following child:

64   iii.   PATRICIA CATHERINE RITCHHART was born on 12 May 1953. She married RONALD WARD, son of James Edward WARD and Rose SCHLEGEL. He was born on 27 Jan 1953.

47. **DELBERT BUSH[7] RITCHHART** (Alonzo Francis[6], Wesley[5], Andrew[4], John[3], Christian[2] RITSCHARD, Christian[1] RITSCHHART)[69,79,138] was born on 02 Nov 1910 (Carthage, Missouri)[69,70,79,84]. He died on 18 Feb 1981 in Denver, Colorado, USA[84]. He married **HELEN JANE DEAN** on 01 Aug 1952 in Raton, Colfax, New Mexico, USA (Remarried)[139], daughter of Arthur Spear DEAN and Mary Loretta O'MALLEY. She was born on 06 Aug 1915 in Denver, Adams, Colorado, USA (2:53 p.m., St. Joseph's Hospital)[140,141,142,143]. She died on 28 Oct 1995 in Loveland, Larimer, Colorado, USA[137,142,144].

Notes for Delbert Bush RITCHHART: Was a star football player for the La Junta Tigers High School team playing in the backfield along with his older brother "Dutch." Also played football and baseball at the University of Colorado. He was a left-handed hitting 3rd baseman and played guard and end in College. He earned All-Conference honors in football as a senior. Was drafted by the Detroit Lions and played two years 1936/37. He played center on offense and linebacker on defense at Detroit. As a rookie he intercepted a pass in one game and returned it 96 yards for a touchdown. Following his first year at Detroit he returned to CU to pick up the final credits for his degree in Physical Education.

Married Helen Jane Dean from the neighboring town of Las Animas in 1936 prior to going to Detroit. After playing two years for Detroit he took a coaching position at Delta, Colorado as the head football coach. He also assisted in the other sports. He moved from Delta to Lamar in September 1939, where he also coached football. My earliest recollections are of going to the gym with my dad and having footballs, basketballs and softballs to play with. I recall one night going outside to observe the "blackout drill" required even in Lamar during WW II. Army Air Corps planes flew over the area to evaluate the "blackout."

With the outbreak of the war, he joined the Navy under the V-5 program. He was commissioned an Ensign on Feb 11, 1943 and entered active service on May 23, 1943. The V-5 program was also know as the program for "90 day wonders"—college graduates were commissioned as officers after 90 days training. He took his training at Chapel Hill, N.C. and was assigned as an instructor at St. Mary's Pre-flight training command at St. Marys University outside Walnut Creek, CA. He taught physical fitness and hand-to-hand combat to the pre-flight candidates.

He was later assigned to a Clinton Naval Air Station near Cordell, OK. We lived directly across the street there from a grade school. I recall my brother and I both getting impetigo, which is a rash like ringworm, from the donkeys we used to ride that belonged to neighbors. We lived in a downstairs apartment that we rented from the owners (who I believe lived upstairs). I recall my mom and dad always kept a broom handy in the evenings to kill mice that would run across the kitchen floor.

Following the end of the war, he got out of the Navy on February 20, 1946 and we returned to La Junta where we lived for a short time in an apartment building near downtown. Dad then got a job at Fort Lyon Veterans Hospital where he worked in Special Services, which included sports activities for the patients. Thus, we moved to Las Animas which was much closer to Fort Lyon.

My parents divorced in 1949. They remarried on August 1, 1952 in Raton, N.M. (according to a newspaper article from the *Las Animas Democrat*) for a very short time (a few months as I recall), but again separated. A letter from Grandma Jane to her daughter, Blanche, dated August 1952 indicated that were back together and thinking of remarrying. They were formally divorced again in August 1959.

Notes for Helen Jane DEAN: Mary Hudnall Fioretti was the bridesmaid and Dutch Ritchhart was best man at the wedding. Two weeks later daddy left for Detroit to start the football season.

My parents separated around the fall of 1946 or early 1947. We then moved back to La Junta and lived with Aunt Frances and Uncle Paul near the Junior College in south La Junta. We stayed there until shortly after Mary Jane was born in Feb 1948. We moved back to Las

Animas and they legally divorced in 1949. My mom and dad remarried on August 1, 1952 and we lived in Grandma's house on Locust, but it only lasted a few months. They separated again and then legally divorced for the second time in 1959.

Mother spent time in the Pueblo County Mental Hospital in 1953–54. On one occasion we were traveling through Pueblo to play a high school game (can't remember if it was football or basketball) and the car I was riding with stopped long enough for me to go in to see her. She was receiving some type of shock therapy and I recall seeing several bruises on her arms. She tended to bruise easily and it may have been from injections or the electric shock treatments.

Delbert Bush RITCHHART and Helen Jane DEAN had the following children:

65   i.   DELBERT ARTHUR[8] RITCHHART[188] was born on 08 May 1937 in Las Animas, Bent, Colorado, USA (11:16 a.m.)[189]. He married JOANNE FRANCES SCHMIDT on 28 Nov 1959 in Wilmette, Cook, Illinois, USA, daughter of Frederick Henry SCHMIDT and Frances Lois MCCONNELL. She was born on 12 Mar 1938 in Evanston, Cook, Illinois, USA[190,191,192,193].

66   ii.   DEAN LEE RITCHHART was born on 08 Oct 1940 (Las Animas, Colorado, 11:35 p.m.). He married EVELYN KIRSCHMAN on 25 Jun 1961 (St. Mary's Catholic Church, Las Animas, CO), daughter of Daniel KIRSCHMAN and UNICE. She was born on 04 Aug 1942.

67   iii.   MARY JANE RITCHHART was born on 29 Feb 1948 (La Junta, Colorado (Mennonite Hospital). She died on 27 Apr 1979 (Denver, Colorado of lymphoma (cancer); Rose Memorial Hospital)[194]. She married (1) ELDON JOHNSON about 1970. He was born on 18 Nov 1944. She married (2) JOHN F. HAYES JR. on 24 Oct 1976 in Boulder, Colorado, USA.

48. **PURL FLOYD[7] RITCHHART** (Alvin E.[6], Wesley[5], Andrew[4], John[3], Christian[2] RITSCHARD, Christian[1] RITSCHHART)[137,150,151,152] was born on 17 Jul 1893 (Carthage, Missouri)[152]. He died in Aug 1975 in Forsyth, Taney, Missouri, USA[137]. He married (1) **ELIZABETH***. He married (2) **LAURA PERRY** on 03 Nov 1929 (Carthage, Jasper, Missouri)[153].

Purl Floyd RITCHHART and Elizabeth * had the following child:

     i.   JUNE L.[8] RITCHHART[85] was born in 1919 in Missouri, USA[85].

49. **ETHEL GRACE[7] RITCHHART** (Alvin E.[6], Wesley[5], Andrew[4], John[3], Christian[2] RITSCHARD, Christian[1] RITSCHHART)[89,157] was born in Mar 1898 in Missouri, USA[89]. She died in 1960[89,90]. She married **BENTON ELVIS CEARNAL** on 22 Jun 1924 in Jasper[157]. He was born on 24 Nov 1896[89]. He died in Jan 1972 in Joplin, Jasper, Missouri, USA[89].

Benton Elvis CEARNAL and Ethel Grace RITCHHART had the following children:

     i.   DON[8] CEARNAL.

68   ii.   KATHLEEN CEARNAL was born in 1929[195]. She died on 24 Nov 1997[196]. She married KING BRIDGES in May 1952.

     iii.   ALVIN CEARNAL[89] was born in 1927[89]. He died in 1927[89].

     iv.   WARREN CEARNAL[89] was born in 1925[89]. He died in 1925[89].

50. **CURTIS BURCH**[7] **RITCHHART** (Curtis Andrew[6], Wesley[5], Andrew[4], John[3], Christian[2] RITSCHARD, Christian[1] RITSCHHART)[54] was born on 24 Oct 1916 (Carthage, Jasper Co., Missouri)[54]. He died on 21 May 1993 in Joplin, Jasper, Missouri, USA[54]. He married **LONA LEA DRESSLAER** on 05 Oct 1936 (Jasper County Courthouse/Carthage, Missouri, USA)[54]. She was born on 22 Jun 1914 in Sheldon, Barton County, MO[54]. She died on 14 Mar 2006 in Joplin, Jasper, Missouri, USA.

Curtis Burch RITCHHART and Lona Lea DRESSLAER had the following children:

69   i. CAROLYN[8] RITCHHART[54] was born in Jun 1936[54]. She married WILLIE GENE STEWART on 21 Apr 1962[54].

70 ii. MARILYN RITCHHART was born in Oct 1937[54]. She married MARTIN GROVES on 19 Oct 1963[54].

71 iii. LINDA RITCHHART[54] was born in Aug 1947[54]. She married BOB BARCLAY on 24 Feb 1968[54].

51. **EDNA MAMIE**[7] **RITCHHART** (Franklin Lester[6], Wesley[5], Andrew[4], John[3], Christian[2] RITSCHARD, Christian[1] RITSCHHART)[11] was born on 28 Apr 1900. She died on 18 May 1996 (Carthage, Jasper Co., Missouri)[161]. She married **WALTER MARVIN COMPTON** on 12 Aug 1921 in Mt. Vernon, Lawrence, MO. He was born on 20 Mar 1900 in Lawrence, Missouri, USA. He died on 01 Jan 1968 (Carthage, MO).

Walter Marvin COMPTON and Edna Mamie RITCHHART had the following children:

72   i. DOROTHY BERNICE[8] COMPTON[11] was born on 09 Apr 1923 (Carthage, MO). She married EARL J. REES on 04 Jun 1945 in Galena, Cherokee, Kansas, USA[11]. He was born on 13 Jan 1920[11].

     ii. BOBBY GENE COMPTON[11] was born on 24 Apr 1929. He married NORMA JEAN ROSE on 21 Jun 1951. She was born on 24 Sep 1930.

52. **LESTER CARR**[7] **RITCHHART** (Franklin Lester[6], Wesley[5], Andrew[4], John[3], Christian[2] RITSCHARD, Christian[1] RITSCHHART)[118,162] was born on 21 Jan 1906 in Jasper, Missouri, USA[120,163]. He died on 11 Aug 1995 in Jasper, Jasper, Missouri, USA[118,120]. He married **IRENE MAE TILLER** on 14 Feb 1925 in Jasper, Missouri, USA. She was born on 08 Aug 1907[11,118]. She died on 24 Jan 1998 in Jasper, Jasper, Missouri, USA[118].

Lester Carr RITCHHART and Irene Mae TILLER had the following children:

73   i. RAYMOND RICHARD[8] RITCHHART was born on 25 Jun 1926 (Carthage, MO). He married MARGARETTE DAISY POINDEXTER on 04 May 1948 in Jasper, Missouri, USA. She was born on 07 Jun 1928[11].

     ii. PAUL LESTER RITCHHART was born on 07 Aug 1930. He married (1) JO NAPPIER in Carthage, MO. He married (2) DOROTHY HILL on 23 Dec 1962 in California[197]. He married (3) DELANA HODSON on 10 Jul 1969 (Carthage, MO). He married (4) JOANN MAY.

        Notes for Paul Lester RITCHHART: I met Paul and his brother Raymond, his cousin Dorothy Rees, and his Aunt Bernice Chapman in Carthage, MO in July 1999. They showed us Fasken Cemetery and recalled knowing Uncle Lon (Alonzo Ritchhart), my Grandfather.

74   iii.   RUSSELL RITCHHART was born on 25 Apr 1950. He married (1) DELANA HODSON on 10 Jul 1969. He married (2) CONNIE COLE on 15 Jan 1983. He married (3) KATHY PORTER on 23 Dec 1997.

53.   **CLARENCE LEON**[7] **RICHHART** (Levi William[6], William Z.[5], William[4] RITCHHART, Heinrich (Henry)[3] RITSCHARD, Christian[2] RITSCHARD, Christian[1] RITSCHHART) was born on 22 Jan 1902 in Moweaqua, Shelby, Illinois, USA. He married **MARIE LUCILLE GIRDWOOD** on 09 Nov 1924 in Tarrant, Texas, USA.

Clarence Leon RICHHART and Marie Lucille GIRDWOOD had the following children:

75   i.   JAMES KENNETH[8] RICHHART was born on 09 Jan 1933 in Fort Worth, Tarrant, Texas, USA. He married BETTYE ANDERSON on 20 Jun 1953, daughter of Clifford ANDERSON and Gertrude *. She was born on 26 Jan 1933 in Abilene, Jones, Texas, USA. She died on 22 Feb 2009 in North Richland Hills, Tarrant, Texas, USA.

    ii.   KARL EDWARD RICHHART was born on 17 Jan 1936 in Fort Worth, Tarrant, Texas, USA. He married JUDITH ELIZABETH LYONS on 20 Aug 1955 in Fort Worth, Tarrant, Texas, USA. She was born on 06 Sep 1936 in Gainesville, Cooke, Texas, USA.

Generation 8

54.   **TERESA**[8] **RITCHHART** (Nelson J.[7], Hiram C.[6], Jacob[5], Jacob[4], Jacob[3] RICHHART, Christian[2] RITSCHARD, Christian[1] RITSCHHART)[8] was born on 09 Nov 1963[170]. She married **JOHN ALLEY**.

John ALLEY and Teresa RITCHHART had the following children:

    i.   BRANDON[9] ALLEY[170].

    ii.   ASHLEY ALLEY.

55.   **MICHELLE**[8] **RITCHHART** (Nelson J.[7], Hiram C.[6], Jacob[5], Jacob[4], Jacob[3] RICHHART, Christian[2] RITSCHARD, Christian[1] RITSCHHART)[8] was born on 03 Oct 1967[170]. She married **TIMOTHY DYKE**.

Notes for Michelle RITCHHART: I received a response on GENI.COM in 2009 from Michelle regarding a photo of Hiram (her grandfather) that I had posted on the net. I tried to get back to her; but didn't get any response.

Timothy DYKE and Michelle RITCHHART had the following child:

    i.   Holden[9] Dyke.

56.   **DANIEL**[8] **RITCHHART** (Charles I.[7], Hiram C.[6], Jacob[5], Jacob[4], Jacob[3] RICHHART, Christian[2] RITSCHARD, Christian[1] RITSCHHART) was born in Ross, Ohio, USA. He married **PAULA**.

Notes for Daniel RITCHHART: When I retired from Lockheed Martin and we were planning to drive across county to California, I wrote letters to relatives along the route. I had obtained their names from internet searches in towns where the family had lived. Daniel responded and was our host the day we were in Chillicothe, Ohio. He took us to the farm where we met Renick and Floyd. Wayne was ill and either in a rest home or the hospital.

We also met Fred and spent quite a bit of time with him. He was living just up the road from the farm house and directly across the road from the little one room school that was built on original Ritchhart land. He had taught for years at a government Indian school in Arizona and was probably the only one of the eight brothers who had graduated from college. Fred and Daniel then took us over to Springbank Cemetery where a very large number of Ritchharts were buried. We also met Pearl, Daniel's aunt; and Fred's brother. She came with Daniel to pick us up at the motel. I believe the other brother we met was Nelson. He and his wife were living in the Ritchhart farmhouse. Interestingly Daniel almost didn't answer my letter soliciting someone to respond and meet with us when we came through Chillicothe, but his father encouraged him to answer. Daniel was a deputy sheriff in Waverly (Pike County) about 13 miles south of Chillicothe. His ex-wife Paula was also a deputy. It is almost incredible in this day that 8 out of 8 children born in Chillicothe were still living there between 64 and 81 years later!

Daniel RITCHHART and Paula had the following child:

    i. JOHN W.[9] RITCHHART.

57. **KENNETH FRANCIS**[8] **RITCHHART** (Samuel Clifford[7], Alonzo Francis[6], Wesley[5], Andrew[4], John[3], Christian[2] RITSCHARD, Christian[1] RITSCHHART) was born on 26 Oct 1927 in Rocky Ford, Otero, Colorado, USA[171]. He married (1) **LEONA VIVIAN BARKER** on 24 Aug 1947 in Liberal, Seward, Kansas, USA, daughter of John Cleveland BARKER and Ollie Vivian MORRIS. She was born on 30 Jul 1928 in Grey, Beaver Co.,Oklahoma[172,173]. She died on 24 Apr 1994 in Noblesville, Hamilton, Indiana, USA. He married (2) **DOROTHY JEANNETTE SHEEK** on 09 Aug 1997 in Indianapolis, Indiana, daughter of Ralph Waldo SHEEK and Ruby BILLINGSLY. She was born on 05 Dec 1929 in Indianapolis, Indiana.

Notes for Kenneth Francis RITCHHART: Although I may have met Kenneth when we were children, my first real recollection of meeting him was in July 1999 when Joanne and I were enroute from Washington D.C. to San Diego. Ironically, I had reconnected with him through a chance encounter with his son Kenneth. One day at work, while with Lockheed Martin in Bethesda, MD, a colleague brought me a notice of a military-industrial Intelligence Conference in which an Air Force Colonel Kenneth Ritchhart was to be the key speaker. Remembering that I had a cousin Kenneth, I surmised this was his son. I called him and he related that his father lived in Indianapolis. I attempted to arrange a lunch with Colonel Ritchhart, but we never were able to get together. However, months later when I was retiring and planning the trip back to San Diego, I decided to contact Kenneth and see if we could get together while passing through Indiana. We stayed with them one night and really had a very good time together. His brother Eugene came up from Tennessee, so it was like a mini reunion. Ken's first wife had passed away and he had met and married Jeannette, who had also lost her spouse about the same time as Ken. That sparked a continuing friendship and Ken and Jeannette have been out to the west coast and visited with us twice since then. We have shared a common interest in family history and have exchanged information about the Ritchhart family.

Kenneth Francis RITCHHART and Leona Vivian BARKER had the following children:

76   i. LINDA JOANN[9] RITCHHART was born on 03 Apr 1949 in Manhattan, Pottawatomie, Kansas, USA. She married (1) MORRIS MARK GROSSMAN on 17 Nov 1972 in Woodbridge, Middlesex, New Jersey, USA. He was born on 01 Feb 1936 in Perth Amboy, Middlesex, New Jersey, USA. She married (2) LARRY ROBINSON on 28 Mar 2009 in Florida, USA.

77   ii. KENNETH MICHAEL RITCHHART was born on 28 May 1951 in Kansas City, Wyandotte, Kansas, USA. He married TENA KAREN JACKSON on 14 Feb 1986 in Montgomery, Alabama, USA. She was born on 09 Jul 1958 in Montgomery, Alabama, USA.

78   iii. CHARLES STEVEN RITCHHART was born on 19 Oct 1956 in Anderson, Madison, Indiana, USA. He married (1) SUZANNE LOU WALTON in Anderson, Madison, Indiana, USA. He married (2) PAMELA SUE BENNETTE on 19 Sep 1977 in Anderson, Madison, Indiana, USA. She was born on 28 Oct 1957 in Anderson, Madison, Indiana, USA.

  iv. RONALD EUGENE RITCHHART was born on 21 Aug 1959 in Anderson, Madison, Indiana, USA. He married KEVON JAY ZEHNER on 12 Apr 1982 in Bloomington, Monroe, Indiana, USA. She was born on 11 May 1951 in Vincennes, Knox, Indiana, USA.

79   v. JEFFERY ALLAN RITCHHART was born on 10 Aug 1962 in Anderson, Madison, Indiana, USA. He married ANN MARIE BABIARZ on 26 May 1990 in Lake Tahoe, Nevada. She was born on 20 Nov 1967 in Chico, Butte, California, USA.

58. **ARTHUR AUGUST[8] RITCHHART** (Samuel Clifford[7], Alonzo Francis[6], Wesley[5], Andrew[4], John[3], Christian[2] RITSCHARD, Christian[1] RITSCHHART) was born on 22 Oct 1934 in La Junta, Otero, Colorado, USA. He died on 21 Mar 1993 in Seattle, King, Washington, USA[137]. He married **GERRY LOUISE CONNAWAY** on 22 Dec 1955 in Cedar Rapids, Linn, Iowa, USA, daughter of J. Clarance CONNAWAY and Mabel SEALY. She was born on 26 May 1935 in Stratton, Kit Carson, Colorado, USA.

Notes for Arthur August RITCHHART: I got to know Arthur and Gerry when I was in college at CU. Don't remember exactly how we knew we were both there; but I think my dad knew he was there and told me. He and Gerry were married and lived in "Vetsville" near the baseball field. He had served time in the military and was entitled to the special low income housing for vets. I can recall them having me over for dinner a few times and really enjoying getting to know them. My brother was once stopped for speeding in Colorado and who should the patrolman be—Arthur. I think he might have gotten off with a warning. Especially since he was driving a Volkswagen beetle!

Arthur August RITCHHART and Gerry Louise CONNAWAY had the following children:

80   i. JAMES JOSEPH[9] RITCHHART was born on 09 Mar 1961 in Denver, Colorado, USA. He married CONNIE JEAN RUSHTON on 16 Apr 1988 in Wayne, Illinois, USA. She was born on 12 Apr 1959 in Elmhurst, Du Page, Illinois, USA.

  ii. ELENA SUE RITCHHART was born on 14 Mar 1963.

59. **CLIFFORD EUGENE**[8] **RITCHHART** (Samuel Clifford[7], Alonzo Francis[6], Wesley[5], Andrew[4], John[3], Christian[2] RITSCHARD, Christian[1] RITSCHHART) was born on 23 Feb 1945 in Liberal, Seward, Kansas, USA[68]. He married **WILDENA RUTH COLLINS** on 05 Jun 1965 in Lamar, Prowers, Colorado, USA. She was born on 26 Jul 1947 in Garden City, Cherokee, Kansas, USA.

Clifford Eugene RITCHHART and Wildena Ruth COLLINS had the following children:

81   i.   KEVIN LEE[9] RITCHHART was born on 05 Jul 1966 in Liberal, Seward, Kansas, USA. He married TANDY LYNN DRACH on 12 Jul 1986 in Dodge City, Ford, Kansas, USA. She was born on 09 Nov 1966 in Dodge City, Ford, Kansas, USA.

82   ii. CHANNON LYNNE RITCHHART was born on 20 Feb 1968 in Garden City, Cherokee, Kansas, USA. She married KRIS GRANTON GREGG on 16 Aug 1986 in Odessa, Jewell, Kansas, USA. He was born on 26 Oct 1963 in El Campo, Wharton, Texas, USA.

83   iii. LOGAN EUGENE RITCHHART was born on 03 Jun 1969 in Garden City, Cherokee, Kansas, USA. He married LISA LYNN ASHLEY on 13 Aug 1988 in Oklahoma City, Oklahoma, Oklahoma, USA. She was born on 13 Jul 1962 in Middletown, Butler, Ohio, USA.

84   iv. TRENDA JANELL RITCHHART was born on 02 May 1973 in Garden City, Cherokee, Kansas, USA. She married (1) MARK ALLAN LITTLE on 05 Jun 1993 in Murfreesboro, Rutherford, Tennessee, USA. He was born on 08 Aug 1963 in Kettering, Montgomery, Ohio, USA. She married (2) SCOTT DEAVER.

      v. SHAWN RAY RITCHHART was born on 08 Aug 1974 in Garden City, Cherokee, Kansas, USA. He married AFTON.

60. **MARGARET E.**[8] **RUMSBY** (Mary Lillian[7] RITCHHART, Alonzo Francis[6] RITCHHART, Wesley[5] RITCHHART, Andrew[4] RITCHHART, John[3] RITCHHART, Christian[2] RITSCHARD, Christian[1] RITSCHHART)[174] was born in Jul 1924 in Colorado, USA[175]. She married **CLIFF BARTON** on 04 Apr 1942 in Las Vegas, Clark, Nevada, USA[176], son of Daniel Da Roado BARTON and Winona Rebecca HUNTSMAN. He was born on 21 Apr 1921 in Bigger, Saskatchiwan, Canada[176,177]. He died on 25 Sep 1995 in Rancho Cordova, Sacramento, California, USA[176].

Notes for Margaret E. RUMSBY: I met with Margaret on Aug 27, 2010 at her home in Rancho Cordova, California. We were in the area for Cheryl's 50th birthday celebration. I had only seem Margaret on one occasion that I remember. That was when I was around 6 years old and my dad was in the Navy stationed at St. Marys Preflight Training and we lived in Walnut Creek. I remember meeting two girls who were my cousins; but no other specifics. Margaret would have been about 19 then and Betty would have been 17, so we wouldn't have had much in common. I showed Margaret the Power Point presentation about the Ritchhart family history and some family photos that I had. I had asked her when I called to set up our meeting, if she would gather any photos she had which might be of interest to me. She had several photos that I scanned. I was particularly happy to get a photo of ggrandma Bush as I didn't have a good photo of her. Margaret who was 86, was very alert and seemed to be in very good health. She commented that her sister Betty's health hadn't been too good.

Notes for Cliff BARTON: Cliff Barton's name was given to me by Jack Linehan when I contacted him around 2007 to get any family history data that Betty (Ritchhart) might have left him.

Cliff BARTON and Margaret E. RUMSBY had the following children:

85　i.　DAVID WESLEY[9] BARTON[176] was born on 17 Mar 1944 in La Junta, Otero, Colorado, USA[176]. He married (1) DIANE GILLILAND. He married (2) JANET BRANKLE.

86　ii.　NANCY LEE BARTON[176] was born on 27 Jun 1947 in Bakersfield, Kern, California, USA[176]. She married GLENN POOLE on 01 Jan 1968 in Las Vegas, Clark, Nevada, USA[176].

61.　**BETTY LOU[8] RUMSBY** (Mary Lillian[7] RITCHHART, Alonzo Francis[6] RITCHHART, Wesley[5] RITCHHART, Andrew[4] RITCHHART, John[3] RITCHHART, Christian[2] RITSCHARD, Christian[1] RITSCHHART)[178,179,180,181] was born in Sep 1926 in Fresno, California, USA[182,183]. She married (1) **JAMES FRANKLIN KLEINKNIGHT** on 12 Aug 1946[184], son of Robert Milo KLEINKNIGHT and Martha Ann MECHAM. He was born on 10 Aug 1925 in Kern, California, USA[185]. He died on 25 Apr 1995 in Fresno, California, USA[184,186]. She married (2) **LAURIE D. SWOAP** on 22 Apr 1943 in Raton, Colfax, New Mexico, USA. He was born on 07 Jan 1924 (Southern California)[184]. He died on 19 Feb 1944 in Italy (Killed in WW II)[184].

Notes for Betty Lou RUMSBY: When I tracked down Margaret in early July 2009, she informed me that Betty was also widowed and still lived in the Fresno area. The following day I called Betty and had a very nice conversation catching up on family history.

James Franklin KLEINKNIGHT and Betty Lou RUMSBY had the following children:

87　i.　ROBERT LLOYD[9] KLEINKNIGHT[198] was born on 27 Aug 1948 in Bakersfield, Kern, California, USA[184,198]. He married DEBORAH KENNETT on 30 May 1978 in Fresno, California, USA[184].

88　ii.　STEVE KLEINKNIGHT[184] was born on 09 Oct 1950 in Fresno, California, USA[184]. He married (1) SHERRYL CALABRESE on 10 May 1975 in Fresno, California, USA. He married (2) JANA MILLS on 03 Dec 2005 in Exeter, Tulare, California, USA.

Laurie D. SWOAP and Betty Lou RUMSBY had the following child:

89　i.　LAURIE LEE[9] SWOAP was born on 22 Jun 1944 in Bakersfield, Kern, California, USA[184]. She married JOHN TILSON on 25 Aug 1967 (Southern California).

62.　**PAUL ALAN[8] RITCHHART** (Paul Wesley[7], Alonzo Francis[6], Wesley[5], Andrew[4], John[3], Christian[2] RITSCHARD, Christian[1] RITSCHHART)[175] was born on 16 Apr 1931[187]. He married **BARBARA HALE** in 1972 in Denver, Colorado, USA.

Paul Alan RITCHHART and Barbara HALE had the following children:

　i.　STEPHANIE[9] RITCHHART was born in 1969.

　ii.　ADIKKE RITCHHART was born in 1973.

63. **MARY ELIZABETH**[8] **RITCHHART** (Paul Wesley[7], Alonzo Francis[6], Wesley[5], Andrew[4], John[3], Christian[2] RITSCHARD, Christian[1] RITSCHHART) was born on 19 Jun 1933 in La Junta, Otero, Colorado, USA. She married **FREDERICK CHARLES BOLSINGER** on 18 Jun 1955 in Denver, Colorado, USA, son of Frederick Smith BOLSINGER and UNK. He was born on 30 Jun 1932 in Denver, Colorado, USA.

Notes for Mary Elizabeth RITCHHART: I only remember meeting Paul Allen and Sue a couple times. I always remember her as "Sue." Not sure how that comes from Mary Elizabeth. I think they lived in Denver in around 1948 when we visited them. I remember both of them very positively. I think I met them one other time when I was around 12 or 13.

Frederick Charles BOLSINGER and Mary Elizabeth RITCHHART had the following children:

> i. BRIT ANTHONY[9] BOLSINGER[175] was born on 18 Jun 1956. He married BONNIE MCKAY in Anchorage, Alaska, USA.
>
> ii. JAMIE ANN BOLSINGER was born on 14 Dec 1957. She died on 09 Jul 1988. She married BRAD SMITH in Anchorage, Alaska, USA.
>
> iii. NAN CATHLEEN BOLSINGER[175] was born on 18 Oct 1959 in Denver, Colorado, USA[175]. She married DAVID TRUITT in Anchorage, Alaska, USA.
>
> iv. TINA SUE BOLSINGER was born on 13 Sep 1962 in Denver, Colorado, USA[175].
>
> v. CHRISTOPHER JOHN BOLSINGER was born on 22 Dec 1964 in Mesa, Maricopa, Arizona, USA. He died on 21 Feb 2000 in Anchorage, Alaska, USA.

64. **PATRICIA CATHERINE**[8] **RITCHHART** (Paul Wesley[7], Alonzo Francis[6], Wesley[5], Andrew[4], John[3], Christian[2] RITSCHARD, Christian[1] RITSCHHART) was born on 12 May 1953. She married **RONALD WARD**, son of James Edward WARD and Rose SCHLEGEL. He was born on 27 Jan 1953.

Notes for Patricia Catherine RITCHHART: Cathy contacted me around 2002 in search of details about her Dad, Paul "Dutch" Ritchhart. I gave her quite a bit of information, including the fact she had a step-brother and sister and have been in periodic contact with her. In July 2004 she was in La Junta and met with Paul Allen.

Ronald WARD and Patricia Catherine RITCHHART had the following children:

90   i. CHRISTINE ELIZABETH[9] WARD was born on 24 Oct 1974[135]. She married DAVID PETERSON on Unknown date, son of Duane A. PETERSON and Barbara CARNAHAN. He was born on 23 Feb 1963[135].

> ii. JENNIFER LYNN WARD was born on 29 Feb 1976.

91   iii. SHERI RENEE WARD[135] was born on 17 Jan 1978[135]. She married KELLY FEIKERT, son of Gary FEIKERT and KAREN. She met GABE WATSON.

65. **DELBERT ARTHUR**[8] **RITCHHART** (Delbert Bush[7], Alonzo Francis[6], Wesley[5], Andrew[4], John[3], Christian[2] RITSCHARD, Christian[1] RITSCHHART)[188] was born on 08 May 1937 in Las Animas, Bent, Colorado, USA (11:16 a.m.)[189]. He married **JOANNE FRANCES SCHMIDT** on 28 Nov 1959 in Wilmette, Cook, Illinois, USA, daughter of Frederick Henry SCHMIDT

and Frances Lois MCCONNELL. She was born on 12 Mar 1938 in Evanston, Cook, Illinois, USA[190,191,192,193].

Delbert Arthur RITCHHART and Joanne Frances SCHMIDT had the following children:

92   i.   CHERYL ANN[9] RITCHHART[199,200] was born on 30 Aug 1960 in Honolulu, Hawaii, USA. She married RONALD G SHORT on 22 Sep 1984 in Reno, Washoe, Nevada, USA[199], son of Terry Vern SHORT and Maryann WOOD. He was born on 20 Jun 1958 in Palo Alto, San Mateo, California, USA[201,202].

93   ii.   DEBORA JANE RITCHHART[203] was born on 29 Sep 1961 in Evanston, Cook, Illinois, USA203. She married ERIC STERLING CANTRELL on 24 Sep 1993 in San Diego, California, USA (Eliam Chapel), son of Richard Ellsworth CANTRELL Jr. and Sharon Roxie RALPH. He was born on 10 Nov 1964 in Encino, Los Angeles, California, USA.

94   iii.   LINDA MARIE RITCHHART[204,205] was born on 07 Jun 1964 in San Diego, San Diego, California, USA[204,205,206]. She married DOUGLAS GREGORY WIMER on 18 Mar 1986 in San Diego, San Diego, California, USA, son of Franklin Bernard WIMER and Margery Anne LOEFFLER. He was born on 10 Dec 1960 in Pittsburgh, Allegheny, Pennsylvania, USA.

66. **DEAN LEE[8] RITCHHART** (Delbert Bush[7], Alonzo Francis[6], Wesley[5], Andrew[4], John[3], Christian[2] RITSCHARD, Christian[1] RITSCHHART) was born on 08 Oct 1940 (Las Animas, Colorado, 11:35 p.m.). He married **EVELYN KIRSCHMAN** on 25 Jun 1961 (St. Mary's Catholic Church, Las Animas, CO), daughter of Daniel KIRSCHMAN and Unice. She was born on 04 Aug 1942.

Notes for Dean Lee RITCHHART: Dean was a very good athlete and played football, basketball, and baseball/softball. He was the point guard (the term hadn't been invented then) on the high school championship team in 1958. He played on the Freshman baseball team at the University of Colorado. He then shifted to Denver University and didn't pursue continuing with baseball. After obtaining a business degree from DU he worked at various times for Boeing and then for one of the big 8 accounting firms (I believe it was Arthur Anderson). He married Evelyn before graduating from DU. They spent some time in Wichita while he was with Boeing. They were later in Sacramento for a few years.

They eventually ended up living in the Seattle area for many years. In 2010 they moved back to Las Animas.

An e-mail from Dean on 6/6/02:
Del,

I will properly protect the material and send it to you soon. It is interesting that the CU picture in that book has Leo and my senior coach Bob Decker who was older than the rest of the team on the same team because Bob had just come out of the military. At our last reunion in Las Animas two years ago, we (Dennis Marquez, John Davidson, Lonnie Davis, Lonnie Melton and me) ganged up on Bob and his lovely wife (he married Jean Lowe) and jokingly told him he was NOTHING without us (just ribbing because we loved him)! You judge for yourself. When I was a junior we had 3 wins and 18 losses (our coach was Ray Wheeler who was a great guy and a fantastic player; but not a great coach). I remember one practice when Mike Glassco was reprimanded by Ray for shooting too much. Mike told Ray that I (Dean) shot more than he did and Ray said that he (Ray) would only build his team around Mike when Mike started hitting more shots than me (or something like that). Mike and I never got along too well after that!! Mike was right; I did shoot too much! As a senior after Bob Decker became coach we were 18 and 3 and won the state championship. You tell me coaching isn't key in high school! On the flip side, I remember a day during practice when I was a junior and Ray was our coach. He loved to practice with us. He was not showing off but once I saw him come down the flood on a fast break and take off at the free throw line, sail through the air, and "DUNK IT." I clearly remember that was the most impressive thing I had ever seen. I WAS STUNNED! I did not fully appreciate that feat until years later. Maybe the second most impressive was Dale Curley who was standing below the basket at a practice that I was watching, who grabbed a rebound directly beneath the basket, jumped flat footed directly up and laid the ball above the rim (it was a soft dunk)! He and Ray both could float in the air. Who says white guys can't dunk???

Just for the record, I was called for "goal tending" once against Lamar. I used to practice my timing during set up drills when I was on the rebounding side by timing my jump and grabbing the net and pushing the lay up out the top; anyone of any height can do that with practice. During a game I was beaten on a fast break and (being mad) I went up and grabbed the net and pushed the ball out the top. The officials had to stop the game to get out the rule book to figure out what to call. They called it "goal tending." Now you have another story to tell your friends about your "BIG LITTLE BROTHER." This is a true story and you can ask anyone on my team to verify it. That story could also include the 38 free throws I made in three consecutive games without a miss including 19 of 19 in one game (Trinidad). In March of 2002 in Las Animas a fellow stopped me at Thaxton's grocery store and asked, "aren't you the guy who had that funny dance at the free throw line (you always looked at the floor until you shot, and had a hop that the officials sometime called illegal), but you seldom missed?. Can life get any better than having people remember those things?. My life is complete!

I will send the materials soon; I am sorry it took so long! Dean Ritchhart

Dean Lee RITCHHART and Evelyn KIRSCHMAN had the following children:

95   i.   CORINA K.[9] RITCHHART was born on 20 Mar 1961 in Denver, Colorado, USA. She married STEFAN A. BIRGH on 16 Jun 1984, son of Karl Richard BIRGH and Anna Marta CLAUSEN. He was born on 21 Jun 1957 in Lund, Dalarnas, Sweden.

      ii.   DAVID LEE RITCHHART[175] was born on 11 Jan 1963 in Denver, Colorado, USA.

    iii.   DENNIS DANIEL RITCHHART[175] was born on 11 Jan 1963 in Denver, Colorado, USA.

67. **MARY JANE**[8] **RITCHHART** (Delbert Bush[7], Alonzo Francis[6], Wesley[5], Andrew[4], John[3], Christian[2] RITSCHARD, Christian[1] RITSCHHART) was born on 29 Feb 1948 (La Junta, Colorado (Mennonite Hospital)). She died on 27 Apr 1979 (Denver, Colorado of lymphoma (cancer); Rose Memorial Hospital)[194]. She married (1) **ELDON JOHNSON** about 1970. He

was born on 18 Nov 1944. She married (2) **JOHN F. HAYES JR**. on 24 Oct 1976 in Boulder, Colorado, USA.

Eldon JOHNSON and Mary Jane RITCHHART had the following child:

96   i.   JACQUELINE[9] FITZPATRICK was born on 04 Mar 1965 (Canon City, Colorado, St. Thomas More Hospital). She married STEVEN WIRSZYLA on 25 Nov 1989 (St. Joseph's Catholic Church, Colorado Springs). He was born on 13 Sep 1962.

68. **KATHLEEN[8] CEARNAL** (Ethel Grace[7] RITCHHART, Alvin E.[6] RITCHHART, Wesley[5] RITCHHART, Andrew[4] RITCHHART, John[3] RITCHHART, Christian[2] RITSCHARD, Christian[1] RITSCHHART) was born in 1929[195]. She died on 24 Nov 1997[196]. She married **KING BRIDGES** in May 1952.

Notes for Kathleen CEARNAL: Kathleen contacted Dean Ritchhart in 1992, while she and her husband were visiting the Seattle area. She subsequently sent him a letter (dated Aug 31, 1992) with copies of many pictures that she had of the Ritchhart brothers and their wives. This included my grandfather, Alonzo, whom they called Lon. I tried to contact Kathleen in 2003 only to find out she passed away from cancer on Thanksgiving Day in 1997. Her daughter, Julie, responded to my letter via e-mail (julia.bridges@wellpoint.com).

King BRIDGES and Kathleen CEARNAL had the following children:

i.   JAMIE[9] BRIDGES[108] was born about 1954.

ii. JULIA BRIDGES was born about 1957.

Notes for Julia BRIDGES: Julia responded to my letter in 2003 to her mom, informing me her mother passed away in Nov 1977. She lived in Houston, TX and is either 43 or 46 years old. julia.bridges@wellpoint.com.

I later corresponded with her by e-mail in July 2008. I was attempting to get better copies of the photos that her mother had sent to Dean in 1992.

iii. UNK BRIDGES was born about 1960.

69. **CAROLYN[8] RITCHHART** (Curtis Burch[7], Curtis Andrew[6], Wesley[5], Andrew[4], John[3], Christian[2] RITSCHARD, Christian[1] RITSCHHART)[54] was born in Jun 1936[54]. She married **WILLIE GENE STEWART** on 21 Apr 1962[54].

Willie Gene STEWART and Carolyn RITCHHART had the following children:

i.   DIANE[9] STEWART[54] was born in Jun 1964[54]. She married TREUSDELL.

ii. DOUGLAS STEWART[54] was born in Sep 1965[54].

iii. JEFF STEWART[54] was born in Jun 1967[54].

70. **MARILYN[8] RITCHHART** (Curtis Burch[7], Curtis Andrew[6], Wesley[5], Andrew[4], John[3], Christian[2] RITSCHARD, Christian[1] RITSCHHART) was born in Oct 1937[54]. She married **MARTIN GROVES** on 19 Oct 1963[54].

Notes for Marilyn RITCHHART: I received a phone call from Marilyn on 5 April 2010 as she had looked at my ancestry.com family tree and noted that we shared a common ggrandfather, Wesley. She indicated that she had several documents and photos that might interest me. I also shared some information with her and informed her about The Ritchhart book. It turns out she lives near DFW airport, so I gave her Jim Richhart's phone number as she seemed interested in buying a copy.

Martin GROVES and Marilyn RITCHHART had the following children:

    i. CURTIS RITCHHART[9] GROVES[54] was born in Nov 1965[54].

    ii. JENNIFER GROVES[54] was born in Nov 1967[54].

71. **LINDA**[8] **RITCHHART** (Curtis Burch[7], Curtis Andrew[6], Wesley[5], Andrew[4], John[3], Christian[2] RITSCHARD, Christian[1] RITSCHHART)[54] was born in Aug 1947[54]. She married **BOB BARCLAY** on 24 Feb 1968[54].

Bob BARCLAY and Linda RITCHHART had the following children:

    i. GAYLE RENAE[9] BARCLAY[54] was born in Jun 1969[54].

    ii. BRADLEY BARCLAY[54] was born on 31 Aug 1974[54].

72. **DOROTHY BERNICE**[8] **COMPTON** (Edna Mamie[7] RITCHHART, Franklin Lester[6] RITCHHART, Wesley[5] RITCHHART, Andrew[4] RITCHHART, John[3] RITCHHART, Christian[2] RITSCHARD, Christian[1] RITSCHHART)[11] was born on 09 Apr 1923 (Carthage, MO). She married **EARL J. REES** on 04 Jun 1945 in Galena, Cherokee, Kansas, USA[11]. He was born on 13 Jan 1920[11].

Notes for Dorothy Bernice COMPTON: I (Del Ritchhart) met Dorothy and her two cousins Raymond and Paul in Carthage in July 1999. They remembered Uncle Alonzo (my grandfather Ritchhart).

Earl J. REES and Dorothy Bernice COMPTON had the following children:

97   i. LINDA MARIE[9] REES[11] was born on 31 Aug 1953. She married OSCAR JAMES COPENHAVER on 26 Dec 1971. He was born on 05 May 1952.

98   ii. GREGORY EARL REES[11] was born on 04 Jul 1956. He married SANDRA GAYLE DEONIER on 03 Jul 1976. She was born on 25 Nov 1957.

73. **RAYMOND RICHARD**[8] **RITCHHART** (Lester Carr[7], Franklin Lester[6], Wesley[5], Andrew[4], John[3], Christian[2] RITSCHARD, Christian[1] RITSCHHART) was born on 25 Jun 1926 (Carthage, MO). He married **MARGARETTE DAISY POINDEXTER** on 04 May 1948 in Jasper, Missouri, USA. She was born on 07 Jun 1928[11].

Notes for Raymond Richard RITCHHART: I met Raymond and his brother Paul, their cousin Dorothy Compton and their Aunt Bernice Chapman in Carthage in July 1999. They took us to Fasken Cemetery and told us about their recollections of the family. They remembered "Uncle Lon" who was Alonzo—my grandfather. Raymond had responded to my letter soliciting someone to meet with us on our cross country trip. He and his wife were very nice and the more sophisticated of the five we met with.

Raymond Richard RITCHHART and Margarette Daisy POINDEXTER had the following children:

99   i. DENNIS RAY[9] RITCHHART was born on 21 Dec 1951. He married (1) SUSAN HOENSHELL. He married (2) SANDRA RAE KELLER in Apr 1975. She was born on 02 Apr 1958.

ii. DIAN SUSAN RITCHHART was born on 17 Sep 1955.

iii. LEA ANN RITCHHART was born on 24 Feb 1961.

74. **RUSSELL**[8] **RITCHHART** (Lester Carr[7], Franklin Lester[6], Wesley[5], Andrew[4], John[3], Christian[2] RITSCHARD, Christian[1] RITSCHHART) was born on 25 Apr 1950. He married (1) **DELANA HODSON** on 10 Jul 1969. He married (2) **CONNIE COLE** on 15 Jan 1983. He married (3) **KATHY**

Russell RITCHHART and Delana HODSON had the following children:

i. WILLIAM RUSSEL[9] RITCHHART was born on 31 Dec 1969.

ii. ASHLEY LATISHA RITCHHART was born on 13 Nov 1983.

Russell RITCHHART and Connie COLE had the following child:

ii. ASHLEY LATISHA RITCHHART was born on 13 Nov 1983.

75. **JAMES KENNETH**[8] **RICHHART** (Clarence Leon[7], Levi William[6], William Z.[5], William[4] RITCHHART, Heinrich (Henry)[3] RITSCHARD, Christian[2] RITSCHARD, Christian[1] RITSCHHART) was born on 09 Jan 1933 in Fort Worth, Tarrant, Texas, USA. He married **BETTYE ANDERSON** on 20 Jun 1953, daughter of Clifford ANDERSON and Gertrude *. She was born on 26 Jan 1933 in Abilene, Jones, Texas, USA. She died on 22 Feb 2009 in North Richland Hills, Tarrant, Texas, USA.

James Kenneth RICHHART and Bettye ANDERSON had the following children:

i. JAMES MICHAEL[9] RICHHART was born on 16 Nov 1962 in Fort Worth, Tarrant, Texas, USA.

ii. CLIFFORD LAWRENCE RICHHART was born on 26 Jul 1967 in Fort Worth, Tarrant, Texas, USA.

Generation 9

76. **LINDA JOANN**[9] **RITCHHART** (Kenneth Francis[8], Samuel Clifford[7], Alonzo Francis[6], Wesley[5], Andrew[4], John[3], Christian[2] RITSCHARD, Christian[1] RITSCHHART) was born on 03 Apr 1949 in Manhattan, Pottawatomie, Kansas, USA. She married (1) **MORRIS MARK GROSSMAN** on 17 Nov 1972 in Woodbridge, Middlesex, New Jersey, USA. He was born on 01 Feb 1936 in Perth Amboy, Middlesex, New Jersey, USA. She married (2) **LARRY ROBINSON** on 28 Mar 2009 in Florida, USA.

Morris Mark GROSSMAN and Linda Joann RITCHHART had the following child:

i. DAVID MICHAEL[10] GROSSMAN was born on 30 Sep 1975.

77. **KENNETH MICHAEL**[9] **RITCHHART** (Kenneth Francis[8], Samuel Clifford[7], Alonzo Francis[6], Wesley[5], Andrew[4], John[3], Christian[2] RITSCHARD, Christian[1] RITSCHHART) was born on 28 May 1951 in Kansas City, Wyandotte, Kansas, USA. He married **TENA KAREN JACKSON** on 14 Feb 1986 in Montgomery, Alabama, USA. She was born on 09 Jul 1958 in Montgomery, Alabama, USA.

Kenneth Michael RITCHHART and Tena Karen JACKSON had the following children:

i. CHRISTOPHER MICHAEL[10] RITCHHART was born on 09 Oct 1989.

ii. MICHAEL SCOTT RITCHHART was born on 21 Oct 1992.

78. **CHARLES STEVEN**[9] **RITCHHART** (Kenneth Francis[8], Samuel Clifford[7], Alonzo Francis[6], Wesley[5], Andrew[4], John[3], Christian[2] RITSCHARD, Christian[1] RITSCHHART) was born on 19 Oct 1956 in Anderson, Madison, Indiana, USA. He married (1) **SUZANNE LOU WALTON** in Anderson, Madison, Indiana, USA. He married (2) **PAMELA SUE BENNETTE** on 19 Sep 1977 in Anderson, Madison, Indiana, USA. She was born on 28 Oct 1957 in Anderson, Madison, Indiana, USA.

Charles Steven RITCHHART and Pamela Sue BENNETTE had the following children:
    i. AMY SUE[10] RITCHHART was born on 27 Apr 1975.
    ii. CHRISTOPHER STEVEN RITCHHART was born on 17 Apr 1978.

79. **JEFFERY ALLAN**[9] **RITCHHART** (Kenneth Francis[8], Samuel Clifford[7], Alonzo Francis[6], Wesley[5], Andrew[4], John[3], Christian[2] RITSCHARD, Christian[1] RITSCHHART) was born on 10 Aug 1962 in Anderson, Madison, Indiana, USA. He married **ANN MARIE BABIARZ** on 26 May 1990 in Lake Tahoe, Nevada. She was born on 20 Nov 1967 in Chico, Butte, California, USA.

Jeffery Allan RITCHHART and Ann Marie BABIARZ had the following children:
    i. SHAWN DARRELL[10]OLSEN was born on 30 Oct 1982.
    ii. REBECCA ANN OLSEN was born on 08 Apr 1985.

80. **JAMES JOSEPH**[9] **RITCHHART** (Arthur August[8], Samuel Clifford[7], Alonzo Francis[6], Wesley[5], Andrew[4], John[3], Christian[2] RITSCHARD, Christian[1] RITSCHHART) was born on 09 Mar 1961 in Denver, Colorado, USA. He married **CONNIE JEAN RUSHTON** on 16 Apr 1988 in Wayne, Illinois, USA. She was born on 12 Apr 1959 in Elmhurst, Du Page, Illinois, USA.

James Joseph RITCHHART and Connie Jean RUSHTON had the following children:
    i. RACHEL[10] RITCHHART.
    ii. REBEKAH RITCHHART.
    iii. JAMES RITCHHART.

81. **KEVIN LEE**[9] **RITCHHART** (Clifford Eugene[8], Samuel Clifford[7], Alonzo Francis[6], Wesley[5], Andrew[4], John[3], Christian[2] RITSCHARD, Christian[1] RITSCHHART) was born on 05 Jul 1966 in Liberal, Seward, Kansas, USA. He married **TANDY LYNN DRACH** on 12 Jul 1986 in Dodge City, Ford, Kansas, USA. She was born on 09 Nov 1966 in Dodge City, Ford, Kansas, USA.

Kevin Lee RITCHHART and Tandy Lynn DRACH had the following child:
    i. KRISTA[10] RITCHHART.

82. **CHANNON LYNNE**[9] **RITCHHART** (Clifford Eugene[8], Samuel Clifford[7], Alonzo Francis[6], Wesley[5], Andrew[4], John[3], Christian[2] RITSCHARD, Christian[1] RITSCHHART) was born on 20 Feb 1968 in Garden City, Cherokee, Kansas, USA. She married **KRIS GRANTON GREGG** on 16 Aug 1986 in Odessa, Jewell, Kansas, USA. He was born on 26 Oct 1963 in El Campo, Wharton, Texas, USA.

Kris Granton GREGG and Channon Lynne RITCHHART had the following children:

    i. MATTHEW[10] GREGG.

    ii. ELIZABETH GREGG.

    iii. SARAH GREGG.

    iv. TIMOTHY GREGG.

83. **LOGAN EUGENE**[9] **RITCHHART** (Clifford Eugene[8], Samuel Clifford[7], Alonzo Francis[6], Wesley[5], Andrew[4], John[3], Christian[2] RITSCHARD, Christian[1] RITSCHHART) was born on 03 Jun 1969 in Garden City, Cherokee, Kansas, USA. He married **LISA LYNN ASHLEY** on 13 Aug 1988 in Oklahoma City, Oklahoma, Oklahoma, USA. She was born on 13 Jul 1962 in Middletown, Butler, Ohio, USA.

Logan Eugene RITCHHART and Lisa Lynn ASHLEY had the following children:

    i. TAD[10] RITCHHART.

    ii. ASHTON RITCHHART.

84. **TRENDA JANELL**[9] **RITCHHART** (Clifford Eugene[8], Samuel Clifford[7], Alonzo Francis[6], Wesley[5], Andrew[4], John[3], Christian[2] RITSCHARD, Christian[1] RITSCHHART) was born on 02 May 1973 in Garden City, Cherokee, Kansas, USA. She married (1) **MARK ALLAN LITTLE** on 05 Jun 1993 in Murfreesboro, Rutherford, Tennessee, USA. He was born on 08 Aug 1963 in Kettering, Montgomery, Ohio, USA. She married (2) **SCOTT DEAVER**.

Scott DEAVER and Trenda Janell RITCHHART had the following children:

    i. KARA[10] DEAVER.

    ii. COLBY DEAVER.

    iii. LANIE DEAVER.

    iv. ANDREW DEAVER.

85. **DAVID WESLEY**[9] **BARTON** (Margaret E[8] RUMSBY, Mary Lillian[7] RITCHHART, Alonzo Francis[6] RITCHHART, Wesley[5] RITCHHART, Andrew[4] RITCHHART, John[3] RITCHHART, Christian[2] RITSCHARD, Christian[1] RITSCHHART)[176] was born on 17 Mar 1944 in La Junta, Otero, Colorado, USA[176]. He married (1) **DIANE GILLILAND**. He married (2) **JANET BRANKLE**.

David Wesley BARTON and Diane GILLILAND had the following children:

100   i. DEANNA[10] BARTON[176] was born on 16 Jan 1968 in Sacramento, California, USA[176]. She married RODNEY GOLDEN on 08 Jun 1991 in Grand Prairie, Dallas, Texas, USA[176].

    ii. DANIELLE BARTON[176] was born on 25 Sep 1970 in Madrid, Spain. She married JAMES HARRIS on 13 Feb 1999 in Dallas, Texas, USA[176].

86. **NANCY LEE**[9] **BARTON** (Margaret E[8] RUMSBY, Mary Lillian[7] RITCHHART, Alonzo Francis[6] RITCHHART, Wesley[5] RITCHHART, Andrew[4] RITCHHART, John[3] RITCHHART, Christian[2] RITSCHARD, Christian[1] RITSCHHART)[176] was born on 27 Jun 1947 in Bakersfield, Kern, California, USA[176]. She married **GLENN POOLE** on 01 Jan 1968 in Las Vegas, Clark, Nevada, USA[176].

Glenn POOLE and Nancy Lee BARTON had the following children:

101   i.   JENNIFER[10] POOLE[176] was born on 28 Nov 1978 in Sacramento, California, USA[176]. She married KYLE GRAHAM on 17 Apr 2004.

      ii. HEATHER POOLE[176] was born on 07 Dec 1985 in Sacramento, California, USA[176].

     iii. MEGAN POOLE[176] was born on 24 May 1988 in Sacramento, California, USA[176].

87. **ROBERT LLOYD**[9] **KLEINKNIGHT** (Betty Lou[8] RUMSBY, Mary Lillian[7] RITCHHART, Alonzo Francis[6] RITCHHART, Wesley[5] RITCHHART, Andrew[4] RITCHHART, John[3] RITCHHART, Christian[2] RITSCHARD, Christian[1] RITSCHHART)[198] was born on 27 Aug 1948 in Bakersfield, Kern, California, USA[184,198]. He married **DEBORAH KENNETT** on 30 May 1978 in Fresno, California, USA[184].

Robert Lloyd KLEINKNIGHT and Deborah KENNETT had the following children:

      i.   ANN[10] KLEINKNIGHT.

102 ii. KATHRYN KLEINKNIGHT. She married TRAVIS O'CONNOR.

88. **STEVE**[9] **KLEINKNIGHT** (Betty Lou[8] RUMSBY, Mary Lillian[7] RITCHHART, Alonzo Francis[6] RITCHHART, Wesley[5] RITCHHART, Andrew[4] RITCHHART, John[3] RITCHHART, Christian[2] RITSCHARD, Christian[1] RITSCHHART)[184] was born on 09 Oct 1950 in Fresno, California, USA[184]. He married (1) **SHERRYL CALABRESE** on 10 May 1975 in Fresno, California, USA. He married (2) **JANA MILLS** on 03 Dec 2005 in Exeter, Tulare, California, USA.

Steve KLEINKNIGHT and Sherryl CALABRESE had the following children:

      i.   CURTIS[10] KLEINKNIGHT[184] was born on 02 Apr 1981[184].

      ii. DARREN KLEINKNIGHT[184] was born on 03 Jun 1985[184].

     iii. ERIK KLEINKNIGHT[184] was born on 12 Jun 1989[184].

89. **LAURIE LEE**[9] **SWOAP** (Betty Lou[8] RUMSBY, Mary Lillian[7] RITCHHART, Alonzo Francis[6] RITCHHART, Wesley[5] RITCHHART, Andrew[4] RITCHHART, John[3] RITCHHART, Christian[2] RITSCHARD, Christian[1] RITSCHHART) was born on 22 Jun 1944 in Bakersfield, Kern, California, USA[184]. She married **JOHN TILSON** on 25 Aug 1967 (Southern California).

John TILSON and Laurie Lee SWOAP had the following child:

      i.   JEFF[10] TILSON[184] was born on 06 Dec 1977[184].

90. **CHRISTINE ELIZABETH**[9] **WARD** (Patricia Catherine[8] RITCHHART, Paul Wesley[7] RITCHHART, Alonzo Francis[6] RITCHHART, Wesley[5] RITCHHART, Andrew[4] RITCHHART, John[3] RITCHHART, Christian[2] RITSCHARD, Christian[1] RITSCHHART) was born on 24 Oct 1974[135]. She married **DAVID PETERSON** on UNKNOWN date, son of Duane A. PETERSON and Barbara CARNAHAN. He was born on 23 Feb 1963[135].

David PETERSON and Christine Elizabeth WARD had the following children:

      i.   JOSHUA[10] PETERSON.

      ii. BRETT PETERSON.

     iii. BRIAN PETERSON.

91. **SHERI RENEE**[9] **WARD** (Patricia Catherine[8] RITCHHART, Paul Wesley[7] RITCHHART, Alonzo Francis[6] RITCHHART, Wesley[5] RITCHHART, Andrew[4] RITCHHART, John[3]

RITCHHART, Christian[2] RITSCHARD, Christian[1] RITSCHHART)[135] was born on 17 Jan 1978[135]. She married **KELLY** FEIKERT, son of Gary FEIKERT and KAREN. She met **GABE WATSON**.

Kelly FEIKERT and Sheri Renee WARD had the following children:

    i. CHASE[10] FEIKERT.

    ii. CONNER FEIKERT.

    iii. MOLLY FEIKERT.

Gabe WATSON and Sheri Renee WARD had the following child:

    i. MICHEALA CATHERINE[10] WARD[135].

92. **CHERYL ANN[9] RITCHHART** (Delbert Arthur[8], Delbert Bush[7], Alonzo Francis[6], Wesley[5], Andrew[4], John[3], Christian[2] RITSCHARD, Christian[1] RITSCHHART)[199,200] was born on 30 Aug 1960 in Honolulu, Hawaii, USA. She married **RONALD G. SHORT** on 22 Sep 1984 in Reno, Washoe, Nevada, USA[199], son of Terry Vern SHORT and Maryann WOOD. He was born on 20 Jun 1958 in Palo Alto, San Mateo, California, USA[201,202].

Ronald G SHORT and Cheryl Ann RITCHHART had the following children:

    i. JAMIE ANN[10] SHORT[200,207,208] was born on 06 Apr 1985 in Santa Clara, California, USA[200]. She married JUSTIN PATRICK CHRISTMAN on 19 Sep 2009 in South San Francisco, San Mateo, California, USA (California Golf Club), son of Richard CHRISTMAN and Pamela HOWARD. He was born on 25 Feb 1981 in Fallbrook, San Diego, California, USA[209,210].

    ii. LINDSAY MARIE SHORT[211,212] was born on 12 Mar 1986 in Mountain View, Santa Clara, California, USA[211,212].

    iii. KYLEIGH LYNN SHORT[213,214,215] was born on 15 Jul 1987 in Mountain View, Santa Clara, California, USA[213,215].

93. **DEBORA JANE[9] RITCHHART** (Delbert Arthur[8], Delbert Bush[7], Alonzo Francis[6], Wesley[5], Andrew[4], John[3], Christian[2] RITSCHARD, Christian[1] RITSCHHART)[203] was born on 29 Sep 1961 in Evanston, Cook, Illinois, USA[203]. She married **ERIC STERLING CANTRELL** on 24 Sep 1993 in San Diego, California, USA (Eliam Chapel), son of Richard Ellsworth CANTRELL Jr. and Sharon Roxie RALPH. He was born on 10 Nov 1964 in Encino, Los Angeles, California, USA.

Eric Sterling CANTRELL and Debora Jane RITCHHART had the following children:

    i. RYAN STERLING[10] CANTRELL[216] was born on 25 Oct 1995 in Fresno, California, USA[216].

    ii. SARA NICOLE CANTRELL was born on 12 Dec 1997 in Altoona, Blair, Pennsylvania, USA.

94. **LINDA MARIE[9] RITCHHART** (Delbert Arthur[8], Delbert Bush[7], Alonzo Francis[6], Wesley[5], Andrew[4], John[3], Christian[2] RITSCHARD, Christian[1] RITSCHHART)[204,205] was born on 07 Jun 1964 in San Diego, San Diego, California, USA[204,205,206]. She married **DOUGLAS**

GREGORY WIMER on 18 Mar 1986 in San Diego, San Diego, California, USA, son of Franklin Bernard WIMER and Margery Anne LOEFFLER. He was born on 10 Dec 1960 in Pittsburgh, Allegheny, Pennsylvania, USA.

Notes for Linda Marie RITCHHART: Married on a Saturday at a three o'clock Mass at Sacred Heart Church in Coronado, CA by Father Jerry O'Donnell. Reception dinner was at five o'clock at the Officers Club at NAS North Island on Coronado. The weather was great and everyone had a great time. Ironically, Linda was also born in Coronado, less than a mile from the Church.

Notes for Douglas Gregory WIMER: In researching Doug's ancestors I hit upon a long line tracing their family back to the village of Langensoultzbach which is now in Alsace, France. However, it is only a few kilometers from the German border and research indicates that border has frequently fluctuated over the last few centuries. A contact on the net who had researched Wimer also, suggested the book *History and Genealogy of the Ancestors and some Descendants of Stukely Westcott* by Roscoe L. Whitman as a source of info about Wimers in Pennsylvania.

Douglas Gregory WIMER and Linda Marie RITCHHART had the following children:

    i. VICTORIA ANN[10] WIMER was born on 25 Jul 1994 (Fort Collins. Colorado, Poudre Hospital).

    ii. KURT WIMER was born on 09 Aug 1997 in Fort Collins, Larimer, Colorado, USA.

    iii. CASSANDRA WIMER was born on 09 Aug 1997 in Fort Collins, Larimer, Colorado, USA.

95. **CORINA K.**[9] **RITCHHART** (Dean Lee[8], Delbert Bush[7], Alonzo Francis[6], Wesley[5], Andrew[4], John[3], Christian[2] RITSCHARD, Christian[1] RITSCHHART) was born on 20 Mar 1961 in Denver, Colorado, USA. She married **STEFAN A. BIRGH** on 16 Jun 1984, son of Karl Richard BIRGH and Anna Marta CLAUSEN. He was born on 21 Jun 1957 in Lund, Dalarnas, Sweden.

Stefan A. BIRGH and Corina K. RITCHHART had the following children:

    i. NICOLE EVANNA[10] BIRGH was born on 31 Jan 1988 (Seattle, WA 11:35 p.m.).

    ii. KRISTINA KAY BIRGH was born on 16 Jul 1989 in Seattle, King, Washington, USA.

96. **JACQUELINE**[9] **FITZPATRICK** (Mary Jane[8] RITCHHART, Delbert Bush[7] RITCHHART, Alonzo Francis[6] RITCHHART, Wesley[5] RITCHHART, Andrew[4] RITCHHART, John[3] RITCHHART, Christian[2] RITSCHARD, Christian[1] RITSCHHART) was born on 04 Mar 1965 (Canon City, Colorado, St. Thomas More Hospital). She married **STEVEN WIRSZYLA** on 25 Nov 1989 (St. Joseph's Catholic Church, Colorado Springs). He was born on 13 Sep 1962.

Notes for Jacqueline FITZPATRICK: Adopted shortly after birth by Fitzpatricks. They had two boys who were also adopted. Parents divorced in 1976. Mother, Carol, remarried in 1980 and had a baby boy. Her new married name is Gass. Her father passed away in 1983.

Jackii met Steve in San Diego where he had just gotten out of the Navy. He was originally from New York. He has a sister who lives in Oceanside, California and Jackii has a great-aunt who lives in Lakeside, California.

Steven WIRSZYLA and Jacqueline FITZPATRICK had the following children:

  i. ZACK[10] WIRSZYLA was born in Nov 1994.

  ii. ZOE WIRSZYLA was born about Jan 2000.

97. **LINDA MARIE**[9] **REES** (Dorothy Bernice[8] COMPTON, Edna Mamie[7] RITCHHART, Franklin Lester[6] RITCHHART, Wesley[5] RITCHHART, Andrew[4] RITCHHART, John[3] RITCHHART, Christian[2] RITSCHARD, Christian[1] RITSCHHART)[11] was born on 31 Aug 1953. She married **OSCAR JAMES COPENHAVER** on 26 Dec 1971. He was born on 05 May 1952.

Oscar James COPENHAVER and Linda Marie REES had the following child:

  i. JASON THOMAS[10] COPENHAVER[11] was born on 09 Nov 1973.

98. **GREGORY EARL**[9] **REES** (Dorothy Bernice[8] COMPTON, Edna Mamie[7] RITCHHART, Franklin Lester[6] RITCHHART, Wesley[5] RITCHHART, Andrew[4] RITCHHART, John[3] RITCHHART, Christian[2] RITSCHARD, Christian[1] RITSCHHART)[11] was born on 04 Jul 1956. He married **SANDRA GAYLE DEONIER** on 03 Jul 1976. She was born on 25 Nov 1957.

Gregory Earl REES and Sandra Gayle DEONIER had the following child:

  i. GREGORY SHANE[10] REES[11] was born on 14 Aug 1979.

99. **DENNIS RAY**[9] **RITCHHART** (Raymond Richard[8], Lester Carr[7], Franklin Lester[6], Wesley[5], Andrew[4], John[3], Christian[2] RITSCHARD, Christian[1] RITSCHHART) was born on 21 Dec 1951. He married (1) **SUSAN HOENSHELL**. He married (2) **SANDRA RAE KELLER** in Apr 1975. She was born on 02 Apr 1958.

Dennis Ray RITCHHART and Sandra Rae KELLER had the following children:

103 i. TRAVIS RAY[10] RITCHHART[11] was born on 30 Oct 1976.

  ii. TRISHA RAE RITCHHART was born on 08 Feb 1977.

  iii. DANIEL RAY RITCHHART was born on 28 Sep 1982.

Generation 10

100. **DEANNA**[10] **BARTON** (David Wesley[9], Margaret E[8] RUMSBY, Mary Lillian[7] RITCHHART, Alonzo Francis[6] RITCHHART, Wesley[5] RITCHHART, Andrew[4] RITCHHART, John[3] RITCHHART, Christian[2] RITSCHARD, Christian[1] RITSCHHART)[176] was born on 16 Jan 1968 in Sacramento, California, USA[176]. She married **RODNEY GOLDEN** on 08 Jun 1991 in Grand Prairie, Dallas, Texas, USA[176].

Rodney GOLDEN and Deanna BARTON had the following children:

  i. REILLY[11] GOLDEN[176] was born on 05 Feb 1998[176].

  ii. BRADY GOLDEN was born on 05 Feb 2008[176].

101. **JENNIFER**[10] **POOLE** (Nancy Lee[9] BARTON, Margaret E[8] RUMSBY, Mary Lillian[7] RITCHHART, Alonzo Francis[6] RITCHHART, Wesley[5] RITCHHART, Andrew[4] RITCHHART, John[3] RITCHHART, Christian[2] RITSCHARD, Christian[1] RITSCHHART)[176] was born on 28

Nov 1978 in Sacramento, California, USA[176]. She married **KYLE GRAHAM** on 17 Apr 2004.

Kyle GRAHAM and Jennifer POOLE had the following children:

    i. BAILEY[11] GRAHAM[176] was born on 14 Nov 2006[176].

    ii. TAYLOR GRAHAM[176] was born on 28 Dec 2008[176].

102. **KATHRYN**[10] **KLEINKNIGHT** (Robert Lloyd[9], Betty Lou[8] RUMSBY, Mary Lillian[7] RITCHHART, Alonzo Francis[6] RITCHHART, Wesley[5] RITCHHART, Andrew[4] RITCHHART, John[3] RITCHHART, Christian[2] RITSCHARD, Christian[1] RITSCHHART). She married **TRAVIS O'CONNOR**.

Travis O'CONNOR and Kathryn KLEINKNIGHT had the following children:

    i. SEAN[11] O'CONNOR.

    ii. SAMANTHA O'CONNOR.

103. **TRAVIS RAY**[10] **RITCHHART** (Dennis Ray[9], Raymond Richard[8], Lester Carr[7], Franklin Lester[6], Wesley[5], Andrew[4], John[3], Christian[2] RITSCHARD, Christian[1] RITSCHHART)[11] was born on 30 Oct 1976.

Travis Ray RITCHHART had the following children:

    i. AARON[11] RITCHHART[11] was born in 1991.

    ii. DEVIN RAY RITCHHART[11] was born in 1994.

    iii. DEIDRE RAE RITCHHART[11] was born in 1994.

Sources

1   Bettye Anderson Richhart, *Richhart, Ritchhart, Ritschard, A Swiss-German family from 1500 until 1993.* (North Richland Hills, Tex., B.A. Richhart, 1993), 23.

2   Ethel E. Beieler Gould, *Genealogy of the family of Jacob Blessing I of Pennsylvania and Virginia.* (Woodinville, WA: Vanderloop Communications, 1989).

3   FamilySearch.org, LDS Pedigree Charts, Family History Centers.

4   Ancestry.com, *One World Tree*^{SM} (Provo, UT, USA: The Generations Network, Inc., n.d.), www.ancestry.com, database online. Provo, UT, USA: The Generations Network, Inc.

5   *History of Ross and Highland Counties, Ohio* (Published in 1880), Carlsbad Library.

6   Ancestry.com, OneWorldTree (Provo, UT, USA, The Generations Network, Inc.), www.ancestry.com, Database online. Record for Abraham Ritchhart.

7   Ancestry.com, *Public Member Trees* (Provo, UT, USA, The Generations Network, Inc., 2006), www.ancestry.com, Database online. Record for Elizabeth Messersmith.

8   Martha Gerber Rittinger, *History of Springbank & Yellowbud Communities* (Yellowbud, Ohio, Springbank United Methodist Church, 1999), Allen Co. Public Library.

9   Headstone, Springbank Cemetery, Ross Co., OH, Took photos in July 1999 while visiting Ritchhart family locations.

10   Gearhart, *Revolutionary War Patriots of Ross Co., Ohio* (Chillicothe, Ohio: Sons of the American Revolution , 203).

11   Chart from Raymond Ritchhart, 1999.

12   Bettye Anderson Richhart, *Richhart, Ritchhart, Ritschard, A Swiss-German family from 1500 until 1993.* (North Richland Hills, Tex., B.A. Richhart, 1993), 38.

13   Bettye Anderson Richhart, *Richhart, Ritchhart, Ritschard, A Swiss-German family from 1500 until 1993.* (North Richland Hills, Tex., B.A. Richhart, 1993), 43.

14   Ancestry.com, *Public Member Trees* (Provo, UT, USA, The Generations Network, Inc., 2006), www.ancestry.com, Database online. Record for Andrew Ritchhart. This is probably confused with the date that Joseph Boothe attested to the marriage application which, according to Hamilton County Marriage Records was May 24, 1841.

15   Ancestry.com, *Public Member Trees* (Provo, UT, USA, The Generations Network, Inc., 2006), www.ancestry.com, Database online. Record for Samuel Ritchhart.

16   Ohio Land Records.

17   Ancestry.com, *Public Member Trees* (Provo, UT, USA, The Generations Network, Inc., 2006), www.ancestry.com, Database online. Record for John Ritchhart.

18   Bettye Anderson Richhart, *Richhart, Ritchhart, Ritschard, A Swiss-German family from 1500 until 1993.* (North Richland Hills, Tex., B.A. Richhart, 1993), 23.

19   Ancestry.com, *One World Tree*^{SM} (Provo, UT, USA: The Generations Network, Inc., n.d.), www.ancestry.com, database online. Provo, UT, USA: The Generations Network, Inc.

20   Ancestry.com, *Iowa State Census Collection, 1836–1925* (Provo, UT, USA: The Generations Network, Inc., 2007), www.ancestry.com, Online publication—Ancestry.com, Iowa State Census

Collection, 1836–1925 [database online]. Provo, UT, USA: The Generations Network, Inc., 2007. Original data—Microfilm of Iowa State Censuses, 1856, 1885, 1895, 1905, 1915, 1925 as well various special censuses from 1836–1897 obtained from the State Historical Society of Iowa via Heritage Quest.

21 *Ross Co., Ohio Marriages 1850–99*, Lists by brides and by grooms with the date of the marriage. Found in the Allen County Public Library.

22 Ohio Genealogy Express—Ross Co., Ohio Marriages, www.ohiogenealogyexpress.com/ross/marriages

23 Springbank Cemetery Headstone.

24 George J. Richman, *History of Hancock County, Indiana* (Greenfield, IN, William Mitchell, 1916), Family History Library.

25 Ancestry.com, *Public Member Trees* (Provo, UT, USA, The Generations Network, Inc., 2006), www.ancestry.com, Database online. Record for Sally Coverdale.

26 Ancestry.com, *Public Member Trees* (Provo, UT, USA, The Generations Network, Inc., 2006), www.ancestry.com, Database online. Record for Samuel Ritchhart.

27 Peggy Sapp, Springfield, Ill, *Family Pedigrees 1500–1990* FTM.

28 Ross, Ohio, *Early Marriage Bonds of Ohio—1828*, Daughters of the American Revolution.

29 *Hamilton, Indiana Marriage Records 1837–45*, Allen Co. Public Library, Minister: Craig Moses.

30 Ancestry.com, *Public Member Trees* (Provo, UT, USA, The Generations Network, Inc., 2006), www.ancestry.com, Database online. Record for George Booth.

31 Chart from Kathleen Bridges, August 1992. Bettye Richhart's book lists the child as Collins, which might have been a nickname for Cornelius.

32 Bettye Anderson Richhart, *Richhart, Ritchhart, Ritschard, A Swiss-German family from 1500 until 1993*. (North Richland Hills, Tex., B.A. Richhart, 1993)

33 CD #164, S.D. Mormon library, *Death Records*.

34 1850 Kosciusco, IN census, taken from Bettye Richhart's book.

35 Scott Fellers, Ohio GenWeb by Scott Fellers.

36 *Ross Co. Marriage Records 1876–1900*, Allen Co. Public Library.

37 Ancestry.com, *Public Member Trees* (Provo, UT, USA, The Generations Network, Inc., 2006), www.ancestry.com, Database online.

38 Ancestry.com, *Public Member Trees* (Provo, UT, USA, The Generations Network, Inc., 2006), www.ancestry.com, Database online.

39 Ross Co. Genealogical Society, *Ancestor Charts of Ross Co Genealogical Society*, 977.182 D2 ANC. Carlsbad Library

40 Ancestry.com, 1970 Census, FTM.

41 *1870 Census. Ross Co., Ohio.*

42 *1880 United States Federal Census* (Provo, UT, USA: The Generations Network, Inc., 2005, www.ancestry.com, Online publication. 1880 U.S. Census Index provided by The Church of Jesus Christ of Latter-day Saints © Copyright 1999 Intellectual Reserve, Inc. All rights reserved. Original data—United States of America, Bureau of the Census. Tenth Census of the United

States. Washington, D.C.: National Archives and Records Administration, 1880. Sandusky, Erie, Ohio, ED 121, roll T9_1013, page 234.4000, image 0290.

43   *1880 United States Federal Census* (Provo, UT, USA: The Generations Network, Inc., 2005, www.ancestry.com, Online publication. 1880 U.S. Census Index provided by The Church of Jesus Christ of Latter-day Saints © Copyright 1999 Intellectual Reserve, Inc. All rights reserved. Original data—United States of America, Bureau of the Census. Tenth Census of the United States, 1880. Washington, D.C.: National Archives and Records Administration, 1880. Noblesville, Hamilton, Indiana, ED 40, roll T9_281, page 432.1000, image 0512.

44   Ancestry.com. *Indiana Marriage Collection, 1800–1941* [database online]. Provo, UT, USA: Ancestry.com Operations Inc, 2005. Original data:
Works Progress Administration, comp. *Index to Marriage Records.* Indiana: Indiana Works Progress Administration, 1938–1940.
Jordan Dodd, Liahona Research, comp. Electronic transcription of marriage records held by the individual counties in Indiana. Many of these records are on microfilm at the Family History Library in Salt Lake City, Utah.

45   *1900 United States Federal Census* (Provo, UT, USA: The Generations Network, Inc., 2004, www.ancestry.com, online publication. Original data—United States of America, Bureau of the Census. Twelfth Census of the United States, 1900. Washington, D.C.: National Archives and Records Administration, 1900). Census Place: Carthage Ward 5, Jasper, Missouri; Roll: T623 866; Page: 7B; Enumeration District: 62, birthdate: abt 1843, Birth place: Indiana, Residence date: 1900 Residence place: Carthage Ward 5, Jasper, Missouri.

46   *1920 United States Federal Census* (Provo, UT, USA: The Generations Network, Inc., 2005), www.ancestry.com, Online publication. Original data United States of America, Bureau of the Census. Fourteenth Census of the United States. Washington, D.C.: National Archives and Records Administration, 1920.T625, 2076 rolls). Census Place: Carthage Ward 5, Jasper, Missouri; Roll: T625_922; Page: 6B; Enumeration District: 86; Image: 908, birthdate: abt 1876, Birth place: Indiana, Residence date: 1920 Residence place: Carthage Ward 5, Jasper, Missouri.

47   *1880 United States Federal Census* (Provo, UT, USA: The Generations Network, Inc., 2005, www.ancestry.com, Online publication. 1880 U.S. Census Index provided by The Church of Jesus Christ of Latter-day Saints © Copyright 1999 Intellectual Reserve, Inc. All rights reserved. Original data—United States of America, Bureau of the Census. Tenth Census of the United States, 1880. Washington, D.C.: National Archives and Records Administration, 1880. Census Place: Noblesville, Hamilton, Indiana; Roll: T9_281; Family History Film: 1254281; Page: 432.1000; Enumeration District: 40; Image: 0512, birthdate: abt 1842, Birth place: Indiana, Residence date: 1880, Residence place: Noblesville, Hamilton, Indiana, United States.

48   Ancestry.com, *1850 United States Federal Census* (Online publication; Provo, UT, USA: The Generations Network, Inc., 2005. Original data—United States of America, Bureau of the Census. Seventh Census of the United States, 1850. Washington, D.C.: National Archives and Records Administration, 1850, M432), Year: 1850; Census Place: Noblesville, Hamilton, Indiana; Roll: M432_148; Page: 100; Image: 521, birthdate: abt 1841, Birth place: Indiana, Residence date: 1850 Residence place: Noblesville, Hamilton, Indiana.

49   Ancestry.com, *U.S. National Homes for Disabled Volunteer Soldiers, 1866–1938* (Provo, UT, USA, Ancestry.com Operations Inc, 2007), www.ancestry.com, Database online. Record for Wesley Ritchhart.

50 Ancestry.com, *Public Member Trees* (Provo, UT, USA, The Generations Network, Inc., 2006), www.ancestry.com, Database online.

51 Ancestry.com, *Public Member Trees* (Provo, UT, USA, The Generations Network, Inc., 2006), www.ancestry.com, Database online. Record for Curtis A Ritchhart.

52 Ancestry.com, *Public Member Trees* (Provo, UT, USA, The Generations Network, Inc., 2006), www.ancestry.com, Database online. Record for Alonzo F Ritchhart.

53 Ancestry.com. *Indiana Marriage Collection, 1800–1941* [database online]. Provo, UT, USA: Ancestry.com Operations Inc, 2005. Original data:
Works Progress Administration, comp. *Index to Marriage Records*. Indiana: Indiana Works Progress Administration, 1938–1940. Hamilton Co., IN.

54 Marilyn Groves, Marilyn Ritchhart Groves e-mail of April 2010 (April 6, 2010), Personal files of Del Ritchhart, This came from a baptismal certificate held by Marilyn Ritchhart Groves. She e-mailed me the information. I did not view the certificate first hand.

55 *1920 Federal Census, Carthage, MO.*

56 Susan Bevelhimer, *Hamilton County Will Records 1824–1901* (Cook & McDowell, 1981), Allen Co. Public Library.

57 *1930 United States Federal Census* (Provo, UT, USA: The Generations Network, Inc., 2002), www.ancestry.com, Online publication. Original data United States of America, Bureau of the Census. Fifteenth Census of the United States. Washington, D.C.: National Archives and Records Administration, 1930.T626, 2,667 rolls). Noblesville, Hamilton, Indiana, ED 15, roll 590, page 2A, image 914.0.

58 *1910 United States Federal Census* (Provo, UT, USA: The Generations Network, Inc., 2006), www.ancestry.com, Online publication. Original data United States of America, Bureau of the Census. Thirteenth Census of the United States. Washington, D.C.: National Archives and Records Administration, 1910.T624, 1,178 rolls). 1-Wd Noblesville, Hamilton, Indiana, ED 107, roll 353, part 1, pagse 187A.

59 Bettye Anderson Richhart, *Richhart, Ritchhart, Ritschard, A Swiss-German family from 1500 until 1993.* (North Richland Hills, Tex., B.A. Richhart, 1993), 47.

60 *1870 United States Federal Census* (Provo, UT, USA: The Generations Network, Inc., 2003), www.ancestry.com, database online, 2003. Indexed by Ancestry.com from microfilmed schedules of the 1870 U.S. Federal Decennial Census. Original data: Data imaged from National Archives and Records Administration. Ninth Census of the United States, 1870. M593, 1,761 rolls). Noblesville, Hamilton, Indiana, post office Noblesville, roll 319, page 135, image 270.

61 *1930 United States Federal Census* (Provo, UT, USA: The Generations Network, Inc., 2002), www.ancestry.com, Online publication. Original data United States of America, Bureau of the Census. Fifteenth Census of the United States. Washington, D.C.: National Archives and Records Administration, 1930.T626, 2,667 rolls). Noblesville, Hamilton, Indiana, ED 15, roll 590, page , image 914.0.

62 *1930 United States Federal Census* (Provo, UT, USA: The Generations Network, Inc., 2002), www.ancestry.com, Online publication. Original data United States of America, Bureau of the Census. Fifteenth Census of the United States. Washington, D.C.: National Archives and Records Administration, 1930.T626, 2,667 rolls). Noblesville, Hamilton, Indiana, ED 15, roll 590, page , image 914.0. Record for Charles Ritchhart.

63 *1930 United States Federal Census* (Provo, UT, USA: The Generations Network, Inc., 2002), www.ancestry.com, Online publication. Original data United States of America, Bureau of the Census. Fifteenth Census of the United States. Washington, D.C.: National Archives and Records Administration, 1930.T626, 2,667 rolls). Noblesville, IN.

64 Bettye Anderson Richhart, *Richhart, Ritchhart, Ritschard, A Swiss-German family from 1500 until 1993.* (North Richland Hills, Tex., B.A. Richhart, 1993), 109.

65 Bettye Anderson Richhart, *Richhart, Ritchhart, Ritschard, A Swiss-German family from 1500 until 1993.* (North Richland Hills, Tex., B.A. Richhart, 1993), 41.

66 *Ross Co., Ohio Families Vol II*, Carlsbad Library.

67 Ancestry.com, *California Death Index, 1940–1997* (Provo, UT, USA: The Generations Network, Inc., 2000). Original data: State of California. *California Death Index, 1940–1997.* Sacramento, CA: State of California Department of Health Services, Center for Health Statistics, 19–.

68 Family History from Clifford Ritchhart.

69 Ancestry.com, *One World Tree*SM (Provo, UT, USA: The Generations Network, Inc., n.d.), www. ancestry.com, database online. Provo, UT, USA: The Generations Network, Inc.

70 *1930 United States Federal Census* (Provo, UT, USA: The Generations Network, Inc., 2002), www.ancestry.com, Online publication. Original data United States of America, Bureau of the Census. Fifteenth Census of the United States. Washington, D.C.: National Archives and Records Administration, 1930.T626, 2,667 rolls). La Junta, Otero, Colorado, ED 8, roll 248, page , image 99.0. Record for Dalbert Ritchhart.

71 *1880 United States Federal Census* (Provo, UT, USA: The Generations Network, Inc., 2005, www.ancestry.com, Online publication. 1880 U.S. Census Index provided by The Church of Jesus Christ of Latter-day Saints © Copyright 1999 Intellectual Reserve, Inc. All rights reserved. Original data—United States of America, Bureau of the Census. Tenth Census of the United States, 1880. Washington, D.C.: National Archives and Records Administration, 1880. Census Place: Noblesville, Hamilton, Indiana; Roll: T9_281; Family History Film: 1254281; Page: 432.1000; Enumeration District: 40; Image: 0512, birthdate: abt 1867, Birth place: Indiana, Residence date: 1880, Residence place: Noblesville, Hamilton, Indiana, United States.

72 Ancestry.com, *California Death Index, 1940–1997* (Provo, UT, USA: The Generations Network, Inc., 2000). Original data: State of California. *California Death Index, 1940–1997.* Sacramento, CA: State of California Department of Health Services, Center for Health Statistics, 19–. Birthdate: 3 Nov 1867, Birth place: Indiana, Death date: 27 May 1959, Death place: Stanislaus, California.

73 *1930 United States Federal Census* (Provo, UT, USA: The Generations Network, Inc., 2002), www.ancestry.com, Online publication. Original data United States of America, Bureau of the Census. Fifteenth Census of the United States. Washington, D.C.: National Archives and Records Administration, 1930.T626, 2,667 rolls). Census Place: La Junta, Otero, Colorado; Roll: 248; Page: 6B; Enumeration District: 8; Image: 99.0, birthdate: abt 1868, Birth place: Indiana, Residence date: 1930 Residence place: La Junta, Otero, Colorado.

74 *1870 United States Federal Census* (Provo, UT, USA: The Generations Network, Inc., 2003), www.ancestry.com, database online, 2003. Indexed by Ancestry.com from microfilmed schedules of the 1870 U.S. Federal Decennial Census. Original data: Data imaged from National Archives and Records Administration. Ninth Census of the United States, 1870. M593, 1,761 rolls). Birthdate: abt 1868, Birth place: Indiana, Residence date: 1870, Residence place: Wayne,

Hamilton, Indiana.

75   *1900 United States Federal Census* (Provo, UT, USA: The Generations Network, Inc., 2004, www.ancestry.com, online publication. Original data—United States of America, Bureau of the Census. Twelfth Census of the United States, 1900. Washington, D.C.: National Archives and Records Administration, 1900). Census Place: Preston, Jasper, Missouri; Roll: T623_867; Page: 7B; Enumeration District: 65, birth date Nov 1867, Birth place: Indiana, Residence date: 1900, Residence place: Preston, Jasper, Missouri.

76   *Ancestry Family Trees* (Online publication—Provo, UT, USA: The Generations Network. Original data: Family Tree files submitted by Ancestry members). http://trees.ancestry.com/pt/ AMTCitationRedir.aspx?tid=2906494&pid=-1803570457.

77   Ancestry.com, *Public Member Trees* (Provo, UT, USA, The Generations Network, Inc., 2006), www.ancestry.com, Database online. Record for Grace Azetta Bush.

78   La Junta Newspaper Wedding Announcement (La Junta, Colorado, January 1902), Personal files of Del Ritchhart.

79   *1930 United States Federal Census* (Provo, UT, USA: The Generations Network, Inc., 2002), www.ancestry.com, Online publication. Original data United States of America, Bureau of the Census. Fifteenth Census of the United States. Washington, D.C.: National Archives and Records Administration, 1930.T626, 2,667 rolls). La Junta, Otero, Colorado, ED 8, roll 248, page , image 99.0.

80   June 1880 Census. Indicated she was 7 months old, and her birth month was November.

81   *1880 United States Federal Census* (Provo, UT, USA: The Generations Network, Inc., 2005, www.ancestry.com, Online publication. 1880 U.S. Census Index provided by The Church of Jesus Christ of Latter-day Saints © Copyright 1999 Intellectual Reserve, Inc. All rights reserved. Original data—United States of America, Bureau of the Census. Tenth Census of the United States, 1880. Washington, D.C.: National Archives and Records Administration, 1880. Census Place: Carthage, Jasper, Missouri; Roll: T9_694; Family History Film: 1254694; Page: 479.2000; Enumeration District: 66; Image: 0761. Record for Samuel S. Bush.

82   Ancestry.com, *Public Member Trees* (Provo, UT, USA, The Generations Network, Inc., 2006), www.ancestry.com, Database online. Record for Grace Bush.

83   Ancestry.com, *Public Member Trees* (Provo, UT, USA, The Generations Network, Inc., 2006), www.ancestry.com, Database online. Record for Grace Azetta Bush.

84   Ancestry.com, *Public Member Trees* (Provo, UT, USA, The Generations Network, Inc., 2006), www.ancestry.com, Database online. Record for Grace Azetta Bush.

85   *1920 United States Federal Census* (Provo, UT, USA: The Generations Network, Inc., 2005), www.ancestry.com, Online publication. Original data United States of America, Bureau of the Census. Fourteenth Census of the United States. Washington, D.C.: National Archives and Records Administration, 1920.T625, 2076 rolls). Madison, Jasper, Missouri, image 675.

86   *1930 United States Federal Census* (Provo, UT, USA: The Generations Network, Inc., 2002), www.ancestry.com, Online publication. Original data United States of America, Bureau of the Census. Fifteenth Census of the United States. Washington, D.C.: National Archives and Records Administration, 1930.T626, 2,667 rolls). Madison, Jasper, Missouri, ED 39, roll 1205, page , image 1077.0.

87   *1930 United States Federal Census* (Provo, UT, USA: The Generations Network, Inc., 2002),

www.ancestry.com, Online publication. Original data United States of America, Bureau of the Census. Fifteenth Census of the United States. Washington, D.C.: National Archives and Records Administration, 1930.T626, 2,667 rolls). Census Place: Madison, Jasper, Missouri; Roll: 1205; Page: 2A; Enumeration District: 39; Image: 1077.0. Record for Alvin E Ritchhart.

88   Ancestry.com, *Public Member Trees* (Provo, UT, USA, The Generations Network, Inc., 2006), www.ancestry.com, Database online. Record for Ethel Ritchhart.

89   Ancestry.com, *Public Member Trees* (Provo, UT, USA, The Generations Network, Inc., 2006), www.ancestry.com, Database online. Record for Ethel Ritchhart.

90   Ancestry.com, *Public Member Trees* (Provo, UT, USA, The Generations Network, Inc., 2006), www.ancestry.com, Database online. Record for Ethel Ritchhart.

91   *1910 Federal Census, Madison, Jasper Co., MO.*

92   Ancestry.com, *Public Member Trees* (Provo, UT, USA, The Generations Network, Inc., 2006), www.ancestry.com, Database online. Record for William W Carr.

93   Ancestry.com, *Public Member Trees* (Provo, UT, USA, The Generations Network, Inc., 2006), www.ancestry.com, Database online. Record for Curtis Andrew Ritchhart.

94   *1930 United States Federal Census* (Provo, UT, USA: The Generations Network, Inc., 2002), www.ancestry.com, Online publication. Original data United States of America, Bureau of the Census. Fifteenth Census of the United States. Washington, D.C.: National Archives and Records Administration, 1930.T626, 2,667 rolls). Census Place: Marion, Jasper, Missouri; Roll: 1206; Page: 3A; Enumeration District: 45; Image: 209.0. Record for Curtis B. Ritchhart.

95   Wedding announcement, but no year given., Clippings from Kathleen Bridges.

96   Ancestry.com, *Public Member Trees* (Provo, UT, USA, The Generations Network, Inc., 2006), www.ancestry.com, Database online. Record for Pearl Penny.

97   *1930 United States Federal Census* (Provo, UT, USA: The Generations Network, Inc., 2002), www.ancestry.com, Online publication. Original data United States of America, Bureau of the Census. Fifteenth Census of the United States. Washington, D.C.: National Archives and Records Administration, 1930.T626, 2,667 rolls). Census Place: Madison, Jasper, Missouri; Roll: 1205; Page: 9A; Enumeration District: 39; Image: 1091.0. Record for Frank L Ritchhart.

98   50th Anniversary Newspaper Article.

99   *1880 United States Federal Census* (Provo, UT, USA: The Generations Network, Inc., 2005, www.ancestry.com, Online publication. 1880 U.S. Census Index provided by The Church of Jesus Christ of Latter-day Saints © Copyright 1999 Intellectual Reserve, Inc. All rights reserved. Original data—United States of America, Bureau of the Census. Tenth Census of the United States, 1880. Washington, D.C.: National Archives and Records Administration, 1880. Census Place: Noblesville, Hamilton, Indiana; Roll: T9_281; Family History Film: 1254281; Page: 432.1000; Enumeration District: 40; Image: 0512. birthdate: abt 1873, Birth place: Indiana, Residence date: 1880 Residence place: Noblesville, Hamilton, Indiana, United States.

100   Ancestry.com, *Public Member Trees* (Provo, UT, USA, The Generations Network, Inc., 2006), www.ancestry.com, Database online. Record for Bernise Ritchhart.

101   Ancestry.com, *World War I Draft Registration Cards, 1917–1918* (Provo, UT, USA, The Generations Network, Inc., 2005), www.ancestry.com, Database online. Original data—United States, Selective Service System. World War I Selective Service System Draft Registration Cards,

1917–1918. Washington, D.C.: National Archives and Records Administration, M1509, 4,582 rolls. Registration Location: Jasper County, Missouri; Roll: 1683222; Draft Board: 1. Record for Frank Lester Ritchhart.

102 Ancestry.com, *Public Member Trees* (Provo, UT, USA, The Generations Network, Inc., 2006), www.ancestry.com, Database online. Record for Lester Carr Ritchhart.

103 Ancestry.com, *Public Member Trees* (Provo, UT, USA, The Generations Network, Inc., 2006), www.ancestry.com, Database online. Record for Lester Carr Ritchhart.

104 *1930 United States Federal Census* (Provo, UT, USA: The Generations Network, Inc., 2002), www.ancestry.com, Online publication. Original data United States of America, Bureau of the Census. Fifteenth Census of the United States. Washington, D.C.: National Archives and Records Administration, 1930.T626, 2,667 rolls). El Monte, Los Angeles, California, ED 928, roll 126, page , image 566.0.

105 Ancestry.com, *Military Record of Colorado Soldiers, California Deaths 1940–97.*

106 Ancestry.com, *California Death Index, 1940–1997* (Provo, UT, USA: The Generations Network, Inc., 2000). Original data: State of California. *California Death Index, 1940–1997.* Sacramento, CA: State of California Department of Health Services, Center for Health Statistics, 19–.

107 State of California, *California Voter Registrations 1900–68*, Ancestry.com.

108 Ltr to Dean of August 1992 from Kathleen Bridges.

109 Ltr to Dean of August 1992 from Kathleen Bridges., Freddia listed in journal of Michael Wagner. Did not know exact first name from previous other records.

110 Ancestry.com, *World War I Draft Registration Cards, 1917–1918* (Provo, UT, USA, The Generations Network, Inc., 2005), www.ancestry.com, Database online. Original data—United States, Selective Service System. World War I Selective Service System Draft Registration Cards, 1917–1918. Washington, D.C.: National Archives and Records Administration, M1509, 4,582 rolls. Roll 1683398, draft board 0.

111 *1920 United States Federal Census* (Provo, UT, USA: The Generations Network, Inc., 2005), www.ancestry.com, Online publication. Original data United States of America, Bureau of the Census. Fourteenth Census of the United States. Washington, D.C.: National Archives and Records Administration, 1920.T625, 2076 rolls). Aurora, Lawrence, Missouri, image 8.

112 *1900 United States Federal Census* (Provo, UT, USA: The Generations Network, Inc., 2004, www.ancestry.com, online publication. Original data—United States of America, Bureau of the Census. Twelfth Census of the United States, 1900. Washington, D.C.: National Archives and Records Administration, 1900). Census Place: Carthage Ward 5, Jasper, Missouri; Roll: T623 866; Page: 7B; Enumeration District: 62, birthdate: abt 1885, Birth place: Indiana, Residence date: 1900, Residence place: Carthage Ward 5, Jasper, Missouri.

113 Ancestry.com, *Missouri Marriage Records, 1805–2002* (Provo, UT, USA: The Generations Network, Inc., 2007), www.ancestry.com, Online publication. Original data: *Missouri Marriage Records.* Jefferson City, MO, USA: Missouri State Archives, Microfilm.

114 *1910 United States Federal Census* (Provo, UT, USA: The Generations Network, Inc., 2006), www.ancestry.com, Online publication. Original data United States of America, Bureau of the Census. Thirteenth Census of the United States. Washington, D.C.: National Archives and Records Administration, 1910.T624, 1,178 rolls). Aurora Ward 1, Lawrence, Missouri, roll T624_795.

115 *1910 United States Federal Census* (Provo, UT, USA: The Generations Network, Inc., 2006), www.ancestry.com, Online publication. Original data United States of America, Bureau of the Census. Thirteenth Census of the United States. Washington, D.C.: National Archives and Records Administration, 1910.T624, 1,178 rolls). Noblesville, Hamilton, Indiana, ed , roll T624_353.

116 WPA, *Marriages Hamilton Co, IN 1900–1920*, Indiana State Library.

117 Bettye Anderson Richhart, *Richhart, Ritchhart, Ritschard, A Swiss-German family from 1500 until 1993.* (North Richland Hills, Tex., B.A. Richhart, 1993), 41.

118 Ancestry.com, *Social Security Death Index* (Provo, UT, USA: The Generations Network, Inc., 2008), www.ancestry.com, [database online]. Original data: Social Security Administration. *Social Security Death Index, Master File.* Social Security Administration.

119 *1930 United States Federal Census* (Provo, UT, USA: The Generations Network, Inc., 2002), www.ancestry.com, Online publication. Original data United States of America, Bureau of the Census. Fifteenth Census of the United States. Washington, D.C.: National Archives and Records Administration, 1930.T626, 2,667 rolls). Union, Ross, Ohio, ED 31, roll 1865, image 544.0.

120 *Social Security Death Index*, digital image, The National Archives (www.genealogyBank.com).

121 Ancestry.com, *United States Obituary Collection* (Provo, UT, USA: The Generations Network, Inc., 2006), www.ancestry.com [database online].

122 *Ohio Obituary Index 1830s–2009* (Rutherford B. Hayes Presidential Center, 2009), Ancestry. com.

123 Ancestry.com, *California Death Index, 1940–1997* (Provo, UT, USA: The Generations Network, Inc., 2000). Original data: State of California. *California Death Index, 1940–1997.* Sacramento, CA: State of California Department of Health Services, Center for Health Statistics, 19–.

124 Ancestry.com, *Social Security Death Index* (Provo, UT, USA: The Generations Network, Inc., 2008), www.ancestry.com, [database online]. Original data: Social Security Administration. *Social Security Death Index, Master File.* Social Security Administration. Number: 550-24-3179; Issue State: California; Issue Date: Before 1951. Record for Mary Rumsby.

125 *1930 United States Federal Census* (Provo, UT, USA: The Generations Network, Inc., 2002), www.ancestry.com, Online publication. Original data United States of America, Bureau of the Census. Fifteenth Census of the United States. Washington, D.C.: National Archives and Records Administration, 1930.T626, 2,667 rolls). Census Place: Township 3, Fresno, California; Roll: 117; Page: 6A; Enumeration District: 8; Image: 596.0. Record for Betty L Rumsby.

126 Ancestry.com, *1920 United States Federal Census* (Online publication -Provo, UT, USA: The *1920 United States Federal Census* (Provo, UT, USA: The Generations Network, Inc., 2005), www.ancestry.com, Online publication. Original data United States of America, Bureau of the Census. Fourteenth Census of the United States. Washington, D.C.: National Archives and Records Administration, 1920.T625, 2076 rolls). Census Place: Salt Lake City Ward 4, Salt Lake, Utah; Roll: T625_1865; Page: 13A; Enumeration District: 137; Image: 341, birth date: abt 1919, Birth place: Colorado, Residence date: 1920, Residence place: Salt Lake City Ward 4, Salt Lake, Utah.

127 1930 Census, Fresno, California, Gave ages at marriage as 21 and 17.

128 Ancestry.com, *California Death Index, 1940–1997* (Provo, UT, USA: The Generations Network, Inc., 2000). Original data: State of California. *California Death Index, 1940–1997.* Sacramento,

CA: State of California Department of Health Services, Center for Health Statistics, 19–.

129 Ancestry.com, *California Death Index, 1940–1997* (Provo, UT, USA: The Generations Network, Inc., 2000). Original data: State of California. *California Death Index, 1940–1997*. Sacramento, CA: State of California Department of Health Services, Center for Health Statistics, 19–. Place: Sacramento; Date: 19 Jan 1983; Social Security: 709169267. Record for James Rumsby.

130 1840 Census from "My Genealogy.com."

131 *1930 United States Federal Census* (Provo, UT, USA: The Generations Network, Inc., 2002), www.ancestry.com, Online publication. Original data United States of America, Bureau of the Census. Fifteenth Census of the United States. Washington, D.C.: National Archives and Records Administration, 1930.T626, 2,667 rolls). Census Place: La Junta, Otero, Colorado; Roll: 248; Page: 4A; Enumeration District: 10; Image: 142.0, birth date: abt 1909, Birth place: Colorado, Residence date: 1930, Residence place: La Junta, Otero, Colorado.

132 *Ancestry Family Trees* (Online publication—Provo, UT, USA: The Generations Network. Original data: Family Tree files submitted by Ancestry members). http://trees.ancestry.com/pt/ AMTCitationRedir.aspx?tid=2906494&pid=-76157346.

133 Broderbund Family Archive #110, Vol. 2, Ed. 5, *Social Security Death Index*: U.S., Date of Import: Jul 6, 1998, Internal Ref. #1.112.5.56488.82

134 *1910 United States Federal Census* (Provo, UT, USA: The Generations Network, Inc., 2006), www.ancestry.com, Online publication. Original data United States of America, Bureau of the Census. Thirteenth Census of the United States. Washington, D.C.: National Archives and Records Administration, 1910.T624, 1,178 rolls). La Junta, Otero, Colorado, ed , roll T624_123.

135 Christy Peterson, Christy Ward Peterson's Family Tree (, Jan 2009), GENI.COM.

136 Ancestry.com, *Social Security Death Index* (Provo, UT, USA: The Generations Network, Inc., 2008), www.ancestry.com, [database online]. Original data: Social Security Administration. *Social Security Death Index, Master File*. Social Security Administration. Number: 357-05-8358; Issue State: Illinois; Issue Date: Before 1951. Record for Susie Ritchhart.

137 Ancestry.com, *Social Security Death Index* (Provo, UT, USA: The Generations Network, Inc., 2008), www.ancestry.com, [database online]. Original data: Social Security Administration. *Social Security Death Index, Master File*. Social Security Administration.

138 *Ancestry Family Trees* (Online publication—Provo, UT, USA: The Generations Network. Original data: Family Tree files submitted by Ancestry members). http://trees.ancestry.com/pt/ AMTCitationRedir.aspx?tid=2906494&pid=-1803611891.

139 *Bent County Democrat* Article, Files of Del Ritchhart.

140 *1930 United States Federal Census* (Provo, UT, USA: The Generations Network, Inc., 2002), www.ancestry.com, Online publication. Original data United States of America, Bureau of the Census. Fifteenth Census of the United States. Washington, D.C.: National Archives and Records Administration, 1930.T626, 2,667 rolls). Las Animas, Bent, Colorado, ED 8, roll 230, page , image 619.0.

141 *1920 United States Federal Census* (Provo, UT, USA: The Generations Network, Inc., 2005), www.ancestry.com, Online publication. Original data United States of America, Bureau of the Census. Fourteenth Census of the United States. Washington, D.C.: National Archives and Records Administration, 1920.T625, 2076 rolls). Census Place: Las Animas, Bent, Colorado;

Roll: T625_155; Page: 6B; Enumeration District: 269; Image: 529, birth date: abt 1915, Birth place: Colorado, Residence date: 1920, Residence place: Las Animas, Bent, Colorado.

142   Ancestry.com, *Social Security Death Index* (Provo, UT, USA: The Generations Network, Inc., 2008), www.ancestry.com, [database online]. Original data: Social Security Administration. *Social Security Death Index, Master File*. Social Security Administration. Number: 524-34-6670; Issue State: Colorado; Issue Date: Before 1951. Birth date: 6 Aug 1915, Death date: 15 Oct 1995, Death place: Loveland, Larimer, Colorado, United States of America.

143   Ancestry.com, *U.S. Public Records Index, Volume 2* (Provo, UT, USA, Ancestry.com Operations, Inc., 2010), www.ancestry.com, Database online. Record for Helen J Ritchhart.

144   *Ancestry Family Trees* (Online publication—Provo, UT, USA: The Generations Network. Original data: Family Tree files submitted by Ancestry members). http://trees.ancestry.com/pt/AMTCitationRedir.aspx?tid=2906494&pid=-76072090.

145   Cemetery Plot Records.

146   Ancestry.com, *Social Security Death Index* (Provo, UT, USA: The Generations Network, Inc., 2008), www.ancestry.com, [database online]. Original data: Social Security Administration. *Social Security Death Index, Master File*. Social Security Administration.

147   1930 Census, La Junta, Colorado, Listed Alonzo, Grace, Delbert and Betty. All the others must have moved out by then.

148   Broderbund Family Archive #110, Vol. 1, Ed. 5, *Social Security Death Index*: U.S., Date of Import: Feb 18, 2001, Internal Ref. #1.111.5.143522.195

149   Letter from Betty's husband Jack Linehan dtd Dec 16, 1993., Stated that Betty died on their 48th wedding anniversary.

150   Ancestry.com, *World War I Draft Registration Cards, 1917–1918* (Provo, UT, USA, The Generations Network, Inc., 2005), www.ancestry.com, Database online. Original data—United States, Selective Service System. World War I Selective Service System Draft Registration Cards, 1917–1918. Washington, D.C.: National Archives and Records Administration, M1509, 4,582 rolls. Roll 1683222, DraftBoard 1.

151   *1930 United States Federal Census* (Provo, UT, USA: The Generations Network, Inc., 2002), www.ancestry.com, Online publication. Original data United States of America, Bureau of the Census. Fifteenth Census of the United States. Washington, D.C.: National Archives and Records Administration, 1930.T626, 2,667 rolls). Carthage, Jasper, Missouri, ED 43, roll 1206, page , image 133.0.

152   Ancestry.com, *World War I Draft Registration Cards, 1917–1918* (Provo, UT, USA, The Generations Network, Inc., 2005), www.ancestry.com, Database online. Original data—United States, Selective Service System. World War I Selective Service System Draft Registration Cards, 1917–1918. Washington, D.C.: National Archives and Records Administration, M1509, 4,582 rolls. Registration Location: Jasper County, Missouri; Roll: 1683222; Draft Board: 1. Record for Purl Floyd Ritchhart.

153   Ancestry.com, Missouri Marriage Records, 1805–2002 (Provo, UT, USA, Ancestry.com Operations Inc, 2007), www.ancestry.com, Database online. Record for Purl F Ritchhart.

154   *1920 United States Federal Census* (Provo, UT, USA: The Generations Network, Inc., 2005), www.ancestry.com, Online publication. Original data United States of America, Bureau of

the Census. Fourteenth Census of the United States. Washington, D.C.: National Archives and Records Administration, 1920.T625, 2076 rolls). Census Place: Madison, Jasper, Missouri; Roll: T625_922; Page: 6B; Enumeration District: 78; Image: 675. Record for Alvin E Ritchhart.

155   Obituary from *Garden City Telegram*, July 2, 1994.

156   Obituary for Edyth from *Garden City Telegram*, July 2, 1994.

157   Ancestry.com, Missouri Marriage Records, 1805–2002 (Provo, UT, USA, Ancestry.com Operations Inc, 2007), www.ancestry.com, Database online. Record for Ethel Grace Ritchhart.

158   *1910 United States Federal Census* (Provo, UT, USA: The Generations Network, Inc., 2006), www.ancestry.com, Online publication. Original data United States of America, Bureau of the Census. Thirteenth Census of the United States. Washington, D.C.: National Archives and Records Administration, 1910.T624, 1,178 rolls). Census Place: Madison, Jasper, Missouri; Roll: T624_791; Page: 8A; Enumeration District: 68; Image: 1117. Record for Alvin Ritchart.

159   Ancestry.com, *Missouri Marriage Records, 1805–2002* (Provo, UT, USA: The Generations Network, Inc., 2007), www.ancestry.com, Online publication. Original data: *Missouri Marriage Records*. Jefferson City, MO, USA: Missouri State Archives, Microfilm.

160   Ancestry.com, *Public Member Trees* (Provo, UT, USA, The Generations Network, Inc., 2006), www.ancestry.com, Database online. Record for Maude P Ritchhart.

161   Ancestry.com Family Tree of T. Garrison, listed her birth and death information as well as mother and father.

162   *1920 United States Federal Census* (Provo, UT, USA: The Generations Network, Inc., 2005), www.ancestry.com, Online publication. Original data United States of America, Bureau of the Census. Fourteenth Census of the United States. Washington, D.C.: National Archives and Records Administration, 1920.T625, 2076 rolls). Census Place: Madison, Jasper, Missouri; Roll: T625_922; Page: 7A; Enumeration District: 78; Image: 676. Record for Frank L Ritchhart.

163   Ancestry.com, *U.S. Public Records Index, Volume 2* (Provo, UT, USA, Ancestry.com Operations, Inc., 2010), www.ancestry.com, Database online. Record for Lester C Ritchart.

164   Missouri, County of Jasper, Carthage, Marriage Licenses.

165   Ancestry.com, *Social Security Death Index* (Provo, UT, USA: The Generations Network, Inc., 2008), www.ancestry.com, [database online]. Original data: Social Security Administration. *Social Security Death Index, Master File*. Social Security Administration. Number: 487-10-5986; Issue State: Missouri; Issue Date: Before 1951. Record for Carl Chapman.

166   Carthage, MO newspaper wedding announcement.

167   *1920 United States Federal Census* (Provo, UT, USA: The Generations Network, Inc., 2005), www.ancestry.com, Online publication. Original data United States of America, Bureau of the Census. Fourteenth Census of the United States. Washington, D.C.: National Archives and Records Administration, 1920.T625, 2076 rolls). Census Place: Aurora, Lawrence, Missouri; Roll: T625_932; Page: 3A; Enumeration District: 100; Image: 8. Record for Elenor Ritchhart.

168   *1930 United States Federal Census* (Provo, UT, USA: The Generations Network, Inc., 2002), www.ancestry.com, Online publication. Original data United States of America, Bureau of the Census. Fifteenth Census of the United States. Washington, D.C.: National Archives and Records Administration, 1930.T626, 2,667 rolls). Census Place: Aurora, Lawrence, Missouri; Roll: 1208; Page: 2B; Enumeration District: 1; Image: 634.0. Record for Eleanor M Ritchart.

169   WPA, Births Hamilton Co., IN (WPA).

170   GENI.COM inputs from Michelle Dyke, Inputs in Jan 09 by Michell Ritchhart Dyke on GENI. COM. She has since joined my family site and added her information.

171   Ancestry.com, *U.S. Public Records Index, Volume 1* (Provo, UT, USA, Ancestry.com Operations, Inc., 2010), www.ancestry.com, Database online. Record for Kenneth F Ritchhart.

172   Ancestry.com, *Public Member Trees* (Provo, UT, USA, The Generations Network, Inc., 2006), www.ancestry.com, Database online. Record for John Cleveland Barker.

173   Ancestry.com, *Social Security Death Index* (Provo, UT, USA: The Generations Network, Inc., 2008), www.ancestry.com, [database online]. Original data: Social Security Administration. *Social Security Death Index, Master File.* Social Security Administration. Number: 446-16-1075; Issue State: Oklahoma; Issue Date: Before 1951. Record for Leona V. Ritchhart.

174   Ancestry.com, *One World Tree^SM* (Provo, UT, USA: The Generations Network, Inc., n.d.), www. ancestry.com, database online. Provo, UT, USA: The Generations Network, Inc.

175   Ancestry.com, *U.S. Public Records Index* (Provo, UT, USA: The Generations Network, Inc., 2007), www.ancestry.com, [database online]. Original data compiled from various U.S. public records.

176   Margaret Barton, Letter from Margaret Rumsby Barton (July 2009), Personal files of Del Ritchhart.

177   Letter from Betty's husband Jack Linehan dtd Dec 16, 1993., In the letter Jack indicated that he had called Cliff and Margaret Barton. I assumed that to be Margaret Ritchhart's husband.

178   Ancestry.com, *U.S. Public Records Index* (Provo, UT, USA: The Generations Network, Inc., 2007), www.ancestry.com, [database online]. Original data compiled from various U.S. public records. Record for Bette L Kleinknight.

179   Ancestry.com, *U.S. Phone and Address Directories*, 1993–2002 (Provo, UT, USA, The Generations Network, Inc., 2005), www.ancestry.com, Database online. Record for B L Kleinknight.

180   Ancestry.com, *U.S. Phone and Address Directories*, 1993–2002 (Provo, UT, USA, The Generations Network, Inc., 2005), www.ancestry.com, Database online. Record for B L Kleinknight.

181   Ancestry.com, *California Birth Index, 1905–1995* (Provo, UT, USA, The Generations Network, Inc., 2005), www.ancestry.com, Database online. Birthdate: 10 Jul 1926; Birth County: Fresno. Record for Betty Lou Rumsby.

182   1930 Census, Fresno, California.

183   Conversation with Betty Kleinknight (, July 2009), Personal files of Del Ritchhart.

184   Betty Lou Rumsby, Letter from Betty Lou (, July 2009), Personal files of Del Ritchhart.

185   Ancestry.com, *California Birth Index, 1905–1995* (Provo, UT, USA, The Generations Network, Inc., 2005), www.ancestry.com, Database online. Birthdate: 10 Aug 1925; Birth County: Kern. Record for James Franklin Kleinknight.

186   Ancestry.com, *California Death Index, 1940–1997* (Provo, UT, USA: The Generations Network, Inc., 2000). Original data: State of California. *California Death Index, 1940–1997.* Sacramento, CA: State of California Department of Health Services, Center for Health Statistics, 19–. Record for Jim F Kleinknight.

187   Ancestry.com, *U.S. Public Records Index* (Provo, UT, USA: The Generations Network, Inc.,

2007), www.ancestry.com, [database online]. Original data compiled from various U.S. public records.

188   Ancestry.com, *U.S. Public Records Index, Volume 1* (Provo, UT, USA, Ancestry.com Operations, Inc., 2010), www.ancestry.com, Database online. Record for Ml Delbert A Ritchhart.

189   Ancestry.com, *U.S. Public Records Index, Volume 1* (Provo, UT, USA, Ancestry.com Operations, Inc., 2010), www.ancestry.com, Database online. Record for Ml Delbert A Ritchhart.

190   Ancestry.com, *U.S. Public Records Index, Volume 1* (Provo, UT, USA, Ancestry.com Operations, Inc., 2010), www.ancestry.com, Database online. Record for Joanne S Ritchhart.

191   Ancestry.com, *U.S. Public Records Index, Volume 1* (Provo, UT, USA, Ancestry.com Operations, Inc., 2010), www.ancestry.com, Database online. Record for Joanne S Ritchhart.

192   Ancestry.com, *U.S. Public Records Index, Volume 1* (Provo, UT, USA, Ancestry.com Operations, Inc., 2010), www.ancestry.com, Database online. Record for Joanne S Ritchhart.

193   Ancestry.com, *U.S. Public Records Index, Volume 2* (Provo, UT, USA, Ancestry.com Operations, Inc., 2010), www.ancestry.com, Database online. Record for Joanne S Ritchhart.

194   State of Colorado, Death Certificate.

195   Ltr to Dean of August 1992 from Kathleen Bridges.

196   Ltr from Julia to me (Del) in early 2003 telling me her mother died in 1997.

197   Chart from Raymond Ritchhart, 1999, According to Kathleen's chart the marriage date was 12/23/1963 vice 1962.

198   Ancestry.com, *California Birth Index, 1905–1995* (Provo, UT, USA, The Generations Network, Inc., 2005), www.ancestry.com, Database online. Birthdate: 27 Aug 1948; Birth County: Kern.

199   Ancestry.com, Nevada Marriage Index, 1956–2005 (Provo, UT, USA, The Generations Network, Inc., 2007), www.ancestry.com, Database online. Record for Cheryl Ann Ritchhart.

200   Ancestry.com, *California Birth Index, 1905–1995* (Provo, UT, USA, The Generations Network, Inc., 2005), www.ancestry.com, Database online. Birthdate: 6 Apr 1985; Birth County: Santa Clara. Record for Jamie Ann Short.

201   Ancestry.com, *U.S. Public Records Index, Volume 2* (Provo, UT, USA, Ancestry.com Operations, Inc., 2010), www.ancestry.com, Database online. Record for Ronald G Short.

202   Ancestry.com, *U.S. Public Records Index, Volume 2* (Provo, UT, USA, Ancestry.com Operations, Inc., 2010), www.ancestry.com, Database online. Record for Ronald G Short.

203   Birth Certificate.

204   Ancestry.com, *U.S. Public Records Index, Volume 1* (Provo, UT, USA, Ancestry.com Operations, Inc., 2010), www.ancestry.com, Database online. Record for Linda R Wimer.

205   Ancestry.com, *U.S. Public Records Index, Volume 1* (Provo, UT, USA, Ancestry.com Operations, Inc., 2010), www.ancestry.com, Database online. Record for Linda R Wimer.

206   Ancestry.com, *California Birth Index, 1905–1995* (Provo, UT, USA, The Generations Network, Inc., 2005), www.ancestry.com, Database online. Record for Linda M Ritchhart.

207   Ancestry.com, *California Birth Index, 1905–1995* (Provo, UT, USA: The Generations Network, Inc., 2005. Original data—State of California Department of Health Services, Center for Health Statistics. *California Birth Index, 1905–1995*. Sacramento, CA, USA. Original), Birthdate: 6 Apr

1985; Birth County: Santa Clara, Birth place: Santa Clara, California.

208 *Ancestry Family Trees* (Online publication—Provo, UT, USA: The Generations Network. Original data: Family Tree files submitted by Ancestry members). http://trees.ancestry.com/pt/ AMTCitationRedir.aspx?tid=2906494&pid=-1803611873.

209 Justin Christman, Justin Christman's GENI.COM entries (Oct 2009), GENI.COM.

210 Ancestry.com, *California Birth Index, 1905–1995* (Provo, UT, USA: The Generations Network, Inc., 2005. Original data—State of California Department of Health Services, Center for Health Statistics. *California Birth Index, 1905–1995*. Sacramento, CA, USA. Original). Birthdate: 25 Feb 1981; Birth County: San Diego. Record for Justin Patrick Christman.

211 Ancestry.com, *California Birth Index, 1905–1995* (Provo, UT, USA: The Generations Network, Inc., 2005. Original data—State of California Department of Health Services, Center for Health Statistics. *California Birth Index, 1905–1995*. Sacramento, CA, USA. Original), Birthdate: 12 Mar 1986; Birth County: Santa Clara, Birth place: Santa Clara, California.

212 Ancestry.com, *California Birth Index, 1905–1995* (Provo, UT, USA: The Generations Network, Inc., 2005. Original data—State of California Department of Health Services, Center for Health Statistics. *California Birth Index, 1905–1995*. Sacramento, CA, USA. Original), Birthdate: 12 Mar 1986; Birth County: Santa Clara. Record for Lindsay Marie Short.

213 Ancestry.com, *California Birth Index, 1905–1995* (Provo, UT, USA: The Generations Network, Inc., 2005. Original data -State of California. *California Birth Index, 1905–1995*. Sacramento, CA, USA: State of California Department of Health Services, Center for Health Statistics.Original), Birthdate: 15 Jul 1987; Birth County: Santa Clara, Birth place: Santa Clara, California.

214 *Ancestry Family Trees* (Online publication—Provo, UT, USA: The Generations Network. Original data: Family Tree files submitted by Ancestry members). http://trees.ancestry.com/pt/ AMTCitationRedir.aspx?tid=2906494&pid=-1803611871.

215 Ancestry.com, *California Birth Index, 1905–1995* (Provo, UT, USA: The Generations Network, Inc., 2005. Original data—State of California Department of Health Services, Center for Health Statistics. *California Birth Index, 1905–1995*. Sacramento, CA, USA. Original), Birthdate: 15 Jul 1987; Birth County: Santa Clara. Record for Kyleigh Lynn Short.

216 Ancestry.com, *California Birth Index, 1905–1995* (Provo, UT, USA: The Generations Network, Inc., 2005. Original data—State of California Department of Health Services, Center for Health Statistics. *California Birth Index, 1905–1995*. Sacramento, CA, USA. Original), Birthdate: 25 Oct 1995; Birth County: Fresno, Birth place: Fresno, California.

Generation 1

1. **JOHN HARDIN[1] BUSH**[1] was born about 1776 in Virginia, USA[2]. He died in 1850[1,3,4]. He married **ANN BASS** in 1803 in Kentucky, USA[3], daughter of Daniel Marsh NOE and Jane SMITH. She was born in 1775 in Virginia, USA[1,3,4]. She died on 25 Oct 1853 in Hart, Kentucky, United States[1,3,4,5].

Notes for Ann BASS: The only evidence I have that Ann was married to Henry is because she was listed in the 1850 US Census for Kentucky as a member of John Bush's household. Based on that, I assumed her to be John's mother.

John Hardin BUSH and Ann BASS had the following children:

    i. CATHERINE[2] BUSH[3] was born about 1795 in Kentucky, USA. She died in Kentucky, USA[3].

    Notes for Catherine BUSH: Catherine age 55 was listed as a member of John Bush's family in the 1850 census along with Ann age 75. I assumed they were John's sister and mother because they both had the Bush name. I feel very confident the Ann is his mother—otherwise why would a woman age 75 with the same last name be in his household! Catherine could be a sister-in-law who was widowed, but I chose to assume she was a sister. More research is warranted.

    ii. LANDON BUSH[3] was born in 1800 in Kentucky, USA3.

    iii. DELILA BUSH[3] was born in 1807 in Hart, Kentucky, United States[3]. She died in 1894[3].

  2 iv. JOHN HARDING BUSH JR.[1,6] was born about 1807 in Hart, Kentucky, USA[3,4,7,8]. He died on 19 Jul 1894 in Jasper, Missouri, USA[3,4]. He married ABERGALE ABIGAL WARDRIP in 1839[1,4], daughter of Reese WARDROPE and Catherine WADDLE. She was born on 25 Jan 1812 in Kentucky, USA[9,10,11]. She died on 10 Feb 1883 in Jasper, Missouri, USA[11].

    v. MARY JANE BUSH[3] was born in 1813 in Kentucky, USA[3]. She died in 1880 in Hart, Kentucky, United States[3].

Generation 2

2. **JOHN HARDING[2] BUSH JR.** (John Hardin[1])[1,6] was born about 1807 in Hart, Kentucky, USA[3,4,7,8]. He died on 19 Jul 1894 in Jasper, Missouri, USA[3,4]. He married **ABERGALE ABIGAL WARDRIP** in 1839[1,4], daughter of Reese WARDROPE and Catherine WADDLE. She was born on 25 Jan 1812 in Kentucky, USA[9,10,11]. She died on 10 Feb 1883 in Jasper, Missouri, USA[11].

Notes for John Harding BUSH Jr.: Were listed in the 1880 census as living with their son-in-law, James Logsdon, and daughter, Mary.

The 1870 census listed John H. Bush and his wife Magot (59) with children Shelton (18) and Mary (14). Magot and Abergale could be the same person as the 1880 census listed Abergale as (69) which agrees with the 1870 census age for Magot. In either case the children would have been born late in life (age 41 and 45 for the mother in either case).

Henry Bush is listed in the 1810 census in Hardin Co., KY with a three sons under 10. In 1820 he is listed with three under 10 and one age 10–16 living in the adjacent Hart county. If John was born in 1809 he would have been one years of age in the 1810 census, and 11 in 1820.

The 1880 US Census, Jasper, Missouri lists John (72) and Abegale (69) living with James Logsdon and his wife Mary Bush Logsdon. It was common in those days for older parents to live with their children.

Notes for Abergale Abigal WARDRIP: I speculate that the name could be spelled Abagail or Abigail which is more traditional. The June 1880 showed Abergale and John living with their daughter, Mary and son-in-law James Logsdon in the southeast suburbs of Carthage, MO. Neither Abergale nor John H. could read or write. Also, her last name could be Wardrope vice Waldrip.

In the 1860 census John and Abigail's ages were 60 and 58 respectively. Then in the 1870 census they were 61 and 59 respectively. I think the latter makes more sense. Neither could read or write, so their math might not have been very good either. Also in the 1860 census Mary was listed as being born in Missouri, which makes sense since she was 4 and they were in Missouri. However, in the 1870 census Mary was listed as being born in Iowa.

John Harding BUSH Jr. and Abergale Abigal WARDRIP had the following children:

3   i.   YOUNGER[3] BUSH[2,12] was born about 1829 in Kentucky, USA. He died after 1900 in Ringgold, Iowa, USA[2]. He married ELIZABETH *. She was born about 1840 in Kentucky, USA.

     ii. AMEY BUSH[1,13] was born about 1832 in Kentucky, USA.

     iii. NANCY J. BUSH[2,13] was born about 1834 in Kentucky, USA[2].

4   iv. HENRY B. BUSH[2,13] was born about 1838 in Kentucky, USA[2]. He died in Warwickshire, England[1]. He married MARY J. She was born in 1843 in Indiana, USA[14].

     v.   JACKSON T. BUSH[13] was born about 1839 in Kentucky, USA[2]. He died on 04 Jan 1931 in Barren, Kentucky, USA[1].

     vi. ELISHA BUSH[2,13] was born about 1841 in Kentucky, USA[2].

     vii. WILLIAM A. BUSH[13] was born about 1845 in Kentucky, USA.

     viii. LISA A. BUSH[13] was born about 1847 in Kentucky, USA[2].

5   ix. SARAH E. BUSH[2,13] was born about 1848 in Kentucky, USA. She married JACOB L. BROOKS. He was born in 1834 in Kentucky, USA.

6   x.   SAMUEL SHELTON BUSH[1,13,15,16,17,18,19,20,21,22,23] was born on 27 Jan 1852 in Hart, Kentucky, USA[15,18,19,20,21,24,25]. He died on 08 Jun 1907 in La Junta, Otero, Colorado, USA[20,26]. He married LILLIAN PERDIDA LOGSDON on 19 Apr 1876 in Jasper, Missouri, USA, daughter of George W. LOGSDON and Susan LINDER. She was

born on 01 Mar 1860 in Iowa, USA[11,19,27,28,29,30,31]. She died on 01 Jan 1929 in La Junta, Otero, Colorado, USA[18,32].

7 xi. MARY L. BUSH[33] was born on 29 Jul 1857 in Hart, Kentucky, USA[33]. She died on 18 Mar 1940 in Los Angeles, California, USA[33]. She married JAMES LOGSDON, son of George W. LOGSDON and Susan LINDER. He was born in 1858 in Kentucky, USA[34].

Generation 3

3. **YOUNGER**[3] **BUSH** (John Harding[2]Jr., John Hardin[1])[2,12] was born about 1829 in Kentucky, USA. He died after 1900 in Ringgold, Iowa, USA[2]. He married **ELIZABETH***. She was born about 1840 in Kentucky, USA.

Younger BUSH and Elizabeth * had the following children:

 i. JAMES L.[4] BUSH[12] was born about 1868 in Missouri, USA.

 ii. RICHARD BUSH[12] was born about 1869 in Missouri, USA.

 iii. LAFAYETT BUSH[12] was born about 1871 in Missouri, USA.

 iv. GEORGE W. BUSH was born about 1873 in Missouri, USA.

4. **HENRY B.**[3] **BUSH** (John Harding[2]Jr., John Hardin[1])[2,13] was born about 1838 in Kentucky, USA[2]. He died in Warwickshire, England[1]. He married **MARY J.** She was born in 1843 in Indiana, USA[14].

Henry B. BUSH and Mary J. had the following children:

 i. SARAH[4] BUSH[14] was born in 1862 in Missouri, USA[14].

 ii. FEBA S. BUSH[14] was born in 1864 in Missouri, USA[14].

 iii. ELIZABETH BUSH[14] was born in 1867 in Missouri, USA[14].

 iv. ANNA BUSH[14] was born in 1869 in Missouri, USA[14].

 v. JACOB BUSH[14] was born in 1871 in Missouri, USA[14].

 vi. JAMES BUSH[14] was born in 1874 in Missouri, USA[14].

 vii. DANIEL M. BUSH[14] was born in 1876 in Missouri, USA[14].

 viii. MARTHA F. BUSH[14] was born in 1876 in Missouri, USA[14].

 ix. ADA BUSH[14] was born in 1878 in Missouri, USA[14].

5. **SARAH E.**[3] **BUSH** (John Harding[2]Jr., John Hardin[1])[2,13] was born about 1848 in Kentucky, USA. She married **JACOB L. BROOKS**. He was born in 1834 in Kentucky, USA.

Jacob L. BROOKS and Sarah E. BUSH had the following children:

 i. MARY E.[4] BROOKS was born about 1860 in Missouri, USA.

 ii. LILLY A. BROOKS was born about 1865 in Missouri, USA.

 iii. HARRIOTT E. BROOKS was born about 1866 in Missouri, USA.

 iv. JOHN H. BROOKS was born about 1867 in Missouri, USA.

 v. SAMUEL J. BROOKS was born about 1868 in Missouri, USA.

 vi. WILLIAM R. BROOKS was born about 1871 in Missouri, USA.

vii. MARY S. BROOKS was born about 1873 in Missouri, USA.

6. **SAMUEL SHELTON**[3] **BUSH** (John Harding[2] Jr., John Hardin[1])[1,13,15,16,17,18,19,20,21,22,23] was born on 27 Jan 1852 in Hart, Kentucky, USA[15,18,19,20,21,24,25]. He died on 08 Jun 1907 in La Junta, Otero, Colorado, USA[20,26]. He married **LILLIAN PERDIDA LOGSDON** on 19 Apr 1876 in Jasper, Missouri, USA, daughter of George W. LOGSDON and Susan LINDER. She was born on 01 Mar 1860 in Iowa, USA[11,19,27,28,29,30,31]. She died on 01 Jan 1929 in La Junta, Otero, Colorado, USA[18,32].

Notes for Samuel Shelton BUSH: The wedding announcement in the Carthage, MO newspaper for Grace and Alonzo listed the Bride's father as S.S. Bush, a former resident of Jasper county, who moved to Colorado because of his health. I speculate that his name was Samuel, as Grace and Alonzo named their oldest son Samuel Clifford, and the custom was to name children after their parents and grandparents. Additionally, Clifford Ritchhart listed Grace's father as Shelton Bush. He also listed Samuel Shelton Bush as Lillian (Logston) Bush's father. I think he must have been confused on this, as he was getting on in years when he composed the data. Therefore, I think it is further evidence that Grace's father was named Samuel Shelton. In later research I did find his name in census data for both 1870 and 1880. He died not too many years after moving to La Junta. However, I have been unable to find any record of his burial in La Junta. I found records of his wife and children, but not him.

Clifford remembers he received his grandfathers wallet with $12 in it when his grandfather passed away. In 1910 Clifford would have been about 7 and old enough to remember that. The two years prior to that Clifford and his folks had moved back to Missouri, so the death of his grandfather probably did not occur during that time.

Samuel was born in Hart County, Kentucky which is about half way between Louisville and Bowling Green (ssw of Louisville).

Notes for Lillian Perdida LOGSDON: Thanks to Clifford Ritchhart's family history document we were able to identify GGrandma Bush's name. I had a picture of a headstone in the La Junta Cemetery with the heading of "Turner" but below it was the inscription "Mother" and Lillian P. Bush. Clifford's notes indicated that Grandma Bush had remarried a Mr. Turner after Grandpa Bush passed away. Thus, the reason the name Turner was on the headstone.

They must have married after 1910, as she was living alone and doing private nursing according to the 1910 Census. The 1910 census also confirmed that she had four children, all of whom were still living.

Samuel Shelton BUSH and Lillian Perdida LOGSDON had the following children:

8　　i. ADELL THORNLEY[4] BUSH[9,9,10,23] was born on 15 Jul 1877 in Carthage, Jasper, Missouri, USA[9,10,19,23,35]. She died on 26 Feb 1948 in La Junta, Otero, Colorado, USA[23]. She married JOHN HOLMES SIMONTON on 04 Jun 1902 in La Junta, Otero, Colorado, USA[9]. He was born on 30 Jul 1858 in Mifflinburg, Union, Pennsylvania, USA[9,10]. He died on 26 Jun 1938 in La Junta, Otero, Colorado, USA.

9   ii. GRACE AZETTA BUSH[9,10,18,20,21,25,36,37,38,39,40,41,42,43] was born on 17 Nov 1879 in Carthage, Jasper, Missouri, USA[9,10,19,21,25,36,42,43,44]. She died on 28 Jan 1952 in La Junta, Otero, Colorado, USA[9,42,43]. She married ALONZO FRANCIS RITCHHART on 01 Jan 1902 in La Junta, Otero, Colorado, USA (5 p.m. wedding followed by dinner)[45], son of Wesley RITCHHART and Maria Sibilla WAGNER. He was born on 03 Nov 1867 in Indiana, USA[46]. He died on 27 May 1959 in Stanislaus, California, USA[46,47].

10   iii. WILLIAM ELBERT BUSH[10,48] was born on 27 Jan 1884 in Jasper, Missouri, USA. He died on 14 Oct 1958 in La Junta, Otero, Colorado, USA. He married ELIZABETH ARMINDA BEEDLE on 03 Dec 1904 in La Junta, Otero, Colorado, USA[10], daughter of Simeon Jeremiah BEEDLE and Nancy Jane SPURGEON. She was born on 01 Aug 1880 in Lovilla, Monroe, IA, USA[10,10]. She died on 01 Mar 1966 in La Junta, Otero, Colorado, USA.

11   iv. LESLIE CLYDE BUSH[10,32,49] was born on 09 Jun 1887 in Carthage, Jasper, Missouri, USA[10]. He died on 09 Sep 1940 in La Junta, Otero, Colorado, USA. He married JENNIE MAY AVERY, daughter of Charles Mandell AVERY and Justina MILLER. She was born on 18 Oct 1890 in Coolidge, Hamilton, Kansas, USA[10]. She died on 13 Nov 1944 in La Junta, Otero, Colorado, USA.

7. **MARY L.[3] BUSH** (John Harding[2] Jr., John Hardin[1])[33] was born on 29 Jul 1857 in Hart, Kentucky, USA[33]. She died on 18 Mar 1940 in Los Angeles, California, USA[33]. She married **JAMES LOGSDON**, son of George W. LOGSDON and Susan LINDER. He was born in 1858 in Kentucky, USA[34].

James LOGSDON and Mary L. BUSH had the following children:

    i. VIOLETTA[4] LOGSDON was born about 1875.
    ii. IONA LOGSDON was born about 1877 (Carthage, Missouri).
    iii. INFANT LOGSDON was born in Feb 1880 (Carthage, Missouri).

Generation 4

8. **ADELL THORNLEY[4] BUSH** (Samuel Shelton[3], John Harding[2]Jr., John Hardin[1])[9,9,10,23] was born on 15 Jul 1877 in Carthage, Jasper, Missouri, USA[9,10,19,23,35]. She died on 26 Feb 1948 in La Junta, Otero, Colorado, USA[23]. She married **JOHN HOLMES SIMONTON** on 04 Jun 1902 in La Junta, Otero, Colorado, USA[9]. He was born on 30 Jul 1858 in Mifflinburg, Union, Pennsylvania, USA[9,10]. He died on 26 Jun 1938 in La Junta, Otero, Colorado, USA.

Notes for Adell Thornley BUSH: In Clifford Ritchhart's family history he spelled her name with one "l" (Adel). However, Grace and Alonzo had a child who died in infancy that was named Adell Frances. It is likely she was named after her Aunt and they spelled it with two l's. Later discovery of cemetery records proved this to be correct. I knew my "Aunt Dell" who lived in North La Junta. We used to go visit them. My memories are very vague as I was probably only about 8 or 9 (and I am 65 now), but my memories are fond of Aunt Dell. I am guessing that my father's name Delbert was an offshoot of my Aunt Dell's name, possibly combined with his uncle Bert's name—resulting in Delbert.

Although other sources list her name as Adell, the 1880 census clearly spells her name Adella. I assume either she dropped the "a" from her name or the enumerator made a mistake.

Notes for John Holmes SIMONTON: According to Clifford Ritchhart's family history, Holmes was much older than Adell. He operated a store and was in charge of the Post Office in La Junta where the Bush family settled.

The wedding notice in the newspaper indicated "…many wedding presents were received, among them was a handsome one hundred piece dinner set, presented by Mr. Simonton of La Junta."

John Holmes SIMONTON and Adell Thornley BUSH had the following children:

    i. MYRA LOIS[5] SIMONTON[9,9,9,10,50] was born about 1904 in Colorado, USA. She married CLAUDE OLIVER LLOYD, son of David Stokes LLOYD and Nancy Ellis HENDERSON. He was born on 08 Jul 1908 in Kurten, Brazos, Texas, USA[9,9,51]. He died on 15 Jan 1967 in La Junta, Otero, Colorado, USA[9,9].

    ii. RUTH SIMONTON[50,52] was born in 1907 in Colorado, USA[50,52].

    iii. GRACE SIMONTON[50,52] was born in 1911 in Colorado, USA[50,52].

    iv. MARTHA SIMONTON[50,52] was born in 1918 in Colorado, USA[50,52].

9.   **GRACE AZETTA[4] BUSH** (Samuel Shelton[3], John Harding[2] Jr., John Hardin[1])[9,10,18,20,21,25,36,37,38,39,40,41,42,43] was born on 17 Nov 1879 in Carthage, Jasper, Missouri, USA[9,10,19,21,25,36,42,43,44]. She died on 28 Jan 1952 in La Junta, Otero, Colorado, USA[9,42,43]. She married **ALONZO FRANCIS RITCHHART** on 01 Jan 1902 in La Junta, Otero, Colorado, USA (5 p.m. wedding followed by dinner)[45], son of Wesley RITCHHART and Maria Sibilla WAGNER. He was born on 03 Nov 1867 in Indiana, USA[46]. He died on 27 May 1959 in Stanislaus, California, USA[46,47].

Alonzo Francis RITCHHART and Grace Azetta BUSH had the following children:

    i. SAMUEL CLIFFORD[5] RITCHHART was born on 31 May 1903 in Rocky Ford, Otero, Colorado, USA[53]. He died on 09 Aug 1989 in Canon City, Fremont, Colorado, USA. He married MARIANNA EVALINA GLATZ on 16 Sep 1926 in La Junta, Otero, Colorado, USA, daughter of Edward William GLATZ and Emma Elizabeth HERWIG. She was born on 02 Jan 1908[54]. She died on 29 Oct 1990 in Murfreesboro, Rutherford, Tennessee, USA[54].

    ii. MARY LILLIAN RITCHHART[55,56] was born on 16 Jan 1906 in La Junta, Otero, Colorado, USA[56,57]. She died on 28 Jan 1983 in Sacramento, Sacramento, California, USA[58]. She married JAMES RUMSBY about 1923[59], son of James RUMSBY and Louie KIMBALL. He was born on 01 Apr 1902 in Colorado, USA[60,61]. He died on 19 Jan 1983 in Sacramento, California, USA[60,61].

    iii. PAUL WESLEY RITCHHART[9,10,62,63] was born on 26 May 1908 in La Junta, Otero, Colorado, USA[63,64]. He died in Jun 1964 in Wyoming, USA[65]. He married (1) INEZ JOSEPHINE RITTER about 1930 in Colorado, USA, daughter of Carl Burch RITTER and Dell Reynolds PORTER. She was born on 17 Feb 1908 in Colorado, USA[66]. She died on 06 Dec 1963 in Phoenix, Maricopa, Arizona, USA. He married (2) SUSIE SANTA DELORENZO on 29 Dec 1951[67]. She was born on 02 Sep 1911 in La Junta, Otero, Colorado, USA[9,68]. She died on 03 Feb 1988 in La Junta, Otero, Colorado, USA[69].

    iv. DELBERT BUSH RITCHHART[10,36,70] was born on 02 Nov 1910 (Carthage, Missouri)[10,36,38,43]. He died on 18 Feb 1981 in Denver, Colorado, USA[43]. He married HELEN JANE DEAN on 01 Aug 1952 in Raton, Colfax, New Mexico, USA (Remarried)[71], daughter of Arthur Spear DEAN and Mary Loretta O'MALLEY. She was born on 06 Aug 1915 in Denver, Adams, Colorado, USA (2:53 p.m., St. Joseph's Hospital)[72,73,74,75]. She died on 28 Oct 1995 in Loveland, Larimer, Colorado, USA[69,74,76].

    v. ADELL FRANCES RITCHHART[9] was born in Apr 1915 in La Junta, Otero, Colorado, USA. She died on 01 Jan 1916 (Died as young child prior to 1st birthday.)[77].

    vi. BETTY JANE RITCHHART was born on 04 Jul 1919 in La Junta, Otero, Colorado, USA[36,78,79]. She died on 04 May 1993 in Newark, New Castle, Delaware, USA[80]. She married (1) JOHN T. LINEHAN on 04 May 1945[81], son of Joseph Aloysius LINEHAN and Mary Louise HOLMES. He was born in 1920 in Seymour, New Haven, Connecticut, USA. She married (2) BILLY GLENN about 1939.

10. **WILLIAM ELBERT[4] BUSH** (Samuel Shelton[3], John Harding[2] Jr., John Hardin[1])[10,48] was born on 27 Jan 1884 in Jasper, Missouri, USA. He died on 14 Oct 1958 in La Junta, Otero, Colorado, USA. He married **ELIZABETH ARMINDA BEEDLE** on 03 Dec 1904 in La Junta, Otero, Colorado, USA[10], daughter of Simeon Jeremiah BEEDLE and Nancy Jane SPURGEON. She was born on 01 Aug 1880 in Lovilla, Monroe, IA, USA[10,10]. She died on 01 Mar 1966 in La Junta, Otero, Colorado, USA.

Notes for William Elbert BUSH: Grace's brother W.E. Bush was reported in the obituary to be living in La Junta in January 1952 when Grace passed away. Clifford Ritchhart, in his family history, indicated that Grace had only two brothers, Bert and Les. I assume, therefore, that William's nickname must have been "Bert." It is logical since his middle name was Elbert.

Notes for Elizabeth Arminda BEEDLE: According to date in the *World Family Tree* Vol #33, Elizabeth's last name was Beedle.

William Elbert BUSH and Elizabeth Arminda BEEDLE had the following children:

    i. MISCARRIAGE[5] BUSH[10].

    ii. HAROLD HEBER BUSH[82] was born on 22 Sep 1905 in La Junta, Otero, Colorado, USA[10]. He died on 03 Jul 1921 in La Junta, Otero, Colorado, USA.

    Notes for Harold Heber BUSH: Clifford Ritchhart refers to going deer hunting with his dad, his Uncles Les and Bert, and Bert's son Heber. Clifford said Heber was a little younger than himself. This correlates with Clifford being born in 1903 and Heber in 1905. Since Heber died when he was 16, they must have gone deer hunting prior to 1921.

    iii. PAULINE B. BUSH[83] was born about 1908 in Colorado, USA.

    iv. WILMA BUSH was born on 25 Jul 1910 in La Junta, Otero, Colorado, USA[77]. She died on 01 May 2001 in La Junta, Otero, Colorado, USA.

    Notes for Wilma BUSH: I speculate that Wilma is the daughter of William Bush and Elizabeth Bush, but have no current proof. She was in the same series of burial plots as William, Elizabeth and their son Harold (i.e., Plot 19, Lot 014, spaces 0001, 0002, 0003 and 0004). Based on the inscription on her headstone she died at age 90, thus she would have been born when Elizabeth was 21 and William was 27—which is logical.

    v. RUBY ELIZABETH BUSH[10] was born on 06 Sep 1915 in La Junta, Otero, Colorado, USA[10]. She died on 26 Apr 1969[10].

    Notes for Ruby Elizabeth BUSH: Graduate of Brown's Business College. Undated newspaper article announced she accepted a government stenographic position in Ignacio, Colorado near the Indian reservation.

    vi. CONSTANCE BUSH[10] was born in 1919[10].

11. **LESLIE CLYDE**[4] **BUSH** (Samuel Shelton[3], John Harding[2] Jr., John Hardin[1])[10,32,49] was born on 09 Jun 1887 in Carthage, Jasper, Missouri, USA[10]. He died on 09 Sep 1940 in La Junta, Otero, Colorado, USA. He married **JENNIE MAY AVERY**, daughter of Charles Mandell AVERY and Justina MILLER. She was born on 18 Oct 1890 in Coolidge, Hamilton, Kansas, USA[10]. She died on 13 Nov 1944 in La Junta, Otero, Colorado, USA.

Notes for Leslie Clyde BUSH: Records from the La Junta Cemetery and headstone photos indicate the name Leslie C. Bush; but the plot records record the name as Lester C.

Leslie Clyde BUSH and Jennie May AVERY had the following children:

    i. MARY LESLIE[5] BUSH[84]. She married RICHARD MANN about Jun 1940 in La Junta, Otero, Colorado, USA[84].

    ii. DOROTHY E BUSH[10]. She died on 26 Jan 1999[10].

    iii. JANET M BUSH[10]. She died on 14 Oct 1999[10].

    iv. HELEN BUSH[10].

    v. CLYDE E BUSH[10].

    vi. SAMUEL BUSH was born in 1910 in La Junta, Otero, Colorado, USA. He died in Dec 1910 in La Junta, Otero, Colorado, USA.

    Notes for Samuel BUSH: I have deduced that Samuel was the infant son of Jennie May and Leslie Bush because of the plot records. All three (as well as Lillian P.) are in consecutive spaces. They are in Plot 0015, Lot 014, spaces 0001, 0002, 0003, and 0004.

Sources

1   Ancestry.com, *Public Member Trees* (Provo, UT, USA, The Generations Network, Inc., 2006),

www.ancestry.com, Database online. Record for John Harding Bush.

2   Ancestry.com, *Public Member Trees* (Provo, UT, USA, The Generations Network, Inc., 2006), www.ancestry.com, Database online. Record for John Hardin Bush.

3   Ancestry.com, *Public Member Trees* (Provo, UT, USA, The Generations Network, Inc., 2006), www.ancestry.com, Database online. Record for Ann Bass.

4   Ancestry.com, *Public Member Trees* (Provo, UT, USA, The Generations Network, Inc., 2006), www.ancestry.com, Database online. Record for John H Bush.

5   Ancestry.com, Kentucky Death Records, 1852–1953 (Provo, UT, USA, Ancestry.com Operations Inc, 2007), www.ancestry.com, Database online. Record for Anna Bush.

6   *1870 US Census*, Carthage, Jasper Co., MO, Pg. 25. 7 June 1880 Census. listed age as 72. Thus, if born prior to June, he was born in 1808. If born after June, he was born in 1807.

8   Jerry Jupin; Ancestry.com, 2009. Jupin-Wardrip Family Tree on Ancestry.com.

9   Ancestry.com, *One World Tree*[SM] (Provo, UT, USA: The Generations Network, Inc., n.d.), www. ancestry.com, database online. Provo, UT, USA: The Generations Network, Inc.

11   Ancestry.com, *Public Member Trees* (Provo, UT, USA, The Generations Network, Inc., 2006), www.ancestry.com, Database online. Record for Samuel Shelton "Seth" Bush.

12   *1880 US Census*, Colfax, Harrison Co., Missouri.

13   *1850 US Census*, Hart, Kentucky.

14   *1880 United States Federal Census* (Provo, UT, USA: The Generations Network, Inc., 2005, www.ancestry.com, Online publication. 1880 U.S. Census Index provided by The Church of Jesus Christ of Latter-day Saints © Copyright 1999 Intellectual Reserve, Inc. All rights reserved. Original data—United States of America, Bureau of the Census. Tenth Census of the United States. Washington, D.C.: National Archives and Records Administration, 1880. T9, 1,454 rolls. Jackson, Clark, Missouri, ED 37, roll T9_681, page 153.1000, image 0310.

15   *1880 United States Federal Census* (Provo, UT, USA: The Generations Network, Inc., 2005, www.ancestry.com, Online publication. 1880 U.S. Census Index provided by The Church of Jesus Christ of Latter-day Saints © Copyright 1999 Intellectual Reserve, Inc. All rights reserved. Original data—United States of America, Bureau of the Census. Tenth Census of the United States. Washington, D.C.: National Archives and Records Administration, 1880. Census Place: Carthage, Jasper, Missouri; Roll: T9_694; Family History Film: 1254694; Page: 479.2000; Enumeration District: 66; Image: 0761. Birth date: abt 1853, Birth place: Kentucky, Residence date: 1880, Residence place: Carthage, Jasper, Missouri, United States.

16   *Ancestry Family Trees* (Online publication—Provo, UT, USA: The Generations Network. Original data: Family Tree files submitted by Ancestry members). http://trees.ancestry.com/pt/ AMTCitationRedir.aspx?tid=2906494&pid=-1803570455.

17   *1870 United States Federal Census* (Provo, UT, USA: The Generations Network, Inc., 2003), www.ancestry.com, database online, 2003. Indexed by Ancestry.com from microfilmed schedules of the 1870 U.S. Federal Decennial Census. Original data: Data imaged from National Archives

and Records Administration. Ninth Census of the United States, 1870. M593, 1,761 rolls). Census Place: Marion, Jasper, Missouri; Roll: M593. Record for Shelton Bush.

18   Ancestry.com, *Public Member Trees* (Provo, UT, USA, The Generations Network, Inc., 2006), www.ancestry.com, Database online. Record for Samuel Shelton Bush.

19   *1880 United States Federal Census* (Provo, UT, USA: The Generations Network, Inc., 2005, www.ancestry.com, Online publication. 1880 U.S. Census Index provided by The Church of Jesus Christ of Latter-day Saints © Copyright 1999 Intellectual Reserve, Inc. All rights reserved. Original data—United States of America, Bureau of the Census. Tenth Census of the United States. Washington, D.C.: National Archives and Records Administration, 1880. Census Place: Carthage, Jasper, Missouri; Roll: T9_694; Family History Film: 1254694; Page: 479.2000; Enumeration District: 66; Image: 0761. Record for Samuel S. Bush.

20   Ancestry.com, *Public Member Trees* (Provo, UT, USA, The Generations Network, Inc., 2006), www.ancestry.com, Database online. Record for Grace Azetta Bush.

21   Ancestry.com, *Public Member Trees* (Provo, UT, USA, The Generations Network, Inc., 2006), www.ancestry.com, Database online. Record for Grace Azetta Bush.

22   *1900 United States Federal Census* (Provo, UT, USA: The Generations Network, Inc., 2004, www.ancestry.com, online publication. Original data—United States of America, Bureau of the Census. Twelfth Census of the United States, 1900. Washington, D.C.: National Archives and Records Administration, 1900). Census Place: Madison, Jasper, Missouri; Roll: T623_866; Page: 4B; Enumeration District: 55. Record for Lilian Bush.

23   Ancestry.com, *Public Member Trees* (Provo, UT, USA, The Generations Network, Inc., 2006), www.ancestry.com, Database online. Record for Lillian Perdida Logsdon.

24   *1930 US Census*. Grace listed her father's birthplace as Kentucky.

25   Ancestry.com, *Public Member Trees* (Provo, UT, USA, The Generations Network, Inc., 2006), www.ancestry.com, Database online. Record for Grace Bush.

26   *World Family Tree* Vol 33.

27   La Junta Cemetery Headstone and plot files, 1930 Census Grace lists mother's birthplace as Iowa.

28   *1910 United States Federal Census* (Provo, UT, USA: The Generations Network, Inc., 2006), www.ancestry.com, Online publication. Original data United States of America, Bureau of the Census. Thirteenth Census of the United States. Washington, D.C.: National Archives and Records Administration, 1910.T624, 1,178 rolls). Census Place: La Junta, Otero, Colorado; Roll: T624_123; Page: 18A; Enumeration District: 128; Image: 793, birth date: abt 1860, Birth place: Iowa, Residence date: 1910, Residence place: La Junta, Otero, Colorado.

29   *1870 United States Federal Census* (Provo, UT, USA: The Generations Network, Inc., 2003), www.ancestry.com, database online, 2003. Indexed by Ancestry.com from microfilmed schedules of the 1870 U.S. Federal Decennial Census. Original data: Data imaged from National Archives and Records Administration. Ninth Census of the United States, 1870. M593, 1,761 rolls). Birth date: abt 1860, Birth place: Iowa, Residence date: 1870, Residence place: Marion, Jasper, Missouri.

30   *1900 United States Federal Census* (Provo, UT, USA: The Generations Network, Inc., 2004, www.ancestry.com, online publication. Original data—United States of America, Bureau of the Census. Twelfth Census of thc United States, 1900. Washington, D.C.: National Archives

and Records Administration, 1900). Census Place: Madison, Jasper, Missouri; birthdate Mar 1860, Birth place: Iowa, Marriage date: 1876, Residence date: 1900, Residence place: Madison Township, Jasper, Missouri.

31 *1880 United States Federal Census* (Provo, UT, USA: The Generations Network, Inc., 2005, www.ancestry.com, Online publication. 1880 U.S. Census Index provided by The Church of Jesus Christ of Latter-day Saints © Copyright 1999 Intellectual Reserve, Inc. All rights reserved. Original data—United States of America, Bureau of the Census. Tenth Census of the United States. Washington, D.C.: National Archives and Records Administration, 1880. Census Place: Carthage, Jasper, Missouri; Roll: T9_694; Family History Film: 1254694; Page: 479.2000; Enumeration District: 66; Image: 0761, birth date: abt 1860, Birth place: Iowa, Residence date: 1880, Residence place: Carthage, Jasper, Missouri, United States.

32 La Junta Cemetery Headstone and plot files.

33 Ancestry.com, *Public Member Trees* (Provo, UT, USA, The Generations Network, Inc., 2006), www.ancestry.com, Database online. Record for John Hardin Bush.

34 *1880 United States Federal Census* (Provo, UT, USA: The Generations Network, Inc., 2005, www.ancestry.com, Online publication. 1880 U.S. Census Index provided by The Church of Jesus Christ of Latter-day Saints © Copyright 1999 Intellectual Reserve, Inc. All rights reserved. Original data—United States of America, Bureau of the Census. Tenth Census of the United States. Washington, D.C.: National Archives and Records Administration, 1880.

35 *1880 United States Federal Census* (Provo, UT, USA: The Generations Network, Inc., 2005, www.ancestry.com, Online publication. 1880 U.S. Census Index provided by The Church of Jesus Christ of Latter-day Saints © Copyright 1999 Intellectual Reserve, Inc. All rights reserved. Original data—United States of America, Bureau of the Census. Tenth Census of the United States. Washington, D.C.: National Archives and Records Administration, 1880. Census Place: Carthage, Jasper, Missouri; Roll: T9_694; Family History Film: 1254694; Page: 479.2000; Enumeration District: 66; Image: 0761, birth date: abt 1877, Birth place: Missouri, Residence date: 1880, Residence place: Carthage, Jasper, Missouri, United States.

36 *1930 United States Federal Census* (Provo, UT, USA: The Generations Network, Inc., 2002), www.ancestry.com, Online publication. Original data United States of America, Bureau of the Census. Fifteenth Census of the United States. Washington, D.C.: National Archives and Records Administration, 1930.T626, 2,667 rolls). La Junta, Otero, Colorado, ed 8, roll 248, image 99.0.

37 Clifford Ritchhart's Family History. Two pages listing ancestors and children of Alonso and Grace Ritchhart.

38 *1930 United States Federal Census* (Provo, UT, USA: The Generations Network, Inc., 2002), www.ancestry.com, Online publication. Original data United States of America, Bureau of the Census. Fifteenth Census of the United States. Washington, D.C.: National Archives and Records Administration, 1930.T626, 2,667 rolls). La Junta, Otero, Colorado, ed 8, roll 248, image 99.0. Record for Dalbert Ritchhart.

39 *1880 United States Federal Census* (Provo, UT, USA: The Generations Network, Inc., 2005, www.ancestry.com, Online publication. 1880 U.S. Census Index provided by The Church of Jesus Christ of Latter-day Saints © Copyright 1999 Intellectual Reserve, Inc. All rights reserved. Original data—United States of America, Bureau of the Census. Tenth Census of the United States. Washington, D.C.: National Archives and Records Administration, 1880. Census Place: Carthage, Jasper, Missouri; Roll: T9_694; Family History Film: 1254694; Page: 479.2000;

Enumeration District: 66; Image: 0761, birth date: abt 1879, Birth place: Missouri, Residence date: 1880, Residence place: Carthage, Jasper, Missouri, United States.

40   *1900 United States Federal Census* (Provo, UT, USA: The Generations Network, Inc., 2004, www.ancestry.com, online publication. Original data—United States of America, Bureau of the Census. Twelfth Census of the United States, 1900. Washington, D.C.: National Archives and Records Administration, 1900). Census Place: Madison, Jasper, Missouri; Roll: T623 866; Page: 4B; Enumeration District: 55, birth date: abt 1880, Birth place: Missouri, Residence date: 1900, Residence place: Madison, Jasper, Missouri.

41   *1930 United States Federal Census* (Provo, UT, USA: The Generations Network, Inc., 2002), www.ancestry.com, Online publication. Original data United States of America, Bureau of the Census. Fifteenth Census of the United States. Washington, D.C.: National Archives and Records Administration, 1930.T626, 2,667 rolls). Census Place: La Junta, Otero, Colorado; Roll: 248; Page: 6B; Enumeration District: 8; Image: 99.0, birth date: abt 1880, Residence date: 1930, Residence place: La Junta, Otero, Colorado.

42   Ancestry.com, *Public Member Trees* (Provo, UT, USA, The Generations Network, Inc., 2006), www.ancestry.com, Database online. Record for Grace Azetta Bush.

43   Ancestry.com, *Public Member Trees* (Provo, UT, USA, The Generations Network, Inc., 2006), www.ancestry.com, Database online. Record for Grace Azetta Bush.

44   *June 1880 US Census.* Indicated she was 7 months old, and her birth month was November.

45   La Junta Newspaper Wedding Announcement (La Junta, Colorado, January 1902), Personal files of Del Ritchhart.

46   Ancestry.com, *California Death Index, 1940–1997* (Provo, UT, USA: The Generations Network, Inc., 2000). Original data: State of California. *California Death Index, 1940–1997.* Sacramento, CA: State of California Department of Health Services, Center for Health Statistics, 19–.

47   Ancestry.com, *Public Member Trees* (Provo, UT, USA, The Generations Network, Inc., 2006), www.ancestry.com, Database online. Record for Alonzo F Ritchhart.

48   La Junta Newspaper Obituary.

49   Clifford Ritchhart's Family History, La Junta Cemetary records.

50   *1930 United States Federal Census* (Provo, UT, USA: The Generations Network, Inc., 2002), www.ancestry.com, Online publication. Original data United States of America, Bureau of the Census. Fifteenth Census of the United States. Washington, D.C.: National Archives and Records Administration, 1930.T626, 2,667 rolls). North La Junta, Otero, Colorado, ed 7, roll 248, image 72.0. Record for John H Simonton.

51   *1910 United States Federal Census* (Provo, UT, USA: The Generations Network, Inc., 2006), www.ancestry.com, Online publication. Original data United States of America, Bureau of the Census. Thirteenth Census of the United States. Washington, D.C.: National Archives and Records Administration, 1910.T624, 1,178 rolls). Justice Precinct 3, Brazos, Texas, ed , roll T624_1529.

52   *1930 United States Federal Census* (Provo, UT, USA: The Generations Network, Inc., 2002), www.ancestry.com, Online publication. Original data United States of America, Bureau of the Census. Fifteenth Census of the United States. Washington, D.C.: National Archives and Records Administration, 1930.T626, 2,667 rolls). North La Junta, Otero, Colorado, ed 7, roll 248, image 72.0.

53   Family History from Clifford Ritchhart.

54   *Social Security Death Index*, digital image, The National Archives (www.genealogyBank.com).

55   Ancestry.com, *California Death Index, 1940–1997* (Provo, UT, USA: The Generations Network, Inc., 2000). Original data: State of California. *California Death Index, 1940–1997*. Sacramento, CA: State of California Department of Health Services, Center for Health Statistics, 19–.

56   Ancestry.com, *Social Security Death Index* (Provo, UT, USA: The Generations Network, Inc., 2008), www.ancestry.com, [database online]. Original data: Social Security Administration. *Social Security Death Index, Master File*. Social Security Administration. Number: 550-24-3179; Issue State: California; Issue Date: Before 1951. Record for Mary Rumsby.

57   *1930 United States Federal Census* (Provo, UT, USA: The Generations Network, Inc., 2002), www.ancestry.com, Online publication. Original data United States of America, Bureau of the Census. Fifteenth Census of the United States. Washington, D.C.: National Archives and Records Administration, 1930.T626, 2,667 rolls). Census Place: Township 3, Fresno, California; Roll: 117; Page: 6A; Enumeration District: 8; Image: 596.0. Record for Betty L Rumsby.

58   *1920 United States Federal Census* (Provo, UT, USA: The Generations Network, Inc., 2005), www.ancestry.com, Online publication. Original data United States of America, Bureau of the Census. Fourteenth Census of the United States. Washington, D.C.: National Archives and Records Administration, 1920.T625, 2076 rolls). Census Place: Salt Lake City Ward 4, Salt Lake, Utah; Roll: T625_1865; Page: 13A; Enumeration District: 137; Image: 341, birth date: abt 1919, Birth place: Colorado, Residence date: 1920, Residence place: Salt Lake City Ward 4, Salt Lake, Utah.

59   *1930 US Census*, Fresno, California, Gave ages at marriage as 21 and 17.

60   Ancestry.com, *California Death Index, 1940–1997* (Provo, UT, USA: The Generations Network, Inc., 2000). Original data: State of California. *California Death Index, 1940–1997*. Sacramento, CA: State of California Department of Health Services, Center for Health Statistics, 19–.

61   Ancestry.com, California Death Index, 1940–1997 (Provo, UT, USA, The Generations Network, Inc., 2000), www.ancestry.com, Database online. Place: Sacramento; Date: 19 Jan 1983; Social Security: 709169267. Record for James Rumsby.

62   *1840 US Census* from "My Genealogy.com."

63   *1930 United States Federal Census* (Provo, UT, USA: The Generations Network, Inc., 2002), www.ancestry.com, Online publication. Original data United States of America, Bureau of the Census. Fifteenth Census of the United States. Washington, D.C.: National Archives and Records Administration, 1930.T626, 2,667 rolls). Census Place: La Junta, Otero, Colorado; Roll: 248; Page: 4A; Enumeration District: 10; Image: 142.0, birth date: abt 1909, Birth place: Colorado, Residence date: 1930, Residence place: La Junta, Otero, Colorado.

64   *Ancestry Family Trees* (Online publication—Provo, UT, USA: The Generations Network. Original data: Family Tree files submitted by Ancestry members). http://trees.ancestry.com/pt/AMTCitationRedir.aspx?tid=2906494&pid=-76157346.

65   Broderbund Family Archive #110, Vol. 2, Ed. 5, *Social Security Death Index*: U.S., Date of Import: Jul 6, 1998, Internal Ref. #1.112.5.56488.82

66   *1910 United States Federal Census* (Provo, UT, USA: The Generations Network, Inc., 2006), www.ancestry.com, Online publication. Original data United States of America, Bureau of the

Census. Thirteenth Census of the United States. Washington, D.C.: National Archives and Records Administration, 1910.T624, 1,178 rolls). La Junta, Otero, Colorado, roll T624_123.

67   Christy Peterson, Christy Ward Peterson's Family Tree (, Jan 2009), GENI.COM.

68   Ancestry.com, *Social Security Death Index* (Provo, UT, USA: The Generations Network, Inc., 2008), www.ancestry.com, [database online]. Original data: Social Security Administration. *Social Security Death Index, Master File*. Social Security Administration. Number: 357-05-8358; Issue State: Illinois; Issue Date: Before 1951. Record for Susie Ritchhart.

69   Ancestry.com, *Social Security Death Index* (Provo, UT, USA: The Generations Network, Inc., 2008), www.ancestry.com, [database online]. Original data: Social Security Administration. *Social Security Death Index, Master File*. Social Security Administration.

70   *Ancestry Family Trees* (Online publication—Provo, UT, USA: The Generations Network. Original data: Family Tree files submitted by Ancestry members). http://trees.ancestry.com/pt/ AMTCitationRedir.aspx?tid=2906494&pid=-1803611891.

71   *Bent County Democrat* Article, Files of Del Ritchhart.

72   *1930 United States Federal Census* (Provo, UT, USA: The Generations Network, Inc., 2002), www.ancestry.com, Online publication. Original data United States of America, Bureau of the Census. Fifteenth Census of the United States. Washington, D.C.: National Archives and Records Administration, 1930. T626, 2,667 rolls). Las Animas, Bent, Colorado, ed 8, roll 230, image 619.0.

73   *1920 United States Federal Census* (Provo, UT, USA: The Generations Network, Inc., 2005), www.ancestry.com, Online publication. Original data United States of America, Bureau of the Census. Fourteenth Census of the United States. Washington, D.C.: National Archives and Records Administration, 1920. T625, 2076 rolls). Census Place: Las Animas, Bent, Colorado; Roll: T625_155; Page: 6B; Enumeration District: 269; Image: 529, birth date: abt 1915, Birth place: Colorado, Residence date: 1920, Residence place: Las Animas, Bent, Colorado.

74   Ancestry.com, *Social Security Death Index* (Provo, UT, USA: The Generations Network, Inc., 2008), www.ancestry.com, [database online]. Original data: Social Security Administration. *Social Security Death Index, Master File*. Social Security Administration. Number: 524-34-6670; Issue State: Colorado; Issue Date: Before 1951. Birth date : 6 Aug 1915, Death date: 15 Oct 1995, Death place: Loveland, Larimer, Colorado, United States of America.

75   Ancestry.com, *U.S. Public Records Index, Volume 2* (Provo, UT, USA, Ancestry.com Operations, Inc., 2010), www.ancestry.com, Database online. Record for Helen J Ritchhart.

76   *Ancestry Family Trees* (Online publication—Provo, UT, USA: The Generations Network. Original data: Family Tree files submitted by Ancestry members). http://trees.ancestry.com/pt/ AMTCitationRedir.aspx?tid=2906494&pid=-76072090.

77   Cemetery Plot Records.

78   Ancestry.com, *Social Security Death Index* (Provo, UT, USA: The Generations Network, Inc., 2008), www.ancestry.com, [database online]. Original data: Social Security Administration. *Social Security Death Index, Master File*. Social Security Administration.

79   *1930 US Census*, La Junta, Colorado, Listed Alonzo, Grace, Delbert and Betty. All the others must have moved out by then.

80   Broderbund Family Archive #110, Vol. 1, Ed. 5, *Social Security Death Index*: U.S., Date of

Import: Feb 18, 2001, Internal Ref. #1.111.5.143522.195

81   Letter from Betty's husband Jack Linehan dated Dec 16, 1993, stated that Betty died on their 48th wedding anniversary.

82   1910 Census Otero Co., La Junta, Listed Harold H. Other sources listed name as Harold Heber. Age of 4 agreed with Sep 1905 birthday.

83   *1910 US Census,* Otero Co., La Junta, Listed her age as 2 and born in Colorado.

84   The JJ Ranch on the Purgatory River.

Generation 1

1. **RICHARD[1] DEAN**[1,2,3,4,5,6,7,8,9,10,11,12,13,14,15,16] was born on 02 Sep 1698 (Cripplegate Ward, London, , England)[8,9,10,11,12,14,15,16]. He died on 01 Oct 1747 in , Henrico, Virginia, USA[10,11,12,14,15,16]. He married **SARAH ELIZABETH JORDAN** in 1718[11,13], daughter of Benjamin JORDAN and Sarah HATCHER. She was born in 1700 in Nansemond, Virginia, USA[8,9,10,15,17,18]. She died in 1751 in Henrico, Virginia, USA[1,3,6,7,8,9,10,15,18].

Richard DEAN and Sarah Elizabeth JORDAN had the following children:

2   i.   EDWARD[2] DEAN[1,3,4,5,6,7,8,10,13,16,19,20] was born in 1718 in Henrico, Virginia, USA[1, 3, 4, 7, 10, 19]. He died on 18 Jun 1761 in Antrim, Halifax, Virginia, USA[1, 6, 7, 8, 10, 16, 19]. He married REBECCA ABNEY about 1738 in Henrico, Virginia, USA[1,21]. She was born in 1720 in Henrico, Virginia, USA[22]. She died in 1761 in Halifax, Halifax, Virginia, USA[22].

ii.   CHARLES DEAN[6,12,23] was born in 1722[5]. He died in 1798 in Rockingham, North Carolina, USA[5,12].

iii.   RICHARD DEAN[4,5] was born in Henrico, Virginia, USA[4,5].

iv.   DANIEL DEAN[5,6] was born in 1730[5].

v.   THOMAS DEAN[5,6,12] was born in 1729[5,6,12].

vi.   WILLIAM DEAN[5,6] was born in 1727 in Henrico, Virginia, USA[6].

vii.   JOHN DEAN[5,6] was born in 1725[5,6]. He died in 1765 in Halifax, Virginia, USA[5,6].

viii.   ELIZABETH DEAN[5,6,13] was born in 1718[5,6,13].

ix.   JACOB DEAN[12] was born in 1732[12].

Generation 2

2. **EDWARD[2] DEAN** (Richard[1])[1,3,4,5,6,7,8,10,13,16,19,20] was born in 1718 in Henrico, Virginia, USA[1,3,4,7,10,19]. He died on 18 Jun 1761 in Antrim, Halifax, Virginia, USA[1,6,7,8,10,16,19]. He married **REBECCA ABNEY** about 1738 in Henrico, Virginia, USA[1,21]. She was born in 1720 in Henrico, Virginia, USA[22]. She died in 1761 in Halifax, Halifax, Virginia, USA[22].

Notes for Edward DEAN: A deed book for Halifax County 1767–70 indicates that land was being purchased by two other men that had once been part of a patent Edward had received on 10 June 1760. The land was on Spider Creek.

The *Halifax County, VA Will Book 1752–73* listed an inventory & appraisement for his wife Rebecca as follows: 1 young horse, looking glass, a razor, book, hogs and 2 yearlings. It also included his will dated 2 April 1961, indicating he was "...sick and weak of body..." It further detailed what would be left to his wife and children. Edward's will indicated that his wife was pregnant, which would have been their fifth child.

In October 1763 the court ordered that the Church Wardens of Antrim Parish bind out

Charles Dean, son of Edward and also bind out Joshua, Edward & William, other orphans of Edward. I assume from this that Rebecca must have preceded Edward in death.

The *Halifax County, Virginia Deeds 1767–1772 v.1* indicated the John Dean was selling 20 acres in September 1772 that he had inherited from his father, Edward. The land was on the south side of the head of Spider Creek. The *Vesting Book of Antrim Parish* had a note dated May 1753, that Edward Dean (Deen) was exempt from parish levys due to illness. Edward's will was contained in *Halifax County, Virginia Will Book 1752–1773*. Thus, I am inclined the believe he did die in 1761.

Edward DEAN and Rebecca ABNEY had the following children:

    i. EDWARD[3] DEAN[22,24] was born in 1747 in Henrico or Halifax, Virginia, USA[22].

    ii. CHIARLES DEAN[23] was born in 1753 in Lunenburgh, , Virginia, USA[22]. He died in 1780 (, , Georgia, USA)[22].

        Notes for Chiarles DEAN: His name could be "Charles" vice Chiles. One will book listed him as Chiles and a court record as Charles. I think it is more likely to be Charles.

    iii. JOSHUE DEAN[24,25] was born in 1750 in Lunenburgh, , Virgini a, USA[22]. He died on 23 May 1801 in South, Carolina, Puerto Rico, USA[22].

    iv. WILLIAM DEAN[24] was born in 1759 in Halifax, Virginia, USA[1]. He died after 1830 in Pickens, Alabama, USA[1].

    v. JULIUS DEAN[22] was born in 1744 in Henrico or, Halifax, Virginia, USA[22].

3   vi. JOHN DEAN[2,19,26,27,28,29,30] was born about 1743 in Henrico, Virginia, USA[31]. He died in 1775 in Surry, North Carolina, USA[26,28]. He married KEZIAH SMITH about 1761 in Halifax, Virginia, USA[31], daughter of Gideon SMITH and Eleanor Elizabeth ECHOLS. She was born about 1743 in Halifax, Virginia, USA[31,32]. She died in Nov 1787 in Surry, North Carolina, USA[26,31,32,33,34,35].

Generation 3

3. **JOHN[3] DEAN** (Edward[2], Richard[1])[2,19,26,27,28,29,30] was born about 1743 in Henrico, Virginia, USA[31]. He died in 1775 in Surry, North Carolina, USA[26,28]. He married **KEZIAH SMITH** about 1761 in Halifax, Virginia, USA[31], daughter of Gideon SMITH and Eleanor Elizabeth ECHOLS. She was born about 1743 in Halifax, Virginia, USA[31,32]. She died in Nov 1787 in Surry, North Carolina, USA[26,31,32,33,34,35].

Notes for John DEAN: John appeared to have a lot of problems handling his debts. There were three separate claims against him by other individuals in the *Halifax County, Virginia Court Orders 1759–62*, 975.5661 (2t V.1). He had several other friends vouch that he would pay the debt; but in July 1759 his cosigners delivered him to the court rather than pay his debt, which he obviously had not paid. However, in September 1759 he was in court again for a debt of 18 pounds. Ironically, in June 1761 he was a member of a jury in an assault and battery case. In July 1761 he was again a defendant in a debt case.

Interestingly enough, the plaintiff against John in one case was Nathaniel Abney, whom I am guessing was a relative as John's father was married to Rebecca Abney. In another case in June 1764 Rebecca Dean was the plaintiff against her son, John; but the parties agreed and it was dismissed. I don't think John was a very good character!

A second case brought against John by Nathaniel Abney was dismissed. Another Abney was also a defendant and was also dismissed. In a July 1764 court order John was referred to as John Dean Sr. I have his son listed as Job John, so perhaps he went by John? In March 1765 John and Kezia sold 126.5 acres of land on the north side of the Dan River.

John still appears in court records in August 1769 and September 1772 (both debt cases) in Fairfax County, so he must not have moved to North Carolina until late in life. There were no Deans listed in Volume 3 of the Halifax County, Virginia Will Book which covered 1783–1792. This tends to agree with the fact John died in North Carolina and the fact he sold land in 1772. Ironically he was appointed Sexton of the Antrim Parish at a salary of 400 (pounds I believe) on 17 Jun 1769.

Notes for Keziah SMITH: *Surry County, North Carolina, Wills 1771–1827* contains several references to Keziah and has a summary of her will. In Keziah's will she only listed six children. I believe that one of them (probably Winnie) preceded Keziah in death. Amongst the names John, Job John and Job, I think there is duplication and that some or all might be one in the same. It is very unlikely they would have had two boys both named Job. Additionally, Amasa is indicated as having died between 1850–60, yet she is named in her mother's will in 1787. Suffice to say there is some question about the data associated with the children.

According to "Keziah Smith Dean's Story" submitted to Ancestry.com by Brenda Riggs, Keziah's father died when she was only 12. She and her younger sister were bound out by the church warden to either their uncle Daniel Smith, or to their half-brother William Murphy—it varies from account to account as to who the girls went to. I wonder why the girls were bound out if their mother, Eleanor, was still alive?

Keziah's will was entered into the *Surry County Will Book #2*, page 81. She died in 1787; but her will was made out on 22 May 1780. In 1783 she purchased 50 acres of land and added 50 more the following year.

John DEAN and Keziah SMITH had the following children:

4   i.   JOHN[4] DEAN[2,27,34,36] was born about 1763 in Surry, North Carolina, USA. He died in Wayne, West Virginia, USA. He married HANNAH MARSHALL. She was born in Massachusetts, USA[2]. She died Near Preston, Kentucky[2].

     ii. WINNIE DEAN[37] was born in 1764 in Surry, North Carolina, USA. She died in Floyd, Kentucky, USA.

          Notes for Winnie DEAN: Winnie might have preceded her mother in death as she is not listed in her mother's will dated in Nov 1787.

5   iii. THOMAS DEAN[2,31,34,38] was born about 1765 in Halifax, Virginia, USA. He died in 1832 in Washington, Kentucky, USA[31]. He married SALLY.

6   iv. JOB JOHN DEAN[26,26,26,34,39,40] was born in 1767[33]. He died in 1808 in Washington, Kentucky, USA[26,28]. He married (1) MARY POLLY MAXWELL on 16 Nov 1796 in Washington, Kentucky, USA[26,26,41], daughter of Edward MAXWELL and Jane MONTGOMERY. She was born on 07 Sep 1779 in Surry, North Carolina, USA[26]. She died on 26 Jan 1844 in Livingston, Kentucky, USA[26]. He married (2) SUSANNAH UNK.

     v. KEZIAH DEAN[31,42] was born in 1772 in Halifax, Virginia, USA[2,31]. She died in 1841 in Lawrence, Kentucky, USA[2,31].

    vi. AMASA DEAN[2,31,34,43] was born on 25 Dec 1774 in Surry, Virginia, USA[2,31]. He died between 1850–1860 in Wayne, West Virginia, USA[31].

Generation 4

4.   **JOHN[4] DEAN** (John[3], Edward[2], Richard[1])[2,27,34,36] was born about 1763 in Surry, North Carolina, USA. He died in Wayne, West Virginia, USA. He married **HANNAH MARSHALL**. She was born in Massachusetts, USA[2]. She died Near Preston, Kentucky[2].

Notes for John DEAN: According to Luch Deyoung on her website www.deyoungmatson.com, this John Dean was in the Revolutionary War. John served in the Continental Line of North Carolina, 10th Regiment, Quinn's Company. He enlisted 20 Jul 1778 and served 9 months. However, Footnote. com lists a "John Dean/Deane" as a Pvt in the First Virginia State Regiment in Capt Abner Crump's Company.

There are pay vouchers for Dec 1778 to March 1779 and a payroll roster for Jan 1779. Perhaps this was for Job John Dean or the website was referring to another John Dean. That is likely because this John was in Virginia his whole life.

John DEAN and Hannah MARSHALL had the following children:
      i. HANNAH[5] DEAN[2]. She died in 1830[2].
     ii. LILLIAN DEAN[2]. She died in 1847[2].
    iii. JOBE DEAN was born in 1785 in North Carolina, USA[2]. He died in 1855 in Kentucky, USA[2].
    iv. PENINAH DEAN[2] was born in 1794 in Surry, North Carolina, USA[2]. She died in 1884 in Floyd, Kentucky, USA[2].
     v. MIRANDA DEAN[2] was born in 1797 in North Carolina, USA[2]. She died in 1886 in Pulanski County, Kenturcky[2].
    vi. SARAH DEAN[2] was born in 1805 in Floyd, Kentucky, USA[2]. She died in 1870 in Floyd, Kentucky, USA[2].

5.   **THOMAS[4] DEAN** (John[3], Edward[2], Richard[1])[2,31,34,38] was born about 1765 in Halifax, Virginia, USA. He died in 1832 in Washington, Kentucky, USA[31]. He married **SALLY**.

Notes for Thomas DEAN: I made a calculated assumption that Thomas was the son of John based on multiple references to Thomas in Kentucky and an association with Thomas.

There are many transactions in the *Washington Co., KY Deed Abstracts 1803–11* by Thomas.

Many of them were in some association with Job Dean. I believe this further substantiates the above assumption that Job and Thomas were related.

In 1814 Thomas sold off several parcels of land in Washington County. Not sure what this means; but it could indicate he was planning to move; however, there was a Thomas Dean in the 1830 Washington County Census.

Thomas DEAN and SALLY had the following child:

> i. ANN[5] DEAN[44] was born about 1790[45]. She married JOHN PHILLIPS on 09 Mar 1816 in Washington, Kentucky, USA (Date of License)[41].

6. **JOB JOHN[4] DEAN** (John[3], Edward[2], Richard[1])[26,26,26,34,39,40] was born in 1767[33]. He died in 1808 in Washington, Kentucky, USA[26,28]. He married (1) **MARY POLLY MAXWELL** on 16 Nov 1796 in Washington, Kentucky, USA[26,26,41], daughter of Edward MAXWELL and Jane MONTGOMERY. She was born on 07 Sep 1779 in Surry, North Carolina, USA[26]. She died on 26 Jan 1844 in Livingston, Kentucky, USA[26]. He married (2) **SUSANNAH UNK**.

Notes for Job John DEAN: I speculate that John and Mary may have had additional children named Jesse and Ira (Asa) and perhaps Willis. The book *Red River County, Texas First Settlers* lists Edward, Jesse, Ira, Willis and Levi as being awarded land for being early settlers of the county. Since I only have three children listed for them, and that is a small family for those times, I think it is likely that the above speculation may be valid.

An entry in the *Washington Co., KY Deed Abstracts* in which Thomas and his wife, Sally, made an indenture for Job Dean's "infant heirs" for 80 acres of land. The wording referred to Job as "dec'd" indicating that he had passed away. The transaction was dated 2 April 1804. There may also be two Job Deans.

The *Index of Washington County, KY Deeds* listed Job & Thomas, Job and Wife and Job's infant as Grantors of Deeds. No dates listed.

The *Surry County, N.C. Abstracts of Land Entries 1784–95* notes a Warrant issued by the court to John Dean on May 18, 1805 regarding a Jul 16, 1792 sale of 50 acres by John to Thomas Ross. Even though the name was listed as John Dean, because the dates are after the death of John Dean, I assume it refers to John Dean, his son. Another entry in the Surry County land records noted 50 acres on the West side of Mitchells River at Reedy Fork being granted to "JNO Dean," whom I equate with John Dean (in those times it was common to abbreviate John as JNO).

In *Surry County, North Carolina, Wills 1771–1827* there is reference to the inventory of John Deane's estate by Keziah Deane (wife & administrator). It notes that on 15 May 1783 Job Deane, orphan of John Dean deceased, aged 16, was bound to Zadock Riggs to learn the Art & Mistry of a blacksmith. Later in the same book the will of Kezia Smith Dean leaves all her land to son, John. Son, Thomas gets the livestock and the remainder goes to her children Job, Kezia, & Amasa.

Washington County, Kentucky deed abstract book indicates that on 19 Aug 1799 Willia Gathen, orphan of Reuben was indentured to Job Dean to learn the art of blacksmith.

Interestingly, Job was indentured in May 1783, at the age of 16, to Zadock Riggs to learn the art of Blacksmith. This was occasioned by the death of his father, John. This was in Surry County, N.C.

Job John DEAN and Mary Polly MAXWELL had the following children:

> i. MARTIN[5] DEAN[26,26,46] was born in 1797 in Washington, Kentucky, USA[26,26]. He died in 1809.

7   ii. EDWARD MAXWELL DEAN[26,39,47] was born on 21 Apr 1799 in Kentucky, USA[48]. He died on 14 Feb 1842 in Detroit, Red River, Texas, USA[48,49]. He married SARAH JANE DEAN on 26 Oct 1822 in Washington, Kentucky, USA[26,41]. She was born in 1805 in Kentucky, USA[26,48,49]. She died in Nov 1849 in Detroit, Red River, Texas, USA[26,47].

> iii. ALEXANDER DEAN[26,26,50] was born on 11 Jan 1801 in Marion, Crittenden, Kentucky, USA[26,26]. He died on 22 Mar 1879 in Livingston, Kentucky, USA[26,26]. He married ANNA GATES on 02 Nov 1826 in Caldwell County, Kentucky[51].

Job John DEAN and Susannah UNK had the following child:

> iv. ANNA ELIZABETH DEAN was born in 1793 in North Carolina, USA[2].

Generation 5

7.   **EDWARD MAXWELL[5] DEAN** (Job John[4], John[3], Edward[2], Richard[1])[26,39,47] was born on 21 Apr 1799 in Kentucky, USA[48]. He died on 14 Feb 1842 in Detroit, Red River, Texas, USA[48,49]. He married **SARAH JANE DEAN** on 26 Oct 1822 in Washington, Kentucky, USA[26,41]. She was born in 1805 in Kentucky, USA[26,48,49]. She died in Nov 1849 in Detroit, Red River, Texas, USA[26,47].

Notes for Edward Maxwell DEAN: According to data about 1st Citizens of Texas in *Stopes* periodical, the Deans came to Texas in 1833. The book *Red River County, Texas First Settlers* lists Edward as emigrating on 1 December 1834 to the County. He was the 4th person to file for a land grant and was awarded 1 League and 1 Labor of land.

Headstone marker included Sarah, Alfred and Thomas L. His grave is the oldest marked in the Detroit #2 or Dean Cemetery located between Clarksville and Detroit.

Notes for Sarah Jane DEAN: The *Washington Co., KY Marriages* book listed Sarah's maiden name as Dean. So it is possible Edward Maxwell married a distant cousin.

Edward Maxwell DEAN and Sarah Jane DEAN had the following children:

> i. JOB[6] DEAN[26,39,52] was born on 02 Feb 1824 in Caldwell County, Kentucky[26,39].
>
> Notes for Job DEAN: May also have been known as Edward. Thomas L. Dean's will named six brothers and sisters. Considering that Alfred had already passed away and their were only six remaining brothers and sisters, all others were accounted for except Job to match the sixth name "Edward."

> ii. MARY DEAN was born on 08 Jan 1826 in Caldwell County, Kentucky[26]. She died on 28 Oct 1910. She married JAMES SHARP. He was born about 1825 (est based on

Mary's age).

8   iii. SPEAR CHRISTOPHER DEAN[53,54,55,56] was born on 18 Jun 1829 in Caldwell, Kentucky, USA[39,53,54,55,56]. He died on 11 May 1908 in Weatherford, Parker, Texas, USA[39]. He married SARAH MARSHALL JONES on 12 Jul 1853 in Red River, Texas, USA[57,58], daughter of Erasmus JONES II and Christianna BOND. She was born on 15 Oct 1835 in Murfreesboro, Cannon County, Tennessee[59,60]. She died on 28 Jul 1935 in Abilene, Taylor, Texas, USA[61,62].

    iv. THOMAS LOGAN DEAN[26] was born on 20 Jun 1831 in Caldwell County, Kentucky[26]. He died in Dec 1854 in Red River, Texas, USA[26,48,49].

Notes for Thomas Logan DEAN: Thomas wrote his Will on Nov 21, 1854 and upon his death the following month it was probated on 18 December 1854. It named his brothers and sisters as the recipients of his estate. They were Levi, James, George, S.C., Edward and Mary M. Sharp. This was found in *Pioneers of Red River County, Texas* by Frances Terry Ingmire, call number Gc 976.401 R24i at the Allen County Public Library.

    v. ALFRED DEAN[48] was born in 1833 in Kentucky, USA[26,48]. He died in Apr 1842 in Red River, Texas, USA[48].

9   vi. LEVI DEAN[26,26,39,48] was born on 23 Aug 1838 in Red River, Texas, USA[48]. He died on 25 Jun 1925 in Detroit, Red River County, Texas[39,48]. He married MARTHA M. WILLIAMS in 1866 in Red River, Texas, USA[48]. She was born on 10 Jun 1849 in Lamar, Texas, USA[48]. She died on 24 Dec 1929 in Detroit, Red River County, Texas[48].

   vii. JAMES R. DEAN[39] was born on 13 Apr 1840 in Red River, Texas, USA[26,39]. He died in 1905[39].

10 viii. GEORGE BROWN DEAN[26,39,52,63] was born on 11 Sep 1842 in Red River, Texas, USA[26,39,63]. He died on 27 Jun 1920 in Detroit, Red River County, Texas[39,48,63]. He married (1) WILLIE BAILEY on 09 Nov 1865 in Red River, Texas, USA[48]. She was born on 04 Nov 1842[49,63]. She died on 11 Dec 1871[63]. He married (2) MARY HOLMES PARKS on 31 Oct 1872 in Red River, Texas, USA[48]. She was born on 05 Oct 1852[48,49]. She died on 07 Feb 1894 in Red River, Texas, USA[48,49].

Generation 6

8. **SPEAR CHRISTOPHER**[6] **DEAN** (Edward Maxwell[5], Job John[4], John[3], Edward[2], Richard[1])[53,54,55,56] was born on 18 Jun 1829 in Caldwell, Kentucky, USA[39,53,54,55,56]. He died on 11 May 1908 in Weatherford, Parker, Texas, USA[39]. He married **SARAH MARSHALL JONES** on 12 Jul 1853 in Red River, Texas, USA[57,58], daughter of Erasmus JONES II and Christianna BOND. She was born on 15 Oct 1835 in Murfreesboro, Cannon County, Tennessee[59,60]. She died on 28 Jul 1935 in Abilene, Taylor, Texas, USA[61,62].

Notes for Spear Christopher DEAN: Spear must have run for some office in Weatherford, Texas in 1892 because I have a letter from his wife to their son, Thomas F., dated Nov 25, 1892 in which she says, "Every thing quieted down since the election your Pa was defeated by a large majority."

Middle name listed as Christopher in *The JJ Ranch on the Purgatory*. Also listed as Christopher in the DeyoungMatson web site.

Named in *Pioneers of Red River County, Texas* as a 1st Settler of Red River.

Notes for Sarah Marshall JONES: Family legend indicates Sara was the great Aunt of General George C. Marshall of WW II fame. Thus, the Marshall as a middle name. Making it even more interesting is the fact General Marshall's middle name is Catlett which may also have been the middle name of Sarah's husband, Spear Catlett Dean. Thus, the possibility their was a family connection between not only Sarah and General Marshall, but Spear Dean and General Marshall. However, as noted above, other sources indicate Spear's middle name was Christopher?

Her brothers started the famous JJ Ranch south of Las Animas. In doing research in the Mormon family research center in Park City, UT, I happened to enter Spear Dean and then noticed that there were extensive records regarding the ancestry of his wife, Sara. Someone had obviously done a lot of research about her family and I became the benefactor of all that work.

LDS Family Search records have two listings for Sara Marshall Jones' parents. Both list Erasmus Jones as her father (one having him born in 1799 est in Bedford, VA and the other 1807 est in Chattanooga, Tenn). The first lists her mother as Christian Bond the second only as Christiana, born about 1811 in Chattanooga, Tenn. The second listing also lists all of her siblings, whereas, the first only lists herself. However, the second source lists her birth as 1845 vice 1835 making her 8 at the time of marriage vice 18. None of the ages of her brothers and sisters seem to agree with other sources either. (I later learned there were a father and son, Erasmus I and Erasmus I Jones).

Sara died at her daughter's home in Abilene, TX, but was buried in Weatherford, TX. Interestingly, according to Marshall Dean, when Jim Jones and his brothers first started their cattle drive to Colorado, they departed from near San Angelo, TX which is just southwest of Abilene.

I would estimate she moved from Weatherford, TX to Abilene in 1912, as I have a letter she sent to her grandson, Arthur, in Jan of 1913 saying that his letter had been forwarded to her in Abilene from Weatherford.

From reading her letters, one would assume she was not an educated person. Letters had no periods to separate sentences and spelling was like a child "bead' for bed, two vice to, heare for here, wright for right, "gon a fishen," "fealing good." Yet, words like insurance, Chicago and treatment were correctly spelled. She was 92 at the time.

She had 25 grandchildren, 28 great grandchildren and one great-great grandson at the time of the family reunion for her 96th birthday in 1931. Not all were in attendance, but she related in a letter to Ida Dean those were the figures.

The 1880 census listed she and Spear living next door to Sara's brother George D. and his family.

Spear Christopher DEAN and Sarah Marshall JONES had the following children:

    i. MARSHALL[7] DEAN[61] was born in 1854 in Red River, Texas, USA.

    ii. ERASMUS MAXWELL DEAN[26,64,65,66,67,68,69] was born on 13 Jul 1854 in Red River, Texas, USA[26,69,70]. He died on 22 Apr 1945 in McLennan, Texas, USA[65,69]. He married NANCY FRANCIS J. EDDLEMAN on 07 Dec 1876 in Young, Texas, USA[64,70], daughter of Columbus Ashbury EDDLEMAN and Elizabeth BRANSCOMB. She was born in 1854 in Arkansas[71].

    Notes for Erasmus Maxwell DEAN: Name listed in 1850 Census as Masil, which could be what they called him as a nickname (possibly because his younger siblings couldn't pronounce Maxwell—MY NOTE). Young County, Texas where Nancy and Erasmus were married is about 45 miles northwest of Weatherford, Texas, where Spear and Sarah Marshall Dean lived.

    According to Ed Dean, Max came to Colorado in 1868 (1869 according to other sources) along with the Jones brothers Stephen (and wife), Pete and Jim, of JJ Ranch fame, driving 1100 cattle they had roped and branded. They followed Goodnight's trail made 2 years earlier. They drove 3 days (50 miles) once without water. The West Texas plains were bare from the lack of rain and the streams were dry. They proceeded to the Pecos then north through the foothills to Raton Pass. "Uncle" Billy Wooten controlled the pass & wanted money per head of cattle. The Jones' refused to pay and went east and found another pass to go north to Higbee (also called "Nine mile bottom"). It was October when they came into Calfax County, New Mexico. The weather was cold and snowy. They moved on down the Purgatory (Picketwire) River to Nine Mile Bottom, known today as Higbee, Colorado. They settled in the Higbee area and then in the spring some of the men returned to Texas for more cattle. The trip was quicker this time as the families were not with them and they took a shorter route. The herds were moved to Smith Canyon, which is located 50 miles southwest of Las Animas. The brand used on the cattle was JJ for Jim Jones.

    Thomas Franklin and James Bingham Dean later came to Higbee to help with the JJ Ranch, probably on the first, or later, return to Texas for more cattle. Max's mother's obituary said that a son (unnamed) who was 80 attended the funeral. This was probably Max, as he would have been about 80 then.

    The 1920 Census for Amarillo listed an E.M. Dean living with Fanny Franklin and her husband. I assume he returned to Texas after his Colorado adventures. It is also probably that Fanny had died by then.

    Ed Dean's notes also indicated that Mack Dean killed a man and went to Canada for five years.

11 iii. MARY ELIZABETH DEAN[26,26,26,47,54,72,73,74,75] was born on 06 Aug 1856 in Red River, Texas, USA[74,75,76]. She died on 16 Sep 1942 in Austin, Travis, Texas, USA[76,77]. She married (1) FELIX EZELL SMITH on 14 Sep 1882 in Red River, Texas, United

States[73], son of James Woods SMITH and Sarah Sally A. BRYSON. He was born in Nov 1860 in Texas, USA[78]. He died on 11 Aug 1930 in Austin, Travis, Texas, USA[79].

12   iv.   JAMES BINGHAM DEAN[26,80] was born on 29 Jan 1858 in Red River, Texas, USA[26,81]. He died on 23 Mar 1936 in Las Animas, Bent, Colorado, USA[81]. He married TEXANA EDDLEMAN on 25 Nov 1886 in Bent County (Smith Canyon)[81], daughter of Columbus Ashbury EDDLEMAN and Elizabeth BRANSCOMB. She was born on 12 Sep 1865 in Fort Worth, Johnson, Texas, USA[82,83]. She died in 1946 in Las Animas, Bent, Colorado, USA.

13   v.   THOMAS FRANKLIN DEAN[84,85,86] was born on 15 Nov 1860 in Weatherford, Parker, Texas, USA[84,85]. He died on 29 Jun 1905 in Las Animas, Bent, Colorado, USA. He married IDA JANE BRITTON on 23 Dec 1885 in Las Animas, Bent, Colorado, USA[87], daughter of Thomas Dugan BRITTON and Effie Melissa MOLER. She was born on 13 Nov 1868 in Bernard, Nodaway, Missouri, USA[87,88,89,90]. She died on 18 Oct 1952 in Las Animas, Bent, Colorado, USA.

14   vi.   FANNIE LEE DEAN[26,47,54,91,92,93,94] was born on 25 Sep 1862 in Parker, Texas, USA[26,47,54,94]. She died on 19 Jan 1956 in Amarillo, Potter, Texas, USA. She married FELIX E FRANKLIN. He was born in 1858 in Texas, USA[92]. He died about 1925 in Texas, USA.

     vii.   ANN LAURA DEAN[54,95,96,97] was born on 24 Jun 1864 in Parker, Texas, USA[26,26,54]. She died on 19 Jan 1956 in Amarillo, Potter, Texas, USA[26,26,98]. She married WILLIAM M. LAY on 27 May 1891 in Parker, Texas, USA[99,100], son of Arnold M. LAY and MARY. He was born about 1847 in Texas, USA[101].

     Notes for Ann Laura DEAN: In a letter from her to her brother, Thomas Franklin, dated 1892 she was in Weatherford, TX. Judging from her letter she was better educated than her mother and would have been at least in her 20s, thus she was born before about 1872. She was not married yet, as she signed the letter Laura Dean.

     viii.   LOURETTA DEAN[102] was born on 08 Jun 1866 in Parker, Texas, USA[47]. She died on 19 Aug 1869 in Parker, Texas, USA[26,47].

     Notes for Louretta DEAN: Probably died as a child. Listed as 3 of age in 1870 census; but not listed in 1880 census. Whereas, her other siblings were all listed in order. In *Parker County Cemeteries*, Dean Cemetery (pg. 77) Lou Nettie Dean is listed as being buried within the wall for the Jones family including Spear and Sarah Marshall Jones Dean. Birth and death dates were listed as about 1857 and about 1870. I speculate that Louretta and Lou Nettie are one in the same.

15   ix.   JENNIE DEAN[26,54,103,104,105,106] was born on 16 Jan 1869 in Parker, Texas, USA[26,54,105]. She died on 07 Nov 1942 in Weatherford, Parker, Texas, USA[26]. She married R. L. DAVIS.

     x.   JESSE DEAN[26,47,54,95,107] was born on 10 Dec 1871 in Parker, Texas, USA[26,47,54]. He died on 19 Dec 1900 in Sundance, Crook, Wyoming, USA.

     Notes for Jesse DEAN: Supposedly died in a gunfight in Sundance, Wyoming. Had gotten paid for the winters work and went to town. Was gambling and drinking and was shot by one of the other gamblers. I have letters written by his brother Frank (Sheriff of Las Animas) to officials in Wyoming inquiring about the circumstances surrounding his brothers death. There were responses by the Sundance Sheriff and the rancher who employed Jessie.

    xi. MINNIE DEAN[26,54,108,109] was born on 15 Apr 1873 in Parker, Texas, USA[26,54]. She died on 21 Dec 1967 in Abilene, Taylor, Texas, USA[26]. She married UNK BLAINE.

    Notes for Minnie DEAN: Must have lived in Abilene or somewhere in Texas in 1913, as a letter from Sara Dean to her grandson, Arthur Dean, stated that Aunt Minnie sends her best wishes as well.

    xii. JOSEPHINE DEAN[26,26,54,110,111] was born on 14 Mar 1875 in Weatherford, Parker, Texas, USA[26,54]. She died on 19 Aug in Weatherford, Parker, Texas, USA[26]. She married R. CARTER on 27 May 1898 in Weatherford, Parker, Texas, USA[112]. He was born about 1873.

    Notes for Josephine DEAN: Had a source indicating Josephine died in 1869; but a Wedding Notice from a newspaper article stated that she married in 1898. I choose to believe the newspaper article.

9. **LEVI[6] DEAN** (Edward Maxwell[5], Job John[4], John[3], Edward[2], Richard[1])[26,26,39,48] was born on 23 Aug 1838 in Red River, Texas, USA[48]. He died on 25 Jun 1925 in Detroit, Red River County, Texas[39,48]. He married **MARTHA M. WILLIAMS** in 1866 in Red River, Texas, USA[48]. She was born on 10 Jun 1849 in Lamar, Texas, USA[48]. She died on 24 Dec 1929 in Detroit, Red River County, Texas[48].

Notes for Levi DEAN: Levi's very detailed obituary said he died a mile and half from where he was born. However, an equally detailed obituary for his brother George B. Dean said that the brothers were born in Tennessee and following service for the Confederates in the Civil War they came to Texas. Census data for three different census' confirm Texas as his birthplace. His headstone marker said he died in 1924; but the obituary says 1925, which I believe to be correct. Served as an early Texas Ranger and in the Confederate Army. In 1911 he organized the first state bank, however, he severed relations with the bank in 1923 and became ill shortly after that.

Pioneers of Red River County designates Levi as a 1st Settler of Red River entitled to Second Class Certificates because of arriving there between 2 Mar 1836 and 1 Oct 1837. For this he was given 1280 acres on his month of birth August 2, 1838. Since Levi wasn't born until Aug 1838, his qualifying date for land certificates must have been based on the date his father arrived in Red River County.

Notes for Martha M. WILLIAMS: Obituary indicated she was survived by four daughters.

Levi DEAN and Martha M. WILLIAMS had the following children:

    i. LIZZIE[7] DEAN[48]. She married C. A. MARTIN.

    ii. MARY DEAN[48]. She married J. H. EBRITE.

10. **GEORGE BROWN[6] DEAN** (Edward Maxwell[5], Job John[4], John[3], Edward[2], Richard[1])[26,39,52,63] was born on 11 Sep 1842 in Red River, Texas, USA[26,39,63]. He died on 27 Jun 1920 in Detroit,

Red River County, Texas[39,48,63]. He married (1) **WILLIE BAILEY** on 09 Nov 1865 in Red River, Texas, USA[48]. She was born on 04 Nov 1842[49,63]. She died on 11 Dec 1871[63]. He married (2) **MARY HOLMES PARKS** on 31 Oct 1872 in Red River, Texas, USA[48]. She was born on 05 Oct 1852[48,49]. She died on 07 Feb 1894 in Red River, Texas, USA[48,49].

Notes for George Brown DEAN: According to his obituary George was a very prominent citizen of the county. He and his brother Levi came to Texas after the Civil War. They traveled down the Mississippi River to New Orleans on a cotton boat, bought a pack mule and traveled to Texas. They first went to Lamar County to visit friends they had known from Tennessee and then went on to Red River County and settled on Blossom Prairie. George had acquired considerable land in both Red River and Delta Counties and they even closed the bank the day of his funeral because he was a major stockholder in the bank.

George Brown DEAN and Willie BAILEY had the following children:

     i. J.W. [7]DEAN[48].

     ii. GEORGE B. DEAN JR. He married DUBIE WHEELER MILLER on 15 Apr 1899 in Red River, Texas, USA[48]. She was born on 26 Apr 1861 in Mississippi, USA[48]. She died on 24 Jun 1928 in Detroit, Red River County, Texas[48].

16 iii. SARAH JANE DEAN[48,63,113,114,115] was born on 06 Nov 1866 (Stringtown Community, Red River Co., TX)[48,63,113,114,115]. She died on 07 Oct 1945 in Detroit, Red River County, Texas[48,63]. She married (1) JAMES B. DEAN in 1886 in Red River, Texas, USA[63], son of Joseph Madison DEAN and Isabel Caroline CLEMENT. He was born on 26 Apr 1856 in Deanwood, Crittiton County, Kentucky[48,114]. He died on 01 Oct 1931[48,63,113,115,116]. She married (2) UNK CONLEY.

George Brown DEAN and Mary Holmes PARKS had the following children:

     iv. HOUSTON H. DEAN[48].

     v. MINNIE DEAN[48].

     vi. JAMES W. DEAN[48].

     vii. LISSIE DEAN[48].

    viii. ELLA DEAN[48].

     ix. GEORGE E. DEAN[48].

Generation 7

11. **MARY ELIZABETH[7] DEAN** (Spear Christopher[6], Edward Maxwell[5], Job John[4], John[3], Edward[2], Richard[1])[26,26,26,47,54,72,73,74,75] was born on 06 Aug 1856 in Red River, Texas, USA[74,75,76]. She died on 16 Sep 1942 in Austin, Travis, Texas, USA[76,77]. She married (1) **FELIX EZELL SMITH** on 14 Sep 1882 in Red River, Texas, United States[73], son of James Woods SMITH and Sarah Sally A. BRYSON. He was born in Nov 1860 in Texas, USA[78]. He died on 11 Aug 1930 in Austin, Travis, Texas, USA[79].

Notes for Mary Elizabeth DEAN: Her mother spelled her name as Bettie in a letter dated Nov 25, 1892 to her son Thomas Frank. She must have been married, as the letter said "they have changed Post Office her post office is now Highland Park, Los Angeles County Cala (for California I expect).

The 1880 census listed the oldest daughter, age 23, as "M.E." I speculate it could be Mary Elizabeth. Since Betty is short for Elizabeth, it could be the same person (in fact when I checked the 1870 census, she was listed as Mary E.).

Felix Ezell SMITH and Mary Elizabeth DEAN had the following children:

     i. JAMES EDWARD[8]SMITH[73,74] was born on 20 Jun 1888 in Travis, Texas, USA[73,74].

     ii. ANNIE MARSHALL SMITH[73,74] was born on 04 Dec 1886 in Travis, Texas, USA[73,74].

     Notes for Annie Marshall SMITH: In a letter dated 1994 to Helen Jane Ritchhart, Ed Dean talked about Annie Smith. He said she never married; but was a bit of a family historian. He claimed the Deans came from Normandy, France to southwest England and the name was Den. Apparently Annie's grandfather, I assume on the Smith side, was a lieutenant to Sam Houston. He claimed Annie and her brother, Edward, inherited a land grant south of Austin from Sam Houston. Not sure if it went from Houston to their grandfather and then to them or directly to them. He also claimed Annie gave lots of money to the University of Texas. He also claimed that Annie's research claimed the Deans supposedly founded Concord, Massachusetts. They then went to North Carolina and to Kentucky. My research shows the original Dean (John) came to Virginia from England. The Deans then moved to North Carolina, Kentucky and on to Texas; before coming to Colorado. The Jones side of the family spent time in Massachusetts; but not the Deans (according) to my research.

12. **JAMES BINGHAM**[7] **DEAN** (Spear Christopher[6], Edward Maxwell[5], Job John[4], John[3], Edward[2], Richard[1])[26,80] was born on 29 Jan 1858 in Red River, Texas, USA[26,81]. He died on 23 Mar 1936 in Las Animas, Bent, Colorado, USA[81]. He married **TEXANA EDDLEMAN** on 25 Nov 1886 in Bent County (Smith Canyon)[81], daughter of Columbus Ashbury EDDLEMAN and Elizabeth BRANSCOMB. She was born on 12 Sep 1865 in Fort Worth, Johnson, Texas, USA[82,83]. She died in 1946 in Las Animas, Bent, Colorado, USA.

Notes for James Bingham DEAN: When he was 21, his Uncle Payton came from Colorado and took him, his brother Thomas Frank and four other Texans back with him. According to Ed Dean, they came by train. They understood they were to be cowboys, but Uncle Pete put them to digging ditches to irrigate and build rock fences. They later had a chance to be cowboys and helped on the famous JJ Ranch.

Notes for Texana EDDLEMAN: I have a funeral notice for Mamie Lizzie Eddleman, b. June 12, 1878 in Kent, Iowa and d. in Las Animas on Nov 5, 1964. She could have been a sister of Texana or could have married one of Texana's brothers. She obviously had a Dean connection as Ed and Art Dean were Casket Bearers.

James Bingham DEAN and Texana EDDLEMAN had the following children:

17   i. JESSIE EDWARD[8] DEAN was born on 27 Jun 1887 (Bent County, Colorado)[117]. He died in 1943 in Pueblo, Colorado, USA[118]. He married CLARA WRIGHT on 27 Feb 1924 in Denver, Colorado, USA.

     ii. HARRY DEAN was born about 1888 (Bent County, Colorado). He died about 1905

(Age 12 from appendicitis.)[83].

    iii. ANNIE PEARL DEAN[119] was born in Feb 1891 in Las Animas, Bent, Colorado, USA[120].

Notes for Annie Pearl DEAN: According to Ed Dean's writings.."Pearl was born crippled, cross-eyed and of sound mind at the Vandiver rooming house in La Junta. Her dress caught on fire when she was 12 and she was burned and severely scarred."

    iv. LANETTIE DEAN[121] was born in Apr 1893 in Las Animas, Bent, Colorado, USA. She married JACKSON WHITFIELD RICKMAN.

    v. ROY BINGHAM DEAN was born in Oct 1895 in Las Animas, Bent, Colorado, USA. He married DITA LOU UNK.

Notes for Roy Bingham DEAN: 1900 Census listed his name as either Le Roy or H. Roy. Not sure where the Bingham comes from. According to Ed Dean's letter of 19 March 1998 about family history, Roy was a dentist and he went to Pacheco, Mexico. He described Roy as a person who knew all the presidents of Mexico. Women demanded his presence at parties. He was a brilliant conversationalist, dentist, orthodontist, famous fisherman and writer. I am sure much of that was true; but Ed sometimes "enhanced" his stories about the family.

18   vi. MARSHALL SPEAR DEAN[122] was born on 07 Apr 1897 in Las Animas, Bent County, Colorado[122,123,124,125]. He died in Jan 1976 in Las Animas, Bent, Colorado, USA. He married ELLA PRYOR. She was born on 22 Mar 1897[126]. She died in Jun 1984 in Las Animas, Bent, Colorado, USA.

13. **THOMAS FRANKLIN**[7] **DEAN** (Spear Christopher[6], Edward Maxwell[5], Job John[4], John[3], Edward[2], Richard[1])[84,85,86] was born on 15 Nov 1860 in Weatherford, Parker, Texas, USA[84,85]. He died on 29 Jun 1905 in Las Animas, Bent, Colorado, USA. He married **IDA JANE BRITTON** on 23 Dec 1885 in Las Animas, Bent, Colorado, USA[87], daughter of Thomas Dugan BRITTON and Effie Melissa MOLER. She was born on 13 Nov 1868 in Bernard, Nodaway, Missouri, USA[87,88,89,90]. She died on 18 Oct 1952 in Las Animas, Bent, Colorado, USA.

Notes for Thomas Franklin DEAN: —Came to Colorado in 1879. According to Ed Dean he, along with his brother James Bingham, were brought by his uncle Pete. It seems logical that he would have come on one of the JJ Ranch crew trips back to Texas for more cattle; but some of Ed Dean's notes said it was by train. He and J.B. were put to work digging an irrigation ditch on the Picketwire 1/2 mile south of the Davidson Ranch HQ. Later they broke horses and helped work the cattle on the JJ Ranch. After the cattle and ranch were sold in 1882 to the Prairie Cattle Company they tried to "prove up" on land in Smith Canyon. However, they could not get title to the land and were considered "squatters." Supposedly the Prairie Cattle Company had some enforcers to discourage "squatters" so they moved to Las Animas. One source indicated he tried farming for a while and then later opened a butcher shop. Then in the fall of 1899 he became one of Bent County's first sheriffs. He was elected Sheriff again in 1901 and was in office when he passed away of appendicitis in 1905. —Funeral services held July 1 in the family residence by Rev. H. M.

Pingree. His Father and Mother were still alive and still lived in Weatherford, TX.

In my files I have a series of letters between Frank and people in Sundance, Wyoming (northeast corner near N. Dakota border). His brother Jessie worked on a ranch outside of Sundance and, apparently after getting his seasonal pay, went to town, got drunk, got in a fist fight and eventually it evolved to a gun fight and he was killed. Frank corresponded with the Sheriff, Jessie's employer, and a couple other observers to get the details of how Jessie was killed. It is very interesting reading.

Notes for Ida Jane BRITTON: Came to Colorado in 1881 from Missouri with her parents. This was verified in an article in the Bent County Democrat dated April 23, 1937. She was one of the founding members of The Half Century Club (also called the Pioneer Club) and the paper had interviewed them as to when they came to Colorado. The members had all lived in Colorado for 50 years or more. Supposedly she came here in a covered wagon (I don't have a direct source for that—only word of mouth from my mother).

I was fortunate to have known my "Grandma Jane." She still lived in the house on Locust and when I was about 11 or 12, I would go over weekly and pump her drinking water from the well. She didn't like drinking the faucet water because she said it didn't taste as good. I have a 38 caliber Smith and Wesson pistol that belonged to her. The patent date on it is 1889, but I am not sure when it was made.

She was not a very big woman, probably about 5'4". She was always very pleasant and would always spend some time sitting and talking with me whenever I went to pump water for her.

In 1952 at the Old Settlers contest in La Junta she was 8th among the registered attendees as having lived the longest in Colorado.

Thomas Franklin DEAN and Ida Jane BRITTON had the following children:

19   i.   ARTHUR SPEAR[8] DEAN[127,128,129,130,131,132,133] was born on 22 Oct 1886 in Las Animas, Bent, Colorado, USA[127,130,131,132,133]. He died on 01 Dec 1969 in Las Animas, Bent, Colorado, USA[128,134]. He married MARY LORETTA O'MALLEY on 25 Jul 1911 in Denver, Adams, Colorado, USA, daughter of Walter William O'MALLEY and Mary Elizabeth EARHART. She was born on 14 Nov 1886 in Forest City, Mason, Illinois, USA (Forest City Hospital)[135]. She died on 14 Mar 1961 in Las Animas, Bent, Colorado, USA[136].

     ii.   BLANCHE DEAN[137,138,139] was born on 09 Sep 1892 in Las Animas, Colorado[138,139]. She died on 28 Oct 1972 in La Jolla, California (VA Hospital). She married (1) ISAAK LEPOSKY about 1934 in Yuma, Yuma, Arizona, USA[140], son of Jacob LEPOSKY and Amelia AURBACK. He was born on 13 May 1876 in Tennessee, USA[141]. He died on 17 Dec 1962 in El Cajon, San Diego, California, USA. She married (2) MOAT C. BAUBLITS about 1911 in Las Animas, CO[142], son of Joshua E. BAUBLITS and Clora Alice MURDOCK. He was born on 22 Jul 1884 in Nodaway, Missouri, USA[140]. He died on 09 Sep 1913 in Bent, Colorado, USA (Runaway horse buggy)[140]. She married (3) MAURICE GAINES in Norfolk, Norfolk, Virginia, USA[143], son of

Joseph Richard GAINES and Mary Emma PERRY. He was born in 1895[143].

Notes for Blanche DEAN: Blanche was married three times. First to Tony Baublets. He was killed accidentally when his buggy horse spooked and drug him to death. She then married Dr. Gaines who was later killed. She then married Ike Leposky when Ike was in 80s and Blanche in 70s. Blanche served in WW I as a nurse.

14. **FANNIE LEE**[7] **DEAN** (Spear Christopher[6], Edward Maxwell[5], Job John[4], John[3], Edward[2], Richard[1])[26,47,54,91,92,93,94] was born on 25 Sep 1862 in Parker, Texas, USA[26,47,54,94]. She died on 19 Jan 1956 in Amarillo, Potter, Texas, USA. She married **FELIX E FRANKLIN**. He was born in 1858 in Texas, USA[92]. He died about 1925 in Texas, USA.

Notes for Felix E FRANKLIN: I assume Felix died between 1920 and 1930 since he and Fannie were in the 1920 census; but only Fannie was listed in the 1930 census.

Felix E FRANKLIN and Fannie Lee DEAN had the following children:

    i. JENNIE B. [8]FRANKLIN.

    Notes for Jennie B. FRANKLIN: Found photos of Jennie B. & Irene Franklin in Ida Dean's photo album. Surmised they were the children of Fannie (Dean) Franklin.

    ii. IRENE FRANKLIN.

    Notes for Irene FRANKLIN: Based on photo in Ida and Frank Dean's scrapbook of "Jennie B. & Irene Franklin," I surmised they were the children of Fannie (Dean) Franklin.

15. **JENNIE**[7] **DEAN** (Spear Christopher[6], Edward Maxwell[5], Job John[4], John[3], Edward[2], Richard[1])[26,54,103,104,105,106] was born on 16 Jan 1869 in Parker, Texas, USA[26,54,105]. She died on 07 Nov 1942 in Weatherford, Parker, Texas, USA[26]. She married **R. L. DAVIS**.

Notes for Jennie DEAN: Jennie must have had two girls as in a letter from her mother to Ida Dean in 1929 she related, "Jennie's girls both came home (for Christmas)." The oldest (unnamed) was married and lived 60 miles west (of Weatherford, TX). The other was attending the Univ of Texas in Austin.

R. L. DAVIS and Jennie DEAN had the following child:

    i. CLARA[8] DAVIS.

16. **SARAH JANE DEAN** (George Brown[6], Edward Maxwell[5], Job John[4], John[3], Edward[2], Richard[1])[48,63,113,114,115] was born on 06 Nov 1866 (Stringtown Community, Red River Co., TX)[48,63,113,114,115]. She died on 07 Oct 1945 in Detroit, Red River County, Texas[48,63]. She married (1) **JAMES B. DEAN** in 1886 in Red River, Texas, USA[63], son of Joseph Madison DEAN and Isabel Caroline CLEMENT. He was born on 26 Apr 1856 in Deanwood, Crittiton County, Kentucky[48,114]. He died on 01 Oct 1931[48,63,113,115,116]. She married (2) **UNK CONLEY**.

Notes for Sarah Jane DEAN: Obituary in the *Detroit News Herald* of 11 Oct 1945 on microfilm in the Clarksville Library #45679. I am guessing that Sara Jane was married to a Conley prior to marrying James B. Dean. The *Burial, Cemetery and Death Records for Red River County, Texas* has extensive information about the Deans. In the column about Sara it states that her father and mother were G. B. Dean and Willie Bailey; yet in the section on her husband James B.; it states that he married Mrs. Sara Jane Conley. The Mrs. is also an indication she was previously married.

James B. DEAN and Sarah Jane DEAN had the following children:

    i. STELLA H DEAN[113] was born in May 1887 in Texas, USA[113].

    ii. GEORGE MAT DEAN[113] was born about 1890 in Texas, USA[113]. He died in 1942[48].

    iii. CARRIE M. DEAN[113,144] was born in May 1891 in Texas, USA[113].

    iv. NELLIE DEAN[113,144] was born about 1893 in Texas, USA[113,144].

    v. DIXIE DEAN[113,144] was born about 1899 in Texas, USA[113,144].

    vi. VAN IRVING DEAN[63,113,114,115,144,145] was born on 22 Dec 1908 in Taylor, Texas, USA[63,113,114,115,145]. He died on 26 Jul 1992 in Santa Anna, Coleman, Texas, USA[63,113,114,115,145]. He married Lena Lucille COTTREL on 05 Mar 1949 in Albany, Shackelford, Texas, USA (1st Presbyterian Church)[145], daughter of Charles Robert COTTRELL and Mattie Ann BURNS. She was born on 22 Jan 1911 in Taylor, Texas, USA[114,115,145,146,147]. She died on 05 Jun 2000 in Coleman, Texas, USA[114,115,147,148].

Generation 8

17. **JESSIE EDWARD[8] DEAN** (James Bingham[7], Spear Christopher[6], Edward Maxwell[5], Job John[4], John[3], Edward[2], Richard[1]) was born on 27 Jun 1887 (Bent County, Colorado)[117]. He died in 1943 in Pueblo, Colorado, USA[118]. He married **CLARA WRIGHT** on 27 Feb 1924 in Denver, Colorado, USA.

Jessie Edward DEAN and Clara WRIGHT had the following children:

    i. ROBERT[9] DEAN[117].

    ii. CHARLES MARSHAL DEAN[117].

18. **MARSHALL SPEAR[8] DEAN** (James Bingham[7], Spear Christopher[6], Edward Maxwell[5], Job John[4], John[3], Edward[2], Richard[1])[122] was born on 07 Apr 1897 in Las Animas, Bent County, Colorado[122,123,124,125]. He died in Jan 1976 in Las Animas, Bent, Colorado, USA. He married **ELLA PRYOR**. She was born on 22 Mar 1897[126]. She died in Jun 1984 in Las Animas, Bent, Colorado, USA.

Notes for Marshall Spear DEAN: According to Ed Dean, Marshall was once interviewed by James Michner, who was doing research for his book *Centennial*. Many people claim that much of the material in *Centennial* parallels the development of the cattle industry by the Jones's in Colorado.

Marshall was a very successful rancher in Las Animas, Colorado.

Marshall Spear DEAN and Ella PRYOR had the following children:

20. i. EDWARD PRYOR[9] DEAN was born on 17 Aug 1920 in Colorado, USA[125]. He died on 01 Jan 2006 in Las Animas, Bent County, Colorado[125]. He married CONNIE BOULDIN.

    ii. MARSELLA DEAN was born in 1928[149].

19. **ARTHUR SPEAR**[8] **DEAN** (Thomas Franklin[7], Spear Christopher[6], Edward Maxwell[5], Job John[4], John[3], Edward[2], Richard[1])[127,128,129,130,131,132,133] was born on 22 Oct 1886 in Las Animas, Bent, Colorado, USA[127,130,131,132,133]. He died on 01 Dec 1969 in Las Animas, Bent, Colorado, USA[128,134]. He married **MARY LORETTA O'MALLEY** on 25 Jul 1911 in Denver, Adams, Colorado, USA, daughter of Walter William O'MALLEY and Mary Elizabeth EARHART. She was born on 14 Nov 1886 in Forest City, Mason, Illinois, USA (Forest City Hospital)[135]. She died on 14 Mar 1961 in Las Animas, Bent, Colorado, USA[136].

Notes for Arthur Spear DEAN: In a letter from Ed Dean, the son of grandpa Dean's cousin Marshall Dean, was the following comments about grandpa (Art Dean): "Arthur never forgot a name, everyone in Southeastern Colorado knew him and he became well acquainted with President Roosevelt, who once said on seeing the back of his head, "Stand up Art Dean, I'd know you anywhere." Once, Art Dean and President Roosevelt were visiting and someone announced a Cabinet meeting and Roosevelt said, "Tell them to go to hell, Art and I are visiting." Art was working to get the John Martin Dam approved.

Ed Dean also commented that Art Dean was know as the best storyteller in southeast Colorado. I can back that up. I just wish that I had tape recorded some of the stories or taken notes about some of the tales he used to tell. I recall him talking of cattle drives from "Twin Peaks" near Walsenburg where there was a railroad cattle loading lot to south of Las Animas. That was in the days of an "open range" where there were no fences. He also related some escapades as under sheriff chasing criminals—one being an incident where shots were exchanged.

Grandpa took me golfing on a few occasions to the golf course in La Junta. The group would consist of Wilson R. Brown (who was President of the bank), Shorty Clark (real estate), Grandpa and I. None of them could hit the ball much over 150–180 yards; but it was always down the middle. Meanwhile, I could hit it a ton; but never had any idea where it would go—usually NOT STRAIGHT. Needless to say we spent a lot of time looking for my ball. He used to say "Del, you don't have to swing so hard." But, of course, I never listened! That is probably why I only got invited a few times!

I think the most excited I ever saw him was following the time we played in Grand Junction, Colorado for the state American Legion Baseball Championship. I pitched a shutout, Larry Turner hit a two-run home run (over the fence—most fields we played on didn't have a fence!). He was so excited after the game he could hardly stand it. He had played baseball as a youth and still had his glove and cleats hanging in the basement. One of my regrets is that I didn't save them. The glove wasn't much bigger than a work glove with a single strap between the thumb and index finger—a real classic.

He had a varied background: worked in the Secretary of State's office in charge of brands, was a butcher, was the County Treasurer, was under sheriff of Bent County, was the Postmaster, was very active in the Bent Prowers Cattlemens Association, was a mailman doing rural deliveries (after the Republicans were elected and he got replaced as Postmaster); but throughout it all he was a "cowboy"—a rancher and farmer.

Not until I was an adult did I realize the sacrifices Grandma and Grandpa Dean made for my mom, Dean, Mary Jane and myself. Because of my parents divorce and my mother's alcoholism, they took us in and we lived with them throughout my high school years and my mother continued living with them until both of them had passed away. Thus, there were six of us in a three bedroom, one bathroom house of about 1500 sq. ft Now that I am a grandfather, I realize that was not only an additional expense; but a total loss of any privacy.

Grandpa was also always very good about letting me borrow the car once I got a license and started dating. Because we only had the one car, on nights I borrowed it, that meant they were without one. He also let me drive it back to Chicago at Christmas of 1958, when I drove back to see Joanne and meet her parents. I think he also had a pick up for the farm by then so they weren't totally without transportation.

Grandpa and Grandma were both very well respected in the community. He was always very active in politics and was a staunch Democrat. He actually ran for state assembly when he was in his 80s. I think he knew he wouldn't win; but wanted to bring attention to some issues that he believed in. He was the treasurer of the local Irrigation Water control board for many years.

Grandpa liked to hunt and fish and I remember that Grandma had an agreement with him. If he killed it he cleaned it and she would cook it. But it was clear that she didn't do any cleaning of fish or game! He also liked to play poker and had his periodic night out at the local Elks lodge. When he would get home from the game, having also had a shot or two of bourbon, Grandma would always chide him that she got half his winnings. They would then go through a regular ritual of him claiming he lost and she owed him money and she sticking to her guns that he owed her half the winnings. I think most times she won out because he was know as a pretty good poker player.

He had a great mind for numbers and was always quizzing Dean and I about numbers related to acres in a section and other figures pertaining to land measurements.

He wasn't much for talking on a telephone. Somewhat, because in those days long distance calls were a luxury and something we didn't do very often because of the cost. However, on those occasions when Grandma might call one of their children or vice versa, Grandma would give him the phone to say , "Hi." That is about all he would say. As I recall his typical response was "Hi, how are you all doing? ("Fine") Well that's good, we're doing fine—here let me give you back to Grandma." I doubt that he was ever on the phone more than about 15 seconds!

Grandma was the Catholic in the family; but in her later years, due to poor health, didn't go to church often. When she did go regularly, Grandpa only went twice a year. He would go on Easter and Christmas eve. Mass was always at Midnight on Christmas eve and we kids loved it because we got to stay up. However, Grandpa would go to bed, get up around 11 p.m. and get dressed—go to church with us and then come home and go back to bed.

He would occasionally offer advice and I recall coming home to visit once when I was in the Navy and was undecided about making the Navy a career. He urged me to stay in the

Navy because he thought it would be a better life due to the uncertainties of the economy and the job market at that time. It turned out to be good advice.

Grandpa always wore a Stetson cowboy hat when he got dressed up or a straw hat for work. However, unlike most of today's "cowboy wannabes," he always removed it when indoors or in the presence of ladies. Nothing irks me more than to see men in restaurants or other public places with their hats on! I also don't think I ever saw him in anything but cowboy boots. He had everyday boots and dress boots. I guess he did have golf shoes for golf — but that was one of the few times he didn't have his boots on.

Grandpa also liked cigars and chewing tobacco. In his later years he had to have a cancerous growth on his lower lip cut out. I am sure it was caused by the cigar and chewing tobacco. Grandpa also liked to have his bourbon; but I don't think I ever saw him drink it other than straight—either from a shot glass or from the bottle. He had a very wry sense of humor and the first time Joanne came to visit us in Las Animas before we were married mother asked Grandpa to offer Joanne and I a drink. He went into his room, got the bourbon bottle, came back to the living room and handed it to Joanne. My mother almost died! He knew better; but was testing Joanne a little and also showing a little of his humorous side.

Cause of death. Pneumonia which he contacted in the hospital following a serious fall at home.

Notes for Mary Loretta O'MALLEY: According to Lee O'Malley, Walter O'Malley left his wife and their two children, Walter Lee and Mary when the kids were very young. Later research indicated that Mary Elizabeth died when the children were only 3 and 6 years of age. I later discovered a Petition by D.C. White to be the guardian of Mary and Walter because their mother died in 1892 and the father no longer lived in Mason County and made no effort to raise them. The children were 6 and 4 when their mother died and were formally assigned guardianship two years later. When the children were 15 and 13 they petitioned for their Aunt to take over guardianship.

According to comments from Lee O'Malley, Mary ran away from the McCabe's home (prob in late teens) and went to Denver to go to business school. At the time she and her brother, Walter Lee, were being raised by their Aunt and Uncle, Tom and Sara Jane McCabe. Apparently, Tom wasn't a big believer in education for girls and she wanted to pursue further education. The 1900 census confirmed that Mary and Walter were living with the McCabes, however, they were not there for the 1910 census. She also had an aunt, Katherine Hyland who lived in Denver. Whether that was a factor and she knew her aunt was in Denver is speculation on my part. After she had saved up some money she sent for her brother, Walter Lee, to also come to Denver. If she went to Denver when she was 21 (1907), that would be about right because I am guessing that she met Arthur Dean around 1910–11. She was listed in the 1910 census living in Denver on West 14th St. in a boarding house working as a stenographer. Arthur went to Denver in late 1910 or 1911 (still in Las Animas census in Apr 1910) to work in the Secretary of State's office and moved back to Las Animas with Mary around 1913 or 1914. They were married in 1911. interestingly, in the 1910 census she listed her mother and father being born in NY and Penn. However, that would have been the places of birth of Tom and Sarah McCabe; not her real biological parents who were born in Penn and Illinois (Walter and Mary Elizabeth).

There were a series of letters 1942–1945 from Uncle Lee O'Malley in Peoria, Illinois to his sister, Mary (O'Malley) Dean. They referred to a farm of about 150 acres in Havana, IL which they owned in part with their Aunt Jen (Sara Jane McCabe), who raised them. In April of 1943 the property was apparently deeded over to Lee and Mary. Their was some hint that the property might have also been owned (partially perhaps) earlier by their mother Loretta O'Malley and passed down to them. When I visited the Mason County Area in April 2009, I found the land records in the Mason County Courthouse in Havana. It indicated that Mary and her brother, Walter Lee, sold the land in January of 1946.

Although some info I have indicates she was born in Macon City, IL, I think it must have been Mason City (which agrees with her obituary). It is very close to Havana where she was raised by an aunt and where she and Uncle Lee owned property during WW II. Mother's (Helen Jane's) birth certificate lists grandma's birthplace as Chicago, Illinois. I am certain that was a mistake.

In March of 1954 Grandpa and Grandma Dean drove out to visit Uncle Lee in Mesa, Arizona. I read a letter from grandma to mother (Helen Jane) about their trip. They stayed over night in Show Low, Arizona and drove on in to Mesa the next day. Grandma commented about driving through Salt Creek and Devil's Canyons.

It is interesting to note that neither Grandma's original nor certified copy of her birth certificate lists her middle name.

Arthur Spear DEAN and Mary Loretta O'MALLEY had the following children:

    i. MARY FRANCES[9] DEAN[127,150,151,152] was born on 05 Jun 1913 in Denver, Colorado, USA[127,150]. She died on 05 Apr 1968 in Pittsburgh, Allegheny, Pennsylvania, USA. She married WILLIAM PAUL GALLAGHER in 1942 in Syracuse, Hamilton, Kansas, USA[153], son of Hugh A. GALLAGHER and Mary E. He was born in 1911 in Pennsylvania[154,155].

    Notes for Mary Frances DEAN: A former pharmacist and a resident of Shadyside since 1950, died at her home at 702 Bellefonte St. of a heart attack. Although she was named Mary Frances she always went by the name "Frances." Funeral home H. Samson In Pittsburgh. An article in the *Las Animas Democrat*, dated September 3, 1964 recounted that Frances remembers Hubert Humphrey was in her Pharmacy Class in Denver in 1933. Humphrey was a vice presidential candidate in the 1964 elections. In those days (1933) pharmacy class was three months long. Frances was a practicing pharmacist for several years in Las Animas.

21   ii. HELEN JANE DEAN[127,156,157] was born on 06 Aug 1915 in Denver, Adams, Colorado, USA (2:53 p.m., St. Joseph's Hospital)[127,157,158,159]. She died on 28 Oct 1995 in Loveland, Larimer, Colorado, USA[50,156,158]. She married DELBERT BUSH RITCHHART on 01 Aug 1952 in Raton, Colfax, New Mexico, USA (Remarried)[160],

son of Alonzo Francis RITCHHART and Grace Azetta BUSH. He was born on 02 Nov 1910 (Carthage, Missouri)[128,161,162,163]. He died on 18 Feb 1981 in Denver, Colorado, USA[163].

22 iii. THOMAS FRANKLIN DEAN[127,164] was born on 24 Sep 1917[165,166]. He died on 22 May 1975[167]. He married BESSIE B. RYAN, daughter of Ed RYAN and Hanna HENDERSTAT. She was born on 21 Apr 1920[168]. She died on 28 May 2009 in Lakewood, Jefferson, Colorado, USA[168].

23 iv. JAMES BINGHAM DEAN[127] was born on 06 Jul 1923 (Denver, Colorado, 11:20 p.m., St. Joseph's hospital)[127]. He died on 29 Sep 1993 in Rocky Ford, Otero, Colorado, USA. He married MARILYN STEBBINS on 14 Jun 1949 in Gothenburg, Dawson, Nebraska, USA, daughter of Virge Wilcox STEBBINS and Florence BROOKS. She was born on 08 Jul 1927 in Gothenberg, Nebraska. She died on 06 Feb 2004 in Omaha, Douglas, Nebraska, USA[169].

Generation 9

20. **EDWARD PRYOR**[9] **DEAN** (Marshall Spear[8], James Bingham[7], Spear Christopher[6], Edward Maxwell[5], Job John[4], John[3], Edward[2], Richard[1]) was born on 17 Aug 1920 in Colorado, USA[125]. He died on 01 Jan 2006 in Las Animas, Bent County, Colorado[125]. He married **CONNIE BOULDIN**.

Notes for Edward Pryor DEAN: I interviewed Ed in May of 2005 while he was in a nursing home in Las Animas. He remembered a lot of things very accurately; but was suffering from some degree of dementia as he claimed his Father and Mother were still alive (his dad would have been 108). He related that Michner's wife Mari Sawa was in his class in High School. Her folks ran a Japanese grocery store even before the WW II internment camp was established in Las Animas.

Other sources related that Michner once interviewed Marshall Dean when doing research for the book *Centennial*. Thus, the story of the development of the cattle industry in Colorado as related in the book; closely parallels the JJ Ranch development.

Edward Pryor DEAN and Connie BOULDIN had the following children:

 i. KATHERIN[10] DEAN was born about 1950. She married UNK MOORE.

 ii. DIANA DEAN[170] was born about 1953. She married JIM RICKMAN.

 iii. ALAN JONES DEAN[171,172] was born about 1955.

 Notes for Alan Jones DEAN: When I talked with Allen in May of 2005, he was farming his father's old place in Las Animas. He was going to join me for the interview with his dad; but later canceled due to the press of work on the farm.

21. **HELEN JANE**[9] **DEAN** (Arthur Spear[8], Thomas Franklin[7], Spear Christopher[6], Edward Maxwell[5], Job John[4], John[3], Edward[2], Richard[1])[127,156,157] was born on 06 Aug 1915 in Denver, Adams, Colorado, USA (2:53 p.m., St. Joseph's Hospital)[127,157,158,159]. She died on 28 Oct 1995 in Loveland, Larimer, Colorado, USA[50,156,158]. She married **DELBERT BUSH RITCHHART** on 01 Aug 1952 in Raton, Colfax, New Mexico, USA (Remarried)[160], son

of Alonzo Francis RITCHHART and Grace Azetta BUSH. He was born on 02 Nov 1910 (Carthage, Missouri)[128,161,162,163]. He died on 18 Feb 1981 in Denver, Colorado, USA[163].

Delbert Bush RITCHHART and Helen Jane DEAN had the following children:

    i. DELBERT ARTHUR[10] RITCHHART[173] was born on 08 May 1937 in Las Animas, Bent, Colorado, USA (11:16 a.m.)[174]. He married JOANNE FRANCES SCHMIDT on 28 Nov 1959 in Wilmette, Cook, Illinois, USA, daughter of Frederick Henry SCHMIDT and Frances Lois MCCONNELL. She was born on 12 Mar 1938 in Evanston, Cook, Illinois, USA[175,176,177,178].

    ii. DEAN LEE RITCHHART was born on 08 Oct 1940 (Las Animas, Colorado, 11:35 p.m.). He married EVELYN KIRSCHMAN on 25 Jun 1961 (St. Mary's Catholic Church, Las Animas, CO), daughter of Daniel KIRSCHMAN and Unice. She was born on 04 Aug 1942.

    iii. MARY JANE RITCHHART was born on 29 Feb 1948 (La Junta, Colorado (Mennonite Hospital)). She died on 27 Apr 1979 (Denver, Colorado of lymphoma (cancer); Rose Memorial Hospital)[179]. She married (1) ELDON JOHNSON about 1970. He was born on 18 Nov 1944. She married (2) JOHN F. HAYES JR. on 24 Oct 1976 in Boulder, Colorado, USA.

22. **THOMAS FRANKLIN**[9] **DEAN** (Arthur Spear[8], Thomas Franklin[7], Spear Christopher[6], Edward Maxwell[5], Job John[4], John[3], Edward[2], Richard[1])[127,164] was born on 24 Sep 1917[165,166]. He died on 22 May 1975[167]. He married **BESSIE B. RYAN**, daughter of Ed RYAN and Hanna HENDERSTAT. She was born on 21 Apr 1920[168]. She died on 28 May 2009 in Lakewood, Jefferson, Colorado, USA[168].

Notes for Thomas Franklin DEAN: Social Security death records show his birth date as 24 Sep 1917 vice other records 14 Sep 1917.

Notes for Bessie B. RYAN: Buena Visto, CO, Phone: 303-395-8186 (about 1988)

Thomas Franklin DEAN and Bessie B. RYAN had the following children:

    i. DARROL[10] DEAN[167,180] was born on 05 Jun 1941[167,181]. He died in Oct 2005 in Denver, Colorado, USA[167,182]. He married MARY ANN LANE on 30 Dec 1963 in Los Angeles, California, USA[183].

    Notes for Darrol DEAN: Darrol developed a bad lung condition in his mid-50s and was on oxygen most of the time. He passed away in October 2005 from complications associated with his lung problems.

    ii. CURTIS DEAN was born on 15 Feb 1949. He married Kim.

    Notes for Curtis DEAN: 8807 W. Maplewood Place Littleton CO, Phone: 303-973-2488 (about 1996)

23. **JAMES BINGHAM**[9] **DEAN** (Arthur Spear[8], Thomas Franklin[7], Spear Christopher[6], Edward Maxwell[5], Job John[4], John[3], Edward[2], Richard[1])[127] was born on 06 Jul 1923 (Denver, Colorado, 1120 p.m., St. Joseph's hospital)[127]. He died on 29 Sep 1993 in Rocky Ford, Otero, Colorado, USA. He married **MARILYN STEBBINS** on 14 Jun 1949 in Gothenburg,

Dawson, Nebraska, USA, daughter of Virge Wilcox STEBBINS and Florence BROOKS. She was born on 08 Jul 1927 in Gothenberg, Nebraska. She died on 06 Feb 2004 in Omaha, Douglas, Nebraska, USA[169].

Notes for James Bingham DEAN: Social Security records show death date as Sep 15, 1993. They also have his name as John B. vice James B. J.B.'s headstone reads "John Bingham Dean; but I am sure Liz, his daughter, corrected me that it was James Bingham?

The following article appeared in a March 1941 edition of the *Las Animas Leader*: "John Bingham (J.B.) Dean Captain of the 1940 Trojan Southern Co. Football team, was honored in Denver last week, when he was named on the Associated Press All-tournament Basketball team in division B and chosen to play in the all-star football game to be played Aug. 22 in Denver under the supervision of a number of the nations outstanding grid coaches. J.B. also holds an appointment by the former Congressman William E. Burney of Pueblo, to the U.S. Naval Academy at Annapolis, subject to examinations to be given in April. He is the youngest son of Mr.and Mrs. Arthur S. Dean of this city."

James Bingham DEAN and Marilyn STEBBINS had the following children:

    i. ELIZABETH JANE[10] DEAN was born on 26 Feb 1949. She married UNK GLEASON.

    ii. MARY SUSAN DEAN was born on 26 Feb 1949. She married MARK LINDER.

    iii. JAMES BINGHAM DEAN was born on 04 Feb 1951.

    iv. STEBBINS FRANKLIN DEAN was born about 1953. He died in Mar 2005 in Las Vegas, Clark, Nevada, USA.

    v. AMY ANNE DEAN was born on 09 Feb 1958 in Denver, Colorado, USA. She died on 15 Jun 1980.

Sources

1   FHL Salt Lake, Family Search Pedigree Resource File, CD #112 (FHL Salt Lake City: FamilySearch).

2   Lucy DeYoung, DeYoungMatson Family Tree (Ancestry.com), Ancestry.com

3   Ancestry.com, *Public Member Trees* (Provo, UT, USA, The Generations Network, Inc., 2006), www.ancestry.com, Database online. Record for Richard Dean.

4   Ancestry.com, *Public Member Trees* (Provo, UT, USA, The Generations Network, Inc., 2006), www.ancestry.com, Database online. Record for Richard Dean.

5   Ancestry.com, *Public Member Trees* (Provo, UT, USA, The Generations Network, Inc., 2006), www.ancestry.com, Database online. Record for Richard Dean.

6   Ancestry.com, *Public Member Trees* (Provo, UT, USA, The Generations Network, Inc., 2006), www.ancestry.com, Database online. Record for Richard DEAN.

7   Ancestry.com, *Public Member Trees* (Provo, UT, USA, The Generations Network, Inc., 2006), www.ancestry.com, Database online. Record for Richard DEAN.

8   Ancestry.com, *Public Member Trees* (Provo, UT, USA, The Generations Network, Inc., 2006), www.ancestry.com, Database online. Record for Richard Dean.

9   Ancestry.com, *Public Member Trees* (Provo, UT, USA, The Generations Network, Inc., 2006), www.ancestry.com, Database online. Record for Richard Dean.

10 Ancestry.com, *Public Member Trees* (Provo, UT, USA, The Generations Network, Inc., 2006), www.ancestry.com, Database online. Record for Sarah Elizabeth Jordan.

11 Ancestry.com, *Public Member Trees* (Provo, UT, USA, The Generations Network, Inc., 2006), www.ancestry.com, Database online. Record for Eliza Jordan.

12 Ancestry.com, *Public Member Trees* (Provo, UT, USA, The Generations Network, Inc., 2006), www.ancestry.com, Database online. Record for Richard Dean.

13 Ancestry.com, *Public Member Trees* (Provo, UT, USA, The Generations Network, Inc., 2006), www.ancestry.com, Database online. Record for Richard Dean.

14 Ancestry.com, *Public Member Trees* (Provo, UT, USA, The Generations Network, Inc., 2006), www.ancestry.com, Database online. Record for Richard Dean.

15 Ancestry.com, *Public Member Trees* (Provo, UT, USA, The Generations Network, Inc., 2006), www.ancestry.com, Database online.

16 Ancestry.com, *Public Member Trees* (Provo, UT, USA, The Generations Network, Inc., 2006), www.ancestry.com, Database online.

17 Godfrey Memorial Library, comp., American Genealogical-Biographical Index (AGBI) (Provo, UT, USA, Ancestry.com Operations Inc, 1999), www.ancestry.com, Database online. Record for Mary Eliza Dean.

18 Ancestry.com, *Public Member Trees* (Provo, UT, USA, The Generations Network, Inc., 2006), www.ancestry.com, Database online. Record for Eliza Jordan.

19 Ancestry.com, *Public Member Trees* (Provo, UT, USA, The Generations Network, Inc., 2006), www.ancestry.com, Database online. Record for John Dean.

20   *Ancestry Family Trees* (Online publication—Provo, UT, USA: The Generations Network. Original data: Family Tree files submitted by Ancestry members). http://trees.ancestry.com/pt/ AMTCitationRedir.aspx?tid=2906494&pid=-76093086.

21   *Marriages Henrico Co., Virginia 1680–1808*, Family History Library, Call no. 975.545 V2L.

22   Ancestry.com, *Public Member Trees* (Provo, UT, USA, The Generations Network, Inc., 2006), www.ancestry.com, Database online. Record for Rebecca Abney.

23   *Halifax County, Virginia Will Book 1752–1773*, Family History Library.

24   T.L.C. Genealogy, *Halifax County, Virginia Court Orders 1763–64* (Miami Beach, Fl, , 1998), Family History Library.

25   *Will Book Halifax Co., VA 1752–73*, Allen Co. Public Library.

26   Ancestry.com, *One World Tree*SM (Provo, UT, USA: The Generations Network, Inc., n.d.), www. ancestry.com, database online. Provo, UT, USA: The Generations Network, Inc.

27   FamilySearch.org, LDS Pedigree Charts, Family History Centers.

28   Ancestry.com, *Public Member Trees* (Provo, UT, USA, The Generations Network, Inc., 2006), www.ancestry.com, Database online. Record for Job Dean.

29   Ancestry.com, *Public Member Trees* (Provo, UT, USA, The Generations Network, Inc., 2006), www.ancestry.com, Database online. Record for Job Dean.

30   *Ancestry Family Trees* (Online publication—Provo, UT, USA: The Generations Network. Original data: Family Tree files submitted by Ancestry members). http://trees.ancestry.com/pt/ AMTCitationRedir.aspx?tid=2906494&pid=-100242354.

31   Ancestry.com, *Public Member Trees* (Provo, UT, USA, The Generations Network, Inc., 2006), www.ancestry.com, Database online. Record for Keziah Smith.

32   Brenda Riggs, Keziah Smith Dean's Story (, 31 May 2010), Ancestry.com.

33   Jo White Linn, *Surry County, N.C. Will Abstracts 1771–1827* (Baltimore, MD, Genealogical Publishing Co., 1992), Family History Library.

34   *Will Abstracts, North Carolina*; Family History Library.

35   Ancestry.com, *Public Member Trees* (Provo, UT, USA, The Generations Network, Inc., 2006), www.ancestry.com, Database online.

36   *Ancestry Family Trees* (Online publication—Provo, UT, USA: The Generations Network. Original data: Family Tree files submitted by Ancestry members). http://trees.ancestry.com/pt/ AMTCitationRedir.aspx?tid=2906494&pid=-76093047.

37   *Ancestry Family Trees* (Online publication—Provo, UT, USA: The Generations Network. Original data: Family Tree files submitted by Ancestry members). http://trees.ancestry.com/pt/ AMTCitationRedir.aspx?tid=2906494&pid=-76093024.

38   *Ancestry Family Trees* (Online publication—Provo, UT, USA: The Generations Network. Original data: Family Tree files submitted by Ancestry members). http://trees.ancestry.com/pt/ AMTCitationRedir.aspx?tid=2906494&pid=-76093000.

39   Ancestry.com, *Public Member Trees* (Provo, UT, USA, The Generations Network, Inc., 2006), www.ancestry.com, Database online. Record for Edward Maxwell Dean.

40   *Ancestry Family Trees* (Online publication—Provo, UT, USA: The Generations Network.

Original data: Family Tree files submitted by Ancestry members). http://trees.ancestry.com/pt/
AMTCitationRedir.aspx?tid=2906494&pid=-100250989.

41   Annie Walker Bell Burns, *Washington County, KY Marriages 1792–1825* (Washington D.C., ,
      1934), Family History Library, 976.9493 V28b, pg 27 & 84.

42   *Ancestry Family Trees* (Online publication—Provo, UT, USA: The Generations Network.
      Original data: Family Tree files submitted by Ancestry members). http://trees.ancestry.com/pt/
      AMTCitationRedir.aspx?tid=2906494&pid=-76092966.

43   *Ancestry Family Trees* (Online publication—Provo, UT, USA: The Generations Network.
      Original data: Family Tree files submitted by Ancestry members). http://trees.ancestry.com/pt/
      AMTCitationRedir.aspx?tid=2906494&pid=-76092960.

44   Faye Sea Sanders, *Washington County, Kentucky Deed Abstracts 1792–1803* (Louisville, KY, ,
      1991), Family History Library.

45   Educated Guess.

46   *Ancestry Family Trees* (Online publication—Provo, UT, USA: The Generations Network.
      Original data: Family Tree files submitted by Ancestry members). http://trees.ancestry.com/pt/
      AMTCitationRedir.aspx?tid=2906494&pid=-76072093.

47   Ancestry.com, *Public Member Trees* (Provo, UT, USA, The Generations Network, Inc., 2006),
      www.ancestry.com, Database online. Record for Spears Christopher Dean.

48   Red River County, Texas, *Burial, Cemetery and Death Records for Red River County, TX*; Allen
      Co. Public Library.

49   Gable, *Red River County, Texas Cemeteries*, Allen Co. Public Library.

50   *Ancestry Family Trees* (Online publication—Provo, UT, USA: The Generations Network.
      Original data: Family Tree files submitted by Ancestry members). http://trees.ancestry.com/pt/
      AMTCitationRedir.aspx?tid=2906494&pid=-76072090.

51   *Caldwell County, KY marriages 1809–32*, Allen Co. Public Library.

52   Periodical by a Texas Genealogical Society, *Stirpes*, vol XIII, no. 3, 1973, PERSI.

53   *1900 United States Federal Census* (Provo, UT, USA: The Generations Network, Inc., 2004,
      www.ancestry.com, online publication. Original data—United States of America, Bureau of
      the Census. Twelfth Census of the United States, 1900. Washington, D.C.: National Archives
      and Records Administration, 1900). Census Place: Weatherford Ward 4, Parker, Texas; Roll:
      T623_1664; Page: 20B; Enumeration District: 67, birth date: Jun 1829, Birth place: Kentucky,
      Marriage date: 1854, Residence date: 1900, Residence place: Weatherford Ward 4, Parker, Texas.

54   *1880 United States Federal Census* (Provo, UT, USA: The Generations Network, Inc., 2005,
      www.ancestry.com, Online publication. 1880 U.S. Census Index provided by The Church
      of Jesus Christ of Latter-day Saints © Copyright 1999 Intellectual Reserve, Inc. All rights re-
      served. Original data—United States of America, Bureau of the Census. Tenth Census of the
      United States. Washington, D.C.: National Archives and Records Administration, 1880. Census
      Place: Precinct 1, Parker, Texas; Roll: T9_1322; Family History Film: 1255322; Page: 377.2000;
      Enumeration District: 135; Image: Record for S C Dean.

55   *1850 United States Federal Census* (Provo, UT, USA: The Generations Network, Inc., 2005),
      www.ancestry.com, database online, 2005. Indexed by Ancestry.com from microfilmed schedules
      of the 1850 U.S. Federal Decennial Census. Original data: Data imaged from National Archives

and Records Administration. Ninth Census of the United States, 1850. M432, 1,009 rolls); Census Place: Red River, Texas; Roll: M432_914; Page: 219B; Image: Record for Spere Dean.

56   *1870 United States Federal Census* (Provo, UT, USA: The Generations Network, Inc., 2003), www.ancestry.com, database online, 2003. Indexed by Ancestry.com from microfilmed schedules of the 1870 U.S. Federal Decennial Census. Original data: Data imaged from National Archives and Records Administration. Ninth Census of the United States, 1870. M593, 1,761 rolls). Census Place: Precinct 1, Parker, Texas; Roll: M593_; Record for S C Dean.

57   Frances Bollacker Keck, *The JJ Ranch on the Rurgatory River in Colorado: The Jones Family and the Prairie Cattle Company* (La Junta, Colorado: Otero Press, 2001), 5.

58   *Texas Marriages 1851–1900* (MyFamily.Com).

59   *1900 United States Federal Census* (Provo, UT, USA: The Generations Network, Inc., 2004, www.ancestry.com, online publication. Original data—United States of America, Bureau of the Census. Twelfth Census of the United States, 1900. Washington, D.C.: National Archives and Records Administration, 1900). Parker, Texas, ED 67, roll T623 1664, page 20B.

60   Obituary in *Las Animas Democrat* (or *Leader*?), Mrs. Sarah M. Dean passed away at the home of a daughter in Abilene, Tex., Saturday and funeral services were held Monday afternoon at Weatherford, Texas, with burial at that place. Mrs Dean would have been 100 had she lived until October.

61   *Ancestry Family Trees* (Online publication—Provo, UT, USA: The Generations Network. Original data: Family Tree files submitted by Ancestry members). http://trees.ancestry.com/pt/ AMTCitationRedir.aspx?tid=2906494&pid=-76012137.

62   Ancestry.com, *Texas Death Index, 1903–2000* (Provo, UT, USA, The Generations Network, Inc., 2006), www.ancestry.com, Database online. Record for Sarah Marshall Dean.

63   Ancestry.com, *Public Member Trees* (Provo, UT, USA, The Generations Network, Inc., 2006), www.ancestry.com, Database online. Record for Sarah Jane Dean.

64   Georgia Pratt Cunningham, *Young County, Texas Marriages, Book A* (USGENWEB, July 1997– Jan 2006), Texas State Archives.

65   Ancestry.com, *Texas Death Index, 1903–2000* (Provo, UT, USA, The Generations Network, Inc., 2006), www.ancestry.com, Database online. Record for Erasmus Maxwell Dean.

66   *1870 United States Federal Census* (Provo, UT, USA: The Generations Network, Inc., 2003), www.ancestry.com, database online, 2003. Indexed by Ancestry.com from microfilmed schedules of the 1870 U.S. Federal Decennial Census. Original data: Data imaged from National Archives and Records Administration. Ninth Census of the United States, 1870. M593, 1,761 rolls). Census Place: Precinct 1, Parker, Texas; Roll: M593_1601; Page: 366; Image: 274. Record for E M Dean.

67   Ancestry.com, *Colorado State Census, 1885* (Provo, UT, USA, Ancestry.com Operations Inc, 2006), www.ancestry.com, Database online. Record for E M Dean.

68   *Ancestry Family Trees* (Online publication—Provo, UT, USA: The Generations Network. Original data: Family Tree files submitted by Ancestry members). http://trees.ancestry.com/pt/ AMTCitationRedir.aspx?tid=2906494&pid=-100209074.

69   Ancestry.com, *Public Member Trees* (Provo, UT, USA, The Generations Network, Inc., 2006), www.ancestry.com, Database online. Record for Nancy Francis Fanny Eddleman.

70   Ancestry.com, *Public Member Trees* (Provo, UT, USA, The Generations Network, Inc., 2006),

www.ancestry.com, Database online. Record for Nancy Francis Fanny Eddleman.

71   Ancestry.com, *Public Member Trees* (Provo, UT, USA, The Generations Network, Inc., 2006), www.ancestry.com, Database online. Record for Elizabeth Branscomb.

72   *Ancestry Family Trees* (Online publication—Provo, UT, USA: The Generations Network. Original data: Family Tree files submitted by Ancestry members). http://trees.ancestry.com/pt/ AMTCitationRedir.aspx?tid=2906494&pid=-100185521.

73   Ancestry.com, *Public Member Trees* (Provo, UT, USA, The Generations Network, Inc., 2006), www.ancestry.com, Database online. Record for Mary Elizabeth Dean.

74   Ancestry.com, *Public Member Trees* (Provo, UT, USA, The Generations Network, Inc., 2006), www.ancestry.com, Database online. Record for Felix Ezell Smith.

75   *1930 United States Federal Census* (Provo, UT, USA: The Generations Network, Inc., 2002), www.ancestry.com, Online publication. Original data United States of America, Bureau of the Census. Fifteenth Census of the United States. Washington, D.C.: National Archives and Records Administration, 1930.T626, 2,667 rolls). Census Place: Austin, Travis, Texas; Roll: 2402; Page: 6B; Enumeration District: 15; Image: 247.0. Record for Felix E Smith.

76   Ancestry.com, *Public Member Trees* (Provo, UT, USA, The Generations Network, Inc., 2006), www.ancestry.com, Database online. Record for Mary Elizabeth 'Bettie' Dean.

77   Ancestry.com, *Texas Death Index, 1903–2000* (Provo, UT, USA, The Generations Network, Inc., 2006), www.ancestry.com, Database online. Record for Mary E. Smith.

78   *1900 United States Federal Census* (Provo, UT, USA: The Generations Network, Inc., 2004, www.ancestry.com, online publication. Original data—United States of America, Bureau of the Census. Twelfth Census of the United States, 1900. Washington, D.C.: National Archives and Records Administration, 1900). Census Place: Justice Precinct 6, Travis, Texas; Roll: T623_1673; Page: 18A; Enumeration District: 115. Record for Felix E Smith.

79   Ancestry.com, *Public Member Trees* (Provo, UT, USA, The Generations Network, Inc., 2006), www.ancestry.com, Database online. Record for James Woods Smith.

80   *Ancestry Family Trees* (Online publication—Provo, UT, USA: The Generations Network. Original data: Family Tree files submitted by Ancestry members). http://trees.ancestry.com/pt/ AMTCitationRedir.aspx?tid=2906494&pid=-100182963.

81   Obituary (Las Animas, Colorado, *Bent County Democrat*, 27 March 1936), Personal files of Del Ritchhart.

82   *1930 United States Federal Census* (Provo, UT, USA: The Generations Network, Inc., 2002), www.ancestry.com, Online publication. Original data United States of America, Bureau of the Census. Fifteenth Census of the United States. Washington, D.C.: National Archives and Records Administration, 1930. T626, 2,667 rolls). Las Animas, Bent, Colorado, ed 8, roll 230, image 621.0.

83   *Bent County Democrat* Newspaper, Obituary for Texanna Eddleman Dean, Personal files of Del Ritchhart.

84   *1900 United States Federal Census* (Provo, UT, USA: The Generations Network, Inc., 2004, www.ancestry.com, online publication. Original data—United States of America, Bureau of the Census. Twelfth Census of the United States, 1900. Washington, D.C.: National Archives and Records Administration, 1900). Census Place: Precincts 1, 3–8, Bent, Colorado; Roll: T623 121; Page: 10A; Enumeration District: 3, birth date: abt 1861, Birth place: Texas, Residence date:

1900, Residence place: Precincts 1, 3–8, Bent, Colorado.

85   *1870 United States Federal Census* (Provo, UT, USA: The Generations Network, Inc., 2003), www.ancestry.com, database online, 2003. Indexed by Ancestry.com from microfilmed schedules of the 1870 U.S. Federal Decennial Census. Original data: Data imaged from National Archives and Records Administration. Ninth Census of the United States, 1870. M593, 1,761 rolls). Census Place: Precinct 1, Parker, Texas; Roll: M593_1601; Page: 366; Image: 274, birth date: abt 1860, Birth place: Texas, Residence date: 1870, Residence place: Precinct 1, Parker, Texas.

86   *Ancestry Family Trees* (Online publication—Provo, UT, USA: The Generations Network. Original data: Family Tree files submitted by Ancestry members). http://trees.ancestry.com/pt/ AMTCitationRedir.aspx?tid=2906494&pid=-1803569648.

87   Family Register T.D. Britton & Effie M. Reece.

88   *1900 United States Federal Census* (Provo, UT, USA: The Generations Network, Inc., 2004, www.ancestry.com, online publication. Original data—United States of America, Bureau of the Census. Twelfth Census of the United States, 1900. Washington, D.C.: National Archives and Records Administration, 1900). Census Place: Precincts 1, 3–8, Bent, Colorado; Roll: T623 121; Page: 10A; Enumeration District: 3, birth date: abt 1868, Birth place: Missouri, Residence date: 1900, Residence place: Precincts 1, 3–8, Bent, Colorado.

89   *1910 United States Federal Census* (Provo, UT, USA: The Generations Network, Inc., 2006), www.ancestry.com, Online publication. Original data United States of America, Bureau of the Census. Thirteenth Census of the United States. Washington, D.C.: National Archives and Records Administration, 1910.T624, 1,178 rolls). Census Place: Precinct 9, Bent, Colorado; Roll: T624_112; Page: 3B; Enumeration District: 6; Image: 718, birth date: abt 1868, Birth place: Missouri, Residence date: 1910, Residence place: Precinct 9, Bent, Colorado.

90   *1880 United States Federal Census* (Provo, UT, USA: The Generations Network, Inc., 2005, www.ancestry.com, Online publication. 1880 U.S. Census Index provided by The Church of Jesus Christ of Latter-day Saints © Copyright 1999 Intellectual Reserve, Inc. All rights reserved. Original data—United States of America, Bureau of the Census. Tenth Census of the United States. Washington, D.C.: National Archives and Records Administration, 1880. Census Place: Barnard, Nodaway, Missouri; Roll: T9_706; Family History Film: 1254706; Page: 3.2000; Enumeration District: 249; Image: 0238, birthdate: abt 1868, Birth place: Missouri, Residence date: 1880, Residence place: Barnard, Nodaway, Missouri, United States.

91   *1930 United States Federal Census* (Provo, UT, USA: The Generations Network, Inc., 2002), www.ancestry.com, Online publication. Original data United States of America, Bureau of the Census. Fifteenth Census of the United States. Washington, D.C.: National Archives and Records Administration, 1930.T626, 2,667 rolls). Amarillo, Potter, Texas, ed 10, roll 2384, image 501.0.

92   *1920 United States Federal Census* (Provo, UT, USA: The Generations Network, Inc., 2005), www.ancestry.com, Online publication. Original data United States of America, Bureau of the Census. Fourteenth Census of the United States. Washington, D.C.: National Archives and Records Administration, 1920.T625, 2076 rolls). Amarillo, Potter, Texas, image 1067.

93   *Ancestry Family Trees* (Online publication—Provo, UT, USA: The Generations Network. Original data: Family Tree files submitted by Ancestry members). http://trees.ancestry.com/pt/ AMTCitationRedir.aspx?tid=2906494&pid=-100179690.

94   Ancestry.com, *Public Member Trees* (Provo, UT, USA, The Generations Network, Inc., 2006), www.ancestry.com, Database online. Record for Spears Christopher Dean.

95   1880 Parker Co. Census.

96   *1870 US Census* Parker Co., TX, Listed name as Ann L., whereas was just Lauga in the 1880 census.

97   *Ancestry Family Trees* (Online publication—Provo, UT, USA: The Generations Network. Original data: Family Tree files submitted by Ancestry members). http://trees.ancestry.com/pt/ AMTCitationRedir.aspx?tid=2906494&pid=-100177098.

98   Texas Dept of Health, Bureau of Vital Statistics, Certificate of Death, Ancestry.com.

99   Ancestry.com, *Texas Marriage Collection, 1814–1909 and 1966–2002* (Provo, UT, USA: The Generations Network, Inc., 2005), www.ancestry.com, Online publication. Original data: Dodd, Jordan R, et. al. *Early American Marriages: Texas to 1850.* Bountiful, UT: Precision Indexing Publishers, 19xx; Hunting For Bears, comp. Texas marriage information taken from county courthouse records. Many of these records were extracted from copies of the original records in microfilm, microfiche, or book format, located at the Family History Library;Texas Department of State Health Services. Texas Marriage Index, 1966–2002. Texas Department of State Health Services, Texa; Dodd, Jordan, Liahona Research, comp. (P.O. Box 740, Orem, Utah 84059) from county marriage records on microfilm located at the Family History Library in Salt Lake City, Utah, in published books cataloged by the Library of Congress, or from county courthouse records.

100   *Parker Co, Texas Marriages 1889–93*, Vol II, Allen Co. Public Library.

101   *1910 United States Federal Census* (Provo, UT, USA: The Generations Network, Inc., 2006), www.ancestry.com, Online publication. Original data United States of America, Bureau of the Census. Thirteenth Census of the United States. Washington, D.C.: National Archives and Records Administration, 1910.T624, 1,178 rolls). Justice Precinct 1, Potter, Texas, roll T624_1582

102   *1870 US Census* Parker Co., TX, Listed in 1870 census; but not 1880.

103   *1870 US Census* Parker Co., TX, Listed Sara and Spear plus 7 children.

104   *1870 United States Federal Census* (Provo, UT, USA: The Generations Network, Inc., 2003), www.ancestry.com, database online, 2003. Indexed by Ancestry.com from microfilmed schedules of the 1870 U.S. Federal Decennial Census. Original data: Data imaged from National Archives and Records Administration. Ninth Census of the United States, 1870. M593, 1,761 rolls). Precinct 1, Parker, Texas, post office Fort Worth, roll 1601, page 366, image 274.

105   *1920 United States Federal Census* (Provo, UT, USA: The Generations Network, Inc., 2005), www.ancestry.com, Online publication. Original data United States of America, Bureau of the Census. Fourteenth Census of the United States. Washington, D.C.: National Archives and Records Administration, 1920.T625, 2076 rolls). Census Place: Weatherford Ward 4, Parker, Texas; Roll: T625_1838; Page: 2A; Enumeration District: 64; Image: 729, birth date: abt 1870, Birth place: Texas, Residence date: 1920, Residence place: Weatherford Ward 4, Parker, Texas.

106   *Ancestry Family Trees* (Online publication—Provo, UT, USA: The Generations Network. Original data: Family Tree files submitted by Ancestry members). http://trees.ancestry.com/pt/ AMTCitationRedir.aspx?tid=2906494&pid=-100162755.

107   *1880 United States Federal Census* (Provo, UT, USA: The Generations Network, Inc., 2005, www.ancestry.com, Online publication. 1880 U.S. Census Index provided by The Church of Jesus Christ of Latter-day Saints © Copyright 1999 Intellectual Reserve, Inc. All rights reserved. Original data—United States of America, Bureau of the Census. Tenth Census of the United States. Washington, D.C.: National Archives and Records Administration, 1880. Precinct 1,

Parker, Texas, ed 135, roll T9_1322, page 377.2000.

108 *1880 US Census*, Parker Co., TX, Listed Spear, Sarah and 7 children.

109 *Ancestry Family Trees* (Online publication—Provo, UT, USA: The Generations Network. Original data: Family Tree files submitted by Ancestry members). http://trees.ancestry.com/pt/AMTCitationRedir.aspx?tid=2906494&pid=-100145414.

110 *1880 US Census*, Parker Co. TX, Listed parents plus 7 children, including the youngest, Josephine.

111 *Ancestry Family Trees* (Online publication—Provo, UT, USA: The Generations Network. Original data: Family Tree files submitted by Ancestry members). http://trees.ancestry.com/pt/AMTCitationRedir.aspx?tid=2906494&pid=-100143280.

112 GenealogyBank.com, *Dallas Morning News* article, May 29, 1898. Rev R.C. Armstrong officiated.

113 Ancestry.com, *Public Member Trees* (Provo, UT, USA, The Generations Network, Inc., 2006), www.ancestry.com, Database online. Record for James Buchanan Dean.

114 Ancestry.com, *Public Member Trees* (Provo, UT, USA, The Generations Network, Inc., 2006), www.ancestry.com, Database online. Record for Van Irving Dean.

115 Ancestry.com, *Public Member Trees* (Provo, UT, USA, The Generations Network, Inc., 2006), www.ancestry.com, Database online. Record for Van Irving Dean.

116 Ancestry.com, *Public Member Trees* (Provo, UT, USA, The Generations Network, Inc., 2006), www.ancestry.com, Database online. Record for Joseph Madison Dean.

117 Obituary for Jesse E. Dean.

118 Obituary for Jessie E. Dean, *Bent County Democrat*.

119 *1900 US Census*, Las Animas, CO, Name listed as Annie P. Other sourses listed a Pearl Dean. I assume they are the same person.

120 *1900 US Census*, Las Animas, CO.

121 *1900 US Census*, Las Animas, CO, Listed name as Lanettie; but other sources listed a Nettie Dean. I assume they are one in the same.

122 Ancestry.com, *Public Member Trees* (Provo, UT, USA, The Generations Network, Inc., 2006), www.ancestry.com, Database online. Record for Lydia Ella pryor.

123 Ancestry.com, *Social Security Death Index* (Provo, UT, USA: The Generations Network, Inc., 2008), www.ancestry.com, [database online]. Original data: Social Security Administration. *Social Security Death Index, Master File.* Social Security Administration. Number: 522-18-2007; Issue State: Colorado; Issue Date: Before 1951. Record for Marshall Dean.

124 Ancestry.com, *World War I Draft Registration Cards, 1917–1918* (Provo, UT, USA, The Generations Network, Inc., 2005), www.ancestry.com, Database online. Original data—United States, Selective Service System. World War I Selective Service System Draft Registration Cards, 1917–1918. Washington, D.C.: National Archives and Records Administration, M1509, 4,582 rolls. Registration Location: Bent County, Colorado; Roll: 1544478; Draft Board: 0. Record for Marshall S Dean.

125 Ancestry.com, *Public Member Trees* (Provo, UT, USA, The Generations Network, Inc., 2006), www.ancestry.com, Database online. Record for Edward P Dean.

126 Ancestry.com, *Social Security Death Index* (Provo, UT, USA: The Generations Network, Inc., 2008), www.ancestry.com, [database online]. Original data: Social Security Administration. *Social Security Death Index, Master File.* Social Security Administration. Number: 522-66-6152; Issue State: Colorado; Issue Date: 1963. Record for Ella Dean.

127 *1930 United States Federal Census* (Provo, UT, USA: The Generations Network, Inc., 2002), www.ancestry.com, Online publication. Original data United States of America, Bureau of the Census. Fifteenth Census of the United States. Washington, D.C.: National Archives and Records Administration, 1930.T626, 2,667 rolls). Las Animas, Bent, Colorado, ED 8, roll 230, page , image 619.0.

128 Ancestry.com, *One World Tree^SM* (Provo, UT, USA: The Generations Network, Inc., n.d.), www.ancestry.com, database online. Provo, UT, USA: The Generations Network, Inc.

129 *1930 United States Federal Census* (Provo, UT, USA: The Generations Network, Inc., 2002), www.ancestry.com, Online publication. Original data United States of America, Bureau of the Census. Fifteenth Census of the United States. Washington, D.C.: National Archives and Records Administration, 1930.T626, 2,667 rolls). Census Place: Las Animas, Bent, Colorado; Roll: 230; Page: 3A; Enumeration District: 8; Image: 619.0, birth date: abt 1887, Birth place: Colorado, Residence date: 1930, Residence place: Las Animas, Bent, Colorado.

130 *1900 United States Federal Census* (Provo, UT, USA: The Generations Network, Inc., 2004, www.ancestry.com, online publication. Original data—United States of America, Bureau of the Census. Twelfth Census of the United States, 1900. Washington, D.C.: National Archives and Records Administration, 1900). Census Place: Precincts 1, 3–8, Bent, Colorado; Roll: T623 121; Page: 10A; Enumeration District: 3, birth date: abt 1886, Birth place: Colorado, Residence date: 1900, Residence place: Precincts 1, 3–8, Bent, Colorado.

131 *1910 United States Federal Census* (Provo, UT, USA: The Generations Network, Inc., 2006), www.ancestry.com, Online publication. Original data United States of America, Bureau of the Census. Thirteenth Census of the United States. Washington, D.C.: National Archives and Records Administration, 1910.T624, 1,178 rolls). Census Place: Precinct 9, Bent, Colorado; Roll: T624_112; Page: 3B; Enumeration District: 6; Image: 718, birth date: abt 1887, Birth place: Colorado, Residence date: 1910, Residence place: Precinct 9, Bent, Colorado.

132 *1920 United States Federal Census* (Provo, UT, USA: The Generations Network, Inc., 2005), www.ancestry.com, Online publication. Original data United States of America, Bureau of the Census. Fourteenth Census of the United States. Washington, D.C.: National Archives and Records Administration, 1920.T625, 2076 rolls). Census Place: Las Animas, Bent, Colorado; Roll: T625_155; Page: 6B; Enumeration District: 269; Image: 529, birth date: abt 1887, Birth place: Colorado, Residence date: 1920, Residence place: Las Animas, Bent, Colorado.

133 *1930 United States Federal Census* (Provo, UT, USA: The Generations Network, Inc., 2002), www.ancestry.com, Online publication. Original data United States of America, Bureau of the Census. Fifteenth Census of the United States. Washington, D.C.: National Archives and Records Administration, 1930.T626, 2,667 rolls). Census Place: Las Animas, Bent, Colorado; Roll: 230; Page: 3A; Enumeration District: 8; Image: 619.0. Record for Thomas F Dean.

134 Broderbund Family Archive #110, Vol. 1, Ed. 5, *Social Security Death Index*: U.S., Date of Import: Jul 6, 1998, Internal Ref. #1.111.5.58264.131

135 *Mason Co. Illinois Birth Records*, 977.31 M395.Ma-3 (LA City Library), Original Birth Records, 1877–1900.

136 Ancestry.com, *Public Member Trees* (Provo, UT, USA, The Generations Network, Inc., 2006), www.ancestry.com, Database online. Record for Mary Loretta O Malley.

137 *1900 United States Federal Census* (Provo, UT, USA: The Generations Network, Inc., 2004, www.ancestry.com, online publication. Original data—United States of America, Bureau of the Census. Twelfth Census of the United States, 1900. Washington, D.C.: National Archives and Records Administration, 1900). Bent, Colorado, ED 3, roll T623 121, page 10A.

138 *1900 United States Federal Census* (Provo, UT, USA: The Generations Network, Inc., 2004, www.ancestry.com, online publication. Original data—United States of America, Bureau of the Census. Twelfth Census of the United States, 1900. Washington, D.C.: National Archives and Records Administration, 1900). Census Place: Precincts 1, 3–8, Bent, Colorado; Roll: T623 121; Page: 10A; Enumeration District: 3, birthdate abt 1894, Birth place: Colorado, Residence date: 1900, Residence place: Precincts 1, 3–8, Bent, Colorado.

139 *1910 United States Federal Census* (Provo, UT, USA: The Generations Network, Inc., 2006), www.ancestry.com, Online publication. Original data United States of America, Bureau of the Census. Thirteenth Census of the United States. Washington, D.C.: National Archives and Records Administration, 1910.T624, 1,178 rolls). Census Place: Precinct 9, Bent, Colorado; Roll: T624_112; Page: 3B; Enumeration District: 6; Image: 718, birth date: abt 1893, Birth place: Colorado, Residence date: 1910, Residence place: Precinct 9, Bent, Colorado.

140 Genealogy Report by Dan Muse, discussion list.

141 Ancestry.com, *California Death Index, 1940–1997* (Provo, UT, USA: The Generations Network, Inc., 2000). Original data: State of California. *California Death Index, 1940–1997.* Sacramento, CA: State of California Department of Health Services, Center for Health Statistics, 19–.

142 Dan Muse, "Baublits Family report"; Genealogy Report, May 2010 (San Diego, CA; privately held by Del Ritchhart, San Diego).

143 Bent County History Book Committee, *Bent County, Colorado History* (Holly, Colorado : The Holly Publishing Company, 1986).

144 *1920 United States Federal Census* (Provo, UT, USA: The Generations Network, Inc., 2005), www.ancestry.com, Online publication. Original data United States of America, Bureau of the Census. Fourteenth Census of the United States. Washington, D.C.: National Archives and Records Administration, 1920.T625, 2076 rolls), Red River, Texas.

145 Ancestry.com, *Public Member Trees* (Provo, UT, USA, The Generations Network, Inc., 2006), www.ancestry.com, Database online. Record for Lena Lucille Cottrell.

146 Ancestry.com, *Social Security Death Index* (Provo, UT, USA: The Generations Network, Inc., 2008), www.ancestry.com, [database online]. Original data: Social Security Administration. *Social Security Death Index, Master File.* Social Security Administration. Number: 546-36-4195; Issue State: California; Issue Date: Before 1951. Record for Lena L. Dean.

147 Ancestry.com, *Public Member Trees* (Provo, UT, USA, The Generations Network, Inc., 2006), www.ancestry.com, Database online. Record for Charles Robert "C.R." Cottrell.

148 Ancestry.com, *Texas Death Index, 1903–2000* (Provo, UT, USA, The Generations Network, Inc., 2006), www.ancestry.com, Database online. Record for Lena Lucille Dean.

149 *1930 United States Federal Census* (Provo, UT, USA: The Generations Network, Inc., 2002), www.ancestry.com, Online publication. Original data United States of America, Bureau of the

Census. Fifteenth Census of the United States. Washington, D.C.: National Archives and Records Administration, 1930.T626, 2,667 rolls). Census Place: Rixey, Bent, Colorado; Roll: 230; Page: 7B; Enumeration District: 2; Image: 542.0. Record for Marcella Dean.

150   *1920 United States Federal Census* (Provo, UT, USA: The Generations Network, Inc., 2005), www.ancestry.com, Online publication. Original data United States of America, Bureau of the Census. Fourteenth Census of the United States. Washington, D.C.: National Archives and Records Administration, 1920.T625, 2076 rolls). Census Place: Las Animas, Bent, Colorado; Roll: T625_155; Page: 6B; Enumeration District: 269; Image: 529, birth date: abt 1914, Birth place: Colorado, Residence date: 1920, Residence place: Las Animas, Bent, Colorado.

151   *1920 United States Federal Census* (Provo, UT, USA: The Generations Network, Inc., 2005), www.ancestry.com, Online publication. Original data United States of America, Bureau of the Census. Fourteenth Census of the United States. Washington, D.C.: National Archives and Records Administration, 1920.T625, 2076 rolls). Census Place: Las Animas, Bent, Colorado; Roll: T625_155; Page: 6B; Enumeration District: 269. Record for Frances Dean.

152   *1930 United States Federal Census* (Provo, UT, USA: The Generations Network, Inc., 2002), www.ancestry.com, Online publication. Original data United States of America, Bureau of the Census. Fifteenth Census of the United States. Washington, D.C.: National Archives and Records Administration, 1930.T626, 2,667 rolls). Census Place: Denver, Denver, Colorado; Roll: 236; Page: 22A; Enumeration District: 86; Image: 268.0. Record for Frances Gallagher.

153   Obituary for Frances Dean Gallagher.

154   *1920 United States Federal Census* (Provo, UT, USA: The Generations Network, Inc., 2005), www.ancestry.com, Online publication. Original data United States of America, Bureau of the Census. Fourteenth Census of the United States. Washington, D.C.: National Archives and Records Administration, 1920.T625, 2076 rolls). Census Place: East Pittsburgh Ward 2, Allegheny, Pennsylvania; Roll: T625_1511; Page: 4A; Enumeration District: 93. Record for William P Gallgher.

155   *1920 United States Federal Census* (Provo, UT, USA: The Generations Network, Inc., 2005), www.ancestry.com, Online publication. Original data United States of America, Bureau of the Census. Fourteenth Census of the United States. Washington, D.C.: National Archives and Records Administration, 1920.T625, 2076 rolls). Census Place: East Pittsburgh Ward 2, Allegheny, Pennsylvania; Roll: T625_1511; Page: 4A; Enumeration District: 93. Record for William P Gallgher.

156   Ancestry.com, *Social Security Death Index* (Provo, UT, USA: The Generations Network, Inc., 2008), www.ancestry.com, [database online]. Original data: Social Security Administration. *Social Security Death Index, Master File*. Social Security Administration.

157   *1920 United States Federal Census* (Provo, UT, USA: The Generations Network, Inc., 2005), www.ancestry.com, Online publication. Original data United States of America, Bureau of the Census. Fourteenth Census of the United States. Washington, D.C.: National Archives and Records Administration, 1920.T625, 2076 rolls). Census Place: Las Animas, Bent, Colorado; Roll: T625_155; Page: 6B; Enumeration District: 269; Image: 529, birth date: abt 1915, Birth place: Colorado, Residence date: 1920, Residence place: Las Animas, Bent, Colorado.

158   Ancestry.com, *Social Security Death Index* (Provo, UT, USA: The Generations Network, Inc., 2008), www.ancestry.com, [database online]. Original data: Social Security Administration. *Social Security Death Index, Master File*. Social Security Administration. Number: 524-34-6670;

Issue State: Colorado; Issue Date: Before 1951. Birth date: 6 Aug 1915, Death date: 15 Oct 1995, Death place: Loveland, Larimer, Colorado, United States of America.

159   Ancestry.com, *U.S. Public Records Index, Volume 2* (Provo, UT, USA, Ancestry.com Operations, Inc., 2010), www.ancestry.com, Database online. Record for Helen J Ritchhart.

160   *Bent County Democrat* Article, Files of Del Ritchhart.

161   *1930 United States Federal Census* (Provo, UT, USA: The Generations Network, Inc., 2002), www.ancestry.com, Online publication. Original data United States of America, Bureau of the Census. Fifteenth Census of the United States. Washington, D.C.: National Archives and Records Administration, 1930.T626, 2,667 rolls). La Junta, Otero, Colorado, ed 8, roll 248, image 99.0.

162   *1930 United States Federal Census* (Provo, UT, USA: The Generations Network, Inc., 2002), www.ancestry.com, Online publication. Original data United States of America, Bureau of the Census. Fifteenth Census of the United States. Washington, D.C.: National Archives and Records Administration, 1930.T626, 2,667 rolls). La Junta, Otero, Colorado, ed 8, roll 248, image 99.0. Record for Dalbert Ritchhart.

163   Ancestry.com, *Public Member Trees* (Provo, UT, USA, The Generations Network, Inc., 2006), www.ancestry.com, Database online. Record for Grace Azetta Bush.

164   *1920 United States Federal Census* (Provo, UT, USA: The Generations Network, Inc., 2005), www.ancestry.com, Online publication. Original data United States of America, Bureau of the Census. Fourteenth Census of the United States. Washington, D.C.: National Archives and Records Administration, 1920.T625, 2076 rolls). Census Place: Las Animas, Bent, Colorado; Roll: T625_155; Page: 6B; Enumeration District: 269; Image: 529, birth date: abt 1917, Birth place: Colorado, Residence date: 1920, Residence place: Las Animas, Bent, Colorado.

165   Ancestry.com, *Social Security Death Index* (Provo, UT, USA: The Generations Network, Inc., 2008), www.ancestry.com, [database online]. Original data: Social Security Administration. *Social Security Death Index, Master File*. Social Security Administration, 2005.

166   Ancestry.com, *Social Security Death Index* (Provo, UT, USA: The Generations Network, Inc., 2008), www.ancestry.com, [database online]. Original data: Social Security Administration. *Social Security Death Index, Master File*. Social Security Administration. Number: 522-12-0700; Issue State: Colorado; Issue Date: Before 1951. Record for Thomas Dean.

167   Ancestry.com, *Public Member Trees* (Provo, UT, USA, The Generations Network, Inc., 2006), www.ancestry.com, Database online. Record for Darrol Dean.

168   Ancestry.com, *Social Security Death Index* (Provo, UT, USA: The Generations Network, Inc., 2008), www.ancestry.com, [database online]. Original data: Social Security Administration. *Social Security Death Index, Master File*. Social Security Administration. Number: 524-24-8710; Issue State: Colorado; Issue Date: Before 1951. Record for Bessie B. Dean.

169   Headstone Las Animas Cemetery, Observed during visit to Las Animas in May 2005.

170   Ed Dean interview, May 2005.

171   Ed Dean interview, May 2005, I also talked with Allen on the phone to set up the interview with his father.

172   Ed Dean, Letter from Ed Dean to Helen Jane Dean (1994), Personal files of Del Ritchhart.

173   Ancestry.com, *U.S. Public Records Index, Volume 1* (Provo, UT, USA, Ancestry.com Operations, Inc., 2010), www.ancestry.com, Database online. Record for Ml Delbert A Ritchhart.

174 Ancestry.com, *U.S. Public Records Index, Volume 1* (Provo, UT, USA, Ancestry.com Operations, Inc., 2010), www.ancestry.com, Database online. Record for Ml Delbert A Ritchhart.

175 Ancestry.com, *U.S. Public Records Index, Volume 1* (Provo, UT, USA, Ancestry.com Operations, Inc., 2010), www.ancestry.com, Database online. Record for Joanne S Ritchhart.

176 Ancestry.com, *U.S. Public Records Index, Volume 1* (Provo, UT, USA, Ancestry.com Operations, Inc., 2010), www.ancestry.com, Database online. Record for Joanne S Ritchhart.

177 Ancestry.com, *U.S. Public Records Index, Volume 1* (Provo, UT, USA, Ancestry.com Operations, Inc., 2010), www.ancestry.com, Database online. Record for Joanne S Ritchhart.

178 Ancestry.com, *U.S. Public Records Index, Volume 2* (Provo, UT, USA, Ancestry.com Operations, Inc., 2010), www.ancestry.com, Database online. Record for Joanne S Ritchhart.

179 State of Colorado, Death Certificate.

180 Curtis Dean's GENI.COM Inputs.

181 Ancestry.com, *Social Security Death Index* (Provo, UT, USA: The Generations Network, Inc., 2008), www.ancestry.com, [database online]. Original data: Social Security Administration. *Social Security Death Index, Master File*. Social Security Administration. Number: 524-44-9184; Issue State: Colorado; Issue Date: 1953. Record for Darol E. Dean.

182 Ancestry.com, *Social Security Death Index* (Provo, UT, USA: The Generations Network, Inc., 2008), www.ancestry.com, [database online]. Original data: Social Security Administration. *Social Security Death Index, Master File*. Social Security Administration. Number: 524-44-9184; Issue State: Colorado; Issue Date: 1953. Birth date: 5 Jun 1941, Death date: 6 Sep 2005, Death place: Arvada, Jefferson, Colorado.

183 Ancestry.com, *California Marriage Index, 1960–1985* (Provo, UT, USA, Ancestry.com Operations Inc, 2007), www.ancestry.com, Database online. Record for Darol E Dean.

Generation 1

1. **PETER[1] O'MALLEY** [1,2,3,4] was born about 1835 in Mayo, Ireland[4,5,6,7,8,9,10,11]. He died in 1893 in Manito, Mason, Illinois, USA[7,10]. He married (2) **JULIA MCNALLY** between 1852–1853 in Salem, Wayne, Pennsylvania, USA[12]. She was born in Jan 1835 in Mayo, Ireland[13,14]. She died in Apr 1906 in Manito, Mason, Illinois, USA[7,10,15].

Notes for Peter O'MALLEY: In the 1900 census Walter listed his parent's birthplace as unk, however, in the 1910 census he listed their birthplaces as Mayo County, Ireland. Ballina area (Mayo Co.) residents frequently settled in the Scranton, PA area, which is where Peter settled.

For the longest time I couldn't find any records for Peter and Julia in Pennsylvania, although I know from their daughter Sarah's obituary that they lived in Scranton, PA. Then in March 2005, I put a note on the Ancestry.com message board about searching for Peter and Julia and also listed the names of the children I knew of. Shortly thereafter I received a reply from John Stanley, who was also researching O'Malleys. He found the family; but listed as "Malia" in the 1870 census in Scranton and as "Maloy" in the 1860 census in Salem Township, PA. That was a key breakthrough that led to identifying all the children and will hopefully help me trace Peter back to Ireland. I later noted in the 1870 Census that there were four Malia men living in the 2nd Ward: Anthony (22), Patrick (30), Thomas (25) and Peter (35). Peter and Thomas were almost neighbors (houses 316 & 321 of the survey). I then found Peter O'Maly, Julia and three children in the June 1880 census in Illinois, which must have been just after their arrival in Illinois. Thus the surname evolution was: 1860—Maloy, 1870—Malia, 1880—OMaly thence O'Malley in later years. In checking Scranton City Directories I found the following, but cannot verify any or all are our Peter:
1867—Peter O'Maley, laborer, Providence (Borough)
1868—Peter Malia, laborer, G.R. Mine, Diamond Flats (Home)
1871—Peter Malia, miner, V.S. Mine, (Home) P (could be for Providence)
1871—Peter J. Malia, laborer, G.R. Mine, Diamond Flats
1876–77—Peter O'Malley, laborer, (Home) Water near Oak
1879–80—Peter O'Malia, brakeman, Prospect

In *County Mayo, Ireland Achill Parish, Some Baptismal transcriptions with Index* by William G. Masterson I found the following interesting comments about the O'Malley family name. "…the surname O'Malley, Maley, Malley and Malia may be found under the predominant surname for the family." It appears that Malley was used for several years at the beginning of the records and then it became Maley for a few years and then reverts to Malley.

I think this indicates that they probably moved from the Salem area around 1867 and that he started as a laborer, then worked in the mines and eventually with the railroad. This correlates with the fact he was listed as working for the railroad in the 1980 census in Mason

Co., Illinois. I don't think the 1876–77 Peter is the same person as my Peter.

In conversation with Betsy Smith, she referred to the "famous Grace O'Malley" from Mayo County. I later learned through research that Graine Mhaol: in Irish her name is Gra'aine Ni Mhaile; is the subject of many romantic tales in Ireland. She has been variously described by responsible contemporary writers as "a most famous sea captain" and "nurse of all the rebellions in the province (of Connacht} for forty years." "The name O'Malley may well be said to be Irish of the Irish. It is one of the few O names from which the prefix was never widely dropped. It is not specially numerous, but it is very well known. It belonged exclusively in the past to County Mayo, and this is almost equally true of the present day; over eighty per cent of the births recorded are in Connacht and most of these are in County Mayo. Their particular territory is the baronies of Burrishoole and Murrisk. It may be of interest that the well-known Sir Owen O'Malley, diplomat and author, who claims to be Chief of the Name, insists on his name being pronounced O'Mailey." (*Irish Families* by Edward Maclysaght)

Researching the International & Passenger Records on Genealogy.com I found several Peter O'Malleys listed immigrating from Ireland. The potato blight of late 1845 caused about 77,000 people to leave Ireland. In 1846 the number increased to 106,000 and peaked at almost 250,000 in 1851. It was probably during that time frame that Peter left Ireland. He may have been accompanied by others of his family; but I have not been able to confirm that.

The 1880 Census of 14, 15 June in Mason Co. listed Peter's age as 45. Thus, if his birthdate was prior to June he would have been born in 1835, and if he was born after June he was born in 1834. This disagrees with the 1837 on his gravestone. Likewise, Julia would have been born in 1833 or 34 based on here age of 46 from the Census. However, her gravestone reflects 1835.

I have researched the Philadelphia naturalization records extensively and have been unsuccessful in identifying a Peter O'Malley (or other spelling) who closely correlates. I did find in the Philadelphia Naturalization Record Index by Philby in the FHL a Peter O'Malley who Petitioned for Naturalization on April 21, 1858; but when I found the actual petition, it listed his age as 39. Thus, he would have been born in 1819 which isn't even close to the 1834 to 1837 that is the best estimate of his birth year. I found the petition in the Pennsylvania District Court Records (Philadelphia Co.) Film 965236.

I also found the following in the 1992 *Journal of South Mayo Research Society* (Vol V, pg 12), "The 10 Principal Surnames of County Mayo." O'Malley was one of those and the article stated, "Inland the surname was frequently anglicized as Melia in the last century (i.e., 1800s). In this century (1900s) the variant has frequently been changed back to O'Malley."

Sara's obituary listed her as being one of seven children and that she had outlived all but one of the others.

The *Mason County Marriage Records 1885–1890* listed the marriage of Tom McCabe and Sarah O'Malley. It listed Sarah's parents and listed two spellings for Peter (O'Malley and O'Mally). It also listed Julia's maiden name as McNally vice Downey.

During the time Julia and Peter lived in the Scranton area they must have observed tremendous growth of the area and of the Catholic church. Prior to 1856 there were very few catholics and no church structure in the area. However, in 1856 a priest from the adjoining Carbondale area began saying mass in a small apartment. In 1858 a small church was built. Finally in 1876, after some additional expansion: a cathedral, The Church of St. Vincent de Paul, was built in Scranton.

The borough of Scranton was incorporated in 1856, named after the Scranton brothers who developed the process to make steel rail for the railroad. Although there are huge deposits of anthracite coal in and around Scranton, it was the steel mills that put them on the map. In 1866 Scranton was incorporated as a city, combining with the boroughs of Hide Park and Providence.

I visited Mason County and Sherman on April 17, 2009 in conjunction with a trip to the Allen County Public Library in Ft. Wayne, Indiana. When I go to Sherman I could only find about a four square block area that looked like it might have been part of the original settlement area. The remainder of the surrounding area looked quite upscale and was probably a residential area for many who work in neighboring Springfield. I had this strong feeling that this area just didn't "fit in" with the Mason County area I had just come from visiting over the previous two days. Somehow I couldn't envision Peter and Julia living there. The next day while doing further research in the Lincoln Springfield City Public Library, I learned that there is a Sherman Township in Mason County and after rechecking the 1880 Census confirmed that is where they moved to from Pennsylvania—not the town of Sherman outside Springfield! Thus, my gut feeling the day before was correct.

A very strong naming tradition of the Irish is for sons to name their first born son after their father. Thus, it may be that Peter's father's name was John—the same name as his first born son.

Sherry Dilla, the wife of one of Peter O'Malley's great grandsons, said that there was a story told by her monther-in-law about Peter O'Malley. According to the story, Peter wanted to go back to Ireland and one night got drunk. The next morning when he woke up he was on a ship headed for Ireland. It then took the family a year to raise the money for him to return back to the USA. I asked her if anyone ever said **when** this supposidly happened. She didn't know. This couldn't have happened while they lived in Illinois. It is even hard to imagine happening when he lived in the Scranton area, as the closest port would have been Philadelphia or New York and both were about 125 miles away. I tend to doubt the story; but it might have happened shortly after Peter arrived in this country when he was still living in one of those port areas. My first records of Peter are in Wayne County, Pennsylvania; but he probably arrived in New York or Philadelphia and might have lived there for a while prior to moving to Wayne County.

Notes for Julia MCNALLY: The 1880 Census tends to indicate that the Omalys were living as two families when the June census was taken. Thomas Highland and wife Mary O'Mally Highland were listed in the same household with Michael, Isabella, John, Sarah and Ellen. Peter Omaly and Julia were listed with Walter, Michael and Ella. There seems to be some duplication. The name is still being spelled OMaly and OMally, probably because Peter and Julia could not read or write or didn't care to correct the enumerator (**This was my earlier evaluation; however, I now believe they actually spelled the name Melia or Malia until changing it later**).

The 1900 Census had Julia living with Sara and Thomas McCabe, their 5 children and their niece and nephew, Mary and Walter O'Malley. The census noted that Julia immigrated in 1859. However, that doesn't make sense because first child was John born in 1854 in Pennsylvania. Maybe she was naturalized in 1859?

Somehow in my early research, I determined Julia's maiden name to be Downey. However, the *Mason County Marriage Records 1885–1890* listed the parents of Sarah O'Malley as Peter O'Malley and Julia McNally. Not sure if it was a mistake; but I now believe McNally is more likely than Downey. The 1900 census also lists a John O'Malley, born 1856 married to Catherine O'Malley with children Julia and Daniel. Because the age is a fit, he was born in Pennsylvania, and had a girl the same name as his (possible) mother; I think John is the child of Peter and Julia.

For several years I included Catherine (Katherine) as a member of the O'Malley family. I think I added her because I knew there was a Hyland connection with the O'Malleys and I found a Thomas Hyland from Pennsylvania married to a Katherine whose parents were Irish and she later moved to Denver. However there were supposidly 7 O'Malley children and she increased that to eight. Most importantly, she was not listed with the family in either the 1860 or 1870 census.

Peter O'MALLEY and Julia MCNALLY had the following children:

2 i. MICHAEL[2] O'MALLEY[10,56,57,58,59,60] was born in Aug 1873 in Scranton, Lackawanna, Pennsylvania, USA[10,58,59,60,61,62,63,64]. He married FRANCES L. MOORE. She was born in Feb 1874 in Illinois, USA[65,66,67].

3 ii. JOHN T. O'MALLEY[10,16,17] was born in May 1854 in Salem, Wayne, Pennsylvania, USA[10,18]. He died on 19 Sep 1935 in Kingman, Kingman, Kansas, USA (From notes in Mary Dean's bible)[19]. He married CATHRINE in 1883 in Illinois, USA[20]. She was born in Feb 1862 in Illinois, USA[21]. She died about 1925 in Union, Kingman, Kansas, USA[22].

4 iii. MARY O'MALLEY[10,23,24,24,25,25,26] was born in 1856 in Salem, Wayne, Pennsylvania, USA[10,24,24,27,28]. She died about 1945 in Denver, Colorado, USA[10,29]. She married THOMAS H HYLAND about 1879. He was born in Nov 1859 in England[30].

iv. JOHANNA O'MALLEY[10,31,32] was born in 1861 in Pennsylvania, USA[31,32]. She married JOHN HENRY on 01 Feb 1880 in Manito, Mason, Illinois, USA. He was born in 1847 in Ireland[31,31].

Notes for Johanna O'MALLEY: *The Index for Marriage Records, Mason Co., Ill 1878–1884* listed the marriage of Joanna O. Mala (19) of Easton on 1 Feb 1880 to John Henry (33) of Easton. Service at the Church of Immaculate Conception in Manito. The age fits very closely with Hannah O'Malley as does the location.

Joanna and Hannah are often used interchangeably as variants. She and John were listed in the June 1880 Federal census and her birthplace was listed as Pennsylvania, further correlation that she was the same person as Hannah O'Malley.

5   v.   SARAH JANE O'MALLEY[33] was born on 01 Aug 1864 in Scranton, Lackawanna, Pennsylvania, USA[10,34,35,36]. She died on 08 Dec 1944 in Havana, Mason, Illinois, USA[10,36,37,38]. She married THOMAS J. MCCABE on 05 Jan 1887 (Delavan, Ill; Tazewell County)[39,40], son of Thomas MCCABE and Ellen I. EILLIHER. He was born in 1857 in New York City, NY[33,41,42]. He died on 27 Dec 1937 in Havana, Mason, Illinois, USA[43].

6   vi.   WALTER WILLIAM O'MALLEY[10,44,45,46] was born on 17 Jul 1867 in Scranton, Lackawanna, Pennsylvania, USA[10,46,47,48]. He died on 05 Feb 1937 in St Joseph, Andrew, Missouri, USA[10,49]. He married (1) MARY ELIZABETH EARHART about 1885, daughter of Franklin EARHART and Mary Elizabeth MOZINGO. She was born on 26 Apr 1869 in est Mason Co., Illinois (based on adoption papers)[50]. She died on 06 Mar 1892 in Forest City, Mason, Illinois, USA[51]. He married (2) BESSIE MOREY in 1900. She was born in Jun 1876 in Illinois, USA[52]. She died on 24 Jan 1937 in St Joseph, Andrew, Missouri, USA[53].

    vii.   ELLEN O'MALLEY[10,54] was born in Oct 1869 in Scranton, Lackawanna, Pennsylvania, USA[10,55].

Notes for Ellen O'MALLEY: The 1870 and 1880 Census both list Ella as a member of the family. However, her name is listed as Ellen in 1870 and Ella in 1880. The 1880 census did not list either Katherine, John, Mary or Sara, so I assume they had moved out on their own by then. Sara's obituary listed her as one of seven children. Ella brings the number of children to seven.

There are letters to Mary (O'Malley) Dean from Emma Lefebre of Denver talking about "Aunt Mary" passing away. Emma and Ella might be one in the same.

Generation 2

2.   **MICHAEL² O'MALLEY** (Peter¹)[10,56,57,58,59,60] was born in Aug 1873 in Scranton, Lackawanna, Pennsylvania, USA[10,58,59,60,61,62,63,64]. He married **FRANCES L. MOORE**. She was born in Feb 1874 in Illinois, USA[65,66,67].

Notes for Michael O'MALLEY: Was listed in 1937 obituary for his brother, Walter, as a resident of Havana, IL. However, in the 1944 obituary for his sister, Sarah, he was noted as residing in Ipava (Fulton Co.), which is about 10 miles west of Havana just across the Illinois River.

In a phone conversation with the Manito library they noted there was a *History of Manito* prepared by the Manito Historical Society in 1983. In the book Michael was mentioned in a discussion of the Moore family as having married Fanny Moore. It stated that Michael was born in Pennsylvania and was farming in Fulton County. It mentioned they had three children Floyd, Grace, and John.

The 1900 Census had Michael, Fannie and Floyd in Fulton Co. and they had a servant, Milton Bybe, living with them. I would surmise he was actually a hired hand since Michael's occupation was listed as farmer.

Notes for Frances L. MOORE: 1900 census listed her name as Fannie L. which must have been her nickname. She was born in Illinois, her father in Indiana and her mother in Pennsylvania.

Michael O'MALLEY and Frances L. MOORE had the following children:

7   i.   FLOYD F.[3] O'MALLEY[57,68,69] was born on 16 May 1898 in Fulton, Illinois, USA[70,71,72,73,74]. He died in Oct 1965 in Illinois, USA[75,76]. He married ILA V. about 1925 in Fulton, Illinois, USA. She was born on 08 Apr 1896 in Illinois, USA[77,78]. She died in Sep 1975 in Ipava, Fulton, Illinois, USA[75,76,78].

     ii.   GRACE F. O'MALLEY[57,69] was born in 1906 in Fulton, Illinois, USA[68,79,80]. She married HENRY HOLT.

8   iii. JOHN M. O'MALLEY[57,69] was born about 1910 in Fulton, Illinois, USA[81,82]. He married NEVA SMITH about 1932.

3. **JOHN T.[2] O'MALLEY** (Peter[1])[10,16,17] was born in May 1854 in Salem, Wayne, Pennsylvania, USA[10,18]. He died on 19 Sep 1935 in Kingman, Kingman, Kansas, USA (From notes in Mary Dean's bible)[19]. He married **CATHRINE** in 1883 in Illinois, USA[20]. She was born in Feb 1862 in Illinois, USA[21]. She died about 1925 in Union, Kingman, Kansas, USA[22].

Notes for John T. O'MALLEY: It is difficult to pinpoint the birth year of John, since the 1920, 1930 and 1870 census don't exactly agree. Most likely he was born in 1854, but could have been 1855. Grandma (Mary Dean) has an entry in her bible that "Tommy died Nov 11, 1922." I couldn't find any logical candidates other that John T. Not sure if the T stood for Thomas and he was called Tommy. The dates could be correct. However, a later entry in her bible said "Uncle John O'Malley died Thursday Sept 19, 1935. Got telegram from Uncle Elmer Thur afternoon—Dean & I left here Fri 10:30 a.m. arrived there 7 p.m. Friday night. Funeral was at Kingman, Kansas at 9:30 Saturday morning." Kingman is about 40 mines west of Wichita, so the times Grandma noted make sense. I found he and his wife Kate in the 1920 and 1930 Census. All their 7 children were born there, the first in 1917, so they had lived there quite a few years. They were in Illinois in the 1900 Census, so moved between then and 1917.

John T. O'MALLEY and CATHRINE had the following children:

     i.   JULIA[3] O'MALLEY[83,84,85] was born in Feb 1884 in Mason, Illinois, USA[21,86].
           Notes for Julia O'MALLEY: Still living with her father in 1930 on their farm in Union, Kansas according to 1930 census.

9   ii.   DANIEL O'MALLEY[87] was born in Jan 1886 in Mason, Illinois, USA[21,86]. He married MAGDALENA about 1916. She was born about 1889 in Nebraska, USA.

4. **MARY[2] O'MALLEY** (Peter[1])[10,23,24,24,25,25,26] was born in 1856 in Salem, Wayne, Pennsylvania, USA[10,24,24,27,28]. She died about 1945 in Denver, Colorado, USA[10,29]. She married **THOMAS H HYLAND** about 1879. He was born in Nov 1859 in England[30].

Notes for Mary O'MALLEY: The 1870 census listed a Mary Malia living in the house of Jacob & Elinor Gessner in Scranton, Ward 1 as a domestic servant. Her age was listed as 15.

In her brother, Walter's obituary; listed as a surviving sister Mrs. Mary Hyland of Denver, Colorado. She lived in Denver and probably passed away around 1945. I have a telegram to Mary (O'Malley) Dean from Emma Lefebvre informing that "Aunt Mary" had passed away. It was dated Apr 17; but had no year. I am estimating it was around 1945–49, as Grandma's address was the Palace Hotel which they owned then. Also an earlier letter from Aunt Mary was dated 1943. Further confirming that she was a relative, Grandma Dean (Mary) listed "Mrs. T. Hyland, 1614 E. 29th Ave, Denver in her address book. Since the book had dates in the early 1920s, I am guessing that was close to the date of the address.

Elizabeth Moll's obit references her mother Katherine Hyland; but another obituary source references "Mary Hyland of Denver" as being in attendance. I do know there was a close connection between the Hylands and Mary O'Malley Dean.

Notes for Thomas H HYLAND: Middle initial of J. in father's obit.

In the 1880 Mason Co. Census I found Thomas and Mary listed with Michael Omally (6) and Isabella Omally (5/12) listed as son and daughter. Michael is the same age as Mary's brother Michael. Also listed in the family were John (25), Sarah (19) and Ellen OMally (16) listed as Brother, sister-in-law and blank for Ellen. However, according to all other information I have Thomas and Mary didn't have any children until 1882. The OMallys moved to Illinois in 1880 according to Sarah's obituary, so perhaps having just gotten there they were living in two locations.

In the same census Peter OMaly and Julia are listed with Walter, Ella and Michael, thus, having Ella and Michael listed twice in the census.

Thomas H HYLAND and Mary O'MALLEY had the following children:

i. ISABELLA[3] HYLAND[88] was born in Dec 1880 in Illinois[30].

Notes for Isabella HYLAND: Isabella was listed in the June 1880 for Mason County, Illinois census as being 5 months old. However, since she doesn't show up in later records of the Hyland family, it is probable she died as an infant.

ii. ROBERT E HYLAND[24,24,26] was born in Dec 1881 in Illinois[30].

iii. JULIA B HYLAND[24,24,26] was born in Dec 1884 in Illinois[30].

iv. WALTER C HYLAND[30,89] was born in Aug 1887 in Colorado[30]. He died about 1938 in Denver, Denver, Colorado, USA. He married MARGARET. She was born about 1893[89].

v. NELLIE HYLAND[24,24,26] was born in Sep 1890 in Colorado[30].

vi. WILLIAM W. HYLAND[90] was born in 1902 in Colorado, USA[25].

Notes for William W. HYLAND: The other five children were listed in the 1910 Census; but not William. However, the census said she had 6 living children and there were only five listed.

vii. NORBET HYLAND[26] was born in 1902 in Colorado, USA[26]. He died in Jan 1980 in

Denver, Denver, Colorado, United States of America[91]. He married MARIE E. * in 1928. She was born in 1899[92,93].

Notes for Norbet HYLAND: Was a friend of Mary Dean and mentioned in her bible notes. I believe he was the son of her Aunt, who married Thomas Hyland.

5. **SARAH JANE**[2] **O'MALLEY** (Peter[1])[33] was born on 01 Aug 1864 in Scranton, Lackawanna, Pennsylvania, USA[10,34,35,36]. She died on 08 Dec 1944 in Havana, Mason, Illinois, USA[10,36,37,38]. She married **THOMAS J. MCCABE** on 05 Jan 1887 (Delavan, IL; Tazewell County)[39,40], son of Thomas MCCABE and Ellen I. EILLIHER. He was born in 1857 in New York City, NY[33,41,42]. He died on 27 Dec 1937 in Havana, Mason, Illinois, USA[43].

Notes for Sarah Jane O'MALLEY: Sara moved from Scranton with her parents in 1880, when she was 16, to Mason County, Penn Township. Her obituary stated that she was one of seven children, all who preceded her in death, except Mike O'Malley. She had lived near Forest City until 1919 when she moved to Havana. The 1910 census listed her age as 43, which would mean she was born in 1866 or 67, however, she would only have been 13 or 14 when they moved to Illinois. The 1864 date was based on her death certificate; but that could have been in error.

Sarah and her husband, Tom, raised Mary L. (Dean) O'Malley and her brother Walter Lee O'Malley when the children's mother passed away at the young age of 25. The father showed no interest in raising the children and moved out of the state. The children were actually under guardianship of a Mr. White for about 8 years before coming under the guardianship of Sarah. I think it is likely they were living with Sarah and Tom; but were legally under the guardianship of Mr. White. This happened after Sarah's brother, Walter, abandoned the two children and his wife (Mary Elizabeth).

Lived at 418 Orange for six years, which is about the time her husband died. Probably moved after he died.

Funeral services were conducted by Fr. Blough in the St. Patrick's Catholic church.

Walter O'Malley's 1937 obituary listed Sarah as a resident of Havana, IL.

Notes for Thomas J. MCCABE: According to Lee O'Malley, the reason Mary O'Malley left the McCabes was because Tom didn't believe in educating girls and was extremely strict with Mary and her brother, Lee.

Thomas J. MCCABE and Sarah Jane O'MALLEY had the following children:

i. THOMAS ALEXANDER[3] MCCABE[94,95] was born on 09 Mar 1890 in Pennsylvania, Mason, Illinois, USA.

Notes for Thomas Alexander MCCABE: Provided information for mother's death certificate. Did not know grandmother's maiden name. Thomas' birth listing in *Mason Co. Birth Records* listed him as being the second child born to his parents.

ii. EDNA J. MCCABE[94] was born in 1893 in Mason, Illinois, USA. She married UNK DAHLSTROM.

iii. HELEN NELLIE MCCABE[96] was born in 1895 in Mason, Illinois, USA. She married

UNK EVERSON.

Notes for Helen Nellie MCCABE: May also be known as Helen. 1910 Census did not list a Helen; but other source, such as her sister Sara's Obituary, listed Helen. I assume Helen and Nellie are one in the same since the obituary listed all of the children. Nellie could be a nickname, middle name or first name.

    iv. MARIE MCCABE[94] was born in 1898 in Mason, Illinois, USA. She married UNK FISK.

    v. EDWARD MCCABE[33,94] was born in 1900 in Mason, Illinois, USA.

Notes for Edward MCCABE: His mother's obituary listed him as a resident of Chicago, along with Edna and Helen.

    vi. ISABEL MCCABE[94] was born in 1904 in Mason, Illinois, USA[33]. She married LYLE E. BAKER.

    vii. WALTER L. MCCABE[33,94] was born in 1906 in Mason, Illinois, USA[7,33]. He died in Feb 1933 in Mason, Illinois, USA[97,98].

Notes for Walter L. MCCABE: According to a letter in 1933 from his mother, Sarah, to Mary Dean; Sarah was very saddened by the death of Walter. She was pleased, however, that he had no children and his wife was young. Walter, Thomas, and Sarah are all buried in St. Frederick's Catholic Cemetery in Manito along with Peter and Julia O'Malley.

6.   **WALTER WILLIAM[2] O'MALLEY** (Peter*[1]*)[10,44,45,46] was born on 17 Jul 1867 in Scranton, Lackawanna, Pennsylvania, USA[10,46,47,48]. He died on 05 Feb 1937 in St Joseph, Andrew, Missouri, USA[10,49]. He married (1) **MARY ELIZABETH EARHART** about 1885, daughter of Franklin EARHART and Mary Elizabeth MOZINGO. She was born on 26 Apr 1869 in est Mason Co., Illinois (based on adoption papers)[50]. She died on 06 Mar 1892 in Forest City, Mason, Illinois, USA[51]. He married (2) **BESSIE MOREY** in 1900. She was born in Jun 1876 in Illinois, USA[52]. She died on 24 Jan 1937 in St Joseph, Andrew, Missouri, USA[53].

Notes for Walter William O'MALLEY: Found a wire from Mary O'Malley Dean to her husband, Arthur, saying "Dad died this morning wire me ten dollars." Dated Feb 5, 1937. I assume this to be her father who had run out on her, her brother, Lee, and their mother when they were young kids. According to family sources (and confirmed by census data) he went to St. Joseph, MO and started another family.

In searching *Buchanan County Taxpayers list for 1891–95*, in 1901 a Walter O'Malley is listed in Washington Township, South St. Joseph. Also, he is listed in their 1902 Directory for Washington Township of St. Joseph, MO. His Post Office was listed as Station D St. Joseph.

The June 6, 1900 census confirms his wife as Bessie and that they had been married for less than a year. They lived in a boarding house and he was listed as being employed in the packing business. He listed as unknown where his father and mother were born. In the 1910 Census, he now owned his home in St. Joseph and listed his father and mother as being born in Ireland. Although he listed his birthplace as Pennsylvania, the father of his three children (himself) is listed as being born in Ireland. Must have been a misunderstanding between Walter and the census taker.

Death certificate listed his occupation as laborer and that he was widowed. The person providing the information for the death certificate was listed as Dolphus O'Malley (a son) of 424 Lee Street, St. Joseph, MO. It also stated that he had lived in St. Joseph for 35 years (since 1902). I had a startling discovery in March of 2009. I decided to fill in some holes as to the location of Walter and his family by looking at the 1930 census. Because her name is more unusual, I looked up Bessie and found that she and the two youngest children were living in St. Joseph, Missouri; but Walter was not with them. She was still listed as married, so I entered Walter's name to search the census for him. I found him listed as an inmate in Ft. Leavenworth, Kansas Penitentiary. I later queried the Bureau of Prisons and Corrections and learned he was sentenced in Sep 1929 for violation of the Volstead Act, which was Prohibition. He was selling liquor illegally. His sentence was 1 year and 1 month. He was discharged in July of 1930, 72 days early.

Notes for Mary Elizabeth EARHART: Interestingly the 1870 census listed her mother, father and brother John. If she was born in 1869, as most records indicate, she should have been listed in the census. Not sure what this means. Later information indicates that she was adopted in 1873 (given name Elizabeth Kellaher), so she would have been listed with another family in 1870, as that was prior to her adoption. I have tried to find an Elizabeth Kellaher in the 1870 Census; but wasn't successful. She was listed in the 1880 census as being 11 and living with her mother and stepfather, John Gilmore. That same census listed her birthplace as Illinois and that of her mother as Missouri. However, her adopted mother Mary Elizabeth was listed as being born in Indiana, thus, providing further credence to the fact she was adopted. I find it unusual that the name on the adoption papers was Elizabeth Kellaher and her adoptive mother's name is Mary Elizabeth. I assume they gave her the name Mary so that mother and daughter would have the same name. Adoption papers list her name as simply "Elizabeth Kellaher." The reason given was "the mother of said child is poor and is unable to give the said child that care and education it needs."

Her husband Walter left her after the birth of their two children. I am not sure if that was before or after Mary's death. She died in 1892 when the kids were 6 and 3, respectively. Only through my research did I learn that. Earlier I had speculated that she had mental problems or for some other reason turned over the children to her sister-in-law. I now speculate that after she died, her husband either put the kids up for adoption or turned them over to his sister. I did find records of a custodian having been assigned to Mary and Walter Lee and that later their Aunt, Sara McCabe and her husband Tom, became their legal guardians.

The 1920 and 1930 Census lists Mary and Walter Lee's mother's birthplace as Illinois not New York. Also, the Mason Co. birth records also list her birthplace as Illinois. An earlier reference (which I can't recall right now) listed her birthplace as New York.

In November 2010 I received an e-mail through Ancestry from Wendy Seyller indicating that they recently found copies of Mary Elizabeth's adoption papers. She was adopted by Franklin and Mary Elizabeth Mozingo Earhart. Apparantly her name was Elizabeth

Kellaher. The names of her natural parents were not given in the papers. I have made the case that I am a direct descendent and have a very logical claim to the papers—at least a copy if nothing else. They haven't decided yet whether to give me the originals nor have I received a copy.

If it is true that Mary was adopted, then the black slave heritage of her mother Mary Elizabeth Mozingo Earhart would not have been passed down to her descendents.

Walter William O'MALLEY and Mary Elizabeth EARHART had the following children:

10   i. MARY LORETTA[3] O'MALLEY[99,100] was born on 14 Nov 1886 in Forest City, Mason, Illinois, USA (Forest City Hospital)[101]. She died on 14 Mar 1961 in Las Animas, Bent, Colorado, USA[102]. She married ARTHUR SPEAR DEAN on 25 Jul 1911 in Denver, Adams, Colorado, USA, son of Thomas Franklin DEAN and Ida Jane BRITTON. He was born on 22 Oct 1886 in Las Animas, Bent, Colorado, USA[103,104,105,106,107]. He died on 01 Dec 1969 in Las Animas, Bent, Colorado, USA[108,109].

11   ii. WALTER LEE O'MALLEY[110,111,112] was born on 22 Jan 1889 in Forest City, Mason, Illinois, USA[79,113,114,115]. He died on 04 May 1961 in Phoenix, Maricopa, Arizona, USA[75,114]. He married ELIZABETH KYLE on 28 Nov 1914 in Denver, Colorado, USA, daughter of Thomas D. KYLE and Marian H. WALKER. She was born on 23 Aug 1896 in Leadville, Lake, Colorado, USA[79,116,117,118]. She died in Jun 1921 in Salt Lake City, Salt Lake, Utah, United States[118].

Notes for Bessie MOREY: The 1900 Census lists her as married to Walter O'Malley. They were boarders in a home owned by Charles Scott. Her father was born in Illinois and her mother in "Canada-Eng." She had no children.

Walter William O'MALLEY and Bessie MOREY had the following children:

iii. MARIE O'MALLEY was born in 1901 in St Joseph, Andrew, Missouri, USA. She married BERNARD COOPER.

Notes for Marie O'MALLEY: Listed in father Walter's obit as a surviving daughter—Mrs Bernard Cooper of St. Joseph.

iv. ADOLPHUS O'MALLEY was born in 1904 in St Joseph, Andrew, Missouri, USA[119].

12   v. MINNIE PEARL O'MALLEY[120,121] was born in Sep 1908 in St Joseph, Andrew, Missouri, USA. She died on 16 May 1996[122]. She married FRANK J. DILLA. He was born in 1904 in Missouri[123,124,125].

vi. PETER O'MALLEY was born about 1910 in Missouri, USA[119].

vii. JULIA O'MALLEY was born in May 1919 in Colorado, USA[119,126]. She died on 26 Mar 1931 in Dallas, Texas, USA[127].

Notes for Julia O'MALLEY: An entry in Mary Dean's "black book" stated: "March 26, 1931 Uncle Elmer called from Kingman. Julia O'Malley died of flue day the girls were to start home from Dallas having a real blizzard." I speculate it was this Julia O'Malley.

Generation 3

7. **FLOYD F.**[3] **O'MALLEY** (Michael[2], Peter[1])[57,68,69] was born on 16 May 1898 in Fulton, Illinois, USA[70,71,72,73,74]. He died in Oct 1965 in Illinois, USA[75,76]. He married **ILA V.** about 1925 in Fulton, Illinois, USA. She was born on 08 Apr 1896 in Illinois, USA[77,78]. She died in Sep 1975 in Ipava, Fulton, Illinois, USA[75,76,78].

Notes for Floyd F. O'MALLEY: Was listed, along with his brother John, as a pallbearer at his Aunt Sarah O'Malley McCabe's funeral.

Floyd F. O'MALLEY and Ila V. had the following children:

- i. SARAH F.[4] O'MALLEY[128,129] was born about Dec 1926[129,130].
- ii. CATHERINE B. O'MALLEY[128,131] was born about Oct 1928[128,131].

8. **JOHN M.**[3] **O'MALLEY** (Michael[2], Peter[1])[57,69] was born about 1910 in Fulton, Illinois, USA[81,82]. He married **NEVA SMITH** about 1932.

Notes for John M. O'MALLEY: Was listed (along with his brother) as a pallbearer at his aunt, Sarah O'Malley McCabe's funeral.

John M. O'MALLEY and Neva SMITH had the following children:

- i. MARCIA[4] O'MALLEY[57]. She married UNK LIDWELL.
- 13 ii. VEANNA LU O'MALLEY[57,132,133,133] was born on 06 Mar 1942[132]. She died on 24 Nov 2005 in Spotsylvania, Spotsylvania, Virginia, USA[132]. She married LLOYD C SCHWANEBECK. He was born in Jan 1937[134,134,135].

9. **DANIEL**[3] **O'MALLEY** (John T.[2], Peter[1])[87] was born in Jan 1886 in Mason, Illinois, USA[21,86]. He married **MAGDALENA** about 1916. She was born about 1889 in Nebraska, USA.

Notes for MAGDALENA: According to the 1920 and 1930 census, her parents were both born in Switzerland and spoke French. Thus they probably came from the western portion of Switzerland.

Based on the 1930 census indicating the age at which they were married, the marriage was in 1916.

Daniel O'MALLEY and Magdalena had the following children:

- i. IRENE[4] O'MALLEY[22] was born in 1917 in Kansas, USA.
- ii. EMMETT O'MALLEY[22] was born in 1919 in Kansas, USA.
- iii. ROBERT O'MALLEY[22] was born in 1921 in Kansas, USA.
- iv. WALTER O'MALLEY was born in 1923 in Kansas, USA.
- v. FRANCIS O'MALLEY[22] was born in 1925 in Kansas, USA.
- vi. LEE O'MALLEY[136] was born in Aug 1926 in Kansas, USA.
- vii. BEATRICE O'MALLEY[137] was born in Dec 1928 in Kansas, USA.

10. **MARY LORETTA**[3] **O'MALLEY** (Walter William[2], Peter[1])[99,100] was born on 14 Nov 1886 in Forest City, Mason, Illinois, USA (Forest City Hospital)[101]. She died on 14 Mar 1961 in Las Animas, Bent, Colorado, USA[102]. She married **ARTHUR SPEAR DEAN** on 25 Jul 1911 in

Denver, Adams, Colorado, USA, son of Thomas Franklin DEAN and Ida Jane BRITTON. He was born on 22 Oct 1886 in Las Animas, Bent, Colorado, USA[103,104,105,106,107]. He died on 01 Dec 1969 in Las Animas, Bent, Colorado, USA[108,109].

Arthur Spear DEAN and Mary Loretta O'MALLEY had the following children:

  i. MARY FRANCES[4] DEAN[103,138,139,140] was born on 05 Jun 1913 in Denver, Colorado, USA[103,138]. She died on 05 Apr 1968 in Pittsburgh, Allegheny, Pennsylvania, USA. She married WILLIAM PAUL GALLAGHER in 1942 in Syracuse, Hamilton, Kansas, USA[141], son of Hugh A. GALLAGHER and Mary E. He was born in 1911 in Pennsylvania[142,143].

  Notes for Mary Frances DEAN: A former pharmacist and a resident of Shadyside since 1950, died at her home at 702 Bellefonte St. of a heart attack. Although she was named Mary Frances she always went by the name "Frances." Funeral home H. Samson In Pittsburgh. An article in the *Las Animas Democrat*, dated September 3, 1964 recounted that Frances remembers Hubert Humphrey was in her Pharmacy Class in Denver in 1933. Humphrey was a vice presidential candidate in the 1964 elections. In those days (1933) pharmacy class was three months long. Frances was a practicing pharmacist for several years in Las Animas.

14 ii. HELEN JANE DEAN[75,103,144] was born on 06 Aug 1915 in Denver, Adams, Colorado, USA (2:53 p.m., St. Joseph's Hospital)[103,144,145,146]. She died on 28 Oct 1995 in Loveland, Larimer, Colorado, USA[75,145,147]. She married DELBERT BUSH RITCHHART on 01 Aug 1952 in Raton, Colfax, New Mexico, USA (Remarried)[148], son of Alonzo Francis RITCHHART and Grace Azetta BUSH. He was born on 02 Nov 1910 (Carthage, Missouri)[108,149,150,151]. He died on 18 Feb 1981 in Denver, Colorado, USA[151].

15 iii. THOMAS FRANKLIN DEAN[103,152] was born on 24 Sep 1917[153,154]. He died on 22 May 1975[155]. He married BESSIE B. RYAN, daughter of Ed RYAN and Hanna HENDERSTAT. She was born on 21 Apr 1920[156]. She died on 28 May 2009 in Lakewood, Jefferson, Colorado, USA[156].

16 iv. JAMES BINGHAM DEAN[103] was born on 06 Jul 1923 (Denver, Colorado, 1120 p.m., St. Joseph's hospital)[103]. He died on 29 Sep 1993 in Rocky Ford, Otero, Colorado, USA. He married MARILYN STEBBINS on 14 Jun 1949 in Gothenburg, Dawson, Nebraska, USA, daughter of Virge Wilcox STEBBINS and Florence BROOKS. She was born on 08 Jul 1927 in Gothenberg, Nebraska. She died on 06 Feb 2004 in Omaha, Douglas, Nebraska, USA[157].

11. **WALTER LEE[3] O'MALLEY** (Walter William[2], Peter[1])[110,111,112] was born on 22 Jan 1889 in Forest City, Mason, Illinois, USA[79,113,114,115]. He died on 04 May 1961 in Phoenix, Maricopa, Arizona, USA[75,114]. He married **ELIZABETH KYLE** on 28 Nov 1914 in Denver, Colorado, USA, daughter of Thomas D. KYLE and Marian H. WALKER. She was born on 23 Aug 1896 in Leadville, Lake, Colorado, USA[79,116,117,118]. She died in Jun 1921 in Salt Lake City, Salt Lake, Utah, United States[118].

Notes for Walter Lee O'MALLEY: Had another daughter, Mrs. Joe Miller (Elizabeth I believe) of Salt Lake City.

This was my great-uncle Lee. When his two children were very young his wife passed away. Grandma and Grandpa Dean agreed to raise his son Lee (who they called Jim).

In conversation with his granddaughters, Betsy and Marilee, in 2009; they indicated their grandfather told them he ran away to St. Joseph, Missouri about the time his sister, Mary, left and went to Denver. He was taken in by a Catholic Home for wayward boys and stayed there until his sister made enough money to send for him. According to the stories he told Betsy and Marilee, the McCabes treated him and Mary like slaves. Tom McCabe only let Lee go to school if there wasn't any farm work to do and didn't believe girls needed to be educated.

Betsy and Marilee also related that Walter Lee met Elizabeth Kyle when she was only around 15 years old. He decided then that he wanted to marry her; but had to wait until she was 18 to get married. That tracks with the data, because their first children (twins) was born when Elizabeth was within days of her 20th birthday.

Notes for Elizabeth KYLE: According to Lee O'Malley, his mother died during a flu epidemic right after he was born. He was then raised by Arthur and Mary Dean until he was in his late teens.

According to Betsy and Marilee, Elizabeth became ill with the flu shortly after giving birth to Lee. This developed into pneumonia and let to her death. It was then that Mary Dean and Arthur took Lee and raised him with their children. Elizabeth's father and mother were born in Illinois and Indiana, respectively, according to 1920 census.

Walter Lee O'MALLEY and Elizabeth KYLE had the following children:

17   i. MARION HOWARD[4] O'MALLEY was born on 13 Aug 1916 in Las Animas, Bent, Colorado, USA[158,159,160]. She died on 03 Apr 2007 in Bellvue, Washington. She married JOSEPH HENRY MILLER on 27 Jun 1938 in Salt Lake City, Salt Lake, Utah, USA. He was born on 09 Aug 1914 in Butte, Montana[161]. He died on 24 Feb 2005 in Bellvue, Washington.

18   ii. ELIZABETH WALKER O'MALLEY[118] was born in Dec 1918 in Colorado, USA[114]. She died in May 2007 in Phoenix, Maricopa, Arizona, USA[114,118]. She married ORVILLE RICHARD STINSON. He was born on 02 Mar 1913.

19   iii. WALTER LEE O'MALLEY JR. was born on 02 Mar 1921 in Salt Lake City, Salt Lake, Utah, USA[162]. He died on 15 Dec 2004 (At Sea in the Caribbean)[163]. He married HEATHER ROBERTSON, daughter of William McIntosh ROBERTSON and Muriel CHAMBERS. She was born on 24 Mar 1923 in Rockhampton, Queensland, Australia. She died.

12. **MINNIE PEARL**[3] **O'MALLEY** (Walter William[2], Peter[1])[120,121] was born in Sep 1908 in St Joseph, Andrew, Missouri, USA. She died on 16 May 1996[122]. She married **FRANK J. DILLA**. He was born in 1904 in Missouri[123,124,125].

Notes for Minnie Pearl O'MALLEY: The 1910 St. Joseph, Washington Township census lists a 20 month old daughter who name was very difficult to decipher from the record and looked like "Marinie." In the 1920 Census her name looked more like Minnie and that turned out to be correct. Listed in Walter O'Malley's obit as surviving daughter Mrs. F. J. Dilla of St. Joseph. I was later (2010) contacted by a woman who was married to the son of Minnie and Frank, thus, we were able to verify her name.

Frank J. DILLA and Minnie Pearl O'MALLEY had the following children:

    i. ROBERT[4] DILLA[120]. He married SHERRY.

        Notes for Robert DILLA: Late in 2010 I was contacted by Shelly Dilla through Ancestry.com. He husband, Robert, was the son of Minnie O'Malley Dilla. She and "Bobby" still live in St. Joseph, Missouri. Then in March 2011 I received another piece of correspondence from Shelly indicating that they had some photos of Walter William that I might be interested in. In return I offered to share copies of the prison records that I had obtained about Walter. We also talked on the phone. She said that Walter wasn't a very good father or husband according to stories passed down by her mother-in-law, Minnie. Apparently, his wife, Bessie, left him before his death. I am guessing it might have been when he was in prison. Walter was a bartender for years in the "Blue Blaze Bar" in St. Joseph. Supposedly, according to family stories, he was caught for bootlegging when his still in the basement blew up.

        She related that Bessie, Marie and Minnie are all buried in King Hill Cemetery. However, Walter, is buried in another cemetery that recently received some damage by vandals. Supposedly it is the oldest cemetery in St. Joseph.

        Sherry also said that there was a story told by her monther-in-law about Peter O'Malley. According to the story, Peter wanted to go back to Ireland and one night got drunk. The next morning when he woke up he was on a ship headed for Ireland. It then took the family a year to raise the money for him to return back to the USA. I asked her if anyone ever said **when** this supposedly happened. She didn't know. This couldn't have happened while they lived in Illinois. It is even hard to imagine happening when he lived in the Scranton area, as the closest port would have been Philadelphia or New York and both are about 125 miles away. I tend to doubt the story; but it might have happened shortly after arriving in this country when he was still living in one of those port areas.

    ii. FRANCIS J DILLA[123] was born in 1930[123].

Generation 4

13. **VEANNA LU[4] O'MALLEY** (John M.[3], Michael[2], Peter[1])[57,132,133,133] was born on 06 Mar 1942[132]. She died on 24 Nov 2005 in Spotsylvania, Spotsylvania, Virginia, USA[132]. She married **LLOYD C. SCHWANEBECK**. He was born in Jan 1937[134,134,135].

Notes for Lloyd C SCHWANEBECK: Chart from Ellen says her father's name is William not Lloyd.

Lloyd C SCHWANEBECK and Veanna Lu O'MALLEY had the following children:

    i. ELLEN[5] SCHWANEBECK[57] was born about 1964.

Notes for Ellen SCHWANEBECK: I got in touch with Ellen in January of 2009 based on an O'Malley surname site on Ancestry.com. I e-mailed her and she gave me details about her mother's O'Malley ancestors (which trace back to Peter and Julia's son Michael). She and her mother have also researched the O'Malley line; but also ran into a brick wall trying to trace Peter and Julia back further than Pennsylvania. They have been to Ireland three times and ran into the same problems that I did into getting any help from the Family Research Centers.

    ii. ELIZABETH SCHWANEBECK.

14. **HELEN JANE**[4] **DEAN** (Mary Loretta[3] O'MALLEY, Walter William[2] O'MALLEY, Peter[1] O'MALLEY)[75,103,144] was born on 06 Aug 1915 in Denver, Adams, Colorado, USA (2:53 p.m., St. Joseph's Hospital)[103,144,145,146]. She died on 28 Oct 1995 in Loveland, Larimer, Colorado, USA[75,145,147]. She married **DELBERT BUSH RITCHHART** on 01 Aug 1952 in Raton, Colfax, New Mexico, USA (Remarried)[148], son of Alonzo Francis RITCHHART and Grace Azetta BUSH. He was born on 02 Nov 1910 (Carthage, Missouri)[108,149,150,151]. He died on 18 Feb 1981 in Denver, Colorado, USA[151].

Delbert Bush RITCHHART and Helen Jane DEAN had the following children:

    i. DELBERT ARTHUR[5] RITCHHART[164] was born on 08 May 1937 in Las Animas, Bent, Colorado, USA (11:16 a.m.)[165]. He married JOANNE FRANCES SCHMIDT on 28 Nov 1959 in Wilmette, Cook, Illinois, USA, daughter of Frederick Henry SCHMIDT and Frances Lois MCCONNELL. She was born on 12 Mar 1938 in Evanston, Cook, Illinois, USA[166,167,168,169].

    ii. DEAN LEE RITCHHART was born on 08 Oct 1940 (Las Animas, Colorado, 11:35 p.m.). He married EVELYN KIRSCHMAN on 25 Jun 1961 (St. Mary's Catholic Church, Las Animas, CO), daughter of Daniel KIRSCHMAN and UNICE. She was born on 04 Aug 1942.

    iii. MARY JANE RITCHHART was born on 29 Feb 1948 (La Junta, Colorado (Mennonite Hospital)). She died on 27 Apr 1979 (Denver, Colorado of lymphoma (cancer); Rose Memorial Hospital)[170]. She married (1) ELDON JOHNSON about 1970. He was born on 18 Nov 1944. She married (2) JOHN F. HAYES JR. on 24 Oct 1976 in Boulder, Colorado, USA.

15. **THOMAS FRANKLIN**[4] **DEAN** (Mary Loretta[3] O'MALLEY, Walter William[2] O'MALLEY, Peter[1] O'MALLEY)[103,152] was born on 24 Sep 1917[153,154]. He died on 22 May 1975[155]. He married **BESSIE B. RYAN,** daughter of Ed RYAN and Hanna HENDERSTAT. She was born on 21 Apr 1920[156]. She died on 28 May 2009 in Lakewood, Jefferson, Colorado, USA[156].

Thomas Franklin DEAN and Bessie B. RYAN had the following children:

    i. DARROL[5] DEAN[155,171] was born on 05 Jun 1941[155,172]. He died in Oct 2005 in Denver, Colorado, USA[155,173]. He married MARY ANN LANE on 30 Dec 1963 in Los Angeles, California, USA[174].

    Notes for Darrol DEAN: Darrol developed a bad lung condition in his mid-50s and was on oxygen most of the time. He passed away in October 2005 from complications associated with his lung problems.

  ii. CURTIS DEAN was born on 15 Feb 1949. He married KIM.

  Notes for Curtis DEAN: 8807 W. Maplewood Place Littleton CO, Phone: 303-973-2488 (about 1996)

16. **JAMES BINGHAM[4] DEAN** (Mary Loretta[3] O'MALLEY, Walter William[2] O'MALLEY, Peter[1] O'MALLEY)[103] was born on 06 Jul 1923 (Denver, Colorado, 1120 p.m., St. Joseph's hospital)[103]. He died on 29 Sep 1993 in Rocky Ford, Otero, Colorado, USA. He married **MARILYN STEBBINS** on 14 Jun 1949 in Gothenburg, Dawson, Nebraska, USA, daughter of Virge Wilcox STEBBINS and Florence BROOKS. She was born on 08 Jul 1927 in Gothenberg, Nebraska. She died on 06 Feb 2004 in Omaha, Douglas, Nebraska, USA[157].

James Bingham DEAN and Marilyn STEBBINS had the following children:

  i. ELIZABETH JANE[5] DEAN was born on 26 Feb 1949. She married UNK GLEASON.

  ii. MARY SUSAN DEAN was born on 26 Feb 1949. She married MARK LINDER.

  iii. JAMES BINGHAM DEAN was born on 04 Feb 1951.

  iv. STEBBINS FRANKLIN DEAN was born about 1953. He died in Mar 2005 in Las Vegas, Clark, Nevada, USA.

  v. AMY ANNE DEAN was born on 09 Feb 1958 in Denver, Colorado, USA. She died on 15 Jun 1980.

17. **MARION HOWARD[4] O'MALLEY** (Walter Lee[3], Walter William[2], Peter[1]) was born on 13 Aug 1916 in Las Animas, Bent, Colorado, USA[158,159,160]. She died on 03 Apr 2007 in Bellvue, Washington. She married **JOSEPH HENRY MILLER** on 27 Jun 1938 in Salt Lake City, Salt Lake, Utah, USA. He was born on 09 Aug 1914 in Butte, Montana[161]. He died on 24 Feb 2005 in Bellvue, Washington.

Notes for Marion Howard O'MALLEY: The 1920 census listed her name as Mary H. The 1920 census listed her name as Mary H. The 1920 census listed her name as Mary H.

Joseph Henry MILLER and Marion Howard O'MALLEY had the following children:

  i. JOE[5] MILLER was born on 09 Aug 1939 in Salt Lake City, Salt Lake, Utah, USA. He married MARTHA BETLER about 1962.

  ii. MARILEE MILLER was born on 22 Jul 1942 in Salt Lake City, Salt Lake, Utah, USA. She married KAPSA.

  Notes for Marilee MILLER: I first met Marilee in Feb 2009 when she and her sister, Betsy, came over to our house to discuss family history. She lives here in San Diego, but lived for several years in the Seattle area. She practiced law there as well as after moving to San Diego. She is currently retired. She has a son who lives in Washington D.C. She brought a couple of very interesting photographs. One of Mary Dean with Marion, Elizabeth and Walter Lee O'Malley. It might have been taken when Elizabeth O'Malley was very sick with pneumonia which led to her death. I would suspect she went to Denver to help out her brother, Walter Lee, and then when his wife died she brought Lee home and raised him. He was only an infant at the time. She also had a photo of Frances Dean and Marion Miller; but I had a copy of that one.

   iii. SUSAN MILLER was born on 22 Jan 1944 in Salt Lake City, Salt Lake, Utah, USA. She married KENT WADE.

   iv. JOHN MILLER was born on 28 Mar 1945 in Salt Lake City, Salt Lake, Utah, USA.

   v. MELANIE MILLER was born on 09 Nov 1949 in Salt Lake City, Salt Lake, Utah, USA.

   vi. BETSY ANNA ELIZABETH MILLER was born on 29 Jul 1952 in Salt Lake City, Salt Lake, Utah, USA. She married DOUGLAS WILLIAM SMITH on 21 Jun 1986. He was born on 26 Feb 1958 in Salt Lake City, Salt Lake, Utah, USA.

Notes for Betsy Anna Elizabeth MILLER: Betsy apparently is considered the family historian. She lived in the San Jose area until around 2002 when she and her husband moved to the Seattle area to be near her m other and father, who are in an assisted care facility. I have corresponded with her off and on over the past few years (2000–2006) in an attempt to fill some holes on the O'Malley/ Miller side of the house. She is a Human Resources and Compensation consultant, is a Certified Compensation Professional (CCP) and has her own business.

   vii. MONICA MILLER was born on 02 May 1955 in Salt Lake City, Salt Lake, Utah, USA.

18. **ELIZABETH WALKER**[4] **O'MALLEY** (Walter Lee[3], Walter William[2], Peter[1])[118] was born in Dec 1918 in Colorado, USA[114]. She died in May 2007 in Phoenix, Maricopa, Arizona, USA[114,118]. She married **ORVILLE RICHARD STINSON**. He was born on 02 Mar 1913.

Notes for Elizabeth Walker O'MALLEY: Currently lives in Phoenix (2004).

Orville Richard STINSON and Elizabeth Walker O'MALLEY had the following children:

   i. FRANCIS MARSHAL[5] STINSON was born on 02 Mar 1944.

   ii. ELIZABETH JOSEPHENE STINSON was born on 05 Jun 1949.

   iii. BARBARA ANN STINSON was born in Apr 1950.

   iv. JOAN MARIE STINSON was born on 15 Oct 1956.

   v. KELLY ERIN STINSON was born on 14 May 1963.

   vi. PATRICIA LEE STINSON was born on 21 May 1947. She died on 31 Mar 1990.

19. **WALTER LEE**[4] **O'MALLEY JR**. (Walter Lee[3], Walter William[2], Peter[1]) was born on 02 Mar 1921 in Salt Lake City, Salt Lake, Utah, USA[162]. He died on 15 Dec 2004 (At Sea in the Caribbean)[163]. He married **HEATHER ROBERTSON**, daughter of William McIntosh ROBERTSON and Muriel CHAMBERS. She was born on 24 Mar 1923 in Rockhampton, Queensland, Australia. She died.

Notes for Walter Lee O'MALLEY Jr.: When Lee was 13 days old his mother died from the flu epidemic. He moved to Las Animas and was raised by Arthur and Mary Dean. He was known as "Jim" when he lived with the Deans. His two sisters were older and were put in a convent school. Throughout all his years Lee remained very close to Arthur, Mary and their children. As long as I can remember he always called Mary "Momma."

The following is a note from Lee in June 2004 regarding some research I had written him about regarding the early death of his dad's mother and his dad and Mary being raised by the McCabes:

"Del: You will just have to get used to my writing of "momma" your grand mother and dad (my father). Momma and dad stepped into a rabbit trap when they went to live with the McCabes. Tom McCabe was firmly convinced that education was a waste to farmers. Dad was sent to school only when there was nothing to do on the farm. Momma was never allowed to go to school. He also tried to get control of the money, too. That is why she got away from there first , then sent for Dad.   Lee (Jim)"

Jim grew up as a brother to my mother and has remained very attached to the family ever since. At this time (2000) he resides in the Washington State area; but has been in somewhat bad health lately.

Jim suffered very bad wounds in WW II. He tried acting for a brief time in Los Angles; but ended up in the Aerospace business.

The 1930 census listed Lee with the Deans on Poplar street in Las Animas. His listed age was 9 which agrees with his birth date.

Walter Lee O'MALLEY Jr. and Heather ROBERTSON had the following children:

    i. WALTER LEIGH[5] O'MALLEY was born on 12 Sep 1949.

    ii. MARION ELIZABETH HAWDON O'MALLEY was born on 28 Nov 1956. She married WERNER SREIDANG.

1   *1860 US Census* Salem Township, Wayne Co., Pennsylvania, listed Peter Julia and three childres with the surname MALOY.

2   *1880 US Census* Mason County, Illinois, Listed name as Peter O'Maly along with wife Julia and children Walter, Ella and Michael. Since they had just arrived in Illinois, the other older children perhaps followed later or were staying with friends or relatives at the time of the census.

3   *1870 US Census* Scranton, Pennsylvania, 42, Second Ward. Listed Peter Malia, Julia and five children. Occupation listed as Miner. Joanna and Sarah both listed as going to school. Both Peter and Julia were listed as not being able to read or write.

4   Ancestry.com, *New York Passenger Lists, 1820–1957* (Online publication -Provo, UT, USA: The Generations Network, Inc., 2006.Original data -Passenger Lists of Vessels Arriving at New York, New York, 1820–1897; (National Archives Microfilm Publication M237, 675 rolls); Records of the U.S. Customs Service, R), Year: 1847. Microfilm serial: M237; Microfilm roll: M237_66; Birth date: abt 1832, Arrival date: 24 Apr 1847, Arrival place: New York, New York, Departure place: Galway, Ireland.

5   Lee O'Malley, Letter from Lee "Jim" O'Malley to Helen Jane Ritchhart, Personal files of Del Ritchhart.

6   Sara Jane (McCabe) O'Malley's death certificate. Dec 1944.

7   *Mason Co. Illinois Cemeteries* 977.31 M395 Ma (LA City Library).

8   *1880 US Census* (Ancestry.com), Listed as Peter OMaly and age listed as 45. He would have been born in 1835 if his birthday was prior to June; but in 1834 if his birthday was after June. He his mother and father were all listed as being born in Ireland. Lived in Sherman Township, Mason Co., IL.

9   *1880 US Census* (Ancestry.com), Based on his listed age of 45 in June 1880, he was either born in 1834 or 1835, depending on his BD being after or before June. This disagrees with the 1837 on his headstone.

10   Ancestry.com, *Public Member Trees* (Provo, UT, USA, The Generations Network, Inc., 2006), www.ancestry.com, Database online. Record for Peter O'Malley.

11   Walter O'Malley (son) death certificate.

12   *1930 US Census*, Denver, CO, If their daughter, Katherine was born in 1853, I am assuming they were married in 1852 at the ages of 16 and 18.

13   *1900 US Census* Forrest City Township, Mason Co., Illinois, 977.31 M395 Ma (LA City Library).

14   Illinois, Department of Public Health, Certificate of Death; Mason County Clerk and Recorder of Deeds, Havana, Illinois.

15   Catholic Diocese of Peoria Archives, Letter from Diocese dated March 11, 2009. Research by Sister Lea Stefancova, Archivist. "The day of her death is unknown—there is only a blank space for that in her death record. She died suddenly and without sacraments in April 1906, and is buried at St. Fredrick Cemetery in Manito, IL. Service officiated by Rev. J. McGreevey in St. Patrick's Church, Havana, IL. No burial date was documented (as it is throughout this Death Record Book)."

16   *1870 US Census* Scranton, Pennsylvania, Age 15 working as a clerk in a garage. Living with his

folks.

17 *1930 US Census*, Union Township, Kingman Co., Kansas, 2B. Listed middle initial as T. Daughter, Julia, living with him. Listed as widowed, so wife Cathrine mush ave died between 1920 and 1930.

18 *1930 US Census*, Union Township, Kingman Co., Kansas, Census dates don't agree on his birth year. It is either 1854 or 55.

19 Mary Loretta Dean, 1922–1940, Personal Notes, *The Official Prayer Book of the Catholic Church* (Baltimore, MD: John Murphy Company , 1889); privately held by Delbert Ritchhart, 2011.

20 *1900 US Census*, Allens Grove Township, Mason County, Illinois, Listed them as being married 17 years. Oldest child was 16 born in Feb of 1884, thus, I assume they were married early in 1883 (prior to June–month of 1900 census).

21 *1900 United States Federal Census* (Provo, UT, USA: The Generations Network, Inc., 2004, www.ancestry.com, online publication. Original data—United States of America, Bureau of the Census. Twelfth Census of the United States, 1900. Washington, D.C.: National Archives and Records Administration, 1900). Census Place: Allen Grove, Mason, Illinois; Roll: T623_328; Page: 1A; Enumeration District: 54.

22 *1930 US Census*, Union Township, Kingman Co., Kansas.

23 Obituary for Walter W. O'Malley, Indicated he was survived by a sister Mrs. Mary Hyland of Denver.

24 *1910 United States Federal Census* (Provo, UT, USA: The Generations Network, Inc., 2006), www.ancestry.com, Online publication. Original data United States of America, Bureau of the Census. Thirteenth Census of the United States. Washington, D.C.: National Archives and Records Administration, 1910.T624, 1,178 rolls). Denver Ward 8, Denver, Colorado, roll T624_115.

25 *1920 United States Federal Census* (Provo, UT, USA: The Generations Network, Inc., 2005), www.ancestry.com, Online publication. Original data United States of America, Bureau of the Census. Fourteenth Census of the United States. Washington, D.C.: National Archives and Records Administration, 1920.T625, 2076 rolls). Denver, Denver, Colorado, image 745.

26 *1910 United States Federal Census* (Provo, UT, USA: The Generations Network, Inc., 2006), www.ancestry.com, Online publication. Original data United States of America, Bureau of the Census. Thirteenth Census of the United States. Washington, D.C.: National Archives and Records Administration, 1910.T624, 1,178 rolls). Denver Ward 8, Denver, Colorado, roll T624_115. Record for Thomas H Hyland.

27 *1920 US Census*, Denver, CO.

28 *1870 US Census* Scranton, Pennsylvania, June 21 census listed her age as 11. Thus, if she was born before June 21 she would have been born in 1859 and if born after June 21 she would have been born in 1858.

29 Letter to Mary Dean announcing "Aunt Mary" had died in Denver.

30 *1900 United States Federal Census* (Provo, UT, USA: The Generations Network, Inc., 2004, www.ancestry.com, online publication. Original data—United States of America, Bureau of the Census. Twelfth Census of the United States, 1900. Washington, D.C.: National Archives and Records Administration, 1900). Census Place: Denver, Arapahoe, Colorado; Roll: T623_118; Page: 1B; Enumeration District: 50.

31 *1880 United States Federal Census* (Provo, UT, USA: The Generations Network, Inc., 2005, www.ancestry.com, Online publication. 1880 U.S. Census Index provided by The Church of Jesus Christ of Latter-day Saints © Copyright 1999 Intellectual Reserve, Inc. All rights reserved. Original data—United States of America, Bureau of the Census. Tenth Census of the United States. Washington, D.C.: National Archives and Records Administration, 1880. Sherman, Mason, Illinois, ED 127, roll T9_235, page 421.2000, image 0224.

32 Illinois; *1880 Illinois State Census*; Lincoln Public Library, Springfield, IL.

33 *1920 United States Federal Census* (Provo, UT, USA: The Generations Network, Inc., 2005), www.ancestry.com, Online publication. Original data United States of America, Bureau of the Census. Fourteenth Census of the United States. Washington, D.C.: National Archives and Records Administration, 1920.T625, 2076 rolls). Havana, Mason, Illinois, image 159. Record for Thomas J McCabe.

34 Death Certificate of Sara O'Malley.

35 Havana, Illinois Newspaper, Sara's Obituary (Havana, Illinois, December 1944), Personal files of Del Ritchhart.

36 Ancestry.com, *Public Member Trees* (Provo, UT, USA, The Generations Network, Inc., 2006), www.ancestry.com, Database online. Record for Julia McNally.

37 *Illinois Statewide Death Index 1916–1950*, Death certificate #0048476.

38 Catholic Diocese of Peoria Archives, Letter to Delbert Ritchhart dated March 11, 2009. "She died on December 8, 1944, at the age of 80 yrs. She had been previously married to Thomas J. McCabe (deceased). There were six surviving children. Rev. E. C. Blough administered the last sacraments. On December 11, 1944, after the services in St. Patrick's Havana, IL, she was buried at St. Fredrick's Cemetery, Manito, IL. She was not found in the baptismal records because they start in the 1890's or because she was possibly born and lived in Forest City (Iowa?). (In fact she was born in Pennsylvania—my note). No information on her marriage (1887) was found, since the marriage records of St. Patrick's Havana start in 1892 and of the Immaculate Conception, Maniot, in 1899.

39 *Mason Co. Illinois Marriage Records 1841–1900*; Gen 977.31 M395 Ma-1 (LA City Library).

40 Marriage License for Sarah and Thomas McCabe, The license was issued in Mason County; but the ceremony took place in Delevan, Tazewell County (about 15 m east of Forest City).

41 *Mason Co. Illinois Birth Records* 977.31 M395.Ma-3 (LA City Library), Records listed father's birthplace as NY.

42 Marriage License for Sarah and Thomas McCabe, License listed Thomas age as 28 when they were married. Assuming his birthday to be after Jan 5th (the date of their marriage), he would have been born in 1858. Other sources list it as 1857.

43 *Illinois Statewide Death Index 1916–1950*, Death certificate #0000124.

44 *Mason Co. Illinois Birth Records* 977.31 M395.Ma-3 (LA City Library), Father of Walter Lee listed as Walter Wm. O'Malley.

45 Birth Certificates Mary and Walter Lee O'Malley, Certs 1963 & 2123; book 1, pgs 152 & 164. Walter's certificate listed father as Walter Wm O'Malley but Mary's left out the middle name.

46 *1900 United States Federal Census* (Provo, UT, USA: The Generations Network, Inc., 2004, www.ancestry.com, online publication. Original data—United States of America, Bureau of the

Census. Twelfth Census of the United States, 1900. Washington, D.C.: National Archives and Records Administration, 1900). Census Place: Chicago Ward 23, Cook, Illinois; Roll: T623 273; Page: 3B; Enumeration District: 685, birth date: abt 1861, Birth place: Ireland, Residence date: 1900, Residence place: Chicago Ward 23, Cook, Illinois, Arrival date: 1884.

47   Death Certificate of Walter O'Malley.

48   *1880 US Census* (Ancestry.com), Listed Walter's age as 13, which coincides with an 1867 birth-date. Listed him as being born in Pennsylvania which also coincides with other sources.

49   Missouri State Board of Health, Certificate of Death—Missouri (March 16, 1937), Personal files of Del Ritchhart.

50   Mason, Illinois; digital images, Wendy Seyller.

51   Ltr to Mary O'Malley from her Aunt Jen dtd 7/14/1933, Assuming that Ma Gillmore was in fact the mother of Mary and Walter Lee.

52   *1900 US Census* of Buchanan County, IL, Sheet 9.

53   Walter's Obituary.

54   *1870 US Census* Scranton, Pennsylvania, 42. Age in June of 1870 listed as 8/12 (8 months) and the month of birth as Oct.

55   *1880 US Census* (Ancestry.com), Census listed age as 8 and birthplace as Penn.

56   Brother Walter's obituary, Listed name as Mike; but I am guessing his actual given name was Michael.

57   Ellen Schwanebeck, Correspondence with Ellen Schwanebeck.

58   *1900 United States Federal Census* (Provo, UT, USA: The Generations Network, Inc., 2004, www.ancestry.com, online publication. Original data—United States of America, Bureau of the Census. Twelfth Census of the United States, 1900. Washington, D.C.: National Archives and Records Administration, 1900). Census Place: Isabel, Fulton, Illinois; Roll: T623 302; Page: 3A; Enumeration District: 21, birth date: abt 1874, Birth place: Pennsylvania, Residence date: 1900, Residence place: Isabel, Fulton, Illinois.

59   *1920 United States Federal Census* (Provo, UT, USA: The Generations Network, Inc., 2005), www.ancestry.com, Online publication. Original data United States of America, Bureau of the Census. Fourteenth Census of the United States. Washington, D.C.: National Archives and Records Administration, 1920.T625, 2076 rolls). Census Place: Isabel, Fulton, Illinois; Roll: T625_369; Page: 1A; Enumeration District: 93; Image: 674, birth date: abt 1874, Birth place: Pennsylvania, Residence date: 1920, Residence place: Isabel, Fulton, Illinois.

60   Ancestry.com, *Pennsylvania 1910 Miracode Index* (Online publication -Provo, UT, USA: The Generations Network, Inc., 2000. Original data—Pennsylvania Miracode. Washington, D.C.: National Archives and Records Administration), birth date: abt 1872, Birth place: Pennsylvania, Residence date: 1910, Residence place: Lackawanna, Scranton, PA.

61   *1880 US Census* (Ancestry.com), Listed birthplace as Pennsylvania and age as 7. Since the census was in June, his birthday was probably in the Jan–May period of 1873.

62   *1900 US Census* Fulton County, IL, Listed age as 26 and birthday as Aug 1873. Enumeration date was June 5 and the enum district was 21.

63   *1900 US Census* Fulton County, IL, Enumeration date 5 Jun. District 21. Listed his birthday as

Aug 1873 which agrees with his listed age of 26.

64   *1900 US Census* Fulton County, IL, Listed age as 26 and birthday as Aug 1873. Enumeration date was June 5 and the enum district was 21.Enumeration date 5 Jun. District 21. Listed his birthday as Aug 1873 which agrees with his listed age of 26.

65   *1900 US Census* Fulton County, IL, listed her birthday as Feb 1874 and her age as 26, which all coincides.

66   *1920 United States Federal Census* (Provo, UT, USA: The Generations Network, Inc., 2005), www.ancestry.com, Online publication. Original data United States of America, Bureau of the Census. Fourteenth Census of the United States. Washington, D.C.: National Archives and Records Administration, 1920.T625, 2076 rolls). Census Place: Isabel, Fulton, Illinois; Roll: T625_369; Page: 1A; Enumeration District: 93; Image: 674, birth date: abt 1875, Birth place: Illinois, Residence date: 1920, Residence place: Isabel, Fulton, Illinois.

67   *1900 United States Federal Census* (Provo, UT, USA: The Generations Network, Inc., 2004, www.ancestry.com, online publication. Original data—United States of America, Bureau of the Census. Twelfth Census of the United States, 1900. Washington, D.C.: National Archives and Records Administration, 1900). Census Place: Isabel, Fulton, Illinois; Roll: T623 302; Page: 3A; Enumeration District: 21, birth date: abt 1874, Birth place: Illinois, Residence date: 1900, Residence place: Isabel, Fulton, Illinois.

68   *1920 US Census*, Fulton Co., IL.

69   Manito Historical Society—*Manito History*.

70   Ancestry.com, *Social Security Death Index* (Provo, UT, USA: The Generations Network, Inc., 2008), www.ancestry.com, [database online]. Original data: Social Security Administration. *Social Security Death Index, Master File*. Social Security Administration. Previously knew birth year, but not exact date. The Index agreed with the year, thus I believe it to be correct.

71   *1900 US Census* Fulton Co., Illinois, Listed age as 2 and birthdate as May 1898.

72   *1930 United States Federal Census* (Provo, UT, USA: The Generations Network, Inc., 2002), www.ancestry.com, Online publication. Original data United States of America, Bureau of the Census. Fifteenth Census of the United States. Washington, D.C.: National Archives and Records Administration, 1930.T626, 2,667 rolls). Census Place: Pleasant, Fulton, Illinois; Roll: 514; Page: 1A; Enumeration District: 40; Image: 657.0, birth date: abt 1899, Birth place: Illinois, Residence date: 1930, Residence place: Pleasant, Fulton, Illinois.

73   *1900 United States Federal Census* (Provo, UT, USA: The Generations Network, Inc., 2004, www.ancestry.com, online publication. Original data—United States of America, Bureau of the Census. Twelfth Census of the United States, 1900. Washington, D.C.: National Archives and Records Administration, 1900). Census Place: Isabel, Fulton, Illinois; Roll: T623 302; Page: 3A; Enumeration District: 21, birth date: abt 1898, Birth place: Illinois, Residence date: 1900, Residence place: Isabel, Fulton, Illinois.

74   *1920 United States Federal Census* (Provo, UT, USA: The Generations Network, Inc., 2005), www.ancestry.com, Online publication. Original data United States of America, Bureau of the Census. Fourteenth Census of the United States. Washington, D.C.: National Archives and Records Administration, 1920.T625, 2076 rolls). Census Place: Isabel, Fulton, Illinois; Roll: T625_369; Page: 1A; Enumeration District: 93; Image: 674, birth date: abt 1899, Birth place: Illinois, Residence date: 1920, Residence place: Isabel, Fulton, Illinois.

75   Ancestry.com, *Social Security Death Index* (Provo, UT, USA: The Generations Network, Inc., 2008), www.ancestry.com, [database online]. Original data: Social Security Administration. *Social Security Death Index, Master File.* Social Security Administration.

76   Ancestry.com, *Social Security Death Index* (Provo, UT, USA: The Generations Network, Inc., 2008), www.ancestry.com, [database online]. Original data: Social Security Administration. *Social Security Death Index, Master File.* Social Security Administration.

77   *1930 United States Federal Census* (Provo, UT, USA: The Generations Network, Inc., 2002), www.ancestry.com, Online publication. Original data United States of America, Bureau of the Census. Fifteenth Census of the United States. Washington, D.C.: National Archives and Records Administration, 1930.T626, 2,667 rolls). Census Place: Pleasant, Fulton, Illinois; Roll: 514; Page: 1A; Enumeration District: 40; Image: 657.0, birth date: abt 1898, Residence date: 1930, Residence place: Pleasant, Fulton, Illinois.

78   Ancestry.com, *Social Security Death Index* (Provo, UT, USA: The Generations Network, Inc., 2008), www.ancestry.com, [database online]. Original data: Social Security Administration. *Social Security Death Index, Master File.* Social Security Administration. Number: 357-56-5767; Issue State: Illinois; Issue Date: 1973. Birth date: 8 Apr 1896, Death date: Sep 1975, Death place: Ipava, Fulton, Illinois, United States of America.

79   1920 Census, Fulton Co., Ill, Roll T626_248, Pg 6B, ed 8, Image 0099.

80   *1920 United States Federal Census* (Provo, UT, USA: The Generations Network, Inc., 2005), www.ancestry.com, Online publication. Original data United States of America, Bureau of the Census. Fourteenth Census of the United States. Washington, D.C.: National Archives and Records Administration, 1920.T625, 2076 rolls). Census Place: Isabel, Fulton, Illinois; Roll: T625_369; Page: 1A; Enumeration District: 93; Image: 674, birth date: abt 1907, Birth place: Illinois, Residence date: 1920, Residence place: Isabel, Fulton, Illinois.

81   1920 Census, Fulton Co., Ill, Listed John as being 9 years old. The census was conducted 5–7 January, so he was probably born in 1910.

82   *1920 United States Federal Census* (Provo, UT, USA: The Generations Network, Inc., 2005), www.ancestry.com, Online publication. Original data United States of America, Bureau of the Census. Fourteenth Census of the United States. Washington, D.C.: National Archives and Records Administration, 1920.T625, 2076 rolls). Census Place: Isabel, Fulton, Illinois; Roll: T625_369; Page: 1A; Enumeration District: 93; Image: 674, birth date: abt 1911, Birth place: Illinois, Residence date: 1920, Residence place: Isabel, Fulton, Illinois.

83   *1920 US Census*, Kingman, Kansas, Union County, Julia listed as age 35.

84   *1930 US Census*, Union Township, Kingman Co., Kansas, Julia listed living with her father, who was 75. She was 46.

85   Ancestry.com., *Kansas State Census Collection, 1855–1925* (Provo, UT, USA, Ancestry.com Operations Inc, 2009), www.ancestry.com, Database online.

86   *1900 US Census* Allens Grove Township, Mason County, Illinois.

87   *1930 US Census*, Union Township, Kingman Co., Kansas, Daniel and his family of wife and seven children are listed.

88   *1880 US Census* Mason County, Illinois, Pg 15. also listed OMally's as son, dau, brother & sister-in-law.

89   *1930 United States Federal Census* (Provo, UT, USA: The Generations Network, Inc., 2002),

www.ancestry.com, Online publication. Original data United States of America, Bureau of the Census. Fifteenth Census of the United States. Washington, D.C.: National Archives and Records Administration, 1930.T626, 2,667 rolls). Census Place: Denver, Denver, Colorado; Roll: 237; Page: 4B; Enumeration District: 115; Image: 740.0.

90   *1920 United States Federal Census* (Provo, UT, USA: The Generations Network, Inc., 2005), www.ancestry.com, Online publication. Original data United States of America, Bureau of the Census. Fourteenth Census of the United States. Washington, D.C.: National Archives and Records Administration, 1920.T625, 2076 rolls). Census Place: Denver, Denver, Colorado; Roll: T625_159; Page: 4A; Enumeration District: 110.

91   Ancestry.com, *Social Security Death Index* (Provo, UT, USA: The Generations Network, Inc., 2008), www.ancestry.com, [database online]. Original data: Social Security Administration. *Social Security Death Index, Master File*. Social Security Administration. Number: 495-20-2866; Issue State: Missouri; Issue Date: Before 1951.

92   *1930 United States Federal Census* (Provo, UT, USA: The Generations Network, Inc., 2002), www.ancestry.com, Online publication. Original data United States of America, Bureau of the Census. Fifteenth Census of the United States. Washington, D.C.: National Archives and Records Administration, 1930.T626, 2,667 rolls). Kansas City, Jackson, Missouri, ED 80, roll 1195, image 636.0.

93   *1930 United States Federal Census* (Provo, UT, USA: The Generations Network, Inc., 2002), www.ancestry.com, Online publication. Original data United States of America, Bureau of the Census. Fifteenth Census of the United States. Washington, D.C.: National Archives and Records Administration, 1930.T626, 2,667 rolls). Census Place: Kansas City, Jackson, Missouri; Roll: 1195; Page: 26A; Enumeration District: 80; Image: 636.0.

94   *1910 US Census* Mason County, Illinois.

95   Mason County Members of the Church of Jesus Christ of Latter-Day Saints, *Mason Co., Illinois Original Birth Records*.

96   *1910 US Census* Mason County, Illinois, Listed 7 children which is what Sarah had according to census. Did not list Helen only Nellie matched up. I assume they are the same.

97   Probate of Sarah J. McCabe, listed date of death of Walter.

98   Lists Thomas, Sarah and Walter McCabe as being buried in St. Frederick's Catholic Cemetery.

99   Delbert Ritchhart. *Personal Recollections*, 2010 (San Diego, CA; privately held by Del Ritchhart).

100 Colorado, City and County of Denver, Certificate of Marriage; Personal files of Del Ritchhart.

101 *Mason Co. Illinois Birth Records* 977.31 M395.Ma-3 (LA City Library), Original Birth Records, 1877–1900.

102 Ancestry.com, *Public Member Trees* (Provo, UT, USA, The Generations Network, Inc., 2006), www.ancestry.com, Database online. Record for Mary Loretta O Malley.

103 *1930 United States Federal Census* (Provo, UT, USA: The Generations Network, Inc., 2002), www.ancestry.com, Online publication. Original data United States of America, Bureau of the Census. Fifteenth Census of the United States. Washington, D.C.: National Archives and Records Administration, 1930.T626, 2,667 rolls). Las Animas, Bent, Colorado, ED 8, roll 230, page , image 619.0.

104 *1900 United States Federal Census* (Provo, UT, USA: The Generations Network, Inc., 2004,

www.ancestry.com, online publication. Original data—United States of America, Bureau of the Census. Twelfth Census of the United States, 1900. Washington, D.C.: National Archives and Records Administration, 1900). Census Place: Precincts 1, 3–8, Bent, Colorado; Roll: T623 121; Page: 10A; Enumeration District: 3, birth date: abt 1886, Birth place: Colorado, Residence date: 1900, Residence place: Precincts 1, 3–8, Bent, Colorado.

105   *1910 United States Federal Census* (Provo, UT, USA: The Generations Network, Inc., 2006), www.ancestry.com, Online publication. Original data United States of America, Bureau of the Census. Thirteenth Census of the United States. Washington, D.C.: National Archives and Records Administration, 1910.T624, 1,178 rolls). Census Place: Precinct 9, Bent, Colorado; Roll: T624_112; Page: 3B; Enumeration District: 6; Image: 718, birth date: abt 1887, Birth place: Colorado, Residence date: 1910, Residence place: Precinct 9, Bent, Colorado.

106   *1920 United States Federal Census* (Provo, UT, USA: The Generations Network, Inc., 2005), www.ancestry.com, Online publication. Original data United States of America, Bureau of the Census. Fourteenth Census of the United States. Washington, D.C.: National Archives and Records Administration, 1920.T625, 2076 rolls). Census Place: Las Animas, Bent, Colorado; Roll: T625_155; Page: 6B; Enumeration District: 269; Image: 529, birth date: abt 1887, Birth place: Colorado, Residence date: 1920, Residence place: Las Animas, Bent, Colorado.

107   *1930 United States Federal Census* (Provo, UT, USA: The Generations Network, Inc., 2002), www.ancestry.com, Online publication. Original data United States of America, Bureau of the Census. Fifteenth Census of the United States. Washington, D.C.: National Archives and Records Administration, 1930.T626, 2,667 rolls). Census Place: Las Animas, Bent, Colorado; Roll: 230; Page: 3A; Enumeration District: 8; Image: 619.0. Record for Thomas F Dean.

108   Ancestry.com, *One World Tree*[SM] (Provo, UT, USA: The Generations Network, Inc., n.d.), www.ancestry.com, database online. Provo, UT, USA: The Generations Network, Inc.

109   Broderbund Family Archive #110, Vol. 1, Ed. 5, *Social Security Death Index: U.S.,* Date of Import: Jul 6, 1998, Internal Ref. #1.111.5.58264.131

110   Ancestry.com, *World War I Draft Registration Cards, 1917–1918* (Provo, UT, USA, The Generations Network, Inc., 2005), www.ancestry.com, Database online. Original data—United States, Selective Service System. World War I Selective Service System Draft Registration Cards, 1917–1918. Washington, D.C.: National Archives and Records Administration, M1509, 4,582 rolls. Registration Location: Bent County, Colorado; Roll: 1544478; Draft Board: 0, Birth date: 22 Jan 1889, Birth place: Residence date: Residence place: Not Stated, Bent, Colorado.

111   *1920 United States Federal Census* (Provo, UT, USA: The Generations Network, Inc., 2005), www.ancestry.com, Online publication. Original data United States of America, Bureau of the Census. Fourteenth Census of the United States. Washington, D.C.: National Archives and Records Administration, 1920.T625, 2076 rolls). Census Place: Salt Lake City Ward 4, Salt Lake, Utah; Roll: T625_1865; Page: 13A; Enumeration District: 137; Image: 341, birth date: abt 1889, Birth place: Illinois, Residence date: 1920, Residence place: Salt Lake City Ward 4, Salt Lake, Utah.

112   *1930 United States Federal Census* (Provo, UT, USA: The Generations Network, Inc., 2002), www.ancestry.com, Online publication. Original data United States of America, Bureau of the Census. Fifteenth Census of the United States. Washington, D.C.: National Archives and Records Administration, 1930.T626, 2,667 rolls). Census Place: Salt Lake City, Salt Lake, Utah; Roll: 2420; Page: 5A; Enumeration District: 77; Image: 328.0, birth date: abt 1889, Birth place: Illinois, Residence date: 1930, Residence place: Salt Lake City, Salt Lake, Utah.

113 *Mason Co. Illinois Birth Records* 977.31 M395.Ma-3 (LA City Library), Birth information for Mary listed mother's age as 19. (Did the same for Walter Lee; but that not possible).

114 Meeting with Betsy & Mary O'Malley, Meeting in San Diego on Feb 16, 2009 to discuss family history.

115 Ancestry.com, *World War I Draft Registration Cards, 1917–1918* (Provo, UT, USA, The Generations Network, Inc., 2005), www.ancestry.com, Database online. Original data—United States, Selective Service System. World War I Selective Service System Draft Registration Cards, 1917–1918. Washington, D.C.: National Archives and Records Administration, M1509, 4,582 rolls. Roll 1544478, DraftBoard 0. Record for Walter Lee Omalley.

116 *1930 US Census* listed Lee's mother's birthplace as Colorado.

117 *1930 US Census* listed Lee's mother's birthplace as Colorado.

118 Ancestry.com, *Public Member Trees* (Provo, UT, USA, The Generations Network, Inc., 2006), www.ancestry.com, Database online. Record for Elizabeth Kyle.

119 *1930 US Census*, Buchanan Co., MO.

120 Correspondence with "Cottondilla" (Cottondilla was married to the Grandson of Walter and Bessie O'Malley).

121 *1920 United States Federal Census* (Provo, UT, USA: The Generations Network, Inc., 2005), www.ancestry.com, Online publication. Original data United States of America, Bureau of the Census. Fourteenth Census of the United States. Washington, D.C.: National Archives and Records Administration, 1920.T625, 2076 rolls). Census Place: Denver, Denver, Colorado; Roll: T625_159; Page: 4A; Enumeration District: 110.

122 Ancestry.com, *Social Security Death Index* (Provo, UT, USA: The Generations Network, Inc., 2008), www.ancestry.com, [database online]. Original data: Social Security Administration. *Social Security Death Index, Master File*. Social Security Administration. Number: 488-56-6005; Issue State: Missouri; Issue Date: 1965–1966.

123 *1930 United States Federal Census* (Provo, UT, USA: The Generations Network, Inc., 2002), www.ancestry.com, Online publication. Original data United States of America, Bureau of the Census. Fifteenth Census of the United States. Washington, D.C.: National Archives and Records Administration, 1930.T626, 2,667 rolls). Census Place: St Joseph, Buchanan, Missouri; Roll: 1178; Page: 17A; Enumeration District: 48; Image: 1066.0.

124 *1910 United States Federal Census* (Provo, UT, USA: The Generations Network, Inc., 2006), www.ancestry.com, Online publication. Original data United States of America, Bureau of the Census. Thirteenth Census of the United States. Washington, D.C.: National Archives and Records Administration, 1910.T624, 1,178 rolls). Census Place: St Joseph Ward 9, Buchanan, Missouri.

125 *1920 United States Federal Census* (Provo, UT, USA: The Generations Network, Inc., 2005), www.ancestry.com, Online publication. Original data United States of America, Bureau of the Census. Fourteenth Census of the United States. Washington, D.C.: National Archives and Records Administration, 1920.T625, 2076 rolls). Census Place: St Joseph Ward 9, Buchanan, Missouri; Roll: T625_907; Page: 11A; Enumeration District: 125.

126 *1920 US Census*, Denver, CO, Listed on same page as Mary and Thomas Hyland.

127 Mary Dean, Mary Dean's Address Book/diary, Personal files of Del Ritchhart.

128 *1930 US Census*, Fulton Co., Illinois.

129 *1930 United States Federal Census* (Provo, UT, USA: The Generations Network, Inc., 2002), www.ancestry.com, Online publication. Original data United States of America, Bureau of the Census. Fifteenth Census of the United States. Washington, D.C.: National Archives and Records Administration, 1930.T626, 2,667 rolls). Census Place: Pleasant, Fulton, Illinois; Roll: 514; Page: 1A; Enumeration District: 40; Image: 657.0, birth date: abt 1926, Birth place: Residence date: 1930, Residence place: Pleasant, Fulton, Illinois.

130 *1930 US Census*, Fulton Co., Illinois, Pleasant Township. Roll T626_514, Enum dist 40, Supervisor dist 13.

131 *1930 United States Federal Census* (Provo, UT, USA: The Generations Network, Inc., 2002), www.ancestry.com, Online publication. Original data United States of America, Bureau of the Census. Fifteenth Census of the United States. Washington, D.C.: National Archives and Records Administration, 1930.T626, 2,667 rolls). Census Place: Pleasant, Fulton, Illinois; Roll: 514; Page: 1A; Enumeration District: 40; Image: 657.0, birth date: abt 1928, Residence date: 1930, Residence place: Pleasant, Fulton, Illinois.

132 Ancestry.com, *Social Security Death Index* (Provo, UT, USA: The Generations Network, Inc., 2008), www.ancestry.com, [database online]. Original data: Social Security Administration. *Social Security Death Index, Master File*. Social Security Administration.

133 Ancestry.com, *U.S. Phone and Address Directories*, 1993–2002 (Provo, UT, USA: The Generations Network, Inc., 2005), www.ancestry.com, Online publication -Ancestry.com. *U.S. Phone and Address Directories*, 1993–2002 [database online]. Provo, UT, USA: The Generations Network, Inc., 2005.Original data -1993–2002 White Pages. Little Rock, AR, USA: Acxiom Corporation.

134 Ancestry.com, *U.S. Public Records Index* (Provo, UT, USA: The Generations Network, Inc., 2007), www.ancestry.com, [database online]. Original data compiled from various U.S. public records.

135 Ancestry.com, *U.S. Public Records Index* (Provo, UT, USA: The Generations Network, Inc., 2007), www.ancestry.com, [database online]. Original data compiled from various U.S. public records. Record for Lloyd C Schwanebeck.

136 *1930 US Census*, Union Township, Kingman Co., Kansas, Listed his age as 3 8/12. Census dated Apr 25, 1930.

137 *1930 US Census*, Union Township, Kingman Co., Kansas, Listed age as 1 4/12. Census dated Apr 25, 1930.

138 *1920 United States Federal Census* (Provo, UT, USA: The Generations Network, Inc., 2005), www.ancestry.com, Online publication. Original data United States of America, Bureau of the Census. Fourteenth Census of the United States. Washington, D.C.: National Archives and Records Administration, 1920.T625, 2076 rolls). Census Place: Las Animas, Bent, Colorado; Roll: T625_155; Page: 6B; Enumeration District: 269; Image: 529, birth date: abt 1914, Birth place: Colorado, Residence date: 1920, Residence place: Las Animas, Bent, Colorado.

139 *1920 United States Federal Census* (Provo, UT, USA: The Generations Network, Inc., 2005), www.ancestry.com, Online publication. Original data United States of America, Bureau of the Census. Fourteenth Census of the United States. Washington, D.C.: National Archives and Records Administration, 1920.T625, 2076 rolls). Census Place: Las Animas, Bent, Colorado; Roll: T625_155; Page: 6B; Enumeration District: 269. Record for Frances Dean.

140 *1930 United States Federal Census* (Provo, UT, USA: The Generations Network, Inc., 2002),

www.ancestry.com, Online publication. Original data United States of America, Bureau of the Census. Fifteenth Census of the United States. Washington, D.C.: National Archives and Records Administration, 1930.T626, 2,667 rolls). Census Place: Denver, Denver, Colorado; Roll: 236; Page: 22A; Enumeration District: 86; Image: 268.0. Record for Frances Gallagher.

141 Obituary for Frances Dean Gallagher.

142 *1920 United States Federal Census* (Provo, UT, USA: The Generations Network, Inc., 2005), www.ancestry.com, Online publication. Original data United States of America, Bureau of the Census. Fourteenth Census of the United States. Washington, D.C.: National Archives and Records Administration, 1920.T625, 2076 rolls). Census Place: East Pittsburgh Ward 2, Allegheny, Pennsylvania; Roll: T625_1511; Page: 4A; Enumeration District: 93. Record for William P Gallgher.

143 *1920 United States Federal Census* (Provo, UT, USA: The Generations Network, Inc., 2005), www.ancestry.com, Online publication. Original data United States of America, Bureau of the Census. Fourteenth Census of the United States. Washington, D.C.: National Archives and Records Administration, 1920.T625, 2076 rolls). Census Place: East Pittsburgh Ward 2, Allegheny, Pennsylvania; Roll: T625_1511; Page: 4A; Enumeration District: 93. Record for William P Gallgher.

144 *1920 United States Federal Census* (Provo, UT, USA: The Generations Network, Inc., 2005), www.ancestry.com, Online publication. Original data United States of America, Bureau of the Census. Fourteenth Census of the United States. Washington, D.C.: National Archives and Records Administration, 1920.T625, 2076 rolls). Census Place: Las Animas, Bent, Colorado; Roll: T625_155; Page: 6B; Enumeration District: 269; Image: 529, birth date: abt 1915, Birth place: Colorado, Residence date: 1920, Residence place: Las Animas, Bent, Colorado.

145 Ancestry.com, *Social Security Death Index* (Provo, UT, USA: The Generations Network, Inc., 2008), www.ancestry.com, [database online]. Original data: Social Security Administration. *Social Security Death Index, Master File*. Social Security Administration. Number: 524-34-6670; Issue State: Colorado; Issue Date: Before 1951. Birth date: 6 Aug 1915, Death date: 15 Oct 1995, Death place: Loveland, Larimer, Colorado, United States of America.

146 Ancestry.com, *U.S. Public Records Index, Volume 2* (Provo, UT, USA, Ancestry.com Operations, Inc., 2010), www.ancestry.com, Database online. Record for Helen J Ritchhart.

147 *Ancestry Family Trees* (Online publication—Provo, UT, USA: The Generations Network. Original data: Family Tree files submitted by Ancestry members). http://trees.ancestry.com/pt/AMTCitationRedir.aspx?tid=2906494&pid=-76072090.

148 *Bent County Democrat* Article, Files of Del Ritchhart.

149 *1930 United States Federal Census* (Provo, UT, USA: The Generations Network, Inc., 2002), www.ancestry.com, Online publication. Original data United States of America, Bureau of the Census. Fifteenth Census of the United States. Washington, D.C.: National Archives and Records Administration, 1930.T626, 2,667 rolls). La Junta, Otero, Colorado, ED 8, roll 248, image 99.0.

150 *1930 United States Federal Census* (Provo, UT, USA: The Generations Network, Inc., 2002), www.ancestry.com, Online publication. Original data United States of America, Bureau of the Census. Fifteenth Census of the United States. Washington, D.C.: National Archives and Records Administration, 1930.T626, 2,667 rolls). La Junta, Otero, Colorado, ED 8, roll 248, image 99.0. Record for Dalbert Ritchhart.

151   Ancestry.com, *Public Member Trees* (Provo, UT, USA, The Generations Network, Inc., 2006), www.ancestry.com, Database online. Record for Grace Azetta Bush.

152   *1920 United States Federal Census* (Provo, UT, USA: The Generations Network, Inc., 2005), www.ancestry.com, Online publication. Original data United States of America, Bureau of the Census. Fourteenth Census of the United States. Washington, D.C.: National Archives and Records Administration, 1920.T625, 2076 rolls). Census Place: Las Animas, Bent, Colorado; Roll: T625_155; Page: 6B; Enumeration District: 269; Image: 529, birth date: abt 1917, Birth place: Colorado, Residence date: 1920, Residence place: Las Animas, Bent, Colorado.

153   Ancestry.com, *Social Security Death Index* (Provo, UT, USA: The Generations Network, Inc., 2008), www.ancestry.com, [database online]. Original data: Social Security Administration. *Social Security Death Index, Master File*. Social Security Administration, 2005.

154   Ancestry.com, *Social Security Death Index* (Provo, UT, USA: The Generations Network, Inc., 2008), www.ancestry.com, [database online]. Original data: Social Security Administration. *Social Security Death Index, Master File*. Social Security Administration. Number: 522-12-0700; Issue State: Colorado; Issue Date: Before 1951. Record for Thomas Dean.

155   Ancestry.com, *Public Member Trees* (Provo, UT, USA, The Generations Network, Inc., 2006), www.ancestry.com, Database online. Record for Darrol Dean.

156   Ancestry.com, *Social Security Death Index* (Provo, UT, USA: The Generations Network, Inc., 2008), www.ancestry.com, [database online]. Original data: Social Security Administration. *Social Security Death Index, Master File*. Social Security Administration. Number: 524-24-8710; Issue State: Colorado; Issue Date: Before 1951. Record for Bessie B. Dean.

157   Headstone Las Animas Cemetery, Observed during visit to Las Animas in May 2005.

158   *1920 US Census*, Salt Lake City, Dist 137, Division 77.

159   Annotated Photo from Helen Jane Ritchhart listed age of Marian as being 71 and the photo was dated Nov 1987.

160   *1920 United States Federal Census* (Provo, UT, USA: The Generations Network, Inc., 2005), www.ancestry.com, Online publication. Original data United States of America, Bureau of the Census. Fourteenth Census of the United States. Washington, D.C.: National Archives and Records Administration, 1920.T625, 2076 rolls). Census Place: Salt Lake City Ward 4, Salt Lake, Utah; Roll: T625_1865; Page: 13A; Enumeration District: 137; Image: 341, birth date: abt 1917, Birth place: Colorado, Residence date: 1920, Residence place: Salt Lake City Ward 4, Salt Lake, Utah.

161   Photo narrated by Helen Jane Ritchhart. Indicated Joe was 73 on a picture taken in November 1987.

162   Mary Dean, Mary Dean's Address Book/diary, Personal files of Del Ritchhart, entry stating W.L. O'Malley Jr. made First Holy Communion June 2, 1929.

163   Heather O'Malley, Lee's wife. Lee was cremated and his ashes spread at sea near Orcha Island where he lived in his later years.

164   Ancestry.com, *U.S. Public Records Index, Volume 1* (Provo, UT, USA, Ancestry.com Operations, Inc., 2010), www.ancestry.com, Database online. Record for Ml Delbert A Ritchhart.

165   Ancestry.com, *U.S. Public Records Index, Volume 1* (Provo, UT, USA, Ancestry.com Operations, Inc., 2010), www.ancestry.com, Database online. Record for Ml Delbert A Ritchhart.

166   Ancestry.com, *U.S. Public Records Index, Volume 1* (Provo, UT, USA, Ancestry.com Operations,

Inc., 2010), www.ancestry.com, Database online. Record for Joanne S Ritchhart.

167 Ancestry.com, *U.S. Public Records Index, Volume 1* (Provo, UT, USA, Ancestry.com Operations, Inc., 2010), www.ancestry.com, Database online. Record for Joanne S Ritchhart.

168 Ancestry.com, *U.S. Public Records Index, Volume 1* (Provo, UT, USA, Ancestry.com Operations, Inc., 2010), www.ancestry.com, Database online. Record for Joanne S Ritchhart.

169 Ancestry.com, *U.S. Public Records Index, Volume 2* (Provo, UT, USA, Ancestry.com Operations, Inc., 2010), www.ancestry.com, Database online. Record for Joanne S Ritchhart.

170 State of Colorado, Death Certificate.

171 Curtis Dean's GENI.COM inputs.

172 Ancestry.com, *Social Security Death Index* (Provo, UT, USA: The Generations Network, Inc., 2008), www.ancestry.com, [database online]. Original data: Social Security Administration. *Social Security Death Index, Master File*. Social Security Administration. Number: 524-44-9184; Issue State: Colorado; Issue Date: 1953. Record for Darol E. Dean.

173 Ancestry.com, *Social Security Death Index* (Provo, UT, USA: The Generations Network, Inc., 2008), www.ancestry.com, [database online]. Original data: Social Security Administration. *Social Security Death Index, Master File*. Social Security Administration. Number: 524-44-9184; Issue State: Colorado; Issue Date: 1953. Birth date: 5 Jun 1941, Death date: 6 Sep 2005, Death place: Arvada, Jefferson, Colorado.

174 Ancestry.com, *California Marriage Index, 1960–1985* (Provo, UT, USA, Ancestry.com Operations Inc, 2007), www.ancestry.com, Database online. Record for Darol E Dean.

Register Report for Frederic Schmidt

Generation 1

1   **FREDERIC*¹* SCHMIDT** was born in Mar 1822 in Baden-Württemberg, Germany. He died on 13 Oct 1872 in Indianapolis, Marion, Indiana, USA. He married **MARIA ELIZABETH HOLLIDAY** in 1849 in New York, USA. She was born on 08 Jan 1830 in Bavaria, Germany. She died on 04 Mar 1904 in Indianapolis, Indiana.

Notes for Frederic SCHMIDT: For over two years I could not locate Frederic and his wife, Maria, in New York City, even after checking census and City Directory data. Finally in Jan 2006, while at a GRA meeting at the San Diego Family History Center, one of the members helped me look again at the census data. After checking several spellings of Schmidt; she just typed in Frederick S and looked at all the surnames beginning with S. In checking Smith we found that the wife's and son's name and ages in the 1850 census were a match. Yeh! We were both elated!

Was listed in the 1872 Indianapolis City Directory as living at 75 N. Illinois St; but was not listed in either the 1872 or 1873 Directory. His wife and sons, however continued to be listed in the Indianapolis City Directory and Elizabeth, his wife, was listed in a later census as "widowed." I surmise therefore that he passed away in 1872. I later confirmed this in Marion Co. mortality records. However, his name was listed as "Fredrick Schmitt" (having been taken from hand written records a "d" could have been mistaken for a "t." It listed his address as 75 N. Illinois St. which agreed with the census and City Directory.

Since their youngest son Fred was born in NY in 1850 and they were in the Aug 1850 New York Census and the next child, Metilda, was born in Indianapolis in 1852, I surmise they moved to Indianapolis in the 1851–52 time frame.

I did find three Frederic Schmidts listed in the *Passenger & Immigration List* arriving in NY in 1845 and 1846 with dates of birth within a year of his. I needed to research the microfilm further. Having done that, the most likely candidate "Frederic Schmidt," age 24, arrived 8 Nov 1845 in NY from Le Havre on the *Argo*. Place of origin listed as Deutschland. I haven't found the passenger list yet or anything about the *Argo*. Departing from Le Havre makes sense as it is much closer from Württemberg than Bremen. Finally in April 2010 I had the good sense to check the Castle Garden Immigration List. After looking at the time frame 1840–1850, I found about 14 Frederic/k Schmidts. After going through each one individually, I found the 13th to be a butcher, age 22 from Württemberg arriving in NY City on the *Probus* on 18 Jan 1848—it all matched! I was finally comfortable that this was the Frederic that I was looking for. In checking further, however, it appears that Le Havre only has records of passengers for the period 1780 to 1840. Thus, my hopes of finding his parents' names or home village or city weren't helped.

I also found a Friedrich Heinrich Schmidt in the IGI. He was born 7 Feb 1822 in Blamdikow, Württemberg. However, in doing several place name searches, I couldn't find any such place. I ordered (8/2008) the microfilm to check it out (178144), but didn't find any additional information that was helpful.

Notes for Maria Elizabeth HOLLIDAY: The 1880 census listed Elizabeth as the head of household, implying that her husband was either dead or she was divorced. It also listed the areas where she and her husband were from, whereas, the 1930 census for Oscar Schmidt just listed his parents as being from Germany. The 1870 Census listed her as being from Prussia and Frederick from Württemberg.

The 1900 census showed her living with her son, William and that she was widowed. It indicated she had born 13 children of which 9 were alive (Cemetery lot records list Clarence and Elizabeth in graves #2–3, so I assumed they were children). The census also indicated she could read, write, and speak English. It also listed her name as Maria (later I learned her Permit for Burial listed her name as Maria Elizabeth). So she may have been named Maria Elizabeth, but gone by the name Elizabeth—which appears on all other records.

In talking with an assistant at the FHL in Salt Lake, he opined that Elizabeth's original last name was not Holliday because it is not a German name. He suggested that Feiertag or Feyertag might have been her name as it translates to Holliday (vacation) in German. In researching names, I could not find any Hollidays—thus I tend to agree with him. However, I have also checked for Feiertag/Feyertag whenever researching the Schmidt line and haven't found any promising connections.

The 1872 through 1874 Indianapolis City Directories listed "Mrs. E. Schmidt" as a Midwife. Interestingly, the 1887–1890 Directories listed her as a "Physician." Her obituary said that she was "one of the most prominent German charity organization workers in the city…".

Frederic SCHMIDT and Maria Elizabeth HOLLIDAY had the following children:

2   i.   FREDERICK[2] SCHMIDT was born in Jan 1850 in New York, USA. He died in May 1891. He married EUNICE *. She was born about 1850 in Indiana, USA.

     ii. METILDA SCHMIDT was born in 1852 in Indianapolis, Marion, Indiana, USA.

3   iii. CHARLES L. SCHMIDT was born in Jan 1855 in Indiana, USA. He married (2) MATILDA F. SWEET on 08 Jan 1879 in Indianapolis, Marion, Indiana, USA, daughter of John C. SWETT and Matilda ROTHERMEL. She was born in 1854 in Cincinnati, Clermont, Ohio, USA. She died on 15 Mar 1937 in Indianapolis, Marion, Indiana, USA.

     iv. ELIZABETH SCHMIDT was born about 1855 in Indianapolis, Hamilton, Indiana, USA. She died on 12 Aug 1894 in Indianapolis, Marion, Indiana, USA.

     v.   WILLIAM H. SCHMIDT was born in Sep 1856 in Indianapolis, Marion, Indiana, USA. He died on 25 Apr 1904 in Indianapolis, Marion, Indiana, USA. He married SARAH CURRY in 1898. She was born in Jan 1866. She died in Nov 1941.

          Notes for William H. SCHMIDT:

          The 1900 census shows his mother, his brother Edward, and two nephews and two nieces living in his household. I believe the children were those of his brother Fred because their father's birthplace was listed as NY Fred was the only child born in NY.

          William was at one time Marion County Treasurer according to his mother's obituary. According to his mother's obituary, at the time of her death William was in a sanatorium under the care of Dr. Fletcher.

In the book *The Germans in Indianapolis* I found William listed as "a passive member" of The Maennerchor Society. It listed his address which agreed with his 1900 census address. The name translates as "Men's Choir." The group initially promoted music from their homeland; but later turned into both an advocate for classical music and as a social club. It also listed F.H. Schmidt, and Edward; but not sure they were William's brothers.

4   vi.   LOUISA SCHMIDT was born in 1859 in Indianapolis, Marion, Indiana, USA. She died about 1934. She married EDWARD MATHEWS on 07 Nov 1878 in Indianapolis, Indiana.

     v.   CLARENCE SCHMIDT was born about 1861 in Indianapolis, Hamilton, Indiana, USA. He died in Feb 1873.

            Notes for Clarence SCHMIDT: Only by reviewing the burial plot records is their any record of Clarence. Since we know there were 13 children born to Marie Elizabeth, of which only 9 were living in 1900; it is a good assumption she had a couple children die very young or at birth. Clarence was probably one that died young.

5   viii. GEORGE W. SCHMIDT was born in Jan 1864 in Indianapolis, Marion, Indiana, USA. He died on 21 Aug 1943 in Wilmette, Cook, Illinois, USA. He married EMMA * in 1891 in Indianapolis, Indiana, daughter of UNK and Unk #2. She was born in Aug 1863 in Pennsylvania, USA.

6   ix.   LEONORA SCHMIDT was born in Oct 1865 in Indianapolis, Marion, Indiana, USA. She died on 24 Oct 1948. She married PHILIP HEUSER on 24 Jan 1893 in Marion, Indiana, USA.

     x.   EDWARD H. SCHMIDT was born in Mar 1868 in Indiana, USA. He married ELIZABETH S. She was born in 1875 in Michigan, USA.

7   xi.   OSCAR WEBER SCHMIDT was born in Aug 1871 in Indiana, USA. He died on 21 Aug 1943 in Wilmette, Cook, Illinois, USA. He married MARY LOUISE BOLLA in 1897 in Chicago, Cook, Illinois, USA, daughter of William Harry BOLLA and Lucinda Jane GARDNER. She was born in Jun 1873 in Kentucky. She died on 04 Oct 1940 in Chicago, Illinois (Cook county).

Generation 2

2.   **FREDERICK² SCHMIDT** (Frederic¹) was born in Jan 1850 in New York, USA. He died in May 1891. He married **EUNICE ***. She was born about 1850 in Indiana, USA.

Notes for Frederick SCHMIDT: Was still living at home during the time of the 1870 census and listed as a Clerk in Store.

The Indianapolis City Directory listed Fred and C.A. Schmidt as manufactures of Schmidts French Liquid Bluing & Writing Fluid. The address of 175 E. Market St. was the same as their mother's residence. Thus, assume they were working out of the house. The *1878 Polks City Directory* also listed him as a bluing manufacturer; but with an address of 260 Christian Avenue.

Frederick SCHMIDT and Eunice * had the following children:

  i. ISAAC FREDERICK*3* SCHMIDT was born on 02 Sep 1877 in Indianapolis, IN.

  ii. WILLIAM SCHMIDT was born about Aug 1879 in Indianapolis, IN.

8 iii. ARTHUR L SCHMIDT was born in 1881 in Indianapolis, IN. He married EDITH L. about 1907 in Indianapolis, Indiana. She was born about 1885 in Indiana, USA.

  iv. LULU C. SCHMIDT was born in 1882.

  v. BERTHA B. SCHMIDT was born in Dec 1884 in Indiana, USA.

3. **CHARLES L.*2* SCHMIDT** (Frederic*1*) was born in Jan 1855 in Indiana, USA. He married (2) **MATILDA F. SWEET** on 08 Jan 1879 in Indianapolis, Marion, Indiana, USA, daughter of John C. SWETT and Matilda ROTHERMEL. She was born in 1854 in Cincinnati, Clermont, Ohio, USA. She died on 15 Mar 1937 in Indianapolis, Marion, Indiana, USA.

Charles L. SCHMIDT and Matilda F. SWEET had the following children:

  i. NINA E*3* SCHMIDT was born in Jun 1880 in Indiana, USA. She died on 21 Sep 1948 in Indianapolis, Marion, Indiana, USA.

  ii. CHARLES L. SCHMIDT JR was born in Dec 1882 in Indiana, USA.

  iv. MATILDA E SCHMIDT was born in Dec 1882 in Indiana, USA. She married GEORGE O. LEHMAN.

  v. GEORGE G. SCHMIDT was born in Aug 1889 in Indiana, USA. He married ISORA A. UNKNOWN.

9 v. MAY IRENE SCHMIDT was born in May 1892 in Indiana, USA. She married RUSSELL L. BROUSE. He was born in 1889. He died in Jan 1960 in Indianapolis, Marion, Indiana, USA.

  vi. LOUIS SCHMIDT.

4. **LOUISA*2* SCHMIDT** (Frederic*1*) was born in 1859 in Indianapolis, Marion, Indiana, USA. She died about 1934. She married **EDWARD MATHEWS** on 07 Nov 1878 in Indianapolis, Indiana.

Notes for Louisa SCHMIDT: Edward's name is listed as Mathews in the Indiana WPA records.

Edward MATHEWS and Louisa SCHMIDT had the following children:

  i. LOUISE C.*3* MATHEWS. She married UNK MARTIN.

  ii. LEONORE MATHEWS. She died about 1947. She married UNK DORRANCE.

  iii. VIOLA MATHEWS. She died on 01 Jan 1953. She married UNK PATTERSON.

  iv. WILLIAM H. MATHEWS.

  v. OSCAR G. MATHEWS.

  vi. LOUIS E. MATHEWS.

10 vii. EDGAR MATHEWS. He died about 1921. He married MATTIE MCDANIEL.

5. **GEORGE W. SCHMIDT** (Frederic*1*) was born in Jan 1864 in Indianapolis, Marion, Indiana, USA. He died on 21 Aug 1943 in Wilmette, Cook, Illinois, USA. He married **EMMA** * in

1891 in Indianapolis, Indiana, daughter of UNK and Unk #2. She was born in Aug 1863 in Pennsylvania, USA.

George W. SCHMIDT and Emma * had the following children:

    i. OLIVER B SCHMIDT was born in Dec 1891.

    ii. EDDIE J. SCHMIDT was born in Jul 1894.

    iii. ARTHUR E. SCHMIDT was born in Nov 1898.

    iv. ALBERT SCHMIDT was born in Apr 1900.

6. **LEONORA SCHMIDT** (Frederic[1]) was born in Oct 1865 in Indianapolis, Marion, Indiana, USA. She died on 24 Oct 1948. She married **PHILIP HEUSER** on 24 Jan 1893 in Marion, Indiana, USA.

Philip HEUSER and Leonora SCHMIDT had the following child:

    i. METILDA C. HEUSER.

7. **OSCAR WEBER[2] SCHMIDT** (Frederic[1]) was born in Aug 1871 in Indiana, USA. He died on 21 Aug 1943 in Wilmette, Cook, Illinois, USA. He married **MARY LOUISE BOLLA** in 1897 in Chicago, Cook, Illinois, USA, daughter of William Harry BOLLA and Lucinda Jane GARDNER. She was born in Jun 1873 in Kentucky. She died on 04 Oct 1940 in Chicago, Illinois (Cook county).

Notes for Oscar Weber SCHMIDT: According to death certificate, was living with his daughter, Minnie Mae, when he passed away. Have a photo of his headstone that we took when we were at the cemetery in July 1999.

The 1930 Census indicates he was 27 when married. Thus, the wedding must have been after his 1897 birthday and before his 1898 birthday. It also indicated he was not a veteran.

Notes for Mary Louise BOLLA: Obtained the date of death from the Illinois State Death records, but when I ordered the death certificate I found out that this Mary B. (which I thought was Mary Beth) was a window whose husband was Benjamen. Since Mary Beth's husband died in 1943 and was named Oscar, this Mary B was the wrong person.

The 1920 Census from Wilmette indicated Mary's father was born in Prussia and her mother was from New Hampshire. In a letter from Memorial Park Cemetery regarding those buried in the lot purchased by Oscar Schmidt in 1931, it indicated Mary L. Schmidt was in grave three. Her maiden name might have begun with an "L," thus the reason for such a listing.

I surmise her maiden name was Bolla because the 1910 New Trier Census showed a Minnie Bolla (single), identified as Sister-in-law living with them. Also Cora B. Bridwell, another sister-in-law (widowed) was living with them. Cora's middle initial could have been her maiden name (Bolla). I am now (2009) questioning those assumptions. I can only find one Bolla in Kentucky in the 1880 census. I think I would have been able to trace her family if her name was really Bolla. In reexamining the wedding book from Fred and Fran's wedding, one of the guests was "Minnie M. Bolla," who I assume is Mary Beth's sister. They might also have changed the name from a much more difficult name to spell and pronounce? Later, while checking the 1880 census and finding the family listed as "Bollan," I thought I had identified the problem. However, in digitizing the data, the name was mistakenly translated with an "n" on the end. However, after further investigation I found that to be an error. It did, however, account for the family in 1880. I searched the 1880 Census for a Mary, born in Kentucky, with a father born in Germany and a mother born in NH. First choice was Mary L. Bollan! They might have dropped the "n," but I finally filled that hole. Checking further I found Mary, mother, and two of the children in the 1900 census, still living in Louisville; but listed as Bolla. In fact, I found her sister, Minnie, listed in the 1910, 1920 and 1930 census as Bolla.

Oscar Weber SCHMIDT and Mary Louise BOLLA had the following children:

11   i. MINNIE MAE[3] SCHMIDT was born on 16 Jun 1901. She died in Jun 1980 in Pasadena, Harris, Texas, United States of America. She married HARRY N KERR in 1926, son of Isaac N KERR and MILLISSA. He was born in May 1897 in Indiana, USA.

        ii. EDWARD B. SCHMIDT was born in 1906 in Illinois, USA.

        Notes for Edward B. SCHMIDT: Was listed in the 1930 census as being age 25. The census was on April 22, 1930. So if he was born before April, he was born in 1905; but if he was born after April 22, he was born in 1904.

        According to Joanne Ritchhart, her uncle Ed was married 8 or 9 times. He got an early start as the 1930 census showed him living at home at age 25 and that his first marriage was at age 24. Thus, I assume the first marriage didn't last a year!

12 iii. FREDERICK HENRY SCHMIDT was born on 11 Jun 1908 (Evanston, Illinois (St. Francis Hospital)). He died on 22 Nov 1982 in San Jose, Santa Clara, California, USA. He married FRANCES LOIS MCCONNELL on 07 Mar 1936 (Wilmette Baptist Church, Park Ridge, Illinois), daughter of Russell Norman MCCONNELL and Mary Myrtle DYE. She was born on 23 Jul 1910 in Oklahoma City, Oklahoma, Oklahoma, USA. She died on 24 Jan 1978 in San Jose, Santa Clara, California, USA.

Generation 3

8. **ARTHUR L[3] SCHMIDT** (Frederick[2], Frederic[1]) was born in 1881 in Indianapolis, IN. He married **EDITH L.** about 1907 in Indianapolis, Indiana. She was born about 1885 in Indiana, USA.

Notes for Arthur L SCHMIDT: The 1900 census for William Schmidt had a line entry for a nephew born in 1881 who was a apprentice, but lined out the name. I assumed he had been living in the household, but might have recently moved out.

Arthur L SCHMIDT and Edith L. had the following child:

      i. ROBERT R[4] SCHMIDT was born in 1914 in Indiana, USA.

9. **MAY IRENE[3] SCHMIDT** (Charles L.[2], Frederic[1]) was born in May 1892 in Indiana, USA. She married **RUSSELL L. BROUSE**. He was born in 1889. He died in Jan 1960 in Indianapolis, Marion, Indiana, USA.

Russell L. BROUSE and May Irene SCHMIDT had the following children:

    i. BERT W.[4] BROUSE. He married MABLE H. *. She was born in 1911.

    ii. MARY CATHERINE BROUSE was born in 1917. She died on 04 Jun 1973 in Indianapolis, Marion, Indiana, USA.

10. **EDGAR**[3] **MATHEWS** (Louisa[2] SCHMIDT, Frederic[1] SCHMIDT). He died about 1921. He married **MATTIE MCDANIEL**.

Edgar MATTHEWS and Mattie MCDANIEL had the following child:

    i. EVELYN[4] MATHEWS. She died about 1922.

11. **MINNIE MAE**[3] **SCHMIDT** (Oscar Weber[2], Frederic[1]) was born on 16 Jun 1901. She died in Jun 1980 in Pasadena, Harris, Texas, United States of America. She married **HARRY N KERR** in 1926, son of Isaac N KERR and MILLISSA. He was born in May 1897 in Indiana, USA.

Notes for Minnie Mae SCHMIDT: Following the death of her husband, Min lived on their "gentleman's estate" farm north of Chicago in Wisconsin. She had a few sheep and I recall watching their Shetland sheep dog work the sheep. In her later years her daughter, Mary Lou and her husband, Tom, moved her to live near them in Texas.

Harry N. KERR and Minnie Mae SCHMIDT had the following child:

    i. MARY LOUISE[4] KERR was born in Aug 1927. She married TOM DAVIS.

12. **FREDERICK HENRY**[3] **SCHMIDT** (Oscar Weber[2], Frederic[1]) was born on 11 Jun 1908 (Evanston, Illinois (St. Francis Hospital)). He died on 22 Nov 1982 in San Jose, Santa Clara, California, USA. He married **FRANCES LOIS MCCONNELL** on 07 Mar 1936 (Wilmette Baptist Church, Park Ridge, Illinois), daughter of Russell Norman MCCONNELL and Mary Myrtle DYE. She was born on 23 Jul 1910 in Oklahoma City, Oklahoma, Oklahoma, USA. She died on 24 Jan 1978 in San Jose, Santa Clara, California, USA.

Notes for Frederick Henry SCHMIDT: Have a photo of his headstone that we took when we visited the cemetery in July 1999. Attended Dartmouth College where he was a basketball player. Practiced Corporate law in Chicago, Illinois.

Notes for Frances Lois MCCONNELL: According to Social Security records she was born in 1911 vice 1910. That, however, does not agree with the 1930 Census which listed her age as 19. Since the census was in April, prior to her birthday, that would make the census correct. Was a golfer and bridge player. Always told Joanne she wanted to die between her golf and bridge games. She died in her sleep a day after a golf game and she had bridge scheduled for the next day. Her death was likely caused by the stress and work of caring for her husband. Fred was bedridden with an amputated leg from diabetes and was very overweight. In her younger married life she was a John Robert Powers model, having completed the training after Fred's first heart attack.

Frederick Henry SCHMIDT and Frances Lois MCCONNELL had the following children:

13   i. JOANNE FRANCES[4] SCHMIDT was born on 12 Mar 1938 in Evanston, Cook, Illinois, USA. She married DELBERT ARTHUR RITCHHART on 28 Nov 1959 in Wilmette, Cook, Illinois, USA, son of Delbert Bush RITCHHART and Helen Jane DEAN. He was born on 08 May 1937 in Las Animas, Bent, Colorado, USA (11:16 a.m.).

14   ii.   FREDERICK WEBER SCHMIDT was born on 23 Oct 1943 in Evanston, Cook, Illinois, USA. He married JUDY AUSTIN on 16 May, daughter of Richard James AUSTIN and Dorothy Agnes RATTE. She was born on 13 Apr in Vermont, USA.

15   iii.   ELIZABETH JEAN SCHMIDT was born on 29 Aug 1940 in Evanston, Cook, Illinois, USA. She died on 22 Mar 2006 in San Diego, San Diego, California. She met (1) ALBERT CHARLES ESTABROOK, son of William Henry ESTABROOK and Phoebe GAY. He was born on 28 Dec 1929 in Monterey, California, USA. He died on 05 Feb 2007 in San Diego, San Diego, California, USA. She married (2) ARMIN KAMPMAN on 07 Apr 1979 in San Diego, San Diego, California, USA. She married (3) FRED WOLF, son of George Dorr WOLF Jr. and Margaret Winifred HURLBUTT. He was born in Illinois.

Generation 4

13. **JOANNE FRANCES⁴ SCHMIDT** (Frederick Henry³, Oscar Weber², Frederic¹) was born on 12 Mar 1938 in Evanston, Cook, Illinois, USA. She married **DELBERT ARTHUR RITCHHART** on 28 Nov 1959 in Wilmette, Cook, Illinois, USA, son of Delbert Bush RITCHHART and Helen Jane DEAN. He was born on 08 May 1937 in Las Animas, Bent, Colorado, USA (11:16 a.m.).

Delbert Arthur RITCHHART and Joanne Frances SCHMIDT had the following children:
    i.   CHERYL ANN⁵ RITCHHART was born on 30 Aug 1960 in Honolulu, Hawaii, USA. She married RONALD G. SHORT on 22 Sep 1984 in Reno, Washoe, Nevada, USA, son of Terry Vern SHORT and Maryann WOOD. He was born on 20 Jun 1958 in Palo Alto, San Mateo, California, USA.

    ii.   DEBORA JANE RITCHHART was born on 29 Sep 1961 in Evanston, Cook, Illinois, USA. She married ERIC STERLING CANTRELL on 24 Sep 1993 in San Diego, California, USA (Elim Chapel), son of Richard Ellsworth CANTRELL Jr. and Sharon Roxie RALPH. He was born on 10 Nov 1964 in Encino, Los Angeles, California, USA.

    iii. LINDA MARIE RITCHHART was born on 07 Jun 1964 in San Diego, San Diego, California, USA. She married DOUGLAS GREGORY WIMER on 18 Mar 1986 in San Diego, San Diego, California, USA, son of Franklin Bernard WIMER and Margery Anne LOEFFLER. He was born on 10 Dec 1960 in Pittsburgh, Allegheny, Pennsylvania, USA.

14. **FREDERICK WEBER⁴ SCHMIDT** (Frederick Henry³, Oscar Weber², Frederic¹) was born on 23 Oct 1943 in Evanston, Cook, Illinois, USA. He married **JUDY AUSTIN** on 16 May, daughter of Richard James AUSTIN and Dorothy Agnes RATTE. She was born on 13 Apr in Vermont, USA.

Notes for Frederick Weber SCHMIDT: Fred won two gold medals and a bronze in the 1964 Olympics in Tokyo, Japan in the butterfly. He attended Indiana University and got his law degree from Northwestern University. He entered the Navy following graduation and became a Navy SEAL. He participated in the Gemini astronaut recoveries off of Hawaii and was also in the Vietnam war. He left the Navy and entered law practice in San Diego. He later went into real estate development and was a partner in Doerring and Associates.

Fred and Judy later moved to Pagosa Springs, CO around 1988 and were still there in 2005. All their children graduated from Pagosa Springs High School.

Frederick Weber SCHMIDT and Judy AUSTIN had the following children:

    i. ALEXA[5] SCHMIDT was born on 04 Feb 1977 in San Diego, San Diego, CA, USA. She married TOM HEINICKE.

    ii. AUSTIN SCHMIDT was born on 30 Aug 1979 in San Diego, San Diego, CA, USA.

    iii. BRAD SCHMIDT was born on 17 Feb 1982 in San Diego, San Diego, CA, USA.

16   iv. LINDSEY SCHMIDT was born on 17 Jan 1984 in San Diego, San Diego, CA, USA.

15. **ELIZABETH JEAN[4] SCHMIDT** (Frederick Henry[3], Oscar Weber[2], Frederic[1]) was born on 29 Aug 1940 in Evanston, Cook, Illinois, USA. She died on 22 Mar 2006 in San Diego, San Diego, California. She met (1) **ALBERT CHARLES ESTABROOK**, son of William Henry ESTABROOK and Phoebe GAY. He was born on 28 Dec 1929 in Monterey, California, USA. He died on 05 Feb 2007 in San Diego, San Diego, California, USA. She married (2) **ARMIN KAMPMAN** on 07 Apr 1979 in San Diego, San Diego, California, USA. She married (3) **FRED WOLF**, son of George Dorr WOLF Jr. and Margaret Winifred HURLBUTT. He was born in Illinois.

Notes for Albert Charles ESTABROOK: Albert and Betty met in San Jose around 1998 and remained partners until their deaths, about one year apart. Albert grew up in the Monterey area, the son of parents of modest means. Albert started working at a very early age and learned the butcher trade. He served in the Korean war and was stationed in Korea. He later returned to the bay area and lived for many years on the east side of San Jose. He was a railroad hobbiest and also liked restoring old cars. He and Betty moved to San Diego around 2002, having been encouraged by Betty's sister, Joanne, and her husband, Del. They lived in the Rancho Bernardo area. Albert had suffered from cancer before the move; but it had been in remission. Following Betty's death from ovarian cancer in 2006, Al's cancer returned and he eventually succumbed to it in 2007.

Albert and Betty never married, although, they did become engaged around 2004.

Fred WOLF and Elizabeth Jean SCHMIDT had the following children:

17   i. FRED WOLF was born on 30 Jul 1963 in Evanston, Cook, Illinois, USA. He married JODI LYNNE FELTON on 16 May 1987 in Brazos, Texas, daughter of William Albert FELTON Jr. and Diana Darlene FUSON. She was born on 02 Mar 1965 in Brooks, Texas.

    ii. JEFFREY CHARLES WOLF was born in Evanston, Cook, Illinois, USA. He married VALERIE ALICE WASSER on 21 Oct 1995 in Phoenix, Maricopa, Arizona, USA.

Generation 5

16. **LINDSEY^5 SCHMIDT** (Frederick Weber^4, Frederick Henry^3, Oscar Weber^2, Frederic^1) was born on 17 Jan 1984 in San Diego, San Diego, California, USA.

Lindsey SCHMIDT had the following child:

     i. REBECCA^6 SCHMIDT.

17. **FRED WOLF** (Elizabeth Jean^4 SCHMIDT, Frederick Henry^3 SCHMIDT, Oscar Weber^2 SCHMIDT, Frederic^1 SCHMIDT) was born on 30 Jul 1963 in Evanston, Cook, Illinois, USA. He married **JODI LYNNE FELTON** on 16 May 1987 in Brazos, Texas, daughter of William Albert FELTON Jr. and Diana Darlene FUSON. She was born on 02 Mar 1965 in Brooks, Texas.

Fred WOLF and Jodi Lynne FELTON had the following children:

     i. CODY WOLF was born on 17 Aug 1994 in Louisville, Jefferson, Kentucky, USA.

    ii. CAITLIN WOLF was born on 26 Jan 1997 in Spartanburg, South Carolina, USA.

1. **THOMAS**^{1} **MCCONNELL** was born about 1776. He died on 03 Oct 1843. He married **ELEANOR UNKNOWN**. She was born about 1764. She died on 04 Jan 1840.

Thomas MCCONNELL and Eleanor UNKNOWN had the following child:

2   i.   WILLIAM D.^{2} MCCONNELL was born on 07 Jul 1804 in Pennsylvania, USA. He died on Jan 1871 in Clover, Henry, Illinois, USA. He married CATHERINE MORTHLAND before 1835 in Pennsylvania, USA. She was born on 14 Nov 1812 in Pennsylvania, USA. She died on 01 Sep 1905 in Clover, Henry, Illinois, USA.

Generation 2

2. **WILLIAM D.**^{2} **MCCONNELL** (Thomas^1) was born on 07 Jul 1804 in Pennsylvania, USA. He died on 01 Jan 1871 in Clover, Henry, Illinois, USA. He married **CATHERINE MORTHLAND** before 1835 in Pennsylvania, USA. She was born on 14 Nov 1812 in Pennsylvania, USA. She died on 01 Sep 1905 in Clover, Henry, Illinois, USA.

William D. MCCONNELL and Catherine MORTHLAND had the following children:

3   i.   REBECA A.^{3} MCCONNELL was born on 29 Apr 1834 in Mifflin, Pennsylvania, USA. She died on 21 Feb 1859. She married JAMES M. BARTON on 21 Nov 1850 in Juniata Co., Penn.

     ii.   THOMAS SIMON MCCONNELL was born on 16 Apr 1837 in Juniata (then Mifflin) County, Pennsylvania. He died on 19 May 1897 in Clover, Henry, Illinois, USA.

     iii.   ELLEN JANE MCCONNELL was born on 03 Apr 1840 in Juniata (then Mifflin) County, Pennsylvania. She died on 29 Jan 1907 in Coin, Page, Iowa, USA.

4   iv.   JAMES ANDERSON MCCONNELL was born on 25 Jun 1842 in Juniata (then Mifflin) County, Pennsylvania. He died on 06 Dec 1904 in Phoenix, Maricopa, Arizona, USA. He married (1) MARGARET STITT on 29 Oct 1864 in Rock Island, Illinois, USA, daughter of William STITT and Margaret HARMONI. She was born on 25 May 1841 in Amberson, Franklin, Pennsylvania, USA. She died on 13 Apr 1871 in Henry, Illinois, United States. He married (2) MARY M. CONNOR on 10 May 1876. She was born about 1850 in Missouri, USA.

     v.   MARY ELIZABETH MCCONNELL was born on 21 Jan 1847 in Dry Run, Franklin, Pennsylvania, USA. She died on 08 Feb 1929.

     vi.   NANCY C. MCCONNELL was born about 1849 in Juniata (then Mifflin) County, Pennsylvania. She died in 1942 in Salida, Chaffee, Colorado ?.

5   vii.   MAGGIE M. C. MCCONNELL was born on 02 Nov 1852 in East Waterford, Juniata, Pennsylvania, USA. She died on 16 Jan 1930 in East Moline, Rock Island, Illinois, USA. She married JOHN WESLEY BURTON. He was born about 1855 in Schoharie, Schoharie, New York, United States. He died on 29 May 1883 in Henry County, Illinois, USA.

     viii.   WILLIAM DAVID MCCONNELL JR. was born on 26 Jun 1854 in Juniata, Pennsylvania,

USA. He died on 04 May 1940 in Lincoln, Nebraska, USA. He married MAGGIE *. She was born in 1865.

6   ix.   JOSEPH HENRY MARSHALL MCCONNELL was born on 28 Dec 1857 in Clover, Henry, Illinois, USA. He died on 23 Nov 1940 in Clover, Henry, Illinois, USA. He married (1) AMANDA MELISSA PAREGOY about 1888. She was born about 1858 in Ohio, USA. She died on 18 Apr 1927 in Clover, Henry, Illinois, USA. He married (2) AMANDA. She was born in 1859 in Ohio, USA.

Generation 3

3.   **REBECA A.**[3] **MCCONNELL** (William D.[2], Thomas[1]) was born on 29 Apr 1834 in Mifflin, Pennsylvania, USA. She died on 21 Feb 1859. She married **JAMES M. BARTON** on 21 Nov 1850 in Juniata Co., Penn.

James M. BARTON and Rebeca A. MCCONNELL had the following children:
     i.   MAGGIE[4] BARTON was born before 1860.
     ii.   WILLIAM BARTON.
     iii. HENRY BARTON was born before 1860.

4.   **JAMES ANDERSON**[3] **MCCONNELL** (William D.[2], Thomas[1]) was born on 25 Jun 1842 in Juniata (then Mifflin) County, Pennsylvania. He died on 06 Dec 1904 in Phoenix, Maricopa, Arizona, USA. He married (1) **MARGARET STITT** on 29 Oct 1864 in Rock Island, Illinois, USA, daughter of William STITT and Margaret HARMONI. She was born on 25 May 1841 in Amberson, Franklin, Pennsylvania, USA. She died on 13 Apr 1871 in Henry, Illinois, United States. He married (2) **MARY M. CONNOR** on 10 May 1876. She was born about 1850 in Missouri, USA.

Notes for James Anderson MCCONNELL: Illinois Marriages from Ancestry.com indicate a wedding date of Oct 29, 1864. The record is at the County Court Records, film #1428580-1428581.

Notes for Margaret STITT: 1880 Census listed name as Mary and place of birth as Missouri.

James Anderson MCCONNELL and Margaret STITT had the following children:
     i.   MAY[4] MCCONNELL was born about 1874. She died on 19 Jun 1888.
     ii.   FRANCES M. MCCONNELL was born about 1866 in Illinois, USA.
     iii. NANCY LOTTA MCCONNELL was born about 1867 in Illinois, USA.

7   iv.   RUSSELL NORMAN MCCONNELL was born on 22 Nov 1868 in Woodhull, Henry, Illinois, USA. He died on 27 Jan 1965 in Monrovia, Las Angeles, California, United States. He married MARY MYRTLE DYE between 1895–1896 in Oklahoma City, Oklahoma, USA, daughter of Alexander G DYE and Mary Caroline HUDSPETH. She was born on 16 Aug 1874 in Missouri, USA. She died on 09 May 1960 in Los Angeles, Los Angeles, California, USA.

     v.   ARMINDA MINNIE MCCONNELL was born in Mar 1870 in Clover, Henry, Illinois, United States. She died on 19 Jun 1888 in Kewanee, Henry, Illinois, United States.

She married GEORGE ANNIBIL on 09 Sep 1896 in McPherson, Kansas, USA.

vi. LILLY DALE MCCONNELL was born on 18 Dec 1872. She died on 20 Jan 1874 in Woodhull, Henry, Illinois, USA.

vii. WILLIAM STITT MCCONNELL was born on 17 Nov 1871 in Peoria, Peoria, Illinois, United States. He died on 27 Dec 1939 in Nampa, Canyon, Idaho, United States.

5. **MAGGIE M. C.**[3] **MCCONNELL** (William D.[2], Thomas[1]) was born on 02 Nov 1852 in East Waterford, Juniata, Pennsylvania, USA. She died on 16 Jan 1930 in East Moline, Rock Island, Illinois, USA. She married **JOHN WESLEY BURTON**. He was born about 1855 in Schoharie, Schoharie, New York, United States. He died on 29 May 1883 in Henry County, Illinois, USA.

John Wesley BURTON and Maggie M. C. MCCONNELL had the following child:

8   i. JESSIE FAY[4] BURTON was born on 02 Oct 1882 in Cambridge, Henry, Illinois, USA. She died on 16 May 1959 in Naperville, DuPage, Illinois, USA. She married MARTIN VINCENT NUGENT. He was born on 02 Sep 1877 in LaSalle, LaSalle, Illinois, United States. He died on 22 Jan 1939 in Ft. Myers, Lee, Florida, USA.

6. **JOSEPH HENRY MARSHALL**[3] **MCCONNELL** (William D.[2], Thomas[1]) was born on 28 Dec 1857 in Clover, Henry, Illinois, USA. He died on 23 Nov 1940 in Clover, Henry, Illinois, USA. He married (1) **AMANDA MELISSA PAREGOY** about 1888. She was born about 1858 in Ohio, USA. She died on 18 Apr 1927 in Clover, Henry, Illinois, USA. He married (2) **AMANDA**. She was born in 1859 in Ohio, USA.

Joseph Henry Marshall MCCONNELL and Amanda Melissa PAREGOY had the following children:

9   i. NELLIE M.[4] MCCONNELL was born about 1890 in Illinois, USA. She married ELVIN JEFFRIES. He was born in 1891 in Kentucky, USA.

ii. BLANCHE W. MCCONNELL was born about 1892 in Illinois, USA. She married ? ROSE.

10 iii. DAISY P. MCCONNELL was born about 1894 in Illinois, USA. She married EARL E HUNGATE. He was born in 1891 in Missouri, USA.

11 iv. GRACE OLIVE MCCONNELL was born about 1896 in Illinois, USA. She married JAMES T. LASHBROOK on 05 Feb 1913 in Henry, Illinois, USA. He was born on 02 Jun 1887 in Illinois, USA.

12   v. FRANK ERNEST MCCONNELL was born on 12 Nov 1896 in Henry County, Illinois, USA. He died on 22 Aug 1968 in Cambridge, Henry, Illinois, USA. He married NORMA BESS POPPY on 15 Dec 1920 in Cambridge, Henry, Illinois, USA, daughter of John POPPY and Martha L. She was born about 1895 in Illinois, USA. She died in Apr 1984 in Cambridge, Henry, Illinois, USA.

vi. KATIE L. MCCONNELL was born about 1906 in Illinois, USA. She married MYRON G. STACKHOUSE, son of Frank D STACKHOUSE and Nettie J. *. He was born in 1901.

Joseph Henry Marshall MCCONNELL and Amanda had the following child:

  vii. KATIE MCCONNELL was born in 1906 in Illinois, USA.

Generation 4

7. **RUSSELL NORMAN[4] MCCONNELL** (James Anderson[3], William D.[2], Thomas[1]) was born on 22 Nov 1868 in Woodhull, Henry, Illinois, USA. He died on 27 Jan 1965 in Monrovia, Las Angeles, California, United States. He married **MARY MYRTLE DYE** between 1895-1896 in Oklahoma City, Oklahoma, USA, daughter of Alexander G DYE and Mary Caroline HUDSPETH. She was born on 16 Aug 1874 in Missouri, USA. She died on 09 May 1960 in Los Angeles, Los Angeles, California, USA.

Notes for Russell Norman MCCONNELL: Joyce Liscom wasn't sure of her grandfather's first name, but thought it was Russell or Vincent. Apparently he took Carter's Little Liver pills by the hand full. He believed, "If one was good, then three or four were better." The McConnells were reportedly Scotch-Irish of origin. Joyce related that when she was very young she remembers her grandparents living in Chicago. Since Joyce was born in 1927, the McConnells were probably in Chicago in the 1930-40 time frame. Searching the 1930 census revealed extensive, previously unknown, info about the family.

Grandpa McConnell was a lawyer (listed as "commercial lawyer" in the 1930 census) and all of his life lobbied against income tax. He was very much against government controls. Today he would probably be a member of the Libertarian Party. His father was born in Pennsylvania and his mother in Illinois.

The 1930 census indicated that they rented their house in Wilmette for $200 per month. The next door house was worth $25,000. A very high price in 1930. They also owned a radio.

The *California Death Index* listed a Russell McConnell, SSN 320-22-7402 issued in Illinois, b. 11/22/1868, d. Jan 1965 in Los Angeles where he lived at 90042 Los Angeles, Los Angeles, CA. That address was on the same block as his son Arthur who died in L.A. in July of 1972. Valerie Wolf obtained a copy of his Social Security application which stated he was born Norman Russell McConnell, but changed it to Russell Norman.

Notes for Mary Myrtle DYE: According to Joanne and Joyce Liscom Davies their grand-mother had very bad osteoporosis.

In the 1930 census her father was listed as being born in Ohio and her mother in Missouri. Apparently at one time Myrtle took up the name of her stepfather (McMurtry). The *California Death Index* lists her mother's maiden name as McMurtry.

Russell Norman MCCONNELL and Mary Myrtle DYE had the following children:

  i. ALBERT[5] MCCONNELL was born between 1896-Jun 1900 in Oklahoma City, Oklahoma, Oklahoma, USA. He died before 18 Jun 1900.

13 ii. EDITH MCCONNELL was born on 17 Apr 1897 in Oklahoma City, Oklahoma, Oklahoma, USA. She died on 21 Mar 1988 in Butte, California. She married (1) EARLY CARLTON CRABTREE, son of David Carlton CRABTREE and Georgia Ann

BARNETT. He was born on 17 Apr 1895 in Allen, Ponotoc, OK. He died on 10 Dec 1943 in North Hollywood, Los Angeles, California, United States. She married (2) UNK KIRKPATRICK. She married (3) UNK BOYAJIAN.

14 iii. VINCENT DYE MCCONNELL was born on 03 Aug 1898 in Oklahoma City, Oklahoma, Oklahoma, USA. He died on 25 Dec 1969 (Elgin, Kane, Illinois 60120). He married MARGARET ATTWOOD about 1922.

15 iv. MARY CAROLINE MCCONNELL was born on 20 Oct 1902 in Oklahoma City, Oklahoma, Oklahoma, USA. She died on 19 Nov 1988 in Petaluma, Sonoma, California, USA. She married WILLIAM MARTIN LISCOM, son of Jason Fred LISCOM and Amelia SCHROEDER. He was born on 15 Mar 1897 in Illinois, USA. He died on 31 Oct 1957 in Los Angeles, California, USA.

      v. CARLTON MCCONNELL was born about 1903. He died between 1908–21 Apr 1910 in Oklahoma, USA.

Notes for Carlton MCCONNELL: According to Joyce Liscom (Caroline McConnell's daughter) Carlton was riding his bike and was hit and killed by a drunk driver. When Carlton's mother talked with her minister for consolation he said it was God's will that this happened. Apparently, that was when she decided to become a Christian Scientist because she could not comprehend God's will being to have an 8-year-old killed by a drunk driver.

16 vi. RUSSEL NORMAN MCCONNELL JR. was born on 16 Dec 1904 in Oklahoma City, Oklahoma, Oklahoma, USA. He died on 06 Nov 1990 in Alameda, Alameda, California, USA. He married (1) MAURINE. She was born about 1904 in Illinois, USA. He married (2) INEZ.

     vii. ARTHUR E. MCCONNELL was born on 17 Jun 1907 in Oklahoma City, Oklahoma, Oklahoma, USA. He died on 24 Jul 1972 in Los Angeles, California, USA.

Notes for Arthur E. MCCONNELL: The death indexes for both Arthur and his father, Russell, listed their addresses as in the same block in Los Angeles, Los Angeles, CA.

17 viii. FRANCES LOIS MCCONNELL was born on 23 Jul 1910 in Oklahoma City, Oklahoma, Oklahoma, USA. She died on 24 Jan 1978 in San Jose, Santa Clara, California, USA. She married FREDERICK HENRY SCHMIDT on 07 Mar 1936 (Wilmette Baptist Church, Park Ridge, Illinois), son of Oscar Weber SCHMIDT and Mary Louise BOLLA. He was born on 11 Jun 1908 (Evanston, Illinois (St. Francis Hospital)). He died on 22 Nov 1982 in San Jose, Santa Clara, California, USA.

8. **JESSIE FAY*4* BURTON** (Maggie M. C.*3* MCCONNELL, William D.*2* MCCONNELL, Thomas*1* MCCONNELL) was born on 02 Oct 1882 in Cambridge, Henry, Illinois, USA. She died on 16 May 1959 in Naperville, DuPage, Illinois, United States. She married **MARTIN VINCENT NUGENT**. He was born on 02 Sep 1877 in LaSalle, LaSalle, Illinois, United States. He died on 22 Jan 1939 in Ft. Myers, Lee, Florida, United States.

Martin Vincent NUGENT and Jessie Fay BURTON had the following children:

      i. MARY VELMA*5* NUGENT was born on 14 Aug 1909 in Chicago, Cook, Illinois, USA.

She died on 20 Jan 1984 in Roswell, Chavez, New Mexico, United States.

ii. MARTIN BURTON NUGENT was born on 13 Dec 1907 in Illinois. He died on 14 Jun 1960 in Chicago, Cook, Illinois, USA.

9. **NELLIE M.**[4] **MCCONNELL** (Joseph Henry Marshall[3], William D.[2], Thomas[1]) was born about 1890 in Illinois, USA. She married **ELVIN JEFFRIES**. He was born in 1891 in Kentucky, USA.

Elvin JEFFRIES and Nellie M. MCCONNELL had the following children:

i. LUCILLE[5] JEFFRIES was born in 1914.

ii. CHARLES JEFFRIES was born in 1916.

10. **DAISY P.**[4] **MCCONNELL** (Joseph Henry Marshall[3], William D.[2], Thomas[1]) was born about 1894 in Illinois, USA. She married **EARL E HUNGATE**. He was born in 1891 in Missouri, USA.

Earl E HUNGATE and Daisy P. MCCONNELL had the following children:

i. EVERETT[5] HUNGATE was born in 1914.

ii. DONALD HUNGATE was born in 1916.

iii. MARIE HUNGATE was born in 1919.

iv. WAYNE HUNGATE was born in 1921.

v. BETTY J HUNGATE was born in 1925.

vi. BILLY D HUNGATE was born in 1928.

11. **GRACE OLIVE**[4] **MCCONNELL** (Joseph Henry Marshall[3], William D.[2], Thomas[1]) was born about 1896 in Illinois, USA. She married **JAMES T. LASHBROOK** on 05 Feb 1913 in Henry, Illinois, USA. He was born on 02 Jun 1887 in Illinois, USA.

James T. LASHBROOK and Grace Olive MCCONNELL had the following children:

i. DOROTHY M.[5] LASHBROOK was born in 1915 in Illinois, USA.

ii. JAMES M. LASHBROOK was born in Nov 1918 in Minnesota, USA.

iii. RICHARD LASHBROOK was born in 1926 in Minnesota, USA.

12. **FRANK ERNEST**[4] **MCCONNELL** (Joseph Henry Marshall[3], William D.[2], Thomas[1]) was born on 12 Nov 1896 in Henry County, Illinois, USA. He died on 22 Aug 1968 in Cambridge, Henry, Illinois, USA. He married **NORMA BESS POPPY** on 15 Dec 1920 in Cambridge, Henry, Illinois, USA, daughter of John POPPY and Martha L. She was born about 1895 in Illinois, USA. She died in Apr 1984 in Cambridge, Henry, Illinois, USA.

Frank Ernest MCCONNELL and Norma Bess POPPY had the following children:

i. ROBERTA[5] MCCONNELL was born about 1921 in Illinois, USA.

ii. GERALDINE MCCONNELL was born about 1923 in Illinois, USA.

iii. MARVIN L. MCCONNELL was born in Feb 1926 in Illinois, USA.

Notes for Marvin L. MCCONNELL: The census data definitely looks like Marion; but the obit for his father's death was Marvin?

Generation 5

13. **EDITH**[5] **MCCONNELL** (Russell Norman[4], James Anderson[3], William D.[2], Thomas[1]) was born on 17 Apr 1897 in Oklahoma City, Oklahoma, Oklahoma, USA. She died on 21 Mar 1988 in Butte, California. She married (1) **EARLY CARLTON CRABTREE**, son of David Carlton CRABTREE and Georgia Ann BARNETT. He was born on 17 Apr 1895 in Allen, Ponotoc, OK. He died on 10 Dec 1943 in North Hollywood, Los Angeles, California, United States. She married (2) **UNK KIRKPATRICK**. She married (3) **UNK BOYAJIAN**.

Notes for Edith MCCONNELL: According to Joyce Davies, Edith's first husband died young from an ulcer-related problem. They lived in Chicago, but moved to California in the San Fernando Valley after he died. Joyce thinks Edith later remarried. There are conflicts on her husbands' names. Joyce thought her first husband's name was Carlson Crabtree, but Jackie said she first knew Edith as Kirkpatrick. Jackie said she then married a doctor named Boyejian. It appears that she was married three times. In order they probably were Carlson Crabtree, Kirkpatrick and Boyejian.

According to Joyce, Edith was very successful in real estate in the San Fernando Valley. Joyce remembers Edith's house in Cleveland as being very large and having a large basement playroom for the kids with a concrete floor. To dress up the basement playroom Edith did stencils of kids playing on the walls. According to family stories Edith never talked until she was three years old, but "once she started she never stopped!"

Early Carlton CRABTREE and Edith MCCONNELL had the following children:

    i. BETTE JEAN[6] CRABTREE. She married LLOYD BICKING.

        Notes for Bette Jean CRABTREE: Signature as Betty Ann Crabtree in Wedding Book for Schmidt wedding. Joyce Davies gave me the name as Betty Jean Crabtree.

    ii. KATHRYN CRABTREE. She married BILL CROWDER.

        Notes for Kathryn CRABTREE: Signature in Schmidt Marriage Book listed her name as Cathryn Crabtree vice Kathryn as given to me by Joyce Davies.

Notes for Unk KIRKPATRICK: According to Jackie Liscom, Edith probably married Mr. Kirkpatrick after her first husband passed away. Jackie related that Edith's last name was Kirkpatrick when she first met her (which was probably about the time she and Les were married).

Notes for Unk BOYAJIAN: This was probably Edith's third husband according to Jackie Liscom. He was a doctor.

14. **VINCENT DYE**[5] **MCCONNELL** (Russell Norman[4], James Anderson[3], William D.[2], Thomas[1]) was born on 03 Aug 1898 in Oklahoma City, Oklahoma, Oklahoma, USA. He died on 25 Dec 1969 (Elgin, Kane, Illinois 60120). He married **MARGARET ATTWOOD** about 1922.

Notes for Vincent Dye MCCONNELL: The 1930 Census showed Vincent and his two children living with his parents in Wilmette. It also indicated that he was a widower and that he was a veteran of WW I.

Vincent Dye MCCONNELL and Margaret ATTWOOD had the following children:

   i. JACK V.[6] MCCONNELL was born about 1922.
   ii. PATRICIA MCCONNELL was born on 25 Mar 1925 in Cook County, IL. She died in Apr 1991 in Elgin, Kane, Illinois, United States of America.

15. **MARY CAROLINE**[5] **MCCONNELL** (Russell Norman[4], James Anderson[3], William D.[2], Thomas[1]) was born on 20 Oct 1902 in Oklahoma City, Oklahoma, Oklahoma, USA. She died on 19 Nov 1988 in Petaluma, Sonoma, California, USA. She married **WILLIAM MARTIN LISCOM**, son of Jason Fred LISCOM and Amelia SCHROEDER. He was born on 15 Mar 1897 in Illinois, USA. He died on 31 Oct 1957 in Los Angeles, California, USA.

Notes for Mary Caroline MCCONNELL: Was always referred to as "Aunt Carol" by Joanne. She passed away at the age of 85 in California.

According to her daughter, Joyce, Carol was a Phi Beta Kappa. Was also a Pi Beta Phi in college as was Joyce. She also practiced the Christian Science Religion as do Joyce, Joanne and Jackie Liscom.

Notes for William Martin LISCOM: According to Jackie Liscom, William served in France in WW I and returned to attend the University of Illinois. He and his brother Les played in a band to earn money in college. He played the violin.

William Martin LISCOM and Mary Caroline MCCONNELL had the following children:

18   i. MARY JOYCE[6] LISCOM was born on 31 Jan 1927 in Los Angeles, California, USA. She died on 15 Nov 2010 in Marblehead, Essex, Massachusetts, USA. She married DON DAVIES. He was born on 28 Dec 1926 in Minneapolis, Anoka, Minnesota, USA.

19   ii. LESLIE MARTIN LISCOM was born on 30 Jan 1929. He died in 1999. He married JACQUELINE YARBROUGH. She was born on 17 Jan 1929.

20   iii. JOANNE LISCOM was born on 23 Apr 1937 in Cleveland, Cuyahoga, Ohio, USA. She married ROBERT L. PAWLO on 06 Aug 1960 in Orange, California, USA, son of Floyd Anthony PAWLO and Annabelle Marie DRANE. He was born on 09 Jun 1934 in Bridgeville, Allegheny, Pennsylvania, USA.

16. **RUSSEL NORMAN**[5] **MCCONNELL JR.** (Russell Norman[4], James Anderson[3], William D.[2], Thomas[1]) was born on 16 Dec 1904 in Oklahoma City, Oklahoma, Oklahoma, USA. He died on 06 Nov 1990 in Alameda, Alameda, California, USA. He married (1) **MAURINE**. She was born about 1904 in Illinois, USA. He married (2) **INEZ**.

Notes for Russel Norman MCCONNELL Jr.: Social Security Death Index revealed his birth and death dates and SSN. Was confirmed by his mother's maiden name being Dye.

Russel Norman MCCONNELL Jr. and Maurine had the following child:

   i. ROBERT[6] MCCONNELL was born in Dec 1928 in Illinois, USA. He married JOANNE *.
   Notes for Robert MCCONNELL: According to Jackie Liscom, Bob had been in the Korean War and had a metal plate in his head from an injury. She indicated he was no longer alive (Aug 2003).

17. **FRANCES LOIS**[5] **MCCONNELL** (Russell Norman[4], James Anderson[3], William D.[2], Thomas[1]) was born on 23 Jul 1910 in Oklahoma City, Oklahoma, Oklahoma, USA. She died on 24 Jan 1978 in San Jose, Santa Clara, California, USA. She married **FREDERICK HENRY SCHMIDT** on 07 Mar 1936 (Wilmette Baptist Church, Park Ridge, Illinois), son of Oscar Weber SCHMIDT and Mary Louise BOLLA. He was born on 11 Jun 1908 (Evanston, Illinois (St. Francis Hospital)). He died on 22 Nov 1982 in San Jose, Santa Clara, California, USA.

Frederick Henry SCHMIDT and Frances Lois MCCONNELL had the following children:

    i. JOANNE FRANCES[6] SCHMIDT was born on 12 Mar 1938 in Evanston, Cook, Illinois, USA. She married DELBERT ARTHUR RITCHHART on 28 Nov 1959 in Wilmette, Cook, Illinois, USA, son of Delbert Bush RITCHHART and Helen Jane DEAN. He was born on 08 May 1937 in Las Animas, Bent, Colorado, USA (11:16 a.m.).

    ii. FREDERICK WEBER SCHMIDT was born on 23 Oct 1943 in Evanston, Cook, Illinois, USA. He married JUDY AUSTIN on 16 May, daughter of Richard James AUSTIN and Dorothy Agnes RATTE. She was born on 13 Apr in Vermont, USA.

    iii. ELIZABETH JEAN SCHMIDT was born on 29 Aug 1940 in Evanston, Cook, Illinois, USA. She died on 22 Mar 2006 in San Diego, San Diego, California. She met (1) ALBERT CHARLES ESTABROOK, son of William Henry ESTABROOK and Phoebe GAY. He was born on 28 Dec 1929 in Monterey, California, USA. He died on 05 Feb 2007 in San Diego, San Diego, California, USA. She married (2) ARMIN KAMPMAN on 07 Apr 1979 in San Diego, San Diego, California, USA. She married (3) FRED WOLF, son of George Dorr WOLF Jr. and Margaret Winifred HURLBUTT. He was born in Illinois.

Generation 6

18. **MARY JOYCE**[6] **LISCOM** (Mary Caroline[5] MCCONNELL, Russell Norman[4] MCCONNELL, James Anderson[3] MCCONNELL, William D.[2] MCCONNELL, Thomas[1] MCCONNELL) was born on 31 Jan 1927 in Los Angeles, California, USA. She died on 15 Nov 2010 in Marblehead, Essex, Massachusetts, USA. She married **DON DAVIES**. He was born on 28 Dec 1926 in Minneapolis, Anoka, Minnesota, USA.

Notes for Don DAVIES: Don was put up for adoption by his 16-year-old mother when he was just months old. His name was Judson Miner, but his adoptive parents changed his name to Don Davies and had a new birth certificate issued.

Don DAVIES and Mary Joyce LISCOM had the following children:

    i. DRUANNE[7] DAVIES was born on 01 Jul 1952 in Los Angeles, California, USA. She married TOD FORMAN.

    ii. DONNA JOANNE DAVIES was born on 15 Jul 1957 in Hollywood, CA. She married SABRA PERKINS.

19. **LESLIE MARTIN**[6] **LISCOM** (Mary Caroline[5] MCCONNELL, Russell Norman[4] MCCONNELL, James Anderson[3] MCCONNELL, William D.[2] MCCONNELL, Thomas[1] MCCONNELL) was born on 30 Jan 1929. He died in 1999. He married **JACQUELINE YARBROUGH**. She was

born on 17 Jan 1929.

Notes for Leslie Martin LISCOM: According to his wife, Jackie, Les played the violin and was in the Hollywood Bowl Symphony while still in his teens. He later played the trombone and was in the band in Korea. He put together a quartet which sang on a Horace Heidt show from Korea on the radio. They competed with other Divisions and won 1st place. He enjoyed playing the trombone for the rest of his life.

Notes for Jacqueline YARBROUGH: Was a Pi Phi in at UCLA with Joyce Liscom. She met her future husband, Les, through Joyce. Joyce had asked that Les and Jackie be paired in a sorority/fraternity exchange because they both had horses.

Leslie Martin LISCOM and Jacqueline YARBROUGH had the following children:

     i. WILLIAM LESLIE[7] LISCOM was born on 26 Dec 1954.

     ii. DAVID ARTHUR LISCOM was born on 07 Aug 1956.

     iii. JILL CAROLINE LISCOM was born on 12 Nov 1958. She married EDWARD KRAMER.

20. **JOANNE[6] LISCOM** (Mary Caroline[5] MCCONNELL, Russell Norman[4] MCCONNELL, James Anderson[3] MCCONNELL, William D.[2] MCCONNELL, Thomas[1] MCCONNELL) was born on 23 Apr 1937 in Cleveland, Cuyahoga, Ohio, USA. She married **ROBERT L PAWLO** on 06 Aug 1960 in Orange, California, USA, son of Floyd Anthony PAWLO and Annabelle Marie DRANE. He was born on 09 Jun 1934 in Bridgeville, Allegheny, Pennsylvania, USA.

Robert L PAWLO and Joanne LISCOM had the following children:

     i. DANA[7] PAWLO was born on 11 Nov 1961 in San Francisco, California, USA. She married JIM KATZ.

     ii. MELINDA PAWLO was born on 06 May 1964 in San Francisco, California, USA.

     iii. RON PAWLO was born on 26 Aug 1967 in San Rafael, Marin, California, USA. He married ROBYN HACKBARTH. She was born on 02 Jun 1968.

     iv. BRENDA PAWLO was born on 21 May 1970 in San Rafael, Marin, California, USA. She married HOWARD SPEAR.

     v. CAROLYN PAWLO was born on 23 Nov 1971 in San Rafael, Marin, California, USA. She married ANDREW TEAFF. He was born on 21 Jun 1974.

Acknowledgment

Without the countless items that my mother and her mother saved over their lifetimes, that eventually found their ways into my hands; this book might not have been possible. Although, my mother and my brother, sister and I lived with my grandmother and grandfather throughout my junior high, high school and college years; I don't recall my grandmother making any conscious effort to save letters, photographs and other memorabilia. However, throughout the last five years or more of my mother's life she would give me a box or two to take home with me each time I visited her. I would humor her, take them home and store them somewhere in the garage—usually not even bothering to open them. If I did open a box it was only for a cursory look. As the years went by I accumulated 6 or 8 mid-size packing boxes of this "stuff." Fortunately the boxes even survived a couple moves.

My brother, likewise, received boxes from my mother. Later, knowing my interests in family history, he passed copies of most of the significant items along to me.

Even after I finally developed an interest in genealogy, these boxes remained unopened for at least another five years. Finally, mostly in response to my wife's insistence I clean out some of the "junk" in the garage; I started going through the boxes. The contents were a combination of items my grandmother saved and those my mother saved; perhaps due to an inherited trait, with which I seem to have also been inflicted.

I had to take care in going through the boxes to ensure that I carefully examined every item; because mixed in with these treasures were instructions for the microwave, the blender, the washing machine and almost every appliance my mother ever owned. I once grabbed a hand full of these instruction books and was releasing them into the trash can when I noticed something that looked a little different. It was my grandparents original marriage certificate!

My grandmother kept an address book; but it didn't just contain addresses, it had birthdays, death notices, and notes about other significant family events. This was in one of the boxes. Also, was a photo album; but instead of photos it had every letter my mother had written to my grandmother during the two and a half years we lived in California and Oklahoma while my dad was in the Navy during the final years of WW II. Those were my 1st and 2nd grade years in school.

My great grandfather was sheriff in 1900 and received notice from Sundance, Wyoming that his younger brother, Jessie, had been shot in a gunfight. He was curious about the details and wrote both the rancher Jessie worked for and the local sheriff asking how it happened. In one of the boxes were three letters that he received explaining the circumstances surrounding the shooting death. Also in the boxes, were almost all of my grandfather's report cards from the time he was in the 1st grade through high school! There were also obituary articles and mortuary cards for numerous family member deaths, drivers licenses, social security cards and even left over ration books from WW II.

Needless, to say these items are not only keepsakes; but provided a wealth of information about the lives of many of my ancestors. They also further stimulated my interest in delving further into my family's past. Thus, I owe a big debt of gratitude to my deceased mother and grandmother for collecting all that "stuff" and passing it along.

I hate to admit it; but I just discovered another of those boxes in the garage a month ago. I skimmed through it; but have to go back through in more detail to enter all the date in my family history database. It never ends!

I want to also thank my editor, Dona Ritchie, without whose editing and technical skills I could not have completed the book!

Others whom I want to recognize for contributions they have made which have aided in the writing of this book are the following:

Ed Dean
Mary Dean
Beatrice Frye
Marilee Miller Kapsa
Lee O'Malley
Leigh O'Malley
Bettye Richhart
Dean Ritchhart
Kenneth Ritchhart
Eugene Ritchhart
Ulrich Ritschard
Betsy Miller Smith
Jeff Wolf
Valerie Wolf
Jackii Wirszyla
Allen County Public Library
Family History Center, San Diego
Family History Library, Salt Lake City
Los Angeles Public Library

I would be very remiss if I didn't acknowledge the patience and understand of my loving wife, Joanne, over all these years. She has been dragged through cemeteries, and met many of my distant relatives, most of whom we will see only once in our lives. She has been very understanding about the time and money I spend doing family research, buying books, software and subscriptions; as well as attending genealogy conferences and meetings. Finally, after asking once or twice, "When do you get done with all this genealogy stuff?" she has gracefully accepted the answer: "I will never be done researching family history—it has no end!"

References and Resources

Richhart, Ritchhart, Ritschard A Swiss-German Family From 1500 Until 1993; Bettye Anderson Richhart, 1993.

Economic Crisis in Germany, Rudiger Hachtmann (translated by James Chastain).

The New World Book published by Halberts Family Heritage.

The Great Hunger: Ireland 1845–1849 by Cecil Woodham-Smith, Penguin Books, 1962.

History of Ross and Highland Counties Ohio, Published 1978 by Unigraphic in Evansville, IN. Originally published in Cleveland, OH by Williams Bros. in 1880. Includes reprint of Index originally published separately.

County Mayo, Ireland Achill Parish, Some Baptismal Transcriptions with Index by William G. Masterson.

The JJ Ranch on the Purgatory River by Frances Bollacker Keck, Otero Press, La Junta, Colorado. 2001.

Las Animas Leader, Lee Roy Boyd column, March 1949.

Writings of Ed Dean to Helen Jane Ritchhart, around 1970.

The Timechart History Of America, Designed and edited by DAG Publications Ltd., published by Barnes & Noble, Inc., 2003.

Conquistadors to the 21st Century—A History of Otero and Crowley Counties Colorado, by Frances Bollacker Keck, Otero Press, La Junta, Colorado. 1999

The Surnames of Ireland, Edward MacLysaght, Irish Academic Press, 1980.

The Great Hunger: Ireland 1845–1849, Cecil Woodham-Smith, Penguin Books, London, England 1991

The Germans of Indianapolis, George Theodore Probst. Revised edition by Eberhard Reichmann (Indianapolis German-American Center and Indiana German Heritage Society, Inc., 1989)

Index of Individuals